FABIAN SOCIALISM AND
ENGLISH POLITICS
1884–1918

FABIAN SOCIALISM
AND
ENGLISH POLITICS
1884 – 1918

BY

A. M. McBRIAR

Senior Lecturer in History in the University of Melbourne

CAMBRIDGE
AT THE UNIVERSITY PRESS
1962

PUBLISHED BY

THE SYNDICS OF THE CAMBRIDGE UNIVERSITY PRESS

Bentley House, 200 Euston Road, London, N.W.1

American Branch: 32 East 57th Street, New York 22, N.Y.

West African Office: P.O. Box 33, Ibadan, Nigeria

CAMBRIDGE UNIVERSITY PRESS

1962

PRINTED IN GREAT BRITAIN BY WILLMER BROTHERS & HARAM LIMITED

CHESTER STREET, BIRKENHEAD

To
JOHN LLOYD
whose arguments began
this inquiry

CONTENTS

CONTENTS

PREFACE

THIS book is concerned mainly with Fabian doctrine and only incidentally with the history of the Society or with the Fabians as individuals. Its aim is to expound Fabian Socialism in an historical and critical way and then to attempt an estimate of its influence in the politics of London government and the policies of the Liberal Party, the Independent Labour Party and the Labour Party between 1884 and 1918. I have treated the Tracts and other official publications of the Fabian Society as the authoritative source of the doctrine, but I have also taken the view that any narrow or exclusive definition of 'true Fabianism' based on these official publications alone would be so minimal as to be futile, and so, while I am aware of the dangers, I have not hesitated to invoke the opinions of individual Fabians at places where they throw light on the ideas accepted by the Society as a whole. The method used to determine 'influence' is to discover how far the policies adopted by other organizations resembled those advocated by the Fabians, and where that proves to be the case, to ask again whether the policies were adopted as a result of persuasion by the Fabians or as a result of other, or more general, pressures. This historical method has its limitations in solving the problem of 'influence', but I believe it can go some way towards solving it.

To Professor R. H. Tawney's kind encouragement during his visit to Australia is due the appearance of this study as a book. It was originally completed in December 1948 as an Oxford thesis; and Chapter VIII (which I am grateful for permission to republish) appeared as one of the essays in *The Webbs and their Work*, edited by Margaret Cole (London, 1949). I have to thank so many people for help in writing both versions that I hope they will not believe my gratitude any the less if I do not list their names. I cherish particularly affectionate memories of that merry band of Australians in London who in the last frantic rush of December 1948 helped me to write in footnotes which were left off copies by the typist. To Professor G. D. H. Cole and Mrs Cole, Drs Jack and Barbara Tizard and Mr K. D. Gott I owe thanks even beyond those due to other kind friends, for without their aid and encouragement I should almost certainly not have been able to complete the work. I also want to take this opportunity of expressing my thanks to Associate-Professor Kathleen Fitzpatrick and Professor R. M. Crawford for all that their teaching and friendship has meant to me.

Grateful acknowledgements are due to the Fabian Society for allowing me to inspect its records and to quote from its publications, and to all authors and publishers who have given me permission to use extracts from their books. I am indebted particularly to the Passfield Trustees and Messrs Longmans Green and Co. Ltd. and to the Society of Authors and the Public Trustee for permission to quote from the works of Sidney and Beatrice Webb and George Bernard Shaw.

MELBOURNE   A. M. McBRIAR

March, 1962

CHAPTER I

THE ORIGIN OF THE FABIAN SOCIETY AND OF ITS SOCIALIST DOCTRINE

ORIGIN OF THE FABIAN SOCIETY

THE sturdy old Radical, J. Morrison Davidson, in his book *The Annals of Toil*[1] dealt succinctly with the origin of the Fabian Society:

The Fabian Society was founded in London in 1883. Its virtual founder was my brother, Dr Thomas Davidson of New York, author of the *Philosophy of Rosmini-Serbati, Aristotle and Ancient Educational Ideals*, the *Parthenon Frieze*, etc. He had just returned from Rome where he had discussed affairs with His Holiness the Pope, and was in a frame of mind to regenerate mankind on lines which did not appear to me—who was then doing all I could to prevent the G.O.M. from throttling Ireland—very promising.

Dr Thomas Davidson, if we may judge from the tributes to his memory by those who knew him,[2] must have been a remarkable man. A classical scholar, philosopher and linguist, with original educational views, he also fancied himself as a medieval wandering scholar who had wandered into the late nineteenth century. Wherever he went, travelling in Europe or America and enjoying the company of the wise and the great, he gave lectures and often gathered around himself a band of enthusiastic disciples. His general philosophical opinions appear to have changed considerably at different times, but he had been particularly influenced by the ideas of the Italian Roman Catholic philosopher, Antonio Rosmini-Serbati.[3] Eventually Davidson built a scheme for the regeneration of society on the basis of progressive and at times somewhat extravagant educational theory and practice. It was as a teacher that he was chiefly remembered by those he influenced. Havelock Ellis, who knew him well, has paid tribute to him in these warm, but not uncritical, words:

[1] J. Morrison Davidson, *The Annals of Toil, being Labour History Outlines, Roman and British* (Wm. Reeves, London, 1899). p. 427.

[2] An account of Davidson's life and opinions will be found in William Knight (ed.,) *Memorials of Thomas Davidson* (T. Fisher Unwin, London, 1907). See also William Clarke's article 'A Modern Wandering Scholar' in the *Spectator*, 6 October 1900, and Hubert Bland's paper 'The Faith I Hold' (a lecture to the Fabian Society) reprinted in E. Nesbit Bland (ed.), *Essays by Hubert Bland* ('Hubert' of the *Sunday Chronicle*) (Max Goschen, London, 1914), pp. 213–33.

[3] Antonio Rosmini-Serbati (1797–1855) was founder of a religious order, The Institute of the Brethren of Charity, usually known as Rosminians. He tried to reconcile traditional Catholic teaching with the modern philosophy of his time but, after a long struggle between Rosminians and Jesuits, forty propositions of his philosophy were condemned by Pope Leo XIII in 1887. Davidson's Fellowship of the New Life was in some respects a Protestant and secular equivalent of Rosmini's Institute of the Brethren of Charity.

Doubtless he was not a scholar in the scientific sense of the term. He recalls rather those men of the Renaissance of whom Giordano Bruno was the supreme type, wandering philosophers who spent their lives going from one great centre of thought to another, devoured by intellectual passion, equally eager to learn and to teach. . . . The enthusiasm with which he advocated more or less unfamiliar and impossible ideals could not fail to exert a stimulating influence on all those who came to hear him. He helped to teach those who listened to him to think, even though it were to think that he was wrong! Few men, indeed, of his time were permitted to play a part so like to that of those early Greek philosophers whom he loved so greatly. . . .[1]

When Dr Davidson was in London in September 1882, he gathered around him a number of people, amongst whom were some who were later to become prominent in the Fabian Society—Frank Podmore, Edward R. Pease, William Clarke, and Hubert Bland—as well as other less well known Fabians like Miss Dale Owen, the grand-daughter of Robert Owen; some, such as J. L. Joynes and H. H. Champion, who were later to be better known as members of the Social-Democratic Federation; and others, including Havelock Ellis, Percival Chubb and Dr Burns-Gibson, who were to remain in the Davidson group. Altogether, the Fellowship of the New Life seems to have had originally about thirty members, with a general attendance at its meetings of about half that number. In the second month of its existence Davidson suggested the group should take its name, and constitute itself a society for the purpose of leading a 'new life'. His aim[2] seems to have been a group which would progress gradually to a utopia, by a change taking place in several stages. At first, the members were to meet regularly (so far as their 'continuing at their present avocations' would permit) and were to live lives of simplicity and mutual help in accordance with certain general ethical and religious principles. They were to attempt to realise in their own selves the 'new life' based on unselfishness, love and wisdom. Ultimately, the members were to draw together into a community (in Blooms-bury[3] or, perhaps, Peru) where the 'new life' could be lived in common, and by their example encourage others to do the same, and so promote a gradual change in society. The aim was social change, but the Fellowship's method was individualistic: the social change was to be brought about by the perfecting of the individual character. It was a 'utopian' group. However, right from the start some of its members were rather sceptical about the practicality of Dr Davidson's methods and (as Bernard Shaw was later to put it) modestly feared that the ideal society 'would have to wait an unreasonably long time if post-

---

[1] Knight, op. cit. pp. 46–7.

[2] Ibid. pp. 21–5, for the rules drawn up by Davidson himself.

[3] The Fellowship of the New Life did eventually establish a co-operative residence in Bloomsbury. It was not a success. There is an account of it in G. Elton, Life of James Ramsay MacDonald (Collins, London, 1939), vol. 1, pp. 64–5. J. R. MacDonald was Secretary of the Fellowship of the New Life in 1892–3 and was for some years on its Executive. See also E. R. Pease, The History of the Fabian Society (Allen & Unwin, London, 1925), pp. 35–6.

poned until they personally had attained perfection'.[1] Davidson objected to the socialist views put forward by these younger members and held firmly to his opinion that it was only possible to remove the evils of the world by individual change of heart, or, at most, by voluntary co-operation.[2]

Dr Davidson therefore did not, even virtually, found the Fabian Society, nor did he approve of it when it had been founded. The Fabian Society came into existence when the members who disagreed with Davidson separated to form a new group. The fission was decided upon at a meeting of the original body held on 4 January 1884;[3] the old group continued on the lines approved by Dr Davidson and retained the name of the Fellowship of the New Life, while the new group called itself the Fabian Society; and the two groups were quite separate as organizations, though some members of the Fabian Society remained in the Fellowship. There seems to be no doubt that the members who withdrew to form the Fabian Society were already Socialist or socialistically inclined, even though they may not have decided the exact form of their Socialism, and even though such later 'Fabian Essayists,' who were to play so great a part in formulating Fabian doctrine, as Sidney Webb, Bernard Shaw, Sydney Olivier, Graham Wallas, William Clarke, and Annie Besant, were not foundation members of the Society.

The best known of the original members were Frank Podmore, Edward R. Pease, and Hubert Bland. Podmore, a graduate of Oxford University and a clerk in the Post Office, played an active part in establishing the Society, but did not continue his activity after the first years of its existence. He retired in 1888 from the Fabian Executive and devoted himself to literary work, producing penetrating studies of spiritualism and an excellent biography of Robert Owen. His friend, Edward Pease, who had also come to Socialism through the Radical and Positivist movements, was destined to have a longer and closer association than any other person with the organisation he had helped to found. Pease, who had served as the Society's honorary Secretary in 1886, was appointed as General Secretary in 1890, after he had retired from an unsuccessful career as a stockbroker; he held the post until the outbreak of the Great War, and became honorary Secretary again after that and continued in office until 1939. Shrewd, hard-headed, sceptical, determinedly unimaginative and Philistine, steadfastly moderate in his politics, Pease made the perfect Secretary.

Hubert Bland was a complete contrast to the scholarly Podmore and the efficient, self-effacing Pease. Both in his opinions and his private life, he was, indeed, a lustier character than most of his Fabian colleagues. His religious

---

[1] Tract 41.
[2] Davidson's views of the 'economic question' are shown best in a lecture read before the New York Fellowship of the New Life: *The Moral Aspects of the Economic Question* (Wm. Reeves, London, 1888). See also Knight, *op. cit. passim.*
[3] Pease, *op. cit.* p. 33; and Minute Book of the Fabian Society.

beliefs swung from Roman Catholicism to Atheism and back again, his politics were a strange blend of Toryism and Marxism, and he entertained no little scorn for worthy and respectable liberals like Pease and Sidney Webb. As a political observer and commentator he was extraordinarily sharp and perceptive. Assertive, with the bearing, the moustache and monocle of a Prussian military officer and a shrill voice, he made himself the leader in the Fabian Society of the group which was antagonistic to the Liberal Party and which wanted the formation of a new, independent Socialist Party. Many amongst a younger generation of Fabians were influenced by him and enjoyed their visits to the unorthodox household of Bland and his wife, Edith Nesbit, the author of the children's stories. In the 'eighties Bland was beginning to make his name as a journalist after having abandoned a career in a bank and failing as a business man. He remained honorary Treasurer of the Fabian Society from 1884 to 1911.

George Bernard Shaw, then a young Irishman trying unsuccessfully to enter London's literary world as a novelist, joined the Society nine months after its foundation. He had already met Sidney Webb at a debating society and Sydney Olivier at the meetings of a Radical organisation, the Land Reform Union, and he persuaded his new friends to join in May 1885. Both Webb and Olivier were upper division clerks in the Colonial Office, which they had entered through the new system of open competitive examinations, Olivier from Oxford, Webb after evening study at London University. These young colleagues and friends were an incongruous pair. Olivier was tall, massively built, with the appearance of a handsome Spanish grandee. There was something spacious, grandiose and vague in his manner; he was an involved and imprecise speaker, though sometimes profound. Sidney Webb was short and rotund, of the same physical type as the Emperor Napoleon III, his peculiar impressiveness owing nothing to physical beauty. It was the quality of his mind which commanded attention—his prodigious learning, his concentration and incisiveness, his systematic, logical, precise exposition. Although he was no orator, he was, in his early days at least, an effective lecturer, and he shone in discussion. In committee work he was brilliant, at once flexible and forceful, abounding in ideas and persuasiveness and excelling in the art of putting the sense of a meeting into words. Olivier was to continue in the Colonial Office and to have a distinguished career in that Department; but Webb, after his marriage to Beatrice Potter in 1892, retired from the Civil Service, at his wife's suggestion, to devote himself to writing and to politics. This decision resulted in the production of a series of superb historical works by the Webb 'partnership', but the unpropitious nature of Liberal politics confined Webb's political activities to the local government level until after the First World War.

Olivier, in May 1886, brought into the Society Graham Wallas, who had

4

been his friend since their student days at Oxford. Wallas had bec
teacher; and teaching, in schools, in University extension courses
London School of Economics continued to be his primary intere
short forays into municipal politics. A tall, languid man, Wallas alwa
more 'academic' than his Fabian colleagues, his mind delighting in p
of an abstract and theoretical nature, but self-doubting, sluggish and deep-
pondering, sometimes to the point of intellectual entanglement. He was a
superb teacher, and he was led, both by his love of his occupation and by his
genial and easy-going disposition, into devoting much more time to his
students and friends than to his own creative work; yet his *Life of Francis
Place* (1898) and his *Human Nature in Politics* (1908) were pioneer studies
which in their respective spheres remain as significant, if not as substantial, as
the greatest works of the Webbs do in theirs. Wallas was steeped in the teaching
of Bentham and John Stuart Mill, and he retained the strongest affection for
the egalitarian, republican and secularist Radicalism in which he had been
brought up. He finally left the Fabian Society in 1904, when he disagreed with
its views on the tariff question.

Annie Besant came to Socialism after a notable career as fighter, orator and
publicist in the cause of Radicalism and Secularism. Her inspiration, as she
confessed frankly and honestly in her *Autobiography*, was a 'religious' passion
for martyrdom; she devoted herself to helping struggling and unpopular
movements to success, and once the fight began to be successful, she took up
another cause. By the 1880's Annie had helped to launch Bradlaugh on his
parliamentary career; her interest in Secularism was waning and her interest
in Socialism had been aroused. She was persuaded to join the Fabian Society
in May 1885 by Bernard Shaw, the witty young author she had begun to
patronise. Annie Besant was the Society's most notable convert up to that
time; she belonged to an older generation (she was thirty-eight in 1885, while
the other leading Fabians were in their later twenties) and, because of her
contacts in the Radical world, she was able to precipitate the Fabians into
the very heart of London's Radical politics. Although later Fabians were
inclined to be unkind and unappreciative, Annie Besant did a great deal for
the Society in its early years, and her part in organising the Bryant and May's
match girls' strike in 1888 gave dramatic impetus to the movement of
'New Unionism,' so significant in its consequences for the labour movement
as a whole. Then suddenly, in 1890, she abandoned the Fabians to champion
Madame Blavatsky and Theosophy, a cause which took her to India and
occupied the remainder of her long life.

William Clarke, who had been a member of the Fellowship of the New Life
but had not originally gone over to the Fabian Society (though he had attended
a few of its early meetings), joined it in February 1886. Clarke was a graduate
of Cambridge and like Wallas and Olivier and Webb he had been interested

5

in Radical politics from his undergraduate days. An Emersonian, greatly interested in America and its literature, personally shy, retiring and scholarly, he was repelled by loud-mouthed and dogmatic Socialist propaganda and even by the flamboyance of some of his Fabian associates, particularly Bernard Shaw. His delicate health increased his natural inclination to withdraw from the world and active politics; it also fostered his pessimistic and distrustful attitude towards social progress, which contrasted strongly with the robust optimism of most Fabians in the early days of the Society. Clarke was obliged to expend more effort in preparing his material than other leading Fabian speakers and writers, but he made himself a clear and convincing lecturer, and a leading journalist on the staff of the *Spectator*. He retained his membership but withdrew from active participation in the Fabian Society in the early 'nineties, and died in 1901, disillusioned and cynical about the course of English politics, but (as an Emersonian) hoping that all would come right in the long run.

The leaders of the Fabian Society were not, then, exactly a band of bosom friends untroubled by differences. Bernard Shaw has claimed, with much truth, that it was he who kept them together, by acting as lightning-conductor.

In the Fabian Cabinet . . . [he wrote], there was considerable strife of temperaments; and in the other Socialist societies splits and schisms were frequent; for the English are very quarrelsome. I believe that some of my own usefulness lay in smoothing out these frictions by an Irish sort of tact which in England seemed the most outrageous want of it. Wherever there was a quarrel I betrayed everybody's confidence by analyzing it and stating it lucidly in exaggerated terms. Result: both sides agreed that it was all my fault. I was denounced on all hands as a reckless mischief-maker but forgiven as a privileged Irish lunatic.[1]

The early Fabian Society was, no doubt, a body of 'middle-class' or 'bourgeois' intellectuals. In the early years the 'only genuine working-man' amongst them was W. L. Phillips, a house-painter. Most of them were teachers, journalists, and clerks in private and government employment;[2] a number of them had had a university education. Later on, in the early 'nineties, some working-class leaders joined the Society, and there have even been one or two moments when the Fabians dreamt of becoming a mass party,[3] but for most of its existence the Society has openly acknowledged and even boasted of its middle-class intellectual and exclusive character.[4]

The story of the particular circumstances of the founding of the Fabian Society needs to be placed in a wider setting to explain why the Society came

[1] Quotation from G. B. Shaw, *Sixteen Self Sketches* (Constable, London, 1949), p. 68. For general biographical material see Bibliography.

[2] Pease, *op. cit.* pp. 48, 63

[3] These occasions were connected with periods of rapid growth in the Society's membership in the early nineties, and after 1906.

[4] Tract 70 is an excellent example of this

into existence when it did. The eighteen-eighties was a period of economic depression after the 'golden age' of Victorian capitalism, and Socialist doctrines of one kind or another, widely current on the Continent, were once again finding an audience in England. We shall see presently how deeply concerned the Fabians were with the problems of unemployment and poverty, and how Fabian ideas developed by way of criticism of the Socialist doctrine current at the time. The 'consciousness of sin' on the part of the upper and educated classes which Beatrice Webb has described,[1] is partly accounted for by the jolt to Victorian complacency by the depression of the 'eighties, and by an awareness of possible consequences of the extensions of the franchise to working-men which had taken place since the Reform Act of 1867.[2]

It does not seem necessary to look for any special degree of unemployment amongst the middle-class to help explain the origin of the Fabian Society. The Fabians were a very small group not notably motivated by personal interest. While some of them, like Shaw and Bland and Clarke were struggling journalists at that time, others were successful professional or business men; Webb and Olivier were comfortably enough established as civil servants, and Wallas as a teacher. Idealistic considerations, amongst which the lecturing, writing and personal example of William Morris was a powerful element, provided the main inspiration which made Socialists of the Fabians.

One general aspect of the 'Great Depression' of the 'eighties, however, may well have had an important and immediate effect upon the Socialism of that time. The fact that there were rising real wages for those in employment, but a great deal of unemployment,[3] probably helps to explain its separation into the intensely 'proletarian' hunger-marching Socialism of the Social Democratic Federation and the very 'middle-class' Socialism of the Fabians, and its small intermediate appeal (at least till after the time of the Dock Strike and the New Unionism) to the comparatively well-fed workers.

ORIGIN OF FABIAN DOCTRINE

Fabianism derived from two mainstreams of thought. The first was the English Liberal tradition, transmitted through the later writings of John Stuart Mill, and in the turbulent condition London Radicalism had reached in the eighteen-eighties. This stream had absorbed as a tributary much of Positivist doctrine flowing from France. It was disturbed by, but had not yet fully

[1] B. Webb, *My Apprenticeship* (Pelican Books, London, 1938), vol. I, p. 204 *et seq.*

[2] This has been treated very fully by R. D. Howland, *Fabian Thought and Social Change in England,* 1884–1914 (unpublished typescript thesis in the London Library of Social and Political Science), and also in many other histories of this period.

[3] H. L. Beales, 'The "Great Depression" in Industry and Trade,' *Economic History Review,* October 1934, vol. v; G. H. Wood, 'Real Wages and the Standard of Comfort since 1850,' *Journal of the Royal Statistical Society,* March 1909, vol. LXXXII, pp. 91–103; J. H. Clapham, *An Economic History of Modern Britain,* (C.U.P. 1932), book iii, pp. 450–3

absorbed, some of the doctrinal currents from Germany.[1] The other main-stream was the Socialist one, especially its most powerful current, Marxism. Fabianism drew from these streams, and endeavoured to turn Liberalism particularly, as by far the stronger of them in England, to a new course. In the succeeding chapters we will examine in detail what was taken, and what the new direction was.

The derivation of Fabian ideas from the Liberal tradition has always been stressed by historians, and the Fabians themselves insisted on it, sprinkling their writings plentifully with footnotes and other references to John Stuart Mill,[2] the contemporary Liberal economists and other respectable authors. But the influence of Marx on Fabianism has been denied. Many writers have claimed that Fabian Socialism was a pure outgrowth of English Liberalism, uninfluenced by Marxism. This view has been put forward by Fabians, particu-larly those of a later generation who came into the English Socialist movement through the Fabian Society or through the Independent Labour Party and Labour Party, by-passing the Marxist influence of the Social Democratic Federation.[3] It has been shared by nationalists favourable to English Socia-lism, who do not want it soiled by contact with 'foreign' doctrines.[4] It has even been espoused by Marxists anxious to prove that the Fabians knew not the Master.[5] But the initial Marxist influence on the Fabian Society is a reason why the Fabians took up a definitely Socialist standpoint, why they did not content themselves with a left-wing Radical position. And the recognition of this influence helps us to see Fabianism as part of a world-wide tendency in Social Democracy; it prevents Fabianism from appearing a unique, separate and insular phenomenon.

There were tangible links between the early Fabians and the Democratic

[1] Two attempts (neither of them sufficiently comprehensive) to assess the influence of positivism in England are J. E. McGee, *A Crusade for Humanity* (Watts, London, 1931) and an unpublished M.A. thesis by T. Nyland, *The English Positivists* (in the British Library of Social and Political Science). The German influences I have in mind are both philosophical (especially on theorists such as T. H. Green, D. G. Ritchie, and R. B. Haldane) and historico-economic. More will be said of the German 'Historical' school of economists in a later chapter.

[2] Shaw, in his Epilogue to Pease's *History of the Fabian Society (op. cit.* p. 274) is inclined to dispute the influence of Mill. That may be true of *him*, but we must beware of taking Shaw as a typical Fabian. Anyway, even there Shaw admits the importance of the influence of Mill on Webb, and after all, Webb's influence on the Fabian Society was much more pronounced than Shaw's. See M. A. Hamilton, *Sidney and Beatrice Webb* (Sampson Low, Marston & Co. London, 1932), p. 17 for the background to Webb's devotion to Mill.

[3] e.g., P. Snowden, *An Autobiography* (Ivor Nicholson & Watson, London, 1934), vol.I, pp. 62-3; C. R. Attlee, *The Labour Party in Perspective* (Gollancz, London, 1937), pp. 21, 26, 34.

[4] This attitude is carried to extreme lengths in M. A. Hamilton's remark that William Morris left the S.D.F. because he, 'in that a typical Briton', could not believe in Marxism (Hamilton, *op. cit.* p. 11). A great deal of nonsense has been written about Morris's relation with Marxism solely on the basis of an anecdote in which he confessed he was not an expert in Marxist economics.

[5] John Strachey (in his Marxist days) in *What are we to do?* (Gollancz, London, 1938), pp. 77-8.

Federation, which, founded in 1881 as a left-wing Radical body, had adopted a Marxist programme by 1883 (though it did not change its name to Social Democratic Federation until August 1884). Well-known S.D.F. names, like J. L. Joynes and H. H. Champion, appear in the early Fabian lists of members,[1] and of the first Fabian executive of three, two (Hubert Bland and Frederick Keddell) were members of the Democratic Federation. In the early days, Bernard Shaw, Graham Wallas, and Annie Besant, if they were not actually members of the Federation, at least often spoke for it, and we find the names of Olivier, Webb, and Stewart Headlam among a gathering of 'those who have taken an interest in the work [of the Democratic Federation] or were known to be in sympathy with its aim', reported in *Justice*, the Federation's newspaper, of 19 January 1884.[2]

The choice of the name 'Fabian'[3] for the Society may be thought in itself to demonstrate their cardinal principle of gradualness. But the point is weakened by the explanatory note attached to the title page of the first pamphlet: '... For the right moment you must wait, as Fabius did most patiently, when warring against Hannibal, though many censured his delays; but when the time comes you must strike hard, as Fabius did, or your waiting will be in vain, and fruitless.' Striking hard appears not to have been ruled out, the 'Fabian' tactic at this stage was for the purpose of taking counsel, discussing, working out their views.

The truth seems to be that, in these early years of the Socialist revival of the 'eighties, there was no hard and fast cleavage between the different Socialist groups; and the early Fabian Society had not yet formulated a body of doctrine peculiar to itself. Not only was there overlap and interchange between the Fabians and the S.D.F.; we find much the same group of people active in the Christian Socialist movement. Sydney Olivier, for instance, before he joined the Fabian Society, was one of the managing group of the journal *The Christian Socialist*.[4] Again, some of the early Fabians were associated with Anarchists. Mrs Charlotte M. Wilson, the wife of a well-to-do stockbroker, who was elected to the Fabian executive in December 1884, was a follower of Prince Kropotkin and for some years edited the Anarchist paper *Freedom*.[5]

---

[1] Minute Books at Fabian Society's Head Office, London. It is unfortunately not easy to check which of the original members of the Fabian Society had actually been members of the S.D.F., for vital S.D.F. records have been destroyed, and at least some of the Fabians were not so ready in later years to admit to their early 'indiscretions' as Hubert Bland was. H. M. Hyndman, *Further Reminiscences* (Macmillan, London, 1912), p. 212.

[2] *loc. cit.* and see generally H. M. Hyndman, *The Record of an Adventurous Life* (Macmillan, London, 1911), pp. 295-6, 334.

[3] '... as Mr Podmore explained in allusions to the victorious policy of Fabius Cunctator' (Minutes of the first meeting of F.S., and Pease, *op. cit.* p. 34). It is always taken for granted that the name of the Fabian Society derived from Q. Fabius Maximus (Cunctator); quite a different view of the early Fabians would emerge if it derived from K. Fabius Vibulanus. The motto is also supposed to have been written by Podmore (Pease, *op. cit.* p. 39).

[4] Pease, *op. cit.* p. 25.   [5] *Ibid.* p. 49.

The initial views of the Society were not at all clear. The Society's first Tract, which went to the press in April 1884, and which was drafted by W. L. Phillips, bore the title *Why are the Many Poor?* Though it argued that the Capitalist system produced inequality, and that the remedy lay in Socialism, it said nothing at all of the means of effecting the change to Socialism. That topic was then being debated in the earliest of the fortnightly lecture-discussions amongst members of the Society which were being held on Fridays in each others' houses. The second of these was a lecture on the Democratic Federation, which led to the resolution (moved by Bland): 'That whilst not agreeing with the statements and phrases used in the pamphlets of the Democratic Federation, and in the speeches of Mr Hyndman, the Society considers that the Democratic Federation is doing good and useful work and is worthy of sympathy and support.'[1] The Society's Tract No. 2, also issued in 1884, was a *Manifesto*, obviously drafted by Shaw, but the resolutions in it were discussed and passed separately by the Society, and several of them have a decidedly revolutionary flavour, in particular, one declaring: 'That we would rather face a Civil War than such another century of suffering as the present one has been.' E. R. Pease, for one, could remember objecting to this proposition,[2] but it was carried by a majority of the members. Indeed, if one were to judge merely by the Tracts, it would not seem that the situation had altered as late as 1886, when Tract No. 4, *What Socialism Is*, was issued. This Tract was divided into two parts, setting forth 'Anarchist' and 'Collectivist' views, for, it was said, these two trends had become clear and distinct in Continental Socialism, whereas 'English Socialism is not yet Anarchist or Collectivist, not yet definite enough in point of policy to be classified.' Mrs Wilson wrote the Anarchist case for this Tract, while the Fabian Collectivists contented themselves with reprinting an extract from the writings of the German Marxist, Bebel.[3]

All this does not amount to a demonstration that all the early Fabians were

---

[1] *Ibid*. p. 38. Other lectures mentioned in the Minutes of the Fabian Society (unfortunately the early Minutes are of a purely 'business' kind, and there is no record of what was said) include these: Miss C. Haddon, 21 March 1884 spoke on 'The Two Socialisms' (a note had been added later in Olivier's handwriting that this was devoted to a comparison of the socialism of the S.D.F. and that of the Fabian Society; but it is extremely doubtful if this was so—Olivier was not a member of the F.S. at this time, and it looks like an attempt to ante-date Fabian socialism); a paper on 'Surplus Value' was read on 20 June 1884; one on 'English Voluntary Socialism' on 4 July 1884; Mrs Wilson spoke on 'Anarchism' 7 November 1884; Miss Dale Owen on 'New Harmony' 5 December 1884; Bland on 'Revolutionary Prospects' 2 January 1885.

[2] *Ibid*. p. 43.

[3] Actually, the Fabians had applied to Engels to write this section of the Tract, but Engels had declined. G. Mayer, *Friedrich Engels* (Chapman & Hall, London, 1936), p. 251 attributes his aloofness to the fact that the Fabians 'rejected the class-war'. This was hardly true in 1886. Engels was interested only in proletarian movements, and refused to take the London Socialist 'Sects' (as he called them) seriously. No doubt he was particularly wary of lending the support of his name to what was the most insignificant and bourgeois of them all at this time.

revolutionary and believed in the possibility of 'a tremendous smash-up of existing society, to be succeeded by complete Socialism'.[1] Some, like Pease, Olivier, Webb and William Clarke, were sceptical of, if not hostile to, the more extreme doctrines of the S.D.F. from the beginning; others, like Keddell, Bland and Shaw, were at this time favourably disposed. What is demonstrated, however, is that the Fabian Society was influenced to no small degree by the Marxism of the S.D.F. in its earliest days. The disagreements between the S.D.F. and the Fabian Society were, as Shaw has said, 'latent and instinctive'[2] rather than positively doctrinal at this stage.

The belief that the Fabians were unaquainted with Marxist writings, or ignored them,[3] is also incorrect. This can be illustrated in detail later when the different aspects of Fabian theory and their derivation are considered, but it is worth noticing at this point what Marxist works were read by them, as shown by writings and records of discussions, and by the earliest edition of a reading-list for Fabians prepared by Graham Wallas and published in 1891.[4] None of Marx and Engels' philosophical writings appear to have been known to them, nor any of their writings which dealt in a purely theoretic way with the problem of historical causation.[5] What were available to them were Volume I of *Capital* (Eng. ed. 1886), and several of Marx and Engels' actual historical writings and expositions of 'scientific socialism'; namely, *The Communist Manifesto* (Eng. ed. 1848 and 1888), *The Civil War in France* (1871), *Socialism: Utopian and Scientific* (1892), and *The Conditions of the Working Classes in England in 1844* (Eng. ed. 1892). In addition the interpretations of Marxism given by H. M. Hyndman's in his *England for All* (1881), and *Historical Basis of Socialism in England* (1883) were quite familiar to the members of the Society. The particular kind of Marxist works in currency amongst the Fabians had an effect on the development of their own theory, as will be shown later.

What was the basis of the 'latent and instinctive' hostility of the Fabians to the S.D.F., which Shaw has mentioned? To say that the explanation lies in the fact that the Fabians were a group of 'middle-class intellectuals' while the S.D.F. had pretensions towards being a 'proletarian' organization is partly true but not perhaps very enlightening until the issues are made clearer. After all, some of the prominent leaders of the S.D.F. at this time might also be described as 'middle-class intellectuals'—Hyndman himself, William Morris, and H. H. Champion, to select a few principal names. Why did not the

---

[1] G. B. Shaw in Tract 41.
[2] *Ibid.*
[3] e.g. J. Strachey, *What Are We To Do?* (Gollancz, London, 1938), pp. 77–8
[4] Tract No. 29.
[5] This is not surprising. Most of them—*German Ideology, Critique of Political Economy, Ludwig Feuerbach*, and *Anti-Dühring*—were available only in German, where they were available at all, at that time.

Fabians follow the example of these men and join the S.D.F. instead of founding a separate organization? The answer lies to some extent in the character of Hyndman, who appears to have been a difficult leader to work with, but to a still larger extent in the violent and dangerous public reputation of the S.D.F. To be prominent in the S.D.F. one needed to possess that revolutionary zeal which overcomes fear of dismissal from employment, or a good private income or both. Most of the Fabians were less well situated financially than some of the S.D.F. leaders. In the way of social position, they had more to lose than their chains, yet not enough to emancipate them from the fear of loss of 'face' and loss of economic security while the Capitalist system endured. Speaking at street corners, taking up collections, organizing public processions and selling radical newspapers in the street were activities that appealed to only a minority of them.[1] Furthermore, the S.D.F.'s pretensions towards being a mass party (though in fact its membership remained pretty small until the dock strike of 1889[2]), caused it to be more passionate and more dogmatic in its written and spoken propaganda. It failed to provide that critical and educated discussion of social theory which the young men who formed the Fabian Society required. Many of the leaders of the S.D.F. who were their intellectual compeers were of an older generation.

The difference in the emotional atmosphere of the two groups may be captured in two entertaining fragments of reminiscence. The first by Bernard Shaw:

... it was at this period we contracted the habit of freely laughing at ourselves which has always distinguished us, and which has saved us from becoming hampered by the gushing enthusiasts who mistake their own emotions for public movements. From the first, such people fled after one glance at us, declaring that we not serious. Our preference for practical suggestions and criticisms, and our impatience of all general expressions of sympathy with working-class aspirations, not to mention our way of chaffing our opponents in preference to denouncing them as enemies of the human race, repelled from us some warm-hearted and eloquent Socialists, to whom it seemed callous and cynical to be even commonly self-possessed in the presence of the sufferings upon which Socialists make war. But there was far too much equality and personal intimacy among the Fabians to allow of any member presuming to get up and preach at the rest in the fashion which the working-classes still tolerate submissively from their leaders. We knew that a certain sort of oratory was useful for 'stoking up' public meetings; but we needed no stoking up, and, when any orator tried the process on us, soon made him understand that he was wasting his time and

[1] Shaw, Wallas and few other Fabians did some outdoor speaking for the S.D.F. in the early days. But there were frequent complaints in the Fabian Society that Fabians were backward in outdoor speaking, selling pamphlets in Hyde Park, etc., even for the F.S. itself. See H. M. Hyndman, *The Record of an Adventurous Life*, pp. 334–5 for an amusing description of the selling of *Justice*. Pease, *op. cit.* pp. 22–3, for Fabian distaste for S.D.F. activities and their incompatibility with employment. Note that Morris, Hyndman and Champion all had independent sources of income.
[2] G. Elton, *England Arise* (Cape, London, 1931), p. 83.

ours. I, for one, should be very sorry to lower the intellectual standard of the Fabians by making the atmosphere of its public discussions the least bit more congenial to stale declamation than it is at present. If our debates are to be kept wholesome, they cannot be too irreverent or too critical. And the irreverence, which has become traditional with us, comes down from those early days when we often talked such nonsense that we could not help laughing at ourselves.[1]

Hear now Henry M. Hyndman,[2] the S.D.F.'s leader. He writes:

. . . at a conference on unemployment . . . Macdonald[3] opened the discussion. Shaw thought he had closed it with one of his clever, satirical speeches directed towards the destruction of all enthusiasm in the gathering, whether this was intentional on Shaw's part or not. The chairman, whoever he was, thought also that the business of the meeting had concluded with Shaw's speech, and Shaw himself was quite convinced it had. Not so Macdonald. He claimed the right of reply. This was challenged by the chairman and supported by Shaw. Some dissension arose thereupon, but Macdonald very properly insisted upon his right and obtained his hearing. Then Shaw for once in his life had the opportunity of listening to such a rush of conclusive argument, thorough exposure and bitter ridicule turned upon himself, as he has experienced in speech or in writing few times in his life. Macdonald was in no humour to spare a man who brought heartless chaff and fine-chopped literary ribaldry into a discussion upon such a terrible subject to the whole working-class as unemployment. As Macdonald spoke, you could see the families starving, and their homes made desolate by the relentless and ruthless system of profitmongery that Shaw thought a fitting subject for jest. The audience sat at first in breathless silence and then Macdonald turned on Shaw. He simply ripped up Shaw's middle-class quips, and pseudo-economic fantasies, and threw the fragments at him, one after the other. He laughed heartily at Shaw's assumption of superority and obvious overrating of himself, and made the whole of those present laugh with him, not with Shaw. Winding up in a serious vein, he showed why, as a member of the working-class and a skilled tradesman himself, he knew that the question of unemployment lay at the root of all real change for the better, so long as Capitalism and Wagedom dominated society. Not the most skilled, thrifty, and sober worker and wage-earner present but by a turn of bad trade or a bout of ill-health might be reduced to almost hopeless misery, and be forced to join the great army of those whom Shaw's class had sucked wealth out of when toiling and stigmatized as loafers and wastrels when the 'labour market' was overstocked. I have never heard what Shaw thought of the trampling that befell his devoted carcass on this occasion, and I am convinced that his contemptuous attitude and joking were merely a pose. But he has never tried this sort of thing again with a working-class audience since Macdonald thus fell foul of him and offered up his smart witticisms as a sweet-smelling sacrifice on the altar of genuine conviction.

THE FABIANS BREAK WITH THE S.D.F.

This 'latent and instinctive' hostility of the Fabians was sufficient to keep them in a separate organization. But that organization, as we have seen, had

[1] Shaw, Tract 41.
[2] *Further Reminiscences* (ed. cit.), pp. 264–5.
[3] James Macdonald of the S.D.F., not James Ramsay MacDonald.

some close links with the S.D.F., and it is doubtful if these would have been so completely severed had it not been for a series of external events. The formulation of a distinctive Fabian doctrine was begun about the time of their break with the S.D.F. The causes of the breach are therefore interesting.

Some historians have put the formulation of Fabian doctrine prior to the final breach with the S.D.F. by suggesting that Sidney Webb, when he joined the Society in May 1885, immediately gave it a new doctrine and a new direction. The minutes of the Fabian Society record that Webb's first lecture to it, given before he joined, on 20 March 1885 was entitled 'The Way Out', and on this basis it has been assumed that he 'brought them down to earth' from their previous debates mainly upon abstract subjects.[1] This, however, seems unlikely. There is no record of what he said in 'The Way Out' lecture; but there are fairly lengthy reports of two other early lectures given by Webb to the Society in the journal *The Practical Socialist*, and these reports present a very different picture of Webb from that of the efficient practical man, with his mind already made up, telling his associates not to be silly. In fact they show him just beginning to find his way as a Socialist. The first of these lectures was an account of the Positivist social remedy so favourable that Webb was actually obliged to deny in discussion that he himself was a Positivist.[2] The tone of the second lecture entitled 'An Appeal to the Unconverted,' is surprisingly ethical and emotional, and is somewhat reminiscent of the speeches of William Morris,[3] except that Webb did not believe that revolution, or force of any kind, would be required in the advent of Socialism. He thought a change of opinion would accomplish all, carrying that sentiment very far indeed: 'As regards objections,' he is reported to have said, 'we need not trouble to deal with the selfish one of the man who says merely he means to keep what he has got. Dawning conscience and increased social intelligence will bring the sons of such men over to our ranks'. But the most remarkable passage is the following one:

Socialism is more than any Socialist, and its principles more than any system or scheme of reform. The Fabian Society has no such plan or scheme; we preach Socialism as a faith, as a scientific theory, as a judgment of morality on the facts of life. Socialism suffers if identified with any particular scheme, or even with Collectivism itself. In this, as in many other cases, we find the public are so much concerned with details, that they miss the principle: they cannot see the forest for the trees. Indeed, it is no more fair to identify Socialism with Collectivism than it would be to identify Christianity with Primitive Methodism or with the teachings of the Plymouth Brethren.

[1] M. A. Hamilton, *Sidney and Beatrice Webb: a study in contemporary biography* (Sampson Low, Marston & Co, London, n.d.), p.23.

[2] *The Practical Socialist*, vol. 1, No. 2, February 1886.

[3] R. H. Tawney in the article 'In Memory of Sidney Webb' in *Economica*, November 1947, p. 253, has remarked on Webb's 'unexpected' admiration of Morris.

In this same lecture, Webb was again inclined to treat Positivists and Anarchists as kinds of Socialists.[1] While, therefore, it seems clear that Webb, from his earliest Fabian days, was no revolutionist, it is most unlikely that his 'Fabianism' was already worked out and promptly stamped upon the Society as soon as he entered it; nor did any change in the Society's attitude occur immediately after his joining.[2] Fabian theory was worked out after the Fabians had been finally estranged from the S.D.F. by the incident of 'Tory gold' and the unemployed riots of 1886 and 1887.

The Fabians were not unaffected by the first split which occurred in the S.D.F. in December 1884, when the group led by William Morris, comprising both Anarchists and those directly under the influence of Friedrich Engels, had broken with Hyndman and gone to form the Socialist League. This event did not, however, separate the Fabian Society from both bodies, but merely served to divide those Fabians who had kept their membership of the S.D.F. After it, some Fabians (like the Fabian Secretary of that time—Frederick Keddell) remained members also of the S.D.F., while others (like the Blands) became also members of the Socialist League. But this split soon bore fruit in political action. Much has been made of the personal antagonisms between Hyndman on the one side and Morris and the 'Engels group' on the other in explanations that have been given of the split and these personal antagonisms certainly existed, strongly; but there were real political differences of opinion, too. The S.D.F. was divided in its views on the wisdom of standing candidates for Parliament, and the group that seceded under Morris's leadership included those who regarded such a move as useless (because Parliament was a 'bourgeois instrument' and nothing but the corruption of those elected could come of it) and those who regarded the action as premature.[3] In the following year, when the S.D.F. did put up candidates for Hampstead and Kennington (as well as John Burns at West Nottingham) in the General Election of November 1885, the Socialist League's view about prematurity was sufficiently confirmed. The S.D.F. candidates in London polled respectively twenty-seven and thirty-two votes. To make matters worse, it became widely known that the expenses of these two S.D.F. candidates had been paid by the Conservative Party to split the vote of the Liberals.

'Tory Gold' outraged the London Radicals. The Fabian Society and the Socialist League, both seeking to free themselves and Socialism generally from the taint, lost no time in passing resolutions condemning the S.D.F.'s action: '... the Socialist League views with indignation ... trafficking with the honour

---

[1] *The Practical Socialist*, vol. I, No. 6, June 1886. This lecture, somewhat altered, was published as a pamphlet. It was printed by The Leaflet Press, London, 1888. There is a copy in the British Library of Social and Political Science.

[2] Pease, *op. cit.* p. 47.

[3] E. Belfort Bax, *Reminiscences and Reflections of a Mid and Late Victorian* (Allen & Unwin, London, 1918), pp. 77–81.

of the Socialist Party . . . repudiates the tactics of the disreputable gang concerned in the recent proceedings', declared the Socialist League's resolution; '. . . calculated to disgrace the Socialist movement in England', said the Fabians. Hyndman was not the man to take these resolutions without a retort in kind, and from that time the Federation and *Justice*, its newspaper, treated the Fabian Society and the League as hostile bodies. A general sorting-out followed, so far as the Fabians and the S.D.F. were concerned. Fabians who had preserved their membership of the S.D.F. resigned from it, while Frederick Keddell, who hitherto had been secretary of the Fabian Society, resigned from the Society and went entirely over to the S.D.F. The unwarlike Pease was elected secretary in Keddell's place, while Webb was elected to fill the vacancy on the executive, also caused by his resignation.[1]

It was shortly after this affair that the first 'Fabian' journal appeared, in January 1886. *The Practical Socialist*, edited by Thomas Bolas, gives the fullest accounts of Fabian meetings (better than the Society's minute books) and forms the chief source of information of their doings in the years 1886 and 1887. In the first number of *The Practical Socialist* there is a report of a Fabian meeting addressed by Mrs Annie Besant on 'How Can We Nationalize Accumulated Wealth', where sharp exchange took place on the merits and possibilities of revolutionary methods. Two members of the S.D.F. at the meeting (John Burns was one of them) urged revolutionary action, and Mrs Besant retorted vigorously: 'Force indeed! What is your revolutionary strength in London; may we not gauge it by your fifty votes or so, at the late election—and bought and paid for with Tory Gold? . . .' The 'Tory Gold' incident brought home to all the Fabians—even to those of them not naturally inclined to favour slow and peaceful methods—the need for thinking in a realistic and not a romantic way about the actual strength and popularity of Socialism in the England of their time. In this, they were greatly helped by Mrs Annie Besant, whom they acknowledged to know, through her association with left-wing Radicalism and Bradlaugh, 'more of the views of the (educated) working-class than all the other leading Socialists put together'.[2]

The events of 1886 and 1887 completed the conversion of those Fabians who may still have needed converting from revolutionary methods. The unemployed riots of those years were at first encouraging, later disillusioning, to the revolutionists amongst all the Socialist groups. Hubert Bland has stated that, although he did not really believe Hyndman's confident prediction that the social revolution would occur in 1889, the anniversary of the French Revolution, he 'more than half hoped it might be true'. 'Personally,' he added, 'I gave the capitalist regime at least ten years of life.'[3] In these years the S.D.F.

---

[1] Pease, *op. cit.* p. 52.
[2] Bland's article in *The Practical Socialist*, vol. I, No. 10, October 1886.
[3] E. Nesbit Bland (ed.), *op. cit.* p. 223.

rehabilitated itself. 'Tory Gold' was forgotten in its vigorous and courageous, if largely ineffectual, leadership of the London unemployed. The situation appeared revolutionary enough to the S.D.F. Engels, who had seen a revolution or two in his time, was cynical and sneered at Hyndman and his followers.[1] But less experienced people might be forgiven for thinking that a revolutionary epoch had dawned at the outset of that grim and exciting time, with its hunger marches, the parades of the workless to the churches, the meetings in Hyde Park and Trafalgar Square, culminating in the two major incidents—the window-smashing in Pall Mall on 'Black Monday' (8 February 1886), which led to the arrest, trial, and acquittal of Hyndman, Champion, Burns, and Williams of the S.D.F., and 'Bloody Sunday' (13 November 1887) when Burns and Cunninghame Graham led the demonstration in Trafalgar Square in defence of the right of public meeting there and were forcibly dealt with by the police.[2] The outcome of these events was to confirm the Fabians in their anti-revolutionary position and their opposition to the S.D.F.

The Fabian Society as a whole took practically no part in the unemployed agitation. It was still little more than a drawing-room discussion group, and its chief contribution to the unemployment situation was the production of its 'first typically Fabian' document.[3] This was a report, prepared by a committee consisting of Bland, Hughes, Podmore, Stapleton, and Webb on 'The Government Organization of Unemployed Labour.'[4] The report is an interesting document; the work of several hands, it is a hotch-potch of the diverse opinions in the Society at this time. A section written by Webb contains economic doctrines so tender of private enterprise that it raises at least some doubt whether the author ought to be classed as a Socialist at all at this stage. E. R. Pease in his *History* admitted that the report showed 'immature judgement' but also claimed that it first pointed the way to higher Fabian things.[5] The Society's doubts at the time about its collective attitude were revealed when it was not accepted by the members as a regular Fabian Tract, but merely issued as a report printed for the information of members. When people were 'in so hot a temper on the social question'[6] the Society had not yet fully made up its mind whether the existing government was a fit body to receive Fabian instruction.

Apart from this report, the Fabians as a group did no more than many

---

[1] Letter, Engels to Bebel, 15 February 1886, in *Correspondence of Marx and Engels* (National Book Agency, Calcutta), p. 392. See also p. 369.

[2] For a contemporary account from a near-Fabian point of view see *Our Corner* for April 1888.

[3] Pease, *op. cit.* p. 57.

[4] *The Government Organization of Unemployed Labour:* Report made by a committee to the Fabian Society and ordered to be printed for the information of members (Geo. Standring, London, 1886).

[5] Pease, *op. cit.* p. 59.

[6] Shaw, Tract 41.

C

Radical Clubs. The Society affiliated to the Socialist Defence League and the Law and Liberty League, which took up the tasks of defending freedom of speech and the right of public meeting and of raising contributions for the defence of Socialists and others arrested by the police. But a few individual Fabians played a more active part. Mrs Besant, though she disapproved strongly of revolutionary methods, was in the thick of the fight, leading the Radicals in yet another struggle in defence of freedom of speech. Shaw was present at some of the 'incidents', observing how a relatively small number of trained men scattered a numerous mob like chaff, and himself playing a discreet rather than valorous role.[1]

As a result of their observation, even the 'left-wing'[2] Fabians, like Shaw and Bland, had decided about the unemployed that (in Bland's words): '. . . these unhappy people, though not without their importance in any quasi-political movement, are *not* the people to make a political revolution, or even to carry a great reform. The revolt of the empty stomach ends at the baker's shop'.[3] Indeed, other Socialists less susceptible than the Fabians to conversion from revolutionary methods, were suffering disillusion at this time.[4]

All the Fabians definitely abandoned the revolutionary idea, though the degree of reluctance with which they did so varied. Bland, summing up the situation in an article in *The Practical Socialist* of October 1886, gave his opinion that the hope of revolution arising out of the 'increasing misery' of the working–class and a revolt of the unemployed was futile. He still thought it 'not unlikely' that there would be an armed struggle before Socialism could finally be established, but such a struggle would be hopeless until the Socialists had much greater forces, and had taken at least the outworks of the Capitalist citadel. What was necessary, in his opinion, was the abandonment of revolutionary phraseology, a split with those who talked it, and the creation of a party that could win the adherence of the 'well-fed and educated workers', that could press for Socialist measures, build up Socialist strength and weaken the conservative position. Socialists, he claimed, should devote themselves to the difficult and detailed thinking out of constructive legislation. Clearly in Bland's view the political revolution, the armed clash, had become the final act in a long process of gradual change—the last desperate stand of the possessing class, when its position had become hopeless.

[1] A. Henderson, *George Bernard Shaw, Man of the Century* (Appleton-Century-Croft Inc., New York, 1956), pp. 233–4.
[2] I use the expression 'left-wing' with due reservation. At other times and on other matters (e.g. their attitude to the Boer War) Shaw and Bland could not be called 'left-wing'.
[3] *The Practical Socialist*, October 1886. Article on 'The Socialist Party in relation to Politics.'
[4] M. Beer, *A History of British Socialism* (G. Bell & Sons, London, 1929), vol. II, p. 264. See especially H. H. Champion in *Justice*, 14 August 1886. cf. Engels on street fighting in his preface to Marx's *Class Struggles in France*.

Shaw at this time rejected revolutionism even more decisively. He was to put his epitaph on it into his Fabian essay entitled 'The Transition to Social Democracy.'[1]

Let me, in conclusion [he wrote there], disavow all admiration for this inevitable, but sordid, slow, reluctant, cowardly path to justice. I venture to claim your respect for those enthusiasts who still refuse to believe that millions of their fellow creatures must be left to sweat and suffer in hopeless toil and degradation, whilst Parliaments and vestries grudgingly muddle and grope towards paltry instalments of betterment. The right is so clear, the wrong so intolerable, the Gospel so convincing, that it seems to them that it *must* be possible to enlist the whole body of workers—soldiers, police-men and all—under the banner of brotherhood and equality; and at one stroke to set Justice on her rightful throne. Unfortunately, such an army of light is no more to gathered from the human product of the nineteenth century civilization than grapes are to be gathered from thistles. But if we feel glad of the impossibility; if we feel relieved that the change is to be slow enough to avert personal risk to ourselves; if we feel anything less than acute disappointment and bitter humiliation at the dis-covery that there is yet between us and the promised land a wilderness in which many must perish miserably of want and despair; then I submit to you that our institutions have corrupted us to the most dastardly degree of selfishness. The Socialists need not be ashamed of beginning as they did by proposing militant organization of the working-class and general insurrection. The proposal proved impracticable and it has now been abandoned—not without some outspoken regrets—by English Socia-lists. . . .

The more 'right-wing' Fabians probably did not share these regrets, nor did they need to be won away from revolutionary methods. Webb at no time seems to have had much patience with the S.D.F. Marxists; Pease would not have assented to the proposition that revolution, if possible, would be right;[2] Annie Besant, though she had associated with the S.D.F. in the early days, brought with her strong sympathies with Liberal-Radical ideas and methods into the Society, and she had early gone into print recommending 'evolu-tionary' Socialism; and J. C. Foulger had, earliest perhaps of all the Fabians, attacked Hyndman, in a very able article in the journal *Today*, for his advocacy of revolution.[3] A unified, distinctively 'Fabian' view of Socialism emerged only after the 'left-wing' group of members had broken with Marxism, but those who most closely maintained their ties with Liberal-Radicalism had already begun to think along evolutionary Socialist lines.

THE FABIANS BREAK WITH THE SOCIALIST LEAGUE

The breach with the S.D.F. and the doctrine of revolution did not solve all differences within the Fabian Society. This can be seen in the pages of *The Practical Socialist*, which properly should be called the journal of the 'right-

[1] G. B. Shaw (ed.): *Fabian Essays in Socialism* (Walter Scott, London, 1889), pp. 200–1.
[2] Pease, *op. cit.* p. 43, (demurring to Tract 2)
[3] *Today*, vol. II, July–December 1884.

wing' group amongst the Fabians rather than a Fabian journal as it was not issued by the Society itself. *The Practical Socialist* did not take the subtitle 'A monthly review of evolutionary or non-revolutionary socialism' until its thirteenth number (of January 1887), but its character was plain from the first. In the first number, all the contributors deplored the revolutionism of the S.D.F., but disagreed sharply in their definition of the true methods of 'practical socialism'. The editor quoted Lord Salisbury and passages from the conservative *Evening News* with approval, where Socialism was equated with extensions of State interference. Another writer[1] put forward a view popular in the Socialist League, that Socialists should content themselves with making the ethical claim that only those who were actual producers should share in the rewards of production, and not worry about ways and means of achieving it; ways and means, he declared, were 'bridges provided for those who will not cross by them because they have not been persuaded that they would be better on the other side of the river than this one. Persuade them, and they will cross over if they have to swim for it. This persuasion, then, seems to be the most *practical* thing that the Socialists can, at present, take in hand'. The 'Notes' column maintained that anyone who exposed an administrative abuse or took any measure to improve public administration prepared the way for Socialism, because distrust of the State's administrative efficiency was a great obstacle to the progress of Socialist doctrines. Yet, in the same number, Mrs Charlotte Wilson had an article recommending Anarchism.

These differences were to be ironed out by the strengthening of the Fabians' ties with the Radicals, and a breach with the Socialist League and the Anarchists, developments which took place in 1886. In separating from the S.D.F. the Fabians had repudiated revolution; in separating from the Anarchists and the Socialist League, the Fabians were repudiating 'Impossibilism' (the contemporary jargon term for the rejection of constitutional methods) in all its forms.

By 1886 the Anarchists were already beginning to make progress in the Socialist League, though it was not until 1888 that they had become so strong in it that the 'Engels group' was expelled and formed the independent Bloomsbury Socialist Society out of one of the League's branches. In 1889 Morris himself was deprived of the editorship of the League's paper *Commonweal* by the Anarchists, and in the following year Morris and his personal followers abandoned the League altogether to the Anarchists and went to form their own small Hammersmith Socialist Society. But the beginnings of this development could be discerned already in the latter part of 1886, and the Fabian leaders found themselves meeting sharp criticism from the Anarchists both within the Fabian Society and from those in the Socialist League who occasionally attended their meetings.[2] Eventually, the Fabians decided to

[1] W. K. Burton.   [2] Shaw, Tract 41.

bring the issue to a public debate. In September 1886 invitations were sent out to 'all Socialist bodies in London'[1] to debate a resolution: 'That it is advisable that Socialists should organise themselves as a political party for the purpose of transferring into the hands of the whole working community full control over the soil and the means of production, as well as over the production and distribution of wealth,' together with an amendment proposed by William Morris adding the following words:

But whereas the first duty of Socialists is to educate the people to understand what their present position is and what the future might be, and to keep the principle of Socialism steadily before them, and whereas no Parliamentary party can exist without compromise and concession, which would hinder that education and obscure those principles, it would be a false step for Socialists to attempt to take part in the Parliamentary contest.

The issue, as will be seen, was not directly a discussion of Anarchism, because Morris's rider was sufficiently wide to find support amongst anti-Parliamentarians who were not Anarchists (like Morris himself). The issue was really, in the Socialist jargon of the time, between 'Possibilism' and 'Impossibilism';[2] the debate was between the Fabian leaders and the S.D.F. (which had sent along speakers to this meeting) on the one side and the root-and-branch anti-Parliamentarian section (including the Anarchists) of the Socialist League on the other. The Fabian leaders claimed that the result of this debate was to convince them of 'the advisability of setting to work by ordinary political methods and having done with vague exhortations to Emancipate the Workers'.[3] Nevertheless, the issue with Mrs Wilson and the Fabian-Anarchists was not settled at once. It was solved temporarily by a compromise arrangement: at the end of 1886 a Fabian Parliamentary League was formed, which members could join or not join as they chose.

The *Manifesto* of this Fabian Parliamentary League, dated February 1887, contained the first clear statement of Fabian tactics as they later came to be understood. Its preamble also suggests another factor which persuaded the Fabians to take an active part in politics, when it pointed to the success of Socialist parties abroad. The 'progress of the Socialist party in the German Reichstag, in the legislatures of the United States, and in the Paris Municipal Council' were said not only to have 'proved the possibility' of parliamentary action by Socialists, but to have 'rendered it imperative' for English Socialists to do likewise. The *Manifesto* showed a determination to take a full part in politics at all levels, and stressed the importance of work in the municipalities, which was later to become so distinctive a feature of Fabian activity.

[1] Report in *Today*, October 1886.
[2] The use by the Fabians of these terms indicates their familiarity with the theoretical divisions amongst French Marxists at this time. Fabian policy soon came to resemble that of the French 'Possibilistes' quite closely in some respects.
[3] Shaw, Tract 41, Pease, *op. cit.* p. 67.

This compromise arrangement with the Fabian-Anarchists did not last long. A little over a year later, in April 1888, about the same time as Shaw's refutation of Anarchism was written,[1] the Parliamentary League was turned into the Political Committee of the Society—the first move in its reabsorption, as the Society as a whole came to accept its principles. The Anarchists became converted, or left the Society;[2] Mrs Wilson herself retained nominal membership, but for the next twenty years devoted herself to Anarchist work outside the Society, returning in 1908 to active membership to found the Fabian Women's Group.

FABIAN TIES WITH LONDON RADICALS

The repudiation of anti-Parliamentary doctrines and the acceptance of 'Possibilism' was partly promoted by, and in turn strengthened, Fabian ties with the Radicals. Significantly, *The True Radical Programme*[3] was the name of the sole Tract produced by the Parliamentary League in its year of existence.

A conference of Radical and Socialist clubs and societies promoted by the Fabian Society was held over three days in June 1886. Its object was 'to discuss the present commercial system, and the better utilisation of national wealth for the benefit of the Community'.[4] The Conference was modelled on the Industrial Remuneration Conference, which had been held a year previously, and in which Shaw and Glode Stapleton had taken part as Fabian delegates;[5] and the hand of Mrs Annie Besant can be detected in its organization. The powerful support and strenuous activity which Annie Besant devoted to the Fabian Society in its early days[6] has hardly been done justice by the Society's official historian. Mrs Besant came into the Society as a well-known figure in Radical and Secularist circles, and as editor of Freethought journals and newspapers, she was able to give the Fabians valuable publicity. She was determined, perhaps a little prematurely, to drag the Society from its drawing-room obscurity into the public view, and set it forth as the chief exponent of non-revolutionary Socialism. She wrote pamphlets,[7] and articles in the journals,[8]

[1] 'A Refutation of Anarchism': first published in *Our Corner* of May, June and July 1888. Later revised in 1893 and issued as Tract 45 under the title *Impossibilities of Anarchism*.
[2] Tract 41.   [3] Tract 6.   [4] *Our Corner*, July 1886.
[5] *Industrial Remuneration Conference: The Report of the Proceedings and Papers read in the Prince's Hall, Piccadilly, under the Presidency of the Rt Hon. Sir Charles W. Dilke Bart, M.P. on the 28, 29 and 30 January 1885* (Cassell & Co. Ltd), 1885. This contains a report of Shaw's speech.
[6] See Report of the Special Committee appointed in February 1906 to consider measures for increasing the scope, influence, income and activity of the Society, together with the Executive Committee's Report and Resolution thereon. Printed privately, the Fabian Society, London, November 1906. There is a tribute to the work of Mrs Besant at p. 32 (in Exec. Reply).
[7] *Modern Socialism* (Freethought Publishing Co. 1886).
[8] The early Fabian Tracts were also published in Mrs Besant's journal *Our Corner*.

she debated the merits of Socialism in public against Bradlaugh and Foote and other great platform 'draws',[1] she proposed the resolution of 5 February 1886, which permitted the setting up of branches of the Fabian Parliamentary League,[2] and subsequent reports in *Our Corner* tell of these branches being formed after speeches by Mrs Besant. The Fabian conference of June 1886 was part of her campaign to make the Fabians known to a wide circle of Radical Clubs and Secular Societies.[3]

Mrs Besant's object was achieved, and the Fabian Conference of 1886 'signalized' the Society's 'repudiation of political sectarianism'.[4] The S.D.F. refused to take part, but fifty-three other societies, Socialist, Secularist, and Radical, sent delegates. The Socialist League, the Socialist Union,[5] the Guild of St Matthew, and the Anarchist Group of Freedom were represented; so were the Land Restoration Leagues of England, Scotland, and Ireland, and Land Nationalization Society, the National Secular Society, the leading Radical Clubs of London and its environs, and the Socialist Societies of Sheffield, Bristol, and Edinburgh. Many papers were read, mostly devoted to an assault on private property in land. Peasant proprietorship found scant favour, and there was a fairly general insistence on the need for gradual change to a better order. But some were for single-tax, and others against it; most were eventually in favour of full land nationalization, but Bradlaugh thought the problem could be solved by his Parliamentary Bill to force proprietors to use their land, or give it up to the community; many favoured compensation or some measure of relief for landlords, but the representatives of the Woolwich Radical Club thought the poor not the rich deserved compensation. Sidney Webb presented a survey of the doctrines of economic rent. When, during the next two days, Socialism was discussed, the divergence of opinion increased. The advantages of Socialism and individualism were debated, and profit-sharing devices and co-operation were brought into the argument as alternative schemes. John M. Robertson of the National Secular Society read a paper on taxation, which the Fabians found interesting. Finally, William Morris excited hot controversy by a paper in which he maintained the hopelessness of political action. On the other hand, Dr Pankhurst from the Chair, noting 'the growing urgency of labour questions' recommended 'union between Democrats and Socialists',

---

[1] 'Why I am a Socialist' Bradlaugh v. Annie Besant. 'Is Socialism Sound?' Verbatim report of a four nights' debate between Annie Besant and G. W. Foote. Revised by both disputants (Progressive Publishing Co. London, 1887).

[2] *Our Corner*, March 1886, Fabian Notes Column, (It is true this move was premature, and the existence of these branches was brief. Shaw, Tract 41).

[3] *Our Corner*, March 1886 for the text of the invitations.

[4] Shaw, Tract 41.

[5] This was another breakaway group from the S.D.F. It published a paper *The Socialist* (1st issue, July 1886). J. Ramsay MacDonald was a member of its 'managing and editing Committee'.

and Annie Besant spoke strongly in favour of the 'use of political means to obtain the objects of Socialism'.[1]

Bernard Shaw declared that the conference revealed that the Fabians 'had nothing immediately practical to impart to the Radicals and they had nothing to impart to us'.[2] That may have been so, if the emphasis is purely upon the practical; although Shaw admitted that the Fabians gained some important ideas from J. M. Robertson's paper on taxation.[3] Most of the Fabians had come to Socialism through Radicalism and all were familiar with Radical programmes. The conference's main use was to make the Fabian Society known; it had little to impart because the Fabians had absorbed so much of Radicalism and were only beginning to formulate their own programme. Their Tracts published after 1887 show that they had definitely adopted Radical political methods, and that they had taken up certain specific Radical demands with the object of pressing them further in a Socialist direction. Fabian propaganda for the next few years was mainly directed towards the Radical Clubs of London. *The True Radical Programme* is the title of Fabian Tract No. 6 of 1887. In short, the Fabian Society by 1887 decided to take up the task which the Democratic Federation had originally set itself but had abandoned after three years for the path of extreme Socialism: the task of winning the London Radical Clubs to an advanced progressive programme.

THE FIRST STATEMENTS OF THE FABIAN PROGRAMME

At the time when the infant Society entered properly into the political life of London, Radicalism was in ferment. Manhood suffrage had been achieved by the Reform Acts of 1884-5, and there was a general feeling that the Radicals would have to look around for new worlds to conquer. Joseph Chamberlain had shown one way with his 'Unauthorised Radical Programme,' but the official Liberal Party refused to be moved. The Fabian Tract of 1887 had as its purpose an examination of the official Liberal-Radical Programme of Nottingham, October 1887, which it declared to be rather less Radical than Lord Randolph Churchill's 'Tory Democracy' (though Lord Randolph was not treated with any favour on that account). Consequently the Fabians put forward certain practical measures as essential to a 'True Radical Programme.' These measures, amplified and modified by Tracts No. 8 (of 1889) and No. 11 (of 1890), represent the sum and substance of Fabian political demands of the first period. The many other Tracts issued between 1887 and 1891 were really

---

[1] There is a short report of the conference in *Our Corner* for July 1886, and a fuller one in *The Practical Socialist*, July 1886. The MS. report is in the British Library of Social and Political Science (R. (Coll.) Misc. 98), but unfortunately Webb's and Robertson's papers have been removed from the file. However, it is possible to gain some idea of what they said from the report of the discussion. This is a valuable document in the history of London Radicalism.

[2] Tract 41.   [3] *Ibid.*

nothing but restatements of one or more of these demands, either in the same or more elaborate terms.[1]

Almost none of the individual items in their programme actually originated with the Fabians. Each of them, taken separately, could be discovered in the programmes of one or other of the Radical or Socialist bodies of the time. What novelty there was rested in their combination into one programme, and in the design of bridging the gap between Radicalism and Socialism. This bridge was provided by their taxation proposals—by their conclusion that taxation of unearned incomes was the way to arrive at Socialism without great fuss. Certainly this was merely an extension of the Radical proposal (popularised by Henry George) for dealing with the landlords. No doubt the Fabians had their attention drawn to the possibility of using taxation as a means of redistribution of incomes by some of the Radicals of the extreme left-wing. The Democratic Federation in its *Socialism Made Plain* of 1883 had also demanded progressive taxation on incomes over £200 without, however, attaching any more general importance to it. But the claim that the path to complete Socialism lay through taxation (coupled with gradual extensions of State and Municipal enterprise) provided a degree of novelty lacking in their other practical proposals. Even their 'municipalization' proposals, usually regarded as so distinctive of Fabianism were, as will be shown later, taken over from a section of the London Radicals.

The development of Fabian doctrine in each of its aspects will be dealt with in subsequent chapters, and the views expressed in these early programmes will provide the starting-place of these discussions. Nevertheless, it may be convenient to conclude this chapter with a very brief outline of their main proposals, as set forth in the Tracts published between 1887 and 1891. Their proposals may be classified under four headings:

(1) Extension of democracy and the improvement of the machinery of democratic government.

(2) Extension of government powers to improve community welfare (especially the welfare of the working-class).

(3) Positive government action to promote equality.

(4) Other miscellaneous items.

The Fabians' proposals for the extension and improvement of democracy ranged widely, from the monarchy and Parliament down to the lowest local government bodies. A tinge of polite Republicanism lay behind the demand

---

[1] Tracts 30 to 37 are simply sections of Tract 8 printed separately; Tract 10 is a summary of the main points of Tract 8; Tracts 20 and 21, and 25 to 28 cast points of Tract 8 into the form of 'questions for candidates'; Tract 17 gives a more detailed argument for one of the points of Tract 8; Tract 18 does for Bristol what Tract 8 did for London; Tracts 9 and 14 cast points of Tracts 6 and 11 into the form of parliamentary Bills (probably this effective propaganda idea came from a debating-club 'The Charing Cross Parliament' in which the Fabians as members of the 'government' had to bring 'Bills' before the 'House').

for the abolition of 'all hereditary legislators', while Chartist echoes were awakened by their demand for annual parliaments. Elections for the House of Commons were to be made fully democratic—on the basis of universal suffrage, with a 'second ballot' on Continental lines to avoid split votes. Right from the outset, the Fabians demanded the extension of the suffrage to women. This was probably one of the Society's most daring proposals at this time. While there was nothing specially new in the demand, the Fabian Society must have been one of the first *political* societies to make it part of its pro-gramme.[1] Members of Parliament, indeed the members of all governing bodies, were to be paid, so that working-class people could participate fully, and election expenses too were to be borne by the State. Local Government was to be democratized, systematized and simplified. The Local Government Act of 1888, and subsequent enactments of the 'nineties, provided many of the Local Government reforms that the Fabians, along with other Radical groups, were seeking.

Their proposals for the extension of government powers to improve com-munity welfare were of two kinds: the enlargement of existing powers, and the creation of certain new ones. The Fabians urged the extension of the Factory Acts to prevent sweating, and an increase of Government activity in the spheres of housing, health, education, poor relief, etc. At that time the most controversial Fabian proposal along these lines was that for a legal eight hours day. This proposal, general amongst all Socialist bodies and in some Labour-Radical circles, dating back to the Owenite period, and first raised at a Trade Union Congress in 1879 by Adam Weiler, an old Marxist,[2] appears to have commended itself to the Fabians after Tom Mann's first lecture to the Society in April 1886.[3] The Fabians' original and controversial addition was a method for enforcing it, Webb's device of 'Trade Option', which will be described later.

Additional powers obviously were required for any positive Socialist action, even though the action of this kind envisaged by the Fabians in their pro-grammes of this period is fairly limited. They called for the 'nationalization' only of railways, canals, and coal-mines, and the 'municipalization' of certain main services, such as water supply, gas, docks, markets, and tramways. Apart from these, the Fabian 'Socialism' of this early period consisted mainly in calling upon Local Government to make some provision for the unemployed. With this end in view, Local Government Authorities were to be given power to aquire land compulsorily, to engage in all branches of industry 'in fullest

---

[1] The Fabian Society as a whole from its earliest days supported woman suffrage, though a few individual Fabians were opposed, Bland for instance; see Doris Langley Moore, *E. Nesbit: a biography* (Ernest Benn, 1933), p. 259. Tract 2 of 1884 states the principle: 'That men no longer need special privileges to protect them against women, and that the sexes should henceforth enjoy equal political rights.'

[2] S. & B. Webb, *History of Trade Unionism* (Longmans, 1907), p.375.

[3] *Practical Socialist*, May 1886.

competition with private industrial enterprise' and provide 'free and honour-
able municipal employment' for the unemployed. The most optimistic view of
municipal employment is that in Mrs Besant's lecture in the famous *Fabian
Essays* volume, which is largely taken up with a scheme for 'County Farms',
combining some of the ideas in the early Fabian 'Report on the Government
Organization of Unemployed Labour' with those favoured by certain clergymen.[1] The plan was for the County Councils to put the unemployed to work
in county farms and municipal workshops. The optimistic way in which
these concerns were expected to compete with private enterprise and drive it
out of business brought a shadow of an older form of Socialism, that of Louis
Blanc, into Fabian theory. Mrs Besant's County Farms did not long hold
favour in the Fabian Society, but the idea of municipal enterprise competing
with private enterprise and beating it at its own game, persisted much longer.

The Fabians hoped for Government action to promote equality through
education and through taxation. At the lowest level of the educational scale
they expressed their approval of compulsory education, demanding that it also
be made free, and adding that poor Board School children should be provided
by the State with one good meal a day. In the higher ranges of education, they
urged that the State should provide an adequate 'scholarship ladder' to
university level, so that able students should not be hampered by poverty.
Educational opportunity would 'level up', while taxation would 'level down'.
Heavy taxation of unearned incomes was envisaged: 'How high do we want to
tax it? Twenty shillings in the pound will satisfy us. But we will take an
instalment to begin.'[2] The National Parliament was to impose a steeply
progressive income tax and high death duties, while the municipalities were to
be allowed to impose land taxes and death duties on land values.

There was a form of Radical egalitarianism, however, to which the Fabians,
as Socialists, were unalterably opposed. This was the Chamberlain-Collings
'three-acres-and-a-cow' proposal. The Fabians expressed their hostility to any
plans for creating a class of peasant proprietors in England. As an alternative,
they proposed municipal ownership of land, and its lease in small-holdings and
allotments. The Fabians also opposed the Leasehold Enfranchisement Bill of
1891, which was intended to empower leaseholders of houses built on land let
for ninety-nine years to purchase the freehold at a valuation. They looked on
this proposal as the urban equivalent of the three-acres-and-a-cow.

A couple of other 'miscellaneous' items of Fabian policy of this period also
need to be mentioned. These are their attitude to Irish Home Rule and to the
Army. Home Rule for Ireland was a major demand of the Radicals; the
Fabians supported it, giving as a reason that Irish affairs were being used by

---

[1] Rev. Herbert V. Mills, *Poverty and the State: or Work for All*, 1886. See also General
Booth, *Darkest England and the Way Out*.
[2] Tract 6.

politicians as an excuse for neglecting or avoiding measures of social reform in England. Amongst the series of 'questions to Parliamentary Candidates' attached to Tract 11 was one asking the candidate whether he would oppose any settlement of the Irish land question which did not leave the matter to be dealt with by an Irish Parliament.

The Fabian attitude to the army was expressed not in any of the publicly issued Tracts of this time, but in their 'Report on Government Organization of Unemployed Labour.' Like the Social Democratic Federation, they favoured a National Militia, recruited by compulsory service, to replace the standing army. The idea behind the S.D.F.'s demand was simply to replace the forces of the State by the citizens in arms (a principle more revolutionary in theory than in practice). The Fabians, however, justified their plea for the same measure on the somewhat vaguer ground that compulsory military service would promote 'the growth of social consciousness'. Later on, after the Boer militia had put up a brave showing against the British regular army, the Fabians were to revive this proposal in a celebrated Tract.[1]

Such was the Fabian policy of the first period, 1887-1891; we have now to see the theory that justified it, and its subsequent development and modification.

[1] *Fabianism and the Empire* (1900).

CHAPTER II

FABIAN ECONOMICS AND SOCIOLOGY

ORIGIN OF THE FABIAN THEORY OF RENT

THE earliest contribution of the Fabians to social theory was in the field of economics;[1] consequently we shall begin with it, although it is the most difficult and indigestible part of their doctrine. Discussion of the sources of the doctrine can profitably be interwoven with the exposition and criticism, for, in general terms, its sources are fairly obvious. In its first stages, Fabian thinking derived from the Ricardian-Benthamite school, in the state to which it had developed immediately after the death of John Stuart Mill. When the Fabians came to it, that school had been not greatly disturbed by the criticism of Marx, and no more than jolted by the astonishing irruption of Henry George, barging into Utilitarian-Radical circles in England (as Morley said) like a dinosaur into Pall Mall. Stanley Jevons, with his 'final utility' (or marginal utility) theory, was pointing a new way out of the difficulties into which the Labour theory of value had led the Classical School of economists. At the same time, or soon after, Fabian thought was strongly influenced by the fundamental criticism of theoretical economics deriving from Auguste Comte, expressed by his disciples, the English Positivists, and the somewhat similar criticism coming from the English followers of the German Historical School.

Amongst these influences, that of Henry George was almost certainly of least theoretical importance. His main views were already present, in rather more acceptable theoretic form, in English Liberal-Radicalism; and the Natural Rights philosophy, in which, as an American, he presented his ideas, was indeed considered as extinct as a dinosaur in English intellectual circles in the 'eighties. It was as an agitator and propagandist that George was

---

[1] A preliminary question no doubt arises here: is it possible to speak of 'Fabian economics' at all? The only obligation of members of the Society was to subscribe to its Basis, and to take some part in the activities of the Society, and in one of its Tracts (No. 70) it was specifically declared that the Fabian Society 'has no distinctive opinions on the Marriage Question, Religion, Art, abstract Economics, historic Evolution, Currency, or any other subject than its own special business of practical Democracy and Socialism'. The reason for this statement will be discussed later; for the moment all that is necessary is to show that it denies too much. Though there was always some division of opinion in the Society on abstract economics, we can in fact discover a clear point of view expressed in Fabian Tracts and other publications, and referred to by leading members of the Society as 'Fabian Economics'; as an example, E. R. Pease writes in his *History* (*op. cit.* p. 246): '... the Fabians, throwing over Marx's inaccurate term "surplus value" base their socialism on the Law of Rent, because, as they allege, this law negatives both equality of income and earnings in proportion to labour ...' Is it possible, in any case, to have distinctive views on Socialism and Democracy without having a good deal to do, at least by implication, with abstract economics?

influential. His eloquent writings and lectures brought many young men of the 'eighties, including some Fabians, to think along lines which were to lead them to Socialism. Furthermore, Henry George's picturesque manner of presenting economic theory no doubt influenced the form of some Fabian propaganda. Bernard Shaw's contribution, the 'Economic Basis,' in *Fabian Essays* resembles closely in some of its features a chapter in *Progress and Poverty*,[1] although, it must be added, Henry George's chapter itself is simply a variation on an older theme.[2]

As a starting-point in their Socialist thinking for some Fabians Henry George cannot be overlooked; but in thinking socialistically they discovered that the person they had then to confront was Karl Marx, either at first hand, or as relayed, rather imperfectly, through Hyndman and the stalwarts of the Social Democratic Federation. Edward Pease says: 'I find that my copy of the French edition of *Das Kapital* is dated 8 October 1883; but I do not think that any of the original Fabians had read the book or had assimilated its ideas at the time the Society was founded.'[3] That no doubt is true, of the time of Society's *founding;* but the leaders of the Society at least did not long remain in ignorance. The most important time in the working out of a distinctively Fabian point of view was the period when meetings were held of the group which called itself the Hampstead Historic Club. This began as a Marxist reading circle at the house of Mrs Charlotte Wilson early in 1885 and later met in other places, and finally at the Hampstead Public Library. The meetings were continued for several years. At the club, *Capital* was read out from the French translation, until the company fell to disputation. And Shaw tells us what their arguments were about:

F. Y. Edgeworth as a Jevonian, and Sidney Webb as a Stuart Millite, fought the Marxian value theory tooth and nail; whilst Belfort Bax and I, in a spirit of transcendent Marxism, held the fort recklessly,[4] and laughed at Mill and Jevons. The rest kept an open mind and skirmished on either side as they felt moved. . . . The controversy raged at Hampstead until Bax shook the dust of the heath off his boots; and the Historic Club, having had enough of impassioned disputes as to whether the

[1] H. George, *Progress and Poverty*, Bk. IV, Ch. 2.
[2] 'Political economists are fond of Robinson Crusoe . . .' K. Marx, *Capital* (Everyman), p. 50. And cf. Ch. 2. of Ricardo's *Principles*.
[3] Pease, *op. cit.* pp. 24–5.
[4] What Shaw made of the Labour Theory of Value in his Marxist days may be seen in his *An Unsocial Socialist*. The volume *Bernard Shaw and Karl Marx: a Symposium* edited by R. W. Ellis (Random House, N.Y. 1930) is also useful as a neat anthology of Shaw's articles dealing with this subject. It is apparent that Shaw was fundamentally mistaken in at least one aspect of Marx's value theory. He contended in his article in *Today* of May 1889 that Marx's admission that labour was sold at its value could be used to conceal or deny the fact of surplus value; but this overlooks the distinction Marx drew, and which Engels claimed was his main original contribution to the value theory, between labour and labour-force (or labour-power). Certainly if it were held that labour was sold at its value then surplus value could not arise, but with the selling of the worker's entire labour-force the situation is quite otherwise.

value of Mrs Wilson's vases was fixed by the labour socially necessary to produce them, by the cost of production on the margin of cultivation, or by the 'final utility' of the existing stock of vases, insisted on passing to the later chapters and dropping the subject.[1]

These discussions, continued at the Hampstead Historic Club, had begun earlier for some Fabians, when the Rev. Philip H. Wicksteed, a disciple of Jevons, had contributed an article to the socialist journal *Today*,[2] of October 1884 in which he had criticised Marx's value theory from the Jevonian point of view. In this article, he argued that Marx had fallen into error in his elimination argument at the beginning of *Capital*, where he excluded all things but abstract human labour as the possible measure of value. Wicksteed contended that amongst the excluded things was 'abstract utility', which exchangeable goods also have in common. Following then the Jevonian argument, he suggested, by the 'law of indifference', 'the abstract utility of the last available increment of any commodity determines the ratio of exchange of the whole of it'. Having substituted this theory for Marx's variation of the Classical value theme, Wicksteed went on to attack the Marxist 'surplus value' theory, saying that, if it could be shown that the value of labour-force is not determined by the amount of labour required to produce it, then Marx had failed to show 'any immanent law of capitalistic production by which a man who purchases labour-force at its value will extract from its consumption a surplus value'. To this article, Shaw had replied in the January 1885 number of *Today*. His reply was not so much a defence of Marx and the labour theory of value, as a light skirmishing assault on the Jevonian theory which Wicksteed had suggested as an alternative. Unfortunately, Shaw's objections to the use of the utility concept were of a kind that the Jevonians, in formulating their theory, must already have considered, though he did not fail to emphasise the importance of the supply side in the determination of value. Wicksteed's rejoinder (April 1885) was brief and he wound up by recapitulating his main point:

Only a single word in conclusion [he wrote], on the importance of this controversy. It is not a mere question of abstract reasoning (although, if it were, that could hardly be urged in its disparagement by an admirer of Marx). It affects the whole system of economics, and more particularly Marx's economics. In admitted contradiction to apparent facts, and without (at present) any attempt to remove the apparent contradiction, Marx by sheer logic attempts to force us into the admission that 'profits', 'interest', and 'rent' *must* have their origin in the 'surplus value' that results from purchasing 'labour force' at its value and selling wares at their value. The key-stone of the arch is the theory of value adopted by Marx, and I have tried to show that it is not sound. . . .

Wicksteed's criticism raised the question whether the theory of surplus value was necessarily dependent upon the labour theory of value—a most serious

[1] Article: 'Bluffing the Value Theory,' in *Today*, vol. II, No. 66, May 1889.
[2] *Today* was at that time edited by Belfort Bax and J. L. Joynes; later Hubert Bland took over the editorship.

problem for Socialists. The theory of surplus value was Marx's attempt to prove even in the 'very Eden of the innate Rights of Man'—the capitalist economists' state of perfect competition—the workers would be cheated of the full fruits of their labour by the capitalists.[1] The theory was not invented by Marx, but taken over, together with the labour theory of value from earlier writers. Marx's special contribution was the removal of a logical difficulty in reconciling the surplus-value theory, which was current amongst unorthodox and socialistic economists, with the labour theory of value, which was generally accepted at that time. Marx's economic theory is a rigorously worked out logical system. The labour theory of value and the theory of surplus value are used as a key in his analysis of 'the laws of motion' of capitalist society. They enable him to demonstrate that the 'contradictions' of capitalism, which produce its 'movement', are to be found in its productive base and relations of production, and are therefore incapable of superficial remedies. From his analysis of these 'laws of motion' follow his predictions concerning the fate of capitalism: recurrent crises, and the 'increasing misery' of the working-class, which will eventually lead the system to its doom. Wicksteed claimed that, by bringing forward an entirely different theory of the determinant of value, he had struck away the foundation of Marx's arguments and brought the whole edifice down in ruins.

What reply could Socialists make to Wicksteed's claim? Some modern writers have argued that the theory of value is not an important or essential part of Marx's theoretical structure, and that the more 'scientific' parts, dealing with the 'laws of motion' of capitalism, may be considered independently of it.[2] As we shall see, this view has some affinities with the attitude eventually taken up by the Fabians, though it tends to be more radical than theirs. We may be confident that Marx himself would have repudiated it; in fact, the modern attitude is the product of more than one generation of economic thinking in which the discussion of theories of value (in the Marxist

[1] On this, see M. Dobb, *Political Economy and Capitalism* (Routledge, London, 1946) *passim* and K. Popper, *The Open Society and Its Enemies* (Routledge, London, 1945), vol. II pp. 159–62. In emphasising that both the classical value theory and Marx's theory in vol. I of *Capital* were conceived as operating in ideal capitalist conditions, and that the later volumes of *Capital* are concerned with the modifications necessary to bring the 'model' into relation with the real world, these writers have thrown new light on the alleged 'discrepancy' between the first and third volumes of *Capital*. Sir Alexander Gray, *The Socialist Tradition Moses to Lenin* (Longmans, London, 1946), pp. 317–21 makes great play with earlier writers on the subject.

[2] Popper, *op. cit.* vol. II, p. 159. J. Robinson, *An Essay in Marxian Economics* (Macmillan, 1942), p. 27. The Classical Labour Theory of Value derives from Natural Rights philosophy, and Locke's justification of private property. A person is entitled to the things he 'mixes his labour' with in producing; in an ideal capitalist society things exchange at their true values, therefore a person is entitled to what he gets by exchange. The Jevonian theory (insofar as it is a theory of value and not merely a theory of price) is strictly Utilitarian; it assumes that where in a free capitalist society money is paid, equivalent goods or services have been rendered.

sense) has been pushed into the background; in the 'eighties, when the value theory was very much the centre of controversy, such a view would have been almost inconceivable in any full sense, though there are some incidental anticipations of it arising from the discussions amongst the early Fabians. In the circumstances three courses remained open to the Socialists of that time: to ignore the whole thing (which many of them managed to do for a considerable while, if we may judge from the lack of replies to Wicksteed in *Today*); to maintain that the Jevonian theory was unsatisfactory, as the orthodox Marxists eventually did;[1] or to create a new theory of 'surplus value', which the Fabians strove to do.

But how far did the Fabians accept Marx's theory of value? And if they did not, should they have been disturbed by Wicksteed's criticism of it? The answer seems to be that some of them were at first attached to the Marxist theory, while some, from the beginning, were not. Of the principal formulators of the Fabian creed, Shaw and Wallas obviously began with some sympathy for the Marxist theory, while Webb preferred Mill's value theory to Marx's. But as Socialists, all the Fabian leaders wished to preserve some kind of theory of 'surplus value', for they realised that Socialists are bound to attempt to show that even the ideal capitalist society is unjust as part of their argument that the remedy for the ills of existing society lies in moving away from it rather than towards it. Consequently, those Fabians who were hostile to the Marxist theory from the first were really in exactly the same position as those who were put into intellectual difficulties by Wicksteed's criticism.

This leads to a further question: How far did the Fabians accept the Jevonian theory of value, which Wicksteed thought should replace the labour theory? This question is usually not asked, because it is generally assumed that the Fabians did accept it. But the evidence adduced mostly comes from Shaw, and from the fact that the economic essay in *Fabian Essays* (written by Shaw) embodied the Jevonian theory. Certainly, there was something whole-hearted about Shaw's conversion to it.[2] In 1887 he was using it to belabour Hyndman at a Fabian Society lecture (18 February 1887), and again for the same purpose in the pages of the *Pall Mall Gazette* (May 1887), and then, passing from disciple to master, he wrote a fine review of *Capital* for the *National Reformer* of 7, 14, and 21 August 1887, criticising Marx's work from

[1] H. M. Hyndman, 'The Final Futility of Final Utility' in *Transactions of the National Liberal Club Political Economy Circle*, vol. II, pp. 119–33. See also J. H. Levy (ed.), *A Symposium on Value* (P. S. King & Son, London, n.d.), which contains essays by Bax, Hyndman, Shaw, Wicksteed, and others. The ablest defence of Marx on this issue by a modern economist is M. Dobb, *Political Economy and Capitalism* (Routledge, London), *passim*, esp. chs. I and V.

[2] Shaw and Wallas became members of a circle at the house of the stockbroker Beeton, which later expanded into the Royal Economic Society. Wicksteed gave instructions in Jevonian economics there, and Alfred Marshall was also a member of the group. Archibald Henderson, *George Bernard Shaw: His Life and Works: A Critical Biography* (Hurst & Blackett, London, 1911), pp. 158–9.

D

the Jevonian point of view. Graham Wallas, too, appears to have changed from Marx's theory to Jevons', though there are hints in his writings of an even more radical and modern criticism of the value controversy. Wallas declared, in an article entitled 'An Economic Eirenicon' (contributed to *Today* of March 1889): 'The great "value" controversy can really be resolved into the fact that Marx and Jevons are using the same word ('value') in different senses, and expound different but quite consistent laws.' He went on to suggest that the ambiguous term 'value' might be dropped by economists as 'plenty of terms exist for the various meanings which have been attached to "value"— such as "rates of exchange", "normal rates of exchange", "total utility", "final utility" . . . "labour cost", and "normal labour cost".' In reaching this conclusion Wallas had pointed out that the 'ratio of exchange' had both a demand and a supply side to it, and while Marx, assuming demand, had emphasized the supply side, Jevons and Wicksteed, assuming supply, had fixed their attention on the demand side.

It seems to me therefore [he continued], that Marx's essential proposition is in no way inconsistent with that of Jevons and Mr Wicksteed. Marx, I repeat, states the ratio of exchange between commodities varies with (or in Mr Wicksteed's language 'is a function of') the amount of labour necessary on the average to produce either of them. Wicksteed states that it is also a function of the amount of each commodity already possessed by the parties to the exchange. . . . And not only may these two statements both be true, but any number of other economists might also be right in declaring that the ratio of exchange is a function of any number of other variants which affect all commodities more or less, e.g. their weight, or the season of the year in which they are produced.

This still left the question whether one theory was more useful than the other, so Wallas finally gave some reasons for preferring slightly the Jevonian theory (the mathematical treatment in Jevons; the difficulty of disentangling labour costs as an independent variable from other factors, etc.)[1]

Where Sidney Webb is concerned, it is not easy to decide how far he found it necessary to change from Mill's theory of value, which he had upheld at the Hampstead Historic Club, to Jevons'. He was to some extent influenced by the new doctrine, and made use of the marginalist concepts, but his writings do not appear to touch on the most fundamental aspects of the value question, and what he has to say in them would not be inconsistent with a mere restatement of the Millite value theory in the light of marginalist refinements. In any case, it is not true to say (as has been said[2]) that the Fabians, or at any rate, their

[1] Other hints of an extremely radical view of the value issue were to be seen in an article by Edward Carpenter, skirmishing on the outskirts and rather impatient of the knock-about controversy between Hyndman and Shaw; he warned both Fabians and Marxists of some of the metaphysical traps of the value discussion and went so far as to suggest that 'the value of the value theory' was not great. 'The Value of the Value Theory' in *Today*, June 1889.
[2] e.g. J. Strachey, *What Are We To Do?* (Gollancz, London, 1938), p. 80.

leaders, swallowed whole the economics of Jevons and the Marginal Utility School. At the most, some Fabians adopted Jevons' theory of value but his theory of value only. Certainly the Fabians did not adopt the Marginal Utility School's theory of distribution. Instead, they developed their celebrated 'theory of rent', which, they claimed, was a new theory of 'surplus value', more accurate and sounder theoretically than Marx's.[1] It could certainly be maintained that the Fabian Theory of Rent is quite independent of any theory of value, in the sense that it could still stand whether one adopted a labour theory of value, or a cost of production theory or a marginal utility theory. How far the Fabians realized this, it is difficult to tell. Shaw probably did not; Webb probably, and Wallas almost certainly did. In Shaw's articles in *Fabian Essays*, the Jevonian theory of value and the Fabian theory of rent are both made part of the one story, whereas in Webb's various expositions of the theory of rent no value theory is specifically mentioned.

Wicksteed's criticism of Marx, then, was an important factor in the development of the new Fabian theory. There is every indication that the Fabians were acutely alive to the problem created by his attack. But it is by no means the whole explanation. It is conceivable that the Fabian theory of rent might have been developed in any case by those Fabians who disagreed with Marx's theory from the outset. In this sense we can say only that Wicksteed made the Fabians feel the need for a new argument for Socialism and made those Fabians, whom he persuaded that Marx was wrong, willing to accept it. An important additional factor, of course, was that Fabians had by 1886 repudiated the S.D.F., and Marx's theories (much against the wishes of Marx and Engels) had come to be connected in the public mind with the politics of the S.D.F. The S.D.F. had failed signally in its attempts to win the London Radical Clubs, and Marxism was associated with that failure. This also helps to explain why the Fabians chose to repudiate Marx, rather than to interpret him in a moderate direction as the German 'Revisionists' did. Marxism would only have been a hindrance to the Fabians in their attempts to permeate the Radicals; on the other hand, the doctrines of Ricardo, Mill and George were well-established among these people, while the Fabians' acquaintance with the Jevonian theory gave that up-to-date note which the Society always affected in its propaganda. When the Fabian economic doctrine emerged, it appeared as an attempt to create a new theory of 'surplus value' by an extension of the Radical theory of rent.

THE TIME WHEN THE RENT THEORY WAS FORMULATED

The publications which put forward the Fabian theory of rent date from 1888. The principal one of these was Webb's article in the *Quarterly Journal of Economics* for January 1888 when the theory was advanced in reply to an

[1] Shaw, 'Bluffing the Value Theory,' in *Today*, May 1889.

article contributed to the April 1887 number of the journal by Francis A. Walker, the President of the American Economic Association.[1] And so far as the Fabian Tracts are concerned, the first to show the changed theory is No. 7, *Capital and Land*, written by Olivier, which was also published in 1888. The two Tracts published in the previous year *Facts for Socialists* (by Webb) and *The True Radical Programme* (by Shaw),[2] do not raise the value issue. Indeed *Facts for Socialists*, that most successful Fabian pamphlet, had in its early editions quite a Marxist tone because of its plentiful quotations from orthodox economists saying that 'labour is the only source of wealth'.

But there is reason to believe that the theory was formulated before 1888. It seems most probable that the theory was worked out at the meetings of the Hampstead Historic circle and of the Society itself in the latter part of 1886 or the early part of 1887. At any rate, Olivier led a discussion on the subject at a meeting of the Society held on 19 November 1886.[3] The credit for thinking out the theory is usually given to Webb, sometimes to Webb and Olivier jointly.[4]

THE IMPORTANCE OF THE THEORY

Before going on to give an outline and criticism of the Fabian theory of rent, a few words may perhaps be said about the importance of this theory in the eyes of its formulators. There can be no doubt that Webb, Shaw, and Wallas considered this theory a great contribution to socialist thought, and not only when they first worked it out. In his introduction to the 1920 reprint of *Fabian Essays*, written 'in the light of thirty years of subsequent experience', Webb says: 'It is perhaps significant that the part of the book which comes most triumphantly through the ordeal of such an examination is, throughout, the economic analysis. . . . Tested by a whole generation of further experience and criticism, I conclude that, in 1889, we knew our Political Economy, and that our Political Economy was sound.'[5] Wallas similarly referred, in his later years, to the importance of the theory of rent in Fabian thought,[6] and Shaw, most recently of all, has written to the same effect.[7] The doctrine has been spoken of as 'the very corner-stone of collectivist economy'[8] and in other

[1] On 10 July 1889 Webb gave his article, in a slightly altered version, as a lecture to the Political Economy Circle of the National Liberal Club, *Transactions*, vol. I (ed. J. H. Levy), (P. S. King & Son, London, 1891); it was also reprinted, again changed in form, as one of the essays in S. and B. Webb, *Problems of Modern Industry* (1898); some parts of the argument were also reproduced (along with much quotation from Marshall) in S. and B. Webb, *Industrial Democracy*, 1897.

[2] Pease, *op. cit.* p. 289 for authorship.

[3] *Practical Socialist*, vol. I, No. 12, December 1886. See also Olivier's criticisms of Marx in his articles 'Perverse Socialism' in *Today*, vol. vi, August, September and November 1886.

[4] Graham Wallas, *Men and Ideas* (Allen & Unwin, London, 1940), p. 103

[5] Preface to the 1920 edition of *Fabian Essays*.

[6] Wallas, *Men and Ideas*, p. 104.

[7] G. B. Shaw, *Everybody's Political What's What* (Constable, London, 1944), p. 22.

[8] S. and B. Webb, *History of Trade Unionism* (Longmans, London, 1920 edit.), p. 162.

terms that can leave no doubt that its originators always considered it of fundamental importance.

THE THEORY OF RENT SUMMARIZED

The following is an attempt to extract a summary of the Fabian theory of rent, mainly from the writings of Sidney Webb:

(1) The return to the labour of the ordinary unskilled worker, employed with the minimum of capital on the worst soil at that time in use, and in the worst natural circumstances will be the measure of the wages of all unskilled workers. (This 'economic datum-line' 'it will be convenient to call "economic wages".')

(2) Assuming ('as Ricardo and apparently Karl Marx[1] always did') an unregulated increase in population, 'economic wages' will equal the minimum produce upon which the average unskilled worker will maintain himself sufficiently long to rear a generation to replace him (allowing that this minimum involves an habitual and historic standard).[2]

(3) On the 'margin of cultivation' without skill or capital, the whole of the product is 'economic wages'. Any larger product obtained elsewhere by an equivalent amount of labour must be the result of the employment of more advantageous land, of more effective labour, or of capital.

(4) This additional product, or 'surplus value',[3] may be divided as follows:

[1] If Webb meant by this that Marx, like Ricardo, had adopted the Malthusian doctrine of population, he was wrong. See M. Dobb, *Political Economy and Capitalism* (1946 edit.), p. 124.

[2] Webb noted (most fully in *Industrial Democracy*, vol. II pp. 633–43) the untenable nature of the older doctrine that wages tended to subsistence because higher wages would lead to a higher birthrate, but he suggested that this was because 'prosperous and thrifty artisans' were resorting to birth-control (p. 638); he pointed to the infant death rate in Bethnal Green as evidence that 'much truth unfortunately remains' in the Ricardian subsistence theory ('The National Dividend and Its Distribution' in *Problems of Modern Industry*). In the same article he stressed the habitual and historic element in his version of the subsistence theory ('The position of the margin of cultivation is itself partly determined by the "standard of comfort" which each social grade does not willingly abandon'). cf. Shaw in the first Fabian Essay on grades in subsistence: 'If you have to give your footman a better allowance than your wretched hewer of matchwood, it is for the same reason that you have to give your hunter beans and a clean stall instead of chopped straw and a sty.' (1889 edit. p. 19). Trade Unions, by minimum wage demands, can raise the level of subsistence (*Transactions of P.E. Circle of National Liberal Club*, pp. 81–3).

[3] The Fabians differed amongst themselves on the question whether to use the term 'surplus value' to show the relationship of their concept to the older Socialist one. Thus Pease, (*op. cit.* p. 246) says 'the Fabians, throwing over Marx's inaccurate term surplus value . . .'; but Shaw in his first contribution to *Fabian Essays* does not hesitate, in a footnote on p. 27 (1889 edit.), to identify 'rent' in the Fabian sense with Marx's 'surplus value'; Webb prefers the term 'surplus product', (e.g. Tract 15). The Fabians in early disputes with the Marxists (see, e.g., Olivier's articles mentioned in footnote 3, p. 36) took the view that Marx's 'surplus value' theory emphasised the exploitation of the individual worker, and therefore represented the social conflict as a conflict between working-class and middle-class, whereas the theory of 'rent' demonstrated the social conflict to be one between producers and idlers. This ingenious argument was perhaps valid against the 'vulgar Marxists' of the S.D.F., who tended to identify Marx's 'working-class' with manual workers; but it involved a misinterpretation of Marx, and the Fabians later do not seem to have presented the argument in this form.

(a) 'Economic rent' is the extra product due to the greater advantages of the site.

(b) 'Rent of ability' is the extra product due to the superior skill or ability of the worker over the unskilled worker.[1]

(c) 'Economic interest is the extra product due to the use of more or superior quality capital.[2]

(d) 'Rent of opportunity' or 'Profits' is the extra product due to 'adventitious advantages'.[3]

(5) These 'rents' would arise in any society where land, ability, and capital varied in quality, but the feature of capitalist society is that the main part of the rents is appropriated by the owners of the means of production. The more skilled worker, through his quasi-monopolistic position, may get a share of the 'rent of ability', but never all of it.[4] In any case skill is often the result of better education received by the children of landlords and capitalists and thus also indirectly a result of private ownership of the means of production.[5]

THE NATURE OF FABIAN RENT THEORY

What the Fabians have attempted to do is fairly clear. They have extended the Ricardian theory of rent in such a way as to embrace the returns to other factors of production, especially the return to capital, and so have attempted to create a new 'surplus value' theory which, while not necessarily dependent on a marginal utility theory of value, is quite compatible with it. The Ricardian theory had been an effective weapon in the hands of the land nationalizers and Henry Georgeites. Could it be extended and used for the same purpose against the capitalist too?

To discover whether it could or not, it is necessary to observe how the land reformers made use of the Ricardian theory. According to the theory, rent was a differential return from more fertile land over land at the margin of cultivation. If society's demand made it necessary for worse land to be cultivated, then the price of the product must be sufficiently high for the marginal farmers —those who cultivated under the most unfavourable conditions—to make a

---

[1] The 'exercise of abilities as superintendant or director of agriculture or industry' and 'the administration of capital and the organization of industry' are considered by the Fabians to be in the nature of work of a skilled kind (Tract No. 7).

[2] 'Economic interest' as here used is defined as an 'amount of produce' and carefully distinguished from 'rate of interest'. See 'The National Dividend and Its Distribution' *loc. cit.* where Webb distinguishes four senses of 'interest'. He is led by his theory to deny that the accumulation of capital depends solely, or even mainly, on the *rate* of interest (p. 226). Shaw in his Fabian Essay makes a similar distinction (pp. 20–1).

[3] The example given in 'The National Dividend and Its Distribution' is a 'windfall' resulting from a 'temporary monopoly' due to 'the possession of capital, in a certain form, at a particular point of time and space', (p. 218).

[4] This seems to be the position taken in the chief work on 'Rent of Ability,' Shaw's *Socialism and Superior Brains: a Reply to Mr Mallock* (Tract 146).

[5] This point is made by Webb in Tract 69.

living. More fertile land would yield a surplus, at such a price, to its 'landlord'. If the landlord were the farmer himself, he would himself receive this surplus, but if the land were leased by the landlord to others who did the work, then the landlord (or series of landlords) of the superior land would be able to extort the difference between the marginal land and their more favoured piece, as rent. Furthermore, with the increase in population and the pressure to extend to even more inferior land, the difference between the better land and worse would increase, and rents would tend to rise. Continual 'increments' would be added to rent automatically, owing nothing to the action of the land-lord, but everything to the expansion of the community. While Ricardo him-self, in his *Principles*, did not make any ethical recommendations as a result of his conclusions about rent, his disciples did not let the matter rest there. The conclusion was soon drawn that the landlord's 'unearned increment' ought to be nationalized or confiscated by means of taxation. The argument was stated most bluntly of all by Henry George, and by the time Shaw gave his witty variation on this theme in *Fabian Essays*, the Ricardian theory was undoubtedly well-known in Radical circles. One thing needs to be noticed, however, before considering the Fabian extension of this theory. The landlord is particularly vulnerable to the attack along Ricardian lines because it is clear that land is as a rule, neither produced nor destroyed by the landlord's activities. Rent is therefore not a payment necessary to bring land into existence, and, if the theory is accepted, it would appear that the landlord is being paid for some-thing that he has done nothing to earn.

The Fabians were by no means the first theorists to extend the Ricardian rent theory to other factors of production; they merely completed the process. The tendency to extend the theory was common to many of the later econo-mists in the 'Classical School' of economic thinking, and to some of the socialist theorists whose doctrines derived from that school. There is certain similarity, for instance, between the extension of the rent concept by the German socialist economist Johann Karl Rodbertus (who, however, was more critical of Ricardo) and the Fabian extension of it. Yet there is no evidence that the Fabians were familiar with Rodbertus's works at the time they formu-lated their doctrine;[1] indeed the differences between Rodbertus and the Fabi-ans which passed without comment by them make it certain that their theory was developed quite independently. Of more importance to the Fabians than any of their socialist predecessors were the Liberal economists in the Ricardian tradition who were inclined to extend the theory of rent. Alfred Marshall's summing-up of this trend of thought was not published in his *Principles*[2] until

[1] Rodbertus had died in 1875, but Edward Gonner's *The Social Philosophy of Rodbertus* did not appear till 1899. Rodbertus has attracted very little attention in England.

[2] Marshall's views were usually known long before he published them, and it is probable that the Fabians were aware of them, especially as some of the Fabians attended a discussion group of which Marshall was also a member (see footnote 2, p. 33). This is also suggested

after the Fabian theory had been given to the world. The Fabians' immediate predecessor in this line of thought was Francis A. Walker, the President of the American Economic Association.

The Liberal economists' aim in extending the 'differential rent' theory was of course quite different from that of the Fabians. They had no wish to use it to prove that capital and other factors received an 'unearned increment'; the rent theory seemed theoretically useful to them for quite other purposes. F. A. Walker was no fundamental critic of the capitalist system, but an advocate of 'high wages and high profits'; his purpose in extending the rent theory was to account for high business profits in a perfect economic model (always a vexed question for theoretical economists). The question of the justification of high business profits had become important for Walker, because he had helped to destroy the Wages Fund Theory which had maintained that the share of the national dividend the workers received could by no means rise. At the end of his article on business profits, which provoked Webb's reply, he observed: 'If this be correct we see how mistaken is that opinion of the wages class, which regards the successful employer of labour—men who realise large fortunes in manufactures or trade—as having in some way injured or robbed them. . . .'[1]

In this article in the *Quarterly Journal of Economics* of April 1887, Walker maintained that business profits were a kind of 'rent'—a differential return going to the better entrepreneur because of his superior ability. It was rooted in human nature; it sprang from natural differences in ability and so would arise even in a perfect system. Walker therefore used the phrase 'Rent of Ability.' The theory of distribution propounded by Walker thus contained the following propositions. Wages represent the return to the 'marginal' worker; rent is the differential return arising because of a piece of land's superior fertility; interest is the marginal rate paid for hiring capital; and profits are the differential return arising because of an entrepreneur's superior ability. Sidney Webb first put forward the Fabian theory of rent in the *Quarterly Journal of Economics*[2] in the discussion which followed the publication of Walker's article. Webb may perhaps be regarded as 'completing' this trend in economics in the way that Marx 'completed' the labour theory of value trend.

In his article, Webb quoted approvingly from what he called 'Mr George's eloquent but ill-judged onslaught' the opinion that the laws of distribution have 'no common centre', and he proceeded to argue that Walker (and earlier writers) had spoken of interest as a *rate*, while at the same time speaking of

by Webb's comment on the *Principles* when it appeared: 'It is a great book; nothing new— showing the way, not following it . . .' B. Webb, *My Apprenticeship* (Pelican, 1938), p. 458. It has been suggested that Marshall was influenced by the Fabian theory. (P. W. Fox and H. S. Gordon, 'The Early Fabians—Economists and Reformers,' *Canadian Journal of Economics and Political Science*, XVII, August 1951, p. 312). This seems to me unproven and unlikely.

[1] Q.J.E. I, p. 279.
[2] *Op. cit.* II (1888), pp. 188–208 and 469–72.

rent, wages, and (in Walker's case) profit, as a *quantity of produce* apportioned to the factor of production concerned. If, Webb contended, the Theory of Distribution were given a 'common centre', and a quantity of produce spoken of in each case, then 'economic interest' (as distinguished from the rate of interest—the market price of new capital seeking investment) should be regarded as a differential return arising as between the factory which works with better machinery and that which works with marginal capital.

Webb also made some subsidiary, but vital, changes in other parts of the theory. He retained the concept of 'rent of ability', but gave it a new meaning. It was applied not only to entrepreneurs but to all skilled workers, with the entrepreneur, *qua* entrepreneur, treated as a salaried employee, not, as with Walker, an employer. Neither were 'profits' treated by Webb as necessarily connected with 'rent of ability'. By 'profits' he understood also windfalls, resulting from the 'possession of capital in a certain form at a particular time' and similar adventitious advantages, and he suggested the use of the term 'rent of opportunity' to cover them. Thus Webb sought to give a 'common centre' to the laws of distribution and to 'complete' the extension of the Ricardian rent theory.

CRITICISM OF THE EXTENSION OF THE RENT THEORY

In stressing the lack of a 'common centre' to the laws of distribution, Webb placed his finger on a problem which has accupied the attention of theoretical economists both before and since his time.[1] That the Classical theories relating to rent and to the return to capital were based on different assumptions could readily be shown. It was, however, debatable whether they needed to be, or could be, reduced to the same basis; and debatable too, which assumption should be chosen as the basis. Wicksteed's solution was the exact opposite to the Fabian: Wicksteed tended to bring the return to land under the same laws of distribution which applied to interest and the returns to the other factors of production. Other economists have maintained that the Ricardian theory applies uniquely to land, or at least to land under special conditions (such as where the land has no alternative or competing use).[2] It is impossible to enter fully into this much debated problem here: we can only point out a major difficulty for Webb's solution of the problem, as any kind of socialist argument.

As Socialists, the Fabians had sought to demonstrate by their theory of rent that the capitalist was in the same position as the landlord was claimed to be in by the Land Reformers. But is this claim substantiated? The 'punch' which the Ricardian theory had in the hands of the Land Reformers lay in two things.

[1] See generally the paper by F. A. Fetter and discussions upon it in American Economic Association *Publications*, 3rd series, vol. V, 1904, pp. 176–240.
[2] D. Buchanan, 'The Historical Approach to Rent and Price Theory,' *Readings in the Theory of Income Distribution*, selected by a Committee of the American Economic Association, (Blakiston, Philadelphia, 1949), pp. 599–637.

Primarily, in the claim that the landlord's income was 'unearned', and only secondarily in the claim that it was differential and tending to increase automatically. But the separate character of these two elements was not immediately obvious in the case of land. The two claims became telescoped into one by the theory of rent. It seemed only necessary for the Land Reformers to show that rent was a differential return to make it apparent that the differential return was also unearned. The actual creation of 'the original and indestructible qualities of the soil' was something the landlord did not do.

Even so, the Ricardian argument has been hotly contested. How much of 'rent' in real life, as opposed to the economists' definition, is due to the 'original and indestructible powers of the soil', and how much to improvements made by the landlord? Is the more recently worked land always, or even often, inferior in quality? These questions become even more forceful when the theory of rent is extended to interest.

Admitting that the return on fixed capital may be described in terms of the rent theory, and that there would be a differential return to firms employing better capital equipment,[1] admitting that (in the cases where the entrepreneur is a salaried employee) the return goes to the shareholders, does it follow that this return is unearned? Is not this better capital itself created by the capitalist's saving or by his 'abstinence' from immediate consumption? Does not the shareholder participate somewhat in the functions of 'risk-bearer', even where the actual decisions are made by a salaried manager? It seems that the basic element in the theory of rent as applied to land becomes extremely doubtful when the theory is extended to interest, and without the 'unearned' aspect, the 'differential' aspect is singularly ineffective as a socialist argument. When Walker extended the theory of rent, and spoke of profits as being a differential rent of ability, he was not seeking to argue that profits were unearned, but just the opposite—that they were earned by superior ability.

THE REAL FABIAN CASE

When we search for a less questionable argument for Socialism in Fabian writings, we need to turn aside from Sidney Webb's more abstract articles to the Society's popular Tracts, and chiefly to the early Tract, *Capital and Land*,[2] which Pease tells us was written by Sydney Olivier. This pamphlet, which was addressed to a Radical audience familiar with land nationalization and single tax propaganda, devoted, it is true, the major portion of its space to proving that landlords and capitalists were really 'in one boat'. But towards the end it raised the question whether capital is not productive, and if it is, whether the

---

[1] And waiving some important objections to Webb's application of concepts like the Law of Diminishing Returns to capital (see esp. pp. 218-9 of *Problems of Modern Industry*, new ed. 1920, Longmans, Green & Co.)

[2] Tract 7.

capitalist is not entitled to interest as his reward for creating capital by saving. The answer made in the Tract was quite explicit. It agreed that capital is productive, when used in conjunction with the other factors of production; it admitted further that present capital is brought into existence by capitalists abstaining from taking out a claim which they have upon society and deferring their claim to a future date; and, finally, it admitted that the accumulation of capital is a necessary social activity. But it denied that the existence of capitalists as a class is thereby justified.[1] Three main reasons were given for this. First, that 'saving' is an activity which could be done by the community collectively, and not by private individuals. Second, that little or no sacrifice is involved for a rich man to save, and the higher proportion of saving is done by the rich—in fact, so far as 'service' is concerned, the greater service may be rendered to the capitalist, for 'saving' really represents a bargain whereby a wealthy person may arrange to consume at a later date what he cannot conveniently consume immediately. Thirdly, that the nature of the bargain made by the capitalist is a peculiarly unjust one: by investing, the capitalist acquires 'a lien for a perpetual annuity, an enduring tribute from the workers for the use of that which only their using can keep from perishing, while he (the capitalist) retains all the time his claim to the original 'saving' undiminished'.[2]

Such arguments seem more serviceable than the theory of rent in marooning the capitalist 'in the same boat' as the landlord—levelling the charge that, *qua* capitalist, he is an idle and useless member of the community living on an 'unearned income' at the expense of the other members of the community, who do the work. *Qua capitalist* is important. This or that capitalist may be doing other work of social utility, but interest is paid to him, as rent is paid to the landlord, in his capacity as 'an absolutely idle person'. His management and control functions are carefully distinguished from his capitalist functions. The 'exercise of abilities as superintendent or director of agriculture or industry' and the 'administration of capital and the organization of industry' are treated as services, and their reward in the nature of salaries for useful work. Indeed 'savings out of earned incomes' are distinguished from 'savings out of unearned incomes'. Until the Socialist State is capable of doing all the 'saving' itself,

[1] For the detailed working out of the Fabian attitude to 'interest' the following articles and reports are important:
Practical Socialist, January 1886 (Podmore and Marson in a discussion of a talk by Annie Besant), February 1886 (Webb in discussion of his paper on Positivism), June 1886 (Annie Besant on Interest), August 1886 (Notes column), December 1886, (Review of a pamphlet by Caroline Haddon on Interest), May 1887 (Article by G. B. Shaw); *Our Corner*, September-October 1887 (two Articles by Shaw on Interest).
[2] The same argument is implicit in the section 'Capitalism' of Shaw's 'Economic Basis of Socialism' article in *Fabian Essays*, where 'saving' and 'abstinence' are referred to as 'a gleam of humour which still enlivens treatises on capital'. Shaw does not deny that capital performs a useful and necessary function (cf. *Intelligent Woman's Guide* (Pelican), p. 108), and so the ethical problem shifts again to the question whether capitalists perform a necessary function.

persons saving out of earned incomes could be given 'such reward as we give individualist inventors in their patent rights' providing 'that which society has maintained and fructified invariably pass to society within a limited period'. (Presumably, this means that persons saving out of wages would be entitled to receive some interest and to reclaim their principal, but that right of inheritance would be strictly limited). As for the 'saving' out of 'unearned incomes', this should be taxed into public hands.

In Fabian economic doctrine there are, then, the theory of rent, which claims, amongst other things, that the return to capital is a differential return, increasing by 'unearned increments', and also other arguments, contending that the capitalist is the recipient of an 'unearned income'. Now, if the theory of rent requires these other arguments to bolster it up as a socialist case, might it not be that the other arguments are sufficient in themselves, and the theory of rent redundant?

HAS THE THEORY OF RENT ANY USE AT ALL?

At first sight, there seems much to be said for discounting the rent theory altogether as a useful or practical argument for Socialism in Fabian doctrine. Although its originators apparently regarded their rent theory of great importance, they only found it necessary to expound it in very few of their publications. Of the 212 Tracts published by the Fabian Society up to 1924, not more than five actually mention the theory of rent, and in all save one of these the argument turns upon the point that the income is unearned and not at all upon its differential nature. That last remaining Tract, however, may reveal that the theory has some practical significance. It is called *The Impossibilities of Anarchism* and it is by G. Bernard Shaw.[1]

As we have already remarked, Socialists have considered it necessary not only to prove that an existing state of affairs is unjust (though, of course, they devote a great deal of propaganda to setting out the facts of present inequality and its evil effects on social life) but also to prove that the best possible arrangement, retaining the private ownership of the means of production, would be unjust, and (many Socialists have added) because unjust, unstable too. This is necessary, because very few even of orthodox economists have defended capitalism *as it is*, but only in some ideal form. Marx's labour theory of value and theory of surplus value, and the Fabian theory of rent were attempts to show both that inequalities would necessarily result even under ideal capitalist conditions and also that these inequalities would necessarily get worse and worse. Marx's theories of 'movement of capitalism' were attempts to explain the course which this getting worse and worse would take, but the Fabians did not feel it necessary to carry their analysis to these lengths. Why, then, was it necessary to go so far in the first place as to construct a theory of rent? On the

[1] Tract 45.

44

orthodox economists' own terms it could easily be shown that the price system measures only 'effective' demand (i.e. demand made effective by the possession of money to pay for the articles demanded) and not necessarily demand that is socially desirable. Shaw, in his article in *Fabian Essays*, made this point: 'The moment a price is to be had for a luxury, it acquires exchange value, and labour is employed to produce it. A New York lady, for instance, having a nature of exquisite sensibility, orders an elegant rosewood and silver coffin, upholstered in pink satin, for her dead dog. It is made; and meanwhile a live child is prowling barefooted and hunger-stunted in the frozen gutter outside.'[1] Similarly it could be shown, just as the price system fails to compare the intensity of consumers' needs but only measures their 'effective demand', it also fails to compare the degree of one producer's 'sacrifices' with another's. Most Socialists would maintain firmly, despite sophistical objections to the comparison of 'sacrifices', that the 'sacrifice' involved in saving out of a large income is almost no sacrifice at all, especially when compared with the sacrifice of a labourer who has to work long hours for a meagre wage. Finally it could be suggested that such a system, which, historically, began with a state of inequality, would at least perpetuate that inequality. One socialist, at any rate, has relied on these arguments alone for his case against 'ideal' capitalism.[2]

But, at this stage, the arguments of the individualist Anarchists come into play, and the Fabians were acutely alive to the theoretical problem raised by their arguments. This may be seen from Shaw's *Impossibilities of Anarchism*, first produced in 1888, when the Anarchists were active in the Socialist League, and rewritten and issued as a Tract by the Society in 1893, when some of the provincial Fabian Societies were in need of guidance about their attitude to the Anarchists. Shaw's paper contains a criticism both of individualist Anarchism and Anarchist Communism, but it is the first of these only that is of interest here. Shaw began by pointing out the connexion between individualist Anarchism and orthodox Liberalism—that Anarchism is a logical extension of the Liberal economic creed. Individualist Anarchists, he said, admitted the difficulty of having a beginning point of capitalism in inequality, so they declared: 'Destroy the money-monopoly, the tariff-monopoly, and the patent monopoly. Enforce only those land titles which rest on personal occupancy or cultivation; and the social problem of how to secure to each worker the product of his own labour will be solved simply by everyone minding his own business.'[3] Briefly, their contention was that equality should first be established, and then *laissez faire* would work justly and properly. Against them, Shaw argued that even if their recommendations were carried out differential returns would automatically arise and lead to inequality once more,

[1] *Op. cit.* (1889 ed.), p. 22.
[2] Douglas Jay, *The Socialist Case* (Faber & Faber, 1937).
[3] Benjamin R. Tucker paraphrased by Shaw in Tract 45.

though the system began in a state of equality. If some degree of equality were to be preserved, it would be necessary to have some kind of state machine at least to appropriate and distribute the differential 'rents'.[1] Is not the theory of rent useful in this case? Shaw claimed that it is. In fact, he went further and claimed that the theory of rent is the only effective answer to this kind of Anarchism, and any 'side-stepping' of the theory of rent leads to a recrudescence of Anarchism.[2]

There is undoubtedly something in this argument, in the sense that some theory of distribution which demonstrated inequalities of return in the way the theory of rent claimed to do would be a useful counter to individualist Anarchism. But it is significant that Shaw manages to state his case without expounding the theory of rent in full. It would seem that the arguments which are effective against the individualist Anarchists are not all those contained in the theory of rent, but rather the assumptions upon which that theory is built: the assumptions, particularly, that inequalities are natural, and equality, though desirable, artificial.

In general, then, the Fabian theory of rent may be said to have given a certain logical completeness to an abstract theory. In the form in which it was presented by Bernard Shaw in *Fabian Essays* and by Webb in his articles, it has not interested theoretical economists greatly. His 'exposition somewhat lacked the rigour that economists demanded if deductive argument were to carry conviction', a favourably-disposed critic wrote of Shaw's articles,[3] and, to a lesser extent, the same might be said of Webb's. The type of theory of distribution propounded by the Fabians, however, influenced J. A. Hobson, and in his formulation it has represented an important minority view in academic circles.[4] The theory is, and has remained, essentially an abstract one. The Fabians regarded it a merit of their 'surplus value' theory, when compared with Marx's, that they had separated out the elements of 'surplus value' into three (or four) 'rents'. But when they produce the later editions of their *Facts for Socialists*, or any other statistical data, they do not seem to find their finespun distinctions of much use. In *Facts for Socialists*, for instance, the total

---

[1] After this, Shaw proceeds to join battle with the Anarchist-Communists concerning the nature of the state. This is discussed in a later chapter.

[2] e.g. Pease, *op. cit.* p. 282 (Shaw's appendix).

[3] M. Dobb, 'Bernard Shaw and Economics,' in *G.B.S.* 90 (edited by S. Winsten), (Hutchinson, 1946), p. 133.

[4] F. A. Fetter, Amer. Econ. Assn. *Publications*, 3rd series, vol. I, 1904, p. 176 *et seq.* J. A. Hobson was obviously influenced by the Fabian theory, although for personal reasons, he failed to acknowledge his indebtedness fully (J. A. Hobson, *Confessions of an Economic Heretic* (Allen & Unwin, London, 1938), pp. 45 *et seq.*). The rent theory is much more adaptable to a Radical-Liberal than a Socialist cause. However, as evidence of the 'neutrality' of the rent doctrine, it is worth noticing that the American economist, J. B. Clark, anything but a Socialist, began formulating his Theory of Distribution, which also extended the Ricardian analysis to the other productive factors, about the same time (see especially his 'Distribution as Determined by a Law of Rent,' *Q.J.E.* v, (1890–1), pp. 289–318).

national income is simply divided, fairly roughly, into the amount paid in wages and salaries on the one hand, and this is set against the amount paid in rent and interest on the other.

What happened with the Fabian attempt to give a new theory of surplus value as a 'basis' for their socialism seems to be this: they scrapped Marx's theory, which was a claim of right and a logical construction rolled into one, and in its place they put forward a theory which (though they did not recognise it) really separated out the claim of right from the logical construction. But the theory of rent, their logical construction, can hardly be said to be a theory having practical usefulness, and, despite claims for it, its real importance in Fabian Socialism seems negligible.

THE FABIANS AND THE 'LAW OF MOVEMENT OF CAPITALISM'

While the Fabians were well acquainted with some of Marx's works, it might be claimed that they ignored the dynamic part of Marx's socialist economics— his 'Law of Movement of Capitalism'—his theory of the trade cycle. And since a few important modern writers have tried to rehabilitate this aspect of Marx's theory,[1] it may perhaps be worth while considering how true this claim is.

In the first place, it is certain that the Fabians were aware of this feature of Marx's theory. Bernard Shaw wrote in the review of *Capital* which he contributed to the *National Reformer:*[2]

To Marx, capitalism, with its wage-slavery, is only a passing phase of social development, following primitive communism, chattel slavery, and feudal serfdom into the past. He never loses consciouness of this movement; and herein lies one of the secrets of the novelty and fascination of his treatment. He wrote of the nineteenth century as if it were a cloud passing down the wind, changing its shape and fading as it goes; whilst Ricardo, the stockbroker, and De Quincey, the high Tory, sat comfortably down before it in their office and study chairs, as if it were the great wall of China, safe to last until the Day of Judgement, with an occasional coat of whitewash.

If the Fabians forgot this aspect of Marx, Hyndman was always there to remind them, with his constant jokes about Jevons' 'sunspot' theory of crises that Shaw, after a while, found rather tiresome. In his article in *Today* of May 1889, Shaw, in a controversial manner as sharp as Hyndman's own, declared roundly that his acceptance of Jevons' theory of value did not imply that in his view Jevons was better than Marx in other respects, and in particular, he said he did not hold with the 'sunspot' theory of the trade cycle. Unfortunately Shaw did not enlarge on the subject.

[1] e.g.: J. Robinson, *An Essay in Marxian Economics* (Macmillan, 1942);
P. M. Sweezy, *The Theory of Capitalist Development*, (O.U.P., N.Y., 1942);
M. Dobb, *Political Economy and Capitalism* (Routledge, London, 1937).
[2] First notice, *National Reformer*, 7 August 1887. (Shaw's remarks are not fair or accurate concerning Ricardo).

47

Of course, Marx's 'Law of Movement of Capitalism' was a complex of laws, not a single law. It contained elements—such as the 'increasing misery' of the proletariat, and the increasing concentration of industrial control in fewer hands—which the Fabians made use of, and which are discussed in a later chapter. But it also contained a theory of the trade cycle, which the Fabians appear to have ignored. They may have discussed his analysis of the causes of cyclical fluctuation in capitalist economy at the meetings of the Hampstead Historic circle, but there is no record of this, and it seems unlikely, as they were by no means reticent about giving their conclusions to the world. It is perhaps of some significance that even one of the finest analyses of *Capital* published by a latter-day Fabian as late as 1925[1] gave almost no consideration at all to Marx's attempts at a causal analysis of cyclical fluctuation. And *Fabian News* of May 1895 virtually confessed that the Society had no definite views on the subject when it made a rather curious remark about J. A. Hobson's *Evolution of Modern Capitalism:* '. . . when the author deals with Trusts and Combines, and explains his theory of general over-production and excess of savings, he is traversing new ground. We cannot pretend to sit in judgement on this explanation of the depressions of trade. It is unquestionably an attractive one, and we see no flaw in the author's argument. But we cannot yet venture upon the mental revolution which its acceptance would require . . .'

Though the Fabians had little to say about the causes of crises, they were not completely without interest in the subject. They had an empirical interest. That is, they were aware from their historical and statistical studies of the recurrence of crises, and they assumed that these would go on occurring. But they also assumed that crises were becoming less frequent and less severe. E. R. Pease, reviewing Professor Edwin Jones' book *Economic Crises* wrote:

Earlier in the century crises were more frequent and more intense. Our own view is that the commercial system, as it grows old and well established, gets over the period of crisis which in its youth seriously affected its health. Certainly it appears that the commercially younger countries, France and America, have suffered of late far more than we have. Professor Jones does not put the matter this way, though he suggests it in his final sentence, 'The extinguishment of crises will come through the general economic evolution, rather than as a result of the application of specific remedies'.[2]

An optimistic and comfortable belief; but the Fabians did not fold their hands. If they were not interested in probing causes, they had an interest in remedial measures. This sprang from their practical concern with the unemployment problem and developed gradually. In their earliest publications dealing with unemployment the Fabians proposed measures to be taken by the Government when unemployment had already become severe. But

[1] A. D. Lindsay, *Karl Marx's Capital* (World's Manuals, O.U.P., London, 1925).
[2] *Fabian News*, May 1901.

by the time of the Minority Report on the Poor Law (1909) the Webbs, in conjunction with A. L. Bowley, had worked out a plan for the 'prevention of destitution'. Their plan amounted to a counter-cycle policy, and its basis was the recommendation that government investment should increase whenever statisticians observed that the trade cycle was beginning to enter a bad phase. The Minority Report also suggested that the reason why crises had become less frequent and severe 'in the last twenty years' was that the development of municipal enterprise already acted partially in this direction.[1] The Fabians thus helped to formulate a principle that was ultimately to have profound effects on economic thought when its full theoretical implications had been worked out. However, they were worked out by professional economists, not by Fabians.

A reason may be suggested why the Fabians did not follow up Marx's attempts to give a causal analysis of cyclical fluctuation. Marx was a revolutionist and a Hegelian. As a Hegelian, he was concerned to show how the 'inner contradictions' of capitalism were bringing about its destruction. As a revolutionist, he was interested in periods when revolutionary situations develop, and he believed there was a close correlation between these revolutionary periods and industrial crises. The Fabians' political interest was quite different. They desired a gradual and continuous development towards socialism without catastrophic change, and economic crises were to them a manifestation of the injustice and suffering caused by capitalism, but more a social nuisance than periods when the 'death-knell of capitalism' might sound. They concerned themselves with the stabilizing effects of a counter-cycle policy and rejected an analysis which attempted to prove that the 'contradictions of capitalism' could not be overcome save by complete change.

All the things which Marx's unifying philosophy had bound closely together fell to bits and pieces at the Fabian touch. Marx had placed his egalitarian ethics in the centre of a 'theory of exploitation' and had tried to use that theory of exploitation in an analysis of the way in which the trade cycle was leading capitalism to its doom. The Fabians separated off his theory of value and showed preference, at least, for Jevons', disconnected the theory of surplus value and elaborated it into a theory of rent, thereby unwittingly separating out the ethical demand from the rest of the argument, and finally they ignored Marx's trade cycle theory because it did not interest them.

FABIAN SOCIOLOGY

When all this has been said, we have still not come to the Fabians' real contribution to social science. It has been necessary to devote so much space to the theory of rent because of the part it played in the development of Fabian doctrine, and because it has been regarded by the Fabian leaders as more

---

[1] *Minority Report* (1909) *on the Poor Law*, pp. 1195-8.

important than it really is. But when we think of the large number of Fabian Tracts that never mention it at all, and when we look at the shelves of fat volumes by the Webbs on social and economic matters that we have not yet considered, we may allow that a Fabian could rightly object to any over-emphasis of it. Indeed Professor R. H. Tawney, writing of the Webbs, has declared: 'They were out of sympathy . . . both with the tradition of abstract speculation which descended from Ricardo and with the attempt of some socialists to turn its batteries against itself by employing, as in the case of the labour theory of value, analogous methods to create a system of counter-doctrine.'[1] Enough has been said to show that this is hardly true of Sidney Webb in the early days of the Fabian Society. Yet it certainly seems true of the Webbs' work of a later time and also later of the Society, which, in 1896, could declare that it 'had no distinctive opinions on . . . abstract economics'.[2]

How did this change come about, and to whom was it due? According to Bernard Shaw, a series of lectures on the Chartist Movement which Graham Wallas gave to the Society in 1888 turned Webb and the Fabians away from the 'old abstract deductive economics' to the 'modern historical concrete economics'.[3] This is plausible. Graham Wallas often made a deep impression as a fertile and original thinker on those who heard him lecture. But it seems unlikely that Wallas's lectures in this case had the effect Shaw claimed for them. 'Abstract economics' were still occupying the Fabians' attention after these lectures had been given; and, so far as we may judge from rather imper-fect records of them,[4] the lectures were a straightforward historical account of the Chartist Movement, without any *methodological* novelty about them.[5] The change in Fabian outlook was not the result simply of studying history; it was the consequence of using the historical method specifically upon those problems which economists had previously discussed in terms of their abstract deductive models. Amongst the Fabians, the pioneer of this method was Beatrice Webb.

Already in 1886 and 1887, before she had met any of the leaders of the

---

[1] R. H. Tawney, 'Beatrice Webb, 1858–1943,' *Proceedings of the British Academy*, vol. XXIX, 1945, p. 14 of offprint.

[2] Tract 70.

[3] Pease, *op. cit.* p. 277 (appendix by Shaw).

[4] Shaw, *ibid.* says that the lectures were 'not effectively published'; but a summary version of them may be found in *Our Corner*, August and September 1888.

[5] Later, after he had left the Fabian Society, Graham Wallas did become a pioneer of the new methods of Social Psychology in his works *Human Nature in Politics*, (1908) and *The Great Society*, (1914). But these works, so far as I can see, had little or no influence upon the Fabian Society. Indeed, it is difficult to see how they could have had any; for although they are full of striking observations, the methodology seems highly eclectic, tentative and unsystematic, and much involved with purely definitional problems. Perhaps the Webbs had Graham Wallas' works in mind when they allowed that people 'not unnaturally' might be 'sceptical of the practical utility for everyday life of an exploration of the origins, in animal instinct, religious emotion, or humanistic ideals, of social relations that they prefer to take for granted'. *Methods of Social Study* (Longmans, London, 1932), p. 242.

Fabian Society, Beatrice Potter (as she then was) had been studying economics and growing more and more dissatisfied with the abstract and deductive methods of the established economists.[1] She had come under the influence of Charles Booth, who delighted in 'upsetting generally accepted views, whether the free-trade orthodoxy of Manchester capitalism, at that time in the ascendant, or the cut and dried creed of the Marxian socialist'.[2] Booth was at that time already stating quite clearly his view that: 'The *a priori* reasoning of political economy, orthodox and unorthodox alike, fails from want of reality. At its base are a series of assumptions very imperfectly connected with the observed facts of life. We need to begin with a true picture of the modern industrial organism. . . .'[3] Booth himself had been powerfully influenced by the *Positive Philosophy* of Auguste Comte and by the criticism of orthodox political economy made by the English Positivists, and perhaps also by the ideas of the German Historical School of Schmoller, that, by the end of the 'seventies and beginning of the 'eighties, had begun to find their way into England.

Beatrice Potter also became sensitive to the new influences: she sympathized warmly with the new criticism of the abstract economists, and stressed the need for empirical observation of actual social conditions; she joined Booth in his social survey, and later came to criticise him for the purely 'static' nature of his investigation and his neglect of the 'historical method' of analysing the 'actual processes of birth, growth, decay, and death of social institutions'.[4]

Already in 1886-7, Beatrice Potter had written two papers on the 'Rise and Growth of English Economics' and 'The Economic Theory of Karl Marx,' which she had submitted to friends for their comments.[5] The paper on Marx is of no great interest; but the other essay is important, as it foreshadows the direction which the whole of the Webbs' later studies were to follow. In it she argued that profit-making 'big business' is historically, and even today, only one form of wealth producing institution, yet Ricardian political economy studied it to the exclusion of other social institutions where motives other than profit-making predominate; what is more, it was studied in an abstract and deductive way, relying on certain assumptions about human behaviour and about the way society works that were, to say the least, imperfectly based on actual observation. Going on to give examples of cases where so-called 'friction' was more important than the Ricardian 'law', she argued that what was needed was a study of the history of social institutions as they actually exist,

[1] B. Webb, *My Apprenticeship* (Pelican), p. 338.
[2] *Ibid.* p. 268.
[3] C. Booth, 'Conditions and occupations of the people of the Tower Hamlets 1886-7,' quoted in B. Webb, *op. cit.* p. 270.
[4] B. Webb, *op. cit.* pp. 292-4.
[5] These papers were never published in full, but the gist of them is given in the appendix to *My Apprenticeship*. The summaries show some signs of the later revision, but the contents of the first paper can be verified by reference to Herbert Spencer's comments and her diary remarks on Spencer's replies. B. Webb, *op. cit.* pp. 340-2.

not in any assumed perfection of development, but in all the changing phases of 'health or disease' that they have actually passed through.

Whether competitive profit-making or capitalism promotes greed and oppression, and depresses public spirit—like the analogous accusations that State employment favours slackness and lessens initiative, and that vocational organization furthers exclusiveness and state technique [she wrote] *are all alike questions to be investigated* . . . I believe that we have here a most fruitful field for enquiry. We might discover that each type of organization (or absence of organization), each social institution, has its own peculiar 'social diseases', which will lead to senility or death unless arrested—arrested, possibly, by the presence or the development of another and complementary social institution.[1]

Beatrice Potter at this stage was very far from being a Socialist; the only Socialists she had met were members of the S.D.F., and they had inspired in her feelings of distrust and hostility. She regarded herself as an objective, unbiased social scientist, and she reacted strongly to any signs of what she considered political prejudice in others. When her friend and former tutor Herbert Spencer made some—perhaps basically sound[2]—objections to her criticism of orthodox economics, but expressed his objections in a question-begging way that revealed his political bias, his objections merely served to confirm Beatrice Potter in her own views. Spencer maintained that it was necessary first to have a science of 'normal' economic relations, so that 'pathological' social states could be given a 'course of treatment' to readjust them to 'normal', and Beatrice committed to her diary some short comments which showed how clearly she recognized the way in which ethical statements were confused with scientific in the use of the word 'normal'.[3]

I have no intention of presenting a course of treatment [she wrote] and his reference to it proves that his observation and reasoning on social subjects are subordinate to a *parti pris* on the art of government. . . . The first step surely is to find out what are these ['normal'] relations. . . . But, as I understand Ricardo's economics, he does not attempt to discover, he merely assumes. It is possible that his assumptions may turn out to be an account of normal action, but he does not prove that his assumptions represent fact. But then he does not seem to think that proof is necessary. . . . The object of science is to discover what is; not to tell us according to some social ideal what ought to be.[4]

---

[1] *Ibid.* p. 484.
[2] It was a pity that Spencer did not use some 'neutral' science like ballistics to demonstrate the importance of 'perfect models'.
[3] *Ibid.* pp. 340–2.
[4] Intellectual detachment remained characteristic of her attitude for a long time afterwards. Only very gradually did she move towards Socialism, and even when, after her marriage to Sidney Webb, she joined the Fabian Society in 1893, she was for a long time worried lest such a definite political affiliation might affect her scientific work. Beatrice Webb saw herself primarily as a scholar, a scientific investigator of social problems, and her advocacy of reform came eventually as a result of her investigation. (Tawney, *op. cit.* p. 5).

How Beatrice Potter served her 'apprenticeship' first with the Charity Organization Society, then as a rent collector in the East End of London, and finally as one of Booth's collaborators in his great survey, *The Life and Labour of the People of London*, has been told magnificently by herself and repeated by others. Her 'apprenticeship' complete, it was significant that her first independent research should have been a study (pointed to in her critical comments on the economists) of the 'life-history' of the British Co-operative Movement. In 1890, just before she completed her brilliant little work on Co-operation, Beatrice Potter had met Sidney Webb. On 27 July of that year, as Beatrice recorded in her diary, Sidney Webb remarked after reading Marshall's 'new book': '. . . it is a great book; it will supersede Mill. But it will not make an epoch in economics. Economics has still to be remade. Who is to do it? Either you must help me to do it; or I must help you. . . .'[1]

This determination to refashion economics no doubt sprang from a conjunction of Beatrice's theoretical criticism of the abstract methods of the economists with Sidney Webb's desire to give economics a socialistic slant. But Sidney Webb's interests and capabilities were perhaps also leading him to desert abstract economics for more concrete studies even before he met Beatrice. His 'historic sense' had already been shown in his contribution to *Fabian Essays* and in his *Socialism in England*, while his ability in collecting effective factual information and his interest in Local Government had been displayed in *Facts for Socialists*, *Facts for Londoners*, and *The London Programme*. The second great work to which the Webbs turned—their *History of English Local Government*—derives from Sidney Webb's interests. But Beatrice Webb's turning away from abstract economics was more deliberate and reasoned, and the first problems which the Webb 'partnership' investigated were ones she had already begun or projected. Her study of Co-operation had led her to the conclusion that Trade Unions were as necessary a complement to Consumer's Co-operation as to capitalist production,[2] and so, early in 1889, she had decided to make the British Trade Union Movement her next field of inquiry.[3] May we than ascribe the Fabians' reassessment of the role of Trade Unionism and Co-operation in the Labour Movement primarily to Beatrice Webb?

It is tempting to do so. The *Fabian Essays*, which had been published in 1889, embody the older Socialist attitude to Trade Unionism and Co-operation. Both movements were almost completely ignored, and at least one of the passing references was hostile.[4] Their shortcomings on these subjects were fully acknowledged by Sidney Webb in a preface to a later edition.[5] The

[1] B. Webb, *op. cit.* p. 458.
[2] *Ibid.* p. 437.
[3] *Ibid.* p. 442.
[4] Co-ops treated as transfigured joint-stockism, *Fabian Essays*, 1889 ed. pp. 88–9.
[5] Preface to the 1920 edition of *Fabian Essays*.

recognition of the importance of these two movements, it might be said, has formed the basis of all later Fabian political recommendations. Was it not after Sidney Webb became acquainted with Beatrice Potter that the Fabian attitude changed so greatly?

While Beatrice Webb's investigations, accomplished or planned, were to a considerable extent responsible for the change, other influences were making in the same direction. The 'New Unionism' by 1889 was causing Socialists to reconsider the significance of Trade Unionism in the Labour Movement and in political and economic life generally. In fact, Sidney Webb had already become acquainted with the literature of Trade Unionism, for it was to him that Beatrice Potter had turned when she wanted advice on the subject.[1] Pease suggests also that the Fabian Essayists had already, early in 1889, modified their uncompromising opinions about Co-operation after a meeting with some of the Co-operative leaders.[2] But undoubtedly Beatrice Potter's work on Co-operation exercised a strong influence upon the Fabians, and the time was obviously ripe for the investigation of Trade Unionism by the Webb 'partnership'. The conclusions that Beatrice Potter had arrived at in her paper of 1887 were included in the preface to the Webbs' *Industrial Democracy*, where it was said that no useful conclusions, theoretic or practical, could 'be arrived at by arguing from "common notions" about Trade Unionism; nor even by refining these into a definition of some imaginary form of combination in the abstract'. 'Sociology, like all other sciences', the Webbs continued, 'can advance only upon the basis of a precise observation of actual facts'.[3] The view of the Webb partnership had become influenced by the criticisms of 'abstract economics' made by the followers of Comte and the German Historical School. Sociology, the Webbs had come to believe, had to be built up gradually, from the groundwork of a study of the life history of institutions.

Since the 'eighties the dispute about the relative merits of the 'historical' and 'deductive' methods in economics has produced a library of literature. In the light of later discussions, the Webbs' reasons for abandoning that method of economic theorizing which involves drawing logical conclusions from assumptions appear somewhat hasty and inadequate. While it is true that this method loses its interest and importance if the economic 'models' constructed in this way bear little relation to the real world, it is not *necessary* that economists' assumptions must first be obtained by induction from historical or sociological observation in the strict sense. The relationship between sociology and economics is more complicated than the Webbs allowed, and one cannot avoid the conclusion that they were less concerned to argue the matter out, than to find a reason for escaping to a type of inquiry more congenial to themselves. In the

[1] B. Webb, *My Apprenticeship*, p. 455.
[2] Pease, *op. cit.* p. 92.
[3] S. and B. Webb, *Industrial Democracy* (Longmans, 1897), p.v.

FABIAN ECONOMICS AND SOCIOLOGY

process, they did discover a new and fruitful field of investigation; but we must
notice some of the effects which their acceptance of the historical method had
upon their own works and also upon those produced by the Fabian Society.

First, the completeness of the Webbs' rejection of 'abstract economics' needs
to be emphasized. A fairly comprehensive modern bibliography of economic
theory[1] mentions only two minor works of the Webbs (and of one of them
Sidney Webb is only the editor) written after 1890. Certainly the Webbs did
not hesitate to touch on matters of abstract economics or the pronouncements
of economists relevant to the institutions they were studying historically—they
make masterly use of the opinions of economists to bolster their own social
and political arguments[2]—but they obviously did not consider it worth while
to construct a system or to raise their arguments to an independent theoretic
plane. Theoretical economists in return perhaps ignored the Webbs more than
they should have done. The flow of discussion upon economic theory did not
abate because the Webbs turned away from it.

The second important result of the Webbs' espousal of sociology is the
extent to which they were led to write *history* rather than *economics*, even if
their descriptions of the workings of contemporary social institutions are included under the head of economics. Their works which definitely pointed a
new way in sociology, as opposed to those which were merely histories, are
comparatively few. *Industrial Democracy* did in fact represent a careful analyti-
cal account of Trade Unions, explaining how they worked and what effects
they had upon the community. It was, in short, a superb example of applying
historical methods to the study of one of the subjects that had occupied the
attention of economists, and applying them in such a way that the work has
become one of permanent reference for economists. On the other hand, the
Webbs' *History of Trade Unionism* is most emphatically a *history*. So also is
their most extensive work, which occupied them from 1898 to 1930—their
*English Local Government from the Revolution to the Municipal Corporations
Act*. It is certainly most important history: it is the history of institutions which
had never been so adequately or systematically studied before; institutions,
moreover, that were to become more important in people's eyes after the
Webbs had written. But for all that it is history and not economics. And there
was perhaps just a small grain of truth in H. G. Wells' taunt that their 'study
of the methods of Dogberry and Shallow' was not likely to be of much use for
Socialists.[3]

The Webbs might have retorted to Wells, had they wished, that even history

[1] H. E. Bateson, *A Select Bibliography of Modern Economic Theory* 1870–1929 (Routledge, London, 1930). (This bibliography of course excludes works of descriptive economics
or economic history).
[2] Many examples could be given, but an excellent one is the essay 'The Regulation of the
Hours of Labour' reprinted in *Problems of Modern Industry*.
[3] H. G. Wells, *Experiment in Autobiography* (Gollancz, London, 1934), vol. 1, p. 258.

55

has its uses. Some knowledge of the history of the institutions they are trying to change is important to reformers. The importance of the historical development of Local Government and Trade Union institutions in that 'spontaneous undergrowth of social tissue' which the Webbs saw as growing, ultimately, into Socialism is difficult to deny. In fact the Webbs have declared specifically that, setting out with the intention merely of describing 'the organization and working of the existing Local Government Authorities, with a view to discovering how they could be improved', they found themselves driven to trace their history in order to understand them more fully.[1]

Nevertheless, a distinction must be made between the Webbs' work as members of the Fabian Society and the interests they pursued outside the scope of the Society—just such a distinction as must be made in the case of Shaw, Podmore, and many of the other members, even if it is more difficult to make this distinction where the Webbs are concerned. And we observe that the Webbs' excursions into history have not been followed slavishly by the Fabian Society. The need for the Society's propaganda to keep mainly to contemporary issues has been realized, and, apart from a few Tracts, professedly of a historical or biographical character, the 'historical background' to the Fabian Society's practical recommendations has usually been dealt with briefly enough.

The third result of the Webbs' view of sociology had greater influence upon the Society as a whole. The Webbs believed that a general view of the working of society could only be constructed after a great deal more of their kind of research had been done. With this approach, they tended to see and analyse institutions separately, rather than in terms of a whole system. The 'abstract' economists, with all their faults, had at least avoided this danger, as one of their major purposes in 'building their models' had been to consider the effect upon the system as a whole of a change in one part of it. To say that the Webbs did not consider the system as a whole would be an overstatement (especially when we think of such a work as *Industrial Democracy*)[2]; but perhaps it is an overstatement not without some illumination. The Webbs were the main advocates (amongst socialists) of 'piecemeal social engineering', and both their own writing, and the Fabian Tracts published between 1890 and 1914, show a preoccupation with the pieces only. Until the outbreak of the First World War had revealed to the Webbs and the Fabians the dangers of concentrating on some aspects of social life and ignoring the influences of other aspects, they produced no over-all picture of the 'condition of England'. Nor was it until after the First World War that the Webbs attempted a full sketch of the reorganization of political institutions that Socialism in Great Britain might

[1] S. and B. Webb, *English Local Government: Statutory Authorities for Special Purposes* (Longmans, London, 1922), p. 350.
[2] See the final section of *Industrial Democracy*.

require.[1] As the Webbs themselves remarked, in 1921, they had 'been investigating and describing democratic institutions for nearly thirty years' before they 'published any volume dealing with the National Government or the Political State'.[2] The well-known old jeer at the Fabians, that they reduced socialism to a mere matter of 'gas and water', has something to it, even if the Fabians were able to retort effectively that they achieved results more tangible than mere talk by concentrating on limited and definite objectives.

The Webbs did not 'remake economics'. Their *Industrial Democracy* did indeed seem to point a new way for economics, but this kind of study was not followed up in any of their subsequent major works, save only *The Consumers' Co-operative Movement*, which made a similar analysis of the functions of the Co-operatives. In the main, their historical interests, already apparent in their *History of Trade Unionism*, came to overwhelm their interest in economics. The Webbs' 'sociology' consisted in writing the history of the structure and functions of organized groups within the State, whether these groups were voluntary associations, like Trade Unions or Co-operatives, or compulsory, like Local Government bodies. But economics has traditionally been concerned only with the structure and functions of the system whereby wealth is produced and distributed, and generally only with contemporary matters. Certainly only a fraction of all the Webbs' writings would be considered by most economists as falling within their sphere of interest. The rest would probably be classified as a new and important kind of history. In seeking to widen the scope of economics, the Webbs 'passed into otherness' and became historians. In the Fabian Society, the Webbs' interests had a negative rather than positive effect. That is to say, the Society's publications did not reflect the Webbs' historical interests to any great extent, but the Society followed them in refusing to adopt any general 'system' of economics, and concentrated on piecemeal reforms.

A CODA: EQUAL INCOMES UNDER SOCIALISM?

Some detailed, practical points of Fabian economics will be dealt with in a later chapter. This section will be concluded with one final general issue, which was, however, a personal view of Bernard Shaw's rather than a doctrine of the Fabian Society. This is Shaw's much-discussed proposal for equality of incomes. The earlier, and apparently still un-repudiated *official* Fabian view was that Socialism did not involve equality of incomes.[3] It was not until 1910 that Shaw announced his conversion to the contrary opinion, and it is noteworthy that this occurred at a time when the younger Fabians were beginning to claim that the older Fabian Collectivism had been practically adopted by the Liberal

[1] *A Constitution for the Socialist Commonwealth of Great Britain* was published in 1920.
[2] Quoted Tawney *op. cit.* p. 14.
[3] Tract 70.

Government. There was a need to find a new faith to preach, and Shaw found it in his principle that Socialism involved equal incomes. Later, he was to put this point very strongly when he wrote 'Socialism means equality of income and nothing else.'[1] After 1910 Shaw made the preaching of this doctrine one of his main tasks, and apparently he was able to make a number of converts among the members of the Society.[2]

The most comprehensive statement of Shaw's views on this matter was given in the *Intelligent Woman's Guide*, where he said of the new doctrine: 'As far as I know I was the first Socialist writer to whom it occurred to state this explicitly as a necessary postulate of permanent civilization; but as nothing that is true is ever new I dare say it had been said again and again before I was born.'[3] In his last statement at any rate he was quite right; one does not need to go further than the 1895 annual conference of the Independent Labour Party to find the idea being put forward by a Dr G. Rome Hall.[4]

The difficulty with the new doctrine seems to be that Shaw does not always make it clear whether equality of incomes is an ideal to be attained ultimately by a Socialist Society or a principle capable of application fairly early in its existence. In the rapid 'elimination argument' at the beginning of the *Intelligent Woman's Guide*, six other possible solutions are rejected as unreasonable or unjust, and we are left with equality as the only acceptable way. The argument is highly entertaining, but not one that would be likely to convince an opponent. Its main merit, as is often the case with Shaw's writing, is that its challenging 'reasonableness' leads one to examine commonly accepted assumptions. It is not true to say that Shaw completely ignored the problem of 'incentive payments': he does point out that other things besides money are important incentives,[5] and in the last analysis, he suggested the Socialist State might use an unequal distribution of leisure as an incentive,[6] though without inquiring how far the disadvantages produced by an unequal distribution of leisure might parallel those of an unequal distribution of incomes. In his later works Shaw appears to have agreed that equality of incomes is rather an ideal to be worked towards than an easily established principle, or an essential condition of a Socialist State.[7]

The main interest in the doctrine of equality of incomes lies in the theoretical contradiction which seems to arise between it and the Fabian theory of rent. In one sense, of course, it might be maintained that equality of incomes is a carrying to its logical conclusion of the belief that all 'rents' including 'rent of ability' are 'unearned'. But Shaw gives us two main reasons for rejecting

---

[1] G. B. Shaw, *The Intelligent Woman's Guide* (Pelican), p. 103.
[2] Pease, *op. cit.* p. 203.
[3] *Op. cit.* p. 468.
[4] Report of the 1895 Annual Conference of I.L.P. p. 8.
[5] *Intelligent Woman's Guide* (Pelican), p. 85.
[6] *Ibid.* pp. 89-90.
[7] G. B. Shaw, *Everybody's Political What's What* (Constable, London, 1944), p. 356.

FABIAN ECONOMICS AND SOCIOLOGY

alternative schemes and accepting equality: because you can't 'measure anyone's merit in money';[1] and because 'it is quite impossible to find out how
much each person has produced'.[2] Yet the theory of rent, if it means anything
at all, means that the contribution of the factors of production is at least
theoretically capable of being measured. There also appears to be an element
of 'merit' at least in a negative sense in the Fabian theory of rent—in that it is
suggested that those who live by receiving rent do not really deserve any
reward.

[1] *Intelligent Woman's Guide* (Pelican), p. 44.
[2] *Ibid.* p. 38.

59

CHAPTER III

FABIAN HISTORICAL AND
POLITICAL THEORY

ORIGINS

THE Fabians, in a Tract which they issued as a statement of their views to the 1896 meeting of the Second International, denied that the Society had any collective views on 'historic evolution'.[1] This did not mean that the subject had not been debated in the Society, nor that the Fabian leaders had not approached a measure of agreement on the subject; it merely meant that considerable differences of opinion still existed amongst the Society's members. These differences were never finally compounded, and the Society's statement can be accepted with reservations. Even the views on 'historic evolution' which were held by some of the leaders were never stated with the precision of (for comparison) their views on economics. Nevertheless, a general tendency in Fabian thinking may be discerned in the publications of the Society, and it is too important to be overlooked.

Although the outlines of a new theory of history may be seen in the writings of leading Fabians, it was not made explicit as a theory of history: their views were expressed mainly in a critical and eclectic way. This is not surprising when we reflect that the Fabians grew up in the shadow of the great philosophies of history which had been formulated earlier in the nineteenth century. The philosophies of history or sociologies of Comte, Spencer, Hegel, and Marx[2] (not to mention those of Buckle and lesser figures) had all become familiar to the Fabians' generation of English intellectuals, and one can hardly blame them if they were somewhat overwhelmed by this outpouring of the cornucopia. Darwin's extension of the evolution theory to the world of nature reinforced a principle which had already been applied to history by Hegel, Marx, and even earlier theorists. Darwin's works came as a revelation to some of his younger contemporaries—as Bernard Shaw has wittily recounted[3]—and the thought of a whole period took reflected glory from the science of biology.

At a time when the conceptions of Evolution and of the Social Organism had, as Sidney Webb wrote, 'penetrated to the minds . . . even of our professors of Political Economy',[4] it was only to be expected that the Fabians would avail themselves of these ideas to justify their programme. The extent to which

[1] Tract 70.
[2] This is not a chronological arrangement of the names, but rather the order in which they became generally known in England.
[3] G. B. Shaw, Preface to *Back to Methusaleh*.
[4] *Fabian Essays*, 1889 ed. p. 46.

60

they did so may be seen in several theoretical Tracts written for the Society at different times by Sidney Webb, and also in *Fabian Essays*—and not only in Webb's contribution to that work.

If the views of social development set forth in *Fabian Essays* were not stated systematically enough to be dignified by the name of philosophy of history, they at least imply fairly strong opinions about historical causation, for the advent of Socialism was treated as inevitable (at least in the long run). An evolutionist outlook was common to all the essays, whether they dealt with economic theory, history, industry, ideas of property, politics, or even morality. And the explanations given in the *Essays* of this evolutionary process show that the Fabians were believers in multiple causation in history (as indeed everybody is, at the first level). In their explanations of the inevitable coming of Socialism, they emphasized, amongst intellectual factors, these: the Spirit of the Time (*Zeitgeist*); the continuing momentum of the ideas which the fall of the Bastille had spread throughout the world; the influence of modern writers in revolt against *laissez faire;* and the consciousness of the masses that Individualism had failed to provide a decent social life. The political causes they stressed were the 'irresistible' progress of Democracy; the competition of the political parties for popular favour; and the practical political needs of a more collectivist type of society. Amongst economic factors, they gave major importance to the growth of trade as a solvent of the 'feudal synthesis', and to the Industrial Revolution which had 'left the labourer a landless stranger in his own country', which had produced the unemployment problem, and was leading ultimately to the separation of capitalist and entrepreneurial functions and to the diminution in numbers of the real controllers of economic power, through the development of combinations and monopoly.

This list of explanations reveals the influence, to some extent, of all their great predecessors. They probably borrowed the concept of the *Zeitgeist* from the Neo-Hegelians but their debt to Hegel does not seem great, as the term is not exclusively Hegelian, and there was nothing specifically Hegelian about the way the Fabians used it, in fact they used it only as a vague metaphor. The influence of Comte was strongest upon Sydney Olivier,[1] but his essay owed more to Marx than to Comte in the statements about historical causation embedded in its primarily descriptive outline. Webb too was influenced by Comte both directly and through John Stuart Mill,[2] but his historical essay also fails to give as much causal weight to pure science and philosophy as Comte would have required.[3] Indeed Webb's emphasis suggests that, like

[1] Margaret Olivier (ed.) *Sydney Olivier, Letters and Selected Writings* (Allen & Unwin, London, 1948), pp. 9, 55 *et passim.*
[2] *Ibid*, p. 9.
[3] For Comte's view on historical causation see his *Positive Philosophy* (H. Martineau trans.) (John Chapman, London, 1853), vol. II, esp. pp. 156–7.

Herbert Spencer, he attached more importance to 'opinion' than to philosophical notions as the motive force in historical change.[1] '. . . it is through the slow and gradual turning of the popular mind to new principles that social reorganization bit by bit comes', Webb wrote in one place.[2] Other features in the *Fabian Essays* which derived from Spencer's sociology were the view that progress is differentiation (specifically credited to him) and, in part from Spencer also, the questionable analogy between society and an organism[3] and its corollaries. But the whole direction of Spencer's sociological and political thought was too remote from that of the Fabians to allow him to exert any but a very general influence.[4] As for the influence of Marx, this was more direct and more pervasive, and requires closer analysis.

The clearest example of the influence of Marx's historical theory on Fabian doctrine may be seen in Tract No. 15, *English Progress Towards Social Democracy*, written by Sidney Webb. There are striking similarities to the argument of the historical sections of *The Communist Manifesto*. The sketch given of the course of history emphasized the struggle for the 'surplus product' as the underlying economic characteristic of social evolution; the stages of slavery, serfdom, and proletarianism were rapidly reviewed; and the solution was seen in the political evolution of the working-class and the termination of private control of the means of production by the gradual progress of collective ownership.

Fabian Essays also reveals a number of elements taken over from Marxist theory. In addition to the emphasis on the role of the working-class in bringing Socialism into existence, the doctrines of the narrowing of the numbers of the capitalist class and the increasing misery of the working-class can both be found there, even if the conclusions drawn from them were not Marxist ones. Webb noted the tremendous spread of joint stock organizations and the reduction of the capitalist to a coupon-clipper; both Shaw and Mrs Besant spoke of the rapidly increasing army of the unemployed;[5] William Clarke, drawing mainly on his knowledge of American conditions, anticipated that the growth of great trusts in industry would crush out smaller competitors.[6] When Clarke delivered his essay as a lecture to the Fabian Society, he quoted extensively

[1] Most succinctly stated in H. Spencer's *Reasons for Dissenting from the Philosophy of M. Comte* (Williams & Norgate, London, 1884).

[2] *Fabian Essays* (1889 editn.) p. 34 (cf. also *Methods of Social Study*, p. 251).

[3] Probably the Fabians, especially Webb, took the idea from Darwin and Spencer, but it was of course a very old view refurbished, and they might have had it from other sources. In particular, Comte had stressed the biological analogy, and Hegelian influence tended in the same direction.

[4] J. Rumney, *Herbert Spencer's Sociology: a Study in the History of Social Theory* (Williams & Norgate, London, 1934), gives a good outline of the direction of Spencer's thinking.

[5] At the time *Fabian Essays* was published, the English economy was recovering from the slump of the 'eighties and unemployment in the later 'eighties was diminishing.

[6] English conditions before 1914 would not have been at all satisfactory for Clarke's purpose. H. Levy, *Monopolies, Cartels and Trusts in British Industry* (Macmillan, London, 1927).

from the *Communist Manifesto*,[1] but the quotation was deleted when it was published.

Both the *Essays* and other Tracts show that the Fabians gave considerable weight to the explanation of future social development in terms of the 'contradiction' between the potential power of the working-class and its social condition. This view was expressed firmly enough when in 1892 Sidney Webb, cross-examined before the Royal Commission on Labour, was asked why he considered Socialism 'the economic obverse of democracy'. He answered:

It appears to me that if you allow a tramway conductor a vote he will not for ever be satisfied with exercising that vote over such matters as the appointment of the Ambassador to Paris, or even the position of the franchise. He will realize that the forces which keep him at work for sixteen hours a day for three shillings a day are not the forces of hostile kings, or nobles, or priests; but whatever forces they are he will, it seems to me, seek so far as possible to control them by his vote. That is to say, he will more and more seek to convert his political democracy into what one may roughly term an industrial democracy, so that he may obtain some kind of control as a voter over the conditions under which he lives.[2]

DEPARTURES FROM MARX

If the Fabians' debt to Marx's historical writings was considerable, their departures from him were also of great importance. The fact that the Fabians were impressed by Marx's historical writing, and took something from it, does not of course mean that they accepted his historical theory in any full sense. In the early days of the Fabian Society, they were saved from a considerable amount of theoretical controversy and took a more favourable view of Marx as an historian, because they approached him not through his theoretical statements of his conception of history, but through his actual historical writings.[3] When, later, the Fabians were brought into contact with the theoretical expositions of the materialist conception of history, their reactions were distinctly unfavourable. Some of the more eminent Fabian spokesmen believed Marx's meaning to be both rigid and crude. The Webbs thought that Marx was attempting to impose a transcendental pattern on historical facts; they considered his theory of history 'merely one hypothesis amongst many . . . which appears to describe some of the phenomena of social evolution . . . but not others'; they apparently believed he was seeking to reduce all causes to economic ones. Graham Wallas went further, and thought that Marx was attempting to reduce all historical motivation to economic motives.[4] Marx's meaning

---

[1] See report in *Today*, vol. x, p. 186.
[2] Royal Commission on Labour, 17 November 1892, Minutes of Evidence, 4th Report, vol. xxxix, p. 266.
[3] See ch. I (p. 11) above.
[4] For the Webbs' view, see *Methods of Social Study* (Longmans, London, 1932), footnote to p. 14; for Graham Wallas' view, *Men and Ideas* (Allen & Unwin, London, 1940), p. 105.

is still a much-disputed question, but it seems likely that these are misinterpretations of Marx himself though perhaps not of some of his followers.[1] These Fabian reactions reveal a common confusion between theories of history (or philosophies of history)—the broadest and most general observations about the hierarchy of importance of historical causes—and what might be called 'first level' statements about historical causation (which are the only statements that interest historians who are dealing with the history of a particular period). However, since the Fabians accepted such interpretations, it was sensible to stress, as they did, the importance of non-economic causes, and to warn practising historians against the dangers of having only one hypothesis.[2] So far as historical *method* is concerned any particular theory of history is, as the Webbs point out, only one hypothesis amongst others, and the best advice about method for a person writing the history of a particular period is of the kind given in the Webbs' *Methods of Social Study*—one of the more valuable works written on that subject. But *Methods of Social Study* does not contain a theory of history. The Webbs—and the Fabian Society too —believed that they did not need to subscribe to one.

They hardly seem justified in such a belief when they also indulged in prediction of the future development of society. To say that there are many causes, all inter-acting, is not a very helpful statement, if the generalizations derived from a study of history are to have any predictive value. Historical causes must be capable of being grouped into some order of importance, if a study of the past and present is to provide any assistance in estimating the future. To predict the coming of Socialism with any confidence it is necessary either to list the causes making for Socialism and those making against it and to establish that those making for it are more likely to prevail, or to have some theory of history which, in effect, performs the same operation. In the *Fabian Essays*, the coming of Socialism was predicted, and a number of causes given; but the relative importance of the causes, or their relation one to another, was not considered in any systematic way, though some hints were thrown out, and implicitly the Marxist 'weighting' of the importance of the causes was to a considerable extent accepted. Of course, it is only fair to remember that *Fabian Essays* was a propaganda work, but no more satisfactory treatment of the problem is to be found anywhere else in Fabian writing. They could have extricated themselves from their dilemma by dropping the idea of the inevitability of Socialism, but this they were never quite willing to do, although their

[1] Wallas' interpretation depends upon a 'psychologism' quite foreign to Marx's type of thought (this question has been discussed very ably by Karl Popper in his *The Open Society and its Enemies*, chs. 14 and 15); the Webbs' interpretation, though more justified, depends on a confusion of what I have called 'first level' and more general or philosophical statements about historical causation.

[2] S. and B. Webb, *Industrial Democracy* (Longmans, 1911 ed.), p. x (this may not refer specifically to the Marxist hypothesis); *Methods of Social Study*, pp. 14-15, 61 (this does).

writings after the First World War show that their faith in progress had been shaken.[1]

The Fabians also had objections to the Marxist 'class-war' or 'class-conflict' doctrine. All of them were concerned to maintain that Marx's revolutionary conclusions were not valid for the democratic age, and, while it was open to them merely to say that the class-conflict could now be solved by constitutional means, they usually went further than this, and cast some doubt upon Marx's premises. There always seems to have been a considerable amount of disagreement between individual Fabians about the length to which they would go in criticizing Marx's premises, a disagreement which finally prompted the declaration in Tract 70 that the Society as a whole had no views on 'historic evolution'.

It is sometimes said that the Fabians denied the existence of a class-conflict in society. But this generalization is usually based upon the fact that the Fabians abandoned the use of the Marxist terms 'class-war' and 'class-struggle', and abandoning the terms does not necessarily mean denying the thing. By and large, the Fabians did not develop any alternative definition of class, but used the term very much in the same way as Marx: that is to say, they used it sometimes to mean broad groupings defined strictly in terms of the ownership or non-ownership of the means of production, sometimes more loosely to mean occupational groupings within these broad categories. Some Fabians did make minor criticisms of Marx's categories by pointing to the difficulties of drawing precise boundaries between classes; but leading Fabians at any rate were not guilty of the rash argument that classes did not exist because their boundaries were unclear.[2] The only major significant addition to, or revision of, Marx's use of terms made by the Fabians lay in their recognition of the growth of the managerial class of 'white-collar workers' since Marx's time.[3] Furthermore the Fabians did not deny that there were conflicts of interest between the classes. In fact, a recognition of these conflicts of interest is an essential part of Fabian, as it must be of any socialist theory; and the Fabians at different times have enlarged upon the conflicts caused by capitalist relations of production. What, then, was the point of their renunciation of the Marxist terms? Simply that they wished to deny the Marxist contention that the class-struggle was the engine for bringing Socialism into existence.

The Fabian theorists had recourse to several different arguments to achieve this purpose. The first, and least satisfactory argument was of the 'We-are-all-Socialists-now' type. It perhaps had its uses as a weapon of propaganda, but it met with derision even amongst the Fabians themselves. Nevertheless, some Fabians at times employed it. The impression created in Sidney Webb's contri-

[1] 'Although change is inevitable, progress is not,' the Webbs wrote in *A Constitution for the Socialist Commonwealth of Great Britian*, p. 98.
[2] *Methods of Social Study*, p. 15.
[3] e.g. Tract 41; G. B. Shaw, *Essays in Fabian Socialism* (Constable, 1932,) p. 158.

bution to *Fabian Essays* was that everyone, willy-nilly, was being swept along into Socialism. Even persons and movements professedly anti-socialist were extending the sphere of State activity, and approving its extension. In a famous page, Webb catalogued first the activities which the State already engaged in, and then the things it registered, from hawkers to places of worship. State intervention and control, Webb implied, was increasing and would continue to do so. Webb has been reproached, not only by later critics[1] but even at the time by his Fabian colleagues,[2] for his naivety in equating 'State intervention' with 'Collectivism' and both with 'Socialism'—for believing that *any* extension of State authority must be a step in the direction of Socialism. Perhaps the charge is not quite without foundation, but too much can be, and has been, made of it. After all, Webb did know what he meant by Socialism,[3] and if he forgot to apply his touchstone to test if any particular measure of State intervention was 'socialistic' he had other Fabians, like Hubert Bland, to remind him to do so. The 'We-are-all-Socialists' type of argument was only useful, as Bland said, as 'a good method of scoring a point off an individualist opponent in a debate before a middle-class audience';[4] it was designed to free men's minds from '*laissez faire* panic' about making use of State power.

The second argument used by the Fabians against the Marxist position might be considered a 'revision' of Marx rather than a complete departure from him. In this argument the Fabians agreed with the Marxists that the chief factor in producing the new Society would be the awareness of the working-class that Socialism served its real interests; they agreed also that the present antagonisms of class interests would do something to promote this 'class-consciousness'. But the Fabians denied that this awakening would come simply or automatically, and denied that the expression of these antagonisms in a militant or revolutionary way could assist the advent of Socialism. Thus they envisaged a larger role for education, propaganda, and persuasion and less for 'the practical experience of the working-class struggle'. They were also inclined to treat strikes, lock-outs, and unemployed unrest as nothing but manifestations of the injustice of Capitalism, or a warning of the unpleasantness and chaos that might ensue if Fabian advice were not heeded.

A third argument, used by some Fabians, especially Bernard Shaw, was a radical departure from the Marxist 'class-struggle' position. Shaw denied that

---

[1] A. Gray, *The Socialist Tradition, Moses to Lenin* (Longmans, London, 1946), p. 395.
[2] Hubert Bland in *Fabian Essays* (1889 ed.), p. 212.
[3] S. Webb, *Socialism in England* (Swann Sonnenschein, 1890), p. 10: 'On the economic side, Socialism implies the collective administration of Rent and Interest, leaving to the individual only the wages of his labour by hand and brain. On the political side, it involves the collective control over, and ultimate administration of, all the main instruments of wealth production. On the ethical side, it expresses the real recognition of fraternity, the universal obligation of personal service, and the subordination of individual ends to the common good.'
[4] *Fabian Essays* (1889 ed.), p. 213.

the alignment for and against Socialism bore any real relation to the confront-
ation of classes as seen by Marx. The conflict between bourgeois and proletarian might produce industrial unrest; it would not produce Socialism. In
the struggle for Socialism, it was not true that the bourgeoisie was in one camp
and the proletariat in the other. Not only was socialist theory itself the product
of middle-class thinkers in revolt against the environment in which they had
been brought up; the lines of the struggle for and against Socialism did not
run between the classes, but cut right through them, from richest to poorest.
Bernard Shaw, in elaborating this argument, made lively fun of what he called
'the crude Marxian melodrama of "The Class War; or the Virtuous Worker
and the Brutal Capitalist".'[1] Shaw maintained that the anti-Socialists could
count on the support of large sections in every class who had a stake in the
maintenance of the capitalist system—quite apart from the support of the
stupid, the deceived and the corrupt. 'If the unearned incomes of the rich
disappeared,' Shaw wrote, 'places like Bournemouth would either perish like
the cities of Nineveh and Babylon, or else the inhabitants would have, as they
would put it, to cater for a different class of people. . . .'[2]

All three of these arguments are implicit in Fabian criticisms of the Marxist
class-struggle doctrine from the late 'eighties, but each of them received
different emphasis at different times and by different spokesmen. At the time
of *Fabian Essays* the first two of these arguments were emphasized; the third
was barely yet noticeable. It was not until about the middle 'nineties, by which
time the Fabians were thoroughly disillusioned with the progress of Socialists'
attempts to persuade the English working-class, that Bernard Shaw advanced
the third argument strongly.

Even more important in the *Fabian Essays* than the criticism of basic
Marxist concepts, was the elaboration of an evolutionary interpretation of
history to oppose to Marx's revolutionary interpretation. The account given
by several of the Essayists of the evolution of Capitalism into Socialism, which
was spoken of many years later as 'the inevitability of gradualness', had about
it something of predeterminism, and all the more so, when some of the moving
causes of the *Zeitgeist* were not made as clear as they might have been. It was
their version of Salvation by Faith, and they never quite got rid of it, though
in later years they laid more stress on the doctrine of Salvation by
Works. Not that the Salvation by Faith doctrine ever led the Fabians to sit
down and fold their hands.[3] While in the *Essays* they saw the progress of
Socialism as an inevitable tendency, the Fabians thought of themselves as

---

[1] Shaw's position was most clearly stated in his three articles on 'The Class War' which
appeared in the *Clarion* of 30 September, 21 October and 4 November 1904.
[2] G. B. Shaw, *The Intelligent Woman's Guide* (Pelican, London, 1937), p. 352.
[3] Paradoxically, the doctrine of Salvation by Faith in its various guises in the history of
Europe seems to have stimulated its votaries to vigorous action rather than to have promoted
resignation.

turning the unconscious tendency into a conscious one, because, Webb thought, consciouness of the change would make it come more easily, more tidily and more quickly. Bland also spoke of 'turning instinct into self-conscious reason', without being so optimistic about the political effects of doing so. The importance of preaching was also defended on the somewhat more dubious grounds (dubious, that is, for the *Zeitgeist's* existence)[1] that the *Zeitgeist* is 'only the sum of individual strivings and aspirations' and does not work except through the efforts of individual men.

By one or two of the Fabian Essayists the evolutionary interpretation of history was carried to considerable lengths. An attempt was made to brush away some of the political revolutions which had occurred in the course of history. The French Revolution of 1789 was spoken of, by William Clarke, as a mere incident in a process which had been loosening the fabric of French civilization through several generations. Mrs Besant in a similar way spoke slightingly of 'transient riots which merely upset thrones and behead kings'. Such remarks of course beg the questions: What *was* the relation of these political upheavals to the social revolution? Ought the political revolution not to have occurred? Did it not make any difference to the course of history?. . . The only one of the seven Essayists who seems clearly to have faced the problem was Hubert Bland, and he, the 'Tory-Marxist' among the Fabians, had a peculiar view of evolution and constitutionalism leading up to revolution, which was not shared at that time by his colleagues—though it was later adopted also by Bernard Shaw.[2] Bland had earlier,[3] as well as by implication in his contribution to *Fabian Essays*, declared that the barricades were the 'last ditch of despair', therefore the Socialists should use constitutional methods to make sure the people who resorted to the barricades would be the anti-Socialists, making their last stand. He might very well have given an interpretation of the English Revolution of the seventeenth century and of the French Revolution of the eighteenth century in analogous terms to these, but did not bother to elaborate his view into a theory of history.

However, the main point of the evolutionary interpretation and the idea that nature and history do not make jumps, was to emphasize the 'need' for the change to Socialism to be peaceful. As a general interpretation of history its validity seems more than doubtful. This appears to be admitted by Webb in another place, for while he insisted that the changes to Socialism would

---

[1] *Fabian Essays* (1889 ed.), pp. 50, 132. If the *Zeitgeist* does not work except through the efforts or volition of individual men, the problem of Free Will and Determinism is raised. If it is only the sum of individual strivings, it seems an effect rather than a cause of social change. Despite the Hegelian terminology, it is clear that the Fabian *Zeitgeist* is more like Spencer's Public Opinion. The preaching of individuals and minorities changes Public Opinion, which then produces a social change. Whether this is a sound device for describing even democratic social change seems dubious.

[2] G. B. Shaw, Preface to 1908 reprint of *Fabian Essays*.

[3] Article in *Practical Socialist*, October 1886.

necessarily be democratic, gradual, constitutional and peaceful in England, he made no such prediction about countries where democratic institutions were absent. In the case of Russia, he admitted that the absence of democracy made it impossible for the socialist movement to be other than revolutionary.[1] One suspects that the evolutionary interpretation of history really served to avoid the question whether the Fabians' opposition to revolution was based on moral or on politico-scientific grounds. To say that history is necessarily evolving gradually made it seem that no choice of methods was involved. The question might have been posed in these terms: is your opposition to revolution based on moral grounds (i.e. on the feeling that, in a democratic State people ought not to promote a revolution, even to attain Socialism), or is it purely on scientific grounds (i.e. on the prediction that a revolution, if provoked, would not be successful in establishing Socialism, leading to a different view if this prediction could be proved wrong)? Had the question been put in this way, the Fabians might have found themselves divided into those revealing themselves as Democrats first and Socialists only second, and those who were Socialists first and Democrats second.[2] Bland and Shaw, seem explicitly to have taken the second position, while others, like Edward Pease would certainly have taken the first. But with the confusion introduced by the avoiding of the moral issue, it was not at all clear where some others of the Fabians stood. Perhaps, however, it is rather harsh to speak thus of 'avoiding of the moral issue' for it was not deliberate evasion; in the 'eighties all the Fabians had high hopes of the newly-won democracy and thought it would lead straight to Socialism; they felt revolution was an outmoded and unnecessary expedient, and even those who would have objected to revolution on moral grounds were equally convinced of its impracticability. The importance of the issue lay in the future: not until the question of their attitude to the Russian Revolution of 1917 arose did the differences amongst the Fabians become apparent.

Other practical reasons against revolutionary methods were given in *Fabian Essays*. To demonstrate the need for slow change the Essayists directed attention away from the political to the technical and social aspects. Shaw in his 'Transition' essay ridiculed the idea that Socialism could be established in one exciting day by referring to the difficulty of converting first and third class railway carriages all into second class ones. Elsewhere, William Clarke dwelt on the length of time it took for feudal institutions to be transformed into capitalist ones, and hinted that this change could only be presented in dramatic revolutionary form by an historian who ruthlessly telescoped the length of time it all really took. Such arguments, frequently repeated in later Fabian writing,

[1] S. Webb, *Socialism in England*, p. 8; cf. *Fabian Essays*, p. 35.
[2] Some Fabians might attempt to escape this dilemma by saying that Socialism *is* an extension of Democracy; but this would be avoiding a real problem by a definition.

69

were no doubt effective answers to young and romantic S.D.F. hotheads, but it is doubtful if they really touched the more serious Marxist points. The second Fabian argument raises once again the whole question of the relation of social change to political revolution; Marx did not deny the first was slow, but insisted that the latter occurred at a 'nodal point' in the process. The other Fabian argument also did not meet squarely the Marxist contention that the seizure of power was the first thing, and railway carriage conversion came after that.[1] To a considerable degree, Fabians and Marxists were using words in a different way in the argument. Marxists were inclined to say that Socialism is established when Socialists come to power (with the idea of pretty speedy change occurring thereafter); Fabians said Socialism is established when all important industries are socialized, and, at least in the 'eighties, they did not seem extremely impatient about the time it was to take.[2] In another sense, however, there is a real and not merely verbal dispute involved. It arises out of a different placing of optimism and pessimism in Marxist and Fabian theory. Marx, impressed by the extempore administration of the Committee of Public Safety of 1793-4 and of the Paris Commune of 1871, was inclined to treat administrative difficulties with scant respect, while the Fabians, as public servants and practical administrators, made much of these difficulties. The Fabians, on the other hand, were optimistic about the ease with which the opposition to Socialism could be overcome, and refused to take seriously the Marxist preoccupation with the dangers of counter-revolution.

That the majority of Fabians did not expect opposition to Socialism to be formidable, at least in the long run, was revealed in many places in *Fabian Essays*. 'We need not seriously anticipate that the landlords will actually fight' said Shaw, speaking of probable municipal action to take over the land, and elsewhere he remarked of 'the proprietary class successively capitulating'. Mrs Besant spoke of trusts as easy to capture. Clarke spoke of power falling 'from the weak hands of a useless possessing class'. The attitude was characteristic of all the Essayists, except Bland, who in an article of remarkable political prescience described the 'stubborn barriers' that could be thrown in the path of socialist advance. The reason for the optimism of the majority of the Fabians lay partly in their hopes of the new democracy, and their anticipation of the diminishing numbers of the capitalist class, and partly in their expectation that the moral outlook of Socialism would penetrate the whole community. Perhaps, also, they relied on English political traditions. In the *Essays*

---

[1] Webb however acknowledged the Marxist argument in a footnote quoted from Hyndman at p. 32 of *Fabian Essays* (1889 ed.). Shaw also acknowledged the point to some extent in his preface to the 1908 reprint of the Essays, but he reinforced his own position with the better arguments that force may be the midwife of Chaos as well as of Socialism, and in any case a good deal of the conversion could be done by 'evolutionary methods' before Socialists came fully to power, thus making the path to Socialism easier.

[2] Bland engaged in a brief exchange with Webb and Mrs Besant on the degree of gradualness *Fabian Essays*, (1889 ed.), pp. 214-5.

the only reference to British national character and Parliamentary tradition is a rather satirical one, by Shaw, where he assures everybody that the Fabian proposals 'bear the stamp of the vestry so congenial to the English mind' and 'at no point do they involve guillotining, declaring the Rights of Man, swearing on the altar of the country, or anything else that is supposed to be essentially un-English'—but elsewhere, by the Webbs, more serious tribute was paid to the same characteristics.

Such were the arguments by which the Fabians sought to supplant in Socialist theory a conception of history that had been associated with a catastrophic and revolutionary outlook. Their tentative moves towards the elaboration of a theory of history which would prove both the necessity of Socialism and the necessity for its gradual advent cannot be considered satisfactory, but most of the reviews of *Fabian Essays* when it first appeared gave the Fabians credit for having demonstrated the possibility of attaining Socialism by democratic means.[1] Their arguments provided important starting points in the criticism of Marxism, and helped to inaugurate the Revisionist movement in Germany, for Eduard Bernstein, when he was in England, learnt much from the Fabians.

Fabian historical theory did not develop greatly. The main subsequent tendency was for the Fabian theorists to become more sceptical of ideas of inevitability, progress and prediction. Bernard Shaw eventually abandoned these notions almost completely; and most of the other Fabian leaders, even the Webbs, followed to some extent, with more caution and misgiving, in his wake. Their development in this direction can be discussed more adequately in the next section.

THE FABIANS AND THE DEMOCRATIC STATE

The Fabian Society began with high hopes of the democracy that had been gained by the Reform Bills of 1884-5. Most of the members of the early Fabian Society had been Radicals, that is to say, members of the extreme democratic wing of the Liberal Party. One or two individuals, perhaps, had not moved on to Socialism from Radicalism, but the tone of the Society in its early days was certainly set by those who had. Hubert Bland claimed to be an exception; he declared in his confession of faith that he became a Socialist because, as a Tory, he was disgusted with the triumph of democracy under Liberal auspices. 'Democracy,' he said, so far as he was concerned, 'stood for all that was bumptious, unidealistic, disloyal in the deeper sense of the word, anti-national, and vulgar'.[2] If this truly expressed the opinions he held in the eighteen-

---

[1] A useful press-cutting file of reviews and notices of *Fabian Essays* has been preserved in the head office of the Society.
[2] 'The Faith I Hold,' *Essays by Hubert Bland*, edited by E. Nesbit Bland (Max Goschen, London, 1914), p. 213.

71

eighties, then it is remarkable that Bland should have remained in a Society which had so vigorous a programme for extending the very democracy he despised. But even in Bland's case there is reason for discounting the statement, at least a little. No doubt he was an unusual person, and had some odd views judged by general Fabian standards; he was always somewhat given to trampling upon the hooves of his colleagues' golden calves; but this confession of faith was made in 1907 when criticisms of democracy were becoming fashionable amongst one or two other Fabians. Allowing Bland to be a doubtful case, what of Bernard Shaw? Has not Chesterton declared Shaw to be no democrat, but fundamentally an Irish aristocrat?[1] But again, Chesterton was writing in the twentieth century, and while his assessment may be true 'in a deeper sense' of Shaw's nature, and true of the Shaw of the twentieth century, it is certain that Shaw in the 'eighties and early 'nineties of the last century had embraced democracy in no half-hearted fashion.

The earliest political programmes of the Society make clear the extreme character of its democratic outlook. It demanded (as has been described earlier) extensions of the franchise far beyond anything the men who controlled Liberal Party policy were willing to put forward in their Nottingham programme of 1887.The Fabians expected the enfranchisement of the working-class to force, democratically and gradually, the adoption of collectivist and socialist measures. This enthusiasm for the new democracy of 1884-5, and the hopes built upon it, coloured the propaganda of all left wing groups. Even the Social Democratic Federation, not to be outdone in demanding reforms, put forward claims for 'complete democracy', including the election of all officers and administrators by universal suffrage, proportional representation, the Initiative and Referendum, and 'legislation by the people in such wise that no legislative proposal shall become law until ratified by the majority of the people'.[2]

FABIAN 'THEORY OF THE STATE'

The early Fabians do not appear to have considered it necessary to write an elaborate defence of democracy. Democracy was triumphing. They could, and did, take it for granted. They merely needed to urge its efficacy as a means for bringing about Socialism against those, like some Anarchists and Marxists, who were disposed to deny it. So far as Webb is concerned, one gets very strongly the impression that if he had been asked for his 'Theory of the State' he might have replied in much the same way as he is supposed to have done to Haldane, when the two of them were working out a constitution for the

[1] G. K. Chesterton, *George Bernard Shaw* (John Lane, the Bodley Head, London, 1910), p. 52.
[2] See programme of S.D.F. for 1884 and 1893 quoted in Beer, *op. cit.* pp. 267–8. Also H. Quelch, *The Social Democratic Federation: Its Objects, Its Principles, and Its Work* (Twentieth Century Press, 1907).

University of London. Haldane is said to have asked Webb: 'What is your idea of a university?' and Webb to have replied: 'I haven't any idea of a university. . . . Here are the facts. . . .'[1] Similarly one feels that the question about the State might have elicited from him a vast amount of factual information about the relation between County Councils and central government departments. But not all the Fabians had minds like Webb's, and Shaw particularly was willing to answer the semi-philosophical question about the 'essential nature' of the State in the traditional manner.

The Fabians stood at the parting of the ways, at the point where the modern attitude to the State diverged from the Liberal-Radical attitude of the nineteenth century. To most modern students, coming to the subject for the first time, the Anarchist view of the State, or the Marxist view that the State will eventually 'wither away', seem quite incomprehensible, or at least Utopian optimism of the most extravagant kind. Yet these views were a natural and reasonable development from the Liberal theory which by the nineteenth century had become the predominant view in Western Europe. Beginning in the late seventeenth century, gathering force in the eighteenth, and triumphing in the nineteenth, the Liberal principles had overthrown conservative views which tried to identify State and Society or which allowed the State too large a measure of interference. The Liberals had carefully separated the conception of the State, the coercive agent of society, from the conception of civil society: they saw civil society as a self-acting co-operative mechanism, and they sought to reduce interference of the State to a minimum. The Liberals believed that the State always would retain a minimal role in defence and in the protection of life and property. The Anarchists, with higher immediate hopes, and the Marxists, with higher ultimate hopes, for the development of human nature, envisaged the 'withering away' of the State—of central, organized, coercive power—altogether.

The Liberal conception of the State remained plausible so long as the State remained undemocratic (i.e. remained an 'organ of class oppression') with the Liberals as an opposition group, or so long as the principles of *laissez faire* were, by and large, regarded as desirable. It was, of course, still possible, though difficult, to hold to the Liberal view of the State after the advent of a large measure of democracy, so long as one did not abandon a basically *laissez faire* position—as was demonstrated by John Stuart Mill. But Mill himself was abandoning this position in his later years, and once this had been done, a complete reassessment of the attitude to the State became imperative. Mill's Liberal successors turned for help to the works of Hegel and Comte. Hegel was, perhaps, the better choice. Comte, at a time when theorists were still talking of the diminishing power of the State, had brilliantly predicted that the role of the State of the future would be not less, but greater; but both

---

[1] Quoted M. A. Hamilton, *Sidney and Beatrice Webb*, p. 131.

73

the practical proposals and the tone of Comte's *Positive Polity* repelled many Liberals.[1] Hegel, always divided in his loyalties between his youthful enthusiasm for the French Revolution and his later respect for his Prussian masters, had endeavoured to bridge the gulf between Liberalism and the State-worship of the old order; and so the theorist of backward Germany of the early nineteenth century was discovered to have a political message for the English Liberals of the 'seventies and 'eighties.

The restatement of Liberalism by Thomas Hill Green, Bernard Bosanquet, and Edward Caird was a development parallel to, rather than one which promoted, Fabian political thinking. Some leading Fabians, notably Sydney Olivier and Graham Wallas, were at Oxford at the time T. H. Green flourished there, but they do not appear to have come under his influence to any extent. The influence of the Liberal-Hegelians on Fabian thought came rather later, through D. G. Ritchie, who was a member of the Fabian Society from 1889 to 1893, through Sidney Ball, who led the local Fabian Society in Oxford, and through the Webbs' contacts with R. B. Haldane. By then, the Fabians had already set their feet on the new path.

The first pieces of political philosophizing, which quite explicitly put forward the Fabian view of the State against views which treated the State with distrust and hostility, were Bernard Shaw's articles against the Anarchists. These were first published in 1888[2] and given, in somewhat revised form, as a lecture to the Society in 1891, and published as a Fabian Tract with the punning title *The Impossibilities of Anarchism* in 1893.

The Anarchists were the particular object of Shaw's attack, and the main point he was making against them was the need for the existence of a central authority, armed with coercive power. But many of his points were also a criticism of the Marxist 'theory of the State'. Though he expressed the warmest sympathy with the view that the State is an 'organ of class oppression' so long as it is undemocratic and admitted that the democratic State retained this character to some degree while the electors continued to choose capitalists and landlords for ruling positions, and though he described most elaborately the ways in which capitalism and inequality corrupted even the democratic State, Shaw nevertheless argued that a great change had occurred with the advent of democracy. The democratic franchise opened the way for the election of working-class representatives and Socialists. As for the coercive aspect of the State, there is, Shaw maintained,

a fine impartiality about the policeman and the soldier, who are the cutting edge of the State power. They take their wages and obey their orders without asking questions.

[1] See J. S. Mill's reactions to Comte's *Positive Polity* in his *Auguste Comte and Positivism* (Trübner, London, 1865), part II *passim*, and his *Autobiography*, (World's Classics, O.U.P., London, 1944), p. 180.
[2] Serially, in *Our Corner*, May, June and July 1888.

If those orders are to demolish the homestead of every peasant who refuses to take the bread out of his children's mouths in order that his landlord may have money to spend as an idle gentleman in London, the soldier obeys. But if his orders were to help the police to pitch his lordship into Holloway Gaol until he had paid an Income Tax of twenty shillings on every pound of his unearned income, the soldier would do that with equal devotion to duty, and perhaps with a certain private zest that might be lacking in the other case.

Consequently, he claimed that the task of Socialists was not to attack the State as such, but to use the constitutional methods, and the democratic machinery, for achieving their ends. It was simply a matter of persuading the people to use the power they already possessed.

Bernard Shaw, more versed than some of his colleagues in Anarchist and Marxist doctrine, thus put the Fabian case against their critics of the Left. It remained for Sidney Webb to make explicit their relation to John Stuart Mill, when he delivered a series of six lectures on Democracy to the Society, justifying the position taken in Fabian publications against certain extreme forms of democracy—the Referendum, the Initiative, and the election of public officials by direct popular vote—which were being advocated by the S.D.F., some members of the I.L.P., and some left-wing Liberals.[1]

WEBB'S SIX LECTURES ON DEMOCRACY OF 1896

The six lectures which were given at fortnightly intervals from 2 October to 11 December 1896, were entitled 'The Machinery of Democracy.'[2] The first dealt with 'Primitive Expedients.' Webb began it by pointing out how recent a phenomenon democracy was in the modern world. He then dallied briefly with the question whether democracy was based on natural rights, but he preferred to give no decision, merely making some remark to the effect that, whatever the general validity of the Natural Rights doctrine, it was no help in deciding whether a particular individual should or should not have a vote for a Rural District Council. He then proceeded to discuss the 'primitive expedient' of government by public meeting, with particular reference to the experiences of Uri and other Swiss cantons, and certain Trade Unions, like the London Society of Compositors, finally giving his verdict against mass meetings as a method of democracy. Webb claimed that mass meetings resulted in the Swiss cantons being controlled in fact by leading families, and Trade Unions by the established officials; that mass meetings were at the mercy of orators; that crowds were not aggregates of individuals, but had their own psychology, the study of which was only in its infancy. The utmost function he would allow to a mass meeting in the machinery of democracy was (perhaps) the ratification or rejection of a policy already well prepared for it.

[1] A. M. Thompson, *Here I Lie: The Memorial of an Old Journalist* ('*Dangle*'), (Routledge, London, 1937), pp. 131–2 for some useful information on the point.
[2] Reported in *Fabian News*, November and December 1896, and January 1897.

The second lecture discussed the 'Appointment of Officers.' Here Webb used the metaphor of the organic nature of Society. Society was an organism, he held, and each 'cell' should be specialized to do its own work. Devices like rotation of office were based on the erroneous assumption that one person could govern as well as another. Rotation of office was a device that had been tried in the United States and in some minor positions in the English Trade Unions, and it had not been successful. Popular election of executive officials was another device for securing control, but Webb deemed it unsatisfactory because it led to the election of the best-known man rather than the best man. And as the best-known man was often the retiring official, election was not usually an effective means of exercising popular control. Webb contrasted the Amalgamated Society of Engineers' method of electing their secretary unfavourably with the Cotton Operatives' method of selecting officials by examination. He thought the best method of selecting executive officials was selection from a short list of persons who had obtained a certain standard in a competitive examination.

In the third lecture he came directly to the main question of the Referendum and the Initiative. Proposals for 'Direct Legislation' (he said) were relatively new: they were not discussed by Tocqueville or Mill, but derived, he claimed, from the later followers of Saint-Simon. Webb discussed the various forms of these methods of 'Direct Legislation' as they had been used in France and Switzerland, and in the English Trade Unions,[1] coming to the conclusion that the Referendum and Initiative, far from giving the people control over the Executive, tended in practice rather to give the Executive more power over the people, and that in any case they were very unsatisfactory methods of discovering what the people really wanted, as too many extraneous elements could enter into them. The failure of the Referendum and the Initiative as democratic methods did not reveal popular incapacity for government, Webb maintained, but rather revealed that society requires division of labour. The collective, popular will can only express broad general principles in non-technical language on matters affecting the whole nation. Much modern legislation was technical, detailed, and dealt with matters affecting only a section of the nation. The mass of the electors could only judge such laws by results, and not in anticipation. 'Legislation is as much a distinct craft as shoemaking.'

This led on to the fourth lecture in praise of Representative Democracy. Webb claimed that representative institutions solved the problem of electing people who would devote their time to legislation (i.e. become specialists in it). The most modern Trade Unions, like the Cotton Operatives and the Miners' Federation, Webb claimed, had adopted representative institutions

[1] Cf. article on 'Primitive Democracy in British Trade Unionism,' *Political Science Quarterly*, September 1896.

very similar to those of the British Parliament. Should the representative be merely a delegate? Webb thought not. The elector knew where the shoe pinched, but often not the right method of relief. The representative, as a specialist, could teach his electors as well as learn from them.

The fifth lecture on the 'Sphere of the Expert' repeated much that had already been said in the second one. The problem was how to secure the services of the expert, yet make him subject to popular control. Examinations and adequate selection committees were the only ways of choosing experts on the basis of their expertness. Their places should be permanent, their pay sufficient, and a Socialist State should not neglect the distribution of honours as incentives and rewards.

The final lecture dealt with Federation. It was a principle to be approved wherever there was 'dual loyalty', though it usually did involve undue representation of smaller bodies. Webb supported the principle of Federation in the Trade Union world, contrasting the Engineers somewhat unfavourably with the Cotton Operatives.

FABIAN VIEWS ON DEMOCRACY AND MILL'S 'REPRESENTATIVE GOVERNMENT'

A comparison of the principles embodied in this series of lectures — amplified with other statements of Fabian views at that time—with J. S. Mill's *Representative Government* reveals many similarities and only a few differences. If Webb had written out his political ideas in full on the same lines as Mill's *Representative Government*, Webb's book would have approximated remarkably closely to Mill's.[1] The differences between the Fabians and Mill sprang chiefly from their desire to allow government a positive role in economic affairs, and to foster the supremacy of the working-class rather than to balance the interests of worker and capitalist. The question of the franchise was a main point of departure. The Fabians would certainly have disagreed strongly with Mill when he approved a property basis for the franchise in local government. Desiring the full enfranchisement of the working-class, they rejected the restrictions that Mill would have placed on the franchise, and strongly upheld, against him, voting by secret ballot and the payment of members of governing bodies. Mill's principle of no representation without taxation, particularly, ran strongly counter to the Fabians' plans to impose taxes mainly on 'unearned

---

[1] There are eighteen chapters in *Representative Government*, and of these eighteen I consider that the Fabians would have endorsed at least nine of them fully (viz. chs. 2, 3, 4, 9, 12, 14, 16, 17, 18); of the other nine, the Fabians would have agreed generally (with slight reservations) to three of them (viz. chs. 1, 5, 6); in two cases their disagreement and agreement with the proposals in the chapter would have been about evenly balanced (viz. chs. 7, 15); in another two cases they would have disagreed with Mill in their earlier days and later come to agree with him (viz. chs. 11, 13); while in the case of the two remaining chapters they would have wholly disagreed with one (viz. ch. 10), and mainly disagreed with the other (viz. ch. 8).

incomes'. The Fabians also gave no support to most of Mill's 'fancy franchise' schemes; their only demand was for a 'second ballot' or some scheme for allotting preferences and avoiding a split vote. While the Fabians would not, perhaps, have objected in principle to Mill's scheme for giving extra weight to the intellectual elite (they were always considerably worried by the problem of getting more intelligence into the democratic framework), they were quite opposed to the plural voting methods advocated by Mill. And though the Fabians agreed with Mill about the need for respecting the rights of minorities, they rejected the device of proportional representation after a study of its practical effects.[1]

Apart from the franchise question, however, the Fabians' views of the machinery of democracy were those of Mill, except in two matters, where they at first differed from Mill, and later came to agree with him. A short experience in local administration soon convinced them that their earlier demand for 'annual Parliaments' was impracticable, and from the 'nineties onwards we hear no more of it. As for the House of Lords, the Fabians, up to 1918, were in favour of its complete abolition. In 1918, however, Webb produced Fabian Tract 183, which suggested a possible future for the 'Other House' as a Committee of Experts, elected by the parties of the House of Commons in proportion to their strength, and retiring from office when the House of Commons which appointed them was dissolved. This was much akin to one of Mill's suggestions, but with some additional emphasis on the supremacy of the Lower House. Later, when the Webbs produced their plan for 'a Consitution for the Socialist Commonwealth of Great Britain' with its two Parliaments—Social and Political—the total abolition of the House of Lords was again recommended by them. But the 'Constitution,' unlike Tract 183, was not published as a Fabian Society document.

GENERAL APPROVAL OF MACHINERY OF GOVERNMENT

By 1896 the Fabians expressed themselves as fairly content with the democratic machinery of England. A few more reforms, and they were willing to declare themselves satisfied. '. . . When the House of Commons is freed from the veto of the House of Lords and thrown open to candidates from all classes by an effective system of Payment of Representatives and a more rational method of election, the British Parliamentary system will be, in the opinion of the Fabian Society, a first-rate practical instrument of democratic government' they declared in Tract 70 (drafted by Shaw). This was after the Liberal Party's Local Government Act of 1894 (the Parish Councils Act) had created an administrative system for rural England out of the chaos which had existed before. From 1894 the Fabian Society began (with a Tract on the Parish

[1] Tract 211 summed up earlier Fabian views.

Councils) issuing Tracts which explained how the machinery of democracy worked, and which urged the working-class to take advantage of it.

The Fabian Society set itself up as a voluntary information bureau, and undertook to answer questions connected with the working of democratic institutions. The Fabians were well satisfied with the way the machinery of English Government was developing, and were optimistic about its democratic and socialistic possibilities. Revolutionary Socialists and Anarchists who talked vaguely of the Communes of the Future were firmly told by the Fabians that 'these apparently strange and romantic inventions were simply city corporations under the Local Government Board', despite their horrified protests that the Fabians were reading the conditions of the present system into Socialism. In fact, the Fabians set themselves to do in politics what Shaw from 1892 had commenced to do for the English stage — to deflate romanticism. The State, to the Fabians, meant simply men in the existing offices; and they refused to envisage any great transformation in human nature or democratic institutions with the coming of Socialism. The democratic part of Social Democracy in England meant the existing machinery of British Government, only slightly improved. 'Industrial Democracy' meant the functions already performed by Trade Unions. The 'romantic' Socialists were shocked; they felt something had been missed out in this ruthless translation of their dreams into such precise empiricism. The Marxists, the Syndicalists, the Guild Socialists reacted violently to this 'arid' creed, but the Fabian Society as a whole showed little sign (at least before the Great War) of being persuaded they had missed out anything.

THE FABIANS ABANDON REPUBLICANISM

One of the institutions of British government to which the Fabians, from the time of Queen Victoria's Diamond Jubilee, became increasingly reconciled, was the institution of a constitutional monarchy. There is no doubt that most of the early Fabians began as Republican Radicals. The majority of the Society's members were probably still Republican at the time of the Jubilee, and when the Executive proposed a subscription to the Jubilee decorations, they were stopped by a majority vote at a Members' Meeting.[1] It is true the Society was never actively or vehemently Republican; but the Fabians, like the other Socialists, began in an atmosphere of Republicanism, where it was taken for granted that Socialism implied Republicanism. It is not easy to decide at what stage the majority of the Fabians gave up their Republicanism. There was no official pronouncement about it, but from the 'nineties onward there were no more demands from the Fabians for the abolition of 'all hereditary' institutions. It is difficult to decide how far Shaw and Bland, in a

[1] *Fabian News*, June 1897.

controversy they conducted with Belfort Bax in the *Saturday Review* of 1900, were expressing a view that was shared by other members of the Society. Certainly there was no correspondence from indignant Fabians repudiating the suggestion in Shaw's letters that the Fabians as a group were in favour of constitutional monarchy in England, and that they, as a group, denied that there was any necessary connection between Socialism and Republicanism. 'Why have we been plunged into all this immoderate letter-writing, to the confusion of the quiet readers of the *Saturday Review*? Because a writer therein made the heterodox remark that a man could be a Socialist without being a Republican. It was true; . . . Mr Bax owed it to his orthodoxy to contradict it. *I* owe it to my Fabian heterodoxy to confirm it,' Shaw wrote.[1] Bland, more cautiously, refrained from speaking in the name of the Fabian Society, when he declared: 'To the Socialism of Mr Shaw, of myself, of a growing number of Englishmen who take the trouble to think about these interesting matters, a monarchy will be no obstacle for the next three centuries. Therefore on certain fitting occasions, and in festive moods, we are quite willing to sing "God Save the Queen".'[2]

The reasons advanced by Shaw and Bland for their attitudes are worth considering, and so also are Bax's arguments to the contrary, for the controversy was ably conducted on both sides. In the first place Shaw attempted to argue that Socialism always had been anti-Republican, because even Marx and Hyndman had had to advance their economic case against Republicans and to show that Republicanism was no panacea for the present ills of society. Bax had no difficulty in disposing of that: both Marx and Hyndman (after he became a Marxist) obviously were Republicans; all that either of them had argued was that Republicanism alone was no remedy.[3] Shaw next urged that Republicanism, like 'Cosmism as opposed to Deism' or heterodox views on marriage, had nothing to do with the 'specific doctrine' of Socialism: 'There is nothing to prevent a respectable citizen who utterly abhors all these things . . . from joining a Socialist Society tomorrow.' Bax, in reply, thought nothing 'worthy of the name of Socialism'[4] which did not represent a movement of the working-classes for their own emancipation and which (he set the standard high) did not express itself in the economic sphere as Communism, in the political sphere as Republicanism, in the religious sphere as Atheism, and in the world-political sphere as Internationalism.[5] Another reason given by Shaw was that Republicanism does not 'reduce the capacity of the people for idolatry', whereas constitutional monarchy channels off some part of public idolatry that might otherwise be dangerous: 'Deprived of its Queen, it would

[1] *Saturday Review*, vol. xc, p. 619.
[2] *Ibid.* p. 586.
[3] *Ibid.* p. 553.
[4] *Ibid.* p. 520.
[5] *Ibid.* p. 533.

do what the French nation has done, idolize some British Boulanger and worship the honour of the army. For my part,' said Shaw, 'I prefer the Queen;' and he then went on to contrast the disastrous political effect arising from the idolatry of Gladstone with the comparative harmlessness of the idolatry of a constitutional monarch.[1] Bax replied to this that monarchy did not channel off public idolatry: '. . . I would ask, if monarchy is such a specific against hero-worship, how Mr Shaw explains the Gladstone cult to which he refers, and which certainly had a longer life in England than the Boulangist in France.'[2] It is a little surprising, however, that the question, whether constitutional monarchy was in fact any barrier to the advent of Socialism, was not argued at length; an assertion on one side was simply met by the contrary assertion on the other.

It is well-known, of course, that the institution of constitutional monarchy was defended in two major works, of a much later date, written by Bernard Shaw and Sidney Webb. The retention of the monarchy was proposed in *A Constitution for the Socialist Commonwealth of Great Britain*, while in *The Apple Cart*, King Magnus was shown in very favourable contrast with the popularly elected politicians. The older leaders of the Fabian Society certainly accepted constitutional monarchy. What of the Society as a whole? It would be going too far to suggest that the support of constitutional monarchy became an article of Fabian faith; it became rather one of those matters on which the Society spoke with no collective voice.

That Republicanism was disappearing in Radical circles had been noticed by Hubert Bland as early as 1888, in his contribution to *Fabian Essays;*[3] by the time of the Jubilee its ebb was becoming obvious to all. The Fabians, sensitive to the change in public sentiment, were prepared to cast aside such extraneous beliefs, clinging to the socialist 'essence'. The disappearance of their opposition to hereditary monarchy also coincided in point of time with an interest by leading Fabians in the new Imperialism.

THE STABILITY OF FABIAN DOCTRINE AND LATER DEVIATIONS

So far as the majority of Fabians was concerned, the Society's politica doctrine remained substantially what it was in the middle 'nineties. Edward Pease in 1915 observed that the views of democracy set forth in Tract 70 remained those of the Society as a whole;[4] and, judging by the Society's official pronouncements, this seems correct. Prominent Fabians, such as R. C. K. (Sir Robert) Ensor and A. D. (Lord) Lindsay were always active in defence of democracy as it is embodied in British constitutional practices.[5]

[1] *Ibid.* pp. 519–20.   [2] *Ibid.* p. 553.
[3] *Fabian Essays* (1889 ed.), p. 203.   [4] Pease, *op. cit.* p. 251.
[5] See, e.g. R. C. K. Ensor's lecture on 'Liberty' reported in *Fabian News* of January 1909; and A. D. Lindsay's *Essentials of Democracy* (O.U.P., 1940) and *The Modern Democratic State* (O.U.P., 1947).

G   81

However, individual Fabians, such as Hubert Bland, Bernard Shaw, Mrs Emily C. Townshend, and a few others, diverged from the orthodox Fabian position into paths of fundamental criticism. As Bernard Shaw and Sidney Webb were always the principal Fabian spokesmen, it may be worth while to trace the course of their later development, while remembering that their later views did not commit the Fabian Society as a whole.

SHAW AS A CRITIC OF DEMOCRACY

In his letters to the *Saturday Review* on constitutional monarchy, Bernard Shaw suggested that even Democracy was not an 'essential' part of Socialism.[1] This was new, even for Shaw. He had not voiced this opinion in either of the two theoretical Tracts that he had written for the Society before 1900. On the contrary, up to 1896, Shaw had been as emphatic as Webb about Socialism being the 'counterpart' of Democracy. It seems possible to date this tendency in Shaw's writing to the years immediately after 1896. It was the outcome of a certain kind of cynicism, which passed under the name of 'realism', always present to some extent amongst the Fabians. A little of it was salutary, in an age when the optimism of Socialists far outran their powers, and was useful in bringing the romantically-inclined down to earth. But in an age of disillusion and pessimism it could prove dangerous. Shaw has always been something of an expert in illusions and disillusioning: what he did not learn of that from his father's paradoxical methods of instruction, he probably got from Ibsen.[2] In the early days of Fabianism, up to about 1896, he chiefly concerned himself with exposing the 'illusions' of the Marxists and Anarchists. By 1897 Marxism and Anarchism in England were horses too dead or dying to be worth attacking much longer, so Shaw began a gadfly attack on the earlier Fabianism itself.

The background to this change of attitude on Shaw's part was both personal and political. From his writings and plays it is apparent that the years 1894-1896 were, for Shaw, years of crisis in his thought and his art. He had taken seriously to playwriting from 1892, when he completed an earlier manuscript which he had begun with William Archer, and gave it to the world as *Widowers' Houses*. His other two 'Unpleasant Plays' in the realist style followed in 1893 and 1894. They were not successful. *Widowers' Houses* had only two performances at a small theatre; *The Philanderer* was not acceptable to any theatre-manager; and *Mrs Warren's Profession* was banned by the censor. Shaw

---

[1] *Saturday Review*, vol. xc, p. 520.

[2] Shaw's father's amusing methods of Biblical instruction are told by Shaw in his autobiographical prefaces and repeated by most of his biographers. His *Quintessence of Ibsenism* shows what Shaw gained from Ibsen. It is by no means as great a critical work as his *Perfect Wagnerite*, for Shaw seems incapable of plumbing the depth of Ibsen's fundamental pessimism—his feeling that reforms, though necessary, lead to unhappiness. See also a particularly interesting letter from Shaw to Hyndman, quoted in A. Henderson, *Bernard Shaw, Playboy and Prophet* (Appleton, New York, 1932), p. 189.

FABIAN HISTORICAL AND POLITICAL THEORY

appeared to be having as unsuccessful a beginning as a playwright as he had
had as a novelist. He determined, consequently, to give the public what it
wanted: romantic drama—but with a difference. The 'Pleasant Plays' followed:
Arms and the Man (1894), *Candida* (1895), *The Man of Destiny* (1896), *You
Never Can Tell* (1897). The moral of every one of them was the need to look
at the reality behind romantic and conventional illusions, whether in love,
family life, or military glory. Gradually, not without checks and disappointments, these plays overcame the prejudices of critics, actor-managers, and the
British play-going public. The process took sufficiently long to confirm Shaw
in his contempt for the public taste.[1]

More important than Shaw's personal disappointments, probably, was his
political disillusionment. Shaw, like many other Fabians, had been swept up by
by the wave of optimism following the success of the New Unionism in the
early 'nineties, which had culminated in the founding of the I.L.P. In the three
succeeding years the optimism was dashed. The Trade Union movement did
not respond to the political situation in the way Shaw had hoped; even the
New Unionism itself seemed unsteady; 1895 saw the sweeping Conservative
victory in Parliament and the stalemate of the Progressives on the London
County Council. The reforms demanded by the Fabians had made very little
headway up to the end of the nineteenth century, and Shaw was not alone in
his disillusionment. William Clarke, according to his friend's biographical
note, died in 1901, cynical and pessimistic: '. . . the slowness of the march of
progress seemed almost . . . to chill his blood'.[2] The distressing state of affairs
in Ireland undoubtedly had its effect upon Shaw more than on other Fabians,
and, at the end of the century and in the first years of the new century, the
Fabians were to find themselves associated with the Conservatives and estranged from their Radical and Labour allies on the three major issues of Metropolitan Borough Councils, Education, and Imperialism. To crown all, Shaw
became aware that the progress of Capitalism in England during the 'nineties
had been far from producing the social effects predicted on the basis of the
depression of the 'eighties. He wrote in 1904:

By throwing up fabulous masses of 'surplus value', and doubling and trebling the
incomes of the well-to-do middle classes, who all imitate the imperial luxury and
extravagance of the millionaires, Capitalism has created, as it formerly did in Rome,
an irresistible proletarian bodyguard of labourers whose immediate interests are
bound up with those of the capitalists, and who are, like their Roman prototypes,
more rapacious, more rancorous in their Primrose partisanship, and more hardened
against all the larger social considerations, than their masters, simply because they
are more needy, ignorant and irresponsible.[3]

[1] This theme is worked out interestingly by E. Strauss in *Bernard Shaw: Art and Socialism*
(Gollancz, 1942,) pp. 33–7.
[2] H. Burrows and J. A. Hobson (eds), *William Clarke: a Collection of his Writings*
(Swann Sonnenschein, 1908), p. XIX.
[3] 'The Class War,' in the *Clarion*, 30 September 1904.

To a person so susceptible as Shaw to political tendencies, it was not a period favourable to a continued faith in the earlier and simpler Fabian doctrine. Shaw, though basically an optimist, lacked the invincible patience of Webb, Pease, and others amongst his Fabian colleagues.

In 1896 and 1897, almost immediately after Shaw had set down the classic, official view of the Fabian Society on democracy,[1] he published a couple of essays in which his criticisms of that view can be seen emerging. In his essay on 'The illusions of Socialism,'[2] a brilliant analysis of the uses and abuses of what nowadays pass by the name of 'myths', he incidentally declared that the 'wage-earners are far more conventional, prejudiced, and "bourgeois" than the middle-class'; that 'there is not a single democratically constituted authority in England . . . which would be more progressive but for fear of the popular vote'; and that the main hindrance to Socialism was the 'stupidity of the working-class'. These observations were soon to be elaborated in his subsequent major works: in the preface to *Three Plays for Puritans* and, above all, in the 'Revolutionists' Handbook' epilogue to *Man and Superman*.

Of course, it is necessary to be cautious in assessing the extent to which Shaw abandoned democracy. As we have noted, Socialists (Fabian as well as other) have always claimed that democratic institutions are to some extent corrupted by capitalist influence. Consequently, not *all* the criticisms Shaw might make of contemporary democracy can be taken as showing a change of attitude from his earlier Fabianism. Only those criticisms are relevant which indicate that he had come to think that democracy was 'corrupted' to such a degree that democratic methods could not change the social system fundamentally. Then, presenting even greater difficulty, is the distinction that must be drawn between the artist Shaw and Shaw as a Fabian. Shaw remained a romantic under his self-imposed puritanical discipline. In his plays he tended to 'let off some steam' that would be checked if he were writing as a responsible pamphleteer. Naturally, Shaw also declined to accept responsibility for the utterances of all his characters. His personal opinions must be sought in his articles, his prefaces and the general purport and moral of his plays. This distinction needs to be noted but not overdone for, in actual fact, a fundamentally consistent point of view was sustained in Shaw's artistic as well as in his purely political works.

Even while keeping these cautions in mind, however, it can be shown that Shaw did overstep the limits of the earlier Fabian view of democracy. Not only did he suggest that democracy is impotent before capitalist influence on government, but he even went further, and criticized democracy itself, suggesting methods by which freedom of electoral choice ought to be limited.

[1] In Tract 70.
[2] Edward Carpenter (ed.), *Forecasts of the Coming Century* by a Decade of Writers (W. Scott, Clarion and Labour Press, 1897). See also Shaw's article in F. Whelen (ed.), *Politics in 1896* (Grant Richards, London, 1897).

Shaw's increasing criticism of democracy went along with his particular development of the 'Superman' and 'Life Force' philosophy, with a flavouring of 'Decline-of-the-West' interpretations of history. It is perhaps a pity that this comes earliest to its fullest fruition in the 'Revolutionists' Handbook' epilogue to *Man and Superman*, for the question immediately arises whether Shaw can properly be saddled with the views of 'John Tanner.' No doubt the 'Revolutionists' Handbook' expresses stronger opinions than Shaw would have employed if he had been issuing a political manifesto of his 'own' in 1903, but there is equally little doubt that the substance of the views are consistent with those that he had already begun to put forward in earlier essays and letters, and are also similar to views that he expressed in later works. The ambiguity of 'authorship' merely enabled Shaw to express his doubts more vigorously and shockingly than he might otherwise have done.

The chief object of Shaw's attack was the Fabian belief in Progress.[1] He did not doubt that there was something to progress towards, even if it were no greater millennium than 'the levelling up of all men to the point attained already by the most highly nourished and cultivated in mind and body'.[2] But he doubted if mankind as it was at present could ever get there. The earlier Fabians and Marxists had placed their faith primarily in the might of democracy and the working-class. This faith Shaw had lost. The working-class in general was ignorant, prejudiced, easily misled. Manhood suffrage had merely substituted 'election by the incompetent many for appointment by the corrupt few'.[3] The coming enfranchisement of women would make things no better.[4] There was no evidence for supposing that the working-class would be more favourably disposed to Socialism than any other class. The earlier Fabians had placed some hope in permeating the ruling class. This hope also Shaw now pronounced illusory. 'Why are the Fabians well spoken of in circles where thirty years ago the word Socialist was understood as equivalent to cut-throat incendiary? Not because the English have the smallest intention of studying and adopting the Fabian policy, but because they believe that the Fabians, by eliminating the element of intimidation from the Socialist agitation, have drawn the teeth of insurgent poverty and saved the existing order from the only method of attack it really fears.'[5] Reformers of the Fabian kind could always delude themselves that they were progressing, when they were merely

[1] *Man and Superman* (Penguin, 1946), p. 247.
[2] *Ibid.*
[3] *Ibid.* p. 272 (cf. also pp. 242–3).
[4] Shaw did not, of course, use this as an argument against woman suffrage. He always supported it. But his observation in *The Intelligent Woman's Guide* (Pelican), p. 443 is typical 'I could not be forgiven for warning the suffragettes that votes for women would probably mean their self-exclusion from Parliament, and that what they needed was a constitutional law that all public authorities should have a representative proportion of women on them, votes or no votes.'
[5] *Man and Superman* (Penguin), p. 249.

patching up, never satisfactorily enough, the effects of 'long-continued retrogression' of the kind that had brought many an earlier empire to destruction before it had passed beyond the stage of being merely a 'commercial civilization'.[1]

What was Shaw's solution? A return to the method of violence? No: he continued to think the method of revolution impossible and futile.[2] The only solution was that man's nature should be changed.[3] If man as he was had proved incapable of governing himself intelligently it became necessary to produce Supermen.[4] How was this to be done? A new religion to change men's mental outlook? Selective breeding? Or the choosing as rulers of the nearest existing beings to Supermen by the use of some 'anthropometric method'? From 1903 Shaw investigated the possibilities of all three of these suggestions. One assumes that not all were equally seriously meant, though Shaw's trouble always was that his fantastic humour has prevented him from being taken as seriously as he intended.

Selective breeding was the solution chiefly canvassed in the epilogue to *Man and Superman*. But Shaw was very well aware of the objections to it, and, despite the fanfare, the practical proposals emerging from this startling idea are, as is so often the case with Shaw, moderate enough: a State Department to study the problems of human genetics; possibly a public conference on the subject; the removal of economic and class barriers to any person's choice of a mate; the removal of enforced celibacy (as of school mistresses); perhaps the endowment of motherhood; increased facility of divorce; but for the rest, 'we shall still have to trust to the guidance of fancy (*alias* the Voice of Nature) . . .'[5] These recommendations for race improvement became a constant feature of Shaw's propaganda thereafter.[6]

But has not Shaw defeated his own case by admitting that we do not know what kind of person the Superman is to be?[7] Of what use are the methods for obtaining the Superman if his nature is unknown? The concept 'higher' involves a criterion, and would it not be cosmic optimism, far outrunning the political optimism that Shaw derided, to assume that whatever came later *must* be 'higher'? Shaw was perhaps not free from this cosmic optimism, but actually his criteria for the Superman can be discovered elsewhere in his

[1] *Ibid.* p. 252.

[2] *Ibid.* p. 250. Cf. 1908 Preface to *Fabian Essays*. Elie Halévy is wrong in interpreting *Major Barbara* in a revolutionary sense: *History of the English People: Epilogue* 1895-1905: *Imperialism and the Rise of Labour* (Ernest Benn, London, 1951), pp. 361-2.

[3] *Man and Superman* (Penguin), p. 252.

[4] *Ibid.* p. 227 *et seq.*

[5] *Ibid.* pp. 231, 234, 265, 266, 268 (cf. Fabian Tract 149).

[6] The discussion of 'race improvement' was very much in the air at the time *Man and Superman* was written. See Beatrice Webb's comments in *Our Partnership*, p. 278, on Metchnikoff's *Nature of Man*.

[7] *Man and Superman* (Penguin), p. 228.

writing. Obviously, the Superman must be more intelligent than present-day man, and particularly more intelligent in managing political affairs. Later, when Shaw was older, he suggested in *Back to Methusaleh* that this might be achieved by long life. This was, however, not the end of the process, and the end was left somewhat, though not completely, nebulous: evolution apparently goes on past the long-lifers to 'whirlpools in pure intelligence'. Such remote prospects do not seem very helpful; more immediately important, perhaps, was Shaw's belief that there have been in the past and are in the present men and women with Superman potentialities.[1] He has given some examples in the characters of his plays. They would be rulers like his Mommsenite Caesar not like Cleopatra, like Major Barbara (after she had learnt the secret of power), like the brothers Barnabas not like Burge and Lubin, like St Joan (if she had greater knowledge of the world), like King Magnus (if his power were greater). . . . Even when Shaw shares up Superman qualities amongst different characters in the one play, it is easy to detect the qualities he admires: thus, in *John Bull's Other Island*, we are made to appreciate the energy of Broadbent, the clear-sightedness of Larry Doyle, the 'religious' passion for world-betterment of Keegan (though in each of these characters these qualities go along with corresponding defects). The clear-sighted intelligence that sees the world as it really is and rejects shams, whether moral, political, or aesthetic; the energy and organizing ability which gets things done and overcomes opposition; the passion for subordinating one's petty and personal interests to the call of a higher purpose: these are the characteristics Shaw obviously wishes to secure in his rulers. There is nobility in the idea and much fine poetry. But how were these qualities to be secured in flesh and blood rulers? Was Hubert Bland right when he wrote: 'We know who these rare persons are (*quoram pars magna sum*); they meet on alternate Fridays at 276 Strand, and in a few short weeks, they will offer themselves for re-election to the Fabian Executive.'?[2]

These criteria—vague as they are—perhaps do make it possible to consider Shaw's other methods of producing or discovering the Superman—the 'religion' and the 'anthropometry'. His views on religion developed slowly in the series of 'minor' plays which fell between the three 'major' works of 1903, 1904, and 1905 and the three 'major' works of 1917, 1921, and 1923.[3]

His first hopes seem to have been of a purged and rationalized Christianity. Shaw was well aware of the difficulties. What he wanted was to separate the 'essential faith' (as he understood it) from the barbaric 'nature myth' and the

---

[1] Supermen apparently need superwomen for mates. Shaw has had fun at the expense of his own ideas in his *The Millionairess*.
[2] *Fabian News*, February 1899.
[3] Major and minor are here used in inverted commas, because the words refer to the intention rather than the achievement. *Heartbreak House* is a more pretentious play than *Pygmalion*, not a better one.

87

rites associated with it. Christianity without 'Crosstianity' was the way he put it. In the preface to *Androcles and the Lion* Shaw stated at length what in his opinion was the 'essence' of Christianity that should be preserved and what was inessential and ought to be dispensed with. His purging was severe—the divinity of Christ is one of the beliefs which was thrown out, for instance. What remained comprised a set of ethical precepts for social and individual conduct together with a belief in a Higher Purpose, which apparently 'is willing and not willing to be called by the name of God'. The preface to *Androcles* is assuredly more Rationalist than Christian, and more Deist than either. Later, Shaw came to realize that this 'purging and rationalizing' need not confine itself to Christianity, but could be done to any of the advanced religions with satisfactory results, and in his *Adventures of the Black Girl in her Search for God*, he specifically pictured himself as an Irishman digging potatoes in Voltaire's garden. Already before that time, he had set forth his own religious and philosophical position at some length in *Back to Methusaleh* (1921), and it is clear that though Shaw was right in including his ideas in the same general category as Voltaire's, yet Voltaire's Deism differs in certain important respects from his. Voltaire's Deity is a First Cause, beneficent, but static and remote. Shaw's Life Force is certainly a First Cause, ultimately beneficent no doubt, but ignorant, entangled in Matter, and only slowly evolving through Mind (created out of the Life Force's conflict with Matter) to full intelligence and self-knowledge. Following in the footsteps of Samuel Butler, Shaw brought together Deism and a Lamarckian evolutionary theory. But he was not a systematic philosopher, and hardly ever went deeply into the awful theoretical problems which would be raised by an attempt to justify his beliefs.[1]

It might almost be said that Shaw defeated his own object by his own inner conflict between his Rationalism and his Mysticism. On the one hand he appears to have desired to reduce all established systems of religion to a series of ethical precepts of which he approved. In this, of course, he was like Voltaire. But, also like Voltaire, he wanted to retain something of metaphysics. Voltaire wished to do this for two reasons: he wanted a First Cause (that was all the metaphysical cause he thought necessary); and he wanted a guarantee that men—ordinary men like his debtors and solicitor[2]—would keep the social rules, and he thought they would not do this unless they believed in a religion (philosophers could keep them and not believe). Shaw's reasons were very different. He realized that materialists could find explanations in chance, but he disliked explanations which 'banished Mind from the Universe';[3] Shaw

---

[1] Some of the problems are raised by C. E. M. Joad in his article in *G.B.S. 90: Aspects of Bernard Shaw's Life and Work* (ed. S. Winsten), (Hutchinson, 1946), pp. 74-6. For the views of Voltaire expressed here see particularly the article 'Atheism' in his *Philosophical Dictionary*.

[2] Politicians and rulers are treated in the class of ordinary men—very ordinary men—by Voltaire.　　　　　　　　　　　　　　　　[3] Preface to *Back to Methusaleh*.

wanted things ordered intelligently, and presumably thought one could not get intelligence into the Universe unless the Universe had an intelligent purpose.[1] Again, Shaw had been an atheist in his earlier days, and he was quite prepared to agree that atheists kept the ordinary social rules as well as religious people. But he came to think that those who were striving to make the world better needed something of religious faith, particularly a faith that convinced them they were helping on a great cause (hence his evolutionary purpose of the Life Force). Ordinary rationalism would encourage people to make terms with the world as it existed, would persuade Major Barbara to succumb to money and gunpowder, or Lavinia to sacrifice to the Roman Gods, whereas (Shaw apparently believed) religion spurred their consciences (even where their personal interests and lives were at stake) to do battle with the established state of things and 'do the will of God', to strive for the 'God that is not yet.' It is interesting that Shaw demanded a metaphysical creed of this sort after he abandoned a 'scientific' salvation by faith in the working-class. Shaw's Deism-in-motion was an attempt to satisfy these demands of his mystical nature, and also the demands of his otherwise severely Rationalist intellect, but it may be wondered whether the result has not fallen flat between these two stools.

There remains still Shaw's third method of obtaining his Superman. It was a method which (though he did not recognize it) brought him back in a quite curious way to the ideas of Mill in *Representative Government*. Mill would not have liked the talk about 'Supermen,' but he was concerned with much the same problem—how to give extra weight to intelligence in a democratic government; and he had a scheme for giving intellectuals extra votes (with a pretty broad and arbitrary method of deciding who the intellectuals were). This method would have been too crude for Shaw, who would certainly have objected to some of the classes of people to whom Mill was ready to grant extra votes. In any case Shaw, as a political realist, would have recognized that 'one person one vote' was a principle too well established by his time to be easily upset. In a later work, Shaw advised his 'Intelligent woman' to cling fast to her vote and this principle as it was the individual's real protection against abuse of power by the government.[2] Consequently, Shaw tended to devise methods of selecting the *candidates* for election, rather than to hope for any scheme for differentiating the powers of the electors.

This element had been present in Shaw's thought ever since he wrote in the *Man and Superman* epilogue: 'If the less mind could measure the greater as a footrule can measure a pyramid, there would be finality in universal suffrage. As it is, the political problem remains unsolved . . . Government presents only one problem: the discovery of a trustworthy anthropometric method.'[3] It

---

[1] This desire for metaphysical certainty of salvation is one of the most interesting features of the *Back to Methusaleh* preface.

[2] *Intelligent Woman's Guide* (Pelican), vol. II, p. 424.

[3] *Man and Superman* (Penguin), p. 272.

became a more important feature after the First World War. Up to that time, Shaw had been mainly concentrating on the more long-term questions of how to produce more 'Supermen'; after the war, the growing urgency of the political situation (which is reflected in the more topical-political character of Shaw's plays of that period) brought to the fore the more immediate problem of selecting as rulers the existing persons resembling the 'Superman' most closely. (This discussion, consequently, takes us rather outside the period covered by this book, but it is perhaps worth while to round off the point). In one of his last works, Shaw estimated (on the authority of Stanley the explorer) that five per cent of the total population are 'capable of some degree of government'.[1] He suggested that this five per cent should be selected by examinations of various sorts (written examinations, personal interviews, medical tests, and perhaps improved 'intelligence tests'),[2] and 'empanelled' in various degrees, as capable of such and such ruling work.[3] Their 'empanelling' should not entitle them to assume power automatically.[4] This was where election was to come in. Shaw believed that for all ordinary occasions of government Nature would provide his ruling types in sufficient numbers to give the general populace a choice from amongst the empanelled persons.[5] Presumably elections would take place at regular intervals, as at present, to give the electors a chance to change the rulers for others within the panel.

Who were to be the examiners, and what were to be the subjects in which the examinees were to be proficient? Here Shaw's answers were not nearly so clear-cut. Obviously, he wanted his rulers to be clear-sighted, energetic and good. This means they must know. . . . ? Shades of Plato! Elementary mathematics,[6] statistics,[7] some economics (especially the 'Theory of Rent'),[8] some history,[9] enough science at least to be critical of its pretensions,[10] some appreciation of the social importance of art[11]. . . these were some of the things Shaw suggested. But that was not all: a person may know all these things and yet be a scoundrel. So Shaw also made the profession of the 'creed and catechism' of his type of religion compulsory for rulers.[12] A person, he wrote,

may be qualified intellectually for the top panel; but unless he can not only grasp opportunities but create them without mistaking himself for Jehovah or 'a tin Jesus' he had better be left in private life. As I see the world, the statesman must be religious; but he must discard every element in his religion that is not universal. . . . Above all, he must not look to God to do his work for him. He must regard himself as the fallible servant of a fallible God, acting for God and thinking for God because God, being unable to effect his purposes without hands and brains, has made us evolve

---

[1] *Everybody's Political What's What* (Constable, London, 1944), p. 47.
[2] *Ibid.* pp. 54, 309 *et seq.*   [3] *Ibid.* p. 53.
[4] *Ibid.* p. 46.   [5] *Ibid.* p. 352.
[6] *Ibid.* p. 312.   [7] *Ibid.* p. 244 *et seq.*
[8] *Ibid.* p. 313.   [9] *Ibid.* p. 366.
[10] *Ibid.* p. 200 *et seq.*   [11] *Ibid.* p. 183.
[12] *Ibid.* p. 329.

our hands and brains to act and think for Him. . . . A ruler must not say helplessly 'Thy Will be done': he must divine it, find out how to do it, and have it done. . . . He must face the evil in the world, which apparently reduces the goodness of God to absurdity, as but the survival of errors originally well intended. He must treat life as everlasting, but treat his contemporaries as ephemeral mortals having no life beyond the grave to compensate them for any injustices they may suffer here and now. . . .[1]

And the examiners? Are they to be rulers who have already been selected, or specialists in the different subjects who have not qualified in the 'comprehensive' type of examination required of rulers? (Shaw made it clear that expertness in a special subject is not to qualify a person for inclusion in the ruling panel).[2] Shaw, although he had a good deal to say one way and another about examinations, did not make this point clear. Yet is it not vital? Would it not make a world of difference to the possibility of misuse of political power—or is the 'religion' of the rulers assumed to be an adequate safeguard? It is surprising Shaw had nothing to say on this subject, when he went into such details as the need for giving the rulers a power (to be exercised sparingly) of admitting a few persons to the panel as *bona fide* practitioners whose competence has been established in the course of events' in case the examiners make a mistake.[3] The only other advice about machinery that Shaw had to give the rulers was that they should ruthlessly scrap the party system (against which Shaw had an inveterate hatred) and heed the advice of the Webbs in the *Constitution for the Socialist Commonwealth* to conduct the central Parliamentary business 'as in our municipalities'.[4]

Are Shaw's rather Platonic proposals to be considered anti-democratic? The answer, as Shaw was well aware, depends on one's definition of democracy. For democracy as it exists at present Shaw expressed contempt. But at least there are certain features of Shaw's political requirements that may be spoken of as democratic in the way that those, for instance, of the parallel system of Plato's *Republic* are not. In the first place, the people are allowed some choice of rulers, within the panel. Again, Shaw contemplated a large State, and consequently gave his general approval to associations within it. Thirdly, although Shaw restricted the governing functions to his selected rulers, he was emphatic that popular criticism must be as free as possible, and to secure this he proposed popular Parliaments or Congresses consisting of an equal number of men and women with critical, though not legislative, powers:

When the law becomes an instrument of oppression, as laws often do, especially before they have been amended in the light of the experience of their working, it is the Everymans who know where the shoe pinches. For them there must be congresses in which they can squeal their complaints, agitate for their pet remedies, move reso-

[1] *Ibid.* p. 329.   [2] *Ibid.* p. 312.
[3] *Ibid.* p. 353.   [4] *Ibid.*

lutions and votes of confidence or the reverse, draft private Bills and call on the Government to adopt and enact them, and criticise the Government to the utmost with impunity. And as such congresses must be attended by the rulers, who could not possibly conduct the business of the country if they had to listen to Mr E. and Mrs E. and Miss E. 'ventilating their grievance' for longer or oftener than a few weeks every two years, a day-to-day ventilation must be effected by the newspapers and pamphlets, which should have the same privileges as the congresses. Thus what we call freedom of congress, freedom of speech, freedom of agitation, freedom of the press, are democratic necessities. As they should be as representative of the Everymans as it is possible to make them, congresses should be picked up haphazard like a jury or by some other method that makes party selection impossible. The legislators and rulers should, on the contrary, be as unrepresentative of Everyman as possible, short of being inhuman.[1]

It was, no doubt, not at all necessary that Shaw should have identified his political recommendations with the practice of any existing State. Yet, in the inter-war period, he became more and more impatient with the 'muddling' of governments of Western Europe, and after a brief flirtation with Fascism,[2] which he later emphatically repudiated, he moved gradually towards an identification of his views with the political practice of the U.S.S.R. He eventually claimed that his 'panel of rulers' was (at least to some extent) achieved by the Russian Communist Party, and his religion (to some extent) by 'Marxist philosophy,' and in other ways he came to approve the existing structure of Soviet government, not (as some other Fabians have done) as a necessary transitional stage for that country towards democracy in the Western sense, but as a structure which points the way to the 'new democracy' of the future.[3]

The development of Shaw's views has been dwelt on at some length, both because of its intrinsic interest and because it does represent one influential trend in Fabian thought—the trend that tended to repudiate Liberalism and become obsessed by the problem of securing 'expertness' in government. *Our Partnership* reveals that this trend was not absent from the minds even of those Fabians who refrained from carrying criticisms of democracy to the lengths Shaw has done.[4] But it is at once necessary to point out again that Shaw was in this a very untypical member of the Fabian Society. Shaw, even in his old age (perhaps especially in his old age) was looked upon as an impish figure, standing well to the left of the main body of Fabian members.

[1] *Ibid.* pp. 52-3.
[2] His play of this period is *On the Rocks;* see also *Bernard Shaw and Fascism* (Favil Press, London, 1927).
[3] *Everybody's Political What's What*, p. 339. This 'identification' was a fairly late development. It is not apparent as late as the Pelican edition (1937) of the *Intelligent Woman's Guide.*
[4] H. G. Wells made the remark that his 'order of the Samurai' would 'pander to [Beatrice Webb's] worst instincts'. Note the use of Wells' idea in a footnote to p. 1131 of *Soviet Communism* (Gollancz, 1937).

LATER DEVELOPMENT OF THE WEBBS

The Webbs, more particularly Sidney Webb, were not easily moved from the older Fabian attitude—at least, not until their disillusionment with the Labour Party in 1931 and their subsequent studies in Russia caused them to take a favourable view of the 'Vocation of Leadership' (and, even then, it deserves to be pointed out, their views were by no means *wholly* favourable.[1]) Previously Sidney Webb had 'mocked at Shaw's Supermen' and constantly insisted on the efficacy of Parliamentary representative democracy for bringing about Socialist change. In their work, *A Constitution for the Socialist Commonwealth of Great Britain* the Webbs wrote: 'It might be imagined, from the vigour with which we have criticized the machinery of political Democracy in Great Britain, that we shared in the reactionary opposition to democratic institutions which is, for the moment, common to plutocratic and academic circles. Quite the contrary.'[2]

The Webbs' *Constitution* was an attempt to restate their attitude to the machinery of English democracy at the end of a considerable period of controversy and criticism within the Society; and it was produced only shortly after the end of the period covered by this work, it may serve to round off our discussion. The *Constitution* was of course not a publication which received the endorsement of the Fabian Society as a whole. But, as the Webbs' first general outline of the machinery of their Socialist State, it is an important document.

The most notable feature of the *Constitution* was their proposal to divide Parliament into two organizations: the 'Political Parliament' and the 'Social Parliament'. Both were to be elected, for a fixed term of years, 'proportionately to the population, directly by the people and not through any intermediate body' on the basis of universal franchise.[3] The 'Political Parliament' was to retain control over foreign and colonial affairs, and over the powers of order and justice. It was to be 'the State as envisaged by Marx and the Benthamites'. It should retain the trappings and procedure of the present House of Commons, and its affairs would be conducted by means of the Cabinet system. The 'Social Parliament', on the other hand, can best be described as an enlarged London County Council for all England. It was to have power over economic, social, and cultural activities, including the sole power of levying taxes. It would exercise supervision over the nationalized services. Its

---

[1] S. and B. Webb, *Soviet Communism: A New Civilization* (Gollancz, 1937), p. 1132. The Webbs were accused of being 'anti-democratic' before 1931 of course; but so many of these accusations rest on personal innuendo or statements isolated from the general context of their thought that it would be tedious to pursue them. The Webbs were always concerned with the problem of obtaining an efficient bureaucracy, but, I think, within a democratic framework.

[2] *Op. cit.* (Longmans, 1920), p. 86.　　　　　　　[3] *Ibid.* pp. 115, 120, 128.

business was to be conducted by a system of standing committees, which would elect their own chairmen; and these chairmen would not need to agree with each other in policy or accept any responsibility for the work of other committees than their own. The Social Parliament would therefore dissolve only when its term of office expired, or when decided by a majority vote of its members.

The Webbs of course realized the difficulties which would be created by this division of power, and the disputes that were likely to arise, particularly over the allocation of finance. They attempted to devise machinery for coping with those possible deadlocks, by giving power to the judiciary to decide between the two Parliaments legal questions of disputed territory and, for solving political disputes, they arranged a whole series of measures, ranging from Joint Committees and Conferences of the two Parliaments, through decisions by the 'aggregate vote of members of the two Parliaments in joint session assembled', to—as a last resort—an appeal to the electorate by a double dissolution.

As a revelation of the essentially Liberal-Democratic basis of Fabianism, the importance of the Webbs' *Constitution* lies less in the actual machinery they proposed, than in their reason for thinking such complicated machinery was necessary. What was their purpose? It is apparent that the Webbs had become alarmed at the tendencies towards an over-centralized State, and their purpose was to devise a system of 'checks and balances'. They declared the division of Parliament into two Assemblies would not only be more efficient than the present 'over-loaded' Parliament which was increasingly unable to cope with its new duties, but also that this plan would provide 'a new safeguard for personal freedom'.[1] In the first place, they claimed that the Social Parliament would enable the representatives of the citizen-consumers to exercise a more effective control over nationalized enterprises. Secondly, they thought their scheme would enable the coercive functions of the State to be separated from its economic functions. Where coercive power and economic power is in the hands of the same body, the government is tempted to use State force to break strikes and enforce economic discipline in nationalized enterprises. Under their system of divided control, the 'Social Parliament' was to have no coercive power without the consent of the 'Political Parliament,' and a similar check was imposed on the 'Political Parliament' because, while it would be 'free to conduct the nation's international relations and to direct its armed forces for the maintenance of law and order', it would 'have to come to the "Social Parliament" for whatever funds' it seemed necessary to expend for the duties entrusted to it.[2]

The same purpose of protecting 'the personal liberty of the citizen, which, from the very nature of things, is, in the densely populated, highly organized

[1] *Ibid.* p. 140   [2] *Ibid.* pp. 142-3

modern community, always in danger'[1] underlay the Webbs' plans for a
'Unit-bookcase system' for combining areas of local government. They were
alarmed at the tendency of services to overlap municipal boundaries, and thus
require central control. The older Fabianism had relied on 'municipal socialism' to prevent the socialist State from becoming over-centralized. The Webbs'
new system was an attempt to devise a highly adaptable machinery for coping
with 'boundary problems' and so keeping the larger part of socialized enterprise out of the hands even of the 'Social Parliament.'[2]

One other problem which the Webbs faced in their *Constitution* also reveals
their democratic outlook—the problem of freedom of the Press.[3] They were
hostile both to an 'official' Press and to individual proprietorship of large and
influential newspapers. Whether this difficult problem is really capable of
being solved in the way they proposed—the control of newspapers by consumers' co-operatives, with the 'continuous subscribers' electing the 'managing
committee'—may be doubted, but at least the Webbs showed themselves deeply
appreciative of the problem of liberty involved.

It seems a great pity that the Webbs' *Constitution* has so often been dismissed as a 'Utopia', or left altogether unread, because of its rather repellent
style. The solutions it proposes are open to much debate, but it shows a constant preoccupation with the danger that 'if the present powers of the Crown,
the Cabinet, the House of Commons, and the Civil Service were to be applied
to the ownership and administration of industrial capital, the individual might
easily find himself practically helpless'.

POLITICAL TACTICS

The word 'permeation' was adopted by the Fabians in the 'eighties to describe
their political tactics. It was a term which had some flexibility of meaning, and
one which in the course of Fabian history was used flexibly. In its most general
sense, it meant that Fabians should join all organizations where useful Socialist work could be done, and influence them. There was nothing especially
novel in that: even the S.D.F. 'permeated' organizations which it considered
worth influencing. The thing which distinguished Fabian permeation from
that of the S.D.F., in this broad sense of the term, was that the Fabians took
a hopeful view of some organizations which the S.D.F. abandoned as 'bourgeois' and incorrigible. Taking a broad interpretation of the meaning of
Socialism and having an optimistic belief in their powers of persuasion, the
Fabians thought that most organizations would be willing to accept at least
a grain or two of Socialism. It was mainly a matter of addressing them
reasonably, with a strong emphasis on facts, diplomatically, with an eye to
the amount of Socialism they were prepared to receive, and in a conciliatory

'*Ibid.* p. 128.   [2] *Ibid.* p. 238.   [3] *Ibid.* p. 271.

spirit. In its general sense, 'permeation' was meant as an antithesis of the S.D.F.'s narrow, uncompromising tactics, and dogmatic, abusive propaganda. The importance of permeation lay less in this general meaning, however, than in its application to party politics. The issue was raised early by a writer in *The Practical Socialist* of January 1887,[1] who pointed out that the Fabians were divided about political tactics. He classified them into three groups: first, those who wished for a Socialist Party entirely distinct from any existing party; second, those who preferred to make use of the existing Liberal-Radical Party, forming its left-wing; and third, those (the writer called them 'flabby-minded persons') who wanted to hold aloof from any party, without forming a party of their own, but supporting any party, or any Member of Parliament, who seemed for the time being to be promoting Socialism. The Manifesto of the Fabian Parliamentary League of 1887[2] embodies all three of these policies and bears out this opinion of divided views in the Society.

Lip-service was still being paid to the third of these views, that the Fabian Society supported any politician advocating Socialism indifferently of his party, in the phrasing of the Manifesto in which the Society declared its policy to the 1896 Conference of the Second International.[3] But it had never had any practical application. Perhaps there was little reason in the 'eighties 'for regarding the Tory Party as any more hostile to Socialism than the Liberal Party', but the tone of the Fabians' discussion of Lord Randolph Churchill's programme did not suggest that the Tory Democrats had acquired much merit in the eyes of the Fabians by being more 'socialistic' than the Liberals. In fact, the Fabians had few links with the Conservatives, and the few Fabians like Hubert Bland, who had been Conservative before their conversion to Socialism, could see little hope for Socialism in the Tory Party. Most Socialists predicted that the Tory Party would end by becoming heir to the doctrines and practices of Whiggery. On the other hand, the majority of Fabians, including many of the Society's leading members, had been Radicals, and the possibility of capturing the Liberal-Radical Party for a socialistic, if not Socialist, policy did not appear in the 'eighties and early 'nineties so hopeless a venture as later history makes it seem.[4]

After the emergence of the Labour Party in English politics, there was a tendency for Fabians to argue that they had always envisaged the emergence of such a party, and 'permeation' had meant pressing the Liberals as far as they would go beforehand, and afterwards influencing the Labour Party with Socialist ideas while not neglecting such influence as could still be brought to bear upon the Liberals. In support of this interpretation, Hubert Bland's

[1] J. Brailsford Bright: article on 'English Possibilists.'
[2] Tract 6.
[3] Tract 70.
[4] This is discussed more fully in ch. ix, below.

contribution to *Fabian Essays* was cited as the expression of a common Fabian view in 1888.[1] This, however, was not the case. When Bland gave his paper to the Fabian Society, he was acting as spokesman of the 'official opposition' within the Society. The policy being pursued by the majority of the Society is expressed in Sidney Webb's writings of the time, as for example in the last few pages of his *Socialism in England,* where he hoped that the Liberal Party would suffer a change of heart and really become the party of the workers.

Bland attacked this view and, by direct implication if not by name, its principal advocates Webb and Graham Wallas. He gave excellent reasons for thinking that the policy of permeating the Liberals, while necessary so long as a real Socialist Party did not exist, would prove futile in the long run. He looked forward to the formation of a new Socialist Party independent of the older parties. He did not, of course, envisage the sort of Labour Party which emerged in 1900, with the Socialists submerged by the Trade Unionists; but neither did he confine himself to Hyndman's narrow idea of a Socialist Party. The view of the 'opposition' group of Fabians was of a broad-based Socialist Party supported by Trade Unions—such a one as the I.L.P. failed to become in the early 'nineties.

The antagonism between the 'permeators' and the 'independents' was a permanent feature of the Fabian Society and continued right through its history until the Society moved definitely into the ambit of the Labour Party at the end of the First World War.

---

[1] See the interpretation of 'permeation' given by Shaw during his debates with the Wells in 1906. Olivier rightly declared Shaw's interpretation to be 'largely imaginary', *Fabian News,* March 1907.

CHAPTER IV

FABIAN COLLECTIVISM

THE Socialism advocated by the Fabian Society is State Socialism exclusively. . . . England now possesses an elaborate democratic State machinery . . . the opposition which exists in Continental Monarchies between the State and the people does not hamper English Socialists. For example, the distinction made between State Socialism and Social Democracy in Germany . . . has no meaning in England.[1]

This statement from Tract 70, so characteristic of the Fabian view of the State, also sums up briefly their collectivist position. It is perhaps best to begin the discussion of Fabian collectivism by considering what was excluded.

REJECTION OF UTOPIANISM

Edouard Pfeiffer, a French historian[2] of the Fabian Society, has considered that the rejection of Utopian Socialism was the first development in the working out of the Society's doctrine. The terms 'Utopian Socialism' or 'Utopianism' are used by Socialists in two senses: meaning either the advocacy of the founding of Socialist colonies, or the drawing up of detailed blue-prints of the future Society.

So far as the first sense is concerned, there is much to be said for Pfeiffer's view, if we think of the days of the Fellowship of the New Life as part of the history of the Fabian Society. But the breach with the Fellowship, which actually led to the founding of the Society, marked the time when the Fabians put behind them any ideas of gathering together in a small colony, either in Peru or London, to lead the 'New Life' in common. In their theoretical works, the Fabians always denounced the founding of Socialist colonies as futile as a means of changing society in general, and liable to be disillusioning and disastrous for the enthusiasts who participated in them. Shaw's withering phrase, 'The establishment of Socialism by private enterprise,'[3] epitomized Fabian hostility. But the Fabians were not content with general denunciations; some of the Society's members made studies of Utopian Socialist colonies and gave the reasons, psychological and economic, for the failure which seems to have been the general fate of such schemes. They were anxious to demonstrate that the disaster which overtook these enterprises was due to special psychological and economic circumstances which would not arise in the kind of Socialist

---

[1] This last sentence is usually overlooked by those who accuse the Fabians of being 'Bismarckian Socialists.'

[2] Edouard Pfeiffer, *La Société Fabienne et le mouvement socialiste anglais contemporain*, Thèse pour le doctorat, Faculté de droit de l'Université de Paris (V. Giard et E. Brière, Paris, 1911), p. 32.

[3] Tract 70; cf. also Tract 51, *Socialism: True and False* (by Sidney Webb).

State which they envisaged, and they undoubtedly had some success in this. Podmore and Aylmer Maude took the lead in these investigations. Podmore, on one occasion at least, lectured the Society on the Socialist communities of America,[1] and in his biography of Robert Owen discussed the Owenite schemes. Aylmer Maude wrote a work on the Doukhobors.

The Fabians were inclined to extend the meaning of this first sense of Utopianism to include schemes for establishing 'national workshops' or 'labour colonies' as a remedy for the unemployment problem. With such schemes, declared Sidney Webb, 'the Utopia-founder comes in more dangerous guise'.[2] No doubt these strong words were prompted by the fact that Mrs Annie Besant and some of the early Fabians had flirted with these ideas. They were repudiated as 'an extreme instance of Utopia founding', because it was unimaginable that 'a Parliament of landlords and capitalists' would vote the necessary capital, or, even if it did, that such a scheme would work. The idea that the gathering of 'a mixed crowd of unemployed' into a co-operative enterprise offered a 'hopeful way of ushering in a Socialist State', wrote Sidney Webb, 'argues . . . a complete misconception of the actual facts of industrial and social life'.

What of the second kind of Utopianism, the 'duodecimo edition of the New Jerusalem', as Marx called it? This the Fabians sedulously avoided. They busied themselves with the administrative problems of the here and now and the very immediate tomorrow. But could they avoid altogether the challenge that a Utopian might hurl back at his Socialist opponents, the challenge that if they were honest, they should give an outline of the 'just society' which was their end? It may be inexpedient to give a detailed picture of the objective, for the more detailed it is the fewer people will agree with it, but is it right to avoid it? Should one persuade people to help along a social change unless one has a fairly precise idea of the objective? The Marxist answer, frequently made, to this question consists in drawing a distinction between general social prediction, which is claimed to be possible, and detailed social prediction, which is not possible. The Fabian answer, in effect, was a more 'reformist' or 'social-engineering' one: they merely wanted this institution and that in society changed in this or that way, while they accepted the rest as it was.

REJECTION OF ANARCHISM

After a struggle, which has been described, the Fabians separated themselves from the Anarchists. Their main opponents were not the Individualist Anarchists[3] but the Communist Anarchists of the Socialist League. The fundamental Fabian objection was to the Communist Anarchists' view of human nature

[1] Report in *Practical Socialist*, vol. 1 No. 4, April 1886.
[2] Tract 51. The following quotes in the paragraph are also from this Tract.
[3] See ch. 2, pp. 45-6 and ch. 3, pp. 74-5 above.

and their conception of voluntarism as an adequate basis of society. 'Could the institution of property as we know it ever have come into existence unless nearly every man had been, not merely willing, but openly and shamelessly eager to quarter himself idly on the labour of his fellows and to domineer over them whenever the mysterious workings of the economic law enabled him to do so?' asked Shaw.[1] To be sure, an Anarchist might attempt an evolutionary account of the development of morals which would answer this particular question, but asking it reveals the Fabian (and almost universal) view that man is not yet good enough for Anarchy. The Fabians recognized the need for some 'external compulsion to labour' at least until everyone accepted 'a social morality . . . that we have failed as yet to attain'.[2] They also stressed the administrative problems which made the continued existence of a central State authority necessary. Anarchism, moreover, was a doctrine appropriate to countries where small-scale production predominated; in England, large-scale enterprise had 'come to stay'.[3]

REJECTION OF SYNDICALISM

Syndicalist doctrine in its modern form began emerging from near-Anarchist sources in France in the early 'nineties,[4] and nearly twenty more years were to elapse before it had any considerable influence in England. However, ideas of a Syndicalist type were current, though not widespread, in England in the middle 'nineties and attracted the attention of the Fabians. The name given to these doctrines at that time was 'Trade Sectionalism', and, as Sidney Webb showed,[5] they had a long history, dating back to one of the schemes propounded by Robert Owen. In their Tracts, articles, and books of the middle and late 'nineties, the Fabians insisted on the need for 'community control' as opposed to control by particular groups of workers over their own industry—the 'mine for the miners or the sewer for the sewer-men', as William Clarke satirically phrased it.[6] Beatrice Webb's early study of the history of self-governing co-operative workshops also gave the Webbs and other leading Fabians an ineradicable prejudice against ideas of 'workers' control' in industry. Her survey was taken to have proved that self-governing workshops could provide neither the managerial ability, nor the knowledge of the market, nor

[1] Tract 45. [2] Ibid.
[3] Tract 51 (S. Webb). Notice, however, that Bernard Shaw (perhaps because he had been himself attracted by Anarchism in his earlier days) was in the 'nineties the chief Fabian critic of Anarchism. Shaw's The Perfect Wagnerite is an extremely interesting interpretation of The Ring as an Anarchist allegory.
[4] Even in France, Syndicalism was not full grown until the early years of the twentieth century.
[5] Tract 51.
[6] William Clarke, 'Limits of Collectivism' in Contemporary Review, February 1893; see also Tracts 51 and 70; S. and B. Webb, History of Trade Unionism (Longmans, 1894), pp. 145–8; Problems of Modern Industry (Longmans, 1920), pp. 269–72.

the workshop discipline which was necessary to efficient production.[1] This, combined with general Fabian objections to revolutionary methods and Sidney Webb's arguments against Trade Sectionalism, provided the basis of the Webbs' later criticism of Syndicalism. Sidney Webb's principal objection to the Owenite scheme was that particular Trade Unions would become 'simply the head offices of huge companies owning the entire means of production in their industry, and subject to no control by the community as a whole'.[2]

Although Syndicalism was preached more vigorously in England from 1903, it did not become influential until the years of unrest before the First World War. In 1910 a conference of Syndicalists was held at Manchester and the Industrial Syndicalist Education League was formed to propagate their ideas. The new movement found able leaders in Tom Mann and Ben Tillett. Tom Mann had recently returned from Australia, where for some years he had played an active part in a Labour movement considerably influenced by the Industrial Workers of the World. The series of monthly pamphlets which he edited provided the chief Syndicalist propaganda of 1910—11; the influential pamphlet *The Miners' Next Step*, produced by a group of young members of the South Wales Miners Federation appeared in 1912; and from 1912 Syndicalist views found wider currency through the columns of the *Daily Herald* and the monthly *Syndicalist*.[3]

The Webbs' article on Syndicalism was published in August 1912 as a supplement to the periodical *The Crusade*. It had four main parts—the cause of the rise of Syndicalism, an exposition of the 'essence' of Syndicalist theory, their objections to Syndicalism, and the 'underlying truth of Syndicalism'. They attributed the rise of Syndicalism to working-class and labour intellectual disillusionment with existing institutions which aimed at altering the social order, in particular with Trade Unionism and the Co-operative Movement, and with Collectivist and Reformist methods of reform (extending sometimes to disillusionment with Democracy itself). They saw the 'essence' of Syndicalism in the revival of certain revolutionary beliefs of Marxist and Anarchist origin. The theory of the class-war had been revived in an absolute form; the working-class was declared to be in a continuous state of war with its capitalist employers, and workers were exhorted to organize in 'one big union' for each industry ('industrial unionism') to carry on this war relentlessly, resorting to strikes and other means of increasing wages and decreasing hours of work until all the employers' profits were extracted.[4] How far

[1] Beatrice Potter, *The Co-operative Movement in Great Britain* (Swann Sonnenchein, 1891), ch.v.   [2] Tract 51.
[3] Also in *The Syndicalist Railwayman, South Wales Worker, University Syndicalist*, etc.
[4] As the Webbs did not say anything at this point about Syndicalist opposition to Collectivism the following quotation from *The Miners' Next Step* is interesting:
'*Nationalization of Mines*. Does not lead in this direction [of eliminating the employer] but

ordinary moral rules could be set aside in this war of the classes was not altogether clear, but at least some Syndicalists advocated deliberate sabotage and wrecking. The culmination of this action was the General Strike which would lead to the Social Revolution. The Syndicalists had not given much thought to the organization which was to replace the State: the Trade Unions were to assume power on the morrow of the Social Revolution and were to transfer to themselves the few useful functions 'which create the illusion as to the great utility of government': but there might be a Central Production Board, or even some form of State composed of delegates elected from the Trade Unions. The Trade Unions would organize the management of industry on democratic self-governing lines, abolish the wages system, and restore to the worker the full product of his labour.

The Webbs argued first that Syndicalism was impracticable, and second that, even if practicable, it was not desirable. They predicted that the Syndicalists would find difficulty enough in getting the majority of workers enrolled in the new Trade Unions, and immense difficulty in persuading them all to carry on unrelenting class-war over a considerable length of time; they argued that the General Strike was less likely to produce a transfer of power than to produce a great deal of misery for the workers themselves and political reaction. Assuming, however, the success of the General Strike and the emergence of a Syndicalist society, the Webbs refused to believe it would be possible to abolish the wages system or to introduce democracy in industry, in the sense of giving the worker all he produced or of making him not liable to orders from a manager and remoter authorities.[1] Neither would the new society be able to dispense with a state. 'Something very like wages' would need to be paid, just as the great Trade Union monopolies would need to be brought together by 'something very like a Parliament'. The Syndicalist society would require a bureacracy to deal with all the other governmental needs of a complex society besides production, such as foreign affairs, education, police, and sanitation.

A particularly shrewd blow was struck by their observation that a Syndicalist society would 'rob the workers of their Trade Unions', by making them the controlling authority. Possibly those elected to positions of power would be more liberal in their attitude than the present employers, but it was doubtful if the workers would, even then, consider them liberal enough. Unless a new

simply makes a national trust with all the force of the Government behind it, whose one concern will be to see that the industry is run in such a way as to pay the interest on the bonds with which the Coalowners are paid out. As they feel the increasing pressure we shall be bringing on their profits, they will cry loudly for Nationalization. We shall and must strenuously oppose this in our interests, and in the interests of our objective.'
[1] For Sidney Webb's own interpretation of the 'abolition of the wages system' slogan, see Tract 51. He says it means the replacement of a wage 'fixed solely by the competitive struggle' by one 'deliberately settled according to the needs of the occupation and the means at the nation's command'.

crop of organizations sprang up in place of present Trade Unions, the workers would be unprotected.

The Webbs also had some more general objections: they thought Syndicalism, in its abstention from political action, and its contempt for the Trade Union methods of collective bargaining and legal enactment, futile and wrong; they doubted the right of the Syndicalists to attempt to force all workers into Trade Unions and even doubted the right of industrial unions to crush craft unions out of existence; and they considered some of the methods of 'class warfare' adopted by the Syndicalists, and the 'egotistic materialism' of Syndicalist doctrine, liable to produce 'bad citizenship', not auguring well for the future society.

The Webbs' final remarks on the 'underlying truth of Syndicalism' left the impression that, in their opinion, no truth underlay it which was not the common property of all Socialism. The 'truth' was said to be the worker's opposition to being 'a mere "hand" or "tool" in capitalist enterprise'. To do justice to Syndicalism the Webbs ought to have added 'or in Collectivist enterprise'. But there are signs that they appreciated this point, for, after stressing the 'importance of the consumer' against the Syndicalists, they concluded their article by describing the methods of control which the Collectivist State of the future would employ to avoid becoming a 'horrid tyranny', with centralization of power, knowledge, and authority. This could be done by making local authorities more important—more important, perhaps, than the central government itself—and by allowing the individual producer and co-operative enterprise their own spheres outside the State-controlled economy.

This article was not issued by the Fabian Society or under its auspices, but there is little doubt that it expressed an attitude to Syndicalism which had the approval of all but a minority of the younger members of the Society. This was shown when the arguments were repeated, with very little modification,[1] in the 'Report of the Committee of the Fabian Research Department on the Control of Industry'[2] which was published as a supplement to the *New Statesman* of 14 February 1914.[3]

REJECTION OF GUILD SOCIALISM

Guild Socialism was claimed by some of its advocates to occupy a position half-way between Syndicalism and Collectivism,[4] but the distance looked to the Collectivists more like three-quarters from themselves and only one-

---

[1] The modification consisted in a better recognition of the variety of Syndicalist views.

[2] Beatrice Webb was Chairman of this Committee. The printed copy of her opening address is interesting as illustrating Webb methods of research.

[3] See pp. 27–9 of Supplement. This Report is also severely critical of profit-sharing and co-partnership schemes, of self-governing workshops, producers' co-operatives and Trade Union ventures in industry.

[4] See, e.g., G. D. H. Cole, *The World of Labour* (Macmillan, London, 1928), pp. 367–8.

quarter from the Syndicalists, and it is difficult not to agree with them. In its intellectual aspect, the Guild Socialist movement can be said to have been the product of ex-Fabians.[1] For a number of years it exercised a strong appeal amongst left-wing Fabians who had been influenced by Syndicalism, but who were unable to give complete assent to Syndicalist doctrines.[2] Feeling ran high in the Society. The dispute was characterized by much rudeness on the part of the insurgents, and exasperatingly good manners on the part of the 'Old Guard' Fabians, until eventually it led to the split in 1915. But relations between the Fabians and Guild Socialists were never completely broken. They co-operated in the Fabian Research Committee (later Labour Research Department); and in 1920 the Fabian Society devoted a week of its summer-school to a discussion of Guild Socialism, published a lecture given by G. D. H. Cole on the subject as a Fabian Tract,[3] and also published R. H. Tawney's Guild Socialist work *The Sickness of an Acquisitive Society*.

Criticism of Guild Socialism from a Collectivist point of view was expressed from time to time in Fabian publications before 1918,[4] but it was presented in its most systematic form by the Webbs at the end of their *Consumers' Co-operative Movement*.[5] The Webbs admitted that Guild Socialism was 'better informed' than Syndicalism, and coped with the more obvious objections to the earlier creed. At least the Guildsmen had no simple plan of replacing municipal government by Trades Councils and the National State by the T.U.C.; they were careful to allow a place for national and local government and the consumers' co-operative movement, even if in a changed form. Nor were the majority of the Guildsmen revolutionists: most of them sought to achieve their ends by the gradualist method of 'encroaching control', which involved persuading the Trade Unions first to reorganize themselves along the lines of industrial unions, and then to convert themselves into 'Guilds' by bringing into their ranks the clerical and managerial workers as well as the manual workers. These 'Guilds' would have the task of encouraging the workers to win by various means a greater and greater share in the actual control, management, and direction of the workshop, eventually usurping the authority of the capitalists and appointed managers, and achieving self-government in industry.

The Webbs did not trouble themselves overmuch with the more philosophic and theoretical aspects of Guild Socialism[6], though they did have something

---

[1] E.g. A. J. Penty, S. G. Hobson, G. D. H. Cole.
[2] Especially university Fabians.
[3] Tract 192.
[4] E.g. *New Statesman*, 3 March 1917, p. 523.
[5] S. and B. Webb, *The Consumers' Co-operative Movement* (Longmans, London, 1921), pp. 448-62. (The quotations in this section which follow are taken from this work).
[6] This was an important aspect of Guild Socialism. The Webbs' *Constitution for the Socialist Commonwealth of Great Britain* does seem to show the influence of the writings of G. D. H. Cole in the form (though not the content) of their presentation.

to say about their conception of 'democracy in the co-operative common-wealth'. They seized immediately on the works of G. D. H. Cole, as the ablest exponent of Guild Socialism, and examined his practical proposals, stressing the effect these would have on the Consumers' Co-operatives. And they refused to dismiss his project lightly as Utopian merely because of the intricate elaboration of the machinery he had been led to propose. 'Anything beyond the most superficial description of social organization, even of the existing social organization amongst which we live, becomes bewilderingly elaborate.'

Aside from the specific criticisms of Guild Socialism in relation to the co-operative movement, their general objections were on four grounds: that it would weaken the control by the consumer to a degree which was undesirable; that producers' control was impracticable; that Guild Socialism had certain other minor disadvantages when contrasted with a system of democratic Collectivism; and that Guild Socialism was not likely to succeed because social development did not appear to be moving in that direction.

They began by attempting to demonstrate that in G. D. H. Cole's Guild Socialist State the organizations representing the consumers had merely con-sultative powers, or a control through a hierarchy of communes so remote and roundabout as to be ineffectual. This state of affairs they considered extremely undesirable. 'We understand by Democracy the principle of the rule of a community according to the will of the majority of the members of the community;' in the Guild State 'all the several specialized parts of the mental and physical environment of the community [would be] determined by the desires and wills of relatively small fractions of the community (namely, the workers engaged in each department) instead of by the community itself'; this would be government by 'peculiarly "interested" oligarchies'.

Guild Socialism they considered to rest basically on 'producers' control, and a revival of the idea of the 'self-governing workshops'. Even in the Con-sumers' Co-operative Movement the Guild Socialists envisaged a 'complete exchange of the positions now occupied in the Co-operative movement by the committee of management or board of directors, and the committee repre-senting the co-operative employees'. Consequently, the Webbs elaborated their objections to these ideas. They insisted that, whereas co-operative ex-perience had shown that 'democracies of consumers' had been notably suc-cessful in competition with capitalism, even under unfavourable conditions, producers' co-operation, on the other hand, had almost universally failed, although the 'experiment has been made in literally thousands of instances, extending over nearly a century, in almost every occupation, in various countries, often under apparently most promising conditions'.

They found the reason primarily in the 'homely adage that no man can be trusted to be judge in his own case'. The function of a vocation is not to be an end in itself, but to serve the community: goods and services are produced for exchange; but the self-governing workshop almost invariably comes to consider its own function as of more importance than the community thinks it. Producers' Co-operatives are always tempted to exact a profit from the consumers like any capitalist concern; yet their members also exact pay above the average, better hours and conditions. Producers' Co-operatives develop vested interests, and are constantly tempted for their members' convenience to maintain existing processes unchanged and discourage innovation; they forget the demands of the community; they prefer to increase their members' incomes by restricting membership and limiting output, rather than by increasing efficiency and production. In the self-governing workshop there is a failure of discipline: the direct election of officials of any kind has proved disastrous wherever it has been tried, in Trade Unions, Co-operatives or local authorities; it is a matter of psychology—the manager needs to have authority behind his orders, and elected managers think more of the producers than of the consumers; there arise endless disputes about who is 'entitled' to jobs. And finally, another practical objection to any simple form of workers' control is that the workers in any workshop are not one homogeneous mass; they are divided into grades in different numbers, and the smaller and more exclusive divisions would object strenuously to having their conditions prescribed for them by the numerically greater lower grades. The Webbs concluded their argument by pointing out that all this did not mean that 'democracies of producers' were not necessary, or that they did not have a proper sphere of activity. But they made it clear they thought this sphere was confined to Trade Union and Professional Association functions. They carried their argument to the length of criticizing the Industrial Unions on which the Guild form oi organization was based: 'It is, however, indispensable, in our view, that any such organization should be vocational;' the objective of greater quantity and quality of producers' control over a vocation could best be achieved by 'intensification of this tie of specialized vocation, transcending geographical limits'.

Whatever arguments may be found [they wrote], in favour of a large and inclusive organization on the lines of industries and services for the purposes of the class struggle, or in resistance to the capitalist, it does not seem that the essential purpose of vocational organization will be promoted by any form of organization that included, in one and the same body, masses of men and women of different callings, even within a single industry or service. . . .

At the end, the Webbs declared they were willing to see some cautious experiments in producers' control, providing 'that the consumers' society should in all cases retain the ownership of the enterprise, with the right to terminate the experiment and resume full control of administration, either at a specified date, or whenever the resumption seems to be required in the public interest'. But 'we do not ourselves look with much hope to any of these experiments . . .', they added.

The difficulties of demarcation between the Guilds themselves, and between the Guilds and other organizations such as Co-operatives, the difficulties of separating 'ownership' from control, and the difficulty of price-fixing were further problems. The Webbs remarked that the Guild Socialists were unlikely to be successful, even in persuading the majority of Trade Unions to convert themselves into Guilds.

Most of the Guildsmen thought that the Webbs took too gloomy a view of producers' control, and that the complicated Guild Socialist schemes[1] had made adequate provision for protecting the interests of consumers. Some of them remained unshaken.[2] But the Webbs considered their criticisms were borne out by the failure of the experiment of the Building Guilds, and by the experiences of the U.S.S.R.[3]

It is at first somewhat surprising to discover that there is no detailed plan for the nationalization of a service in Fabian literature until 1910.[4] There were, of course, demands for nationalization of certain central services before that date, but no detailed discussion of what, administratively, such nationalization would involve. Why not? Partly because nationalization was hardly 'practical politics' in the pre-war years, but also because the preoccupations of Fabian Collectivism for the first twenty-five years of the Society's existence were first, the extension of existing regulatory and protective functions of the State for the benefit of the working-class and the community as a whole, and secondly, municipalization, so far as they envisaged the direct transfer of services to social control.

(1) The national minimum

From the mid 'nineties, the Fabians used the slogan 'The National Minimum' to describe the political and social policy they were putting forward, a policy they considered to be merely an extension of a long series of State interventions which had regulated factory conditions and public health. It was gradually becoming recognized, they claimed, that the State had a duty to preserve certain standards below which no citizen should be allowed to fall. When they advocated each particular extension of this policy the Fabians usually entered

[1] See G. D. H. Cole, Guild Socialism Restated (G. Bell & Sons, London, 1919), for the most elaborate statement of Guild Socialism.

[2] G. D. H. Cole, Co-operation, Labour and Socialism (6th Blandford Memorial Lecture).

[3] S. and B. Webb, Soviet Communism: A New Civilization, two vols. in one (Gollancz, 1937), pp. 607–8.

[4] Tract 150.

the theoretical arena to defend their attitude against the champions of the policy of leaving things alone.

'The National Minimum' slogan was coined by the Webbs in their *Industrial Democracy*, the great work in which, besides describing and analyzing the functions of trade unions, they also defended trade unionism against its opponents. Writing in the 'nineties, the Webbs were traversing a well-fought field in their assault on what remained of earlier attempts to show that trade unions were harmful and 'contrary to the principles of political economy'. But they carried the argument further, maintaining that for the most part trade union practices were positively beneficial, not only to their own members, but to the community in general. In particular, the trade union practice of the 'common rule' stimulated efficiency; it encouraged the employment of the best workmen and the introduction of better machinery and organization; and if it did put an end to 'parasitic' trades, which kept men in employment at standards incompatible with health and vigour, that was a good thing too. And if the 'common rule' was beneficial, would not a 'minimum wage' have similar effects? The case for the minimum wage was argued in *Industrial Democracy*, and was at the same time presented in Tract form by H. W. Macrosty.[1]

A very large amount of Fabian propaganda—probably the greater part of it—was devoted to such arguments in favour of items of their 'national minimum' policy. Their advocacy of extensions of the factory acts, their campaign against sweating, their demands for arbitration and the eight hours day and for the extension of the principle of workers' compensation, their support for old age pensions, for the reform of the poor laws, for improved housing conditions, and for the extension of educational facilities all fitted into this policy of raising the status of the under-privileged. Although the Fabians regarded these demands as socialist in tendency, each one of them had widespread support outside socialist ranks. Propaganda in favour of them could, and usually did, take the form less of inventing new arguments than in marshalling arguments from other sources—an activity in which the Fabians were expert. The degree of novelty and Fabian influence in different aspects of this 'national minimum' policy is discussed in later chapters.

(2) *Municipal socialism*

It was not only considerations of what was 'practical politics' that led the Fabians to concentrate on 'Municipal Socialism' in the early days. The ideal of Fabian Collectivism was never an intensely centralized State. The Fabians prided themselves that they had a proper appreciation of the manifold, rather than unified, nature of the Socialist State. Local government was their

---

[1] Tract 83, (1897). Note also that Tract 72 of 1896 (by Sidney Ball) presented the case in ethical terms for the maintenance of minimum standards.

first discovery, at the time of the establishment of the London County Council, and perhaps in their enthusiasm they over-emphasized its Socialist possibilities. They admitted, of course, that certain services (like railways) were essentially national in character, and would need to be under the control of the central government, but they had high hopes of municipal enterprise. Later, they also insisted on the importance of Consumers' Co-operatives and Trade Unions, maintaining that both would find a place in the State of the future, and still later allowed the picture to become more complicated, with a fringe of private enterprise around the main block of municipalized and nationalized industry,[1] and, in agriculture, the letting-out of small holdings by the municipalities.[2] It is not surprising that Webb indignantly repudiated the accusation that he desired the 'Servile State' and 'one employer'.[3]

The problems which Webb and the Fabians encountered in making their recommendations for improvements in the machinery of local government are described in a later chapter.[4] But some of the conclusions may be anticipated here insofar as they throw light on their Collectivism. Webb and the Fabians eventually came to recommend neither rigid centralization nor complete decentralization in local government, but a balance between them. They favoured the simplification of government machinery, by the absorption of *ad hoc* authorities into the ordinary machinery of local government, but they desired a system which would give the higher authorities supervision over the lower only through a measure of financial control, leaving them otherwise autonomous. The 'municipalized' services would be controlled by council committees. The Fabians also recommended 'direct employment',[5] that is, the use under the local government committee of a manager with power to employ and dismiss workmen; the committee confining itself to the control of general policy, finance, and terms of employment, to see that Trade Union or 'model' conditions were observed.

(3) *The consequences of gradualism*

The Fabians' acceptance of 'gradualism' set the particular questions: What enterprises should first be socialized? By what means should socialist control be extended? In what form should private enterprise exist alongside State enterprise?

Their earliest answer to the first of these problems was determined by their association with Radicals and Municipal Reformers. They hoped much from the development of municipal enterprise. 'Municipal enterprise and Radical

[1] Tract 70.
[2] Fabian Socialist Series, No. 2, *Socialism and Agriculture* (1908) contains a number of Fabian Tracts dealing with agriculture.
[3] *Crusade*, August 1912, Supplement p. 152.
[4] See chapter VIII, below, for a full discussion of the following observations.
[5] See especially Tract 84.

finance' was declared by Bernard Shaw to be the early Fabian programme. Those public utilities vital to the community were destined first for municipal ownership and the Fabians were willing to confine their demands at the beginning to those backed by a considerable body of Radical opinion. Railways, canals, and coal-mines by their nature required central control and 'nationalization'. Later the list grew considerably though there appears to have been no rigid order of priority. Enterprises that had become organized in the form of trusts,[1] and those controlling services which directly affected the health and well-being of the community,[2] had a high place, but some of their demands are not easy to classify in either of these categories,[3] and the Fabians were evidently always ready to press for any widely supported scheme of socialization.

'Radical taxation' meant graduated taxation, falling most heavily on the higher income groups and particularly upon 'unearned incomes', together with higher, graduated death duties. Indirect taxation, because its incidence was usually regressive, should, they thought, be made as light as possible on necessities, heavy on luxuries. In addition, the Fabians concurred in the Radical demand for the taxation of ground values. It became a constant complaint with them that local rates fell only upon the occupiers, and allowed the owners, the ground landlords, who were better able to pay, to escape. The Fabians recognized how municipal 'Progressivism' was hampered by the legitimate fear of rising rates on the part of occupiers who could ill afford to pay them.[4] They therefore proposed a separate tax on 'owners' of property (or more generally on all persons receiving emoluments from property in the form of rent) in addition to, and at least partly in substitution for, the rate paid by the occupiers. They also supported proposals for a municipal death duty on realty, and the introduction of the principle of 'Betterment' (a special rent-charge imposed by a local authority in cases where improvements carried out by it increased the value of the adjacent property). Sidney Webb, in his evidence before the Royal Commission on Labour, showed that the Fabians had in contemplation a time when national and municipal taxation would extinguish 'unearned incomes'. To a hostile question about the lengths to which he would go in taxing occupying owners of property, he blandly replied:

I should contemplate that the amount which that occupying owner would have to pay in rates would become very considerable, might even amount to what one would call the economic rent of that property. If the community wanted those services, and

[1] Tract 124 (Many Liberal-Radicals of course agreed that 'monopolies' should be socialized).
[2] e.g. Water supply (Tract 34), Milk (Tract 90), Slaughter-houses (Tract 92), Bakeries (Tract 94).
[3] e.g. Steamboats.
[4] See 'Report and Resolutions of the Special Committee appointed to consider Socialist Representation in Parliament,' transmitted by the Executive Committee to members for discussion at a meeting on Friday, 24 January 1908, p. 6.

if the community was not acting arbitrarily, if the taxation was equal all round and if it was arrived at gradually, I confess I should view with equanimity the result that the man might have to work for his living.[1]

The Fabians believed that the extension of municipal and State enterprise and the increase in taxation of unearned incomes would be a slow and gradual process. Now and again, they even hinted that 'complete Socialism' in the sense of a society where every industry is socialized never would come, and perhaps would not be desirable. Ever since the point was put forward in Tract 70, it has been a constant, if a not greatly emphasized, feature of Fabian doctrine that even in a society which was mainly socialist private enterprise might have a function in pioneering new inventions.[2] Outside the socialized and planned economy of the Fabian State, a fringe of small, new and speculative ventures carried on by private entrepreneurs for profit might always, apparently, be permitted to exist, at least until they had established themselves sufficiently to be incorporated into the socialist framework.[3]

Another 'consequence of gradualism' was the matter of compensation. Should the present owners of industry be compensated on its transfer from private to public ownership? The logical conclusion of the Socialists' attempts to prove that the incomes of landlords and capitalists were 'unearned' would seem to be that they deserved no compensation. Yet, clearly, if socialization were to come piecemeal and peacefully, compensation would be expedient. The early Fabians endeavoured to escape from this dilemma by writing into their first 'Basis' that socialization should be 'carried out without compensation (though not without such relief to expropriated individuals as may seem fit to the community)'.[4]

This compromise appears to have satisfied the first generation of Fabians, but when, after 1906, a new generation began to surge into the Society, its amendment was canvassed and the older members found themselves obliged to explain what they had meant. The report of the discussion at a meeting in 1907 throws some light on the subtle distinction between 'compensation' and 'relief', which at least one recent historian of socialism has found curious.[5] The mover of the amendment advocating deletion (F. W. Hayes) argued

that in every particular case our Tracts advocate compensation and the mention of the extreme principle of non-compensation, which we did not in practice advocate, interfered with our propaganda amongst the middle-classes. H. G. Bentley

[1] Royal Commission on Labour, 17 November 1892, Minutes of Evidence, 4th Report, vol. xxxix, p. 263.
[2] Cf. S. and B. Webb, *Constitution for the Socialist Commonwealth of Great Britain*, pp. 147–8, 268.
[3] The early Fabians did not give much thought to the problems of running a 'mixed economy'.
[4] Basis of the Fabian Society (until 1919); quoted Pease, *op. cit.* p. 284.
[5] Sir Alexander Gray, *The Socialist Tradition, Moses to Lenin* (Longmans, London, 1946), p. 387.

seconded, and urged that the idea of confiscation prevented people from joining Socialist societies. Sidney Herbert opposed, arguing that any change would show that we were out of sympathy with other Socialists. Cecil Chesterton also opposed, contending that we wanted a bar to keep out those who call themselves Socialists because they want to be kind to the poor. Dr Clarke said that even Conservative Governments in Parliament had passed laws repudiating compensation. Sydney Olivier, on the other side, urged that the Basis was objectionable as a whole.[1] Bernard Shaw opposed the amendment, maintaining that payment to expropriated individuals is not compensation to expropriated classes. The phrase proposed to be deleted, allowing relief to expropriated individuals was the only item in the Basis likely to reassure the middle-class doubter. H. G. Wells supported the alteration. Fabianism now meant the slow, humane process of evolution. The Basis was drawn up in the old revolutionary days. It should be changed to fit changes of Socialist opinion. H. T. Muggeridge was firm for no compensation. Dr Guest regarded the phrase as a bad one, though he was a revolutionary Socialist, which did not mean an advocate of violence. Mrs Townshend supported the proposal to amend. Gerald Bishop said he had tried his hand at a redraft, and had discovered its difficulties. After a reply by F. W. Hayes the vote was taken. The supporters of the resolution numbered about twenty-seven, while the opponents were several times more numerous.[2]

The final defence of the old distinction was given by Sidney Webb in December 1908, at a lecture in Essex Hall. He felt obliged to explain at length how the clause had come to be in the 'Basis', as the minutes of the Society were imperfect. It was a compromise that had finally been arrived at by a committee of fifteen over a meal in a restaurant. Webb said he had originally opposed the insertion of this sentence, but 'Mr Headlam had overborne him', and he had eventually been convinced that Mr Headlam was right. The term 'compensation' had two associations which it was desirable to avoid: an ethical association with the claim that persons had a moral right to the perpetuation of unearned incomes, and an historical association with payment only for expropriation of, or injury to, interests in land. The Fabian attitude embodied three principles: first, that the State should pay when it took over services, and not haggle too much over the price;[3] second, that the State should recoup its expenditure by increasing taxes on unearned incomes; third, that the State should extend 'consideration and relief—or as it is often termed, compensation' to all persons (including workmen) injuriously affected by changes made for the public benefit.[4] Such relief where practicable should

[1] Olivier was at this time a supporter of the changes recommended by H. G. Wells, which included a complete revision of the Basis.

[2] *Fabian News*, March 1907.

[3] 'It is always wise to buy rather than delay. The manorial rights of Manchester were refused by that town in 1808 as too dear at £90,000. In 1846 they were gladly bought for £200,000. Mr Smith's proposal to buy the London Waterworks for £30,000,000 was rejected in 1880 as ruinous, and in 1904 we had to pay £50,000,000 for them . . .'

[4] 'The new spirit was seen when the Greenwich Tunnel was made in 1897, and the London County Council paid compensation to the watermen whose occupation was destroyed'.

take the form merely of 'life allowances to those whose reasonable expectations had been upset, provision for the aged or for children, and generally the prevention of needless suffering'.[1]

Webb's speech revealed in a couple of places that he was not particularly wedded to the distinction between 'compensation' and 'relief', providing that the points he had made were understood. It is not surprising, therefore, that after this time the Society soon gave up the distinction. In the following year (1909) E. R. Pease's Tract *Capital and Compensation*[2] was published by the Society. It declared 'compensation' to be 'possible and proper' at the stage when the State took over the *administration* of capital (i.e. when a particular industry was nationalized or municipalized), but to be 'impossible' when the *ownership* was taken over (i.e. when the rights of the property-owners were finally extinguished). In the same fashion as Webb, this Tract argued that the extinction should be accomplished by increased income tax or death duties,[3] or by the granting of life annuities rather than perpetual annuities at the time of nationalization. Since the publication of *Capital and Compensation* the Fabians have usually made no more bones about using the word 'compensation', though of course they have continued to make their point about the need for extinguishing this 'compensation' in the long run.

(4) *Banking and Credit Policy*

Little requires to be said of Fabian views on this topic before 1918. One Fabian Tract had been published on the subject—No. 164, *Gold and State Banking: A Study in the Economics of Monopoly*, written by Pease, and it had been touched on in Sidney Webb's Preface to J. Theodore Harris's book on the Guernsey Market currency.[4] They show that the Fabians, like most Socialists, were profoundly suspicious of any credit schemes that professed to be able to 'solve' the problem of capitalism. In this matter, the Fabians were 'orthodox' —perhaps too much so.[5] On the other hand, they recognized that there was a connection between unorthodox ideas about money and socialist ideas, extending back to Robert Owen, and they were anxious to discover what grain of truth might lie behind the older Socialists' claims. Both Webb and Pease declared this grain of truth to be simply the proposition that a correctly managed paper currency could satisfactorily replace gold, because the security

---

[1] *Fabian News*, January 1909.
[2] Tract 147.
[3] The complete confiscation of the wealth of those dying without children or dependents was mentioned as a possibility.
[4] J. T. Harris, *An Example of Communal Currency* (P. S. King & Sons, London, 1911).
[5] This was mainly a post-War discussion. T. A. Knowlton, *The Economic Theory of G. Bernard Shaw* (Maine U.P., 1936), discusses the orthodoxy of the views on credit and banking in Shaw's *Intelligent Woman's Guide*. See also G. D. H. Cole, *Economic Tracts for the Times* (Macmillan, London, 1932), pp. 89–120 for some remarks about the extent to which Socialists have ignored the credit problem. *Fabian News*, April 1923 is interesting for an attack on J. A. Hobson in a review.

of the credit system did not depend on gold but on the total wealth of the community.

The Fabians recommended the nationalization of banking, but on grounds much the same as those for the nationalization of any other service. They did not, as post-war Socialists tended to do,[1] put the demand for nationalization of banking as one of the first items on their plan for socialization. Nevertheless, they did not fail to urge in a general way that the 'power' as well as the 'profit' of banking should be in the community's hands. Banking, they claimed, was becoming a monopoly. The only special argument, however, was that a State monopoly bank could reduce bank interest charges by supplying its services at 'cost' and through other internal economies which they assumed would be the consequence of unification. But even this argument was merely a special application of a more general Fabian argument about the advantages of socialized enterprise.

(5) Nationalization

Nationalization, when it was thought of at all in the early days of the Fabian Society, was seen in fairly simple terms as the purchase of the assets of the undertaking by the State, and the appointment of a Minister to conduct it, as the Post Office is conducted, under Civil Service control.[2] This is shown by plans for nationalizing the mines, one of their earliest demands for the nationalization of a service. Their full plans did not find expression in Tract form until 1913, and *The Nationalization of Mines and Minerals Bill* became the second of the Society's Tracts giving a detailed scheme of nationalization. The Tract[3] took the form of a Bill drawn up by the Fabian lawyer, Henry Schloesser (later to become better known as the Rt Hon. Sir Henry Slesser) for the Executive Council of the Miners' Federation. The Bill had been introduced into the House of Commons on 9 July 1913. It provided for the acquisition (by purchase)[4] of ownership by the State and direct management by a Minister of Mines and a staff appointed by him and under his control. No details of organization or management were given; and the only discussion of the status of workers was a provision safeguarding their right to take part in politics and in Trade Union activities.

The uncompromising 'State Socialism' of this Bill and Tract excited the strenuous opposition of the Syndicalists,[5] and the progress of Syndicalist and Guild Socialist ideas amongst the Trade Unions during the War years completely changed the character of the discussion when the question of the

---

[1] G. D. H. Cole, *Economic Tracts for the Times*, p. 90.
[2] *Ibid.* p. 285.   [3] Tract 171.
[4] No compensation for royalties, wayleaves, etc. Purchase on basis of average output for previous five years; assessed by Mines Commission of eight members (three each nominated by Mining Association and Miners' Federation and two by the T.U.C.); payment in three per cent. government stock.
[5] Debates in Annual Conferences of Miners' Federation 1912-1913.

nationalization of mines was again raised at the end of the War. At the 1918 Annual Conference of the Miners' Federation the resolution calling for State ownership of the coal mining industry also demanded 'joint control and administration by the workmen and the State'. The M.F.G.B.'s Bill (again drawn up by Slesser though not this time altogether approved by him personally), which was submitted in 1919 to the Sankey Commission, provided for the control of the nationalized industry by a Mining Council, consisting of twenty members, ten appointed by the Government and ten appointed by the M.F.G.B., under the Presidency of a Minister of Mines, who was also to be responsible to Parliament for the Council's affairs. In addition, it proposed District Councils (half of whose members were to be appointed by the Mining Council and half by the M.F.G.B.) and Pit Committees (appointed half by the District Councils and half by the M.F.G.B.) Thus the Miners' plan envisaged a half share in control of the industry by the Union at the highest level, and an increase in the Union's influence as the scale of authority went lower, until at the pits something approaching workers' control would be operating. As a concession to the consumers, the government was empowered to appoint a Fuel Consumers' Council, which would have a purely advisory function.

Even Webb and other Fabians who had been appointed Miners' representatives on the Sankey Commission[1] did not propose so uncompromising a 'State Socialist' measure as that in the Tract of 1913. They still proposed that the control of the industry should be in the hands of a Minister of Mines, but he was to have an advisory National Mining Council, consisting of representatives from District Mining Councils, equally representing the miners, consumers, and experts (technical, commercial, and administrative). At the pit level, executive power was to be in the hands of a manager advised by local mining councils.

It must not be thought, however, that the proposals of the Fabians on the Sankey Commission represented the Fabian Society's first venture away from a rigid 'Post Office' conception of nationalization. The *Nationalization of Mines and Minerals Bill* Tract of 1913 was, as has been said, the second full-length Tract of the Society on nationalization. The Society's first Tract of this kind had been Emil Davies' *State Purchase of Railways: A Practicable Scheme*,[2] published in 1910, and in certain respects, the plan of administrative machinery put forward in this Tract anticipated the plan for the mines agreed to by the Fabian and Labour members of the Sankey Commission.[3]

[1] Sidney Webb; R. H. Tawney; Sir Leo Money.   [2] Tract 150.
[3] In this Tract, Davies did not advocate complete nationalization of all railways, as he did not think this was 'practical politics' at the time, but he suggested the purchase of one of the smaller and worse-run lines to prove by experiment the advantages of State ownership (his suggestion was for the purchase of the 'South Eastern and Chatham' and 'London Brighton and South Coast' railways) and he was confident that the experiment would prove a success and lead to an expansion of State ownership.

Davies's outline of management and administration was based on the Swiss system, and was influenced by the structures which had been set up for the Port of London Authority and the Water Board. It differed from the two London Authorities, however, in retaining for Parliament control over the annual budget and power to alter the conditions, wages, and terms of employment of the workers. He proposed the appointment of a Minister of Railways (or the inclusion of the duties in one of the existing portfolios) to ensure responsibility to the House of Commons, and the actual management of the enterprise by a committee of five experts under the general supervision of a 'Railway Council'—three to be selected by the Railway Council and two nominated by the Minister of Railways. The five experts were to be a railway director, a trained business organizer, a lawyer, a financier, and 'another individual . . . to be a connecting link between the railway administration and the Minister of Railways'. The 'Railway Council' was to be made up of representatives of County Councils and County Boroughs served by the nationalized railways, together with representatives from Chambers of Commerce and Chambers of Agriculture (with a membership of more than 100) in the area, and representatives of local branches of the Amalgamated Society of Railway Servants '*pro rata* the number of employees'. Altogether, this plan shows that some Fabians, as early as 1910, appreciated the need of balancing government control with a measure of consumer and employee representation, though the efficiency of this particular scheme, and in particular the relation between the 'Railway Council' and the expert managing committee would seem to require more discussion than was accorded them in the Tract.

The disputes concerning the structure of socialised undertakings, which were so much a feature of the post-war years, and which were (temporarily) solved by the conversion of Mr Herbert Morrison and other Fabians from the view that *ad hoc* Boards were 'capitalist soviets'[1] to the opinion that they were (even without provision for workers' representation on them) fit organs of Socialism, fall largely outside the period of this work.[2] In these earliest Fabian Tracts on nationalization, the problems were implicit, and the Fabians were deeply concerned about them by the end of the war period. Our discussion can perhaps be concluded with some remarks about the suggestions put forward by the Webbs in their *Constitution for the Socialist Commonwealth* for the control and administration of socialized undertakings. These proposals show them to have been greatly influenced by the Sankey Commission.

In their 'Constitution,' the Webbs were still of the opinion that 'only half a dozen or so [of industries] will need to be organized and directed nationally'.

---

[1] *Fabian News*, April 1925.
[2] See G. D. H. Cole's essays 'Public and Semi-Public Concerns' and 'The Essentials of Socialization' in his *Economic Tracts for the Times*.
[3] S. and B. Webb, *Constitution for the Socialist Commonwealth of Great Britain*, p. 168.

They still hoped that most services could be provided by local government.[1] Nevertheless, they recognized elsewhere that local government had not developed to the extent that was once imagined possible.

It was often assumed a generation ago [they wrote] that the bulk of the new work of government would fall, not to Parliament and the Cabinet, but to the Local governing bodies, and that the expansion of the function of these local Authorities would relieve the congestion of public business at Westminster. The Local Authorities have indeed grown by leaps and bounds ... but their expansion has effected nothing in relief of the national government.[2]

Provision was therefore made in the 'Constitution' to cope with a vast expansion of work by the central government.

The new 'Social Parliament' was designed for the purpose of exercising a control which the present House of Commons, with its jumble of activities and congestion of business, could not provide. In form it was to be similar to the London County Council, with separate Standing Committees for each service, advised by a special Civil Service research department.[3] The Committees were to control general policy not day to day administration of the nationalized services.[4] Administration was to be in the hands of a National Board, appointed by the Social Parliament on the advice of the Standing Committee.[5] The Board was to have (on the model of the National Mining Council recommended by the Sankey Commission) equal tripartite representation of managers, workers, and consumers, under the chairmanship of the chief executive officer.[6] Where possible, the organization was to be supplemented by District Councils, constituted on the same lines as the Board and Works Committees (the latter however, to be entirely workers' committees, not composite bodies, and having, not managing functions, but the 'right to confer' with the management).[7] Selection Committees for making appointments, and Discipline Committees with power of dismissal, both with workers' representation, were also envisaged.[8] Trade Unions were to be fully recognized, and machinery provided for collective bargaining and wage fixing.[9] The management of the Boards was also recommended to encourage the formation of voluntary consumers' committees, and make full use of their suggestions and advice.[10]

So keen had the Webbs become for this type of socialized organization that they recommended a miniature copy of it to local government bodies for their 'municipalized' services.[11]

Fabian Collectivist ideas show that the Webbs and their followers were

[1] *Ibid.* p. 238.
[3] *Ibid.* p. 174.
[5] *Ibid.* p. 176.
[7] *Ibid.* p. 181.
[9] *Ibid.* pp. 185–6
[11] *Ibid.* pp. 233–4.

[2] *Ibid.* p. 74.
[4] *Ibid.* p. 169.
[6] *Ibid.* p. 177.
[8] *Ibid.* p. 183–4.
[10] *Ibid.* p. 187

insistent on the advantages of the large-scale, organized State, and yet that they were by no means unmindful of the problem of liberty under Socialism. Their early rejection of visionary and anarchist schemes was matched in later years by their extreme suspicion of 'producers' control', but in their own way they attempted to avoid the rigidity of extreme centralization, and the danger of 'one employer' through a large measure of considerably decentralized 'municipalization'. Later, the Collectivists may be considered to have yielded a little ground before Syndicalist and Guild Socialist criticism, but only a little. There was more of Guild Socialism in the phraseology of the *Constitution for the Socialist Commonwealth* than in its practical recommendations. Its bias was still predominantly for 'Consumer-Democracy', although a certain measure of workers' representation on the higher administrative bodies had been conceded. In assessing the Fabians' concern for liberty under Collectivism, it is also necessary to observe that they would allow Trade Unions to remain unfettered, and that in the *Constitution for the Socialist Commonwealth* the division of Parliament into 'Political' and 'Social' Parliaments was at least partly designed to separate the political-coercive power of the State from its economic power. Finally (as will be discussed later) the Fabians hoped that a well-organized Society would increase freedom outside working-hours, by reducing the time spent on 'necessary social tasks'.

CHAPTER V

THE FABIANS, IMPERIALISM, TARIFF REFORM, AND WAR

THE BOER WAR: FABIANISM AND THE EMPIRE

THE international complications of the years immediately preceding the Boer War took the Fabians by surprise, and in the last years of the nineteenth century and the first years of the twentieth they were forced by the march of events to make a statement of their views on Imperialism and Tariff Policy. Until these issues were positively thrust upon them, the Fabians had simply not bothered about international affairs, even to consider their relation to England's domestic economy. Coming into existence in the atmosphere of optimism, born of a long Victorian peace, the Fabian Society had taken a distinctly insular view. It is true that for a while, under Mrs Besant's regime, a few facts about the progress of Socialism in foreign countries had been published in the 'Fabian Notes' column in *Our Corner*, but these had ceased to appear long before the 'Fabian Notes' column was discontinued in that journal. In any case these notes had been about the internal affairs of foreign countries and not about international relations. Before 1895 the only 'foreign' problem in which the Fabians had interested themselves was Irish Home Rule. They had been in favour of Home Rule, but were at first inclined to adopt the rather simple view that the affair could easily be settled, and was merely being used as a means for diverting attention from domestic reform.[1]

The Fabians began to consider Imperial affairs seriously only after the time of the Jameson raid. Events in South Africa were briefly referred to in the *Report on Fabian Policy* of 1896, and after 1896 Dilke and several other persons

---

[1] A section on Irish Home Rule has not been included, because the Fabian Society as a collective body fought as shy as it could of this explosive issue. The few Tracts, such as No. 99 which mention it suggest that the majority of Fabians were in favour of Home Rule within the Empire, and were not in sympathy with Republican Nationalism. This certainly was the view of Bernard Shaw, who in his individual capacity had a great deal to say about Ireland. See especially his preface to *John Bull's Other Island;* his *How to Settle the Irish Question* (Constable, London, 1917); his *Peace Conference Hints* republished in *What I Really Wrote about the War*, (Standard ed., Constable, London, 1931), p. 319 *et seq.* and his *Irish Nationalism and Labour Internationalism* (Labour Party Publication, London, 1920). Shaw's pronouncements upon Ireland were eminently rational—and rather out of touch. There is an interesting change from his hostility to partition in the earlier pamphlet to his modified approval of it in the later one.

The Webbs' view of the Irish situation was put most unguardedly in a letter they wrote to Graham Wallas when they were on honeymoon in Ireland in July 1892: 'We will tell you about Ireland when we come back. The people are charming but we detest them, as we should the Hottentots, for their very virtues. Home Rule is an absolute necessity in order to depopulate the country of this detestable race.' Quoted in Janet Beveridge, *An Epic of Clare Market* (G. Bell & Sons, London, 1960), p. 9.

were invited to address the Society on Empire problems. Even then the Fabians avoided a full scale discussion of Imperialism until the Boer War was about to break out.[1] According to Edward Pease, 'the whole of the Society, with few exceptions, had scouted the idea of war' almost up to the moment when it was declared by President Kruger on 11 October 1899.[2] However, another potent reason for avoiding the 'Imperialist' issue was, no doubt, the fear of it as a dangerous subject, calculated to split the Society. The differing sympathies of individual Fabians were already, before the outbreak of war, becoming apparent. William Clarke contributed to the *Progressive Review* in February 1897 (the year in which he finally resigned from the Fabian Society)[3] a brilliant, anti-Imperialist article under the title 'The Genesis of Jingoism;' later, he was to become one of the most vehement opponents of the Boer War. On the other hand, Sidney Webb had come closely into contact with Haldane and Rosebery in his work on the L.C.C., and was thought to be drifting into the camp of the Liberal Imperialists, and Shaw and Bland with him.

Once war had broken out, the issue could no longer be evaded. The division in the Society which resulted from it has been described as one in which 'the left and right wings of the Fabians joined hands in opposition to the centre'.[4] The 'left-wing' comprised old Marxists like Walter Crane, the artist, together with leaders of the I.L.P. who were also Fabians, such as J. Ramsay Mac-Donald, S. G. Hobson, and G. N. Barnes. The 'right-wing' of the Fabian Society were 'progressive' Liberals, such as Dr F. Lawson Dodd, Clement Edwards, Dr John Clifford, and Will Crooks. Both the Imperialist and Education controversies at the end of the century were bringing together left-wing Socialists and left-wing Liberals, despite the differences in their views of political tactics. They found themselves ranged against the 'old-guard' Fabians, led by Webb, Shaw, and Bland, no less than against the Liberal Imperialists.

In the first clash of opinion a Members' Meeting held on 8 December 1899 showed the Society to be completely divided. A lengthy resolution was moved

[1] The following is a complete list of lectures on international questions given to the Society from 1896, as reported in *Fabian News:*

Fabian News	March 1896	Bertrand Russell on 'Lessons from Germany in Independent Labour Politics.'
„	„ July 1896	Liebknecht on 'German Socialism'.
„	„ October 1896	Trenwith (Labour Party leader in Victorian Parliament) on 'Australian Labour'.
„	„ August 1897	Speeches at luncheon to Premier of New Zealand.
„	„ November 1897	E. E. Williams on 'Socialism and Protection'.
„	„ December 1897	Dilke on 'The Empire'.
„	„ December 1898	W. A. S. Hewins on 'Imperial Policy in Relation to the Social Question'.
„	„ February 1899	Sidney Webb on 'Some Impressions of Australasia'.

These were all until October 1899 when a series of lectures on the Empire was organised.

[2] Pease, *op. cit.* p. 128

[3] See obituary notice in *Fabian News*, June 1901. This declares, however, that Clarke had 'practically' retired from the society in the early 'nineties.

[4] Pease, *op. cit.* p. 129.

by S. G. Hobson, and an equally long amendment by Shaw on behalf of the Executive. Despite their length, it seems worth while reproducing both of them in full as a reflection of fundamental points of view in the Fabian Society at the crucial moment. Hobson's motion read:

That, in view of the character and tendencies of political and economic ideas which have principally conduced to the present South African War;

In view, namely, of their antagonism to industrial Democracy at home and of the prejudice which their extension threatens to a settlement, acceptable to Socialists, of the Transvaal economic situation and of pending commercial problems in other foreign countries and British possessions;

This Society deems it essential to the furtherance of its own special aims that its attitude in regard to the war should be clearly asserted and that its methods of future attack upon capitalist commercialism should be widened in the light of this incident.

That as it was not the franchise quarrel that really made the war, but on the one hand the aim of establishing British supremacy from the Cape to the Zambesi, on the other the set purpose of the Republics at all costs to maintain their independence, this Society is not called upon to criticize either the Outlanders' political claims or the Boers' policy in regard thereto.

That the phase of Imperialist passion that has overrun this country of recent years, and is the chief cause of the war, has distracted the attention of the nation from domestic progress, has debased the conscience and lowered the democratic spirit of the English people, has effected a sinister co-operation between professional financiers and the military power; and threatens to involve us in political responsibilities which mean the establishment of militarism as the predominant element in our public life and the paramountcy of the interests that withstand the advance of Socialism.

The Fabian Society therefore formally dissociates itself from the Imperialism of Capitalism and vainglorious Nationalism, and pledges itself to support the expansion of the Empire only in so far as that may be compatible with the expansion of that higher social organization which this Society was founded to promote.

Shaw's amendment proposed to replace Hobson's motion with the following:

That in view of the character claimed for the South African War by the Government as a disinterested struggle to secure democratic institutions for the Outlanders of the Transvaal, the Fabian Society ventures to remind the public:

(1) That the time has gone by for regarding the acquisition of a Parliamentary vote alone as worth a war. If it were, about a third of the adult male population of these islands, and all the adult women, would be justified in resorting to armed revolution.

(2) That Democratic Institutions in the modern sense imply:

(a) the recognition of public rights in the natural resources of the country, and the effective safeguarding of these rights against speculators to whom concessions may be granted for commercial purposes;

(b) the protection of the wageworkers by legislation making due precautions for their health and safety compulsory.

(3) That the country is therefore entitled to expect that in the event of this war being carried to a successful issue, the Government will take steps to:
   (a) secure public rights in the valuable mines of the Rand by either placing them in public hands or else exacting in royalties the full economic rent to be expended on public works for the development of the country, after recoupment of a reasonable share of the expenses of the war;
   (b) insist on a stringent Mines Regulation Act for the protection of miners.

(4) That failing the above Imperial precautions, the only effect of victory will be to deprive the Transvaal of its present institutions under the Boer Republic, and make it a prey of the commercial speculators of all nations and races whose avowed object is to make private fortunes out of the mines without regard to the public welfare. Such a result would expose the British Government to the charge of being the dupes of these speculators, and of having spent the nation's blood and treasure, and outraged humanity by a cruel war, to serve the most sordid interests under the cloak of a lofty and public-spirited Imperialism.

(5) And finally, since the spokesmen and newspapers of both our political parties, without a single exception, declared before the war that the constitutional grievances of the Outlanders must be remedied in any case, every member of these parties, whether he approves of the war or believes that it might have been avoided by more skilful diplomacy, is bound to insist that the advance in liberty and good government for which we are professedly fighting shall not be lost sight of in the hubbub of party recrimination, theatrical patriotism, and financial agitation.

The Fabian Society pledges itself to do its utmost to recall public opinion to the realities of the situation as set forth above, and to press them on both political parties as matters which demand and admit of complete unanimity among disinterested and politically conscientious Englishmen.[1]

It may be observed that, in S. G. Hobson's resolution, the word 'Imperialism' has the sinister significance that it so often bears today, as a result of Liberal and Marxist propaganda. In contrast with 'Imperialism' Hobson speaks of 'the expansion of the Empire . . . in so far as that may be compatible with the expansion of that higher social organization which this Society was founded to promote'. In Shaw's amendment, on the other hand, the word 'Imperialism' is used in an approving sense, coupled with the adjectives 'lofty and public-spirited', and contrasted with 'sordid interests'. Usually 'Jingoism' was the word of disapprobation with Shaw and those of his way of thinking—the word used to designate the 'sordid interests' of 'theatrical patriotism and financial agitation'.[2] Deep divisions lay beneath this difference in the use of terms. The motives which underlay a whole recent phase of Empire expansion, and the questions of approving or disapproving government policy and popular sentiment of the 'nineties, were in dispute. The 'Little England' Liberals, who had been brought up in distrust of the 'Imperialist' adventures of Disraeli, and who viewed the later expansion (and its exploita-

[1] *Fabian News*, December 1899 and January 1900 for the resolutions.
[2] The use of 'Imperialism' in an approving and 'Jingoism' in a disapproving sense comes out clearly in most of the speeches of the 'centre' Fabians at this time; the (rather poor) review of J. A. Hobson's *Imperialism* in *Fabian News*, February 1903, is also an example.

tion by Chamberlain in Conservative interests) with deep suspicion, were coming together with left-wing Socialists to produce that hostile interpretation of Imperialism which was eventually to be so brilliantly expressed by J. A. Hobson. The 'Greater Englanders' of all types, whatever they conceded to the criticism of their opponents, wished 'Imperialism' to be understood in a favourable sense; they had a distinct bias in favour of large units of government; and they believed in the superiority of British (or at least, European) institutions, and felt that European rule could benefit 'backward' peoples. It is unlikely that these differences amongst the Fabians could have been settled by an agreement about the use of terms, though the final paragraph of S. G. Hobson's resolution pointed a way out of the impasse.

In their immediate attitude to the war, the two resolutions were in sharp opposition. Hobson's resolution is decidedly pro-Boer, setting aside the question of the Outlanders' franchise as unimportant, and declaring the issue to be one between the independence of the Boer republics and the aim of establishing British supremacy from the Cape to the Zambesi, with the (not quite clearly stated) implication that the first thing is good, the second bad. In Shaw's amendment, despite his mocking remarks about the Outlanders' franchise as a motive for war, the assumption is that the war against the Boers will (must ?)[1] be 'carried to a successful issue'. His amendment is concerned chiefly with recommending to the British government things it should do after its victory.

Neither the resolution nor the amendment was carried at the Members' Meeting. Shaw's amendment, despite support from Bland and other members of the Executive, was decisively rejected by a vote of fifty-eight votes to twenty-seven, on a show of hands. But the supporters of the amendment managed to carry a 'previous question' motion by a narrow margin of fifty-nine votes to fifty on a division. Thereupon, the Executive agreed to appeal to all members of the Society through a postal referendum, which was taken in February 1900. The question submitted was: 'Are you in favour of an official pronouncement being made now by the Fabian Society on Imperialism in relation to the War ?' Arguments were prepared for the 'Yes' and 'No' cases. The 'Yes' case urged that the Society should make a pronouncement on 'a crisis produced by causes antagonistic to its aims'; that the 'Imperial fetish' was an 'invention of aggressive capitalism and militarism'; that 'practically the whole of the International Socialist movement' was opposed to the war and Imperialism; and that social reform would be hindered by the expenditure on war. The 'No' case did not put up any arguments for Imperialism, but maintained that no pronouncement should be made by the Society because it was a subject 'outside the special province of the Society'; that the war, having commenced, could not be solved by a Fabian declaration; and that the only effect of a declaration would be to

[1] The moral question involved here will be discussed later in the chapter.

123

split and damage the Society itself.[1] When the votes were returned, there was a narrow majority for No—259 against 217.[2]

'It was said at the time and has constantly been alleged since,' wrote Pease, 'that the Society had voted its approval of the South African War, and had supported imperialist aggression and anti-democratic militarism . . . no such statement is correct'.[3] He was right, strictly speaking: the Society had only voted in favour of not making a pronouncement against Imperialism. Very few of those who had urged a 'Yes' vote left the Society over this issue—about fifteen altogether (though these included some leading figures in the Labour movement at that time).[4] But it is not difficult to understand why the Fabian Society got the reputation that Pease complained of, not only amongst the public at large, but in the opinion also of an eminent historian.[5]

In the same month in which the Fabian referendum was taken, Shaw 'trailed his coat' at one of the largest public meetings the Fabians had ever had at Clifford's Inn Hall. In this speech, Shaw attacked 'Gladstonian Liberalism,'[6] and boldly claimed that a Fabian must necessarily be an Imperialist, because Fabian Socialism and Imperialism both were based on 'a sense of the supreme importance of the Duties of the Community, with State Organization, Efficient Government, Industrial Civil Service, Regulation of all private enterprise in the common interest, and dissolution of Frontiers through international industrial organization', whereas the older Liberalism placed its faith in 'the Rights of the Individual, with the central conception of Liberty presiding over Free Trade, Competition, Nationality, Jeffersonian Democracy, Peasant Proprietary, the small Master in trade, and the small State in politics'. This correlation of Fabianism with Imperialism was bound to remain in people's minds when they forgot that Shaw went on to argue that Imperialism did not mean uncritical acceptance of every act of the Imperial government— a statement which he attempted to demonstrate by giving four different surveys and forecasts of affairs in South Africa, each leading to a different judgment of the war, from frank pro-Boerism to the most enthusiastic patriotism,

---

[1] For the full resolutions see *Fabian News*, February and March 1900; Pease, *op.cit.* p. 128 *et seq.*

[2] *Fabian News*, March 1900.

[3] Pease, *op. cit.* p. 131.

[4] They included J. R. MacDonald, J. F. Green (both of the Executive Committee of the F.S.); G. N. Barnes and Pete Curran (both future Labour M.P's.); Walter Crane; H. S. Salt; Mrs J. R. MacDonald; and Mrs Pankhurst.

[5] E. Halévy, *History of the English People; Epilogue; Imperialism and the Rise of Labour* 1895-1905 (Ernest Benn, London, 1951), p. 105.

[6] 'Gladstonian Liberalism' was the whipping horse of the Fabians at this time. It was represented by them as the ideology which was causing neglect of the interests of the community and resistance to Fabian reforms. Sidney Webb praised Lord Rosebery for casting off 'Gladstonian rags' in his article 'Lord Rosebery's Escape from Houndsditch' in the *Nineteenth Century* of September 1901. Cecil Chesterton, at that time a Fabian, also entered the fray with his book *Gladstonian Ghosts* (Brown Langham, London, 1905).

and all, he declared, consistent with sound Fabianism and Imperialism.[1] Those who used the word 'Imperialism' in a different way from Shaw were bound to misunderstand him.

Despite the referendum vote against making a pronouncement about Imperialism, the Executive in fact decided to issue a Tract, after the most vigorous anti-Imperialists had left the Society.[2] *Fabianism and the Empire* was most carefully prepared; it was intended to satisfy as many members as possible. Bernard Shaw prepared the first draft, and proofs were sent out to every member for correction and amendments; the final draft was discussed and voted upon at an open meeting. Pease is full of praise of Shaw's skill in carrying out this supreme feat of Fabian compromise.[3] One's admiration of the skill is increased on observing how much of Shaw's own view was incorporated into this collective Tract, in the teeth of the large anti-Imperialist minority of Fabians.

One of the ways in which Shaw imported his ideas into the Tract was through the confusion of ethical recommendations with descriptive statements. In the Tract, statements about what ought to happen and the circumstances in which Imperialism would be justified are mixed up, often in an extremely confusing way, with statements about what in fact was happening in the world. A few sentences from the beginning of the Tract may be taken as an example: 'The problem before us is how the world can be ordered by Great Powers of practically international extent. . . . The partition of the greater part of the globe among such powers is, as a matter of fact that must be faced, approvingly or deploringly, now only a question of time.'[4] In this passage, the second part is certainly a statement of what was happening, but why, an opponent might have asked, should the 'problem before us' be limited merely to the administrative one of how this could be carried out with the least fuss? Many people were considering at the time how this development could be stopped.

Should the Fabians be classified as Imperialists after the publication of *Fabianism and the Empire?* A great deal depends on how one interprets the views expressed in the Tract, and the way the label is to be used. The Fabians themselves repudiated the term 'Imperialism' insofar as it meant that the Society supported the policy of the Government in the South African War, as was shown in a letter released to the press on behalf of the Executive Committee by the Secretary at the end of January 1902. It ran:

Sir,—Statements have appeared in the press to the effect that the Fabian Society is in favour of the policy of the Government in South Africa, or, as some have put it, of

---

[1] By omitting the final part of this speech, Halévy gives an impression of it that is not quite fair to Shaw and the Fabians; Halévy *loc. cit.* See *Fabian News*, March 1900 for a satisfactory report of it.
[2] The reason why the Fabians issued *Fabianism and the Empire* is discussed in ch. IX, p. 254 below.　　　　　　　　　　[3] Pease, *op. cit.* p. 135.
[4] *Fabianism and the Empire* (Grant Richards, London, 1900), p. 3.

'Imperialism'. Will you permit me to say that the statement, in either form, is incorrect? Every shade of opinion in relation to the war is represented amongst the members, and the Society has therefore, on two occasions, by vote of its members, declined to formulate any collective opinion one way or the other. The only authoritative expression of its views is the Manifesto entitled *Fabianism and the Empire*, published in October 1900, which, as stated in the preface, represents the general views of the Society as a whole, but is not binding on any individual members.— Yours, etc., Edw. R. Pease, Secretary. 28 January 1902.[1]

Nevertheless, the views expressed in *Fabianism and the Empire* do range the Fabians on the Imperialist side and not on the opposite side. Providing certain qualifications are made, it does not seem that at the time they were unfairly labelled 'Imperialists'. Their basic criterion emerges in this statement:

The value of a State to the world lies in the quality of its civilization, not in the magnitude of its armaments. . . . There is therefore no question of the steam-rolling of little States because they are little, any more than of their maintenance in deference to romantic nationalism. The State which obstructs international civilization will have to go, be it big or little. That which advances it should be defended by all the Western Powers. Thus huge China and little Monaco may share the same fate, little Switzerland and the vast United States the same fortune.[2]

Once again, there is the uncomfortable mixture of 'is' and 'ought'. What does the sentence which begins 'There is therefore no question' mean? Little States *do* get 'steam-rollered' because they are little; perhaps they *ought* not. . . However, the intention of the passage is clear, especially when it is taken in its context in the pamphlet. The Fabians apparently regarded it as justifiable for a country of 'higher civilization' to take over 'backward' countries, but not for countries of lower civilization to grab countries of higher civilization which are less powerful. This point was made by an instance that Czarist Russia would not be justified in grabbing Switzerland, but 'if Switzerland were to annex Russia and liberalize her institutions, the rest of Europe would breathe more freely'.[3] The test of a higher civilization is nowhere precisely defined, but it apparently meant Western European countries and the U.S.A. as against African and Asiatic countries.

In the case of China, the Fabians realized that the question whether its civilization was 'lower' or 'higher' than Western civilization was a debatable one. Consequently they furnished another argument for Western intervention in this instance: 'Without begging the question as to whether the Chinese civilization is a lower or higher one than ours, we have to face the fact that its effect is to prevent Europeans from trading in China, or from making railway and postal and telegraph routes across it for the convenience of the world in general.'[4] Thus the Fabians also relied on the doctrine of the rightfulness of Free Trade and the progress of Western commercial civilization.

[1] *Fabian News*, February 1902
[3] *Ibid.*

[2] *Fabianism and the Empire*, p. 46.
[4] *Ibid.* p. 44.

Now the notion that a nation has a right to do what it pleases with its own territory without reference to the interests of the rest of the world, is no more tenable from the International Socialist point of view—that is from the point of view of the twentieth century—than the notion that a landlord has a right to do what he likes with his estate without reference to the interests of his neighbours. . . . [In China] we are asserting and enforcing international rights of travel and trade. But the right to trade is a very comprehensive one: it involves a right to insist on a settled government which can keep the peace and enforce agreements. When a native government of this order is impossible, the foreign trading power must set one up.[1]

This was said to be 'the common historical origin of colonies and annexations'.[2]

The analogy between a state in the international scene and a landlord in a state suffered from the obvious defect that there was no international body with power comparable to the state's rightful authority over landlords and other citizens. And while it is true that the establishment of a government by a trading power has frequently been in fact the origin of colonies and annexations, the Fabians were also justifying such action by using words like 'right'. The Fabians at the time of the publication of *Fabianism and the Empire* were Free Traders, and they honestly were thinking in terms of 'right', because they also recommended that the policy of the 'Open Door' in China should be balanced by an 'Open Door' in Australia for Chinese immigrants.[3]

Thus the Fabians in their *Fabianism and the Empire* manifesto not only recognized that the world was being divided up amongst the Imperialist powers, but in a general way they approved and justified the tendency. They seem to have been of the opinion that the states of Western Europe could and would benefit 'less developed' communities by taking them over or ruling them, at least for a while.

But if the majority of the Fabians were, and some of them admitted themselves to be, Imperialists, nevertheless they were always careful to say they were not Jingoes. They meant several important things by this distinction. Above all, they meant that their vision was not clouded by hysterical patriotism, and that they were under no 'romantic illusions' about the causes of Imperial expansion. The growth of modern Empires was recognized by them to be often caused by pressure from interested capitalist groups, though the Fabians did not subscribe to any monistic economic interpretation. They did not deny the anti-Imperialists' claims that there were links between commercial adventurers and the Press and persons influential in the government, but, the Fabians believed, the press and state were made use of only because they

[1] *Ibid.* p. 44–5. [2] *Ibid.* p. 45.
[3] *Ibid.* p. 48–50. Three years later, as we shall see, some Fabians were allowing that Free Trade might be called into question, and the principle of the Open Door in the Empire for Chinese immigration was also being attacked especially by Cecil Chesterton. But the Fabians did not revise these general principles, as perhaps they should have done.

lacked information. As they put it in the pamphlet: '. . . a ring can get at the Press, not because the Press is corrupt, but because it is ignorant. The Press can get at the government for exactly the same reason'.[1] If the government had an efficient administrative service, if it had 'Imperial Institutes' on the spot, combining administrative and research functions, to supply the home government and press with accurate information, and perhaps also to exercise some positive control over the traders, these evils could be eliminated.

The Fabians entertained no 'romantic illusions' that Imperial rule was perfect, or even, in existing circumstances, that it was necessarily beneficial to the ruled. Empire administration, they thought, needed reform, and they were prepared to expose and castigate mistakes in policy. Shaw's withering attack on the British administration for the Denshawi outrage in his preface to *John Bull's Other Island* is the most outstanding example in all Fabian literature; but *Fabianism and the Empire* was also outspoken about mistakes of policy, especially those in South Africa. The Fabian analysis of the causes of the Boer War led the Society to an attitude hostile both to Kruger and to the British capitalists.[2] While Britain was actually at war, the majority of the Fabians 'recognized the British Empire had to win the war, and that no other conclusion to it was possible'.[3] But they recommended that at the conclusion of the war, far-reaching reforms in administration should be introduced: the South African mines should be nationalized—or Imperialized; but wide powers of self-government should be granted in South Africa.[4]

A distinction of another kind was also being made by the Fabians when they claimed that they were not Jingoes. When they approved the control of countries of 'lower civilization' by those of 'higher civilization' they were rating the standard of Western European civilization above that of others, but they did not believe England's was so much higher than that of her other Western neighbours—France, Germany, Italy, or America—as to justify Englishmen entertaining 'the chivalrous feeling' that it was 'their highest duty to save the world from the horrible misfortune of being governed by anyone but . . . young men fresh from the public schools of Britain'.[5] The Fabians' standard of 'higher civilization' was a European standard.

Again, the distinction between Imperialist and Jingo finds some justification in their attitude to nationality and self-government. Though they showed little sympathy for the independence of small and insignificant nations, especially if they were 'backward' socially or politically, they showed great respect for the

[1] *Ibid.* p. 9.
[2] *Ibid.* pp. 22–31.
[3] Pease, *op. cit.* pp. 128–9.
[4] *Fabianism and the Empire*, p. 31 *et. seq.*
[5] G. B. Shaw, *What I really Wrote about the War*, p. 28. Though this quotation comes from a later work, the attitude is implicit in *Fabianism and the Empire*. There is nothing in *Fabianism and the Empire* about a possible clash between European powers arising out of the dividing-up between them of 'backward' areas.

128

principle of nationality, and favoured decentralized Home Rule for all national groups which were capable of it, within the large-scale Empires. In this, they went far: wide powers of self-government were commended for Australasia, for Canada, and for South Africa, with the one proviso that the interests of the aboriginal natives should be protected by the Imperial government. For this purpose, they approved the retention by the Crown of certain powers of veto over the legislation of Colonial governments, until a responsible 'Imperial Council' should be established in London, to which the powers could be transferred. They did not recommend self-government, however, as a universally valid principle in the existing state of the Empire. While they wished for a steady progress for the colonies up a ladder to self-government within the Empire, they recognized that different institutions were necessary for the different parts of the Empire depending on their degree of development. They did not think India was ready for Parliamentary institutions for instance, but they were in favour of other democratic measures, including the development of education facilities, the 'Indianization' of the Civil Service in increasing stages, the multiplication of provincial councils with limited powers, and a 'wise development of the self-government inherent in the village councils'.[1] When colonies had progressed to the level of self-government, the Fabians hoped for the development of federal unions of self-governing states, and trusted that moral ties and the bonds of mutual advantage would hold such Commonwealths together.[2] Thus the Fabians desired a continuous movement in the British Empire towards what was later to be called a 'Commonwealth of Nations.'

The final answer to the question whether the Fabians were Imperialists should perhaps be either: 'Yes, *in the sense used in 1900*, but . . .' or 'No, *not in the modern sense of the word*, but. . . .' It was the left-wing Liberal and Marxist use of the word that triumphed in Socialist ranks, and the Fabian usage went down before it. When J. A. Hobson's book *Imperialism* appeared, a review in *Fabian News* stoutly maintained that Hobson had confounded 'Imperialism' and 'Jingoism,' and had attributed to Imperialism all the evils which really sprang from Jingoism, whereas the Fabians had always been careful to draw a distinction between them.[3] When the pessimism of the Hobsonites appeared to be justified by the outbreak of the First World War, Hobson's usage of the term 'Imperialism' became popular amongst Socialists, and the Fabian distinction forgotten. Even the Fabians themselves succumbed, as can

[1] *Fabianism and the Empire*, pp. 17–21. Cf. the passage on 'Archer and India' in Bernard Shaw's portrait of William Archer in his *Pen Portraits and Reviews*, Standard Ed. (Constable, London, 1932), pp. 27–9, which brings out sharply Shaw's own attitude.
[2] *Ibid.* pp. 4, 21.
[3] See above, p. 122, J. A. Hobson's systematic criticism of the Fabian position was presented in his article 'Socialistic Imperialism' in *International Journal of Ethics*, vol. XII, (1901–2).

be seen from Shaw's writings. In his *Commonsense About the War* of 1914, Shaw, although he adopted a great measure of the Hobsonite analysis,[1] nevertheless continued to call the people he disliked 'Junkers' or 'Militarists' or 'Jingoes.' In his *Peace Conference Hints* published in 1919, when he reviewed the happenings of the past, he used the expression 'Jingo-Imperialists.'[2] In the *Intelligent Woman's Guide* the 'Jingo' was dropped, and 'Imperialism' used in the Hobson manner.[3] By that time, the Fabians had found 'Commonwealth of Nations' a more fitting term to describe the kind of Empire-organization they had, throughout, approved.

The Fabians had made their general approach to Imperialism clear in *Fabianism and the Empire*, but the pamphlet was, by usual Fabian standards, a slight piece. A booklet of 101 pages could hardly hope to deal satisfactorily with the huge problems it touched, even if every page had been devoted to those problems; in fact, the problems of London crowded out those of Empire as a whole. Forty-two of its pages dealt with 'Home Affairs,'[4] and those consisted mostly of a restatement of the Fabian municipal programme. A direct link was made between these 'Home Affairs' and more general Imperial issues only in two matters. First, a warning was given about the emigration of too much capital, leading to the reduction of Britain to a *rentier* nation with a 'bought' and apathetic working class—thereby inviting the fate of the Roman Empire. Secondly, events in South Africa were said to have demonstrated the superiority of a militia over a professional army, and the Fabians renewed a demand they had made long before for the universal military training of young men without removing them from civil life or requiring them to live for long periods in barracks, thus providing a militia which could be supplemented with specialist forces of volunteer soldiers.

Obviously the Fabians did not feel particularly comfortable in their new role of advisers on Imperial affairs. They drew the moral 'that what the British Empire wants most urgently in its government is . . . brains and political science',[5] but many years were to elapse before the Fabian Society itself was willing to follow up this suggestion and to undertake detailed research into Imperial problems. *Fabianism and the Empire* was a *pièce de circonstance* and the Fabians appear to have been happy to turn away from it and return to their 'proper business' of domestic reform. 'We are no longer thinking about Jingoism and Militarism' wrote Pease in 1908, reviewing the posthumous collection of William Clarke's writings, and saying why he found some of the articles 'a trifle out of date'.[6]

---

[1] Hobson was referred to by name, *What I Really Wrote about the War*, p. 55.
[2] *Ibid.* p. 294.
[3] *Intelligent Woman's Guide* (Pelican, London, 1937), ch. 40.
[4] See p. 254 below for an explanation of the peculiar structure of the pamphlet.
[5] *Fabianism and the Empire*, p. 93.
[6] *Fabian News*, July 1908.

'FABIANISM AND THE FISCAL QUESTION'

When the Fabians were confronted, in 1903, with Chamberlain's Tariff Reform issue, their reaction was even more equivocal than their reaction to the Imperialist controversy. Again, the drafting of their Tract on this difficult subject was left to Bernard Shaw. Again, it was submitted to members and many amendments were incorporated in it. Again, Shaw managed to carry the final draft 'with practical unanimity',[1] though one prominent dissentient—Graham Wallas, who had been somewhat in disagreement with the other Fabian leaders over their education policy—was led by his opposition to this Tract to resign from the Society.[2] *Fabianism and the Fiscal Question* began by observing: 'The ease with which Mr Chamberlain has reopened a question which for fifty years has been marked off by all parties as closed in English practical politics is perhaps the severest blow the triumphant Whig anti-Socialism of the nineteenth century has yet received. The establishment of Free Imports seemed as stable and final as the disestablishment of the Irish Church, of Purchase in the Army, of duelling, and of property qualification for the franchise.'[3] But in fairness it must be noted that Whig anti-Socialists had by no means been the only adherents of Free Trade; the Fabian Society, too, had taken Free Trade for granted, and, like most other Labour, Radical, and Socialist organizations, had treated the earlier 'Fair Traders' as enemies.[4]

Considerable argument about the merits of Free Trade and Protection took place within the Society before *Fabianism and the Fiscal Question* was accepted. Sidney Webb opened the debate in June 1903 with a cautious speech.[5] He defended the older position of the Society, and 'could see nothing in our economic, industrial, or fiscal situation that made it necessary, or even desirable, to revolutionize our fiscal system', but he thought, 'it might be inferred that the Prime Minister and the Colonial Secretary would not have raised so

---

[1] Pease, *op. cit.* p. 160.

[2] His letter of resignation appeared in *Fabian News*, February 1904.

[3] Tract 116. Contrast the following from *Fabianism and the Empire*, p. 50: 'Socialism has demolished the Manchester School and discredited the Free Trade Utopia of its economists and dreamers; but all the King's horses and all the King's men can no more set up import duties again than Napoleon could bring back the marquises.' Napoleon, of course, did to some extent 'bring back the marquises', though the restoration of the title was left to Louis xviii.

[4] Benjamin H. Brown, *The Tariff Reform Movement in Great Britain* 1881-95 (Columbia U.P., 1943), for an interesting study of the relations of the 'Fair Traders' with Labour.

[5] Cf. Beatrice Webb, *Our Partnership*, p. 269: '[Hewins' action] has necessitated Sidney flying the free trade flag. He would have preferred to keep quiet and not take part, but that is impossible in view of Hewins' and G.B.S.'s indiscretions'. For the Webbs' real attitude, *ibid.* p. 267; 'To Joe's specific proposals—a tax on food and eventually "protection all round", we are, as at present advised, opposed, as politically impractible, unnecessarily costly to the consumer, and likely to lead to international friction and internal uncertainty. We do not agree, however, with the extreme hostility to these proposals ... Sidney, at present, inclines towards bounties on colonial imports as a likely compromise between the British consumer, the British manufacturer, and the colonial producer.'

large an issue, and one likely to be so disruptive of their own party, without information convincing them of the necessity of taking some action in consolidating the Empire'. The tenor of Webb's speech was against tariffs,[1] but its cautious and tentative character invited rather than stilled criticism. The publication of W. J. Ashley's *The Tariff Problem* seems to have had a considerable influence in moving the Fabians somewhat from their Free Trade position. This work was reviewed in *Fabian News* of November 1903, when it was spoken of as 'the ablest and most interesting presentment we have seen of the case for preferential tariffs'. It found especial favour with the Fabian reviewer, because 'Free Trade arguments are recognized to the full and recourse to defensive tariffs is regarded as provisional only. They may be looked upon as the props to a cathedral to prevent collapse while an alteration is being made to the foundations'. The reviewer appeared disturbed at the author's 'taking the incidental references to Free Trade in our *Fabianism and the Empire* as our final word on the present crisis and our only "alternative" to Preferential Tariffs'.

The full-scale attack on the Fabians' earlier attachment to Free Trade was launched within the Society by Robert Dell. He argued that Free Trade was historically the counterpart of *laissez faire*, in that both placed reliance on the natural working of the economic system. Socialists, who believed in the opposite principle of the conscious control of the economic system, needed to look at the facts, including the character of the country's exports and imports, and to consider whether the most desirable results were being obtained. The fact was, he argued, that English capital was going abroad to build up foreign (and mostly protected) industry, while the staple trades of the country had been stagnant or declining for twenty years. The restoration of English agriculture was the most immediate need; but in general, Dell urged, 'import duties ought to be levied with great care and to vary very much; the decision should be vested in a permanent expert body, and the government should consciously control foreign trade and resolve on expert advice what trades to encourage and what not . . . cheapness was not the only consideration; the quality of the commodities and the conditions under which they were produced must also be considered . . .' because '. . . there was every fear that if the present tendencies continued unchecked England would merely become the pleasure ground of the English-speaking peoples, living on tourists and rich men whose fortunes were made and invested in other countries and producing little or nothing. Collectivism would not check the tendency, its remedies were directed to another class of evils, and a collectivist state would find itself face to face with the same difficulties that we had to face at present'.[2] Sidney Webb, in replying, pointed out that Free Trade was not necessarily proved a bad policy because it was established by men who believed in *laissez faire*, and that arguments

[1] *Fabian News*, July 1903. [2] *Ibid*. December 1903.

showing that trades were declining did not necessarily prove that Protection was the remedy.[1] The debate was continued by Pease,[2] whose bias seemed on the whole towards Free Trade, and later by Cecil Chesterton, who turned the question towards the allied problem of the free immigration of Chinese labour into the Colonies, a proposal which had been favoured in *Fabianism and the Empire*, but which Chesterton opposed.[3]

In the circumstances, the difficulties of drafting a Tract which would satisfy the majority of Fabians were enormous. At a members' meeting held on 22 January 1904, Shaw explained the troubles they had encountered in trying to 'formulate the collective opinion of the Society on this long and debatable subject', and said he had endeavoured 'to incorporate as much as possible the whole of the many suggestions already sent in, excepting those which were incompatible with the general lines of the Tract'. The Tract was then discussed page by page. At the end, Graham Wallas, supported by Aylmer Maude, moved that the Tract as amended be not printed, but they were defeated by a large majority.

Fabianism and the Fiscal Question, considered as a publication designed to bridge the deep divisions amongst the Fabians themselves, is a masterpiece; considered as a manifesto presenting to the world an easily-grasped solution, it is a failure, and it has proved the least popular of all Shaw's pamphlets.[4] Like *Fabianism and the Empire*, its main weakness lies in a confusion between analysing what is occurring and recommending a policy. Although the sub-title of the fiscal Tract is 'An alternative policy', it is not clear from the text whether the Society's recommendations are an alternative to Chamberlain's policy, or to Free Trade policy, or to both. The ambiguity was exploited by Shaw to attack both the Chamberlainites and the Free Traders. A scarifying analysis was given of the arguments and appeal of both policies. Neither side emerged unscathed from criticism, but it would be a nice point to decide which got the worst of it. On the whole, the impression was given that the Fabians expected Chamberlain to sweep the country with his policy, bad as it was. The attack on the Liberal Party was a bitter one: though some of the Conservatives were referred to as nincompoops, the Conservative party was at least said to have given up Conservatism in despair of competing with the Liberals on that score. The working-class was upbraided: its failure to strike out for itself was seen as making it generally an adherent of outmoded Liberal doctrines, though particular sections of it would, for selfish reasons, fall a prey to Chamberlain's propaganda. The elements of the Fabians 'alternative policy' were stated to be nationalized or 'Imperialized' merchant shipping to provide cheaper transport rates, railway nationalization for the same purpose, a reformed Consular service along the lines suggested in the *Fabianism and the Empire* Tract, improved

[1] *Ibid.*
[2] *Ibid.* (his review of Armitage-Smith's book).
[3] *Ibid.* April 1904.
[4] Pease, *op. cit.* p. 160.

facilities for technical education, a system of 'bounties' and research investigations into Britain's resources. But it was no longer suggested, as it had been in *Fabianism and the Empire*, that Fabian reformers accepted the context of a general policy of Free Trade. Rather was it hinted now that policies of Free Trade or Protection involved no question of principle for a Socialist, that the problems were exceedingly complicated, and that no abstract principle could furnish a guide. This, while eminently sensible in a general way, stopped far short of practical proposals. Their only recommendations directly on the fiscal question were that Socialists and Labour men should demand a minimum wage varying according to the price level, and see to it that any revenue produced as a result of any tariff that might be imposed would not be used in reduction of taxes on unearned incomes.

THE ISSUES NEGLECTED, 1904-11

After they had expressed their collective views in these Tracts, the Fabians turned once more to what they considered their 'proper business' of domestic reform. From 1904 to the very end of 1911 the Society's attention was almost entirely absorbed in internal English problems. A list of the topics discussed in the meetings of the Society during these years reveals that the Fabian Society in its official capacity gave almost no further thought to Empire or foreign problems. A rare lecture by a visiting Dominions politician, a couple of talks by Fabians who had been on an Empire tour, one or two lectures on India, an occasional vigorous protest at Czarist tyranny and a 'somewhat small audience'[1] to hear Mr Spencer Wilkinson advocate compulsory military training in 1909—these were all.[2] Nothing at all on international relations. The pessimists were not only ignored, they were mocked: Pease, reviewing J. A. Hobson's *Crisis of Liberalism* in May 1910, wrote:

Mr Hobson was born too late to possess the cheerful self-confidence of the Victorian Liberals, and he has failed to acquire the robust optimism of the convinced Socialist. Hence his outlook on politics is what he himself calls 'the coldly sceptical spirit' of the end of the last century. At every turn the bogey of truculent Imperialism stares at us from his pages. Liberalism has reached a 'crisis' (as it does every second year or so), 'the competitive struggle is fraught with growing hazard' (growing ever since the peaceful days of the South Sea Bubble). . . .[3]

Bernard Shaw frankly confessed, in a sentence equally applicable to his colleagues, that until 1913, he 'had been too pre-occupied with my colleagues

---

[1] *Fabian News*, June 1909.

[2] Olivier's *White Capital and Coloured Labour*, which appeared in 1906, must be mentioned also. But it was, significantly, published by the I.L.P. and not by the Fabian Society. Olivier was at this time supporting H. G. Wells and was somewhat estranged from the 'old guard' Fabian leaders.

[3] *Fabian News*, May 1910.

of the Fabian Society in working out the practicalities of English Socialism, and establishing a Parliamentary Labour Party, to busy myself with foreign policy'.[1]

THE FIRST WORLD WAR: THE FABIAN ATTITUDE

The first Fabian lecture which considered the danger of war between England and Germany was given in December 1911 by William Stephen Sanders, who had made a closer study than most Fabians of German conditions and the German Socialist movement. Sanders began by apologizing for his 'temerity in tackling such an important and difficult problem as that of our relations with another country', because 'foreign policy as far as England was concerned had always been considered the sacred province of government which should not be interfered with either by the people or Parliament'. He approved the demands the Labour Party was making for more Parliamentary control over the Foreign Office and for more publicity of its actions. In Sanders' opinion, the strained relations between England and Germany had developed through 'a variety of causes arising from the remarkable political, commercial, and industrial development of the German Empire during the last forty years'. Trade rivalry had produced hostile feelings amongst the commercial, military, and intellectual circles in both countries. The Boer War, and the German demand for a big navy had inflamed this feeling. And 'in recent years English diplomacy appeared to the Germans to have been directed to the checking and humiliating of their country, culminating in the Morocco incidents, while other nations had been permitted to acquire territory and influence without earnest protest on our part'. This gave the German Anglophobes the opportunity of representing England as an enemy jealous of German power. But opposed to these factors making for war, Sanders saw hopeful signs that peace would be maintained. The 'German people in the mass were a sober, peace-loving people who had no great love of military glory;' the heavy cost of armaments and its burden in taxes was bringing a reaction against the jingoists; and the growing influence of the Social Democratic Party, which desired peaceful relations with England, would restrain the militarists. Sanders concluded that England's foreign policy should be directed less by fear and hostility to Germany and more by the desire to arrive at an understanding with her.[2]

The discussion opened by Sanders was not followed up at the time. Not until 1913 did the Fabian Society address itself seriously to Socialist responsibilities in the international field.[3] The approach of the Triennial International

[1] Shaw, *What I Really Wrote about the War*, p. 4. His first letter to the press on international affairs in this collection is to the *Daily Chronicle* and dated 18 March 1913.

[2] *Fabian News*, February 1912.

[3] This seems remarkable in view of the close friendship between the Webbs and Haldane, but the Webbs were greatly occupied with internal affairs until 1911, and they were absent on a world tour during 1911–2. At all events, the Fabian Society as a body displayed little interest in the worsening international situation.

135

Socialist Congress made necessary some discussion of the issue, for the Congress held in Copenhagen in 1910 had called for reports by the member nations to the next Congress on the possibility of organizing a general strike against war. The Emergency International Socialist Congress held in Bâle in November 1912 reminded member organizations of their obligations in the matter, and the Fabian Executive appointed a small committee of three members to consider the policy it should adopt. Two members of the committee were 'in direct disagreement with one another' and the other 'was neutral'. The Executive therefore decided that the two with decided opinions—the Australian historian, Dr Marion Phillips and the Oxford historian, Mr R. C. K. Ensor—should address the Society.[1]

The character of these two important lectures and the positive recommendations embodied in them, were in sharp contrast. Dr Phillips' was short, direct, not theoretical, militant; Mr Ensor's was carefully prepared, theoretical, long-term, moderate. Dr Phillips favoured the strike against war, while Mr Ensor was content with a little more (but not full) publicity for foreign office affairs.

Dr Phillips began her lecture by saying that, up to this time, the Trade Unions had taken very little interest in foreign affairs, and that 'the same was the case with the Fabian Society'. The Labour Party had passed some 'splendid resolutions' but these had not much affected the indifference of the Party's rank and file. Only the I.L.P. and the Women's Labour League, in Dr Phillips' opinion, had paid serious attention to the problem of international peace. Her main argument in favour of supporting the proposal for a general strike against war at the International Socialist Congress was the paramount need for removing the feeling of apathy and helplessness amongst the rank and file of the Labour Movement in face of the growing menace of the international situation, by setting before them a definite course of action with which the threat of war could be fought. Peace propaganda which had no practical action to suggest—action that provided 'an outlet for excitement' to counteract 'the fascinating hysteria of war'—was futile. Before this consideration, objections to the policy went down, though Dr Phillips admitted some of these to be not unimportant. Difficulties of organization could be overcome provided the miners and transport workers could be brought to support the policy. As for the objection that such a policy would involve a 'sectional tyranny' over society, this supposed 'that a tyranny of trade unionists would be worse than the present tyranny of the diplomatist'.

R. C. K. Ensor's lecture began with an historical analysis of the attitude of Socialists to foreign policy. He thought it 'doubtful whether any view of foreign policy could be so far deduced from the principles of Socialism that only Socialists could hold it'. Socialism had grown up as an opposition creed

[1] Dr Phillips' speech was given in May 1913; Mr Ensor's not till October of the same year. *Fabian News*, June and November 1913.

in countries where the proletariat and its Socialist champions had no part in officering the State, or the Army, or in administering the Colonies. Consequently, all these things had come to be regarded by Socialists as essentially linked with Capitalism, their enemy. But in democratic countries, the anti-State attitude was being increasingly abandoned by Socialists, and their views on imperialism and militarism also required revision in the light of that abandonment. The stage which the conflict between the old and new views had reached could be seen in the International Socialist Congresses and the manifestos of the International Socialist Bureau. These revealed a confusion between two opposite views: 'Cosmopolitanism'—the view that nations are unrealities, patriotism absurd, and all wars caused by capitalism, and 'Internationalism'—the view that nationality is real and precious, patriotism a duty, and that war, representing in the main genuine conflicts of national interests, can only be abolished by finding a substitute for it. Ensor considered Cosmopolitanism, which underlay the idea of 'international solidarity of labour', to be unsound: it was not an attitude to which anyone who passed from opposition to office could remain loyal, except by becoming 'disloyal to the interests of our country and of peace'. Men of affairs everywhere recognized this fact, and Cosmopolitanism rendered a disservice to Socialism by repelling them. Modern Socialists should adopt the principle of Internationalism, 'first clearly enunciated by Kant', which implied that attachment to one's nation was 'of supreme human and moral value' but 'that other people's attachment to theirs was no less',—that one should be a true patriot, but rejoice that nations were many, not one. It also implied a recognition that there could be conflicts of *national* interests.

Ensor then went on to describe 'the four chief attitudes' towards conflicts of national interests, which he labelled the 'Pacifist,' the 'Pugnacious,' the 'Sentimental' (or 'Crusading' or 'Interfering'), and the 'Official' (or 'Policy of National Interests'). While on different occasions there might be 'elements of good in all four', nearly all the trouble was caused by the Pugnacious and Sentimental attitudes, while 'a judicious blend' of the Pacifist and the Official attitudes 'supplied most of what was needed for a wise Internationalism'. Socialists were not commonly entrapped by the faults of the Pugnacious school, but they could be by the Sentimental—making alliances on the basis of their approval of the ally's internal political structure, or acting as the armed missionary of social progress. Such a policy had brought disaster to the French Revolutionaries; and it would be foolish, Ensor suggested, to estimate the national advantages or disadvantages of England's treaties with Russia and France on the basis that Russia was a tyranny and France republican and progressive. Pacifism in its full sense was incompatible with nationhood, but in its valuable sense it meant an insistence that war should not be entered upon by any nation that could justly avoid it, that no money should be spent on armaments which could be dispensed with, and that no State to which arbitration was open should refuse it. The Official attitude was that of diplomats everywhere. 'It was based on historical observation of the things which had in fact made some Powers great and brought others low.' It involved making alliances to protect national interests.

Ensor advocated, though with caution, more popular interest in, and control of, diplomacy. At present, questions of foreign policy were decided by governments: popular feeling had little to do with the making either of treaties or wars, though 'Governments regularly whipped it up through the press, so as to look as if it had.' The same was true in Britain: 'the House of Commons ... did not influence, and it did not deserve to influence, foreign affairs, because it was almost wholly indifferent to and ignorant of them, in this faithfully reflecting the electorate'. Cabinet control over the Foreign Secretary also was slight. But in advocating more popular control over foreign policy, Socialists (Ensor thought) should remember that too much popular control could have its disadvantages. They should 'not forget either the indifference or the peculiar bellicosity of the British masses, nor the proneness of all democracies, through personal irresponsibility, to acts of international bad faith'; they should also remember that Cavour had been able to do great things for Italy by secret diplomacy that he could never have done if all his plans had been known. Ensor finally suggested the setting up of a Standing Committee of the House of Commons on Foreign Affairs. All parties should be represented on this Committee in proportion to their strength; it should meet regularly, and the Foreign Secretary should attend to make statements and answer all questions; proceedings should be public, except in certain cases where the Minister desired them to be private. This Committee would keep a check on the Foreign Secretary, and form a nucleus of members in Parliament who would make foreign affairs a special study. The next step would be 'a policy of Home Rule all round' to set the Imperial Parliament free to consider central and imperial business only, and thus allow problems of foreign policy a degree of attention which their importance deserved.

These speeches of Dr Marion Phillips and Mr Ensor are useful as marking the extremes of militant dissatisfaction with the existing management of foreign policy on the one hand, and of moderate justification of it on the other, that were to be found in the Fabian Society before the First World War.[1] Between these extremes, a number of intermediate positions were taken up by the Society's members. For instance, Shaw's attitude, as shown in letters he began writing to the newspapers from 1913, resembled Ensor's in that he had no faith in the expedient of the general strike against war, and that he fully

[1] Although Ensor had justified very ably the attitude that was to be adopted by the majority of Fabians during the war, the views which had been expressed at the meetings of the Second International were mainly those of Keir Hardie and the I.L.P.

accepted Ensor's principle of 'Internationalism' as against 'Cosmopolitanism', and demanded no more extensive changes in the Foreign Office. But Shaw had no faith in Sir Edward Grey, and was full of contempt for the policy—or (as he alleged) lack of policy—that England was pursuing, and for the persons responsible for it. Both before the war and later Shaw persisted in believing that the war might not have broken out if the British government had made it quite clear that if Germany attacked France, England would combine with France against Germany, and if France attacked Germany, then England would combine with Germany against France.[1] In letters to the Press from March 1913 he called upon the Foreign Office to announce publicly that this was England's position. Nor was Shaw so willing as Ensor to justify an alliance with Russia. To him, as an old Socialist, the Russia of the Czars was an 'obsolete and abominable despotism with which no western State could decently associate'.[2] Russia had ever been, in Socialist and Radical eyes, the centre of reaction in Europe,[3] and, after the outbreak of war, Shaw deeply offended those who were finding new virtues in Russia by giving a ruthless analysis of the economic and political motives of the English and French alliance with her.[4] To this extent, Shaw fell into Ensor's 'Sentimental' category (a curious title for a category that included Shaw). He was apparently influenced also in his view of international alliances by the concept of 'higher' and 'lower' civilizations which had been embodied in the *Fabianism and the Empire* Tract.

Upon the outbreak of the war, the Fabian Society held a discussion at Essex Hall, which was opened by R. C. K. Ensor. The division of opinion amongst the members was extreme. Ensor, in his opening speech, said that Socialism had collapsed before Armageddon—not that anyone conversant with the facts had supposed that the German government would ever have been influenced by Socialist meetings. Actually, the German Socialists by their tirades against Czarism had helped on the cause of the German war-mongers. They forgot 'that as soon as you start agitating, not against the sins of your own Government, but against the domestic sins of some other country's Government, you are sowing the seed of international war'. When war broke out, and national existence was placed at stake, the Socialists simply 'had no alternative but to join in the fighting'. Socialist slogans about the cause of war were untrue or useless. Non-resistance as a policy was futile. In fact, the Socialist parties in each country, though they formed 'reservoirs of popular pacific feeling', had no way out of the situation that others had not: their position was analogous to that of the Christian churches. No one could blame Socialists for rallying to their nation in time of war, except insofar as they acquiesced in a national guilt. The German Socialists had deliberately acquiesced in the crime against Belgium. Ensor saw the hope of peace not in any

[1] Shaw, *What I Really Wrote about the War*, pp. 11, 16, 39 *et seq.*
[2] *Ibid.* p. 3.   [3] *Ibid.* p. 80 *et seq.*   [4] *Ibid.* p. 84 *et. seq.*

specific action on the part of Socialists, but in a world-concert of 'satisfied' Great Powers. 'If a victory by the Allies were followed by a reasonable satisfaction of the historic needs of the Russian Empire, this idea would cease to be Utopian. The presumable reduction in the number of Great Powers was to be regretted; but this and many other calamities were inherent in the great calamity of war'.

A short record which was kept of the ensuing discussion demonstrates, more vividly than any comment or description, the division of opinion within the Fabian Society at that fateful moment. It reads:

Clifford Allen defended the action of Germany, and declared that the German policy was a defensive one and that the violation of Belgian neutrality was a necessary part of that policy. The armament mongers created an atmosphere of war. International Socialism was not dead, but only temporarily checked.

Aylmer Maude agreed with Ensor. He had hoped that an international force would be created to back the decisions of the Hague tribunal. He contended that England had taken the right course in standing by Belgium.

W. Stephen Sanders stated that the policy of Germany was avowedly aggressive and not defensive. Neither the German army nor navy on their present scale were necessary for defence. The Social Democrats in the Reichstag had always voted before the war against the military budget because they were convinced that aggression was the purpose of the Government. Bebel had informed them in 1907 that the German navy was being built to attack England at the first opportunity. England could not have adopted any course than the one she had taken.

A. J. Marriott agreed that England had to go to war, but thought that the reasons for her intervention were not those which the public accepted.

C. E. M. Joad held that the only consistent attitude for international Social Democracy was that of non-resistance.

Dr Clarke expressed astonishment that anyone could defend Germany's attack on Belgium. Something might be said for Austria, but German diplomacy was indefensible.

S. Salzedo argued that Germany had a good case for her action, having regard to the menace of Russia.

Dr O'Brien Harris urged that England should be honest in stating her motive for taking part in the war. She did not believe that we had taken up arms simply for the sake of Belgium.

Mrs Samuel said that the British Government may not have been so much concerned about Belgium as they declared, but nevertheless the German treatment of that country was sufficient justification for England going to war.

Jack Gibson held that once war was entered upon it was impossible for most people not to accept the position that their own country, 'right or wrong', must be supported, and the contest fought through.

Graham Wallas agreed with the previous speaker. He urged, however, that the present war might end in a long, bitter struggle like that of the Thirty Years' War, or a deadlock, neither side being the victor. It would be wise to prepare for this contingency, and men willing to find a way to peace (as for instance, the representatives of International Socialism) should foregather at some 'wayside inn', even before the war was at an end.

J. C. Squire also held that the various sections of the international Socialist movement should get into touch with one another at the earliest opportunity. He defended certain of the proposed terms of peace already put forward by a group of English Radicals.

R. C. K. Ensor, in his reply, emphasized the crime committed against Belgium by Germany, and the impossibility of trusting the latter country again. He also pointed out the difficulties of compulsory arbitration, unless the deciding factors were 'satisfied' Great Powers.[1]

The Fabian Society as a whole, as might be expected, 'made no pronouncement and adopted no policy'[2] on the First World War. Its members were left free to take up their own attitude. The one attempt, made at a Members' Meeting on 12 March 1915, to obtain from the Society a pronouncement of policy, was defeated. Aylmer Rose, Herbert Morrison, C. E. M. Joad, and Alan Trangmar proposed a 'Stop-the-War' resolution, which was met by an Executive amendment declaring: 'That, in all the circumstances of the case, the present is not a suitable moment for initiating any international campaign to stop the war'. The amendment was declared not carried when the voting for and against was fifty either way, and the resolution proper was overwhelmingly rejected when put to the vote. The reason for the close vote on the amendment was that it was opposed by some Fabians who, like Shaw, thought that its passing 'might lead to a misunderstanding'.[3] The majority of the Fabians followed the Labour Party in supporting the war. Sidney Webb, for instance, declared in his election address to the London University in 1918: 'World calamity as I hold war to be, I have never wavered, from Lord Grey's exposition of the case on 3 August 1914, in my conviction that this nation had no alternative, either in honour or in safety, but to take up the challenge . . . and pursue the struggle resolutely to the end, until aggressive militarism was overthrown.'[4] A minority of Fabians, led by Clifford Allen, followed the I.L.P. in its opposition to the war.

Those Fabians who felt sufficiently detached, in a time of intense passion, from violent partisanship, no doubt found pleasure in Shaw's coolly rationalist and critical *Commonsense About the War*,[5] but it hardly found general favour even in the ranks of the Fabian Society. It is easy to see why Shaw's attitude annoyed most people at that time. On the one hand, he claimed that the war having begun, it was necessary to fight until the Germans were defeated. On the other, he ruthlessly rejected all (or nearly all)[6] English claims to moral superiority. After an analysis of the causes of the war, and of the events leading up to it, in terms with which Lenin himself would not greatly have disagreed,

---

[1] *Fabian News*, November 1914.   [2] Pease, *op. cit.* p. 234.
[3] *Fabian News*, April 1915.
[4] Quoted in M. A. Hamilton, *Sidney and Beatrice Webb*, p. 220.
[5] Reprinted in *What I Really Wrote about the War*.
[6] Shaw did admit that Militarism and 'Junkerdom', rampant in the Allied Nations as well as in Germany, was worse in Germany. *What I Really Wrote about the War*, pp. 103–4.

Shaw dismissed the sort of policy that Lenin was recommending to Socialists as hopeless, except, perhaps, 'in a defeated conscript army if its commanders push it beyond human endurance'.[1] Shaw advised Englishmen to fight the war, but to fight it without illusions. He claimed positive advantages for such a policy. The stripping of the British case to its hard core of national survival and prestige, Shaw claimed, strengthened it. People were saved the mental perplexity of relying on weak reasons for fighting that could easily be refuted by the other side, and, more important still, they would fight and make peace uninfluenced by the foolish and vindictive passions aroused by presenting the war as a crude melodrama in which England was the hero and Germany the villain. Germany ought to be defeated, not smashed or dismembered; Czarist Russia had to be checked—it was a militarist autocracy far worse than Germany; measures for extensions of democracy and Socialism needed to be pressed even during the war, for only the victory of democracy and socialism would eliminate the most potent causes of war.

During the war, many of the older Fabians found their services useful in the War-Emergency Workers' National Committee, a national association set up by Trade Union, Co-operative, Labour Party, and Socialist bodies. Among the Fabians on it were Arthur Henderson (its chairman), Sidney Webb, Miss Mary Macarthur, Miss Margaret Bondfield, Dr Marion Phillips, Miss Susan Lawrence, W. C. Anderson, Ben Cooper, Ben Tillett, W. Stephen Sanders, and J. S. Middleton (its Secretary). Sidney Webb was particularly active on this organization which brought him even closer in touch with many of the other Labour leaders. Also Sidney Webb replaced W. Stephen Sanders as the Fabian nominee on the Labour Party Executive (a change which was to have an important influence on both the Fabian Society and the Labour Party) when Sanders took up active war service. Many of the same people were also members of the Cabinet Emergency Committee for the Prevention and Relief of Distress. Beatrice Webb was appointed a member of the Committee for London; Sidney Webb was a member of the Committee for Urban Housing and the Committee for Statistical Enquiry as to Unemployment and Distress in London; Sir Sydney Olivier a member of the Committee on Rural Housing; Miss Mary Macarthur, Miss Susan Lawrence, Miss Margaret Bondfield, and Dr Marion Phillips were members of the Central Committee for Women's Employment; Arthur Henderson and Miss Mary Macarthur were members of the Executive Committee of the Prince of Wales's Fund. The few Fabian Tracts that were produced during the war years were the outcome of activities on these bodies; *War and the Workers. A Handbook of some immediate measures to prevent unemployment and relieve distress* by Sidney Webb;[2] *The War; Women; and Unemployment;*[3] and, also by Sidney Webb, *When Peace Comes. The Way of Industrial Reconstruction.*[4]

[1] *Ibid.* pp. 23-4.   [2] Tract 176.   [3] Tract 178.   [4] Tract 181.

The Fabian Society itself also maintained an active life during the war. The standard of its lectures remained high, and the large percentage of them devoted to the study of the history and political conditions of other European countries suggests that the Fabians were making up for their previous neglect. The Fabian Research Department remained active, and two of its reports had special reference to the war. The Fabians had lost no time after the outbreak of war in commencing research into the possibilities of a supra-national authority for the post-war world. In January 1915 a discussion, led by Miss Mabel Atkinson, was held amongst the Fabian members on the problems of establishing such an authority.[1] In July 1915 two reports, prepared by Leonard Woolf for the Research Department, were published as *New Statesman* Supplements, and in the following year were issued in book form under the title *International Government*. The work consisted of an analysis of all the approximations to international government that actually existed, and some proposals for a future supra-national authority. These proposals envisaged an International Council consisting of representatives of the governments of sovereign and independent States, together with an International High Court for dealing with legal or justiciable disputes, and a Permanent Board of Conciliators for mediation of issues that were not justiciable, and an International Secretariat. It involved an undertaking by the member-nations that all disputes would be submitted to the Council through one or other of its subordinate bodies, and an undertaking that in no circumstances would they proceed to aggression within a period of twelve months of making their submission. All the member-nations were to agree to make common cause, even to the extent of war, against any nation breaking the covenant. Such was one of the earliest foreshadowings of post-war international authorities.

The other publication of the Research Department was *How to Pay for the War*, edited by Sidney Webb. It consisted of four fairly detailed schemes for the nationalization of three main industries and the expansion of one already under public control, together with a scheme for the reform of taxation. 'It has been a matter of reproach,' declared a review in *Fabian News*, 'that the Society has busied itself too exclusively in working out projects of social amelioration along the line of establishing and enforcing a National Minimum of Civilized Life, to the neglect of projects of nationalization. This volume to some extent relieves us from the reproach'.[2] The proposals in the volume were for an extension of the activities of the Post Office, for the development of war-time control over railways into full-scale nationalization of railways and canals, and the nationalization of coal-mines and the insurance companies. The section entitled 'A revolution in Income Tax' proposed a better graduation of the tax in favour of lower incomes, and the 'revolutionary suggestion' that tax should be assessed upon family not individual incomes.

[1] *Fabian News*, February 1915. [2] *Ibid.* August 1916.

In August 1916, in response to a request from the International Socialist Bureau, the Fabian Society drew up a short Report on Peace Terms,[1] which reveals a further development of their views. The first item in the Report was a demand for a supra-national authority on the lines suggested in their *International Government* book. The prevention of future war, the Report declared,

will not be obtained merely by any increase in the Democratic control over the foreign policy or treaty arrangements of the various State Governments, desirable as such Democratic control would be. It will not be secured by any restriction of national armaments, or by a Government monopoly of the manufacture of guns, munitions or ships of war, however advantageous such proposals may be. Nor will war be prevented by the adoption of universal Freedom of Trade, Freedom of Commercial Enterprise, or Freedom of the Seas. It will only be prevented by the deliberate establishment of some way of settling disputes among States, or conflicts among peoples, other than that of resorting to armed force.

Other proposals in the Report were that the territorial mutilation of Germany should be opposed; that Germany and Austria should be compulsorily disarmed, as a prelude to limitation of armaments by the Allies; that territorial changes should be determined on national grounds, save in the few instances where 'the geographical and strategic requirements' of other States needed to take precedence of nationalist aspirations;[2] that each country should be allowed to choose its own economic policy;[3] that all governments should prepare against a post-war depression by providing public works of various kinds 'not as relief works for unemployed workmen, but as accessions to the ordinary capitalist demand for labour—these public enterprises being set going from time to time in exact correspondence with the capitalist demand, so as to maintain at an unvarying level the aggregate demand for wage labour in the country as a whole'; and, finally, that an International Commission should be appointed to distribute an Indemnity Fund amongst those who had suffered in the war.

Though the Fabian Society as a whole favoured the establishment of a supra-national authority, there were divisions of opinion among Fabians on its nature. Should the new League of Nations include all the nations of the earth, or should it be a smaller body of 'politically homogeneous constituents'?

[1] The Report is given in *Fabian News*, September 1916.
[2] The instance given was that of an outlet to the sea. In such cases 'properly organized and humanely arranged' transfers of population might be carried out. Opposition was expressed to punitive transfers of territory, and also to plebiscites for determining nationality as useless and dangerous.
[3] The Fabians had in mind here chiefly the question of protective tariffs. They still showed something of a Free Trade bias, but allowed that every case must be judged on its own merits. See also *Fabian News*, November 1916 (review by S. Webb of J. A. Hobson's *The New Protectionism*); *ibid.* February, April, and May 1917 (R. C. K. Ensor, S. Webb, and Emil Davies on 'War Lights on Free Trade and Protection').

International Government[1] envisaged an almost full international body, comprising at least the eight great powers of Britain, U.S.A., France, Germany, Italy, Austria, Japan, and Russia, fifteen other States of Europe and eighteen other American States, China, Persia, and Siam, with provision for the admission of others. Bernard Shaw, however, favoured the other view: he did not think a League of all nations would work. He declared the League's 'constituents must be either republics or constitutional monarchies in which the monarch has much less personal power than an American President would have if he were elected for life. It must have a well-developed Labour Movement, Socialist movement, and Science movement. And it would have to be prepared for the formation of other Leagues of Nations in the yellow world, the Indian world, perhaps in the Slav world and the Spanish-Indian world . . .';[2] Briefly, Shaw wanted a League consisting only of the countries of 'higher civilization', principally, the United States, Great Britain, France, and Germany. This was a curious projection of Shaw's 'European-consciousness' into the post-war world; but that world was to be more suddenly changed than he anticipated. Needless to say the League of Nations, in the form it was established, was not as the Fabians had desired. Their attitude to it, consequently, was one of support mixed with criticism.[3]

[1] Fabian Committee and L. S. Woolf, *International Government* (Fabian Society and Allen & Unwin, London, 1916), pp. 77-9, 238-9.
[2] Shaw, *What I Really Wrote about the War*, p. 328.
[3] Tract 226.

CHAPTER VI

FABIAN PHILOSOPHY AND IDEALS

Is there a philosophy of Fabianism? As a general rule, it was the practice of the Fabian Society to disavow any distinctive philosophy.[1] One of the chapters in *Fabian Essays* and a couple of the Fabian Tracts are concerned with philosophical problems, but these, like the few other Tracts dealing with religion and art, are signed by their authors. The attitude of the Society always has been that these matters were the private concern of its individual members. At first sight, therefore, it seems impossible to speak of a Fabian philosophy; it is necessary to speak of the philosophy of Bernard Shaw, of Stewart Headlam, of Hubert Bland or of the other individual members. And certainly a very wide range of belief and disbelief was to be found in the Society, where atheists co-operated on practical political issues with ardent churchmen, materialists (Marxists and other) with idealists, all varieties of Christian denominations (from Quakers to Roman Catholics) with militant Rationalists. It might seem therefore that no more can be said about Fabian 'philosophy' than about the Society's views on the marriage question, on which subject, as Shaw once remarked, the Society was 'as open to the strictest Roman Catholic as it was to the most conscientiously polygamous Mahomedan'.[2]

Yet some problems would remain, even if it were completely true that no general Fabian philosophical views could be discovered. Did the Fabians attempt to justify their position on theoretical grounds, or did they simply find it worked as a practical policy? Clearly, if the Fabians could have justified the argument that it was not necessary for a Socialist to subscribe to any particular philosophic system, or to have any philosophic views at all, this would be a matter of first importance. Nor is this all. The term 'philosophy' is a wide one, and while it is true that members of the Fabian Society could, and did, differ profoundly about religion and the nature of ultimate reality, it is by no means so certain that there were not philosophical views of a less metaphysical kind widely accepted in Fabian circles. At least, it may be possible, despite their differences, to make a few cautious generalizations about some philosophic views which influenced the Fabians—and more particularly the early Fabians.

NO VIEWS ON PHILOSOPHY?

It has frequently been claimed, especially by the followers of Marx, that the acceptance of Socialism (or at least the acceptance of a particular brand of Socialism) logically involves the acceptance of a particular 'world view'. And,

[1] See e.g. Tract 70; Tract 132.
[2] Letter against H. G. Wells in *Fabian News*, February 1907.

146

in general, it has frequently been the opinion of persons interested in meta-physics that the acceptance of certain political principles involves the accept-ance of certain metaphysical principles, or, conversely, that the acceptance of a particular metaphysical system leads to certain definite political conclusions. The degree of abstraction or generality of the metaphysical views which are claimed to lead to such political conclusions may vary—for example, from the Marxist argument that idealism leads to non-revolutionary or anti-revolu-tionary politics to, say, the contention of Dr Popper that 'historicism' is in philosophic opposition to the 'Open Society.'

There seems little doubt that the Fabian Society's avoidance of philosophy was intended primarily as a matter of convenience. As such, the attitude was accepted by many members who might have objected strenuously if it had been taken as denying that there were connections between particular political and particular philosophical views. From their own experience, the Fabians observed that people holding the most diverse philosophical views could com-bine in their Society in a specific political programme. Further, they noticed 'as a matter of practical experience English political societies do good work and present a dignified appearance whilst they attend seriously to their proper political business; but, to put it bluntly, they make themselves ridiculous and attract undesirables when they affect art and philosophy'.[1]

Another practical reason for the exclusion of metaphysics from the Fabian creed was undoubtedly their desire to avoid creating barriers to the circulation of their propaganda. The Fabian view was expounded by Shaw many years later in his advice to the Intelligent Woman: 'Even as a professional reformer you had better be content to preach one form of unconventionality at a time. For instance, if you rebel against high-heeled shoes, take care to do it in a very smart hat.'[2]

These 'practical' reasons for the Society's attitude were supplemented by the feeling of many of the early Fabians that metaphysical arguments were not of great importance. Though a number of the leading Fabians later changed their opinions, in the 'eighties many of them (including all the Fabian essay-ists except possibly William Clarke)[3] were, in their attitude to religion, either agnostics or atheists, and most of them had been influenced in philosophic outlook by the anti-metaphysical views of Positivism, either directly through the writings of Comte, or as relayed through Mill and the writings and lectures of Comte's English followers. 'Most of the free-thinking men of that period', one of the Fabians has written of the 'eighties, 'read the *Positive Polity* and

---

[1] Bernard Shaw's Appendix to Pease, *op. cit.* p. 279.
[2] *Intelligent Woman's Guide* (Pelican), vol. II, p. 381.
[3] William Clarke had developed from Scottish orthodoxy to Emersonian ideas: H. Burrows and J. A. Hobson, *William Clarke: a Collection of his Writings* (Swann Sonnen-schein, London, 1908), p. xxvii. Mrs Besant later became a Theosophist and Hubert Bland reverted to Roman Catholicism.

the other writings of the founder, and spent some Sunday mornings at the little conventicle in Lamb's Conduit Street, or attended on Sunday evenings the Newton Hall lectures of Frederic Harrison'.[1] The Fabian leaders rejected both Comte's political recommendations and his 'Religion of Humanity,'[2] but much of the influence of his empiricism and of his scientific outlook remained to reinforce similar influences deriving from the English philosophic tradition. In the circles in which the early Fabians moved, Positive Science, supported by Darwin, Huxley, and Spencer, was enthroned, and Metaphysics rather in disgrace. Thus we come across such statements as the following, in a review in *Fabian News* of a work in which an attempt to define 'justice' was made:

The author . . . sets himself to define justice as a prelude to forming a philosophy of Government. In our view he has undertaken a somewhat thankless task. We are content to leave that excellent word to the tender mercies of Parliamentary orators and newspaper leader-writers. It is a useful word, no doubt, in daily casual talk, but for serious thinking we prefer to leave it alone as an abstraction which belongs to what Comte would call the metaphysical stage of human evolution.[3]

Positivist intellectual influences fostered the Society's neutrality in metaphysical questions, though they were not its main cause. No attempt was made in any of the Fabian Tracts, nor in the writings of the principal Fabian spokesmen, to justify by formal theoretical argument on Positivist lines a renunciation of metaphysical views.[4] From time to time there have been denials directed both against the Marxists and the anti-Socialist Alliance, and prompted by the Fabian policy to 'make it easy for any . . . churchwarden to be a Socialist', that there is any necessary connection between Socialism and Materialism or Atheism. But always, the argument was simply that as a matter of practical experience the Fabian Society had churchgoers and theists within it, whilst

[1] Pease, *op. cit.* p. 18. For the influence of Comte on Olivier, Wallas and Webb see especially Margaret Olivier (ed.), *op. cit.* pp. 9, 62-3. And (for what it is worth) Shaw's tribute to Comtists in his article in *Forecasts of the Coming Century*, p. 153.

[2] Sidney Ball used the expression 'Religion of Humanity' at the end of Tract 72, but in a general not specifically Comtean sense, although the Tract reveals considerable Comtean influence.

[3] *Fabian News*, August 1900.

[4] The Fabians' refusal to attempt such a justification was no doubt politic, but it reduces their interest to a political philosopher. The fact that persons of such diverse philosophic views did co-operate on substantially the same political programme appears to raise an interesting inquiry. Is the connection between politics, and, at any rate, the 'higher' philosophical speculations so 'loose' that it would be possible to hold any metaphysical theory with any political theory? Is the connection between certain types of philosophical theory and certain types of politics a psychological (and historical) rather than a logical connection? What types of philosophical statement are they from which it is impossible to 'deduce' completely opposing political recommendations? In brief, what kind of philosophical and politico-philosophical opinions are incorrigibly political and what kind are indifferent? These questions, facing modern political philosophers, find no answer from the old Fabians. Graham Wallas in *Men and Ideas*, p. 106, recognizes the general problem.

some 'avowed atheists like Charles Bradlaugh or agnostics like Herbert Spencer' had led the attack upon Socialism.[1] It was easy for the Fabians to take up the attitude they did. They were not wholly in revolt against the Liberal-Radical doctrine in which they had been nurtured. Even Bernard Shaw's more flamboyant utterances have a way of exploding in a laugh and dissolving into very moderate proposals. As direct heirs of the Enlightenment in its English Utilitarian branch, the Fabians were fairly satisfied with their philosophical inheritance. They did not, as a group, need to invent a fundamentally new system, but were content to work within the framework of the old, for it opposed no insuperable barriers to their aims. Furthermore, the Fabians were not proposing to behave in a revolutionary or violent manner. They were constitutional, orderly and almost, if not wholly, respectable, and this sort of conduct does not seem to call (in a relatively peaceful age) for special justification. Marxism probably needs a philosophy in a way that Fabianism does not, because Marxists propose to do something that calls much more for justification. There appears to be a certain feeling of badness about revolution in general (certainly very few persons, if any, think revolution is good perpetually; at most some think it is good from time to time or in special circumstances) that seems to demand justification for it of a peculiar kind. While the Marxists need to appeal to moral courage reinforced by a philosophic 'world view', the Fabians could appeal simply to 'common sense' of a practical sort.

It is sometimes said that the Fabians themselves were Utilitarians.[2] This seems to be an overstatement. In the first place, it is in conflict with the Society's refusal to adopt a collective view, and it would certainly be possible to find some Fabians who were not Utilitarians. But even if it is meant to be a description only of the leading Fabians, it still seems doubtful of some of them, though true of others. Consider, for example, four Fabians whose views on this subject are easily discovered: Sidney and Beatrice Webb, D. G. Ritchie (who was writing his book *Natural Rights* at the time he was a member of the Society) and Bernard Shaw.

Certainly, Sidney Webb was a Utilitarian, not only in the general sense that he would have defined Rightness as conduciveness to the greatest common Good, but also, perhaps, in the sense that he was an Altruistic Hedonist Utilitarian, a Benthamite, defining Good again as 'the greatest happiness of the greatest number'. There are some passages in his writings which lend themselves to that interpretation. On the other hand, there are passages which would lead one to think that he was, like his wife, a Utilitarian in the first

[1] Appendix to Pease, *op. cit.* p. 279.
[2] G. D. H. Cole, *British Working Class Politics*, p. 122.

sense, but not in the second. In an illuminating reflection, Beatrice Webb observed:

... Bentham was certainly Sidney's intellectual god-father; and though I have never read a word of him, his teaching was transmitted through Herbert Spencer's very utilitarian system of ethics ... we agree that human action must be judged by its results in bringing about certain defined ends. There is no other sanction we care to accept but results, though we should be inclined to give, perhaps, a wider meaning to results. For instance, the formation of a noble character, the increase of intellectual faculty, stimulus to sense of beauty, sense of conduct, even sense of humour, are all ends that we should regard as 'sanctioning' action; quite apart from whether they produce happiness of one or all, or none. We altogether reject the 'happiness of the greatest number' as a definition of our own end, though other persons are perfectly at liberty to adopt it as theirs. I reject it, because I have no clear vision of what I mean by happiness, or what other people mean by it. If happiness means physical enjoyment, it is an end which does not commend itself to me—certainly not as the sole end. I prefer to define my end as the increase in the community of certain faculties and desires which I happen to like—love, truth, beauty, and humour. Again, I have a certain vision of the sort of human relationships that I like, and those I dislike. But we differ from the Benthamites in thinking that it is necessary that we should all agree as to ends, or that these can be determined by any science. We believe that ends, ideals, are all what may be called in a larger way 'questions of taste' and we like a society in which there is a considerable variety in these tastes.[1]

Beatrice Webb thus carried forward John Stuart Mill's modification of Utilitarianism. While Mill introduced the notion of 'quality' in types of 'happiness', Beatrice Webb dropped the generalized objective of 'happiness' altogether and promoted the 'qualities' to the status of ends. It would have been interesting to know how far Beatrice Webb would have accepted the conclusions of the modern school of Non-naturalistic Utilitarians, but she does not appear to have been acquainted with them. One could foresee difficulties arising out of the apparent incompleteness of her list of 'ends' and also out of the introduction of the notion of 'questions of taste', if these arguments were pressed, although the latter obviously arises out of a laudable desire to preserve individual freedom.

Professor David G. Ritchie in 1891 gave a paper to the Fabian Society on 'Natural Rights,'[2] one of the first sketches for his standard work on that subject. Ritchie in general accepted the Utilitarian criticism of Natural Rights doctrine, but he was not in agreement with the Benthamite position, even as reformulated by John Stuart Mill. Mill's objection—that it was better to be Socrates dissatisfied than a pig satisfied—to the simple Benthamite position seemed decisive to Ritchie. But he sought his solution not in Mill's way, nor in Beatrice Webb's way, but rather in an inclination towards German idealism. Good conduct consists in the development in oneself and others of universal reason, of which the particular self or ego is an imperfect realization.[3]

[1] B. Webb, *Our Partnership*, pp. 210-1.   [2] *Fabian News*, December 1891.
[3] D. G. Ritchie, *Natural Rights* (Swann Sonnenschein, London, 1895), pp. 94-8.

Bernard Shaw showed considerable unwillingness to allow himself to be classified as even a modified Utilitarian in the days before he developed his 'Life Force' philosophy. At the Fabian meeting where Professor Ritchie gave his lecture, Shaw attempted to defend Natural Rights against Ritchie's attack, and statements recur in Shaw's later writings in defence of the doctrine.[1] However, it appears that the 'Natural Rights' defended by Shaw were of a very general kind,[2] and they were defended more on the sophisticated ground that people believed in them, and acted and spoke as if they were possessed of Natural Rights, than that Natural Rights could be proved to exist in fact.[3] They fell into Shaw's category of 'necessary illusions'.[4] In addition, Shaw always opposed a hedonistic ethic, particularly an egotistic hedonist ethic. His aphorisms on this subject are numerous: 'Happiness and Beauty are by-products;' 'Folly is the direct pursuit of Happiness and Beauty.'[5] His discussion of the 'motives' of the Devil's Disciple in the Preface to *Three Plays for Puritans* allows no misunderstanding of his denial of hedonism. Of course, this alone would not necessarily exclude him from being a Utilitarian of Beatrice Webb's variety. But when Shaw had finally worked out his 'Life Force' theory, the question became still more complicated. It is true that Beatrice Webb, whose Diaries show that she was facing the same problems as Shaw, had also come to a mystic belief in 'a Power working for good in the Universe', but she appears to have been content for it to remain remote and undefined. Shaw, on the other hand, was more explicit about the 'Life Force' and made some attempt to work out its relation with his ethical system. Something has already been said of this. Shaw appears to have thought there was a 'higher' and a 'lower' morality, each with a certain validity. The lower morality consists of conventional rules for social and individual conduct, which may very well be justified on some Utilitarian grounds, even such grounds as the greatest convenience of the greatest number. The higher morality springs from the 'Natural Right' of that small minority of men and women ('Supermen'), who have momentarily apprehended the purposes of the Life Force, to break through or ignore the rules of conventional morality. This proceeding is often a cause of inconvenience or unhappiness in society, though really for its good in the end; there is sometimes difficulty in distinguishing Supermen-Saints from criminals, who also break the social rules; consequently, society often treats its Saints cruelly, and Shaw, as his play *St Joan* reveals, was not unsympathetic with the men who have to guard the 'lower' morality. Was Shaw a Utilitarian, then? Up to a point he was; but a mighty unusual one.

---

[1] *Forecasts of the Coming Century*, p. 151; see also Preface to *Three Plays for Puritans*, Epilogue to *Man and Superman*, and Preface to *John Bull's Other Island*.

[2] They needed to be, because Shaw was also opposed to 'absolute morals'. See e.g. 'Death of an Old Revolutionary Hero' in the *Clarion*, 24 March 1905.

[3] *Forecasts of the Coming Century*, loc. cit.

[4] *Ibid.*   [5] Both are from the Epilogue to *Man and Superman*.

Yet another leading Fabian should be considered: Sydney Olivier, who contributed the essay on 'The Moral Basis of Socialism' to *Fabian Essays*, the first of the only three articles of a philosophical nature ever published by the Society. 'The Moral Basis of Socialism' cannot be said to be one of the more successful Fabian works. It is written in a smoothly voluble style, and contains some shrewd and useful observations, but the argument is somewhat confused. Olivier began by insisting that his subject was the moral basis of Socialism, not the Socialist view of the basis of morals. He announced his intention of avoiding meta-ethics[1] altogether, and claimed to resort only to the 'unpretentious methods of empiricism and positive ethical science', renouncing 'the right to appeal to that theologic habit of mind common to Socialists with other pious persons'. He recognized the difficulty of arguing on this basis against those persons who for religious or metaphysical reasons contend that poverty is inevitable or good.[2] But he considered that 'all schools of ethical thought' were coming to approve Socialism, with its objectives of doing away with poverty and ensuring the worker an 'adequate return' for his labour.

Now, it would seem at this point that Olivier should (by the use of the methods of 'empiricism and positive ethical science') have established his claim that 'all schools of ethical thought' were coming to approve Socialism, and shown what ethical reasons they gave for their approval. But he did not do this. He was not content simply with the 'phenomena of current opinion on morality'; he considered that 'we must follow the explanations of ethical speculations into the causes and history of the development of these opinions. By examining the genesis of convictions that this or that kind of action is good or bad, moral or immoral' (he went on) 'we shall be helped to form a judgment as to which appears likely to persist and be strengthened, and which to be modified, weakened, or forgotten. If the claim of Socialism rests on judgments of the latter class, we may know that it is moribund bantling; if they preponderate amongst the obstacles to its credit, we may prophesy encouragingly of it; if it is supported by those judgments whose persistence seems essential to the survival of the individual and society, we may be assured of its realization in the future'.

This is the prelude to a sociological account, not only of the evolution of morals, but also (despite his original intention not to discuss their basis) of their origin. Morality is said to spring from social relations: in the first place, it is those rules which 'tend to preserve the existence of society and the cohesion and convenience of its members', and moral progress is said to consist in two developments: socially, in the extension of a 'common morality' to

[1] Olivier did not of course use the modern term 'meta-ethics', but it is useful in bringing out the sense of his argument.
[2] So Socialists need *some* philosophy? Except where people using such arguments can be ignored as cranks?

ever-widening groups, 'from the family to the horde, from the tribe to the nation, finally to the world', and in the breaking down of barriers—of class, race, etc.—to the recognition that moral rules apply to all alike without distinction; individually, by the extension of 'sympathy' to greater numbers of one's fellow men, and by progress through the restraints of law and convention to the position where one 'perceives it is reasonable to act morally'.

Moral progress is linked with social progress, and at each new stage of social development there are groups and classes of persons whose interests are bound up with the institutions of the old order. The institution of private property in the means of production was once useful and received the sanctions of moral convention, religion, and law; but now it has become 'destructive of the conditions in which alone the common morality . . . is possible'. The essay concludes with an account of the ways in which present-day capitalism favours an injurious 'class morality' against the 'common morality' necessary to the well-being of society; but with the increase of co-operative production, the 'moral ideas appropriate to Socialism' are developing.

Olivier's essay shows the influence of a number of schools of ethical thought. It is indeed the eclecticism of Olivier's thought that is most striking. Positivism, Benthamism, Evolutionism, Kantianism—all contribute something to his argument, but he does not really synthesise them to produce a new ethical theory. And although his sketch of the 'genesis' and 'development' of morals has some interest, it is doubtful if any part of it but the last few pages, where details are given of the actual evils caused by capitalism, would have had much value in convincing an opponent.

Is he a Utilitarian? When he defines morality as rules which tend to preserve society and the cohesion and convenience of its members, he is not only a Utilitarian, but an extremely rigid one. It is almost reminiscent of Godwin's definition in *Political Justice* of morality as a 'system of public advantage'. But it is noteworthy that Olivier was not content simply with this definition, and endeavoured to bring in a personal element with his notion of the extension of 'sympathy'.[1] He is another Fabian who cannot be classified *simply* as a Benthamite, though he certainly has not broken away from the Utilitarian tradition.

It seems fair to conclude that there was a notable variety of ethical opinion to be found amongst the members of the Fabian Society, even if we consider only this small selection of people, who have not been specially chosen to illustrate differences in views. The Fabians here reflected the predominant movement of ideas of their times; they cannot be said to have made any original or important contribution.[2] The attention of the most prominent

[1] He was actually following J. S. Mill in this.
[2] With the possible exception of Shaw, providing one is not thinking of the contribution in an academic or formal sense.

English writers on ethics from the 'seventies to the 'nineties[1] was occupied with attempts to reconcile aspects of the English Utilitarian tradition with ideas deriving from the theory of biological evolution, or alternatively, with attempts to criticize this whole naturalistic and hedonistic position with arguments inspired by Hegelian idealism. The Fabians were drawn only into the fringes of the controversy, but their writing and thinking were coloured by it. The tendency to break away from the Utilitarian school, or at least to modify its basic teachings, was characteristic of the age, and the Fabians were content to follow the lead of other thinkers. This may be observed not only in Olivier's heroic but unsuccessful attempt to unite the jarring elements in *Fabian Essays*, but also in the only other Tract of the period which dealt specifically with ethical questions. Sidney Ball's *The Moral Aspects of Socialism*[2] was mainly concerned to refute the objections that Socialism was 'incompatible with social selection' and that Socialism 'substituted machinery for character'; but it incidentally reflected the main currents of contemporary ethical speculation.

The Fabian Society did not publish another Tract of a primarily philosophical nature until 1917—twenty-one years after the publication of *The Moral Aspects of Socialism*. This pamphlet by A. Clutton Brock, entitled *The Philosophy of Socialism*,[3] may be taken as confirmation that the Fabian Society was not commited to any one school of ethical or philosophical opinion, and as further evidence that it was inclined to follow the philosophical fashions. The Tract advanced the standard of Deontism, Absolute Moral Values, and Religion against Utilitarianism, Relativism and Agnosticism, at a time when these latter opinions were suspected by some people of having had something to do with the misfortunes that had befallen Europe. It was plainly intended to counterbalance the philosophic views which had found expression in earlier Fabian publications, and it is that fact, rather than the originality of the views or the quality of the argument, which gives it its interest.

In conclusion, it is worth observing that the Fabian Society which repudiated any collective views on religious matters even more explicitly and emphatically,[4] nevertheless published six Tracts on Christian Socialism in the period up to the First World War, compared with its two Tracts and one Essay of a philosophical nature. What is more, these Tracts on Christian Socialism proved to be amongst the Tracts with the best and steadiest sale over a long period.[5] All of them were signed by their authors, and with the exception of one, which was an historical study of Charles Kingsley and the Christian

---

[1] I have in mind particularly Herbert Spencer, Leslie Stephen, S. Alexander, T. H. Huxley, A. Sutherland, T. H. Green, and F. H. Bradley.
[2] Tract 72. The article appeared first in the *International Journal of Ethics* for April 1896 and was reprinted as a Fabian Tract (with some changes) in November of the same year.
[3] Tract 180.
[4] e.g. Tracts 70 and 132.
[5] See ch. VII of this work on Fabian propaganda, p. 173, footnote 2.

Socialist Movement,[1] they were all intended to prove to Christians that Christianity and Socialism or Collectivism were compatible. Two of them were reprints of addresses given by the Rev. Dr John Clifford,[2] one a lecture by the Rev. Stewart Headlam,[3] one by the Rev. Percy Dearmer,[4] and one a reprint of extracts from the pamphlet of John Woolman, the eighteenth century New Jersey Quaker, *A Word of Remembrance and Caution to the Rich*.[5] Thus the Fabian Society collectively avoided the responsibility but, nevertheless, reaped the advantages of issuing Tracts on religion. It did not (like the S.D.F.) take upon itself the functions of a Secularist Society, and attempt to persuade religious people to renounce their faith: it contented itself with persuading them to become Socialists, through the words of their co-religionists.

MORAL ASPECTS OF FABIAN SOCIALISM

'Mere nationalization, or mere municipalization, of any industry is not Socialism or Collectivism,' wrote Sidney Ball; 'it may be only the substitution of corporate for private administration; the social idea and purpose with which Collectivism is concerned may be completely absent'.[6] What then were the social ideas that were to inspire the changes in 'machinery' which the Fabians proposed? At the most general level the dispute between Liberals and Socialists is really a dispute about means rather than ends; the Socialist is as likely as the Liberal to state his ends to be Liberty, Equality, and Fraternity—'the freest and fullest development of human quality and power'[7] that is possible in a community. The Socialist merely claims that the means proposed by *laissez faire* Liberalism are unlikely to achieve these ends, and puts forward alternative means to them. However, it is not only the history of religion which shows that there may be importantly different emphases on the three elements of a trinity. Critics have frequently argued that Socialists in general have emphasized Equality and Fraternity at the expense of Liberty.

It may at least be allowed that equality (at any rate, equality in a special sense) is of the very essence of Socialism. Equality of service, or rather, an equal obligation of all able-bodied members to serve the community by 'labour of hand and brain' is a moral duty implicit in Socialists' denunciations of those who 'live by owning'. This moral claim has lent a powerful driving force to Socialist propaganda: it can be illustrated by almost any of the theoretical Tracts of the Fabian Society, from its very first Tract, which asked indignantly, 'What can be said in favour of a system which breeds and tolerates the leisured "masher", who lives without a stroke of useful work ... ?' to the much later one, which in a lighter, but no less deadly vein defined an

---

[1] Tract 174.
[2] Tracts 78 and 139.
[3] Tract 42.
[4] Tract 133.
[5] Tract 79.
[6] Tract 72.
[7] *Ibid.*

'independent income' as 'an abject and total dependence on the labour of others'.[1] Equality of service, in this sense, does not imply that Socialists, Fabian or other, considered that the services contributed to society by individuals would be equal in value, nor that they agreed that individuals should be rewarded equally.[2] Furthermore, the 'ideal principle' of Socialism—the rejection of the right to individual proprietorship of the means of production and of the right to receive rent and interest as a consequence of such proprietorship[3]—is, as we have seen earlier, modified quite seriously when it comes to practical application.[4] But, despite these qualifications, Socialism remains basically a claim for the removal of inequalities caused by private ownership of the means of production.

Behind this narrower ideal of equality looms the vaguer and larger vision of the classless society. Some Fabians questioned the possibility of attaining it, and were content to envisage a Socialist society as one in which classes would be based on status or function and not ownership of land or capital.[5] But however cynical Bernard Shaw and other leading Fabians were prepared to be about the 'inessentials' of Socialism, this piece of disillusionment did not appeal to them. The disenchanting prospect of a class-divided Socialist society drove Shaw to advocate incomes that were absolutely equal, and to propose the 'intermarriageability' test as the criterion for deciding whether a satisfactory degree of equality had been attained.[6] The Webbs' writings, and particularly the denunciations of snobbery and class distinction in Beatrice Webb's Diaries, also leave no doubt that their ideal was some form of classless society, although they shrank from Shaw's extreme proposals. As a body, the Fabian Society did not come to the point of making a choice between the alternative ideals of a Socialist society, one of which, so to speak, institutionalized the *carrière ouverte aux talents*, while the other sought the eventual abolition of all classes; but the leading Fabian spokesmen seem to have preferred the latter.

Equality was probably more important in the hierarchy of Fabian ideals than Fraternity, insofar as Fraternity may be distinguished from Equality. Fraternity, or the spirit of comradeship and general participation, was an ideal rather too romantic and, in its late nineteenth and early twentieth century

---

[1] Tract 107.

[2] See Tract 70.

[3] In disproving these claims of right, Socialists, including the Fabians, have not been content to rely only on the Utilitarian expedient of denying such claims of right in general and discussing the social consequences of individual or collective ownership; they have also tried to establish, by their theories of surplus value or of rent, that the particular claims of right are unjustified.

[4] Compensation; allowing some private enterprise; allowing interest on savings out of earned incomes, etc.

[5] Lecture by Halliday Sparling, *Fabian News*, March 1894.

[6] *Intelligent Woman's Guide* (Pelican), vol. I pp. 68-9; vol. II p. 442.

manifestations, too working-class to dominate Fabian thinking. This is not to say that they lacked it: 'Collectivist' qualities were displayed both in their ameliorative measures to assist the weak and under-privileged in present society, and also in their vision of the future Socialist society; and the members of their own group also shared a sense of common mission with the Labour movement. But Fraternity was an ideal much more emphasized by the Independent Labour Party and the Clarion Clubs, and those Fabians who wished to share fully in the comradely spirit became members of these organizations as well. The Fabian Society for its own part remained resolutely middle class and rationalistic.

What, then, of Liberty? Did the Fabians, in their emphasis on Equality, slip unconsciously towards authoritarianism in their ultimate ideals, and fail to keep the delicate balance between Equality and Liberty? Prominent writers have hinted that they did. Halévy suggested they were influenced by the 'Prussian model' of social organization and social philosophy.[1] 'Well-oiled samurai,' remarked O. D. Skelton.[2] 'Is this . . . the deceitful harmony of Fascism? The law of the beehive?' asked Sir Alexander Gray of a passage in Sidney Webb's Fabian Essay.[3] Something has already been said of the political aspects of these charges, and it remains here to discover the extent to which they were inspired by ideals or ways of thinking which had totalitarian tendencies.

At the outset, it seems necessary to say that there is no difficulty in discovering passages in Fabian literature which show the influence of Hegelian and Platonic philosophy; which imply the acceptance of an 'organic' conception of society and fall without doubt into the category of theories which Dr Popper in his works[4] has labelled 'historicism'. Again, it is easy to choose from Fabian writing passages which show an almost Comtean emphasis on planning, neatness, efficiency, economy, and hygiene. But how strong must these tendencies be for a school of thought to be labelled totalitarian? And are such ideas always totalitarian or is their historical association with it largely fortuitous?

(1) The 'organic' theory of society

The metaphors of 'organism' were employed in several of the Fabian Society's theoretical Tracts;[5] but they were used less lavishly by the Fabians than by other left-wing writers of that period: J. Ramsay MacDonald's works are full

[1] Imperialism and the Rise of Labour (Benn, London, 1951), p. 230.
[2] O. D. Skelton, Socialism: A Critical Analysis (Constable, 1911), p. 289.
[3] Sir Alexander Gray, The Socialist Tradition: Moses to Lenin, p. 397.
[4] The Open Society and its Enemies, and articles in Economica, May and August 1944 and May 1945.
[5] See Tracts 69 and 72 as examples; also Webb's contribution to Fabian Essays. But in the Tracts the biological analogy is in no way essential to the argument: all that was said could have been said without it.

of them. That they were less a feature of the writings of the Webbs and the Fabians was due partly, perhaps, to their early anti-metaphysical bias, and partly to the fact that Sidney Webb's natural tendency in metaphor seems to have been towards the clanking mechanical—'machines', 'ladders', and 'conduit-pipes'. The biologic analogy was, moreover, not confined to theorists of the Left at the end of the nineteenth century. It had come into general fashion in political philosophy at that time and was being put to use equally by those who wished to draw from it radical and conservative conclusions.

Nowadays, after a form of the 'organic' conception of society has been associated with Fascism, the idea is very much out of favour, but it is fairly easy to see what attracted the Fabians to it in the 'eighties and 'nineties. It stressed the claims of society against the untrammelled individualism of *laissez faire* which had obvious analogies, and consequently some theoretic connections, with 'atomism'. Thus Webb wrote:

... the trouble with Gladstonian Liberalism is that, by instinct, by tradition, and by the positive precepts of its past exponents, it 'thinks in individuals'. It visualizes the world as a world of independent Roundheads ... [The Gladstonian Liberals'] conception of freedom means only breaking somebody's bonds asunder. When the 'higher freedom' of corporate life is in question, they become angrily reactionary and denounce and obstruct every new development of common action. If we seek for the greatest enemy of municipal enterprise, we find him in Sir Henry Fowler. If we ask who is the most successful opponent of any extension of the common rule of factory legislation to wider fields of usefulness the answer is Mr John Morley. . . .

A similar purpose was served by a Platonizing tendency, which the Fabians had derived from the English followers of the German philosophers. In what is probably his most extreme utterance of this nature, Sidney Webb speaks of the part played by efficiency in the national struggle for the survival of the fittest, and (in a passage of revealing mixed metaphor) says:

If we desire to hand on to the afterworld our direct influence, and not merely the memory of our excellence, we must take even more care to improve the social organism of which we form part than to perfect our own individual developments. Or rather, the perfect and fitting development of each individual is not necessarily the utmost and highest cultivation of his own personality, but the filling, in the best possible way, of his humble function in the great social machine.[1]

Such a passage would today sound surprising in a left-wing writer—with its heavy overtones of conservatism. Yet at the time it was written, it was being used as a justification for an extreme radical position. The chief recommendation which Webb intended should be derived from it was that people should not assume that social good automatically followed their striving after their

[1] *Fabian Essays*, (1889 ed.) p. 58. It must be emphasized that this is the most extreme statement of its kind in the Webbs' writings, and an early one at that. It could be a paraphrase of a passage in F. H. Bradley's 'My Station and its Duties' in his *Ethical Studies*. London, 2nd ed. 1927, pp. 173-4 (first published in 1876).

own welfare, but should pay great attention to the social good. He was far from any intention to justify the existing state of affairs. 'Organism,' under Darwinian and Lamarckian influence, was thought of as an evolving thing. In the phrase 'filling, in the best possible way, his humble function in the great social machine' great emphasis was given to the words 'the best possible way', and Webb and the Fabians contended, first, that this was not being achieved at the present and, secondly, that it would not be achieved until everyone was 'placed' according to his ability (and not according to birth or wealth), which in turn involved much social reorganization and, in particular, greatly improved educational opportunities.

This example brings out the danger of attempting a political classification of people merely upon the basis of their metaphysical or semi-metaphysical views about society. It seems unfair to hint that Fabians should be classed with Fascists merely because both have held to an 'organic' conception of society. With such general concepts, so much depends upon those intermediate steps which bring them into contact with positive recommendations about contemporary politics, that, by varying these intermediate steps, it is possible to combine the same general concept with quite dissimilar political views. The 'organic' analogy, by itself, seems to be too vague to do much more than to create a feeling of 'togetherness', and the importance of 'the whole'. It would, of course, be possible, with a slight emphasis, to use the conception to suggest the individual was *unimportant* in comparison with the community. But the Fabians would certainly have denied that they had any intention of making such an addition.[1] The historical situation must be taken into account; the Fabians were making use of the organic concept and were stressing the importance of the community because the Benthamites had stressed the importance of the individual at the expense of the community. The organic concept provided a counter to the philosophies of *laissez faire* individualism and of Marxism; against both, it emphasized social unity. That is why the Fabians in their early days espoused it so warmly, without, so far as can be seen, inquiring whether it, too, might be dispensable on the ground that it belonged 'to what Comte would call the metaphysical stage of human evolution'.[2]

(2) *Emphasis on planning, neatness, efficiency, economy, and hygiene*
Much the same can be said of this aspect of Fabian writing. Few today would deny that some planning and a great deal of neatness, efficiency, economy, and hygiene are necessary to civilized life, and still fewer that late nineteenth-century England was greatly improved by their increase. It is once again a

[1] This applies to the quote above from Webb's contribution to *Fabian Essays*. It does not seem nearly so bad in its context. The use of the concept 'social health' in the essay suggests that Webb was also borrowing some of the terminology of Sir Leslie Stephen's *Science of Ethics*.
[2] See footnote 3, p. 148. 'Organism' would seem a more suitable target for the Fabian reviewer's criticism than 'justice'.

question of how much. We may find the dreadful limits on one side described in the blue books on the state of the early factory towns and on the other in Aldous Huxley's *Brave New World*. But the conflict between the 'planners' and the 'anti-planners' in England has usually taken place well within the bounds of these extremes.

Certainly, the Fabians seem well within these bounds, though once again their chief enemy was the *laissez faire* ideal of their Liberal predecessors, so their tendency was rather to emphasize its opposite. One could be reluctant to go as far as the Fabians in state regulation; one could even find isolated passages in their works where a rather naive approval seems to be given to regulation in general;[1] but in looking over their work as a whole it would be unjust to accuse them of being unaware that the problem of liberty was involved. Not only was the Fabian Society as a whole, for the greater part of its existence, engaged in urging hardly more than the 'national minimum' of planning, much of which nowadays finds approval far outside the ranks of Socialists, but the more subtle theoretical aspects of the 'paradox of freedom' were recognized by individual Fabians. 'I entirely agree with the old position that a law is an evil which should be avoided where it can be avoided without greater evil,' said Webb, in answer to a question before the Royal Commission on Labour, 'but of course the case of those who ask for a legal shortening of the hours of labour is that the evil which will result without the law is greater than the evil which the law would cause'.[2]

Nor can the Fabians be accused of taking a naive view of Socialism as the 'New Jerusalem' where the problem of liberty and all the other problems are automatically solved. 'The Fabian Society puts forward Socialism not as a solution of all evils but only of those arising out of the unequal distribution of wealth,'declared Tract 70.' Let it be at once admitted,' wrote William Clarke, 'that if Collectivism makes every human being a mere function of the whole, a mere pin in the wheel, a mere end to others' purposes, then it is impossible, for every strenuous mind will rise in revolt against it. A mechanical uniform civilization, with complete centralization and tremendous intensity of working power, with the general conditions of life very much as they are now, with the exception that no one could starve, would be a very close approximation to hell, whether closer or not than the present system of society I am not prepared to say.'[3] Webb had the same problem in mind when he insisted on the importance of a careful balance of autonomy and centralization in local government. He hoped to avoid over-centralization by an expansion of local government powers through 'Municipal Socialism,' and he hoped to preserve variety of structure in organization within the Socialist State.

[1] E.g. in Webb's Fabian Essay.
[2] Royal Commission on Labour, Minutes of Evidence. Fourth Report, 18 November 1892, p. 283. Cf. Shaw, *Intelligent Woman's Guide* (Pelican), vol. II, p. 314.
[3] In 'Limits of Collectivism,' *Contemporary Review*, February 1893, pp. 263-78.

LIBERTY IS LEISURE

There remains yet another way in which the Fabians sought to increase liberty and which is, indeed, central to their whole Socialist position. Their belief can best be approached from the concept of 'Nature the taskmaster.' 'Once for all', wrote Shaw, 'we are not born free; and we never can be free.[1] When all human tyrants are slain or deposed there will still be the supreme tyrant that can never be slain or deposed, and that tyrant is Nature'.[2] The conflict of Man with Nature is used as an explanation of the origin of society (since co-operative effort is a way of doing Nature's tasks with less labour) and of the fact that complete 'freedom of restraint' could involve a natural (i.e. economic) oppression more intolerable than a social tyranny. The next part of the argument is summed up in Shaw's short and startling question and answer: 'What is liberty? Leisure.' It runs as follows: Nature is a taskmaster that requires certain work to be done, and a certain daily routine to be carried out; work, sleep, feeding, resting, etc. are compulsory; when these daily tasks are done, one has *leisure*—a time in which one may do as one pleases (i.e. be at liberty); the function of society and the purpose of new inventions ought to be to increase leisure and enable it to be equitably distributed.[3]

The objection could of course be raised that this does not exhaust the problem of liberty, in either a political or industrial sense, as Shaw's aphorism, and some of the argumentation with which he has supported it,[4] might suggest. Certainly the Guild Socialists did not think so, when they advocated democracy in industry. Nor need one suppose the Fabians, even Shaw himself, really imagined it did. The idea, however, is important in Fabianism, particularly in connection with the Guild Socialist controversy, because it shows that the Fabians thought mainly of increasing liberty *outside* work by shortening working hours. It shows also that they believed that the State should not regulate its citizens' leisure outside their working hours. And, finally, it is important in Shaw's idea of the place of the artist in the Socialist State: he insists that the State can do no good by regulating or pampering its artists, and the only solution is to give them some employment that will leave them plenty of leisure (which will bring them into contact with community life, and yet leave them free to pursue their art).

The importance of this idea in Fabian thought is so great that it is worth quoting the Webbs' characteristic version of it. At the end of a chapter in which they criticized Guild Socialism, the Webbs concluded:

Equity demands that every healthy adult without exception should put into the common stock of commodities and services at least the equivalent of what he consumes, in order that the world may not be the poorer for his presence. In any

[1] ? 'absolutely free'.   [2] *Intelligent Woman's Guide* (Pelican), vol. ii, p. 304.
[3] *Ibid.*   [4] *Ibid.* p. 305.

rationally organized community, this price should progressively diminish. With every increase in our knowledge, and therefore of our command over natural forces, the amount of time and effort that needs to be spent in the production of the commodities and services by which the community lives must become steadily less. . . . The time and energy thus set free, in every member of the community, for the life and affections of the family, for social intercourse, for the arts and the sciences, and generally for the spiritual development of the individual must necessarily be left at his own disposal. Here we find the sphere for individual decision; for although the beneficial outcome of this development of individual personality is very far from being of value only to the person concerned—is, indeed, ultimately of enormous value to the community as a whole—yet it is, by its very nature, not a service the community can command or enforce; and for the most part, one which it cannot pay for in cash or commodities. . . . Personal beauty and personal charm; the joy of intellectual comradeship; the consolation of self-sacrificing friendship; the play of wit and humour; the highest realms of art, science, and religion cannot be organized, controlled, or produced, either by democracies of producers or democracies of consumers. They are the priceless gifts of individual genius, above and beyond any social organization. . . . Thus, in our view, in the Co-operative Commonwealth of the future, the production of all the needful commodities and services, far from affording the fundamental basis of social organization, will assume a continuously decreasing importance in social life.[1]

Modern automation fits in well with the Webbs' basic conception of social progress; indeed, it would absolve them from the remaining doubts that their socialist state, with its rejection of workers' control in industry, might not allow any more freedom during working hours than the capitalist system. Automation was perhaps most clearly foreshadowed in the scientific utopias of H. G. Wells; but it is only fair to observe that the Webbs and Shaw and other leading Fabians did not subscribe to the more utopian features of Wells' utopias; above all, they did not place any faith in the technocrat ruler. Shaw satirized that Wellsian technocrat superman in his character 'Enry Straker, and he certainly cannot be accused of any naive belief in social salvation through the leadership of engineers or scientists in politics.

The Fabians' idea of 'freedom outside work' shows at all events that they were not 'totalitarian' in the sense of believing that the individual could realize his 'true self' only in communal activity. It shows indeed that Liberty as well as Equality was a principal aim of the Fabians, and that they foresaw and courageously tried to deal with a major problem of the future, even if their faith that people would use their leisure for self-improvement is somewhat redolent of an age before the rise of mass amusements.[2]

[1] S. and B. Webb, *The Consumers' Co-operative Movement*, p. 481.
[2] I have not dealt with the question of the approval expressed by a few (but by very few) Fabians of totalitarian regimes abroad after the war. There are several reasons: first, because the problem arises in the period beyond that covered by this work; second, because the special circumstances of that period have to be considered; third, because theirs was a small minority, not a general Fabian, view; fourth, because even in their cases, it seldom followed that approval of totalitarian regimes in foreign countries meant that such methods were approved for Britain.

CHAPTER VII

FABIAN MEMBERSHIP, TRACT
DISTRIBUTION AND LECTURING

'How far the acquiescence of the public in the enormous extension of State activity and control has been facilitated by the insidious preaching and permeation of the Fabians,' wrote Sir Alexander Gray, 'is a question which it is easy to ask, but which no wise man will venture to answer'.[1] Our reputation for wisdom may be preserved by not putting the question in that way. In the four subsequent chapters an attempt will be made to assess the influence of the Fabians, not upon the public, but upon some public organizations—the London County Council and the political parties—through which the extensions of State activity and control have come. It seems convenient and useful to preface these chapters with one discussing the Society's general propaganda, but, with Sir Alexander Gray's warning in mind, the limits, not to say the limitations, of the inquiry must be made clear.

No measurement of the effects of Fabian propaganda on public opinion is possible by ordinary historical methods. Perhaps in the future records of Public Opinion Surveys may add to the material at the historian's disposal; at present, any estimate he makes must be largely guesswork. Some guesses may be good ones: thus, Max Beer was probably quite correct when he declared of (Sir) Leo Chiozza Money's *Riches and Poverty* (which was not a volume issued by the Fabian Society, although its author was, at the time, a member of the Society), 'of the many books published on the eve of the Labour unrest, none had so notable an effect'.[2] Such guesswork, however, is best left to contemporaries. Its abandonment does not deprive the historian of all resource; he can make some headway by approaching the problem from the angle of the producer rather than the consumer. Works like D. Mornet's *Les origines intellectuelles de la Révolution française* have shown what diligent research can do in tracing the distribution of literature. Given equal industry, and as many years as Mornet's research took, it would be possible to discover at least the quantity of Fabian books, including those of individual Fabians, distributed to the public.[3]

No investigation so full can be attempted here. Still less is it intended to trace the journalistic activities of members of the Society. It is doubtful whether the most painstaking research could track down all these. The articles written by the leading Fabians could, no doubt, be discovered without over-

---

[1] Sir Alexander Gray, *op. cit.* p. 401.
[2] Beer, *op. cit.* p. 353.
[3] A list of the principal writings of Fabian members is given in the bibliography.

much difficulty. We know that Bernard Shaw wrote the music criticisms in the *World* and the *Star*, contributed notes and controversial articles both under his own name and under the pen-name of 'Fabius' to the *Workman's Times* and the *Clarion*, wrote articles for such journals as *Today*, *Our Corner*, the *New Review*, the *Saturday Review* and many others; one day, perhaps, someone may produce a complete bibliography of them.[1] Sidney Webb's weightier writings found their place mostly in the less decidedly left-wing newspapers and journals: the *Star*, the *Speaker*, the *Contemporary Review*, the *Pall Mall Gazette*, and others. Hubert Bland wrote regularly for the *Sunday Chronicle*, and William Clarke was, under Massingham, leader writer of the *Daily Chronicle*, and later an editor of the *Progressive Review*, and he also wrote occasionally for the *Contemporary Review* and the *Spectator*, as well as for American journals. But who will ever trace the writings of all those Fabians unknown to fame who put forward the Fabian case in, or even entirely 'captured', obscure journals and local newspapers such as (to take a couple of instances from the early 'nineties) the *Ratepayer's Chronicle*, or the *Croydon Times?*

The aim of this chapter will be the very modest one of giving, from the Fabian Society's own records, some particulars of the number of its members, and some information concerning the type of propaganda. This may help to give an impression of the importance of the most general side of the Society's activities, before we try to estimate the success of their 'permeation' of particular organizations.

TYPE OF FABIAN PROPAGANDA

The Society's general propaganda, addressed to the public at large, took the form of publishing Tracts, and of organizing lectures, debates, and discussions. The Society was not torn, as the S.D.F. was, between the desire to make itself a mass organization and the opposing desire to become a small body of highly-trained specialists and organizers. The Fabians, making a virtue of necessity, did not attempt to advance their cause by drawing large numbers of people into their organization. The Fabian Society set out to be primarily a body for the study of socialist problems and the publication of the results of the study. This meant a limited membership, and the Fabians were content if they recruited a number of working-class leaders into their ranks to join in these studies and discussions. If there was a dilemma at all for the Society it was whether to make its principal concern the scientific investigation of social and socialist problems at the higher level, or to devote itself mainly to 'educating the masses'. The Society's acceptance of the former role was once again

[1] A bibliography exists in Geoffrey H. Wells' article 'A bibliography of the books and pamphlets of George Bernard Shaw,' *Bookman's Journal*, Supplement, 1925. See also the footnotes to Archibald Henderson's *Bernard Shaw, Playboy and Prophet*, and the fine catalogue of the exhibition to celebrate his ninetieth birthday (National Book League, C.U.P. 1946). There is also a bibliography in German by X. Heydet.

determined more by its composition and character, perhaps, than by careful thought over it. Once only was the problem raised in an acute and explicit manner—by H. G. Wells, in 1906-7, at the time he produced his *This Misery of Boots* pamphlet[1]—but the Society soon forgot it, and continued with the kind of work that Webb had launched it upon in the late 'eighties.

In addition to pamphleteering and providing lecturers, the Society also maintained a library and circulated book-boxes to other organizations; it ran correspondence classes in economics and history, and an information bureau, especially for local government affairs; and it occasionally assisted Parliamentary candidates with finance and canvassing.

MEMBERSHIP OF THE FABIAN SOCIETY

The accompanying chart of the fluctuation of the number of members of the Society from 1890 to 1918 is not satisfactory, as it represents only the membership of the London Society; members of provincial Fabian Societies are not included in the figures unless they happened also to be members of the parent Society. Unfortunately it is not possible to obtain from the Society's records any satisfactory figures over a continuous period of the total membership of provincial Societies. The chart of the figures for the London Society shows a steady increase until 1899; a slight fall until 1904, small increases from then until the beginning of 1906; then a sudden great bound upwards, steadying in 1910, but not reaching its peak until 1913; a considerable fall during the war years reaching its lowest point in 1919, by which time more than half the gain in membership since the beginning of 1906 had been lost; and at that point the numbers steadied again in the immediate post-war years.

We must now take considerably more space to set out the evidence concerning the fluctuations in the membership of provincial Fabian Societies; some information can be gained, unsatisfactory as the available records are and, as we shall see, a noticeable difference would be made to the picture of total numbers if the provincial membership were included.

The growth of provincial Societies in the early 'nineties was rapid—from a dozen in 1890 to forty-two by May 1892. At that time their total membership was estimated at about 1500.[2] The number of provincial Societies reached its highest for the whole period of the Society's history with which we are dealing about the time of the founding of the I.L.P. At the beginning of 1893, there were seventy-two Fabian Societies in the United Kingdom, apart from the London Society. From that high point they declined rapidly.[3] The central

---

[1] See Pease, *op. cit.* ch. IX. Part of Wells' attack on the 'Old Gang' was concerned with the nature of Fabian propaganda, which he claimed was not designed to make converts. Wells wrote *This Misery of Boots* as a sample of the type of propaganda he thought would be more effective.

[2] Annual Report of the F.S. for the year ended March 1893.

[3] The total membership at this time is not recorded (? about 2500).

office did not record what happened to them all. But of fifteen local Societies which disappeared in 1893-4 whose fate has been recorded, eleven joined the I.L.P., two transferred to the S.D.F., and two simply dissolved. There consequently seems no reason for doubting Pease's generalization that the majority of the provincial Fabian Societies merged into the I.L.P.[1]

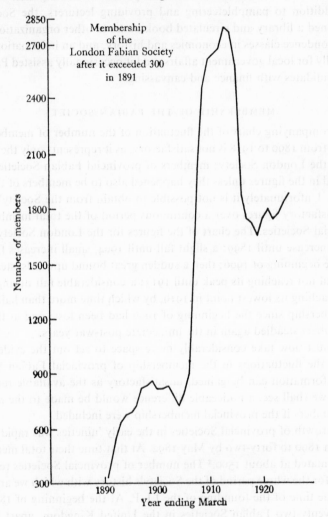

Membership of the London Fabian Society after it exceeded 300 in 1891

At the beginning of 1896, an inquiry by the London Secretary revealed that only eighteen provincial Societies remained, with a total membership of about 540.[2] The decline continued to the end of the century. At the International Socialist Congress of 1896, thirteen local Fabian Societies were represented

[1] Pease, *op. cit.* pp. 102–3.
[2] Annual Report F.S. March 1896.

besides four University Societies.[1] Two years later the number was nine, and four University Societies,[2] and by March 1900, only four provincial Societies, with a total membership of 153, still remained, together with the four University Societies, which had between them sixty-one members and twenty-six 'associates'.[3] There was a small recovery during the year 1900, when the loss of two local groups at Ramsbottom and Waterhouses was offset by the foundation of four other provincial Societies and one more University Society;[4] but the decline continued once again in the following years, reaching its lowest point in 1904-5, when only three Societies were still active, the other three provincial and the three remaining University Societies being on the point of death.[5]

1906 saw the beginning of the revival of provincial Fabianism, though the rise in the following years was more gradual and not so great as it had been in the early 'nineties. Each year new Societies were built up, and the peak was not reached until the beginning of 1913, when there were eleven University Fabian Societies, affiliated to the University Socialist Federation,[6] and thirty-nine provincial Societies. The membership at that time was not definitely known to the central office,[7] but it was estimated to be about 970 members for provincial Societies,[8] while the membership of the University Societies was declared to be 477, and undoubtedly the majority of the Society's total of 323 'associates' was also connected with the University Societies.[9]

A rapid decline in the provincial Societies set in once again during the war years, and it was hastened by the breaking away of the University Societies of Oxford and Cambridge during the Guild Socialism dispute. The decline was steady and continuous and by the beginning of 1918 only eight provincial and three University Societies remained, and of these only the Liverpool and Glasgow Societies were at all active.[10] Only a very slight revival occurred in the post-war years.

The Liverpool Fabian Society was the only provincial Society which maintained a continuous existence from the early 'nineties to 1918. It has had almost as active a career as the London Society itself, but it was always much more closely associated with the I.L.P.[11] Its membership fluctuated between seventy and eighty up to 1904; in 1905 it fell to the low-point of sixty-three, from which it steadily rose (even during the war years) to 155 in 1918. Other provincial Societies with continuous existences of some duration and importance[12] were those at Ramsbottom and Tunbridge Wells founded before the

---

[1] *Ibid.* March 1897.   [2] *Ibid.* March 1899.
[3] *Ibid.* March 1900.   [4] *Ibid.* March 1901.
[5] *Ibid.* March 1905.   [6] Oxford U.F.S. did not affiliate till later in that year.
[7] Article by M. Cole in *Fabian Quarterly*, April 1944, (No. 41), p. 21.
[8] 472 were said to be members of the London Society and 'about 500' not London members.   [9] Annual Report F.S. March 1913.   [10] *Ibid.* March 1918.
[11] Pease, *op. cit.* p. 103; P. Verhaegen, *Socialistes anglais* (Englcke et Larose, 1898), p. 121.
[12] My criterion here is the fairly arbitrary one of eight years' continuous existence, which all those listed enjoyed.

turn of the century, and Glasgow, Edinburgh, Bristol, and Leeds amongst those founded after 1900.

Some additional information may be given of the University Fabian Societies, for the parent Society paid more attention to them than it did to any of the other groups.[1] The records show that from its earliest days the Fabian Society was scheming to increase its influence in University circles.[2] The University Fabian Societies were not established on a permanent basis, however, until 1895, when the Oxford, Cambridge, Aberystwyth (University College of Wales), and Glasgow University Fabian Societies were founded. Considering the necessary fluctuation in the membership of these Societies, their continuity of existence deserves notice. The Oxford Fabian Society was the only one which had no break at all in the continuity of its existence up to 1915. This was probably due to the fact that Sidney Ball remained its permanent President all through the difficult years at the turn of the century.[3] There was a steady decrease in its members from thirty at the time of its foundation to six in 1905,[4] after which time there was a rapid revival, until it had 101 members and fifty-five associates in 1914.[5] It seceded under Guild Socialist influence in 1915. The statistical trend of Cambridge Fabian Society was similar to that of Oxford, but it seems to have been a smaller group: the figures which have been recorded show that it remained approximately three-quarters of the size of the Oxford F.S.[6] It ceased altogether to exist in 1904, and was not reconstituted until 1906. It had seventy members and fifty-eight 'associates' in 1914, and it also dis-affiliated from the Fabian Society in 1915.

Glasgow and Aberystwyth University Societies rivalled, and sometimes surpassed Oxford in size during the period between 1896 and the first years of the twentieth century. At the beginning of 1899 Glasgow with twenty-five members and twenty-one associates,[7] was the largest University Fabian Society. But after that it shared the general tendency to decline, and passed out of existence in 1901, when the few remaining members joined the town Society which was formed in December of that year. Aberystwyth on the other hand, showed a tendency to increase its membership, which at thirty-two in 1902, made it the largest University Society of that year.[8] In the following year, however, there was a sudden decline, said to be due to the loss of members

---

[1] See for example the attitude of Pease, *op. cit.* p. 103.
[2] The Annual Report for 1888 mentioned the setting up of a 'Universities commission'. Fabians frequently gave lectures to undergraduates.
[3] R. C. K. Ensor was Secretary in 1898 and A. D. Lindsay in 1900.
[4] Annual Reports F.S. for this period.
[5] This is the official figure given in the Annual Report for 1914; Professor G. D. H. Cole and other persons who were connected with the Oxford U.F.S. at this time considered the figure far too low; and indeed, there seems little doubt that not all those who played a part in it paid their dues.
[6] Annual Reports F.S. 1899–1903 and 1914.
[7] Annual Report F.S. March 1899.
[8] *Ibid.* March 1902.

leaving College and the failure to recruit more,[1] and the Society collapsed at the end of 1904. Glasgow U.F.S. was reconstituted with thirty members in 1905,[2] but Aberystwyth was not revived until 1912.[3] Prior to 1900 there was also one other University Fabian Society—at Edinburgh. It was founded in 1897, with fourteen members[4] and led a precarious existence for three years, finally disappearing in 1901. A new Society was formed at Edinburgh University in 1907.[5]

In the general revival after 1906, other University Fabian Societies were founded: London (1907),[6] Liverpool and Manchester (1909),[7] Birmingham (1910),[8] and St Andrews (1911).[9] By 1913 all these Societies were affiliated to the University Socialist Federation.[10] But the war and the Guild Socialist heresy played havoc with them. After the war attempts were made to revive the Fabian Societies at Aberystwyth, Edinburgh, Oxford, and Cambridge,[11] but in the course of a year or so all of them became absorbed into wider University Labour Clubs.[12]

It may be concluded that the membership of the Fabian Societies outside London followed the same general trend as the membership of the London Society itself after the turn of the century; but during the 'nineties the trend was quite different, showing a rapid increase in the early 'nineties, with a sudden fall in 1894 and a continuing decrease until 1900. The inclusion of the numbers in provincial Societies in the graph of membership would have balanced the peak after 1906 with a peak nearly as great, and more sudden, in the early 'nineties, and would have emphasised the declining and stagnant condition in the later 'nineties and the first years of the new century.

The rise of provincial Fabianism in the early 'nineties is connected mainly with the rise of the New Unionism and the forces which went to the making of the Independent Labour Party, and its decline was due to the fact that the I.L.P. confronted them with the choice of sinking their identity in the new organization or retaining their own organization and being excluded from the I.L.P. Most of the provincial Societies elected to join the I.L.P., and the London Fabian Society made no struggle to prevent them. The longer, greater, and more general rise in Fabian membership after 1906 is obviously associated with the surprising success of Labour members at the 1906 election, and the revived energy of the Labour movement for which this event provided the impetus. More will be said of this in later chapters.

[1] *Ibid*. March 1904.
[2] Pease, *op. cit*. p. 191. (Only the town society is mentioned in Annual Report for 1904).
[3] Annual Report F.S. March 1913.
[4] *Ibid*. March 1898.   [5] *Ibid*. March 1908.
[6] *Ibid*.   [7] *Ibid*. March 1910.
[8] *Ibid*. March 1911.   [9] *Ibid*. March 1912.
[10] *Ibid*. March 1914.   [11] *Ibid*. March 1919.
[12] *Ibid*. March 1923.

DISTRIBUTION OF FABIAN LEAFLETS

As the Fabian Society did not (except perhaps for one excited moment in 1893)[1] really dream of exercising its influence by drawing large numbers into its ranks, the second chart which shows the total distribution of Fabian Tracts

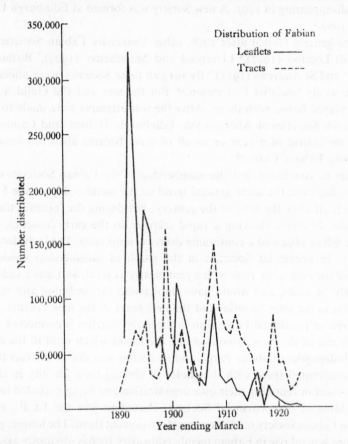

Distribution of Fabian

Leaflets ———

Tracts - - - - -

and leaflets[2] is probably more significant as an indication of its general influence. Some explanation is necessary of the considerable fluctuations. It will be observed that leaflet distribution reached its record peak in the year 1891-2. This was the period immediately before the elections for the L.C.C. and the General Election in which the Fabians gained their first successes. The immense leaflet distribution is mainly accounted for by the publicity given to the different points of Sidney Webb's *London Programme*—each point covered by

[1] See Shaw's hopeful remarks in Tract 41. Contrast those in Tract 70.
[2] Fabian leaflets were usually (but not invariably) also numbered as Tracts. The distinction made here is based on the facts that leaflets were brief—usually only 2-4 pages in length—and were issued free.

a separate leaflet. The Fabian municipal programme was impressed upon London by the distribution of these free leaflets, which laid the foundations of later Fabian influence. This tremendous effort, however, proved a strain on the Society's resources, and the Annual Report for the year ending March 1893 announced that, for the sake of economy, the gratuitous distribution of leaflets would need to be cut down. Nevertheless, a large number had also been distributed between March 1892 and March 1893, though there was a considerable falling off in the following year (but the number remained high by later standards). In the April 1894–March 1895 period, the distribution of leaflets increased once more; the increase was due to propaganda for the elections for the L.C.C., the London School Board, and Parliament, all of which fell in the one year, and for the elections which were impending under the new Parish Councils Act of 1894.

During the first years of Conservative rule after 1895 there was a distinct slump in the number of leaflets distributed by the Fabian Society, with a slight revival before the 1898 L.C.C. election, when a number of the old leaflets dealing with the points of the *London Programme* were brought up to date and reprinted.[1] After this, there was again a falling-off, until the year April 1900–March 1901, when the sharp rise in that year was only partially accounted for by the L.C.C. and Borough Council elections. The Society's local government leaflets on this occasion were devoted mainly to an attempt to persuade the Progressives to go beyond the *London Programme* in the direction of 'Municipal Socialism,'[2] but they did not prove popular. The leaflet with the largest single distribution in this period was not any of those dealing with local government, but the one (drafted by E. R. Pease) entitled *How Trade Unions Benefit Workmen*.[3] This was 'intended for use by Trade Unions desirous of extending their membership', and a blank space was left in it to be filled up by the Union issuing the leaflet if it desired to insert additional information. There were large orders from Trade Unions for it; 74,600 copies were distributed in the April 1900–March 1901 period,[4] and the demand for it continued to be vigorous in the next year also, when 64,000 copies were issued.[5]

After 1902 there was again a great drop in the number of leaflets distributed, as the result of a policy decision. The failure of the latest municipal series had been a shock. These publications had 'involved a great amount of labour and expense', the Annual Report complained, but they 'did not circulate freely, and publications are obviously of value only in so far as they are read by the public', so the Executive decided 'that it is undesirable to issue new leaflets unless in special circumstances'.[6] The fall in leaflet distribution therefore con-

[1] Annual Report F.S. March 1898.   [2] Tracts 94–7, 102.
[3] Tract 104.   [4] Annual Report F.S. March 1901.
[5] *Ibid*. March 1902.   [6] *Ibid*.

tinued unbroken until 1906; there was a continuous but steadily decreasing demand for *How Trade Unions Benefit Workmen*. But in 1906, with the success of the Labour Party at the election and the sudden revival of interest in all things connected with Labour and Socialism, the demand for this leaflet suddenly revived again, and 37,000 copies of it were distributed in the year April 1906-March 1907, as compared with only 17,000 in the previous year.[1] In the year ending March 1908 the distribution of Fabian leaflets rose still further, although since no new leaflets had been prepared, the distribution consisted entirely of reprints of old ones, and once again *How Trade Unions Benefit Workmen* represented the greater part of the total (62,000 out of 95,720).[2]

After 1908, the demand for this particular leaflet seemed temporarily satisfied, and the distribution graph for Fabian leaflets shows a lamentable decline from 1909, with only a feeble revival in the 1914-16 period. The revival in 1914-15 was due to the circulation by the Society of 17,750 copies of a special four-page Memorandum of Suggestions to Local Citizen Committees appointed to deal with distress arising through the war,[3] but the continuation of the revival into 1915-16 was once again due to the issue of 33,000 copies of a new' revised edition of the perennial *How Trade Unions Benefit Workmen*.

DISTRIBUTION OF FABIAN TRACTS

The graph showing the distribution of the Fabian Tracts differs considerably from that of the distribution of leaflets, for the Tract distribution fluctuated with the buyers' demand, whilst the leaflet distribution was dependent largely on the crusading zeal and the internal finance of the Society. The total represented by the graph is arrived at merely by adding together the number of Tracts sold, whatever their price. It is almost needless to say that the penny Tracts sold in thousands, while the number of sixpenny booklets of Tracts disposed of each year was to be reckoned only in hundreds.

The increase in the sale of Fabian Tracts in the early 'nineties appears to have been part of the generally increasing interest in the Society at that time. No individual Tract was singled out in the Annual Reports as having sold exceptionally well, until the year April 1894-March 1895, when Tract 53, explaining the new Parish Councils Act, went through four editions and sold 30,225 copies. 'Few of our penny Tracts have had so large, and none so rapid, a sale,' commented the Executive.[4]

After 1895, there was a sharp and rapid fall in the sale of Tracts, which continued throughout 1896. In the Annual Report for the year ending March 1897, the Executive felt obliged to explain the decline. 'A variety of causes has contributed to this result,' it said.

[1] *Ibid*. March 1906 and March 1907. [2] *Ibid*. March 1908.
[3] *Ibid*. March 1915. [4] *Ibid*. March 1895.

The year has included no important London or general election; public interest has been largely occupied with foreign politics to the exclusion of social and domestic affairs. From all quarters we hear the same story, that the market for political pamphlets is stagnant. In former years we had a practical monopoly of the publication of Socialist Tracts. Now a similar work is carried on by the *Clarion*, the Manchester Labour Press, and other agencies which have advantages over us in the matter of free advertisement. The Fabian Societies throughout the country used to be large buyers of our publications, but few of them now remain. Another cause is the diminished number of lectures, and the fact that our lecturers have largely abandoned the practice of selling Tracts.

While admitting the force of these explanations, it also seems possible that the new Tracts of these years were of such an abstract and theoretical nature as to limit their popularity. Of the seven new Tracts published between April 1895 and March 1897, four are of major importance in the development of Fabian theory[1] (and theoretical Tracts form a small percentage of any complete list of the Society's publications). Apparently Socialist theorizing—at any rate, at that time—attracted attention in only a small circle.[2]

In the following year there was a slight increase in Tract sales, and the change seems to have been brought about chiefly by three new Tracts—two of a practical kind and one of a religious complexion. The Tract on housing[3] was designed 'to assist the movement which has sprung up in various places all over the country for making use of the powers provided by the Housing of the Working Classes Act 1890'; the Tract entitled *Shop Life and its Reform*[4] was purchased for distribution by the Shop Assistants' Union; and the Society's republication of a pamphlet by the eighteenth century New Jersey Quaker, John Woolman, was quickly sold out to the Society of Friends.[5]

But the record year for Tract sales was April 1898–March 1899, and the main cause of it was the publication of *The Workmen's Compensation Act: what it means, and how to make use of it.*[6] Here was a Tract dealing immediately with 'basic economic issues', and which consequently appealed strongly to the British working men and their Trade Union Secretaries. The large Trade Unions ordered supplies for their members, and it was also distributed by the I.L.P. In six months, thirteen editions had been issued, and by 31 March 1899 no less than 120,163 copies of it had been sold.[7]

After 1899, there was a decline which continued until 1905. The apparent

[1] Tracts 69, 70, 72, 75.
[2] Tracts with the largest regular and continuous sale were *Facts for Socialists* (No. 5), *The Workman's Compensation Act* (No. 82), *Cottage Plans and Common Sense* (No. 109), *Houses for the People* (No. 76), *Christian Socialism* (No. 42), and *Socialism and the Teaching of Christ* (No. 78). See Annual Report F.S. March 1903.
[3] Tract 76 and Annual Report F.S. March 1898.
[4] Tract 80.
[5] Tract 79. Annual Report F.S. March 1898.
[6] Tract 82.
[7] Annual Report F.S. March 1899.

recoveries of the 1901–2 period and the 1903–4 period were not caused by an increase in sales, but by a gratis distribution. In 1901 the Hutchinson Trustees[1] agreed to finance a special distribution of Sidney Webb's two Tracts of that year *The Education Muddle and the Way Out* and *Twentieth Century Politics: a Policy of National Efficiency*[2] amongst the graduates of the Universities of London, Glasgow, St Andrews, Manchester, and Wales, and amongst Town Councillors, some County Councillors, and Trade Union Secretaries. 35,000 Tracts were circulated in this way.[3] In 1903, this policy was adopted once again, and 20,000 Tracts were distributed, this time to County Councillors, Urban District Councillors, and County Borough Councillors; the Tracts sent out comprised 10,000 copies of Sidney Webb's *The Education Act 1902: How to Make the best of it*,[4] and the other 10,000 were made up partly of *Twentieth Century Politics* and partly of Tracts selected from the Society's accumulated stocks.[5]

From 1906, another boom in the Tract sale commenced, reaching its peak in the April 1907–March 1908 period, though sales continued at a fairly high level until 1914. This boom in its early stages seems to have been created by a general middle-class interest in Socialism after the 1906 election, as there was no longer a Hutchinson distribution scheme in 1907, and the largest sale of 30,000 copies of the *Workmen's Compensation Act* Tract is not sufficient in itself to account for the increase. The decline shown in the April 1908–March 1909 period would have been somewhat greater had it not been for the free distribution of 10,000 copies of *Parish Councils and Village Life*[6] to chairmen of parish councils and meetings and of rural district councils.[7] Nevertheless, Tract sales continued remarkably high. The minor boom of the April 1911–March 1912 period appears to have been caused solely by the fact that 'the number of Tracts of sixteen pages and upwards published during the year has only once been equalled, and has never been exceeded in the history of the Society'.[8]

With the outbreak of the 1914 War, the Tract sales which had been falling during 1912, 1913, and 1914 dropped suddenly to the lowest level since the beginning of the 'nineties, from which point they climbed, slowly and painfully, during the remaining war years. There was a sudden increase in 1918 at the end of the war, but this was caused chiefly by the purchase of a large

[1] Sidney Webb, E. R. Pease, William Clarke, W. S. De Mattos, and Miss Hutchinson were appointed trustees in 1894 under the will of Henry H. Hutchinson of Derby, a well-to-do Fabian who had contributed substantially to a number of Fabian projects. He left between £9000 and £10,000 to be expended within ten years in furtherance of the objects of the Fabian Society. Miss Hutchinson died fifteen months later and left something under £1000 to a similar body of trustees for a similar purpose. The bequest played an important part in Fabian activity and will be referred to in later chapters. See Pease, *op. cit.* pp. 123–5.
[2] Tracts 106 and 108.   [3] Annual Report F.S. March 1902.
[4] Tract 117.   [5] Annual Report F.S. March 1904.
[6] Tract 137.   [7] Annual Report F.S. March 1909.
[8] *Ibid.* March 1912.

edition of Beatrice Webb's *Abolition of the Poor Law*[1] by the Committee for the Prevention of Destitution and the Standing Joint Committee of the Fabian Society and the I.L.P.[2] The post-war sales statistics, like the post-war figures of leaflet distribution, suggest that the Society was not ready to take advantage of the revival of interest in social questions: very few Tracts were published in these years.

DISTRIBUTION OF 'FABIAN ESSAYS'

The most important book issued by the Society was, of course, *Fabian Essays*. This work, from the time of its first appearance in 1889, had a remarkable sale, which surprised its authors. The first edition of a thousand copies priced at six shillings was disposed of within a month of the book's appearance,[3] and a second thousand copies was issued in March 1890. In September arrangements were made for a shilling edition, which had an extremely lively sale. By March 1892 the total number of *Fabian Essays* issued in all editions had reached the figure of 21,500; by the same month of 1893 the total was 25,000; by 1894, about 28,000; by 1895, over 30,000; by 1896, 32,000; by 1897, 33,000; and when in the April 1897–March 1898 period the sales dropped to only about 500 for the year, the Society thought that the 'demand for this most successful book appears to be nearly satisfied'.[4] By that time, Dutch, Scandinavian, and German translations had appeared. The number of English copies sold between 1898 and 1905 was small—no more than a few hundred copies a year. But in 1906 there was a sudden increase in the sales: in the April 1906–March 1907 period, 1383 copies were sold by the publisher, compared with only 398 copies in the previous year.[5] When this number increased to 2407 between April 1907 and March 1908, the Society decided that the time was opportune for a new edition. Consequently, a sixpenny edition with a new preface by Bernard Shaw was published in 1908, and of the first printing of 10,000, over 8000 copies were sold in four months.[6] By the time of the outbreak of the First World War a total of some 46,000 copies of *Fabian Essays* had been sold in English editions; the volume went out of print during the war, but another edition, with a preface by Sidney Webb, was issued in 1920.

CONCLUSION CONCERNING THE DISTRIBUTION OF WRITTEN PROPAGANDA

The graphs of the distribution of Fabian leaflets and Tracts, taken together, confirm the general trend which has emerged from our analysis of total Fabian membership, that is to say, the 'peaks' of Fabian activity came in the early 'nineties (the beginning of the 'Municipal Socialism' period) and in the years

[1] Tract 185.
[2] Annual Report F.S. March 1919.
[3] *Ibid.* March 1890.
[4] *Ibid.* 1891–8.
[5] *Ibid.* March 1907.
[6] *Ibid.* March 1909.

immediately following the 1906 election. The two intervening years of considerable propaganda activity, 1898 and 1900-1, reflected mainly the publication of one Tract (*The Workmen's Compensation Act*) and one leaflet (*How Trade Unions Benefit Workmen*) respectively, which caught the attention of the major Unions. The 'low points' of the graph are equally significant: 1896, 1902-5, and 1913-8, with the lowest point before 1918, as one would expect, in the middle of the war years. What is unexpected is the even deeper fall in the post-war years, a measure, perhaps, of the 'Old Gang's' success in maintaining control of the Society.

Amongst which sections of the community were the Fabian Tracts and leaflets mainly distributed? Unfortunately, no definite answer can be given. As we have seen, there is occasionally a record of a large number of Tracts being bought by a Trade Union for distribution amongst its members, or by a religious organization, or that the Fabian Society itself sent out copies to members of Parliament or to local government representatives or printed a special supply for one of the Society's parliamentary candidates to distribute amongst his constituents. We know also that the Society advertised its Tracts on the covers of the Annual Conference Reports of the I.L.P. and Labour Party, and no doubt had a considerable sale amongst the members of those organizations. But the task of settling this question in any precise way seems hopeless.

FABIAN LECTURING

The situation is different with the other main avenue of Fabian propaganda—public lectures. Some lists of the lectures given in London and throughout England have been preserved, and it is possible to make some useful generalizations about the kind of organizations and audiences to which they were addressed. It is less easy to say how many lectures were given each year, as attempts were rarely made by the Society to keep a record of the total number. In the first printed Annual Report of the Fabian Society—that for the year ending March 1888—the number of 324 lectures by members of the Society was mentioned, although it was suggested that more had probably been given; a footnote to *Fabian Essays* claims that in the next year (1889) the number of lectures was upwards of 700; in the year ending March 1892, when an attempt was made to keep a record, the total was claimed to have grown to 3339; and in the next year, when no record was kept it was thought to have 'probably exceeded the number recorded in our last Report'.

The lecture-lists which exist make clear the kind of organizations to which the Fabians addressed their lectures. Here is a sample from a list issued in March 1891:

Melvin Road Board School Evening Class: J. F. Oakeshott on
'The Factory System'.

Parish Hall, Sloane Square, Chelsea: Peartree on
'The History and Principles of Poor Relief'.
Battersea Branch National Secular Society: E. Bottle on
'Socialism in Evolution'.
Kentish Town Co-operative Society: G. Wallas on
'The Future of Co-operation'.
Westminster Liberal Association: S. Webb on
'Consequences of Democracy'.
Poplar Co-operative Society: J. F. Oakeshott on
'The Middle Class and Social Reform'.
Working Men's College, Great Ormonde Street: H. Roberts on
'Wages'.
Co-operative Building Society, Camberwell: G. Wallas on
'The Eight Hours Movement'.
Star Radical Club: G. B. Shaw on
'Alternatives to Social Democracy'.
New Debating Society: G. Wallas on
'The Poor Law'.
South Place Institute: Mrs Mallet on
'Reforms for London'.
West Ham Secular Society: J. F. Oakeshott on
'Everyday Ethics'.
Radical Club, North Camberwell: G. B. Shaw on
'Radical Politics'.[1]

This is typical. The early London lecture-lists show that, while the Fabians were prepared to lecture to any group which was willing to hear them, the majority of the lectures were in fact delivered to Liberal Associations, Radical Clubs, Secular Societies, Co-operatives, Working-men's Colleges, Debating Clubs, Trades Councils—in short, mainly to organized associations of Radical working-men.

There was little that was haphazard about the Fabians' arrangements for their lecturers: they tried to organize as scientifically as possible. *Fabian News* the Society's internal news-sheet, originally established to give guidance to the secretaries of local branches, explained carefully, in one of its early issues, the technique of publicity for lectures. The secretaries were advised to prepare and keep a register of all local organizations—working-men's clubs, co-operative societies, political organizations, socialist societies or branches, trade union branches, Church or Chapel Young Men's Associations, Debating societies— that might arrange for lectures. Together with this they should have a full list of local newspapers, a list of addresses of all Socialists and sympathizers in the neighbourhood, as well as the addresses of a dozen or so of the most influential political workers in the main political parties, and a list of all representatives on local governing bodies. The local Fabian branch should then endeavour to

[1] *Fabian News*, March 1891.

obtain invitations to speak to these other associations, and invite their speakers to address the Fabian branch. Whenever a Fabian was lecturing, a notice of the lecture was to be sent to the local press, the *Daily Chronicle, Star, Echo, Labour World and Sunday World, Justice, Worker's Cry*, the *Club and Institute Journal*, to Parliamentary and County Council representatives and candidates for the district, as well as to any other influential persons likely to attend, and handbills were to be sent to other clubs and organizations in the neighbourhood.[1] No doubt these excellent rules were not always followed, but the instructions from the Fabian headquarters left little to be desired in point of thoroughness.

The first heyday of Fabian lecturing occurred in the early 'nineties. By that time the Fabians had been fairly launched into the Radical and Secularist circles; they had worked out in some detail their message for the world in general, and London in particular; and the upsurge of the New Unionism had caused a questioning of older assumptions, and a mental ferment, in which the solutions propounded by the Fabians were eagerly discussed. There was an enthusiasm about the activities of the Fabians in the early 'nineties, springing from a feeling that they were helping in a quickly-moving but peaceful and beneficent change.

From about 1893, however, there were signs of a slackening of interest in the Society's lectures in London. 'In London the lecturing at Clubs and Associations has been steadily continued. A large part of this work is now only preaching to the converted, and not unfrequently small and apathetic audiences discourage the lecturer,' declared the Executive in the 1893 Report. In the following year the Society paid a considerable amount of its attention to the Radical Clubs and Political Associations of the outlying suburbs of London, which had not yet been fully exploited.[2] 'The demand for our lectures in the London Clubs is less than it was a few years ago, and hitherto we have failed to find any equivalent new field for our propaganda,' said the 1895 Report. By 1896 the position had become worse:

A new list of lectures was prepared and printed in September, and with the object of reaching a section of the population hitherto neglected, it was posted to the Secretary of the Debating or Mutual Improvement Society of every Church and Chapel in the London district, and to a large number of Trade Union Branches in London. From the latter a few applications and replies were received, and probably many lectures were arranged by direct communication with the lecturers. But, notwithstanding these efforts, the demand for our lecturers in London seems to be falling off, and the number given, through no fault, so far as we are aware, on our part, is less than it was some years ago. In part, this no doubt is due to the general acceptance by the Progressive Party of the principal practical planks in our programme, and in part to

[1] *Ibid.* June 1891.
[2] Annual Report F.S. March 1894.

the general wave of reaction which has affected London even more than other parts of the country.[1]

From 1896, the Fabians are shown to be experimenting with new means of attracting attention to their lectures. A special committee was set up to make a collection of lantern-slides for illustrated lectures, and a series called the 'The White Slaves of England' was said to be a success.[2] (It is not recorded whether any members of the audience felt they had been attracted under false pretences). But these efforts were defeated by another invention—the bicycle— which completed the decline of the Radical Clubs' interest in political lectures, by removing the audiences entirely.[3] The Fabians do not appear to have been as alive to the possibility of exploiting the invention, by organizing cycling clubs, as were the 'Clarionettes' group in the Independent Labour Party. From this time lectures had frequently to be abandoned because no one came to hear them.[4] By 1900, a phase of Fabian propaganda had come to an end: 'In London, the demand for our lectures so far as known to the officers of the Society has almost ceased. . . . The London Liberal and Radical Clubs, once centres of so much intellectual activity, and constant applicants for our assistance, appear to have in most cases abandoned politics altogether.'[5] From the late 'nineties the Fabian lecturers in London had had to fall back on 'Literary and Social Societies which', a Report grimly remarked, 'attract a class of persons not readily accessible to political education'.[6]

The decline was not so great in the provinces, where the I.L.P. branches opened up a new field for Fabian activity. Nevertheless, the 'Lancashire Campaign' of 1890 was looked back upon as the great time of Fabian lecturing propaganda outside London. This 'Campaign' had been financed by Henry Hutchinson, from whom the Society received so much financial assistance in its early days, and most of the leading Fabians took part. Annie Besant played a vigorous role both in lecturing and in organizing provincial branches, and Shaw, Webb, Wallas, Bland, Clarke, Headlam, De Mattos, and Dell were the other lecturers. Careful preparations were made beforehand for organization and publicity, and within the space of a month, some sixty lectures were delivered in the main cities of the north, mostly at Liberal and Radical Clubs and Co-operative Societies. The reports of the campaign make it clear that ground had been to some extent prepared for the Fabians by the propaganda of the S.D.F. and the Socialist League in the north, although the Fabians addressed themselves to a rather different audience:

The vigorous propaganda in the manufacturing districts of the S.D.F. branches has been carried on by means of outdoor meetings. Its effects upon working-class opinion, especially among unskilled labourers, has been marked and important, but

[1] *Ibid.* March 1896. [2] *Ibid.*
[3] *Ibid.* March 1898. [4] *Ibid.* March 1897.
[5] *Ibid.* March 1900. [6] *Ibid.* March 1898.

179

it has entirely failed to reach the working-men politicians who form the rank-and-file of the Liberal Associations and Clubs, or the 'well-dressed' Liberals who vaguely desire social reform, but who have been encouraged by their leaders to avoid all exact thought on the subject.[1]

In the following year, W. S. De Mattos, who continued as a touring Fabian lecturer in the cities of the north, also referred in his report to the fact that the older Trade Unionists, because of their opposition to the revolutionary socialists, were showing a willingness to invite and encourage the Fabians, and were gradually adopting an 'advanced labour policy, which is scarcely to be distinguished from Constitutional Socialism'.[2] The Lancashire Campaign of 1890 was considered to have been such a success that arrangements were made to put Fabian lecturing in the north of England on a more or less permanent footing. At first De Mattos was given charge of it; later (in 1892) W. H. Utley; in 1893 Hubert Bland, J. R. MacDonald and Halliday Sparling made lecturing tours of the northern cities; and finally, in 1894, when the Hutchinson Trust money became available to the Society, paid lecturers were employed to tour the provinces. Enid Stacy and J. R. MacDonald were the first two 'Hutchinson lecturers' engaged, and in later years the lecturers included Joseph Clayton, H. Snell, S. D. Shallard, J. Bruce Glasier, and W. S. Sanders.

The main reason why Fabian provincial lecturing did not fall off as the London lecturing did—at least not until the early years of the twentieth century (the slump in Fabian provincial lecturing came between 1900 and 1905)—seems to be that after 1893 the Society's activities were carried on largely under I.L.P. auspices. 'The constant demand for lectures in the north of England' was acknowledged in the Society's 1894 Annual Report to be 'due to the growth of the I.L.P. movement and the foundation of a large number of Labour Clubs'. During the year from April 1896 to March 1897, about fifty different towns were visited by the Hutchinson lecturers and 180 lectures were delivered mostly in courses of four connected lectures, and of those 180 lectures ninety-one were delivered under the auspices of I.L.P. branches and clubs, eighteen of Co-operative Societies, only fourteen of Liberal Associations and Clubs, thirteen of Trade Unions, eleven of local Fabian Societies, nine of local S.D.F. Branches, and the other twenty-four under the auspices of a miscellaneous assortment of organizations.[3] At the time when the Society's London lecturers were finding difficulty in obtaining an audience, the attendance at the Hutchinson lectures was said to have 'varied from fifty to as many as 500'.[4] This work continued successfully up to the end of the 'nineties: in the year April 1898–March 1899, the provincial lecturers of the Hutchinson Trust delivered

[1] Quoted Pease, op. cit. p. 96.
[2] Fabian News, July 1891: article on 'The Northern Campaign'.
[3] Annual Report F.S. March 1897.
[4] Ibid. March 1896.

180 lectures to audiences estimated to total between 15,000 and 20,000 persons, 'no small number of whom are town and district councillors, magistrates, trade union officials, teachers, and other persons in positions of authority and influence'.[1]

From 1899, the Fabian provincial lecturing decreased (especially in the north of England), until in 1904 it fell almost to nothing. The immediate reason for this was that in 1899 the Executive decided to use the Hutchinson lecturers and funds in a vain attempt to evangelize Ireland for Fabianism. This attempt was prompted by the creation in 1898 of District and County Councils for Ireland, and it occupied a large part of the last years of the Hutchinson Trust lecturers' work. Although encouraging reports were sent back by Bruce Glasier and other lecturers,[2] the Secretary-historian of the Fabian Society admitted later that there was no sign that the Irish venture had 'any very obvious results'.[3] The Irish Nationalists regarded local government on the English pattern as a concession designed to avoid the granting of full Home Rule; they were mainly interested in capturing the new bodies in order to pass Nationalist resolutions. The Fabians' 'sensible' advice on economic and administrative problems,[4] coupled with their silence or temporizing attitude on what appeared to the Nationalists to be the main issue,[5] were not tactics capable of making an impression in the Irish political scene. Why did they try? Several reasons may be suggested. First, their genuine enthusiasm for local government: county councils had become their main preoccupation in the 'nineties, and they believed that their English experience would be helpful to Ireland. Second, Ireland was new territory for Fabian lecturing. In the English provinces at the turn of the century the I.L.P., because of growing antagonism to the Fabians on important issues, was becoming less willing to be a channel for Fabian influence. Finally, it is possible that leading Fabians had moved so far into the 'Imperialist' camp at this time that they had come to believe that if a system of local government in Ireland could be made to work efficiently it would undermine the support for extreme Nationalism. At all events the Fabians' efforts, and their money, were wasted.

In England, the years between 1900 and 1905 were not a period of intense Fabian propaganda by the spoken word. The regular meetings of the Society continued to be held in London, and the lectures of these years were, in fact, an exceptionally brilliant series, which attracted crowded audiences to Clifford's Inn. On the other hand, many of these lectures at the headquarters of

---

[1] *Ibid.* March 1899.
[2] *Ibid.* March 1900, March 1901, March 1902. *Fabian News,* November 1899.
[3] Pease, *op. cit.* p. 125.
[4] See Tract 99: 'The Fabian Society therefore strongly urges the Irish County elector not to vote on Nationalist or Unionist lines at local elections, but to be guided solely by the candidate's fitness for the special work of the Councils. . . .'
[5] It is significant that one of the first acts of many of the Nationalist controlled councils was to adopt resolutions sympathizing with the Boers.

the Society were given by invited notables from outside the Society's ranks. Of the fifteen lectures given between April 1902 and March 1903 for instance, ten were by guest-speakers.[1] They were years in which fundamental problems of Imperialism, Free Trade versus Protection, Catholic Social policy, Neo-Darwinism and the Social Tendency of the Drama were being debated, and it seems that Fabian members were so concerned in finding a 'new way' for themselves that they had lost much of the energy for propagandizing the old.

The revival came in 1905-6, with the general stir which occurred in the Society when H. G. Wells led the attack on the 'Old Gang'. London groups were organized, suburban lectures were undertaken in conjunction with the I.L.P., provincial Fabian Societies revived and demanded lecturers, and W. S. Sanders was appointed provincial organizer. Such was the growth of the Society that a large proportion of the lecturing needed to be internal: the Fabian Nursery was founded in April 1906, and the Fabian Summer School in July 1907. But a list of lecturers, containing the names of over 200 members in London and the provinces who were willing to address meetings, was prepared and advertized in newspapers and resulted in a large demand from all kinds of organizations, social, political, and religious which were anxious to hear of Labourism and Socialism.[2]

Between 1908 and 1914, the Fabians devoted special attention to provincial lecturing. Bernard Shaw took a very prominent part in the speaking both in the provinces and in London: there is not an Annual Report of the Society between 1909 and 1914 which does not make special mention of the number and importance of the lectures he gave; and he also engaged in a series of brilliant debates with Chesterton and Belloc. An announcement that Shaw was lecturing was a 'sure draw', and could usually be relied upon to swell both the finances and the membership of the groups he addressed. After 1909, the Webbs also toured the provinces lecturing mainly upon the Minority Report on the Poor Law.[3] Other Fabians who took a main share in provincial lecturing were W. S. Sanders, H. H. Schloesser (Slesser), Clifford Sharp, Holbrook Jackson, and H. Beaumont. It is significant that the majority of these lectures were now given to local Fabian Societies,[4] but many were addressed to I.L.P. branches (there was a tendency to send young speakers from the Fabian Nursery to I.L.P. Branches, for practice),[5] and more than ever before to literary and debating societies.

While no complete estimate of Fabian lecturing is possible for these years, it seems almost certain that the quantity was greater than ever before. The Reports for the years ending March 1907 and March 1908 speak of 'unprecedented activity' and 'operations of the Society without precedent in its annals'.

[1] Annual Report F.S. March 1903.   [2] See *ibid*. March 1908.
[3] *Ibid*. March 1910.   [4] *Ibid*. March 1909.
[5] *Ibid*. March 1912.

During 1908, the first enthusiasm had faded somewhat: 'Political, like commercial, growth does not proceed with a uniform steadiness of advance; it has its periods of activity and depression', began the next Report, rather sententiously, '. . . at present popular attention appears to have turned to other topics. . . .' In 1910, the Society's lecturing was 'considerably disturbed by the General Election campaign, and the exhaustion of public interest in political and social subjects which resulted therefrom . . . a large number of engagements had to be cancelled'. But the decline in the quantity of lecturing seems to have been from a high level, and though the fall apparently continued during 1910–11, there was no real slump in the Society's activity. In any case, there seems little evidence of diminished lecturing activity in the remaining pre-war years: if anything, there was probably an increase from the time of the formation in 1911 of the Joint Standing Committee for co-ordinating the activities of the Fabian Society and the I.L.P.[1]

During the war years the Society's lecturing, like its other propaganda activities, necessarily declined, and the emphasis was placed instead on research, though the Fabian Research Department, both before and after its transformation into the Labour Research Department, organized lectures and conferences for the discussion of current problems and these were attended by trade unionists and other delegates. An interesting series of lectures was also continued throughout the war at the Fabian headquarters in London, but the provincial lecturing faded away, the local Societies themselves tended to dissolve, and even at the end of the war the revival was slow.

The survey of Fabian lecturing also tends to confirm the general pattern shown by the fluctuations in total membership and in the distribution of written propaganda, namely, a phase of intense activity in the early 'nineties; followed by a stationary period in the late 'nineties; then a period of sharp decline, or slump, in the years to 1905; this was succeeded by another phase of intense activity which carried on until the war years; then another sharp decline during the war.

THE NATURE OF FABIAN PROPAGANDA

The most striking and obvious quality of the Fabian Tracts is their factual and practical character. This was their great virtue. The Fabians undertook the hard work of detailed research, which other Socialist bodies did not have the time, the patience nor perhaps the ability to do. Even the Fabians' rivals admitted that, on this side, the Fabian propaganda was the best produced in England.[2] It is very noticeable that the more popular propaganda works— Blatchford's *Merrie England* for example—drew upon Fabian sources for such

---

[1] *Ibid.* March 1911, 1912, 1913.
[2] Engels to Sorge 18 January 1893, *Selected Correspondence of Marx and Engels* (National Book Agency, Calcutta), p. 444.

detailed social facts as their authors chose to include in them. *Facts for Socialists* in its various editions, and later more elaborate investigations by individual economists along the same lines, such as (before the First World War) Sir Leo Chiozza Money's *Riches and Poverty* and (after the war) Colin Clark's *National Income and Outlay*, formed the permanent armouries of English Socialists. This care for facts, even those of the drabbest kind, is displayed in all the Fabian publications, whether they deal with the City Guilds, or explain the powers under the Parish Councils Act or suggest what a Health Committee can do. The influence of Sidney Webb, encouraging his fellow members to pursue this dull but useful work, is everywhere apparent. More than that, he even inspired some of the younger members, like the young Cambridge graduate Keeling, with an enthusiasm for it, the kind of enthusiasm which moved him to write: 'By God! If only we could capture a Borough Council or a Board of Guardians we would shift something.'[1] If it were objected that a certain amount of this work seemed far removed from the great changes of Socialism, Shaw was ready to explain to the impatient young members how necessary it was for Fabians to show that Socialists could do more than spout impracticable generalizations, how necessary it was to prove themselves 'safe for all sorts of progressive work'.[2] 'When we go to a Radical Club to inveigh against the monopolies of land and capital,' he would say, 'we know perfectly that we are preaching no new doctrine. and that the old hands were listening to such denunciations twenty-five years before we were born, and are only curious to know whether we have anything new in the way of a practical remedy'.[3]

The Fabians did not confine their task merely to the discovery of facts. They were determined to make the facts 'available'. This aim, so much stressed in the early 'nineties, was in later times perhaps obscured by a greater emphasis on 'research'. It can be illustrated by contrasting the early editions of *Facts for Socialists* with those of the present day: while the recent editions are no doubt even more accurate than those of the 'eighties and 'nineties, they are certainly much less readable. Great care was taken in the drafting of the Tracts in the early days, and in many cases they had the benefit of a literary revision by Bernard Shaw. (In passing, it is worth noting that Shaw and Graham Wallas performed a similar service for the early edition of the Webbs' major works on Trade Unionism). But whether Shaw revised the pamphlets or not—and he performed this function not for all, but only for the more important ones— the Society insisted above all on clarity of presentation. The 'collective' nature

---

[1] E. T. [ownshend] (ed.), *Keeling Letters and Recollections* (Allen & Unwin, London, 1918), p. 31. The enthusiasm and faith inspired by Fabian and I.L.P. Socialism are expressed vividly in a letter written in 1907 to her sister by the young Australian historian Dr Marion Phillips, who had gone to London to study with Graham Wallas. This and other letters of Dr Phillips are now in the possession of Mr M. Bennett of Melbourne.
[2] Tract 41.   [3] *Ibid.*

of the early unsigned Tracts is often overlooked; the technique of their preparation allowed for a criticism by members of their style as well as of their content. In most cases, the original drafts of the Tracts have been preserved,[1] and the comparison of the draft proof with the published Tract is often instructive. After 1900 the number of unsigned Tracts issued by the Society diminished, and after 1905 the vast majority of Tracts were the work of individual members, having only the general approval of the Society.

Their emphasis on the clear presentation of facts helped to lend a cool and rational quality to Fabian propaganda. But other things contributed to it. The Fabians usually[2] avoided emotional appeals, especially those of a sentimental kind. Even where emotion was purified into Art, the Fabians took the view that it should go into print on the responsibility of the individual author, not of the Society.[3] H. G. Wells' *This Misery of Boots* together with a selection of *Ballads and Lyrics of Socialism* and a collection of *Songs for Socialists* remain the exceptions amongst Fabian Tracts. In their desire to avoid highly metaphorical, 'poetic' or oracular utterance, the Fabians tended to develop a precise, empirical prose, with a certain deliberate coldness about it. 'Light, not Heat', was the Fabian motto, and it was a source both of strength and weakness in their propaganda. Of strength, because it gave their works an air of authority, and made them formidable in intellectual circles. Of weakness, because H. G. Wells was probably right when he pointed out to the Fabians that literature having a more emotional appeal would secure a wider circulation amongst the working-class and lower-paid 'salariat'. What is the explanation of the Fabians' avoidance of the emotional appeal? It is true, as Pease says, that the ability to write such pamphlets as *This Misery of Boots* is a vastly rarer accomplishment than the ability to collect detailed social information, and therefore was less capable of being made the basis of the Society's work.[4] No doubt, too, the Fabians in general were 'more grieved by the world's mess than hurt by the world's wrongs'.[5] But it was to some extent a policy deliberately adopted to catch the attention of that class which would dismiss emotional appeals as 'mere propaganda'. The Fabians were very conscious of the importance of the professional and administrative classes in the community: teachers, managers, civil servants, were the groups which the Fabians wished above all to 'permeate',[6] in addition to trade union secretaries, working-class politicians and leaders.

For the same reason, the emphasis of Fabian propaganda tended to be (whatever theoretical reservation some Fabians may have had) on the unity of

---

[1] In the Hutchinson Collection, British Library of Social and Political Science.
[2] At any rate, after about 1890.
[3] Shaw's Appendix to Pease, *op. cit.* p. 278–9.
[4] *Ibid.* p. 183.
[5] Sir Alexander Gray, *op. cit.* p. 400.
[6] See *Fabian News*, January 1895.

society, not on class-conflict; on 'common sense', not the division of interests; on the injustice of the 'system', not the wickedness of individuals or classes. They avoided dogmatic phrases and 'slogan' type of writing, and took care to express in novel words the ideas which they knew would be familiar to their audience. By adopting a 'common sense' standpoint they placed themselves in a strong position for attacking those parts of the earlier social ideology which had become outmoded, and Bernard Shaw, with his consuming wit, his superb eye for contradictions between theory and practice, was here in his element. The Fabians also succeeded, to a remarkable degree, in keeping their literature free from bitter polemics. In this, they were assisted in the early days by the divisions of opinion in their ranks, and a number of attacks which could have given rise to personal bitterness were deleted from draft proofs of Tracts when they were presented for approval of the Society as a whole. But the absence of personal abuse and moral indignation from Fabian writing must be attributed in part to the fundamentally good-natured and optimistic outlook of Webb and Shaw—more particularly of Webb, for Shaw did occasionally allow his pen and tongue to wander from a theoretical criticism to a somewhat personal attack. Sidney Webb, however, was steadfast in his refusal to indulge in personal abuse of others, and in his determination to ignore personal attacks against himself. These qualities were in the main a source of strength in Fabian propaganda. But their attitude was not always without defects: their optimism, their ignoring of divisions of interest in society, sometimes led them to adopt the tone of school-teachers reproving the stupidity of those who declined to accept their advice, and perhaps it also led them occasionally to overrate the amount of good will and to ignore the quantity of positive evil will in the world.

CHAPTER VIII

THE INFLUENCE OF THE FABIANS
IN THE LONDON COUNTY COUNCIL

THE BACKGROUND TO FABIAN MUNICIPAL REFORM

THE Fabian Society was the chief propagandist of the reforms that came to be called 'Municipal Socialism' for at least two decades after the early 'nineties. And within the Society, Sidney Webb was recognized as the man who had first turned his colleagues' attention to the importance of local politics. The Tract *Facts for Londoners*,[1] published in 1889, which was substantially Webb's work, and the influential booklet *The London Programme*, which appeared in 1891 under Webb's own name, formed the basis of a series of leaflets issued by the Society and distributed widely.[2] Sidney Webb had opened the eyes of his fellow-members of the Fabian Society to what was for them a whole new field for propaganda and activity. As a result the Fabians and those who became influenced by them have been inclined to overrate the originality of Webb's proposals for London reform.

The Liberal-Radicals of London in the early 'nineties, however, were not inclined to admit the novelty of the Fabian proposals. The Liberal journal, the *Speaker*, reviewing *The London Programme* in its issue of 3 October 1891 declared: 'On this occasion Mr Webb writes more as a Radical than as a Fabian, and, except on one subject[3] . . . every reform he advocates is certainly included in the programme of every Liberal and Radical in London'. The basic point of this criticism was that the movement for London reform had a long history before the Fabians joined in the campaign. In order to appreciate the role of the Fabians, it is necessary to glance briefly at that history and to observe the point at which they entered.

The movement for municipal reform in London with which we are concerned may be dated back to the time when London had been excluded from the Municipal Corporations Act of 1835 which had reformed the government of the other cities of England. London had been omitted from the Schedule of that Act because the Royal Commision on whose report the legislation had been based took a further two years to complete its researches and present its report on London. The complexity of London government made necessary a

---

[1] Tract 8. [2] Tracts 30-7.

[3] The 'one subject' was Leasehold Enfranchisement, a proposal that leaseholders of houses built on land let for ninety-nine years should be empowered to purchase the freehold at a valuation. It was popular amongst some Radicals, but the Fabians opposed it. They considered it the urban equivalent of the Chamberlain-Collings 'three acres and a cow' (and, indeed, some Liberal leaders intended it so: see references to the 'urban cow' in J. L. Garvin, *Life of Joseph Chamberlain* (Macmillan, London, 1933), vol. II, p. 124).

special report and a separate Bill, though the Commissioners concluded in the 1835 report that they could not find 'any argument on which the course pursued with regard to the towns could be justified which does not apply with the same force to London'. The report was to stand, unimplemented, as the point of appeal for London reformers for fifty years. The delay in giving London the municipal government enjoyed since 1835 by the other cities of England must be explained to a large extent by the opposition of the City Corporation. Jealous of its privileges and estate, the City Corporation has managed to sustain to this day a largely successful opposition to all attacks upon them, and for fifty-three years after 1835 it resisted any large-scale reform of the government of outer London which seemed likely to diminish its authority. The Metropolis Local Management Act of 1855, which established a Metropolitan Board of Works composed of representatives of the local vestries and district boards and of the City Corporation, gave very limited powers to this central body, and evidently intended to keep the Board as far as possible subordinate to its constituent authorities. Though it did good work in drainage, slum clearance and other matters that fell within its competence, the Metropolitan Board of Works could do little more to satisfy reformers than to show how a more powerful central body might terminate an era of Anarchy and Private Enterprise in London government. In general, the local authorities of the metropolis remained limited in size and power—inefficient, undemocratic, sometimes corrupt; the public utility undertakings were necessarily left in the hands of profit-making companies; the administration of the Poor Law, and later, of Asylums and Education were in London, as elsewhere in the Kingdom, in the hands of specially elected authorities—the Poor Law Guardians, the Asylums Board, and the Schools Boards.

A consequence of this lag in reform of London government behind that of the other cities of England was that demands for reform had become general by the eighteen-eighties. Naturally the Radicals had carried their demands furthest, but by the 'seventies the need for reform was so great that many Conservatives, even the august *Times* itself, lent approval to many of the demands.[1] By the time the Fabians entered the scene, the question of London reform had become to some extent a non-party issue, and plenty of ammunition for the reformers had been furnished by reports of Royal Commissions, official committees of inquiry, derelict Bills, and pamphlets and articles by the dozen.

A main division in the ranks of the reformers had also appeared by that time on the question of centralization or decentralization. Should London government be concentrated in the hands of a central authority which would delegate its powers to lesser authorities strictly subordinate to it, or should it be entrusted to several Boroughs federated in a weak central body? The

[1] Particularly in 1874, when *The Times* supported the reform bill of Lord Elcho.

division on this issue ran through the whole history of the reform movement. Whereas the Royal Commission report of 1834 had recommended centralization, a later Royal Commission report of 1854 favoured a decentralized scheme. The Metropolitan Board of Works may be said to have embodied the decentralized principle in its extreme form.

In 1867, the year when the Parliamentary franchise was given to the urban workers, a Select Committee of the House of Commons set forth in its recommendations the minimum demands of all London reformers: that the Metropolitan Board of Works should be enlarged to include justices and directly elected representatives as well as the representatives of the vestries; that the powers of the Board of Works should be increased and its name changed to the Municipal Council of London (these powers were to include control over gas, water supply and railways and uniformity of assessment of rates); that the vestries should be turned into directly elected district governing bodies to be called the 'Common Councils' of the Districts; that the functions of the Boards of Guardians should be absorbed into the new machinery of government; and that the two police forces should be under one control.[1] Nothing was done by the government about these recommendations, and the private Bills introduced by members of Parliament were of no avail. John Stuart Mill in 1867-8 introduced Bills for reform along 'decentralized' lines, which were defeated. In 1869-70 Sydney Buxton's Bills, which were substantially those of J. S. Mill, were referred to a Select Committee and shelved. The vigorous support of *The Times* in 1874 did not enable the Bills on similar lines of Lord Elcho and Sir Ughtred Kay-Shuttleworth to reach a second reading. The last attempt by private members to force the issue was made in 1880 when a group of Radicals—J. F. B. Firth, Thorold Rogers, T. B. Potter, W. H. James, and H. R. Brand—brought in a measure, which differed from the earlier Bills chiefly in the increased powers it sought to give to the central authority. (J. F. B. Firth, a lawyer and politician of great ability, was thereafter to be known as the chief apostle of 'centralization'). Their Bill was prevented by the shortness of the session and lack of Parliamentary time from reaching its second reading, and the reformers decided that their experiences proved that London reform could not be carried through Parliament by private members.

As a result the campaign was transferred outside the House of Commons and transformed into a public Radical agitation intended to force the government to take up the matter. The London Municipal Reform League was founded in 1881 with J. F. B. Firth as its Chairman. It absorbed the earlier Metropolitan Municipal Association of James Beal, which had not achieved

[1] In this background survey, I have drawn considerably from the historical information in the Report of the Commissioners appointed to consider . . . the Amalgamation of the City and County of London . . . (1894). C7493 (ii).

189

much influence; it attracted into its ranks such prominent men as Sir Charles Dilke, Sir Arthur (Lord) Hobhouse, Lord Shuttleworth and Sydney Buxton; and it speedily developed an extensive campaign of propaganda and agitation.[1] The pamphlets and books of J. F. B. Firth stated in clear and persuasive terms its main demands. The campaign of the League led up to Sir William Harcourt's Bill of 1884, which followed closely the lines of reform advocated by Firth with some concessions to the Metropolitan Board and the City Corporation.[2] The Corporation was not conciliated, and fought the Bill fiercely both inside and outside the House of Commons. When the government discovered this opposition to be formidable, and the Municipal Reformers in the House at odds over the question of centralization or decentralization, Harcourt's Bill went the way of its predecessors.

The Local Government Act of 1888, which set up the London County Council, was passed by a Conservative government. The Municipal Reform League claimed it as its victory,[3] but it was in every way a compromise measure brought about more by pressure of general circumstances than the activity of any one group. Two things in particular had precipitated the Act. In the first place, grave charges of corruption had been made against the Metropolitan Board of Works, and these were to a certain extent substantiated by investigations made by a Royal Commission. This provided the justification and the occasion for abolishing the Board. In the second place, the Local Government Act had the more general purpose of setting up County Councils throughout England, and, if separate provision had not been made for London, it would have meant that London would have been divided up between the three counties of Middlesex, Surrey, and Kent, and the confusion of London government increased.[4] The provision for London in the Local Government Act of 1888 was far from being the carefully thought-out reform demanded by the Radical reformers. It dealt only with the most pressing requirements of the situation. This Act setting up Councils throughout England made London as it were incidentally into a separate County, and gave it a County Council in place of the Metropolitan Board of Works, but otherwise made no change. The City Corporation remained untouched, in control of the City proper, and no alteration was made to the smaller authorities—the twenty-five vestries and the fourteen district boards (which managed the fourteen districts into which the fifty-three smaller vestries were grouped). The

[1] John Lloyd, *London Municipal Government: History of a Great Reform*, 1880–1888 (Bedford Press, London, 2nd ed. 1911), *passim*.
[2] See J. F. B. Firth, *Reform of London Government and of the City Guilds* (Swann Sonnenschein, London, 1888).
[3] John Lloyd, *op. cit.*
[4] An additional factor making for the establishment of the London County Council may have been the inadequacy of the Metropolitan Board to cope fully with the housing situation, revealed by the Royal Commission on the Housing of the Working Classes of 1885.

difficult problem of reorganizing these smaller authorities and establishing their formal relationship with the London County Council was avoided, on the ground that the Bill was a general one, dealing with the whole of England, and that detailed provision for London would 'overload' it. The government promised to bring in a more detailed Bill at a later date.

THE SOCIETY'S RELATION TO EARLIER MUNICIPAL REFORMERS

It was at this stage that the Fabian Society entered the municipal arena. Their Tract of 1889[1] was their first real contribution to the struggle for London reform. The Fabian Society as a group had had no share in bringing the L.C.C. into existence, and no member of the Fabian Society was elected to the first L.C.C. 'The Socialist' (as the newspapers of the time were careful to label him) on the L.C.C. was John Burns of the Social Democratic Federation. The emergence of the Progressive Party in the L.C.C. also owed nothing initially to the Fabians. Those who wished to keep party politics out of the L.C.C. accused J. F. B. Firth of having 'created' it, though in fact the party had created itself. A majority of members of the first L.C.C. had been members of the London Municipal Reform League, or were known to be in sympathy with its aims; these members recognized Firth as their theorist and leader, and elected him to the post of deputy-chairman of the L.C.C.; those who did not wish to go so far as the Municipal Reform League's programme were labelled 'Moderates' and thought of as the opposition. At all events the Progressive Party (composed, according to its opponents, of 'Rads', 'Cads', and 'Fads') had emerged in the lifetime of the first L.C.C.

Where then did the Fabians stand in relation to the municipal reformers who had preceded them, and what did Fabianism add that was new? Their predecessors were not only the London Radicals, but also the practical administrators of other cities in England, who had virtually half a century's start on the Londoners. The Fabians, like other London reformers, made it a feature of their propaganda to declare that the reforms they were advocating were neither new nor untried. They took up the attitude that they were demanding for London institutions which had been successful elsewhere, where provincial cities had already introduced them for purely 'practical' reasons and in many cases had gone to the trouble of extending their powers by special Acts of Parliament in order to do so. When they recommended the municipal supply of gas in London, the Fabians did not fail to remark that 170 different towns in England already owned their own gasworks to 'save the cost of shareholders'.[2] Similarly, urging municipal trams for London, they were careful to say that thirty-one towns already owned their own trams, and one (Huddersfield) worked them without any contractor, and was the only tramway working with an eight-hour day for its employees.[3] When they spoke of

[1] Tract 8.   [2] Tract 10.   [3] *Ibid.*

191

the need for an improvement in London's housing situation, they gave instances of what had been done by the local authorities of Liverpool, Greenock, and Glasgow.[1] They contrasted the situation at the London docks in the 'eighties with (as they claimed) 'the already successful' control of the Mersey Docks and Harbour Board of Liverpool, and they went on to declare 'the Clyde, the Mersey, the Tyne, the Wear, the Severn, and the Avon are in the hands of representative public authorities; and Liverpool, Glasgow, Dublin, Bristol, Swansea, as well as most other great ports, have their docks free from private control'.[2] With their demand for the municipalization of London's water supply, the Fabians strengthened their case by showing, not only the example of other places, but also that the Conservative government had actually decided upon the policy in 1879, and that it was only abandoned because of the public outcry which followed the government's decision to pay an outrageous sum in compensation to the shareholders.[3] Their lesser demands were no more original. The abolition of the Guilds of the City and the transfer of their property to the representatives of the people of London, the control by the London County Council over the markets of London, the provision of other amenities, more baths, washhouses, libraries, parks—all these things amounted to a claim that London should enjoy the 'freedom and social activity' of the most progressive provincial cities. Their demands for the simplification of government machinery of London, and for a measure of centralization under the London County Council also followed along the traditional Radical lines in seeking to obtain for London the advantages that other cities of the Kingdom had obtained in 1835.

The Fabians' forerunners as theorists of municipal reform were, principally, J. F. B. Firth and Joseph Chamberlain. A comparison of the works of Sidney Webb and the Fabians with those of Firth make their debt to him quite plain, both in their proposals for reorganizing the machinery of London government, and in their proposals for the control of public monopolies. Firth anticipated the Fabians in demanding the abolition of the rights of liverymen of the City Guilds; he wanted the two police forces of London amalgamated and placed under the control of the elected representatives of London; he recommended that London's central authority should purchase the assets of the water and gas companies, and 'have control of' the markets and tramways and 'give full consideration to' the question of acquiring them, as other cities had done.[4] In one of Firth's pamphlets—*The Gas Supply of London* (1874)— there is an examination, more comprehensive than anything in the Fabian writings, of the different conditions under which the companies' assets had been acquired from the shareholders by other municipalities, leading to some

---

[1] Tract 8.   [2] *Ibid.*   [3] *Ibid.*
[4] J. F. B. Firth, *London Government and How to Reform It*, London Municipal Reform League (Kirby & Endeau, London, 1882), pp. 80-1.

conclusions about the best methods of 'municipalization'. The only major service about which Firth made no recommendation, and the Fabians did, was the London Docks, and the reason for this was that the condition of the Docks was only brought to the attention of reformers by the agitation of the dockers in the late 'eighties.

Wherein lay the novelty of the Fabian proposals? There were some differences, which can best be demonstrated by mentioning Joseph Chamberlain's disagreement with the kind of reforms advocated by Firth. In his Unauthorized Radical Programme of 1885, Chamberlain had attacked Harcourt's Bill of 1884, which was based on Firth's ideas. The difference between these two Radical reformers lay in the old conflict between centralization and decentralization. Firth wanted a centralized system for the Metropolis, with extensive powers in the hands of the central authority and 'District Councils' (to replace the vestries) strictly subordinate to it. Chamberlain, on the other hand, thinking he had learnt from 'practical experience' as mayor of Birmingham that Birmingham was the ideal size for local administration, wanted London split into several 'cities' of that size, federated merely for common purposes in a central body.[1]

Sidney Webb led the Fabians to take, on the whole, a middle position between these champions of centralization and decentralization. This position they maintained, though there were some shifts of emphasis, for Webb tended on different items of policy now towards one side and now towards the other, and he occasionally changed his ground as the result of his experience of London government. Thus at the time he wrote *Facts for Londoners*, Webb was more a disciple of Firth than he was later when he wrote *The London Programme*. In *Facts for Londoners* he recommended that the smaller authorities should be under 'the control, supervision and audit' of the L.C.C. while in *The London Programme* he anticipated that the new 'District Councils' would 'undoubtedly be bodies of independent authority, having power to raise their own rates, expend their own funds and settle their own questions in their own way'.[2] In the latter work Webb had made his discovery that the principle embodied in 'Grants-in-Aid' provided a very satisfactory relationship between higher and lower authorities, giving the necessary degree of central control for ensuring efficiency while also permitting a large measure of local autonomy.[3] Even in *Facts for Londoners*, however, Webb was much less of a centralizer

---

[1] *The Radical Programme*, with a preface by the Rt Hon. J. Chamberlain (Chapman & Hall, London, 1885), p. 233 *et seq.*

[2] *The London Programme* (Swann Sonnenschein, London, 1891), p. 26.

[3] See, for a comprehensive treatment, S. Webb, *Grants-in-Aid: A Criticism and a Proposal* (Longmans, London, 1911); and see also a lecture by Webb to the F.S. reported in *Fabian News*, December 1895, where he approved the 'complicated English system' whereby control was 'purchased' by the central authority, contrasting it favourably with the centralization of French and the decentralization of U.S. local government, and concluding that the 'old Liberal objection' to the English system was wrong.

than Firth. Whereas Firth wanted the functions of the London School Board and the Poor Law Guardians taken over by the new central body,[1] Webb, in his earliest works, showed little objection to the continued existence of these and other *ad hoc* authorities. At that stage, he said nothing against the machinery of the School Board, and he apparently contemplated with approval the establishment of a new *ad hoc* 'Charities Board' or 'Poor Law Council' to take over and 'humanize' the functions of the Guardians and the Asylums Board and to administer public hospitals and other charities. Nor did Webb appear greatly concerned whether the Docks should be taken over by the L.C.C. or by a special public Trust or Board—in fact, in *The London Programme* he expressed a slight preference for a Board.[2] In later years, as we shall see, Webb came back to Firth's point of view concerning *ad hoc* authorities, and came to recommend the transfer to the L.C.C. of the functions of the School Board and the Guardians.[3] But in his attitude to the smaller authorities, Webb did not return to Firth's centralizing view,[4] though he remained equally far from Chamberlain's kind of decentralization.

The middle position taken by the Fabians chiefly distinguishes them from the two chief theorists of municipal reform who preceded them. But the Fabians were Socialists, while Firth and Chamberlain had been Liberals, albeit Radical-Liberals. That made some difference to be sure, but less than might at first be supposed. It was a difference more of ultimate goals than of immediate demands.[5] The Fabians, thinking of Socialism primarily as a long-

---

[1] J. F. B. Firth, *London Government and How to Reform It*, pp. 75, 80.

[2] *The London Programme*, pp. 70, 95.

[3] Although the Fabians came to urge the abolition of the School Board and the Poor Law Guardians and the transfer of their functions to the L.C.C. as a result of practical experience and elaborate investigations into the working of these institutions and not as a result of any objection to *ad hoc* bodies as such, it is interesting to note that the objection to them in principle appeared in their later propaganda. In Tracts 106 and 126 they argued that the principle of electing persons for one particular function was a bad one, and that the tendency in the development of local government in the nineteenth century had been to abolish *ad hoc* bodies.

[4] In one matter only could Sidney Webb and the Fabians be said to have begun and remained as uncompromising 'centralizers'. They considered that overlapping areas for different authorities, and different electoral registers were confusing to the ordinary citizen and they desired their 'centralization' to the extent of basing each of them upon the Parliamentary electoral area so far as was possible, 'regard being had to local sentiment'. Thus in *Facts for Londoners* the Fabians applauded the decision which had made the Parliamentary electoral area the basis of electoral districts of the L.C.C. and they proposed that the same area should (so far as possible) form the District to be governed by the new 'District Councils' when they were set up, and that it should also be used for Poor Law purposes. The Fabians believed that this simplifying of electoral areas would increase the participation of the ordinary citizen in local affairs by fostering a local patriotism.

[5] I do not wish to underrate the importance of this difference. There can be little doubt that the Fabians' presentation of particular reforms as part of a whole scheme of Municipal Socialism gave them a feeling of superiority to the Liberal-Radicals, who lacked so comprehensive an outlook: a feeling of leadership, a feeling of knowing the way the world was going. This was the Fabian 'myth', as important in its more limited sphere as the Marxian 'myth', which it somewhat resembles. One can test its validity either (as a political scientist)

range administrative task, were willing to begin with those concerns that the Radicals were ready to take over. Their Socialism was largely an optimism that these experiments would prove a success and would lead on to extensions of municipal and government ownership and 'trading'. Firth and Chamberlain desired no general inroad into the private ownership of the means of production (though Chamberlain had toyed with the word 'socialistic' in the Unauthorized Programme),[1] but they were willing to take into public ownership certain concerns in the interests of 'efficiency' or because they were monopolies. Other Liberal members of the Progressive Party sometimes justified extensions of municipal activity on the ground that the reform of a few abuses whose existence could not be denied would deprive the Socialists of much of their support. But the usual Progressive attitude was Lord Rosebery's: 'Those things are not Socialism at all. They are a vital necessity for a great city.'[2]

When Sidney Webb was labelled 'a dreamer of dreams', it was his vision of the distant Socialist future that his opponents had in mind. It was the ultimate objectives, rather than the practical proposals of the Fabian Society, that Lord Hobhouse referred to, when he said, speaking at the Eighty Club in 1892, 'Mr Sidney Webb is a gentleman whose ability and uprightness I wish to speak of with every respect, and I have no doubt that when he is returned to the Council he will do excellent work in it. But he does take some very far-reaching views, in which he is not followed by me, and, so far as I know, he is not followed by the majority, or any member of the Progressive Party.'[3] In spite of such protests by Liberal-Progressive leaders the expression 'Municipal Socialism' caught on with the public, for it was a striking expression, and it was popularized not only by the Socialists, but also by the Conservatives and Moderates who hoped by its use to frighten the electors.[4] The resulting confusion may have worked in Fabian interests, but it is no indication that the Progressives were persuaded to go any further along the Socialist path than had been marked out by J. F. B. Firth.

There was, however, a borderline of immediate practical difference between the Fabians and the Radical theorists. The Fabians were confident that the

by examining the causal factors claimed to be influencing the movement of history in that direction, or (as an historian) by looking in retrospect at the extent to which history did move in that direction. But its emotional value for the Fabians and their followers cannot be doubted.

[1] *Op. cit.* pp. 13, 59.
[2] Speech of Lord Rosebery in St James' Hall, 1 March 1898, quoted H. Jephson, *The Making of Modern London: Progress and Reaction* (Bower Bros. London, 1910), p. 206.
[3] *London Government*, Speech by Lord Hobhouse to the Eighty Club, 29 February 1892, Eighty Club, London, 1892, p. 18.
[4] See, as typical of Conservative propaganda, an article in *The Times*, 31 January 1907: 'The whole thing . . . was of purely Socialistic origin. The . . . suggestions quoted above emanated from the Fabian Society and were embodied in a little book called *The London Programme.* . . .'

L.C.C. would be able to manage, as well as own, the concerns it took over, whereas Firth in his writings showed the Liberal distrust of public management. He appeared to be in favour of the municipality letting out its monopoly to a contractor, under fairly strict conditions; but he was cautious and tentative about it, he seemed willing to be open to conviction, and on this point the Fabians may have had some success in persuading the Progressives to their way of thinking. There were, in addition, certain specific 'labour' demands which the Fabians supported enthusiastically and which marked an advance beyond the earlier Radicalism. Socialist and Labour members of the L.C.C. demanded that the municipality should become a 'model employer', that it should grant an eight hours day and 'fair wages' to its employees, and that it should include a clause in all contracts obliging its contractors to do likewise. Another 'labour' demand was that county councillors should be paid, or else council meetings should be held in the evenings so that the working-class men could be councillors. Most of the Progressives, who relied to a considerable extent on the working-class electorate, found that they could agree to these 'labour' demands without moulting too many feathers of their faith in private enterprise.

To stress the similarity of the practical programmes of Fabians and London Radicals is not to settle the question how far the Fabians influenced the Progressives. Originality is far from being the only important element in political influence. Even more important in politics is 'he who says it so long and so loud that he compels mankind to hear him'. And turning to the propaganda activity of the Fabian Society, we observe that Sidney Webb became in a very real sense the successor of J. F. B. Firth as the Progressive Party's theorist. Firth's influence was paramount in the first year of the L.C.C. but his death in an accident occurred in 1889, shortly after the first session of the L.C.C. had come to an end, and his organization, the London Municipal Reform League, over-confident that its work was done once the L.C.C. had been established, faded out of existence soon afterwards. Sidney Webb soon came to fill the place left vacant by his death. Perhaps Webb might have supplanted or at least equalled Firth as a theorist of London reform even had Firth lived. As early as 1887, when the 'United Committee' for advocating the taxation of ground rents and values had been formed by a combination of the Municipal Reform League and the English Land Restoration League, and it desired a statement of its objectives, it was to 'Sidney Webb LL.B., Barrister at Law, Lecturer on Economics at the City of London College' that the Committee went for the drafting of its pamphlet *A Plea for the Taxation of Ground Rents*. But Firth's death removed the most influential rival in this field, and left the way clear for the Fabians.

Sidney Webb's influence with the Progressives really dates from the time of the publication of *The London Programme* in 1891. In that year the Fabian

Society distributed the greatest flood of leaflets it has ever put forth in its whole lifetime, each leaflet dealing with a different point of *The London Programme*. The Fabians' propaganda had the effect they desired. At the time of the second election for the L.C.C. in 1892, the Progressive Party definitely recognized *The London Programme* as the most up-to-date statement of its objectives. In October of the same year the Fabians consolidated their position when the London Reform Union was founded, as the main propaganda body of the Progressive Party, on the basis of a programme which reads like a paraphrase of Webb's booklet.[1] Lord Rosebery, as its first President, made a graceful figure-head for the London Reform Union, but the organization was always well-staffed with Fabians. Sidney Webb in its early days was a member of its Committee, and Tom Mann, who at that time was a member of the Fabian Society and was working closely with the Webbs, became its first Secretary. Later, when Tom Mann retired from this position in 1898, his place was taken by F. W. Galton, who up to that time had been the Webbs' private secretary. Other Fabian names appeared on the Union's list of public lecturers, and there were Fabians on nearly all its sub-committees. The character and format of the pamphlets issued by the London Reform Union bore a marked resemblance to the Fabian Tracts.

There can be little doubt that the Fabians were successful in 'permeating' the Progressive Party. But for the most part it was permeation by consent—or at least, without opposition. Their permeation did not amount to taking the Progressives a great deal further than the left-wing Radicals were already prepared to go. Indeed, when London had lagged so far behind other cities in municipal reform, many Conservatives were willing to go a great part of the distance measured out by *The London Programme*. Webb himself said that *The London Programme* was designed to 'ignore the political differences between Liberals and Conservatives and appeal for the support of all good citizens'. Lord Rosebery, as first chairman of the L.C.C., entertained a similar belief that broad agreement on administrative reforms was possible, and that party politics could be kept out of the County Council. This hope proved too sanguine, but it at least shows there was initially much common ground. Even the anonymous reactionary who wrote the pleasant little pamphlet called *The Doom of the County Council of London* did not suggest that the water, gas, and electric supplies should be left uncontrolled in private hands.[2] It

---

[1] First Annual Report of the L.R.U. London, 1894.

[2] *The Doom of the County Council of London* (W. H. Allen & Co. London, 1892). This delightful pamphlet tells how the L.C.C. in its thirst for power, overreached itself, and in the end, 'the gas, electric lighting, and the water supplies were handed over to the City Corporation, which was confirmed in all its ancient rights and privileges; the tramways and omnibuses and docks were sold to private companies, and the proceeds applied to the reduction of the municipal debt; the care of the parks, and, above all, the control of the Police, were once more vested in the Executive, while the Hotel de Ville became the property of a Limited Liability Company and was transformed into a hotel proper, which was largely patronised

was not until the late 'nineties, when the Fabians began to urge that municipal trading should extend to bakeries, the supply of milk, the selling of intoxicating liquors, to pawnshops, slaughter-houses, and fire insurance[1] that they began seriously to run ahead of the majority of their Progressive colleagues.

FABIANS ON THE L.C.C. AND THE LONDON SCHOOL BOARD

The Fabians have always been a comparatively tiny minority amongst the elected representatives of the governing bodies of London. The Society's first electoral successes had been, not surprisingly, on the London School Board where, from 1888, it had three representatives—Mrs Annie Besant, the Rev. Stewart Headlam, and the Rev. A. W. Jephson. By 1891 the Fabians were reduced from three to one on the School Board: the Rev. Stewart Headlam alone remained on it as representative for Hackney. But by 1891 some Fabians had become members of one or two of the lesser governing bodies of London: E. R. Pease, the Secretary of the Society, had been elected vestryman for Marylebone and Frank Smith vestryman for Chelsea. However, it was not until the 1892 election for the L.C.C. that the Fabians achieved their 'famous victory'.

(1) The London County Council

In estimating Fabian influence it is important to note once again that the Fabian Society had no representative on the first London County Council: the agitation for 'direct employment' of labour, for the eight hours day for Council employees, for a 'fair wages' clause in all Council contracts and other so-called 'socialistic' demands had already been initiated by John Burns and others, on the first Council.[2] The direct participation of the Fabians in the work of the L.C.C. began with the second election of 1892. Amongst the total of 118 elected Councillors, six Fabians were then elected: Sidney Webb for Deptford, Frank Smith for North Lambeth, W. C. Steadman for Stepney, Fred Henderson for Clapham, Will Crooks for Poplar, and F. C. Baum for North Kensington. In addition to these six, Ben Tillett, then a member of the Fabian Society, was elected an alderman by the Council itself. Only one of the Fabian candidates preferred to stand independently of the Progressive Party, and he was defeated.

The results of the 1892 election were in every way characteristic of the Fabian Society's results in later years at the L.C.C. elections. Taking all the election results from 1892 to 1919 inclusive, the Fabian representation averages about six, and indeed continues to do so, even if all the elections from 1892 to the end of the 'twenties are considered. The only serious fluctuations[3] from

by wealthy American visitors. London woke again to life, with a delightful sense of freedom, as though it had escaped the hideous horrors of a prolonged nightmare'

[1] Tracts 85, 86, 90, 91, 92, 94, 96.
[2] William Saunders, *History of the First L.C.C.* (National Press Agency, London), *passim*.
[3] Between 1892 and 1919.

this figure occurred in 1895, when the Fabian representation dropped to three, and in 1907 when it rose to eight. The steadiness of the figure was largely maintained by the regularity with which certain prominent members of the Society were re-elected by the constituencies. Until the 1910 election, all the successful Fabian candidates were members of the Progressive Party, but from 1910 until the last Fabian Progressives finally disappeared at the 1925 election the Fabian representatives on the L.C.C. were equally divided between supporters of the Labour Party and supporters of the Progressives, except in 1913, when the heavy defeat of Labour candidates resulted in only one Fabian Labour but four Fabian Progressive members of the Council. There was a high proportion of working-class Fabians, prominent in the Trade Union and Labour movement, amongst the successful Fabian candidates.

Here are the fortunes of the Fabian Society at the L.C.C. elections in more detail:

In the 1895 election, which marked a slight decline in popular support for the Progressives—the Progressives lost some twenty-three seats and the Progressive and Moderate Parties were returned in exactly equal numbers—the Fabians held three of their seats. Sidney Webb was returned for Deptford, with the largest vote ever obtained by a Progressive to that date; W. Crooks for Poplar; and W. C. Steadman for Stepney. This meant that every Fabian who stood as a Progressive was elected, and each was elected at the top of the poll. The four Fabians who stood as I.L.P. and S.D.F. candidates in opposition to Progressives in no case came near to success.[1]

The 1898 election resulted in a Progressive victory. Twelve Fabians were candidates, and six were elected, four of them at the head of their polls. Of the other six, three were fighting forlorn hopes as Progressives, and the other three stood in opposition to both main parties and only polled small votes. The successful candidates were: Sidney Webb and R. C. Phillimore, both returned for Deptford, Frank Smith for North Lambeth, Will Crooks for Poplar (with a huge majority), W. C. Steadman for Stepney, and Ben Cooper for Bow and Bromley. They were joined in 1900 by J. E. Matthews, elected at a bye-election for St George's in the East.

In 1901 there was an unexpectedly sweeping victory for the Progressives; the Progressives gained fourteen seats, and Independents two at the expense of the Moderates, thus establishing a Council composed of eighty-four Progressives, thirty-one Moderates, and three Independents. The Fabians had seven candidates in the field, but did not manage to keep the recently-won seat. However, they held four of their seats very easily, and Ben Cooper and Will Crooks were each returned unopposed. Frank Smith stood and was elected for Central Finsbury on this occasion, instead of North Lambeth, which he had previously represented.

[1] See *Fabian News*, April 1895.

The Progressives were returned again in 1904 with a scarcely diminished majority, though many, including Webb, were beginning to think that the Progressive programme was becoming 'played out'.[1] In the election the Fabians had four victories and three defeats. Sidney Webb and R. C. Phillimore were once more returned at Deptford, Ben Cooper at Bow and Bromley, and W. C. Steadman at Stepney. Among the defeated was Bernard Shaw (an 'eminently unelectable person'), who had stood for South St Pancras. The number of Fabians on the Council, however, was maintained, because two, Isaac Mitchell and William Sanders, were elected Aldermen by the Council itself.

The electoral tide turned in 1907; the fifteen years of Progressive dominance was to give place to twenty-four years rule by the Moderates, under their changed name of Municipal Reformers. The Fabians did not share in the Progressive debacle; they even increased their numbers to six Councillors and two Aldermen. But the Fabians suffered a major reverse with the defeat of Ben Cooper at Bow and Bromley, where the split vote caused by two Independent Socialist candidatures tipped the scales against him. Sidney Webb and R. C. Phillimore were once more elected for Deptford, while Will Crooks and Frank Smith had a triumphant return for their former constituencies of Poplar and Lambeth North. In addition, Stewart Headlam was elected for Bethnal Green, and R. Bray for Camberwell. Two other Fabians besides Ben Cooper suffered defeat, including one who had stood as S.D.F. All the other Fabian candidates had stood as Progressives.

The 1910 election for the L.C.C. revealed that a change had taken place in the tactics of Fabian 'municipal socialism'. It marked the time when some of the older members of the Society gave up the unequal struggle against the Moderate majority (one or two of them had, by this time, been elevated to the higher realm of Parliament); and it was the first L.C.C. election in which the Fabian candidates were divided between supporters of the old Progressive Party and supporters of the new Labour Party which was just entering the municipal politics of London. Of the nine Fabian candidates, five were elected, two as Progressives, and three as Labour members. Webb, Phillimore, and Crooks did not stand again; the terms of the two Fabian aldermen—Sanders and Mitchell—expired, and they were not reappointed. Stewart Headlam was again elected as a Progressive for Bethnal Green, and R. Bray again as a Progressive for Camberwell North. Frank Smith was also again returned for Lambeth North, but this time he appeared as a Labour Councillor. The other two Fabian Labour Councillors were George Lansbury, elected for Bow and Bromley, and R. C. K. Ensor for Poplar.

The number of Fabians on the L.C.C. stood steady at five after the 1913 election, but there had been many more Fabians in the field, and there was a

[1] *Ibid.* April 1904.

heavy defeat of those standing as Labour candidates. Altogether, thirteen Fabians had stood for election: eight as Labour and five as Progressives. R. C. K. Ensor did not present himself for re-election, and Susan Lawrence was elected for Poplar, but she was the only Labour candidate to be successful. The successful Fabian Progressives were R. Bray (Camberwell), Stewart Headlam (S.W. Bethnal Green), R. C. Phillimore (who had returned once more to his old constituency of Deptford), and Montague Shearman, junior (Bermondsey).

No elections were held during the First World War, but an election was held for the L.C.C. in 1919. In it, the London Labour Party succeeded in increasing its membership from one to fifteen, which represented an increase in Fabian Labour Councillors from one to three. In addition to Susan Lawrence, who was re-elected, Dr L. Haden Guest and Harry Snell were both elected for East Woolwich. Major Attlee was amongst the defeated Fabian Labour candidates. Three Fabian Progressives were also returned: Stewart Headlam (S.W. Bethnal Green), Montague Shearman (South Bermondsey), and W. J. Pincombe (South East Southwark). A. Emil Davies was elected an Alderman by the Council.

Thus, in the period with which this book deals, the Fabians may be reckoned to have always had approximately half a dozen members on the London County Council. Considered in relation to the total membership of the Council this number is minute, but the Fabians contrived to make up in activity and ability what they lacked in numbers.[1]

(2) *The London School Board*

From 1888 until its absorption by the L.C.C. Education Committee in 1903, the Fabians always had at least one representative on the London School Board. In 1888 there were three Fabians on the Board,[2] but in 1891 the Rev. Stewart Headlam was the Society's only representative amongst the twenty-two Progressives, who were in a minority against the thirty-three 'Diggleites'. The 1894 election improved the Progressive position to twenty-six (against twenty-nine), and increased the Fabian members once again to three. Stewart Headlam and Graham Wallas were elected for Hackney and the Rev. W. A.

---

[1] A list of Committees of the L.C.C. on which Fabians served has not been included, as the space it would take hardly warrants it, and the conclusions are incorporated in this chapter. A complete list of Sidney Webb's Committees may be found in my article in Margaret Cole (ed.), *The Webbs and their Work* (Frederick Muller, London, 1949), pp. 85–6. Briefly, the Committees to which the Fabians who had the longest terms of service on the L.C.C. before 1910 devoted their main attention were as follows: *Cooper:* Parks and Open Spaces, Public Control; *Crooks:* Bridges, Parks and Open Spaces, Public Control, Technical Education; *Phillimore:* Appeals, Highways; *Smith:* Asylums, Establishment; *Steadman:* Bridges, Public Health and Housing; *Webb:* Local Government and Taxation, Finance, Parliamentary, Technical Education.

[2] See p. 198, above.

Oxford for Westminster. Some other Fabian candidates who ran as Progressives put up a good showing at the polls, though they were not elected, but the few Fabians who presented themselves as S.D.F. or Labour candidates in no case came anywhere near success.[1]

In the two subsequent elections of 1897 and 1900 the Fabian Society had four members on the School Board. The 1897 election was a Progressive victory—thirty-three Progressives were elected and twenty-two Moderates. The Moderates lost their leader Mr Diggle, and were divided into opposing factions; many of the Moderates were described as 'reactionary only politically' but 'progressive educationally' by a Fabian spokesman who said, 'Mr Diggle had a party of twenty-nine on the last Board; on the new one only nine members would follow him, had he been there to lead.'[2] On this occasion Miss Honner Morten joined Stewart Headlam and Graham Wallas as third representative for Hackney and H. Morgan-Browne was elected for Westminster. In 1900 three Fabians, Kennedy, Headlam, and Wallas were again returned for Hackney, and another, Mrs Miall Smith, for Marylebone.

The influential place held by the Fabians in the educational world in London was, however, more significant than their numbers on the School Board. At one stage in the 'nineties,[3] when Sidney Webb was Chairman of the Technical Education Committee of the L.C.C., Graham Wallas was the Chairman of the School Management Committee of the London School Board, and Stewart Headlam the Chairman of the Evening Classes Committee of the School Board, Fabians were holding three of the most important posts in the educational administration of the metropolis.[4]

---

[1] *Fabian News*, December 1894.
[2] *Ibid.* December 1897.
[3] After the 1897 election.
[4] The results of Fabian candidatures for the other, smaller authorities in London will not be given here, as their activities are not considered in this chapter. Suffice it to say that a number of Fabians have served at one time or another on a Vestry or on a Metropolitan Borough Council which replaced them. Fabian representation, though never large, became fairly widespread after the Progressive victory in the elections of December 1894. For example, at the 1894 election, although a number of the most prominent Fabians who had stood—Bland, Shaw and Sidney and Beatrice Webb—suffered defeat, other Fabians were elected in Hackney, Camberwell, Deptford, Finsbury, Islington, Lambeth, Marylebone, Plumstead, Soho (St Anne's), Woolwich, and Clerkenwell. The Fabian success suffered a check in November 1900, at the first election for the new Metropolitan Borough Councils, when six Fabians were returned as members for six different Borough Councils, but twelve other Fabian candidates were defeated. They retrieved their fortunes in 1903, when twelve Fabians were elected to seven Borough Councils, and only three Fabian candidates were unsuccessful. In Fabian history the most notable of the smaller governing bodies were perhaps the St Pancras Vestry (and later the St Pancras Borough Council) which was graced by the presence of Bernard Shaw for so long as his candidature was uncontested, and the Poplar Board of Guardians, which under the leadership of Will Crooks and George Lansbury, was gradually converted from the strictest to the most generous Poor Law Board in the country, and a model of a 'Labour' Board of Guardians (though the lax administration of the Poor Law was not approved by all Fabians by any means).

(3) *Difficulty of determining Fabian influence*

A principal difficulty in determining the influence which these Fabian representatives had in the activities of the L.C.C. must now be recognized. There is no possibility of giving a detailed account of the Fabians' work on all the committees to which they were appointed, because the available historical records do not allow it. Most of those who played an active part in the L.C.C. in its early days are dead, and have not left detailed accounts of their activities; memories, though they have been helpful at times, have more often proved sketchy and inaccurate; some of the Fabians who took the lead in local government politics, like Sidney Webb, were reticent about their personal role; and the main official historical sources, the heavy tomes of the Minutes of the L.C.C. also tend to eschew personalities. Full justice therefore cannot be done to all the hard committee work of the Fabians, but perhaps we do not require it. Most of the work of the world consists in the routine activities which simply keep things going, and much of the Fabians' committee work too was of this kind; we want to know how far their activities changed the world substantially, how far they managed to push History gently along the path to Municipal Socialism. We know the direction in which they wished the L.C.C. to go: did it go there, and is it possible to make any estimate of the Fabians' share in making it do so?

It is often difficult to separate out the influence of the Fabians in reforms which had support from many different quarters. On such issues as the need for better housing facilities, increased provision for public health, more parks and playgrounds, and better provision for London's education there was a strong body of favourable opinion, much of it of a non-party kind, which the Fabians may have nourished and increased with their facts and statistics but which they could hardly claim to have created. Two examples may illustrate this aspect of Fabian activity: the issues, namely, of the reform of the machinery of London government and education in London.

FABIANS AND THE REFORM OF LONDON GOVERNMENT

From the time London was made a County, and the L.C.C. brought into existence, all parties agreed that some reorganization of the lesser authorities would need to follow. The Gladstone government prepared to tackle the only formidable obstacle in 1893 when it appointed a Royal Commission 'to consider the proper conditions under which the amalgamation of the City and County of London can be effected, and to make specific and practical proposals for that purpose'.

(1) *Amalgamation of City and County and abolition of Guilds*

This Royal Commission was the nearest any government has come to getting rid of the City Corporation and abolishing the City Guilds. When the Commission's report was issued in 1894 its general conclusions were hardly unexpected, as the City Corporation's representatives amongst the Commissioners had withdrawn when the Commission had refused to hear evidence that amalgamation was undesirable. The Commission had taken the view that the terms of its appointment implied that the amalgamation was desirable if it were possible, and that it was merely the task of the Commission to report on the means of accomplishing the amalgamation. Their attitude was appropriately depicted in *Punch's* cartoon of the L.C.C. cook, knife in hand, calling to the Corporation turtle to 'come and be *amalgamated*'. In their report, the Commissioners proposed a new municipal Corporation for London which would take over the functions of both the L.C.C. and City Corporation. It was to be elected triennially, by direct vote, upon the same register as that for the L.C.C., and to consist of councillors, alderman, and a Lord Mayor. The new body, it seemed, was to be a County Council with a Lord Mayor. The Commissioners did not have a great deal to say concerning the relations of the new Corporation with the lesser authorities, but they appeared wary of over-centralization. They contemplated some reorganization of the vestries and district boards as 'District Councils' (of which the old City was to constitute one), but they thought the powers the L.C.C. already exercised over the vestries was sufficient, and ought to be retained, supplemented only by a provision that members of the central Corporation should automatically become members of the District Council in their electorates.

Although some of these recommendations did happen to coincide with some suggestions put forward by the Fabians in their writings, the Commission's proposals would have been the same if the Fabians had never uttered a word on the subject. The Fabians had nothing to do with the Commission, and its report was obviously the conclusion of a long line of recommendations, to which it made reference in its historical sections. The only 'influence' the Fabians may have had was that their preaching and activity provided an excuse for Lord Salisbury to shelve the Commision's report. On 7 November 1894, in the campaign before the L.C.C. election of 1895 Lord Salisbury, calling upon the Moderates to act as a party with Conservative backing, denounced the L.C.C. as 'the place where Collectivist and Socialistic experiments are tried . . . a place where the new revolutionary spirit finds its instruments and collects its arms'. Salisbury came to power in Parliament following the defeat of the Liberals in the election of 1895, and no more was heard of the 'amalgamation' of the City and County.

(2) *The establishment of the Metropolitan Borough Councils*

The reorganizations of the lesser authorities of London thus became a task left for the Conservative government, and Salisbury's famous 'Suicide speech', in which he recommended that fate to the L.C.C., had left no doubt of his attitude to London's local government. When Chamberlain had gone over to the Conservatives he found little difficulty in persuading them to adopt his decentralizing view of London government, after two elections had convinced Lord Salisbury that the L.C.C. was nothing but a hotbed of Radicalism and Collectivism. The violent reaction of the wealthier vestries to the L.C.C.'s plans for equalizing rates provided the opportunity for a Conservative Reform Bill which, under pretext of reorganizing the lesser authorities of London, was really designed to split London into ten 'cities' and deprive the L.C.C. of most of its power. The Progressives fought the original intentions of the Conservative government at the 1898 L.C.C. election under the slogan 'Unification versus Tenification', and won a resounding victory.[1]

The Fabians found themselves in a difficult middle position in this struggle. On the general 'Unification versus Tenification' issue, they supported the Progressives,[2] and when the London Government Bill was originally introduced on the 23 February 1899 the Fabians voted their disapproval along with the majority on the L.C.C.[3] But the Fabians were alarmed lest the opposition should cause the total loss of a reform measure which had much that was good in it, and which might be suitably amended. 'In view of the factious opposition to this Bill, promoted by partisan Liberals and the moribund Bumbledom of the vestries', proclaimed the Fabian Executive,[4] 'members are urged to take every opportunity for putting forward the views of the Society as to the value of the measure'. After the London Government Act 1899 had been passed, *Fabian News* in a leading article[5] claimed a victory, and maintained that the Fabian attitude of support with amendments as opposed to the early tactics of the Liberals and 'Official Progressives' of destruction 'became the attitude of all parties, with the result that the Bill was shorn of most of the bad features'.

It is true the Fabian Society had made its attitude widely known, that it had found some support for it,[6] and that W. C. Steadman as the 'Fabian M.P.' had taken an active part in the Parliamentary debates on the Bill, but it may be doubted if the result was due to any considerable extent to Fabian persuasion. The outcome in general was a compromise between a strong Conservative government and the Progressive Party which had had an overwhelming victory in the 'Unification versus Tenification' issue at the 1898 election. Fabian persuasion was hardly needed to make the Liberals and Progressives take a 'possibilist' attitude to the Bill; however reluctant they

---

[1] See pamphlets of the London Reform Union, especially *The Attack on the L.C.C.* by T. McKinnon Wood.
[2] S. Webb, *Six Years' Work on the L.C.C.: A Letter to the Electors of Deptford* (leaflet) 1898.
[3] L.C.C. Minutes, 1899, pp. 463–87.
[4] *Fabian News*, May 1899.
[5] *Ibid.* August 1899.
[6] See report of the proceedings of the Rotherhithe Vestry in *Fabian News*, May 1899.

were to do so, they had no alternative. The government was determined to force the Bill through, and the most that could be done by the Opposition was to obtain as many satisfactory amendments as possible. The Progressives in general were much less satisfied with their predicament and with the final compromise than the Fabian Executive was, and the Fabians, particularly Sidney Webb, fell out of their favour for rejoicing in it. Even some Fabians were more in accord with the 'official Progressive' than with the 'official Fabian' opinion, it seems, for *Fabian News* was obliged to record a protest from some members at the 'lack of democracy' in the Society: they complained that their point of view on the Bill had not been fully stated.[1]

THE FABIANS AND EDUCATION IN LONDON

(1) *Elementary and secondary education*

At the time when the Fabians first played an active part in the London School Board, a majority of the members of that body were political Conservatives. But the Rev. Stewart Headlam reported to the Society that the votes of the members of the School Board had been 'constantly swayed by the arguments and eloquence of the Progressives, amongst whom Mrs Besant was a tower of strength. This Board [i.e. the one before the 1891 election] was the first important body in England to adopt the principle of a Trade Union Wage Clause, and even the present reactionary body [the Board after the 1891 election] had not gone back upon this reform'.[2] Headlam listed seven reforms that had already been accepted in principle by the Board, despite its Conservative complexion: namely, that elementary education should be free; that special provision should be made for backward children; that the School Board should provide education not only for the children of the poor, but for all children; that meals should be provided in schools; that the size of classes should be reduced; that an 'education ladder' right to the University should be secured for able students; that pianos, baths, and other amenities should be provided in all schools.[3]

If the acceptance of these reforms in principle by the London School Board had led to their immediate adoption, the greater part of Fabian propaganda and activity in the educational field would not have been required. But this did not happen, and the Fabians consequently made a great assault on 'Diggleism'.[4] The Rev. Mr Diggle was the leader of the 'Moderates', and his name had come to signify to the Fabians a policy that was more careful of the

[1] *Ibid.* September 1899.
[2] *Ibid.* June 1894.
[3] *Ibid.*
[4] *Ibid.* (Headlam); *Ibid.* July 1894 (Lowerison); Graham Wallas assisted in the production of *The Case against Diggleism* (Alexander N. Shepheard, London). The Rev. J. R. Diggle's own case was stated in his article 'The Socialist State and Child Distress' in *National Review*, vol. xxvi, December 1895, No. 154.

pockets of the ratepayers than generous to the children for whom the education was provided. In general, however, the Fabian Society paid tribute to the work of the London School Board during the thirty-four years of its existence, and usually recognized that the majority of the School Board members (whatever their party politics) had the interests of London education sincerely at heart. It was the object of the Fabians to assist and hasten the work the Board was already engaged in, and the Fabian programme consisted largely in pressing for these seven reforms already accepted by it in principle.

The Fabians believed that education should be treated as an end in itself. They deprecated the use of School Board elections as a means to any other purpose than the promotion of education. In 1894, Headlam in a speech to the Society emphasized that the School Board had adopted the principle of a Trade Union Wage Clause, and he went on: 'It is therefore unnecessary for Labour men to stand merely or mainly in defence of Fair Wages. Not one-fiftieth part of the work of the Board has any connection with the matter, and the principle is accepted by all save one or two out of the fifty-five members of the Board.'[1] Again, in 1897, the Society carried *nem. con.* the resolution: 'That an election on which the educational opportunities of 750,000 children depend is of too vital importance to be used for electioneering campaigns for propagandist purposes, or for any other object than the securing of the Board most likely to promote the best possible instruction and training of London's children.'[2]

With the sectarian issue which occupied so large a place in the history of the School Board, the Fabians did not greatly concern themselves; but insofar as they did in the early days, their chief spokesmen appear to have been against the teaching of religion (as distinct from social ethics) in State Schools. For some of them this conclusion followed from a general Rationalist attitude that metaphysics should not be forced on any child until it had 'reached what is called in another connection the age of consent'.[3] Graham Wallas was opposed, on Rationalist grounds, to religious education in the schools. But the same practical policy was supported, for quite different reasons, by clergymen in the Fabian Society. The Rev. Stewart Headlam maintained that it was 'not the business of Board Schools to teach religion', that 'parents should choose the parsons they prefer to teach their children religion, and the State should take no part in the matter', and 'above all, we must have no tests for teachers'. He went on, however, to add that while he was personally opposed to the Forster 'Compromise' because it was illogical to 'teach the principles of religion without its doctrines' as 'no intelligible distinction can be drawn between the two', nevertheless he was 'willing to work heartily, for the present, with the supporters of the Compromise' in order to secure better education

[1] *Fabian News*, June 1894.
[2] *Ibid.* August 1897.
[3] See the view put forward later by Shaw in *The Intelligent Woman's Guide* (Pelican) p. 398.

for the people.[1] The Fabian Society, in its collective capacity, made no pronouncement, and the issue caused no division amongst the Fabians until it arose in a new form in the early years of the twentieth century.

Sidney Webb, in a speech he made in 1903, claimed that collectivist principles had brought a new spirit into the educational field. He said that 'ideas of the scope and purpose of public education' had 'enormously progressed since 1832, and even since 1870'.

The first notion was that of charitably bestowing education on the poor man's child for his own good. This led, after forty years' struggle, to the provision of the 'three R's' for everyone alike. Then there came the idea that the object of government was to promote 'equality of opportunity' in the competitive struggle. This led to attempts to put the clever child of poor parents on the same level as the clever child of those who had means—the inference was that it was enough that scholarships should be provided to give the poor boy or girl a chance to gain the higher education already open to the rich. But the really democratic purpose of public education was not to dole out elementary education to all and sundry, nor yet to develop a race of scholarship winners, but to train up the most efficient and most civilized body of citizens, making the most of the brains of all, and, in the interests of the community as a whole, developing each to the 'margin of cultivation'. We must discard the old notion of education free of cost as a grant of charity to the poor; we no longer think that a free opening of all avenues to individual ability is the true ideal. What Collectivists demand is the equipment of the whole body of citizens, each in accordance with his particular aptitudes and capacities, for the service of the community, as far and as freely in each case as the interests of the community require.[2]

It may be doubted whether Sidney Webb was really formulating a new principle, or merely translating into typical Fabian language a principle already accepted by progressive educationists. Many educationists of that time and today, with views as advanced as Webb's, would extend the principle of 'equality of opportunity' in such a way as to include the tremendous expansion of educational facilities for all that he desired. Webb preferred to use the language of 'Collectivism' to make it clear that he wanted no class distinction in education, not even a class distinction tempered by the provision of 'equality of opportunity' for those of 'golden metal' who were discovered (accidentally and surprisingly, it is assumed) amongst the lower class. He was deeply concerned by the wastage of ability which occured when economic pressure forced children to abandon their education for employment at too early an age. His strong feelings were shown in 1909 when he was addressing the Association of Technical Institutes and expressed his firm opinion that 'the proper occupation of youth up to twenty-one is in education and instruction'. The question was asked of him how the community was to get its class of hewers of wood and drawers of water, and Webb angrily replied:

I may be a dreamer of dreams, but I thought that the doctrine that education was only for a part of the nation was buried a hundred years ago: it certainly does not

[1] *Fabian News*, June 1894.   [2] *Ibid.* January 1903.

consort with twentieth century ideas to imagine that there is to be a class of hewers of wood and drawers of water. I want no class of hewers of wood and drawers of water: no class destined to remain there, and prevented from rising, because we do not provide for it. I cannot believe that we are only to provide the means of instruction for a certain limited number of people, who we think will rise, while the rest are to toil for our convenience. For our convenience! Who is to hew? Who is to deliver our bread? *Our* convenience! *Our* comfort! Our comfort is to stand in the way of enabling these people, our fellow citizens, to attain anything better than being mere hewers of wood and drawers of water! I must apologize for having been betrayed into a little heat, but I do object to the notion that, for our convenience, we are to keep people as hewers of wood and drawers of water.[1]

This little speech may be more unguarded, less 'reasonable' than nearly all the rest of Webb's carefully ordered writing and speaking, but it reveals the passion behind his equalitarian views. It would no doubt be an exaggeration to say that the Fabians formulated a new 'principle' in education, but their propaganda and their activity was designed to assist the general movement for larger and better educational opportunities for all.

The Fabians are entitled to their fair share of credit for the services rendered to elementary education by their representatives on the School Board, but to no more than other leading members of the Board. There do not seem to have been any special ways in which the Fabian Society directed or guided the Board's activities. The great change in the organization and control of elementary education, which some Fabians helped to promote, arose rather from their activities in the field of secondary and technical education, where the achievements of Sidney Webb were more spectacular.

Sidney Webb devoted his main attention during the eighteen years he was a member of the L.C.C. to the development of London's secondary education. Webb may indeed be called the creator of the Technical Education Committee of the L.C.C., and the Technical Education Board which grew out of it. Here again the achievement was less a matter of overcoming opposition, than of simply getting the thing done, and Webb did it. By the early 'nineties opposition to the development of technical education under L.C.C. control was slight. There was, of course, the usual dead-weight of apathy and stupidity, but by that time there was sufficient alarm about England's trade and industrial position relative to Germany's—a situation which was freely attributed to the better German system of technical education—to make the path of the reformer smoother than it might otherwise have been. In fact, the first steps had already been taken before any Fabians had been elected to the L.C.C. The Conservative government in 1889 had introduced a Bill to provide for technical education, and the Bill gave the power of levying the rate and of providing this technical education to the County Councils. The London School Board protested, claiming that in London it should have the rating

[1] Quoted: M. A. Hamilton, *Sidney and Beatrice Webb*, p. 120-1.

power. But Goschen, a convinced centralizer who took Germany for his model, forced the Bill through, and it became the Technical Instruction Act 1889. In the following year, as the result of a conflict between the government and the forces of Temperance, the 'whisky money' (the customs duty on beer and spirits levied under the Local Taxation, Customs and Excise Act 1890) was diverted by Goschen from the 'compensation of decayed publicans' to the subsidizing of technical education. Thus both the power and funds for technical education had been placed in the hands of the L.C.C. However, nothing was done about it during the lifetime of the first L.C.C.: the opportunity was wasted in a futile squabble with the City Corporation, when the L.C.C. tried to wrest from the Corporation still more money for educational purposes.

The Fabians determined to end this absurd situation. Shortly after his election Webb moved that a committee be appointed to examine the needs of technical education and the way in which the Council could best make use of its powers.[1] He suggested a list of names for a committee of twenty, in which he included himself and three other Fabian Councillors.[2] When the committee was appointed, it unanimously elected Webb its Chairman,[3] and he held this position until, early in 1893, the Technical Education Committee was converted into the Technical Education Board, with fifteen nominees of other organizations added to the twenty L.C.C. members. Once again this change was made on Webb's advice, to avoid the antagonism of these other bodies to exclusive L.C.C. control, and he became Chairman of the Board, a position which he continued to hold until 1898; he was Vice-Chairman of it in 1899 and 1900, and became Chairman again in 1901 and 1902.

Webb's first action as Chairman was to engage H. Llewellyn Smith to make a full survey of existing facilities and of London's needs for education above the primary level. Then, with the help of A. H. D. Acland, he secured the widest possible definition of the meaning of 'technical education' until, as he said himself, it included 'the teaching of every conceivable subject, other than ancient Greek and Theology'.[4] He also engaged as Secretary of the Technical Education Board a particularly able administrator, Dr William Garnett.[5] Between them, Webb and Garnett directed the Board's activities with such vigour and good management that it not only made an important contribution to the development of London's education; it also provided the answer to those who had argued that the London County Council's control would be less efficient than that of the School Board.

The Technical Education Board's method of dealing with established insti-

---

[1] L.C.C. Minutes, 1892, p. 392.
[2] Baum, Crooks, and Steadman (Baum retired shortly afterwards).
[3] L.C.C. Minutes, 1892, p. 444.
[4] *St Martin's Review*, December 1928: 'Reminiscences' by S. and B. Webb.
[5] B. M. Allen, *Memoir of Dr Garnett* (Heffer, Cambridge, 1933), contains much information about this period.

tutions was almost an object-lesson in Fabian permeative tactics. It preferred to subsidize existing educational institutions, encouraging them to improve and extend their teaching and equipment, rather than to set up new establishments, though new organizations, such as the London Day Training College and the Central School of Arts and Crafts, were created where there was clear need for them. But the general policy avoided delay in building up completely new institutions, avoided the friction which the competition of the new with the old would have caused, and established a 'unity in diversity' by introducing a measure of central supervision and control over otherwise autonomous bodies. In the final report of its ten years' work which the Technical Education Board handed to its successor, the Education Committee, in 1904, it was able to give an impressive list of its work along these lines.[1]

Sidney Webb was still prouder of his achievement in making available to a greater number of young Londoners the 'scholarship ladder' to higher education. When Llewellyn Smith reported in 1892, there was an elementary school roll of 680,000 pupils, yet the total number of scholarships available for them was only about 1000, and many of these had qualifications and obligations attached to them. Webb in 1893 got a resolution passed by the L.C.C. allowing the Technical Education Board to provide scholarships, and shortly afterwards the Board agreed to the award of 500 junior county scholarships annually. These scholarships entitled pupils at elementary schools to further education at secondary or higher grade schools, and, as a wise addition, they provided a maintenance grant of £10 a year 'to compensate parents to some extent for the loss of their children's earnings'. In later years, this 'scholarship ladder' was extended, and at the time the Technical Education Board handed over to its successor in 1904, the number of junior county awards had risen to 600, and there had been added to them 100 intermediate scholarships for pupils of sixteen to nineteen years, five senior scholarships, three teacher's travelling scholarships, thirty art scholarships, some 350 other scholarships for those taking technical, evening or continued instruction, and 800 odd domestic economy scholarships for women and girls.[2] Administratively, the expansion of the scholarship system had the same result as the Board's grants; as Beatrice Webb put it: 'What had previously been a chaos of isolated institutions, largely unaware of one another's existence, became gradually welded—without suppression of local administration by separate bodies of governors —into a graded educational system covering every part of London.'[3]

The administrative success of the Technical Education Board may have helped to convince the officials of the Education Department (not that they needed much convincing) that the control of education should be transferred

---

[1] Chairman's report of T.E.B. 1904 (Archives of County Hall).
[2] *Ibid.*
[3] B. Webb, *Our Partnership* (Longmans, London, 1948), p. 79.

from the School Boards to the County Councils. Beatrice Webb wrote, many years after, that Sidney Webb had decided this step was necessary as early as 1892.[1] If so, he did not take the Fabian Society into his confidence until some years later. It seems altogether more probable that Webb was not a prime initiator of this development, but that he was gradually convinced of the need for it by the investigations of the Royal Commission on Secondary Education of 1894-5, by his practical experience of the difficulties of divided control, and by the arguments of the Education officials of Whitehall, who had to cope with an 'education muddle' over a wider area than London. Certainly the Fabian Society came only slowly to accept the view that School Boards should be abolished. As late as 1897 the Fabian Society, while recognizing that the system of election of the School Board for London 'with its enormous electoral areas and its complicated cumulative vote' was 'costly and troublesome in operation', and failed 'to secure either satisfactory representation of minorities or genuine popular control', did not propose any greater change than that 'the election should take place in future on the widest printed register for the time being in force, and in constituencies identical with those for the Parliamentary and County Council elections'.[2] This was simply a restatement of their old demand for 'one register for all elections'. A similar resolution had been passed by the Fabian Society in 1895 and had been sent to members of Parliament, of the L.C.C., and the School Board;[3] and the principle had been set forth quite clearly eight years earlier still in *Facts for Londoners*.

Mr (Sir Robert) Morant, then an official of the Education Department in Whitehall, is given the credit by historians of education for preparing and launching the attack on the School Board's right to conduct secondary higher grade schools, which led to the Cockerton judgment in 1900 and eventually to the abolition of the School Boards.[4] His action was taken in close collaboration with Dr William Garnett, who persuaded the auditor Cockerton to disallow the payments made by the School Boards,[5] and there can be little doubt that Sidney Webb was aware of the plans. By the later 'nineties the Education Department officials believed that the County Council's administration of technical education had demonstrated adequately that it would be safe to centralize education under their control; Sidney Webb and Dr Garnett, on their side, had had experience of conflicts between the Technical Education Board and the School Board about their areas of authority in secondary education, which wasted time and money.

[1] *Ibid.* p. 63.
[2] *Fabian News*, August 1897.
[3] *Ibid.* November 1895.
[4] G. A. N. Lowndes, *The Silent Social Revolution* (O.U.P., 1937); L. Grier, *Achievement in Education: The Work of Michael Ernest Sadler 1885-1935* (Constable, London, 1952); B. M. Allen, *Sir Robert Morant: A Great Public Servant* (Macmillan, London, 1934.)
[5] L. Grier, *op. cit.* p. 73.

Before the Cockerton case was decided, the question was raised in the Fabian Society. At a Members' Meeting held in May 1899 to discuss the publication of a Tract to be called *The Education Muddle and the Way Out*, Sidney Webb proposed as 'general principles' the abolition of the School Boards and the transfer of their functions to the ordinary local government bodies. The opposition to his proposal was led by the Rev. Stewart Headlam, who was supported to some extent by Graham Wallas. Headlam was a root and branch opponent of the change; Wallas a less strenuous opponent. Headlam believed that the London School Board was well-adapted to its task, that it had done good work, and that the attack on it was unjustified. Wallas agreed with Webb that control of education by the L.C.C. would be better than control by an *ad hoc* body like the London School Board, but he feared that the L.C.C. might be over-worked, and he dreaded the invasion of party politics into the educational field.[1] Wallas's objections increased when it emerged that the Morant-Webb scheme envisaged state aid to church schools, as the bait to persuade the Conservative government to pass a suitable Act.

Webb's arguments which carried the majority of the Fabian Society against the opposition of Headlam and the doubts of Wallas were mainly concerned with administrative efficiency. He pointed out the conflicts which had arisen through the over-lapping jurisdiction of the two authorities, but he also argued more generally that the cleavage between elementary and secondary education was bad for both teachers and scholars: it made elementary teachers feel they belonged to a lower grade, and it prevented scholars seeing that there was an 'organic connection' between elementary and higher schooling. 'School Board members, concentrated on elementary education, get to think of elementary education as more important than all the rest of education, and ultimately regard it as all-important', he said. 'On the other hand, Technical Education authorities, though they may spell technical education with a very big E and a very small T, suffer from absurd restrictions. They have legal power to teach commercial history but not "history"; they can teach Latin to chemists' assistants but to no one else'. He reinforced his case with considerations of expense: two separate bodies meant greater cost with the money being expended on machinery rather than on education itself. Methods of overcoming this were propounded, but Webb considered them unsatisfactory. For instance, it was proposed to hold the School Board election on the same day as the L.C.C. election, but Webb thought that this kind of arrangement had not

[1] For Wallas' views see typescript article 'The Control of Education in London' in L.S.E. Library [Coll. Misc. 162]. M. A. Hamilton, *Sidney and Beatrice Webb*, p. 129, makes the Education Act the main reason for the estrangement between Wallas and Webb. This is not correct. In his letter announcing his resignation from the Fabian Society, Wallas mentioned disagreement on 'minor points' in education policy, but gave his disagreement with the Tariff Tract as the main reason for his resignation: *Fabian News*, February 1904. See also *Fabian News*, June 1899 and January 1903 for Wallas' guarded approval of the new Education Acts.

worked well in America and would result in education getting the 'tail of two tickets'. The best way of ensuring democratic election combined with administrative economy, he argued, was to put education under L.C.C. control; the School Board should give way because it was the less administratively efficient body. The counter-claim, that the L.C.C. was over-worked, he declared to be a 'Moderate bogey'. The L.C.C. was 'capable of doubling its present duties', he said, 'by the simple expedient of halving the size of its committees, which at present were made unnecessarily large . . . only to satisfy the insatiable demand of its members for more work to do'.[1]

The controversy within the Fabian Society was a protracted one and *The Education Muddle and the Way Out* was not published until 1901,[2] after long consideration by a Revision Committee, in which Graham Wallas played a considerable part. The Tract made some concession to the views of the opposition members. It advocated the principle of abolishing the School Boards, but it admitted that the School Boards of twenty or thirty of the largest cities were efficient and probably would prove too strongly intrenched to abolish, and on opportunistic grounds, the Fabians were willing to accept the position. The majority of Fabians came out in favour of the complete abolition only after the Cockerton appeal judgment in May 1901 had dealt its crippling blow to the activities of the more progressive School Boards. After the Cockerton judgment, legislation to mend or end the School Boards became necessary, and Fabians eventually decided for ending.

The sectarian issue played so great a part in the campaign for the Education Acts of 1902 and 1903 that the Fabians' attitude needs to be made clear. The legislation proposed by the Conservative government tied up the issue of County Council control with the support of Church schools out of the rates. The Liberal opposition (to which the Progressive Party in the L.C.C. was officially allied) made itself the defender of the School Boards in the interests of Noncomformity. Sidney Webb managed to persuade the majority of the Fabians to accept the price demanded by the Conservatives in order to achieve the reform, but his attitude cannot be described simply as an opportunistic one, because the consequences for himself were serious, resulting in an estrangement from both the Progressives and the Liberal leaders.[3] The Progressives could not, or would not, understand how the Rationalist Sidney Webb could

---

[1] *Fabian News*, January 1903 for all above quotations. H. G. Wells in his *Experiment in Autobiography*, pp. 67-8, adds a point about the social stigma which still clung to Board Schools that was probably also in Webb's mind: 'In spirit, form, and intention they were inferior schools, and to send one's children to them in those days, as my mother understood perfectly well, was a definite and final acceptance of social inferiority'.

[2] Tract 106.

[3] This estrangement was merely completed by the Education controversy (and, as far as the Radicals were concerned, the Boer War and Tariff controversies). It had been developing since November 1893 when Webb had shocked his Liberal allies by the article 'To Your Tents, Oh Israel!' (discussed in later chapters); Webb's attitude to the Metropolitan Borough Councils had brought him into further disfavour.

ally himself with 'clerical reaction'. Webb's Rationalism was non-militant and completely tolerationist, and he took the view that it was better to have efficient standards even if it involved some subsidy to religious teaching. As he expressed it himself later:

I had seen in the United States and Victoria (Australia) the consequences of such action; I did not like the policy of crushing out minorities. I thought the imposition of 'undenominational Christianity' as unfair to the Jews, Unitarians, and Secularists as the imposition of the Anglican Church catechism on Roman Catholics and Nonconformists, or of Roman Catholic formularies on Protestants. Moreover, I knew that the result would not be the closing of Roman Catholic Schools, but (as in the United States) their continuance entirely at private cost at a still lower level of efficiency, which would be calamitous for the very large and perhaps growing number of children who would resort to them. Above all, I wanted to preserve variety in education, rather than an officially prescribed uniformity—variety in methods of teaching, variety in the subjects taught, and variety in atmospheres. I wanted to leave the door open to new and unthought of experiments in schools.[1]

It is interesting to observe that the argument for subsidizing the Church schools was put to the Fabian Society by a 'non-militant atheist' like Webb, while the strongest opposition came from a Church of England clergyman (not, admittedly, a very orthodox one), the Rev. Stewart Headlam.

Did the Fabians have any influence in the Education Acts of 1902 and 1903? No doubt Fabian influence was slight amongst the causes which induced the Conservative government to bring forward its education Bills. The main explanation would be found in such factors as the failure of the smaller School Boards, the expensiveness of the Board system, the desire for centralization on the part of Sir John Gorst and the officials of the Education Department, the pressure from the Church, and the concern of some of the Conservatives about the state of the denominational schools.[2] But once the Conservative government had decided to introduce these Bills, it found information useful, and Webb and the Fabians ready to supply what was required. Prominent members of Parliament, from both sides of the House, frequented the Webbs' home at 41 Grosvenor Road, for instruction—Balfour and Gorst, Haldane, Asquith and Rosebery.[3] Rosebery was soon to break from the Webbs' influence, and join the Nonconformists' assault on the Education Bill, an event which probably confirmed the Fabians in their opinion that 'the ardour of their [certain Liberal leaders'] hostility to it is due to the fact that it affords an excellent opportunity for uniting the Liberal Party in an effective attack on the Conservative government'.[4] But Haldane refused to vote against the second reading of the Bill, and made a speech expressing sentiments similar to

[1] *St Martin's Review*, December 1928.
[2] G. A. N. Lowndes, *op. cit.* pp. 64, 67, 75, and ch. IV, *passim*.
[3] M. A. Hamilton, *op. cit.* p. 128.
[4] *Fabian News*, June 1902, cf. Lowndes, *op. cit.* ch. V.

Webb's.[1] On the other side, Sir John Gorst applied to the Fabian Society for a number of galley-pulls of *The Education Muddle and the Way Out* before its publication, for instruction of the permanent officials at Whitehall and the Parliamentary draftsmen.[2] The Tract, when it was published, had a good circulation amongst M.P.'s and other influential persons.[3] When the first Bill was actually before the House, the Fabians made some further suggestions for minor amendments and forwarded them to M.P.'s; some of these amendments were ultimately incorporated in the Bill before it became law.

The later Bill dealing with London created more difficulties for the Fabians in their temporary and uneasy alliance with the Conservatives. The whole situation was rather paradoxical: if it had not been for the sectarian issue, the Progressives, nurtured on J. F. B. Firth's centralizing doctrine, should have welcomed the transfer of the School Board's powers to the L.C.C., and the Moderates and Conservatives should have opposed it. Lord Salisbury had only shortly before described the L.C.C. as suffering from megalomania, and Joseph Chamberlain also had insisted that the Council was 'over-worked'. In fact, the government's first proposals for London had been distinctly unfavourable to the L.C.C. Encouraged by the success it had had in setting up the Metropolitan Water Board, the Conservative government proposed, in its original Bill, another such *ad hoc* authority, using the Metropolitan Borough Councils to offset the power of the L.C.C. The new education authority for London was to have ninety-seven members, thirty-six appointed by the L.C.C., an equal number by the Metropolitan Borough Councils, twenty-five to be co-opted experts, and five more (for the first five years) to represent the old School Board.

The proposal raised a storm of protest. The Fabian Society's Executive declared that 'the Government Bill proposed an administrative machinery which would, in the opinion of the Executive, create great friction and be nearly, if not quite, unworkable. The provisions of the Bill as to the formation of the Education Committee of the L.C.C., and as to the powers given to the Borough Councils, would be seriously detrimental to educational efficiency and progress'.[4] The Fabian Society thereupon adopted thirteen resolutions, suggesting definite amendments to the Education Bill, all designed to secure unified control under the L.C.C. The substance of eleven of these resolutions was adopted into the Bill before it finally became law, and one other was practically adopted;[5] but Fabian persuasion was not the only cause of this result. The original Bill pleased nobody. The School Board naturally opposed it; the L.C.C. declared that it would prefer the 'maintenance of the present system' to it, and the Progressives on the Council tacked on a resolution

---

[1] Hansard, vol. cvii, cols. 703–16.   [2] Pease, *op. cit.* p. 144.
[3] *Ibid.* (And see ch. vi hereof, above).   [4] *Fabian News*, June 1903.
[5] For a list of the resolutions and comments, *ibid.*

protesting against 'being required by law to make rates to be applied to the maintenance of denominational schools which are not under public control and in the payment of salaries to teachers, who, while paid wholly out of public money, are subjected to religious tests'.[1] It was plain to the government that it would unite the opposition against its main object by persisting. So the Fabian amendments were adopted, and the L.C.C. became the education authority for London.

The results for Webb personally of carrying his policy through to its conclusion were unfortunate. It meant an estrangement from the majority of the Progressives on the L.C.C.[2] Before the 1904 election, the Webbs, apprehensive of Progressive intentions, were secretly hoping for a Moderate victory![3] This did not occur, and the Progressives revenged themselves by keeping Sidney Webb out of all positions of importance and turning him off the Progressive Party Committee.[4] When the new Education Committee entered upon its duties in 1904, Webb was no longer Chairman. But they did not proceed to the final breach. The Fabians had not abandoned their hopes of influencing the Progressives, and some of the Progressive leaders were reluctant to lose the Fabians' expert knowledge of educational affairs. Consequently four Fabians—Sidney Webb, Graham Wallas, W. S. Sanders, and Susan Lawrence—were appointed to the first Education Committee. In the subordinate position of Chairman of the Scholarships and Higher Education Sub-committee, Webb helped to devise an extension of the 'scholarship ladder'. However, Webb was not happy about the Progressives' attitude to the Education Acts, during the years when the Nonconformist Liberals were agitating for their repeal, and he was not sorry when the position was secured, so far as the L.C.C. was concerned, by the victory of the Moderates (under their new name of 'Municipal Reformers') in 1907, though it must be said that Webb's worst fears were groundless and that the Progressives showed great forbearance in refraining from sabotaging the Education Act. The hope Webb expressed in his *London Education* of 1904, that the new Education Acts would be given a sincere trial for the sake of England's education proved, when feelings had simmered down, not a vain one.

The Fabian Society's next major intervention in the educational field occurred during the campaign to obtain an Act for the provision of meals to schoolchildren. This demand had been prominent in early Fabian propaganda, as well as in that of the S.D.F., but for a number of years in the late 'nineties and in the first years of the twentieth century it had not been vigorously pressed. The Society had come to regard it as somewhat 'impracticable', after

---

[1] L.C.C. Minutes, 1903, p. 622.
[2] The estrangement was particularly from the Nonconformist rank-and-file of the party, less from the old Progressive leaders who respected Webb's integrity and worth.
[3] B. Webb, *Our Partnership*, p. 281.
[4] *Ibid.* p. 308.

hearing a report from Graham Wallas, who had investigated the problem for the London School Board. For various reasons of organization, he had concluded that London was not the best place in which to make the experiment.[1] The demand was taken up by the Society again in 1905 when it issued Hubert Bland's Tract *After Bread, Education*.[2] It was significant that Bland should have written this Tract, because he, through his journalistic activities, was more in contact with the Labour movement in the north of England than many of the other Fabian leaders, and the revival of the campaign for the 'State feeding of school children' owed more to the humanitarian influences from the north than it did to the Fabians. Certainly, the Fabians reinforced it, but the carrying of the Education (Provision of Meals) Act 1906 must be attributed primarily to the I.L.P. men who pressed it upon the Liberals at a favourable moment, during the first flush of victory in 1906. The chief credit must go to F. W. Jowett, who more than any other person was responsible for the Labour Party's Bill.[3] In any case, the importance of the Act must not be exaggerated, though it was the best that could be secured at that time. It was an enabling and not a compulsory measure, and a compromise also between private charity and positive State action. It enabled local authorities to put buildings and facilities at the disposal of voluntary associations providing meals for school children 'unable by reason of lack of food to take full advantage of the education provided for them'; and, if the funds of voluntary associations were insufficient, the authority was enabled (with the approval of the Board of Education) to expend up to the produce of a halfpenny rate in providing these meals itself. So far as the London County Council was concerned, the Fabians were not conspicuously successful in persuading the Municipal Reformers to take advantage of the Act.

(2) *Advanced education*

The Fabian Society made a more decisive contribution to the provision of advanced education in London. 'It is today amazing,' Sidney Webb wrote in 1928,[4]

to think how minute was the provision for economic teaching, and how lacking that for economic research, in the London of the last decade of the century. King's College had a nominal professorship which was suspended.[5] Professor Foxwell held a Chair at University College, but had only a score of students, reported to be 'one-half coloured'. A rather elementary course of lectures (which I had attended in my youth) was annually repeated at the Birkbeck College. That was all that existed in the

[1] Pease, *op. cit.* p. 148; *Fabian News*, February 1896.
[2] Tract 120.
[3] F. Brockway, *Socialism over Sixty Years: the Life of Jowett of Bradford* 1864-1944 (Allen & Unwin, London, 1946), pp. 78-9.
[4] *St Martin's Review*, December 1928.
[5] This was not quite accurate. See Hayek, *Economica*, February 1946, N.S. vol. XIII, No. 49, p. 2.

capital of the British Empire for a population comparable to that of the whole of Scotland (or Belgium or Holland), each of them having several universities. Nor was there any dissatisfaction. The pundits[1] solemnly declared that the existing provision met the entire demand; and as they also suggested, amply supplied the whole need.

The foundation of the London School of Economics in 1895 by the Fabians opened a new era in the study of the social sciences in London.

The 'L.S.E.' began humbly 'in two small hired rooms in John Street, Adelphi destitute even of a promise of endowment, without professor or students, and devoid of any visible chance of academic status'.[2] It had had its origins when the Trustees of the money left under Henry Hutchinson's will for 'the propaganda and other purposes of the [Fabian] Society and its Socialism and towards advancing its objects in any way' had been persuaded by the Webbs to use half the fund to establish a school 'on the lines of the École Libre des Sciences Politiques in Paris'.[3] The use of the money in this way involved some casuistry, as the Webbs were well aware,[4] but it shows how confident the Webbs were at that time of the results of social science. In addition to their general disposition to believe that a scientific study of society would strengthen the case for Socialism, the Webbs at that time were excited by the notion that they had discovered a new approach to economics.

There was certainly no attempt to make the L.S.E. an institution for the teaching of specifically 'Socialist' economics. The first director of the School was W. A. S. Hewins, who had impressed Webb both by his writings and by the plans he had presented for the reorganization of economic teaching in London on the occasion of his unsuccessful candidature for the Professorship of Economics at King's College.[5] Hewins was far from being a Socialist or a Fabian, but like Webb, he was in revolt against orthodox economics and strongly influenced by the Historical School. Later he became a Protectionist and a Conservative M.P.; in 1903 he resigned his directorship of the L.S.E. to become Secretary to the 'Tariff Commission' which was to develop and organize Joseph Chamberlain's propaganda. During their association Webb and Hewins were equally determined to make the L.S.E. the centre for teaching a kind of down-to-earth sociological economics very different from the theoretical and philosophical economics taught at the older centres of learning.[6]

[1] It is not quite clear who Webb meant by 'the pundits'. As Lord Beveridge has pointed out (Margaret Cole (ed.), *The Webbs and their Work*, p. 46), the establishment of a School of Economics in London had already been advocated by T. H. Huxley and the British Association.
[2] Webb, *St Martin's Review*, December 1928.
[3] W. A. S. Hewins, *The Apologia of an Imperialist* (Constable, London, 1929), vol. I, p. 25.
[4] Margaret Cole, (ed.), *The Webbs and their Work*, pp. 43–4. Bernard Shaw at first and J. R. MacDonald and other I.L.P. men later, opposed the use of Hutchinson money to establish an impartial academic institution. Janet Beveridge, *An Epic of Clare Market* (G. Bell & Sons, London, 1960), pp. 27, 41–4.
[5] W. A. S. Hewins, *op. cit.* vol. I, p. 23.
[6] B. Webb, *Our Partnership*, p. 195.

If they showed any bias in their selection, it was an academic rather than political one. But the early lecturers were a most distinguished, and sufficiently various collection of men.[1]

The L.S.E. was finally put on a firm basis when it became part of the University of London. Until this step was taken, its financial affairs required delicate management on the part of its Administrative Committee, of which Sidney Webb was the Chairman and most active member.[2] Additional financial assistance was required from the Webbs' richer friends,[3] and Webb was able to make small grants from the Technical Education Board's 'whisky money'. The permanency and the fortunes of the School were not secured until it became part of the University of London; thereafter (but in part through the activity and persuasion of the Webbs) the L.S.E. received generous endowments. The incorporation of the L.S.E. into the University of London was again due to the influence of Sidney Webb, for the new constitution of the University, which appeared in 1900, after two Royal Commissions, the Act of 1898, and a Statutory Commission, was largely the work of Webb and R. B. (Lord) Haldane. In his autobiography, Haldane has paid handsome tribute to the part played by Webb in the reoganization of the University of London.[4]

Sidney Webb later regarded the constitution of the London University as a compromise between those who wanted to establish a new, unified teaching University, and those who wished to join the existing University, which was purely an examining body, with the existing teaching colleges in London;[5] but it is interesting to observe how much of Webb's own views were embodied in the 'compromise'. Webb's views were set forth in two articles he contributed to the *Nineteenth Century and After* and the *Cornhill Magazine*, that were subsequently recast into a chapter of his book *London Education*.[6] He rejected as impracticable any attempt to organize London University along the lines of Oxford and Cambridge; he did not want for London a residential University capable of taking only an elite, with a bias towards the Classics and the leisurely liberal education of an earlier age. He was far from ignoring the importance of the artistic and cultural side in university education, but his own bias was clearly towards a non-residential, democratic University providing for as many students as possible, with the emphasis on science and vocational training. His concept of science was a wide one, however, and it included the application of the scientific method to social studies, to the study of languages

---

[1] Hayek, *Economica*, February 1946, pp. 5–9; Hewins, *op. cit.* p. 31.

[2] The other members were all Fabians: they were Mrs Webb, Miss Payne-Townshend, Dr William Garnett, William Clarke, E. R. Pease, Sydney Olivier, and Hubert Bland.

[3] Miss Payne-Townshend (later Mrs Bernard Shaw) assisted the L.S.E. in its early days. Later John Passmore Edwards found the money to commence the building on its present site in Clare Market.

[4] R. B. Haldane, *An Autobiography* (Hodder & Stoughton, London, 1929), pp. 124–7.

[5] Margaret Cole (ed.), *The Webbs and their Work*, pp. 45–6.

[6] S. Webb, *London Education* (Longmans, London, 1904), p. 48 *et seq.*

and literature, in addition to the subjects more usually labelled 'scientific', and he emphasized strongly the importance of research as well as of teaching.

This [Webb declared], involves the revival of the older conception of a university course deliberately framed so as to prepare the undergraduate from the outset for the practical pursuit of his profession, but in such a way as to turn him out equipped, not only as a trained professional, but also as a cultivated citizen. The London University, like the universities of Medieval Europe, and modern America, will therefore necessarily take on the character of a technical school for all the brain-working professions of its time—not alone law, medicine, and theology, but also every department of science and learning, from engineering and chemistry to peda-gogy, banking and commerce and public administration. Some may regret this limitation, but the practical men will see in it a great opportunity.[1]

In policy, Webb advocated the organization of the University by faculties, rather than by colleges. This did not mean that there was no place for separately organized institutions and largely autonomous bodies; on the contrary, Webb approved of these and their multiplication, but he insisted that they should all be co-ordinated through the faculty organization. Webb favoured the dispersal of teaching centres as widely as possible through London, but the concentration of post-graduate research students into one or two of the highest colleges. The teaching and research staff should be graded in different levels, and promotion should be strictly by ability, not seniority. The Senate should have real controlling power, and in particular the 'power of the purse' to make its co-ordinating authority real. Furthermore, the Senate should be 'a strong representative body essentially lay in character' to avoid academic vested interests.

Through his collaboration with Haldane and Balfour, Webb's recommend-ations were largely carried into effect in the reorganization of the University of London. From 1900–9, Webb was himself a member of its Senate. The outstanding mark of his influence was the establishment of the Faculty of Economics and Political Science, which included the London School of Economics and appears to have been 'created expressly for the School to dominate'.[2] The School was admitted as one of the Schools of the University in 1900 and its lecturers became teachers of the University. After its admission the Constitution of the School was regularized by obtaining incorporation, in June 1901, as a company 'limited by guarantee and without power of making profits'[3] controlled by a Board of Governors of which the Bishop of London

---

[1] Ibid. pp. 52–3.
[2] St Martin's Review, December 1928.
[3] Article 28 of the Articles of Association reads: 'No religious, political or economic test or qualification shall be made a condition for or disqualify from receiving any of the benefits of the Corporation, or holding an office therein; and no member of the Corporation or professor, lecturer or other officer thereof shall be under any disability or disadvantage by reason only of any opinions that he may hold or promulgate on any subject whatsoever'.

(Mandell Creighton) became the first President and Sidney Webb the Chairman. The course for the degree of B.Sc. (Econ.), devoted to the social sciences, introduced in 1901, became the first university degree of such a kind in England.

Since that time the London School of Economics has gone from strength to strength under the successive Directorships of Sir Halford Mackinder, the Hon. William Pember Reeves, Sidney Webb himself, Sir William Beveridge, and Sir Alexander Carr-Saunders, the Presidencies of Lord Rosebery and Lord Rothschild, and the Chairmanship of the Board of Governors of Sidney Webb from the beginning to 1911, and his successors the Rt Hon. Russell Rea, Sir Arthur Steel-Maitland, and Sir Josiah Stamp. The L.S.E. has become one of the permanent and important colleges of the United Kingdom. But was there, perhaps, an element of defeat in its very success? Has not its successful merging into the educational establishment meant the loss of a good part of the distinctive character that the Webbs originally intended for it? The study of economics at least did not develop in the way that they had hoped; but the rule the Webbs exercised over their creature was light, and perhaps they were satisfied.

MUNICIPAL SOCIALISM

The examples we have considered of the Fabians' influence illustrate their administrative work within the limits of the Progressive policy. The Fabians could have done these things if they had been merely Radicals, not Socialists at all. Of course, when Socialists and Radicals both desired better educational facilities, more scholarships and better municipal government, the Fabians cannot be criticized as Socialists for having pursued these objectives; but are these things *really* 'Municipal Socialism' or Radicalism? The answer must be that they are both, but that 'Municipal Socialism' leads one to expect other things as well.

In their practical suggestions for municipal ownership and administration the Fabians, as we have seen, did not at first press too far ahead of Radical opinion. In *Facts for Londoners* the Fabians confined their demands for socialization to certain specific public services: water, gas, tramways, docks, markets, baths and wash-houses, and cemeteries—the last, which involved free burial, being recommended with the tart observation that 'communism in funerals' was not likely to lead to a 'reckless increase in the demand for graves'. The extent to which the Progressives had already accepted the idea of bringing these services under L.C.C. control before the Fabians had appeared on the scene may be discovered. There is clear evidence of the opinions of seventy-four members of the first L.C.C. (out of 118) on the question of municipalizing the eight water companies, and of them no less than seventy expressed themselves in favour of L.C.C. control, and this number included several who would be classed as Moderates;[1] it is also probable that others whose opinions are not easily traced were also in favour. In the matter of municipalizing the gas companies of London (which competition had reduced to three by the 'eighties—from twenty in 1855), the opinions of seventy-three members are recorded, and of them sixty-five were in favour, while eight were definitely opposed to the change.[2] A measure of the support for L.C.C. ownership, if not of L.C.C. management, of London's fourteen tramway companies can also be given, for this issue was fought out on the first L.C.C. before any Fabians were elected, and the statutory two-thirds of the members of Council voted in favour of purchasing them.[3]

The Fabians could make valid claim to be the originators of the moves for 'Municipal Socialism' in one only of these services. Their pamphlets had been the earliest and clearest of those demanding a Port Authority, and the L.C.C. resolution which began the agitation for it was actually moved by a member of the Society, Ben Tillett.[4] The extension of the L.C.C.'s power over the London docks was acceptable to the Progressives. But this was the one and only substantial extension of 'Municipal Socialism' that the Progressives did accept at the Fabians' suggestion. When, from the late 'nineties, the Fabians at last ventured to recommend extensions in the direction of municipal trading in the supply of liquor, milk, and bread, municipal fire insurance and the municipal ownership of pawnshops, they were severely rebuffed. The weakness of the Fabian position was then exposed. In the enthusiasm and high hopes which attended the early days of the L.C.C. many Fabians, including Sidney Webb, imagined that the first steps in municipalization would be treated as nonparty and soon taken. This was an illusion due to the fact that London lagged so far behind the other cities of the kingdom in municipal administration. As London rapidly caught up, party divisions sharpened when some groups wished to press further forward while others thought 'progress' had gone far enough. At first there was a division into a Progressive Party faced with a weak Moderate opposition, then the development of a strong Moderate Party which soon after took the more appealing name of 'Municipal Reformers', finally in 1910 the emergence of the Labour Party. The Fabians discovered that they were dependent on obtaining the approval of a party if their measures were to be carried, and, for the period we are considering, this meant the approval of

[1] *Dod's L.C.C. Directory*, 1889.
[2] *Ibid.*
[3] L.C.C. Minutes 1891, pp. 1058–9: The amendment, 'That this Council in passing this resolution, has no intention of itself working, or seeking power to work, the Tramways therein referred to', which was tacked to the resolution for acquiring the trams, cannot be taken as expressing the real opinion of the majority of Progressives. It was a tactical move, made necessary because the statute required two-thirds of the members of the Council to be present and voting on a resolution of purchase, and by retiring to the galleries and smoking-room the Moderates could prevent a quorum (see Minutes L.C.C. 1891, pp. 596 and 733) until the Progressives won over sufficient waverers by agreeing to the amendment.
[4] L.C.C. Minutes 1896, pp. 341–2.

the Progressive Party, as the Labour Party was not strong enough. The reasons why the Fabians did not have much success in persuading the Progressives further in the direction of 'Municipal Socialism' are not far to seek. There was always a certain amount of self-delusion about Municipal Socialism, in so far as the Fabians were adapting themselves to Radical demands, not leading the Radicals forward; and the Progressives, while they did not disdain the Fabians' help in demands common to them both, were determined not to be led up the socialist path. Moreover, as time went on, friction developed between the partners, and the Fabians offended the Progressives not only by their attacks on Liberals in national politics, but also by their attitude to the Metropolitan Borough Councils and to the Conservative Party's Education Acts. When by about 1910 the older generation of Progressive leaders who had been brought up on J. F. B. Firth's doctrines had either retired or moved on to the higher sphere of national politics, and the Nonconformists under Scott Lidgett had come into control of the Progressive Party, Fabian influence was practically at an end.

During the 'nineties the Fabians played a fairly active propaganda role in encouraging the Progressives to bring under L.C.C. control the services of water, gas, the markets, the trams, the docks, and in urging or approving such ventures as the L.C.C. Works Department, and the municipal Thames Steam-boats service. It comes as rather a surprise, however, to observe that the personal role of their representatives in the 'socializing' committees of the L.C.C. was neither as prominent nor as active as was Sidney Webb's on the Technical Education Committee. R. C. Phillimore 'worked hard' on the High-ways Committee[1] which controlled the trams, and W. C. Steadman was for a while Vice-Chairman of the Rivers Committee,[2] but the leadership of the 'socializing' part of the L.C.C. programme was taken by non-socialist Pro-gressives like (Sir) John Williams Benn[3] and W. H. (Lord) Dickinson. To a certain extent the Fabians may have considered it wise to remain in the background on these committees.

The campaign to bring these services under L.C.C. control was a long struggle, ending for the most part in defeat for the Progressives—or at least, in a result other than the one they or the Fabians had desired and expected. The Progressives' attempt to acquire the markets met, as in the Spitalfields case (1899–1901), with the fierce opposition not only of the owners, but also of the City Corporation backed by the House of Lords, and was defeated.[4]

[1] S. Webb, *Nine Years' Work on the L.C.C.: A Letter to the Electors of Deptford*, (leaflet).
[2] Vote of thanks to Steadman for his services in this capacity, L.C.C. Minutes 1901, p. 310.
[3] A. G. Gardiner, *John Benn and the Progressive Movement* (Ernest Benn, London, 1925), p. 124. 'John Benn was never a Socialist . . . He was a Radical . . . But the public ownership of public monopolies was an indestructible part of his creed'.
[4] Percy Harris, *London and its Government* (J. M. Dent & Sons, London, 1933), pp. 214–223.

The demand for the municipalization of gas was dropped by the Progressives themselves, in spite of Fabian protests,[1] because they feared that gas would be entirely superseded by electricity.[2] In three services only did the L.C.C. become the controlling authority in a socialist sense: the trams, the Thames Steamboats, and the Works Department. Two of these were ended by the Municipal Reformers when they came to power, and the trams were eventually[3] absorbed into the London Transport Board. The only instance in which socialization came and remained *somewhat* in the way the Fabians had advocated was that of the Port of London Authority—and in that case the Fabians had not recommended L.C.C. control but had approved the example of the Mersey Docks and Harbour Board. In the other cases where the services were socialized, the early Fabian-Progressive plans for L.C.C. control did not eventuate, but *ad hoc* authorities of a new type were developed: the Water Board, the Joint Electricity Committee, and the Transport Board. In the long run, Municipal Socialism succumbed to State Socialism.

However, Municipal Socialism, if only on a very small scale, did have its day in London. Sidney Webb, in his election address of 1901, claimed that the L.C.C. tramways had proved an unqualified success,[4] and historians of the enterprise appear to endorse his claim. In 1894 the Progressives decided to ask Parliament for power to work the tramways[5] (despite the amendment they had agreed to at the time of their acquisition[6]) and a Bill giving the L.C.C. this power was passed in 1896.[7] Under the direct management of the Highways Committee, the service was made more efficient, projects of electrification were carried out, fares were reduced, and the conditions of employees were improved by higher wages and decreased hours of work. Yet the L.C.C. tramways also became profitable undertakings, and survived until they were superseded by other forms of transport, and were taken over by London Transport Board. The lion's share of the credit for the efficiency of London's municipal tramways has rightly been claimed by his biographer for Sir John Benn, but a share of praise is due to the Fabian, R. C. Phillimore.

No such unequivocal success story can be told of the other two L.C.C. undertakings, but the Works Department was important as the L.C.C.'s first venture into 'direct employment'. The experiments which led to its formation

[1] The Fabians continued to issue their Tract 32, and reprinted a second edition of it at the end of the 'nineties.

[2] This was gleefully anticipated by W. J. Devenish, who styled himself the Hon. Secretary of the Anti-One Municipality League, in his pamphlet *Municipal Reform Leaguers: Absolute Centralization Knocked into a Cocked Hat: Firth Dissected* (Judd & Co., London, 1883): 'All his arguments as to Gas and the Central Council have been completely electrified by the electric light', p. 32.

[3] In 1933.

[4] S. Webb, *Nine Years' Work on the L.C.C.* . . . (leaflet).

[5] L.C.C. Minutes, 1894, p. 906.

[6] See footnote 3, p. 223.

[7] Most other great municipalities had possessed this power since 1880.

and its prosperous beginnings helped to convince some timid Progressives that L.C.C. management of the trams would be practicable. Ridiculous as the controversy over it seems at half a century's distance, the Works Department was the very storm centre of the dispute about Municipal Socialism in London. The establishment of this Department was thought to mark the point where Radicalism crossed the boundary into Socialism, where it passed from mere public ownership to public management and the 'direct employment of labour'. The Fabians advocated and defended the move hotly for they saw it as the crucial 'economic heresy',[1] and also as the outcome of the Trade Unions' 'fair wages' policy. John Burns on the first L.C.C. had been chiefly responsible for persuading the Council to include in its contracts a 'fair wages' clause, and when tenders were few and high, Moderates claimed that this was a result of the 'fair wages' policy, while Progressives retorted that contractors were entering into deliberate combination to force the Council to abandon the policy. These disputes led to several experiments in 'direct employment', which resulted in considerable saving when costs were compared with contractors' tenders.[2] The Progressives were convinced, and the Council on a party vote decided, in November 1893, to establish a Works Department with a separate staff under a Works Committee, which to ensure probity, was to consist of an equal number of members of both parties. Sidney Webb, ever ready with such facts, defended the 'principle of eliminating the contractor' on the ground that it was not new, and that Birmingham did it, and so did Liverpool.[3]

The wretched Works Department had to carry on its business for fifteen years under a ceaseless fire of criticism from the Moderates. The position of its successive managers was no easy one, and the record of the Department on the whole seems creditable, though there was a scandal over 'cooked' accounts in 1896-7.[4] The Fabians helped the London Reform Union to defend it during its severest trial in the pamphlet *The Truth about the Works Department*. But the Municipal Reformers (*ci-devant* Moderates) were implacable, and abolished the Department on their accession to power,[5] even though their own auditor reported: 'My investigation leads me to the belief that the present position of the department from a commercial point of view indicates sound and careful management, with efficient and accurate recording of the department's transactions.'[6]

If the Municipal Reformers' abolition of the Works Department was inspired by a fanatical anti-Socialist attitude, their action in getting rid of the

[1] S. Webb, *The Economic Heresies of the London County Council* (leaflet), 1894; *Three Years Work on the L.C.C.* . . . (leaflet), 1895; Fabian Tract 84, *The Economics of Direct Employment*, 1897.
[2] Especially the construction of the York Road sewer.
[3] S. Webb, *Three Years' Work on the L.C.C.* . . . (leaflet).
[4] L.C.C. Minutes, 1896, p. 1255.
[5] *Ibid.* 1908, vol. II pp. 283-94.
[6] *Ibid.* 1907, vol. II p. 1308.

L.C.C.'s Thames Steamboats about the same time could perhaps be justified on the grounds of economy. Yet the establishment of this service had been one of the L.C.C.'s most popular moves, having the support of some of the riverside Boroughs and even of some Moderates on the Council.[1] Though the project was not in origin a Fabian one, the Fabians took up warmly the proposal for a further extension of municipal enterprise, and while the enabling Bill was under consideration by Parliament, the Society produced, in 1900, its Tract No. 97, advocating 'Municipal Steamboats'. After some delay, caused by difficulties in coming to terms with a private company which operated in the summer months,[2] the L.C.C.'s service was inaugurated in June 1905, with a fleet of thirty steamboats. When it appeared, after a winter's experience, that the boats were not a paying proposition, and that they were catering mainly for pleasure-seekers and not workers or business people, the Fabians and Progressives who continued to defend their existence were obliged to change their ground and maintain that it was worth the very small addition to the rates to provide a healthy outing for Londoners.[3] *The Times* was not amused, and launched a thunderbolt against 'Municipal Socialism' and extravagance during the 1907 election campaign; the Steamboats, along with the Works Department, were the chosen sacrifices offered up in the Municipal Reformers' victory.

There were two main reasons—one technical, one political—why the other services which were socialized were not placed under L.C.C. control. The Water Board was brought into existence not because of the technical requirements of the service, but because the Conservative government disliked the L.C.C. as 'a haunt of Radicals and Socialists', and was therefore ready to lend a sympathetic ear to the claims of other interests. Though the presence of the Fabians on the Council may have helped to stiffen the Conservatives in their opposition, the Fabians played no major or independent part in the moves for the expropriation of the water companies. Certainly the Fabian Society supported the Progressive Party by issuing leaflets[4] and calling meetings,[5] and it is true that Sidney Webb was a member of the Water Committee from 1892 to 1895. But Webb did not hold the chairmanship or vice-chairmanship of that Committee, nor is there any evidence that he played a leading part in it. Webb did not serve on the Water Committee after 1895, and no other Fabian was ever a member of it. Special Fabian pressure was not required, because

---

[1] *Ibid.* 1897, p. 1182.
[2] The Thames Steamboat Company, which no doubt had been following with interest the negotiations of the L.C.C. and the government with the water and dock companies, suggested the formation of a Thames Steamboats Trust, with three members appointed by each the L.C.C., the City Corporation, the Thames Conservancy, and itself! L.C.C. Minutes, 1903, p. 838.
[3] S. Webb and R. C. Phillimore, *Fifteen Years' Work on the L.C.C.* (leaflet).
[4] Tracts 34, 81.
[5] *Fabian News*, April 1895.

the majority of the Committee had always been as convinced of the need for 'water municipalization' as the Fabians themselves were. The Committee had been set up by the first L.C.C. with James Beal, a veteran municipal reformer, as its first Chairman;[1] so strong was the support for L.C.C. control of the water companies among the members of the first L.C.C., that doctrinaire objections to the acquisition were treated with scant respect, and even laughed at.[2] Sir John Lubbock (later Lord Avebury) who favoured municipal control of the water companies, but not their purchase and management by the L.C.C. found himself by his own confession in a very small minority on the Committee.[3]

The municipalization was delayed by a suggestion that the L.C.C. should not bother about the water companies, but should render them obsolete by opening an entirely new source of supply through lengthy aqueducts stretching to Wales and the Wye Valley. The investigation of this problem involved a Royal Commission, presided over by Lord Balfour of Burleigh, and its findings[4] led to the decision to proceed with the Bills for the expropriation of the water companies. Unfortunately for the Progressives, the Liberal government under Rosebery fell from power when the Bills had passed their second reading in the House of Commons, and the Conservative government refused to allow them to proceed unless they were amended in a way that had originally been suggested by spokesmen of the City Corporation and certain vestries, namely by substituting control of a Water Trust for control by the L.C.C. itself, and by substituting conditions of purchase more favourable to the companies. The Progressives rejected these terms, and a stalemate resulted, which was not broken until there was a threat of a 'water-famine' in the East End of London. The government then set up another Royal Commission in 1897, under the chairmanship of Lord Llandaff, which in 1900 produced a plan for a Water Board of thirty members, one-third to be nominated by the L.C.C., and the remainder by various other local authorities in and around London. The Progressives were sufficiently indignant at this proposal, but when the government's Bill actually provided for a Board of sixty-nine members, with a representation for the L.C.C. of ten, they gave vent to their anger in a series of resolutions, one of which read: 'That the interests of the people of London in the acquisition and administration of the water-supply are so vital that they ought not to be entrusted to a Water Board nominated by seventy-eight authorities and independent of public control.'[5] The Fabian Society's attitude was more compliant. Its resolution, passed at the time, ran

[1] William Saunders, *op. cit.* p. 45.
[2] *Ibid.* p. 533.
[3] Royal Commission on London Water Supply, 1899–1900, Appendices, vol. XXIX, pt. 1, p. 310.
[4] Royal Commission on Metropolitan Water Supply, 1893, Report, pp. 28 and 71–2.
[5] L.C.C. Minutes, 1902, pp. 182–9.

as follows: 'While regretting that the Government has not made the London County Council the water authority, the executive welcomes the acceptance by the Government of the two cardinal principles that the water-supply should be under public control and that no special payment should be made for compulsory purchase', and it went on to make some polite suggestions for reducing the size of the Board and amending the terms of purchase.[1] The Conservative government did in fact allow a very slight reduction in the size of the Board[2] and a slight increase in the L.C.C.'s representation,[3] but these did not satisfy the Fabians, who joined in the Progressives' futile last minute protest against the London Water Act of 1902.[4]

When the Water Board was established, the merits and defects of control by a Board as contrasted with control by the L.C.C. had been extensively debated, but it does not appear that the nature of the service itself made the choice of a Board necessary. London's water-supply could have been administered by a committee of the L.C.C. (on which other organizations would have had representation) if political considerations had not decided the matter. But in the case of the other main service which was socialized before 1918, London's docks and port, it was clear that technical requirements made direct L.C.C. control impossible. No one really disputed the view that the complexity of the organization of London's docks, their size and their importance to the nation as a whole demanded control by a Port Authority created expressly for that purpose. The committee of investigation set up by the Rivers Committee of the L.C.C. on the motion of Ben Tillett in 1896 found that there were fifty-six authorities having some measure of control over the port of London. The subject had not been investigated for a century (since 1799), and even after four years work, the Committee was obliged to complain that only a Royal Commission could deal with it satisfactorily. The L.C.C. therefore decided to urge the government to take the investigation in hand,[5] and shortly afterwards a Royal Commission was appointed, with Earl Egerton of Tatton[6] as its chairman.

The report of this Royal Commission, which appeared in June 1902, met with the general approval of the Progressives. It confirmed fears that London was likely to lose its 'position relatively to other ports, British and foreign, which it has held so long', and it emphasized the general agreement among many sections of the community that a Port of London Authority should be established. 'It has been shown that there exists in London among shipowners,

---

[1] *Fabian News*, March 1902.
[2] From 69 to 66.
[3] From 10 to 14.
[4] L.C.C. Minutes, 1902, pp. 1874–8. Sidney Webb was appointed one of the L.C.C.'s first representatives on the new Water Board. He was a member in 1904–5.
[5] L.C.C. Minutes, 1900, pp. 222–5.
[6] Earl Egerton later retired and Lord Revelstoke became Chairman.

merchants, and representative bodies a powerful consensus of opinion in favour of the consolidation of powers at present divided, and the creation of a single public authority for the control and improvement of the port. In these circumstances we strongly recommend that such an authority should be constituted.'[1] Though the Royal Commission by no means accepted the Progressives' proposals about the financial and constitutional arrangements of the Port Authority, its recommendations were sufficiently liberal to be acceptable to them.[2] But when the Conservative government introduced its Bill in April 1903, its provisions were much less liberal than those recommended by the Royal Commission, and the Progressives (including the Fabians) immediately took up a more hostile attitude. Once again the bone of contention was the degree of control which the L.C.C. was to exercise. The Conservative government was willing to allow the L.C.C. to appoint only one fifth of the members of the new Authority; the Progressives demanded a clear majority representation.[3] The government's Bill lapsed because the L.C.C. refused to undertake its financial commitments on the government's terms; and a Bill promoted by the Progressives was rejected in Parliament when Bonar Law announced that the government objected principally to the large representation of the L.C.C.[4]

When the matter was taken up again, there had been a change of government both in Parliament and the L.C.C. The Municipal Reformers when they came to power did not dispute the need for a Port Authority. On the contrary, they sent a roving commission from the Rivers Committee to visit other ports in England and abroad, which on its return emphasized the need for action.[5] But the Municipal Reformers were determined to reverse the Progressives' policy: they wanted to keep the representation of the L.C.C. on the new Authority to a minimum, and they wanted correspondingly small financial commitments towards it.[6] They had their way: the Liberal government accepted the situation, and when the Port of London Authority was established in 1908, eighteen of its members, apart from the Chairman and Vice-Chairman, were elected by the payers of dues, wharfingers, and owners of river craft, while ten were appointed by various local government bodies, and of these ten, the L.C.C. appointed only four, two being members of the Council and two not being members of the Council. Thus the Port of London Authority came into being as the Fabians and Progressives had urged, but its composition was not such as they desired. Throughout, the Fabians had supported the Progressives' actions.

---

[1] Report, paragraphs 260 and 261.
[2] L.C.C. Minutes, 1901, pp. 77–82 for L.C.C.'s case to Royal Commission; *Ibid.* 1902, pp. 1073–80 for general approval.
[3] *Ibid.* 1903, pp. 796–807; *Ibid.* 1904, vol. II, pp. 2561–8.
[4] *Ibid.* 1905, vol. I p. 2133.
[5] *Ibid.* 1907, vol. II, pp. 1076–9.
[6] *Ibid.* 1908, vol. I, pp. 469–70.

The debate over the control of electricity brought home to the Fabians the limitations of their earlier Municipal Socialism, and set them for the first time on the path to a re-thinking of their whole position. The significant debate did not occur until the later 'nineties, when the question of bulk supply came to be seriously agitated. Electricity used for purposes of power was the novelty of the 'eighties, and in the infancy of electric lighting it was thought necessary to encourage the creation of many small generating stations. The first Act of Parliament regulating electricity supply was dated 1882, and it gave the Board of Trade power to license either local authorities or companies. The principle of public control was already recognized, for, in the case of companies, the Act granted the local authorities the right of buying them out at the end of twenty-one years. This period was claimed to be too short to render it profitable to the companies, so the Electricity Act of 1888 extended the time to forty-two years (i.e. until 1931). Under these Acts, the local authorities of London which were empowered to set up electricity generating stations, and later to take over the private ones, were the old vestries, and these powers later passed over to the metropolitan borough councils. In general, the vestries left the supply of electricity to private enterprise, though the Fabians on the municipal bodies strove to get them to establish municipal supplies.[1] However, after the creating of borough councils, some municipal plants were established.

The interest of the L.C.C. in the electricity supply of London, and the interest of the Fabian Society in it in a more important way than in that of attempting to persuade the minor authorities to make use of the powers which Parliament had allowed them, dates from about 1898, when there was keen competition for the privilege of supplying electricity in bulk to London and the surrounding districts, and a number of companies promoted Bills in Parliament. They were hampered, however, not only by the competition amongst themselves, and the antagonism of the smaller concerns, private or municipal, that were threatened with extinction, but by the opposition of the Progressive Party which demanded that the L.C.C. should become the authority for supplying electricity in bulk. In this demand the L.C.C. won the approval of the lesser municipal authorities of London in conferences of London local authorities which were held in 1901[2] and 1905.[3] From 1902 the L.C.C. began to introduce Bills into Parliament for the purpose of purchasing the assets of the private companies and providing London with bulk supply.[4] On this issue the Progressives had to encounter the fierce opposition of the Moderates and the 'Industrial Freedom League,'[5] whose most sub-

---

[1] e.g. *Fabian News*, November 1898.
[2] L.C.C. Minutes, 1901, p. 778.
[3] *Ibid.* 1905, vol. I, p. 1128.
[4] *Ibid.* 1903, pp. 464 and 1560; 1906, vol. II, pp. 1055–61.
[5] See G. B. Shaw, *Commonsense of Municipal Trading* (Constable, London, 1904), p. 62.

stantial argument, probably, was that even the area controlled by the L.C.C. was too small for the proper administration of bulk-supplied electricity whereas a company would not be subject to these limitations.

The Fabians were more influenced by this controversy than influential in it. As members of the Progressive Party they voted with their Progressive colleagues in favour of making the L.C.C. the body for providing London with bulk supply.[1] But the Fabians had been made aware of the problems of municipal boundaries involved by H. G. Wells' first paper to the Society in March 1903.[2] The Fabian Society postponed issuing a full pamphlet on electricity until 1905,[3] and by then, at a time when the Progressives were still pressing forward with their Bill in Parliament, the Fabians, inspired by Wells, were talking in terms of the regionalism of the 'New Heptarchy'. Bernard Shaw, too, in his *Commonsense of Municipal Trading* was using electricity as an example of the 'difficulties of municipalization'.[4]

The fate of electricity before 1918 was determined by politics. In the last year of the Conservative government's rule in 1905, it seemed likely that a Bill giving the power of providing bulk supply to a private company would go through. In 1906 when the government was changed, Lloyd George, as President of the Board of Trade, viewed the Progressives' schemes for L.C.C. control with favour,[5] but before a suitable Bill could be passed the Municipal Reformers came to power in the L.C.C. and refused to proceed with the Bill, unless it were amended to allow private enterprise to undertake bulk supply subject merely to the supervision of the Council.[6] The Liberal government declined to support the Bill as amended by the Municipal Reformers, and the London Electricity Supply Act, which was placed on the Statute Book in 1908, proved a weak measure that merely permitted suppliers to link up their systems, in the hope that this would lead eventually to a central generating station. The Act, however, transferred from the boroughs to the L.C.C. the right of purchasing companies' undertakings in 1931. Thus the situation remained until 1918, when the Fabians' earlier doubts were confirmed by the Williamson Committee set up by the Board of Trade in that year which reported 'that it has been conclusively proved that a Municipal or Local Government area is not necessarily, and in fact is rarely, the most economical area of electrical supply'.[7]

---

[1] L.C.C. Minutes, 1906, vol. II, pp. 1055-63.
[2] It was entitled 'The Question of Scientific Administrative Areas in Relation to Municipal Undertakings'.
[3] Tract 119.
[4] Shaw, *op. cit.* ch. VII.
[5] L.C.C. Minutes, 1906, vol. II, pp. 1055-63.
[6] *Ibid.* 1907, vol. I, p. 959.
[7] The Fabians cannot be blamed for the peculiarly complicated structure established in 1925-6, which represented an attempt to retain as much of private enterprise as possible after the practical need for central control had long been recognized.

The Fabians 'New Heptarchy' Tracts of 1905, of which the one dealing with electricity was the first, showed that the Fabians had realized that they were living in an age when administrative space was shrinking and the organization of many services was coming to be national or regional rather than municipal. The regionalism of their 'New Heptarchy' led eventually (after the First World War) to the blessing given by Mr Herbert Morrison and the newer generation of Fabians to the new *ad hoc* authorities which had emerged, as we have seen, partly out of the technical needs of the services themselves and partly out of the compromise of political conflict. The Webbs tried to synthesize the old and the new Fabianism in *A Constitution for the Socialist Commonwealth of Great Britain*. 'Municipal Socialism' of the older Fabian type had come into being too late. It had been, indeed, a reflection of London's lag behind other cities of the kingdom in its municipal services, not a new beacon lighting the dark path to Socialism.

The Fabians deserve a place of honour amongst those men who converted London from one of the worst-governed cities of the British Commonwealth, which it was in the 1880's, to one of the best-governed, which it is today. Their success, however, was greater as administrators within the scope of the Progressive Party's programme, than as propagandists for the extension of municipal activity in new, socialist directions.

CHAPTER IX

THE INFLUENCE OF THE FABIANS
UPON THE LIBERAL PARTY

THE LIBERAL PARTY IN THE LATE 'EIGHTIES

THE Fabian Society ceased to be a drawing-room discussion group and plunged into metropolitan politics about 1887. It was a propitious moment, for Liberal politics were then in a fluid state. The arrival of the Fabians coincided with the end of a period of Radical agitation within the Liberal Party. In 1885 and 1886 Radicalism had lost its leaders with the political annihilation of Dilke and the departure of Joseph Chamberlain with the Liberal Unionists. The party machinery which these Radicals had taken the lead in developing had, by and large, survived the Home Rule split; the question was whether the 'socialistic tendency' which Chamberlain and Dilke had fostered would disappear along with them, or could be given a new impetus.

In London, the years 1885 and 1886 saw the completion of the organization of a network of democratic Liberal caucuses throughout the metropolis, largely through the efforts of W. S. Caine and Renwick Seager. These were eventually federated in the London Liberal and Radical Union, an achievement mainly of Professor Stuart and R. K. Causton. The purpose of establishing these Liberal and Radical Associations was to secure the registration of new voters and to draw them into party activity, and, in order to arouse popular interest, it was provided that every Association should elect one member to its Council for every twenty-five electors in its constituency. But the drive for creating this extremely democratic organization came from a minority of Radical leaders, who soon discovered that their intentions were frustrated by political apathy, and the apathy above all of the working-class districts. Sidney Webb, writing in 1888, maintained that hardly any of the Associations in London had been able to find sufficient Liberals, Radicals, or Irish Nationalists willing to serve to make up their Councils of four per cent of the electorate, even though women and non-voters were admitted. He went further, and alleged that most Liberal Associations in London had not more than a score of active members, and that there was 'probably not one constituency' which had more than fifty people taking an active share in political work, while in at least half a dozen instances the local Associations had simply disintegrated and had had to be reconstituted by the central body.[1] Even allowing for some slight exaggeration for propaganda effect, this does provide a background to Bernard Shaw's later remark that, when he became 'a permeative Fabian in

[1] Sidney Webb, *Wanted a Programme: An Appeal to the Liberal Party* (leaflet), 1888.

the executive of the South St Pancras Liberal and Radical Association', he 'had coolly walked in and demanded to be elected to the Association and Executive, which was done on the spot by the astonished Association—ten strong or thereabouts. . . .'[1]

In addition, there were the Radical Clubs of London. These 'three hundred' (it was supposed) spontaneous organizations were mainly working-class in composition, and the most important of them were united in the Metropolitan Radical Federation, which had refused to become merged in the London Liberal and Radical Union. Only a minority of the members of these clubs joined them for political reasons or engaged in political activity; but that minority was of a very energetic and advanced Radical character, and included many Socialists.[2]

When they saw the Liberal Party's organization apparently wide open to democratic influence, and when they knew it had been deprived so recently of its outstanding Radical leaders, there was every reason why those Fabians who had been Radicals before they were Socialists should consider that permeation tactics might induce the party to adopt an advanced scheme of social reform. It was quite possible to argue at that time that it might be easier to capture the Liberal Party for labour or socialist policy than to defy the established party structure entirely and create a third party. The defection of the Liberal Unionists had meant not only the removal of the Chamberlainites and the Whigs, but also the withdrawal of a number of the 'money bags' from the Liberal Party. This had had the immediate effect of making it impossible for the Liberal Associations to employ paid organizers, but equally, it set a premium on the work of enthusiastic volunteers, and it was thought to have removed a centre of opposition to socialistic proposals. Only the fanatical devotion of the party to the ageing Gladstone, full of his Home Rule schemes and mistrust of social legislation, seemed, in the late 'eighties, a serious impediment. There was a difference of opinion in Fabian ranks at the time concerning the formation of a Labour Party, as we have pointed out elsewhere, but the division was not on the question whether an attempt should be made to push the Liberal Party in a Socialist direction for the time being—all the Fabians were agreed about that—but on the question whether their efforts were likely to be ultimately successful, or whether at a later stage they would be obliged to abandon the Liberals and form a new Labour-Socialist Party. Whatever their expectations of the future, most Fabians in the late 'eighties agreed with Sidney Webb that the time was not ripe for the Society to give much encouragement to the attempts that were being made to form a Labour Party.[3]

[1] G. B. Shaw, footnote to Pease, *op. cit.* p. 112.
[2] Sidney Webb, *Wanted a Programme.*
[3] *Ibid.*

FABIAN ACTIVITY IN THE LIBERAL-RADICAL PARTY

The Fabians began their permeation of the Liberal Party immediately after the announcement of the Party's Nottingham Programme of 1887. This feeble document enraged the Radicals and proved a good starting-place for Fabian criticism. The Society's *True Radical Programme*[1] of the same year was intended to push further along some of the lines laid down in Chamberlain's Un-authorized Radical Programme of 1885. W. T. Stead observed shrewdly, some years later, that 'Mr Sidney Webb . . . aspires to be Mr Chamberlain of London. . . .'[2] The only suggestion which a Chamberlainite Radical of the late 'eighties might have objected to strongly in the Fabian Society's immediate demands of that period was the proposal for a minimum wage and a maximum working day. This demand was the chief one emerging from Labour and Socialist, rather than Radical, sources at that time. Webb's pamphlet *Wanted a Programme: An Appeal to the Liberal Party* (1888) set the tone of the Fabian campaign. It was a call to the Liberal Party to make a bid for the support of the working-class and the Radical Clubs by adopting an advanced Radical and Labour programme of the Fabian type. At the same time the Society instructed its members to join Liberal and Radical Associations and play an active part in them; Fabians were also urged to give lectures to these Associations and to write to the Liberal press, which they did to some effect.[3] The Radicals, on their side, were at first far from hostile to these new allies and willingly provided them audiences and space in influential papers like the *Star*.

The Fabians did a great deal to inspire and urge forward London Radicalism of a socialistic type in the five years from 1887 to 1891. Well-known Fabians can be discovered in positions of influence in Liberal and Radical bodies. Many of them were pluralists: thus Sidney Webb, in 1888, was a member of the Holborn, Westminster, and the London University Liberal and Radical Associations. And the Annual Reports of, say, the Holborn Liberal and Radical Association from 1887 to 1891 give an idea of the extent of Fabian activity. In the first Report (1887) of the Holborn Association, Sidney Webb's name was mentioned amongst the list of 'well-known Liberals and Radicals of the district'[4] who were invited to take a seat on the platform; the Rev. Stewart Headlam appeared as the 'Chairman of the Bloomsbury ward' amongst the officers of the Executive, while in the Report itself special mention was made of the 'very successful discussion groups' which had been held during the year at Headlam's house.[5] The second Report regretted that the

[1] Tract 6, discussed in our ch. I, above.
[2] W. T. Stead (ed.), *The Elector's Guide*, 1892, p. 50.
[3] See ch. VII above on Fabian propaganda.
[4] Report, *cit.* Webb had in fact helped to form the Holborn Association.
[5] *Ibid.*

Nottingham Liberal Party Conference Programme 'contained so little calculated to solve the pressing problem of urban poverty', and urged that the next Liberal Federation meeting at Birmingham should adopt a programme of seven points—points that were identical with those being put forward by the Fabian Society.[1] When, at the time of the third report in 1890, the Association joined the London Liberal and Radical Union, Headlam and Webb were among the representatives it elected to that body,[2] and, in the fourth Report of 1891 there were resolutions adopting the Progressives' 'London Programme,' and urging the National Liberal Federation to declare in favour of the eight hours day and of introducing 'model conditions' in national and municipal employment.[3]

The Annual Reports of other Liberal and Radical Associations which the Fabians permeated tell a similar tale. Thus, the Reports of the Strand Liberal and Radical Association show that there were three Fabians on the Executive Committee—the Rev. Stewart Headlam, the Rev. W. E. Moll, and the Rev. W. A. Oxford[4]—and that these three were among the representatives which this Association elected to the Council of the London Liberal and Radical Union and to the National Liberal Federation.[5] The Report for 1891 mentioned Sidney Webb moving a resolution, following the Liberal Party's adoption of the Newcastle Programme: 'That this meeting congratulates the National Liberal Federation in having declared a Programme, giving prominence to important measures of Social Reform, and it urges the General Purposes Committee to give definiteness to that Programme by the early preparation of Bills dealing with the several proposals especially as regards the extension of the Factory Acts and the Taxation of Land Values.'[6] The Fabians paid an equal amount of attention to the Radical Clubs. Graham Wallas in particular was active and influential in the Metropolitan Radical Federation, and the Radical Clubs were the chief centres of Fabian propaganda by the spoken word. The Fabians abandoned to the S.D.F. the soap-box oratory of the street-corner to casual collections of bystanders, and wisely concentrated their efforts instead on the organized groups of working-men in the Clubs.

The most important post held in the Liberal Party during the 'nineties by a Fabian was Sidney Webb's membership, from 1889, of the Executive Committee of the London Liberal and Radical Union. It was shortly after his election to this position that this organization forwarded to the National Liberal Federation a list of suggestions for the agenda of its 1889 Conference, com-

---

[1] Second Report, Holborn Liberal and Radical Association.
[2] Third Report, Holborn Liberal and Radical Association.
[3] Fourth Report, Holborn Liberal and Radical Association.
[4] Second Report, Strand Liberal and Radical Association.
[5] Third Report, Strand Liberal and Radical Association.
[6] Fifth Report, Strand Liberal and Radical Association.

prising resolutions in favour of extending the powers of the London County Council, providing better housing for the working-class, widening the scope of the factory acts, shortening the duration of Parliament, removing taxes from 'the breakfast table' and imposing them on ground-rents, paying salaries to Members of Parliament, establishing the 'second ballot', and introducing the eight hours working day for government and municipal employees.[1] This programme has a distinctly Fabian appearance, especially the last two items of it. On the other hand, it must be admitted that practically all these demands were common Radical currency at the time, and were by no means new to the leaders of the London Liberal and Radical Union. In the year before Webb was elected to the Executive Committee, J. F. B. Firth had been a member of it, and the programme of Firth's Municipal Reform League had been accepted in 1888 by the London Liberal and Radical Union.[2] This had anticipated most of the points of the 1889 Programme, and others had been anticipated by the Liberal and Radical Union's activity in its 'Housing of the People' campaign.[3]

THE 'NEWCASTLE PROGRAMME': A FABIAN VICTORY?

Pease and Shaw between them have endeavoured to create the impression that the Liberal Party's famous 'Newcastle Programme' of 1891 was Fabian in origin and inspiration.[4] This claim seems an exaggeration of Fabian influence, though it can readily be admitted that the Fabians did much to help forward that Radical aspect of Liberalism of which the Newcastle Programme was the much-acclaimed outcome.

The Newcastle Programme did not make any great change in Liberal Party policy. Every item of it had been adopted by the National Liberal Federation at its annual meetings in 1889 and 1890, and some had been adopted in 1888. The Newcastle Programme gained publicity because it happened to be the statement of Liberal policy issued before the 1892 election,[5] and because Gladstone in 1891 at last gave his blessing to its social demands.[6] But to say that is merely to shift the interest in tracing origins back a couple of years, to the policy adopted by the National Liberal Federation in 1889.

The resolutions adopted by the National Liberal Federation at its annual meeting in 1889 were moved not by Fabians, but by such well-known Liberals

---

[1] Third Report, London Liberal and Radical Union (1889–90).
[2] Second Report, London Liberal and Radical Union.
[3] Ibid.
[4] Pease, op. cit. pp. 111–2, and Shaw's footnote.
[5] See the puff given it by W. T. Stead in his On the Eve: A Handbook for the General Election, (Review of Reviews Publishing Office, London, 1892).
[6] National Liberal Federation, Report of Annual Conference (Liberal Publications Department, London, 1891), pp. 100–15.

as Professor Stuart, C. A. Fyffe, and Sir Wilfred Lawson.[1] All these men were, however, connected with the London Liberal and Radical Union, and the importance of London Radicalism in urging forward these measures must be recognized.[2] But the resolutions adopted by the National Liberal Federation were not identical with those recommended to it by the London Liberal and Radical Union.[3] They contained some additional items, and the most significant addition was the proposal for 'leasehold enfranchisement'—a scheme to which the Fabians were vigorously opposed. There were also two significant omissions: the proposal for a 'second ballot', and, more important, the demand for an eight hours day.[4] Even if Webb had had something to do with drawing up the suggestions put forward by the London Liberal and Radical Union, the resolutions accepted by the National Liberal Federation differed substantially from them, and those proposals which chiefly differentiated the Fabian from other, more general, Radical opinion were not accepted.

At the Newcastle conference itself, it appears that the Fabians, far from gaining a victory, suffered a defeat. Altogether, there were about nine Fabians attending the Conference,[5] but of them only Sidney Webb attempted to speak. He wished to move an amendment to the 'omnibus' resolution on social questions, which was a repetition of the resolution of the previous year, presumably for the purpose of deleting the clause approving leasehold enfranchisement, but he was prevented from putting his amendment by a technicality of procedure.[6]

The Fabians, as part of their campaign for converting the Liberal party into the party of Labour, were also behind a proposal which was put before the Newcastle conference in the name of the Metropolitan Radical Federation, urging the retirement or withdrawal of fifty Liberal candidates in London and the country so that fifty party seats at the next election could be placed at the disposal of direct representatives of Trade Unions and Labour.[7] To this demand Schnadhorst had replied by letter, saying that the National Liberal Federation had always sought to encourage Labour candidatures, and would continue to use its influence in that direction, but that it had no actual power to interfere with local associations' choice of candidates. He ended on a somewhat discouraging financial note: 'I need hardly say that if such candi-

---

[1] *Ibid.* 1889 Report, pp. 7–10.
[2] Prof. Stuart was Hon. Sec. of the L.L. & R.U. See Morley's speech which remarks the importance of London Radicalism in 1890 Conference Report, pp. 51–8. The difference between the programme adopted by the N.L.F. and the Fabian programme can be seen by contrasting the N.L.F.'s resolutions with the obviously Fabian-inspired programme set out in the *Star*, 8 August 1888.
[3] Third Report, L.L. & R.U.
[4] National Liberal Federation, 1889 Conference Report, pp. 9–10.
[5] Mrs Cotton, Mrs Mallet, Mrs E. H. Williams, Sidney Webb, E. L. Manning, R. E. Dell, T. I. Wallas, T. M. Watt, and F. Sydney Morris. *Fabian News*, October 1891.
[6] National Liberal Federation, 1891 Conference Report, p. 96.
[7] *Ibid.* p. 18.

dates are really to represent the labouring classes it is essential that at least some portion of their election expenses should be subscribed by the classes to whom they belong, and I should be glad to have any information you can give me as to the position of your Association in this respect.'[1] In its report to the Newcastle conference the Committee of the National Liberal Federation was even more discouraging:

> The Committee desires to point out that while it is ready to exercise its influence, it has no authority in the selection of candidates. That authority rests in the electors of each constituency through their chosen representatives. In order to secure the selection of Labour candidates and to carry them at the poll it is necessary that there should be a local demand and that the choice should be accepted by all sections of the party. The Committee regrets to observe that in one or two constituencies so-called Labour candidates have been adopted in opposition to well-known and tried Liberal members. Such a policy if persisted in can result in nothing but disaster. It will alienate loyal members of the Liberal Party, and will greatly retard the return of genuine representatives of labour. Nor can it be overlooked that in all these cases opposition is directed against Liberal members and in no single case against a Tory. The return of a large number of labour representatives to the legislature of New South Wales has afforded encouragement to the advocates of a Labour Party independent of all political combinations. It is forgotten that the circumstances of the Colonies and of the United Kingdom are widely different. . . .[2]

The Fabians, then, had an influence on the Liberal Party's Newcastle Programme only in so far as their activity urged forward more general Radical claims. Their influence was one of a number, and perhaps not the most important one. How would it compare, for instance, with that exercised by the labour agitation following the Dock Strike? If these two factors—Fabian propaganda and the Labour agitation following the Dock Strike—were independent, and if it were necessary to decide which was the more important influence on the Liberal Party, the decision would have to go against the Fabians. They were, after all, a small, even if active group, and the Liberal newspapers and spokesmen were prepared at times to speak contemptuously of them, whereas they adopted quite a different tone towards the resolutions of the Trades Union Congresses of 1890 and 1891 at which the New Unionists had gained notable victories.[3] But the two elements are hardly separate. Webb as early as *Wanted a Programme* had recognized that it was the threat of the formation of a third party which would give effect to the Fabian demands, and drive the Liberals to a more Radical policy; Fabian propaganda was based on that assumption. The Liberal Party did move, rather slowly and reluctantly, in the direction of social reform in the early

[1] *Ibid.* p. 20. [2] *Ibid.* p. 21.

[3] The articles in the *Speaker* at the time of the Newcastle Conference and the T.U.C. of 1891 might be taken as typical. For a particularly interesting account of the things uppermost in the minds of Liberals at this time see the speech 'Liberalism and Social Reform' by John Morley at the Eighty Club dinner at St James' Hall, 19 November 1889 (National Press Agency, London), (also included in the 1890 *Handbook of the Eighty Club*).

'nineties; the agitation in the world of labour following the Dock Strike was a potent impetus, but the Fabians had a share in galvanizing London Radicalism, even if they were not mainly responsible for the Newcastle Programme nor successful in forcing the Liberal Party to accept any Fabian measure that went beyond Radicalism.

FABIAN INFLUENCE ON LIBERAL PARTY LEADERS

Gentlemen [said John Morley in a speech to the Eighty Club in November 1889], I do not call myself a Socialist. The name of Radical is good enough for me (loud cheers). If Socialism is the same thing as Communism; if it means the abolition of private property; if it means the assumption by the State of the land—the assumption and administration of all land and all capital; if it means an equal distribution of products, I say that that is against human nature, and could only produce convulsion and disaster (Hear, hear). But if Socialism means a wise use of the forces of all for the good of each; if it means the legal protection of the weak against the strong (Hear, hear); if it means the performance by public bodies of duties which individuals could not perform either so well, or not at all, for themselves, why, then, the principles of Socialism are admitted all over the field of our social activity (Cheers). . . . Gentlemen, do not let us quarrel about nicknames. I have said before to a more popular audience than this, and I say it again—I shall always say it—that if we are agreed upon certain definite ends for today, that is enough for me. Let us achieve the task which is assigned to us: do not let us endeavour to settle millennial problems; let us do what we have to do (Hear, hear).

Continuing, Morley expressed himself in favour of reduction of taxes on the 'breakfast table', of free education, of the provision by School Boards of free meals (on the Birmingham lines) to needy schoolchildren in cases where 'voluntary charity falls short', of the extension of the powers of the municipalities as demanded by the London Progressives, and of the overhaul of Poor Relief. But he declared himself decidedly against any legislative enactment to limit working hours to eight a day or forty-eight a week—warning his listeners specifically against the Fabian plan for 'trade option'—and, while he recognized that fluctuations in wages were the cause of much distress, he said he had 'no panacea'.[1] Morley's speech reveals once more that the dividing-line between Radicals and Socialists was by no means clear-cut on some practical issues, but if the Fabians ever had any hopes of persuading him over to any unequivocally 'Socialist' position,[2] they were speedily to be disillusioned.

[1] *Ibid.* esp. pp. 14, 15–19, 25–6, 28 (cf. Morley's speech at 1890 Conference of the National Liberal Federation). The *Proceedings of the Eighty Club* in the 'nineties are interesting, as revealing a movement of rank and file Liberal parliamentarians towards a Radicalism at least as advanced as Morley's under the combined influence of the propaganda for the Newcastle Programme, the fear that Labour might support the I.L.P. and the persuasion of R. B. Haldane.
[2] R. B. Haldane, in a speech to the Fabian Society reported in *Fabian News*, December 1894, claimed not very convincingly that Morley had been greatly influenced by Fabian propaganda.

Of all the influential men in the Liberal Party, R. B. Haldane stood closest to the Fabians,[1] although the Society also counted among its 'friends' in the Cabinet, when the Liberal Party took office in 1892, Arthur Acland, Asquith, Sir Edward Grey, and Sydney Buxton.[2] The Fabians counted this group as its friends, not simply because they were considered the Radical wing of the Liberal Party, but also because they claimed to have 'influenced' them during the debate on the Leasehold Enfranchisement Bill in 1891. This measure was defeated in the debate of 29 April 1891 by a narrow majority of thirteen in a House numbering 354, and its defeat was made possible by the opposition of a group of Radicals, headed by R. B. Haldane and Sir Edward Grey, who voted with the bulk of the Conservatives. Their decision may well have been influenced by the Fabian leaflet[3] which was sent to all members of Parliament before the debate. At all events, the Fabians prided themselves that they had won over a group of Radicals to a 'Collectivist' attitude to this matter, and set much store by its significance.

Did the Fabians over-estimate their influence with these men? Except in the case of Haldane, they appear to have done so. None of the others in this group was eventually persuaded over from Radicalism to Socialism. Acland and Buxton were, and remained, Radicals of the type of the leaders of the London Progressives in the best days of L.C.C. activity—broad-minded, public-spirited Radicals, unafraid of a little 'Collectivism', but equally unimpressed by the Socialists' more far-reaching demands. Asquith and Grey drifted steadily more and more to the Right, and away from Fabian influence. Only R. B. Haldane, who had been converted by Fabian criticism of his earlier Radicalism,[4] remained throughout fairly intimately associated with Webb and the Fabians, pressing Fabian ideas, or those which he had worked out in conjunction with Webb, gently upon his Liberal colleagues.

THE 'EIGHT HOURS DAY' AS A 'BORDERLINE' BETWEEN RADICALS AND SOCIALISTS

We have seen it is difficult to know where, in the late 'eighties and early 'nineties, Radicalism ended and Collectivism began. 'Radical' was a term which covered a great variety of persons, some willing to go further in a 'Socialist' direction than others. The Fabians were concerned to keep the borderline as blurred as possible; they wished (in their early days, at any rate) to present Collectivism as a 'natural' and 'inevitable' extension of Radicalism. But even the S.D.F., anxious as it was for clear-cut distinctions, included

---

[1] See 1892 *Handbook of the Eighty Club* for a speech by Haldane on 'Social Questions' and a pamphlet by him on the 'The Unearned Increment'. Haldane was a close personal friend of the Webbs.

[2] Editorial, *Fabian News*, September 1892.

[3] Tract 22.

[4] Pease, *op. cit.* pp. 74–5, quoting the *Radical*, vol. II, No. 8, March 1888.

many obviously 'Radical' demands in its programme. Socialists tried to turn moderate Radicals into left-wing Radicals, and to persuade left-wing Radicals to move further forward; and there was considerable disagreement amongst Radicals about which particular measure involved taking the fatal step across the border into Socialism. Some Radicals were inclined to regard such things as the provision of free meals in schools as the borderline case, but this was disputed by others.[1] There was more general agreement concerning the demand for the legal eight hours day. While nowadays this would hardly be thought a 'socialist' proposal, it was a demand originating with the Socialists and at first opposed by leading Radicals as an unwarranted legislative interference with the industrial system. Their opposition was (at least theoretically) to the obligatory reduction of hours by statute, not to the reduction itself. The conflict between Socialists and Radicals occurred over the legal eight hours day for miners; but the extension of this proposal—the demand for a universal legal Eight Hours Day—also served to bring out differences between Fabian and more left-wing Socialists.

The proposal for a general Eight Hours Bill needs only to be mentioned here: its fate will need to be described later. The difference between the Socialist groups concerned the method of implementing a general Eight Hours Act. The original Fabian contribution to the proposal was the device of 'Trade Option'—that is to say, an Act accepting the general eight hours day in principle, establishing it as the legal maximum working day for certain classes of workers (miners, railwaymen, and government servants), and giving the Secretary of State power to bring other classes of workers within the scope of the Act when he was satisfied the majority of workers at the trade desired it. The purpose of 'Trade Option' was to meet the objections to a general Act of those Trade Union leaders who were unfavourable to the eight hours demand. The S.D.F. immediately countered the Fabian 'Trade Option' scheme with their proposal for 'Trade Exemption': the contrary plan, whereby the Act should apply to all classes of workers unless the majority of workers at a trade voted it should not do so. 'Trade Option' and 'Trade Exemption' were long a battleground between the different socialist groups and in the T.U.C.

But the general Eight Hours Bill was far from being 'practical politics' in Westminster. So far as the legislature was concerned, the dispute raged over the Eight Hours Bill for miners. On this particular measure, all Socialists were agreed, but in the wider ranks of Labour there was a division. Though the majority of miners desired an Eight Hours Act, and the miners of central England, of Wales and Scotland ardently supported it, the miners of Durham

---

[1] See report in the *Radical*, vol. I, No. 9, May 1887, p. 68, of debates in the Metropolitan Radical Federation concerning school meals. Also, for an example of what was considered an 'advanced' Radical programme, *ibid*, vol. I. No. 6, p. 46.

and Northumberland were hostile. The main reason for the opposition was that the miners of Durham and Northumberland were a favoured section: the men there worked only seven hours or less 'bank to bank',[1] and they feared that a legislative maximum working-day would become a minimum. But this was not the only reason. A number of influential 'Lib-Lab' Parliamentary representatives were opposed to legislative interference, partly for reasons provided them by the Liberal economists, partly because of a genuine fear that legislation would weaken the Trade Unions, and therefore that Trade Unions should secure the eight hours day without recourse to State intervention.[2]

A Miners' Eight Hours Bill was introduced into the House of Commons by Cunninghame Graham in 1888, 1889, and 1890, but it failed in each session to secure a favourable place in the ballot for opportunities.[3] The Trade Union Congress of 1889, inspired by New Unionism and the decisions of the International Trade Union Congress of the previous year, adopted by a large majority a resolution for a Miners' Eight Hours Act. In the following year the T.U.C. proceeded to advocate a general Eight Hours Bill, and confirmed its decision again at the 1891 Congress. Although the Liberal Party made no definite promises of legal limitation of hours in its Newcastle Programme, it became a major issue during the 1892 election. In W. T. Stead's handbook for the 1892 election[4] all the party leaders gave their opinion of the measure. Only Chamberlain supported it; Morley definitely opposed it, while Salisbury and Gladstone were cautiously disapproving. Even so advanced a Radical as Haldane stressed the difficulties of a Miners' Eight Hours Bill in a speech to the Eighty Club at this time.[5] But the Miners' Eight Hours Bill was a matter on which the Radicals were being pressed forward in a 'Socialist' direction in the early 'nineties, the most important pressure coming from the T.U.C. dominated by the 'New Unionists.'[6] Fabian propaganda reinforced this Labour pressure on the Liberals, and in particular the carefully documented analysis of the problem by Sidney Webb and Harold Cox which appeared in 1891 at the height of controversy must have been very persuasive.[7] When the Bill was first presented to the House of Commons in 1892, the Conservatives were still in power, and it was rejected at its second reading by 272 votes to 160. It was reintroduced before a Liberal House in 1893, and the second reading

[1] More strictly, the hewers. The boys in Northumberland and Durham usually worked ten hours.
[2] See Burt's speech in the 1891 *Handbook of the Eighty Club* for this combination of reasons. The economic ones were that an eight hours day would mean less pay or increased cost of production.
[3] S. Webb and H. Cox, *The Eight Hours Day* (Walter Scott, London, n.d.), p. 22.
[4] *On the Eve*, 1892, esp. pp. 51–2, 59.
[5] 1892 *Handbook of the Eighty Club*.
[6] And pressure on individual representatives from the mining constituencies.
[7] S. Webb and H. Cox, *op. cit.* Webb had also contributed an article to the *Contemporary Review*, December 1889. See also Fabian Tracts Nos. 9, 16, 23, 48.

was carried in 1894, by 281 votes to 194. But in the meantime Gladstone in 1893 had given his blessing to a 'local option' device for overcoming the objections of Northumberland and Durham, which might be said to have carried the 'option' device the Fabians had proposed for a general Eight Hours Bill into the particular Bill for miners. An amendment to this effect was subsequently carried but the Bill in this form was unacceptable to the majority of miners, and it was withdrawn.[1] As a result, the passing of the Miners' Eight Hours Act was put off for fourteen years.[2]

THE LIBERAL GOVERNMENT OF 1892-5 AND THE 'NEWCASTLE PROGRAMME'

The Liberal government, during its period of office from 1892 to 1895, did make an effort to carry out the Newcastle Programme, but the promised measures of domestic reform were only really given effect in legislation from 1894—after the retirement of Gladstone.[3] A few progressive administrative changes were made (too few, in the Fabians' opinion), but the years before 1894 were barren of social legislation, and such measures as were introduced went down in defeat. The inactivity of the Liberal government must be set against the growing power of the left-wing groups in the Trades Union Congress until 1895, and the increasing propaganda for establishing an Independent Labour Party during those years. Even the achievements of 1894—chiefly the 'Parish Councils' Act and Harcourt's Budget—were set in an atmosphere of intestine strife, where personal rivalries for the leadership of the Party intensified the conflict between its Left and Right wings, and threatened it with disaster.

THE FABIAN SOCIETY BETWEEN THE LIBERALS AND THE I.L.P.

In those years, the Fabian Society was divided almost as much as the Liberal Party itself. The Newcastle Programme and the Society's influence on the Progressives of the L.C.C. were considered by some Fabians to have demonstrated the effectiveness of the policy of permeating the Liberals. But at the same time Fabian Societies were spreading throughout the provinces, and many men who were taking the lead in the movement to bring an independent party of labour into existence were joining the Fabian ranks.[4] This intensified

[1] E. Guyot, *La durée du travail dans les mines de Grande Bretagne* (Rousseau, Paris, 1908), p. 33.
[2] *Ibid.* pp. 37–43 for attempts to bring forward a Bill during the Conservative government's rule.
[3] See the contribution of Webb and Shaw to the symposium 'What Mr Gladstone ought to do' in the *Fortnightly Review*, February 1893. This was a foreshadowing of their 'To your Tents, Oh Israel!'.
[4] Keir Hardie, Tom Mann, Ben Tillett, Bob Banner, Fred Hammill, Pete Curran, Fred Henderson, and Robert Blatchford all became members of the Fabian Society in the early 'nineties. 'Fabian Notes' column of the *Workman's Times*, 28 May 1892.

the conflict, always latent in the Society, between 'permeation' and 'independence'. Bernard Shaw flitted lightly between the two groups, endeavouring, with belligerent words and moderate recommendations, to keep the peace between them.

'Stormy debates'[1] took place at Fabian meetings during 1891–2 whenever the question of political tactics arose. Hubert Bland and Robert E. Dell, supported by the newcomers to the Society, such as Joseph Burgess and Keir Hardie, and by the representatives of local Fabian groups, like S. G. Hobson, were conducting a strong campaign to win the Society for the policy of building up a national third party on the basis of independence.[2] William Clarke, Edward Pease, Bernard Shaw, and Sidney Webb all wrote to the *Workman's Times*[3] taking a very pessimistic view of the prospect of founding such a party. The letters of Pease and Webb in particular excited the editor's fury: Pease had said that the situation required 'measures, not men', and Webb had declared that 'the nature of an Englishman seems to be suited only to a political fight between two parties—the party of order and the party of progress'.

Both sides spent much time examining contemporary events for portents favouring their policy, but the omens of 1891–2 were contradictory. At first the balance swung to the side of 'independence'. In 1891 H. W. Massingham and other Fabians were suddenly dismissed by the proprietors of the *Star* who proceeded (as Bernard Shaw put it) 'to Gladstonize' its politics.[4] This was a heavy blow, as the Fabian influence on London Radicalism had been exercised to a very considerable degree through that newspaper. It seemed for a while as though this happening would cause the Fabians to throw their energies behind the campaign for a Labour party. Bernard Shaw delivered a call to battle in two addresses to the Society, which were later printed as Tracts 40 and 41, where he declared that the 'game [of permeation] is played out'. A few months later, however, Massingham had transferred to the *Daily Chronicle* and opened its columns to the Fabians,[5] and they also made a new 'capture' in the *Radical Review*,[6] so 'permeation' was once again restored to favour. The 1892 election for the L.C.C. also resulted in a triumph for the Progressive alliance, and an ignominious defeat of the S.D.F.'s 'independent' candidates.

More difficult to interpret was the result at the General Election of 1892. One Fabian—J. Keir Hardie—was elected out of the seven Fabian candidates.

---

[1] See reports of Fabian meetings in *Workman's Times*, the main source for this period. Joseph Burgess was editor of this paper.
[2] *Ibid.* 12 December 1891, 13 February 1892.
[3] *Ibid.* 23 January 1891, 30 January 1891.
[4] Tract 41. See also *Workman's Times*, 16 October 1891.
[5] William Clarke became its leader-writer.
[6] *Fabian News*, June 1892, *Workman's Times*, 14 May 1892.

This was the first Fabian Parliamentary victory. But was Hardie's victory, and the result of the Labour poll in general, a victory for 'independence' or for 'permeation'? The answers given to this at the time depended on the prejudices of the observer and his method of reckoning. The independent labour men could point out that, even without any national organization behind them, three independent labour representatives—J. Keir Hardie, John Burns, and J. Havelock Wilson—had been elected. Havelock Wilson's was the clearest case, for he had fought and defeated both Liberal and Liberal-Unionist candidates. Furthermore, some other independent Labour candidates had polled extremely well—the best instance being Ben Tillett at West Bradford,[1] who had stood against both Liberal and Conservative candidates and had secured 2749 votes to the 3306 for the Liberal, and 3053 for the Conservative. It was also argued that in the north a large proportion of the votes had come from former supporters of the Tories, and that it was not, as Liberal Party headquarters always supposed, a matter simply of independent Labour candidatures draining away the Liberal vote. On the other hand, the supporters of 'permeation' could point out that John Burns and Keir Hardie, although they had officially rejected Liberal assistance, had in fact been given straight fights against Tories, and that in all other cases where this had happened, Labour polled well, while many independent Labour men (and the 'permeators' tended to include S.D.F. and Scottish Labour Party candidates amongst the 'independents') had secured only an insignificant number of votes.

The failure of the election results of 1892 to make a decision between the value of 'permeation' and 'independence' meant that the attitude of the London Fabians remained divided as before. The *Fabian Election Manifesto*[2] of 1892, although it was one of Bernard Shaw's masterpieces of compromise, had been written shortly after the dismissals from the *Star* and had displayed considerable hopefulness and optimism concerning the independent Labour candidates sponsored by the Society. After the election, Shaw moved more to the side of Webb, Clarke, Wallas and Pease, who were sceptical. Feelings between the two factions in the Society had not been improved by an incident during the election. The independent Labourites had decided to oppose John Morley at Newcastle, because of his hostility to the eight hours day, but Webb and Shaw and other prominent Fabians rallied to the defence of Morley, for they regarded the Labour candidature as hopeless, and likely to result in presenting the seat to the Conservative.[3] Furthermore, a powerful minority amongst the supporters of independent Labour, antagonistic to the Liberals, wished to recommend abstention from voting where no independent

---

[1] A considerable share of Tillett's election expenses had been contributed by the Fabian Society.

[2] Tract 40.

[3] *Workman's Times*, 27 August 1892. Morley's Conservative opponent tried to steal a march by agreeing to support the eight hours' day.

Labour candidate was standing, whereas the Fabian Society always advocated voting for the better man—'there is always a better and worse'—and (as a matter of fact, though not of theory) it took the view that the Liberal was better than the Tory.[1]

The coolness and distrust shown by leading Fabians towards the movement for independence may partly be explained by the degree to which their attention was engrossed by the politics of London. The working-men of London and Southern England who took an interest in politics seem to have been more closely linked with the Liberal Party, and more hostile to the Tories, than was the case in the north. The New Unionism upsurge in London did not produce a political counterpart in an independent labour movement, but subsided again in Progressive Radicalism. In Yorkshire and Lancashire the conditions were different, and, as one shrewd contemporary observer wrote, the Liberal as often as not in the minds of working-class voters was 'associated with the pre-Factory Act horrors, the cotton-famine troubles, the Manningham strike, and the general oppression of "the self-made man who adores his maker".'[2] The gospel of independence found a more receptive audience in the north, with results most surprising to Londoners.

Towards the end of 1892, the *Workman's Times* took in hand the preparations for a Conference at Bradford of the representatives of the scattered independent labour groups, for the purpose of forming a national party. Immediately the two groups amongst the London Fabians rushed into print, for and against. Shaw, in a letter to the editor of the *Workman's Times*, took a pessimistic view, predicting that the new party would not become the party of the entire working-class, but merely of a small section of it, and that its pretensions would result in a repetition of the history of the S.D.F.[3] Shaw's letter provoked a furious reply from a pseudonymous fellow-Fabian in the next issue.[4] Beginning with the taunt: 'If the big guns of the Fabian Society would only spend a little time outside the Liberal Club they might see how wrong are their assumptions', he went on to consider Shaw's question whether there was any difference between the new I.L.P. and the old S.D.F., and answered: 'Not much, except that we have had ten years of Socialist propaganda since the early 'eighties, and what failed then may succeed now, for the simple reason that working-men Radicals are now "permeated" with Socialism. Is there a single Radical Club in London where the majority of members are not Socialists? But what can they do inside the Club?' He contrasted the failure of Deptford Radicals to get a working-man as their Parliamentary candidate with the growth of local I.L.P.'s.

[1] Article by 'Marxian' in *Workman's Times*, 2 September 1893.
[2] 'Marxian' in *Workman's Times*, 9 September 1893.
[3] *Workman's Times*, 8 October 1892.
[4] *Ibid.* 15 October 1892.

The Manchester and Salford Labour Party is beginning to look like a success, and the opportunists, as is their custom, are now patronizing it. But how much of their policy would have been required to call it into life? It is not only the N.I.L.P. that some Fabians object to, but *any* Independent Labour Party. As Shaw mentions (in brackets) Sparling and Utley, I will refer to their opinions. Utley objects to *any* Independent Labour Party. . . . Utley told the Deptford men that they must join the Liberal Associations, and not think of fighting out their cause themselves. Sparling, in a letter to me, said 'If the N.I.L.P. progresses, as I am afraid it will not progress, that is, if it becomes a definite Socialist Party, adequate to the political needs of the workers, the case will be altered.' And why, O Opportunists? Are the Fabian leaders to be Pioneers no longer?[1]

Immediately before the Bradford Conference was called together in January 1893, Pease, as Secretary of the Fabian Society, wrote to the *Workman's Times* saying that the London Society would send delegates to the Conference on condition that this action were not taken as merging the Society in the I.L.P.[2] The Fabians were given this assurance. Had they not been given it, apparently the Conference would have taken place without the representation of the London Society. The provincial Fabian Societies would have attended in any case, as most of them did not approve of the parent Society's attitude. However, with this assurance, a members' meeting of the London Society decided, in spite of further gloomy prophecies by Shaw,[3] to send Bland and Shaw[4] to represent them at the Conference. Bland was not able to go, so his place was taken by De Mattos.

The part played by the Fabians in the Bradford Conference belongs to the history of the Independent Labour Party, and will be told in the next chapter. It now becomes necessary to explain why it was that Shaw and Webb, who gave the Independent Labour Party so cool a reception when it was founded changed their minds a few months later, suddenly launched a shrewd attack upon the Liberal Party and flung themselves enthusiastically behind the cause of independent Labour representation, even at the cost of splitting the Fabian Society and driving out some influential members; and also why this moment of enthusiasm passed, and gave place to bitter disappointment, and a reversion to their former pessimism.

The article 'To Your Tents, Oh Israel!' in the *Fortnightly Review* of November 1893 which was later incorporated into the Tract *A Plan of Campaign for Labour*,[5] created a sensation, though the Liberal newspapers attempted to belittle it.[6] Beatrice Webb in her journal has recorded the dis-

---

[1] For Sparling's view, see 'Fabian Notes Column,' *ibid.* 14 January 1893.
[2] *Ibid.*   [3] *Ibid.* 4 February 1893 (Pete Curran's letter).
[4] Presumably to represent the different points of view.
[5] Tract 49. The article was written by Shaw and Webb, but published in the name of the Fabian Society.
[6] A file of news-clippings relating to 'To Your Tents, Oh Israel!' is preserved in the office of the Fabian Society. The *Workman's Times* tempered its jubilation with caution lest the Fabian action proved another attempt to goad the Liberals rather than a real conversion to 'independence', 11 November 1893.

may amongst the Liberals, including the Liberal friends of the Fabians,[1] at this carefully-documented exposure of the Liberal government's failure to carry out the promises of the Newcastle Programme, especially those which required purely administrative action. It ended with a vigorous call to the workers to withdraw their support from the Liberal Party, and to build up instead an organization for giving the financial and political support of the Trade Unions only to Labour and Socialist candidates. The manifesto led to the resignation from the Fabian Society of some prominent Liberal members,[2] and the Liberal-Radicals never forgave the Fabians for what they considered was a treacherous attack at a time when the Liberal Party was in Parliamentary difficulties.

Beatrice Webb has given two explanations of this change of front: first, that the Fabians were genuinely exasperated with Liberal delay in putting the Newcastle promises into effect, and second, that they were in 'fear of being left behind' by the I.L.P.[3] It is worth elaborating this second point. The Fabians appear to have been impressed by the support shown for the I.L.P. at the time of the Bradford Conference, and by the temperate and efficient tone of the Conference itself; perhaps also by the readiness of many of the I.L.P. delegates to dispense with the services of the London Fabians altogether, if necessary. After the Conference, the Fabians were at pains to emphasize— indeed to over-emphasize—the Fabian contribution to the development of the I.L.P.[4] Inside the Society, the I.L.P. supporters signalized their victory over the Liberal group by carrying an amendment to the Society's constitution[5] and by forcing the unwilling Executive to commence negotiations for 'Socialist Unity' with the S.D.F. and the Hammersmith Socialist Society.[6] A few months later, forced to decide how to act in face of the 'desertion' of the provincial Fabian Societies to the I.L.P., Shaw wrote a letter to the *Workman's Times*, which was definitely a fighting strategic retreat on his part. He declared that the I.L.P. had done well so far but it might still 'go to the bad', for instance by recommending abstention from voting for other parties, therefore the Fabian Society had refused to issue a Tract unreservedly backing the I.L.P., as asked for by some I.L.P. men, until it knew how the I.L.P. was going to turn out. On the main point, he disapproved of the expression 'desertion' to describe the action of provincial Fabians in joining the I.L.P.: he thought Fabians ought to join the I.L.P., and looked forward to the time when there would be 'in every big centre of population in the Kingdom' 'a

[1] B. Webb, *Our Partnership*, p. 110.
[2] Including H. W. Massingham and Professor D. G. Ritchie.
[3] B. Webb, *Our Partnership*, p. 110.
[4] *Workman's Times*, 28 January 1893 (Shaw); 4 February 1893 (replies); 11 February 1893 (Sidney Dark in 'Fabian Notes').
[5] *Ibid.* 29 April 1893. The amendment provided for a referendum.
[6] *Ibid.* 13 May 1893. Shaw and Webb were hostile, and though 'Socialist Unity' might not have come to anything in any case, it was later deliberately sabotaged by Shaw.

Fabian Society with a hundred members all belonging to a Labour Party with five thousand members', when the Fabian task would be 'the congenial work of bringing the Labour Party up to the Socialist mark instead of bringing the Radical wing of the Liberal Party up to the Independent Labour mark'.[1]

The apparent early success of the I.L.P. itself was not, however, the main reason which prompted Shaw and Webb to publish the famous article and Tract. The reason (which did not go unremarked at the time[2]) was the decision of the Trades Union Congress of 1893 to establish a fund for supporting independent Labour-Socialist candidates at both local and parliamentary elections. Here was a real cause for Fabian enthusiasm. In its *Election Manifesto* of 1892 the Society had already advocated a similar plan (though without the 'independent' and 'Socialist' qualifications), and the Webbs' studies had brought home to the Fabians the overwhelming importance of the Trade Unions in the English Labour movement. If this plan were carried out, the I.L.P., backed by the financial power of the organized working-class, might become a political force which would put the Liberals entirely in the shade, especially as the Liberal Party appeared to be in a process of disintegration.

When the full details of the Fabian plan for securing independent Labour and Socialist candidatures appeared in Tract 49 at the beginning of 1894, it appeared, however, that the Fabian Society as a whole had merely swung from the Liberals, but was still far from willing to give exclusive support to the I.L.P. Once again their plan was to obtain Trade Union financial support for *all* Labour and Socialist organizations running candidates, not merely for the I.L.P. The Fabian suggestion was that the Trade Unions could act through the Trades Councils, except in London where there would be a need for separate constituency organizations though the London Trades Council could co-ordinate them. As the Trades Councils were to have the power of selecting candidates, the role of the Socialist parties was presumably to be that of propaganda bodies, and of recommending candidates to the Trades Councils for selection. Perhaps the Fabians had in mind that the majority of those selected would as a matter of fact be I.L.P. men, but the I.L.P. resented this new example of Fabian compromise.

The Fabians' enthusiasm for the scheme was genuine. They considered their financial plan for a contribution of 'one penny per member per annum' would provide funds to finance fifty candidates. But their hopes, like those of the I.L.P., were short-lived. The Trade Union Congress of 1894 showed that the idea of gaining Trade Union support was unfounded, and the I.L.P.'s hopes of gaining exclusive support even more so. This failure meant that the

[1] *Ibid.* 22 April 1893.
[2] *Ibid.* 25 November 1893. Article by 'Autolycus' on relations between F.S. and I.L.P. See also F.S. Annual Report for year ended March 1894, which admits the reason.

inner circle of the Fabian Executive reverted once more to the view that independent Labour action was futile.[1] Even before the I.L.P.'s strength was tried and proved wanting at the 1895 election, leading Fabians had predicted its defeat, and had grown estranged from it.[2] The election result amply confirmed them in their opinion: twenty Fabians went to the poll, fifteen as members of the I.L.P., one without party backing, and four as members of the Liberal Party; none was elected, and Keir Hardie, the Society's only representative in Parliament, lost his seat. After the election, Beatrice Webb wrote:

> To us the result is not altogether unsatisfactory. From our point of view the field had to be cleared. . . . The utter rout, the annihilation, one might almost say, of the Harcourt faction—the hopeless discredit into which such reforms as Local Veto, Home Rule, Church Disestablishment have fallen, clear the field of a good deal of cumbrous debris. On the other hand, the I.L.P. has completed its suicide. Its policy of abstention and deliberate wrecking is proved to be futile and absurd; Keir Hardie has probably lost for good any chance of posturing as an M.P., and will sink into the old place of a discredited Labour leader. So long as the I.L.P. existed as an unknown force of irreconcilables, the more reasonable policy of permeation and levelling-up was utterly checkmated.[3]

So while the Fabian leaders tried to return as best they could to a policy of permeation, Keir Hardie and his more invincibly optimistic followers were left to carry their third party through the difficult period of the late 'nineties.

As an influence upon the Liberal government of 1892–5, the Fabian Society appears to have been effective in so far as it helped on the Radical or the Labour agitation. Fabian influence was indirect, for there was no member of the Fabian Society who was a Liberal M.P. until 1898, when W. C. Steadman was elected for Stepney.[4] Nevertheless, the indirect pressure they were able to exert through the Radical press of London in their agitation for the carrying out of the Newcastle Programme was considerable, even if it is difficult, perhaps impossible, to point to any specific reform which can be attributed without question to Fabian influence. The minor administrative reforms carried out in their departments by Asquith, Buxton, Acland and Haldane had their support and applause, and some of the actions of Lord Rosebery, Lord Ripon, Mundella and Bryce won their approval;[5] but it

---

[1] *Workman's Times*, 2 December 1893: Replies to 'Autolycus' by Shaw and Sparling; the gaining of T.U.C. support was made by them the test of the I.L.P.'s 'ability'.
[2] *Ibid.* 12 May 1894: Sparling writes that the Rosebery faction in the Liberal Party is 'the coming thing' and the Fabian leaders are being drawn into the 'Rosenboom' (as he calls it). B. Webb, *Our Partnership*, p. 122.
[3] B. Webb, *Our Partnership*, pp. 126–7.
[4] Steadman lost the seat again at the 1900 election. In 1906 three Fabians were elected as Liberals; in January 1910, four; in December 1910, four; in 1918, one. The other Fabian Liberal M.P.'s were Percy Alden, H. G. Chancellor, Athelstan Rendall, L. G. Chiozza Money, and J. C. Wedgwood (Wedgwood resigned from the Fabian Society in 1910).
[5] 'To Your Tents, Oh Israel', *Fortnightly Review*, November 1893.

cannot be shown that these reforms were due exclusively or even mainly to Fabian initiative. The Society did claim, however, that the introduction of the eight hours day by the War Office and Admiralty at Woolwich and elsewhere, which followed very shortly after the publication of 'To Your Tents, Oh Israel', was brought about by this exposure of the government's failure to make itself a 'model employer'.[1] It is possible that the Society's action may have hastened the introduction of this reform to some extent, although it was under consideration earlier.

Sir William Harcourt's famous 'death duties' Budget of 1894 illustrates the difficulties and dangers in assessing Fabian influence. This Budget incorporated, if only in a small way, a principle of taxation that the Fabians had long advocated. Yet no love had ever been lost between Sir William and the Fabians: they had repeatedly abused him, in terms calculated to rankle, as an 'extremely well oiled and accurately poised political weathercock',[2] and as a 'Whig' obstructionist of Radical reform, and they had blamed him for the Liberal government's failure to introduce death duties in previous Budgets.[3] Nevertheless, when Sir William Harcourt was drawing up the 1894 Budget, he called extensively on the services of Sir Alfred Milner,[4] then Chairman of the Board of Inland Revenue who was closely in touch with the Fabians. It is fairly certain, however, that the decision to introduce a Radical Budget owed little or nothing to Fabian persuasion, direct or indirect; it was a calculated move by a shrewd politician in the parliamentary game, designed to prepare the way for an impending election by, if possible, trapping the House of Lords into a rash move, by driving a wedge between Salisbury and Chamberlain, and by taking some of the wind out of the sails of the I.L.P.[5] The move failed, perhaps through not being bold enough.

THE FABIANS DURING THE LIBERAL OPPOSITION, 1895–1905

The ten years of Conservative rule, which followed the defeat of the Liberals in 1895, were a period of uncertainty for the Fabians, during which many of the younger members of the Society co-operated with the I.L.P. and accused the older Fabian leaders of 'intrigues' with Liberal Imperialists and even with Conservatives. But inside the Society the tide turned against the I.L.P. men,

[1] Fabian Society Annual Report for year ending March 1894.
[2] *Fabian Essays*, (1889 ed.), p. 209.
[3] 'Sir William Harcourt we pass by for want of words to convey any adequate idea of the impulse he has given the cause of Independent Labour organization by discrediting Liberalism with everyone whose income is less than £500 a year' was the Fabians' comment on the 1893 Budget: *Fortnightly Review*, November 1893.
[4] The Marquess of Crewe, *Lord Rosebery*, vol. II, p. 466 for Rosebery's view that the 1894 Budget was 'the work of Alfred Milner'.
[5] It appears from A. G. Gardiner's *Life of Sir William Harcourt* (Constable, 1923), that Harcourt was susceptible to Radical and Labour pressure of a more general kind; see, for instance, his comments on the Eight Hours Bill in his letter to Lady Harcourt, quoted vol. II, p. 171.

and 'permeation' again became the prevailing tactics. The Society devoted itself mainly to local work, a field of activity in which both the I.L.P. supporters and 'Old Gang' could co-operate fairly harmoniously. Leading Fabians found a useful, if subordinate, role in giving advice in an 'expert' capacity to politicians and administrators; the Webbs' advice was sought by members of both parties in matters of detail concerning local government, education, and labour questions.

In the sphere of national politics, the Fabian leaders Sidney and Beatrice Webb and Bernard Shaw worked closely with Haldane in his manœuvres to reconstruct the Liberal Party. They were drawn deeper and deeper into the factional struggles on the side of the Roseberyites, who were later to be known as the 'Liberal Imperialists'. Haldane was the intermediary, and in the period his influence upon the Fabians was as great as their influence upon him. Haldane attempted to press Fabian Collectivism upon Rosebery, Asquith, and Grey, but he was at least as successful in pressing Imperialism upon the Fabians.

The curious nature of the Society's Tract *Fabianism and the Empire*, which we have noted in an earlier chapter, and the reason why it was issued at all[1] is explained by the Webbs' and Shaw's expectations of the Liberal Imperialists. The fact that *Fabianism and the Empire* was concerned for half its length with domestic rather than Imperial affairs was neither an accident, a quirk of Shaw's, nor merely a sign that the Fabians were preoccupied with domestic reform. The Webbs and Shaw, supported by the majority of Fabians, had concluded at the turn of the century that 'Little England' Liberalism was done for, and they were quite prepared to make a deal with the Liberal Imperialists by which they would accept a broad-minded Imperialism if the 'Limps' would accept a large measure of Collectivism. Rosebery's promises to 'wipe the slate clean' of such features of the Liberal Programme as Home Rule and Church Disestablishment appealed to the Fabians who thought that too much attention to these measures had meant the sacrifice of domestic reforms; and Rosebery's talk of 'national efficiency' was eagerly clutched at and expanded by the Webbs and Haldane to mean such things as improved education and housing. In his article 'Lord Rosebery's Escape from Houndsditch' in the *Nineteenth Century* of September 1901, Sidney Webb praised the ex-Premier for casting off his 'Gladstonian old clothes' and hastened to furnish him with a richly-embroidered Collectivist cloak to hide his nakedness.

One cannot help feeling, in reading *Our Partnership*, that Beatrice Webb, with her *haut-bourgeois* background, and Bernard Shaw, with his social charm, were more at home with the Liberal Imperialists than Sidney Webb was. Sidney Webb does not appear to have been completely happy in the company of 'The Souls', and he had some qualms of Radical conscience

[1] See ch. v, above, for these points.

about the Boer War.[1] Nevertheless, he went along with them.[2] The Fabian 'inner circle' continued to have hopes of the Liberal Imperialists at least until 1902, and 'intrigued' busily on their behalf, bringing together the Liberal Imperialist leaders with promising L.C.C. Progressives and Trade Union officials.[3] After 1902, Beatrice Webb's comments on the Liberal Imperialist group became steadily more critical and disillusioned.

What had gone wrong with their schemes? In the first place, they had grossly under-estimated Sir Henry Campbell-Bannerman. Throughout, they interpreted his central position between the 'pro-Boers' and the Liberal Imperialists as a sign of weakness, when in fact it became a position of strength after the Jingoism of the war years had subsided. It is possible that Campbell-Bannerman's masterly 'waiting' tactics could have been completely upset by the kind of reverse in the Boer War which would have wrecked the Conservative government and brought Lord Rosebery to power. But the central group of Liberals who followed Campbell-Bannerman was always sufficiently strong to make its capture by one of the other groups a decisive factor in the future of the Liberal Party. The Liberal Imperialists and the Webbs entirely neglected to win Campbell-Bannerman. This was, perhaps, impossible for them in any case, for to come to terms with Campbell-Bannerman they would probably have had to recognize his leadership, and the Liberal Imperialists considered they already had a leader in Lord Rosebery. The Webbs also regarded Campbell-Bannerman as an irredeemable Liberal of the old 'Gladstonian' school. Eventually, an alliance was formed between the Campbell-Bannerman group and the pro-Boer group, which proved fatal to the plans of the Webbs and Haldane.[4]

In the second place, the Webbs appear to have under-estimated the continuing importance of the Nonconformist element of the Liberal Party. They came against it during the Education Acts controversy. The Nonconformist opposition to the Acts was exploited by Lloyd George and other Liberals to strengthen the influence of the party throughout the country. The Liberal Imperialist section was hopelessly split upon the issue. While Webb and Haldane supported the Acts, Rosebery, who had been courting Nonconformist support for some time, deserted them, as also did Asquith. The Liberal Imperialists thus presented no united policy, and Webb and Haldane were positively on the unpopular side (from the Liberal point of view) in this controversy from which the Lloyd George-Campbell-Bannerman section of the party drew new strength.

Another powerful reason for the Webbs' lack of success lay in the

[1] B. Webb, *Our Partnership*, p. 218.
[2] *Ibid*. p. 220.
[3] Their activities were rather maliciously satirized by H. G. Wells in his *The New Machiavelli*.
[4] B. Webb, *Our Partnership*, p. 217. Campbell-Bannerman is called a 'weak, vain man'.

FABIAN SOCIALISM AND ENGLISH POLITICS, 1884-1918

personalities of the Liberal Imperialists. This aspect naturally bulks largest in Beatrice Webb's journals of these years. The unstable Rosebery, fearing for his health and his nerve and playing at the best of times a tricky and disingenuous political game, obviously baffled the Webbs, and constantly upset the careful plans they concerted with Haldane. Rosebery was willing to use the Webbs in so far as their ideas served his own ends, but he showed a strong aversion to being 'managed', even for his own good, by them and Haldane, and he appears to have been rather amused by their attempts at it.[1] Asquith disappointed the Webbs more and more as time went on. The apparent change in him was explained by Beatrice Webb at different times in terms of the influence of his wife and society-life, and in terms of the devotion of his real abilities to the Bar rather than to politics. But it is also probable that the Webbs took too sanguine a view of the Collectivist possibilities of Asquith's Radicalism in the 'eighties and 'nineties. The Webbs were often too ready to interpret mere Radicalism in a Collectivist sense. The enthusiasms of Socialism really made little appeal to Asquith's cold and calculating temperament. Sir Edward Grey avoided the Webb influence more easily, by abandoning almost completely an interest in domestic problems and concentrating his attention on foreign and colonial policy.[2]

In addition to this unmanageable group of Liberal Imperialist leaders, the Webbs also, at various times, attempted to come to terms with John Burns, the former Social-Democrat who graduated to Liberal-Radical politics by way of the Progressive Party in the L.C.C. But Burns' jealous egotism made him nearly as suspicious of the Fabians as of most of his other socialist contemporaries. At one time in the 'nineties—in 1893, when the Fabian Society approved the Battersea Labour League's choice of a Liberal as its L.C.C. candidate against an S.D.F. man who was also supported by the I.L.P.[3]— relations between Burns and the Fabians became close.[4] In the same year an article Burns had written on the unemployed was republished as a Fabian Tract.[5] But the Webbs strongly disapproved of Burns' action in 1895, when he revenged himself on the I.L.P. men by conspiring with the Right-Wing Trade Union leaders to smash the I.L.P. influence at the Trades Union Congress; they considered his motives utterly unworthy.[6] From that time, Burns began to follow the path which was to end in the former revolutionary Socialist opposing, as Liberal minister, the recommendations of the Minority Report on the Poor Law.

---

[1] *Ibid.* p. 198.
[2] 'Whatever that may mean', Beatrice Webb commented: a comment significant of the limitation of the Webbs' own interest: *ibid.* p. 227.
[3] *Workman's Times*, 22 and 29 July 1893.
[4] B. Webb, *Our Partnership*, p. 39.
[5] Tract 47.
[6] B. Webb, *Our Partnership*, pp. 48-51.

THE FABIANS AND THE NEW LIBERAL GOVERNMENT, 1905

Well before the Balfour government resigned in December 1905, Lord Rosebery had been abandoned as impossible even by his closest associates; Campbell-Bannerman's leadership was assured, and the Liberal Imperialists were on the defensive, making the so-called 'Relugas Compact'[1] by which they hoped with a threat of non-co-operation to force Campbell-Bannerman to accept them on their own terms. Once he had the distribution of the plums of office in his hands, the new Premier had only momentary difficulty in smashing the 'Relugas Compact'. The terms he offered were generous ones, and brought into the Cabinet representatives of all the Liberal factions. Beatrice Webb wrote 'our friends the Limps have romped into the leading posts',[2] but she forbore to mention that these 'leading posts' were more concerned with foreign policy than with departments capable of being influenced in an important way by Fabian Collectivism. Haldane's appointment as Secretary for War, not the position he would himself have chosen, removed from the sphere of domestic reform their most potent ally. The principal Cabinet posts dealing with home affairs went to the former pro-Boers. Lloyd George, who was not at this time on intimate terms with the Fabians, and John Burns dominated those aspects of domestic policy with which the Fabians were mainly concerned in the pre-war years.

Haldane appointed Sidney Webb to the committee he established to consider his army reforms,[3] but this was a personal matter, rather outside the normal range of Fabian interests. The leading Fabians did not give up hope of influencing other Liberal politicians, and they had some success with the younger Liberals, particularly the Under-Secretaries of the new Cabinet—Winston Churchill, Herbert Samuel, Reginald McKenna, and Walter Runciman.[4] These young men, together with L. T. Hobhouse, J. A. Hobson, H. W. Massingham, and C. P. Scott were responsible for the theoretical statements of the 'New Liberalism' which attracted attention in the first years of the twentieth century. The 'New Liberalism' represented an attempt to establish a theoretical basis for the Radical Progressivism of the late nineteenth century, with its general bias for 'free enterprise', but with a recognition of a field for State and municipal action in the control of public utilities and 'monopolies', and a concession to the demands of Labour and Socialist elements for 'national minimum' standards and greater equality. Winston Churchill put their position succinctly in his remark: 'We want to have free competition upwards; we decline to allow free competition to run downwards.'[5]

The 'New Liberalism' was warmly welcomed by the Fabians, and especially

[1] R. B. Haldane, op. cit. p. 158.　　　　[2] B. Webb, Our Partnership, p. 325.
[3] Ibid. p. 339.　　　　[4] Ibid. pp. 326, 416–7.
[5] Speech at Glasgow 11 October 1906, reprinted in his Liberalism and the Social Problem (Hodder & Stoughton, London, 1909), p. 82.

by the Webbs, whose Socialism about this time was showing a tendency to unravel and allow the 'fringe of private enterprise' to become surprisingly large: 'We don't want to abolish or restrain the development of private enterprise, but, by creating dykes and bulwarks, to control its mischievous effect on the character of the race', wrote Beatrice Webb.[1] Other Fabians agreed, but some with a good deal more scepticism of the 'New Liberalism's' chances of being accepted by the Liberal Party as a whole, or by any important section of it.[2]

To what extent was the 'New Liberalism' influenced by Fabianism? This is no easy question. It could be maintained that the New Liberalism avoided everything in Fabianism that differed from, or went beyond, late nineteenth century Liberal Progressivism, and in this sense it was not influenced by the Socialism of the Fabians. On the other hand, the 'New Liberal' writers had read Fabian works, all of them were in contact with the Fabian leaders, and all were anxious to preserve the Liberal-Labour alliance which seemed threatened by the I.L.P. and the newly-formed Labour Party.[3] Consequently there is a difference in the form, and to a lesser extent in the substance, of 'New Liberalism', when compared with the older Progressivism, which enables one to say that it was influenced by Socialist doctrine of the Fabian kind. There was not merely the use of phrases like 'national minimum standards', and an acceptance of the ideas embodied in such phrases, but a general recognition also of the increased power and importance of Labour in the State, especially of the Trade Unions, and a recognition likewise of the justice of Labour demands for greater material equality.[4]

A gulf still remained, however, between the 'New Liberals' and the Fabians, and they were far to the left of their colleagues in the government. Beatrice Webb's diary shows that the Liberal ministers were willing to receive 'expert' instruction on special points from the Webbs, but were always wary of their advice, even when it concerned particular issues. The Webbs, despite their efforts to present a 'moderate' point of view, were regarded as 'extremists'. Moreover they were listened to with attention only when the demands of organized labour were most formidable in the early days of the new government, and when the young administrators were new to their work and had not yet fallen into the departmental routine. Later, as the attitude of the Liberal politicians hardened, the Webbs were driven gradually into opposition.

The reforms which the Fabians tried to persuade the new Liberal government to accept were set forth in the article 'The Liberal Cabinet: An Intercepted Letter', which was drafted by Sidney Webb, approved by a members' meeting of the Society, and published in the *National Review* for January 1906.

[1] B. Webb, *Our Partnership*, p. 229.
[2] See review of Samuel's book in *Fabian News*, June 1902.
[3] W. Churchill, *op. cit.* pp. 71-84.
[4] *Ibid.* pp. 73, 79-84.

This was an attempt to repeat, in a friendly and joking way, the 'To Your Tents, Oh Israel!' affair. It purported to be a circular letter sent by Sir Henry Campbell-Bannerman to his newly-appointed ministers telling them what reforms were required in each department. To Asquith (Exchequer) were suggested graduated taxes with an abatement on incomes from personal service, the taxation of ground values, certain reforms of grants-in-aid, and the introduction of Trade Union wages, with a 'moral minimum' for government employees. To H. Gladstone (Home Office), the revision of Factory and Truck Acts, the extension of the Workers Compensation Act, the reform of prisons, and the introduction of compulsory arbitration by Trade Boards and minimum wage legislation in certain industries. To Haldane (War), the introduction of compulsory military training for boys under twenty-one, and the extension of the half-time clauses of the Factory Acts to make it possible for boys to undertake this training without interrupting their work or needing to live in barracks. Burns (Local Government Board) was advised to await the report of the Poor Law Commission which had been set up by the previous government, and in the meantime to look to the 'national minimum of sanitation'. Birrell (Education) was urged not to alter too drastically the Acts of 1902-3, and to yield to the Labour demand for the provision of meals for school children. Lloyd George (Board of Trade) was recommended to bring forward a Bill to establish a Port of London Authority, to insist on improvements in the railways, to nationalize canals, and to ensure the collection of proper statistics of home trade. To Buxton (Post Office) the only advice was the provision of higher wages for employees.[1]

It is apparent that most of these recommendations were not 'Socialist' in the narrower sense; some like the extension of the Workers Compensation Act (which the Fabians admitted even the Conservatives were about to enact) were certain to be introduced; all had considerable Radical support; not more than three originated in Fabian or other Socialist circles;[2] and those of the measures which were eventually introduced in no case reproduced Fabian plans in detail, where these had been set forth in their Tracts.

To illustrate these points, two examples may be taken: the establishment of Wages Boards, and the introduction of Old Age Pensions.

(1) *Trade Boards*

In demands for the establishment of wages boards in sweated industries, the Fabians had always been prominent. Beatrice Webb had investigated with Charles Booth the sweated conditions of the tailors in the East End, and later she gave evidence before the Select Committee appointed by the House of

---

[1] There were also a few minor suggestions about the conduct of foreign and colonial affairs.

[2] Port of London Authority, nationalization of canals, and differentiation between earned and unearned incomes, perhaps.

Lords to investigate the sweating system, which reported in 1890 that the evils 'could scarcely be exaggerated'.[1] When no legislative action was taken upon this report, the leadership of a campaign was taken by Sir Charles and Lady Dilke. As early as 1891 Sir Charles advocated minimum wage legislation for sweated trades, and Lady Dilke, in co-operation with Mary Macarthur and other women Labour leaders attempted, largely unsuccessfully, to organize women workers in these trades. In 1894 and 1896, the Fabian Society assisted the campaign with its Tracts *Sweating: Its Cause and Remedy* and *Women and the Factory Acts*,[2] advocating legislative action, and Fabian members were given instructions to persuade all organizations of which they were members to pass resolutions against sweating.[3] In 1897 the Webbs in their *Industrial Democracy* pointed to the working of the minimum wage provisions of the Factories and Shops Act of Victoria, Australia, and put forward the suggestion for a 'national minimum' wage for the lowest-paid workers in all industries. In 1898, Sir Charles Dilke introduced his Sweated Industries Bill in the House of Commons, and thereafter similar measures were presented year after year.

With the return of the Liberals to power in 1906, there was general expectation that they would yield to the widespread demand that had grown up, and, in fact, the Board of Trade immediately commenced an inquiry into the rates of wages in the lowest-paid industries. The result proved even more shocking than had been expected. Scandalously low wages were shown to be paid in the tailoring, cardboard-box making, linen, and jute manufacturing trades and for laundry work.[4] The Anti-Sweating League was immediately formed with widespread support, and Fabian members played an active part in it. Shaw and Wells spoke for it. The Fabian Society produced its Tracts *The Case for a Legal Minimum Wage* (1906) and *Home Work and Sweating: The Causes and Remedies* (1907).[5] The *Daily News* sponsored the campaign, and organized a 'Sweated Industries Exhibit' at the Exhibition in Queen's Hall in 1906, which brought the plight of the workers in these industries to public attention. The Labour Party pressed a Bill upon the Liberals.

After further inquiries into the working of the Victorian legislation, the Select Committee on Home Work, of which Sir Thomas Whittaker was chairman, recommended legislation, and Winston Churchill, as President of the Board of Trade, introduced the Bill which passed into law as the Trade Boards Act 1909. It introduced Trade Boards, from the 1 January 1910, into the tailoring, paper-box making, machine-made lace finishing, and chain-making trades, with a provision for other trades to be brought in by a pro-

---

[1] 5th Report H/L Select Committee on the Sweating System, 1890. This was before Beatrice Webb's marriage and before she had become a Fabian Socialist.
[2] Tracts 50 and 67.
[3] *Fabian News*, May 1894.
[4] Board of Trade: Earning and Hours Enquiry, 1906, vols I—VIII.
[5] Tracts 128 and 130.

visional order of Parliament if the Board of Trade considered the rate of wages paid to be exceptionally low. The legislation substantially followed the Victorian measure.

The Fabians welcomed the passing of the Act, and, although it did not meet all their demands, they envisaged its extension in the future. Their chief point of criticism at the time was that the minimum rates of wages were to be fixed on the basis of 'what the trade would bear', while they considered it should have been fixed on the basis of the wage a worker needed for physical health and efficiency.[1]

(2) *Old age pensions*

Sidney Webb had been amongst the early advocates of old age pensions in England.[2] Bismarck's legislation had been much discussed in both Conservative and Radical circles, and proposals for old age pensions had been put forward by Joseph Chamberlain, Charles Booth and others from the 'eighties and 'nineties. The difference between its various advocates, Socialist and non-Socialist, turned upon such questions as the age-limits, the amount of pension, the method of administering it, and the method of financing it.

The I.L.P., in its 1895 programme, put forward an extremely advanced demand. The Fabian Society, in its first Tract devoted entirely to old age pensions, which appeared in the following year, followed with a scheme that even many Fabian members considered far ahead of anything that was practical politics.[3] However, the Fabian Society put its name to these proposals in order not to lag behind the non-Socialist advocates of pensions. Charles Booth, in articles he had written early in the 'nineties, and in evidence before the Royal Commission on the Aged Poor, had proposed pensions for all at sixty-five, and the Fabians felt they could ask for no less, even if Chamberlain had declared the House of Commons could never be persuaded to vote the money for so generous a scheme.[4] The Fabian Tract therefore demanded universal old age pensions at sixty-five, paid for out of general taxation, and criticized alternative proposals. It altogether rejected plans for subsidies to Friendly Societies; it rejected compulsory state insurance on the ground of collection difficulties, on the ground that the compulsory contributions both of the workers and (ultimately) of the employers would come out of wages, and on the ground that the present generation of aged poor would be unprovided for; and, finally, it dismissed voluntary state insurance as useless. The antagonistic attitude to state insurance became important later.

[1] Addenda to second edition of Tract 130.
[2] See Tract 17 (of 1890).
[3] Pease, *op. cit.* p. 159.
[4] E. Halévy, *History of the English People, Epilogue* 1895–1905, *Imperialism and the rise of Labour*, pp. 233–6.

The Royal Commission on Aged Poor had reported in 1895,[1] and a Parliamentary Committee was appointed in 1896, which sat for two years. In 1898 an Old Age Pensions Act was introduced in New Zealand, and was given publicity in a Fabian leaflet.[2] Charles Booth took the lead in forming the National Committee of Organized Labour for promoting Old Age Pensions for all, with widespread support from Trade Unions, Co-operatives, clergymen,[3] and philanthropists like George Cadbury. The Fabians co-operated. The campaign during 1899 resulted in the appointment of Select Committee of the House of Commons which reported in favour of the New Zealand system, but the matter was shelved on the outbreak of the Boer War. The proposal was taken up again at the conclusion of the war, and the Committee of 1903 reaffirmed, with only a few reservations, the plan of the 1899 Committee. But the Conservative government was unwilling to face the expenditure on old age pensions, and many Conservatives, including Chamberlain, had come to the conclusion that it would need to be made dependent on the establishment of a system of tariffs.

In the meantime, the T.U.C. had steadily pressed the demand, and most candidates included old age pensions in their election promises in 1906, though the Tariff Reformers insisted on a tariff first. The House of Commons on 14 March 1906 unanimously passed a motion in favour of a scheme. After more than a decade of agitation for it, opposition to the scheme as such had been worn down, and delay and government niggardliness remained its only enemies. The Budget of 1907 promised a Bill in the following year, and the T.U.C. in September protested at the delay, demanding 'the payment on 1 January 1909 of pensions of at least five shillings a week to all persons aged sixty or over'. The Fabian Society also issued a new Tract urging the measure,[4] and R. McKenna, the Financial Secretary to the Treasury, consulted the Webbs about the drafting of the bill.[5]

When the Bill was laid before the House in 1908, it was evident that the Webbs' advice had not been taken, at least in the matter of age limits, sliding-scales, and the amount to be paid. The Labour Party was able to secure the modification of the Bill in a more generous direction during its passage through the House, but it was still far from being the measure that the Fabians had desired.

The part played by the Fabians in the passing of these two measures may

---

[1] Sidney Webb had assisted Broadhurst in the preparation of his report. B. Webb, *Our Partnership*, p. 41.
[2] Tract 89.
[3] See article by Stead in *Review of Reviews*, 15 April 1899.
[4] Tract 135.
[5] B. Webb, *Our Partnership*, p. 384. The Webbs recommended to him pensions for all over sixty-five with not less than 10s. a week from property, with a sliding scale from 5s. upwards, income under 5s. not to be taken into account, and no disqualification for pauperism.

be taken as fairly typical of the kind of influence they exercised on the Liberals after the 1906 election. The publication of their Tracts, and their personal influence with politicians and high-placed officials helped in pushing forward demands which had more widespread support. The leadership of the agitation, as in the two cases that have been considered, was often non-Fabian, and the organizations 'non-party' public opinion pressure groups, not of a permanent kind, but set up to promote a specific measure. This kind of agitation and organization became the model for that adopted by the Webbs and the Fabians when they set on foot their greatest campaign of all in the pre-war years—the campaign for implementing the Minority Report on the Poor Law. The story of that campaign must be told at some length, for its results were momentous in the political development of the Society.

THE ROYAL COMMISSION ON THE POOR LAW, 1905-9

In 1905 the Balfour Government set up a Royal Commission to conduct an inquiry into the problem of administering poor relief. There still remains some mystery about the reasons for setting up the Commission at that particular time. It was not an especially bad period of unemployment, and although the 'cyclical' nature of unemployment was becoming recognized, the cycle was not in a bad phase. On the other hand, an election was pending and the government had already passed the Unemployed Workman's Act in the same year, an Act which advanced, if only a small way, in the direction of recognizing that the State had some responsibility for dealing with the causes of poverty. It seems most likely that the appointment of the Royal Commission was inspired by the officials of the Local Government Board, who felt that the principles which should guide them in their administration of the Poor Law had been thrown into a hopeless muddle by this latest piece of social legislation.[1]

The Webbs themselves have described how the English Poor Law had moved from its moorings in the principles which had been laid down by the famous Royal Commission on the Poor Law of 1834.[2] The principle of 'national uniformity' in particular had ceased to have any real application. Under the local control of Poor Law Guardians, elected by the ratepayers in each Poor Law Union, the administration of the law had in some places been made harsher and in others (particularly after the Local Government Act of 1894 had made the elections of Guardians more democratic) more lenient.

---

[1] In this explanation, I have followed that given by the Webbs themselves in vol. II, part II, of their *English Poor Law History* and in *Our Partnership*. I have found no evidence to support the suggestion made by M. A. Hamilton (*op. cit.* pp. 188-9) that the Webbs themselves were responsible for the establishment of the Commission.

[2] B. Webb states the three principles of 1834 to be (i) 'less eligibility' (ii) 'national uniformity' and (iii) 'the workhouse system for the able-bodied', *Our Partnership*, pp. 318-9.

The lenient Guardians made as free use of the system of 'outdoor relief' (assistance given while the paupers remained in their own homes) as the law would allow, though the granting of outdoor relief to the able-bodied poor had been condemned by the 'principles of 1834' as likely to perpetuate and encourage idleness. The harsh Guardians insisted on all paupers entering the workhouse, even when their poverty was due to illness or old age, though the Royal Commissioners of 1834 had recommended the workhouse as appropriate only for the able-bodied poor: the workhouse was intended as a place which would save a man from starvation, but provide bare necessities under conditions so deterrent that the pauper would accept any independent employment offering rather than stay there. The 'General Mixed Workhouses' which housed under the one roof men, women and children, the old, the sick, the feeble-minded along with the able-bodied, were especially appalling.[1] Between the extremes of harshness and leniency, all sorts of variations had occurred in the different Unions, and the officials of the Local Government Board found great difficulty in bringing general rules to bear on the administration of the law.

At a time when social legislation was developing to the point where the new conception of the Welfare State was beginning to challenge the assumptions of nineteenth century Liberalism, the reform of the Poor Law became a crucial problem. Before 1908 the Poor Law was the 'only statutory cash-paying social service in the British Isles';[2] the diverse functions which it performed and the penal restrictions with which it accompanied its aid reflected the State's recognition that it had an obligation to its poorer members and its reluctance to acknowledge more than a minimal role. Could the Poor Law fit in with the new ideas which had already modified it? Should the Poor Law be changed, or the trend of policy which had carried it away from the principles of 1834 be reversed? The government, in so far as it thought about the matter at all, was probably genuinely puzzled about what its attitude should be. But the President of the Local Government Board, Mr Gerald Balfour, was a philosopher who, as Beatrice Webb remarked, 'recognized the public advantage of a precise discrimination between opposing principles',[3] and Mr J. S. (later Sir James) Davy, chief inspector of the Poor Law Division of the Board, was a man of firm views. He adhered strongly to the 'principles of 1834'; to him the Unemployed Workmen's Act of 1905 was the last straw; he and his subordinates decided the 'policy of drift' from the 'principles of 1834' had gone far enough, and that it was time for a complete overhaul of the Poor Law system. Official reaction, combined with genuine

---

[1] The acceptance of poor relief in either of its forms entailed, as a further deterrent feature, pauper status and disfranchisement.
[2] Margaret Cole (ed.), *The Webbs and their Work*, p. 104.
[3] B. Webb, *Our Partnership*, p. 317.

government bewilderment, would explain sufficiently both the setting up of the Royal Commission of 1905 and its mixed composition.[1]

I had extracted from Davy [Beatrice Webb wrote in her diary], in a little interview I had with him, the intention of the Local Government Board officials as to the purpose and procedure they intended to be followed by the Commission. They were going to use us to get certain radical reforms of structure: the Boards of Guardians were to be swept away, judicial officers appointed, and possibly the institutions transferred to the county authorities. With all of which I am inclined to agree. But we were also to recommend reversion to the 'principles of 1834' as regards policy, to stem the tide of philanthropic impulse that was sweeping away the old embankment of deterrent tests to the receipt of relief. . . . Having settled the conclusions to which we are to be led, the L.G.B. officials (on and off the Commission) have pre-determined the procedure. We were to be 'spoon-fed' by evidence carefully selected and prepared; they were to draft the circular to the Board of Guardians; they were to select the Inspectors who were to give evidence; they were virtually to select the Guardians to be called in support of this evidence. Assistant Commissioners were to be appointed, who were to give evidence illustrative of these theories. And, above all we were to be given *opinions* and not *facts.* . . .[2]

She determined to circumvent the officials' plans.

How far was Beatrice Webb successful in influencing the Royal Commission? This is a question which needs to be answered in several stages. There is no doubt that her efforts helped to convert the inquiry from the sort of thing Davy envisaged into a scientific and systematic investigation of all aspects of the Poor Law. Special research was undertaken into the operation of the Poor Law and its effects at her instigation; she played an active part in the cross-examination of the witnesses; and (helped by Sidney) she bombarded the Commission with memoranda on special points. But Beatrice Webb altogether lacked her husband's skill in committee-work, that flexible but tenacious quality which enabled him so often to get his way without in the least offending his colleagues. Beatrice Webb's outspoken and domineering manner, and the unauthorized and sometimes rather unscrupulous methods she used to push her point of view antagonized her fellow-Commissioners. In the end her Minority Report was signed only by the Labour members of the

[1] The Commission had nineteen members, under the chairmanship of Lord George Hamilton, a former Conservative Minister, and a gracious 'Grand Seigneur' to whose capabilities as chairman the Webbs have paid tribute. Allowing for overlap where a member falls into more than one category, they may be classified as follows: nine were responsible in some way—as Poor Law Guardians or high officials of the Local Government Board— for the actual administration of the Poor Law; six were prominent members or supporters of the Charity Organization Society; four represented the Churches; two—George Lansbury and Francis Chandler, secretary of the Carpenter's Union—represented Labour; two were economists; and two—Charles Booth (who was later forced to retire through ill-health) and Beatrice Webb—were social investigators. Report of the Royal Commission on the Poor Laws and Relief of Distress, 1909. Cd 4499. [Hereafter the Report is cited by its number]. In the explanation of the establishment of the Commission, I have followed the Webbs, *English Poor Law History*, vol. II, part II.
[2] B. Webb, *Our Partnership*, p. 322.

Commission and by one convert from amongst the churchmen, the Rev. Russell Wakefield (later Dean of Norwich, and Bishop of Birmingham). Whether more conciliatory and wily tactics would have won over any of the other Commissioners to full support of the Minority proposals may be doubted however, for differing views on the 'deterrence' principle and on the virtues of private charity would have constituted an unbridgeable gulf, even if all personal antagonisms had been set aside.

In the later stages of the Commission, Beatrice Webb was inclined to think that her efforts had been responsible for persuading the Majority to recommend the abolition of the existing Poor Law machinery: the sweeping away of the *ad hoc* Boards of Guardians and the transfer of their functions to other organs of local government.[1] But on her own account of the earlier stages of the Commission, some reservations need to be made.[2] She herself admitted that it was a 'reforming' Commission;[3] even some 'reactionary' officials desired the abolition of the Guardians;[4] and when this question was discussed by the Commission, in October 1907, only two members were 'for the *status quo*'.[5] So far as pure destruction went, there was a great measure of agreement, though the reasons which lay behind this agreement differed. Some officials wanted the Boards of Guardians swept away because they thought many of them had become 'corrupt' and 'lax' and had departed from the 'principles of 1834' under the influence of democratically elected Guardians. Beatrice Webb, at the other extreme, desired their abolition for a number of reasons, one of which was that they imposed a stigma of poverty on everybody who had recourse to their assistance. The Majority of the Poor Law Commission wished to abolish the Guardians in order to make way for new institutions, of a somewhat curious and complicated structure, which would allow a larger share of interference to voluntary charitable organizations.[6]

The central issue of the Commission, however, was its attitude to the 'deterrence principle' or the 'principle of less eligibility', chief of the principles of 1834, and on this issue the difference between the Commissioners emerged. The nature of the deterrence principle was expounded succinctly and ruthlessly by Davy. To make the condition of the person receiving poor relief 'less eligible' than that of the lowest-paid independent labourer, in order to discourage the others, it was necessary that the pauper should suffer first, 'the

[1] *Ibid.* p. 397.
[2] It is possible that Beatrice Webb's activities may have done something to persuade the Majority to transfer the Guardians' functions to committees of the County and County Borough Councils and not to set up a new *ad hoc* authority, so I hesitate to say that she had no influence on the destructive side of the Commission's work.
[3] B. Webb, *Our Partnership*, p. 319.
[4] *Ibid.* p. 322.
[5] *Ibid.* p. 390.
[6] Similarly, the abolition of the General Mixed Workhouse could be recommended, for different reasons, by all shades of opinion from the adherents of the principles of 1834 to those who favoured the complete overthrow of the Poor Law system.

loss of personal reputation (what is understood by the stigma of pauperism); secondly, the loss of personal freedom which is secured by detention in a workhouse; and thirdly, the loss of political freedom by suffering disfranchisement'. In the workhouse, Davy recommended that the 'work should be both irksome and unskilled . . . You have got to find work which anybody can do, and which nearly everybody dislikes doing. . . . You have got to give him something like corn-grinding or flint-crushing, cross-cut sawing, or some work of that sort, which is laborious and wholly unskilled'.[1] A generous spirit might suppose that such a principle could only be justified on the assumption that there was work for everybody if they would go to it or that poverty was in some way the result of the pauper's moral shortcomings. But Beatrice Webb discovered the deterrence principle was supported by hard-headed and hard-hearted administrators who delved not at all into the ethical problem, but who simply took it for granted that 'the poor ye have always with you', and saw the administrative problem as one of keeping paupers off 'the rates'. They believed that poor people would refuse to work at unpleasant employments and prefer to subsist on poor relief unless deterred by the knowledge that they were always worse off when receiving poor relief than the lowest labourer in independent employment. When Davy was asked if he did not think the deterrence principle bore harshly upon men thrown out of work by a trade depression, he answered: 'He [the unemployed man] must stand by his accidents; he must suffer for the general good of the body politic'.[2]

Was Beatrice Webb's campaign against the deterrence principle successful in persuading her fellow-Commissioners? It must not be supposed that the Majority was wedded to harsh views; the Commissioners did not need much persuasion that paupers should be divided into separate categories. There was general agreement that special provision should be made for pauper children and the aged, that those who had fallen into poverty through illness should receive special treatment, and that penalties such as disfranchisement should not be applied to those in receipt of medicine or medical attention. The difference of opinion concerning the non-able-bodied poor really arose on the question whether these categories of pauper should be treated altogether outside the scope of the Poor Law, thus removing from them entirely the stigma of poverty. Beatrice Webb did not succeed in convincing the Majority to take this additional step, despite a long and strenuous fight on behalf of the sick poor.

The main battle was joined on the question of the treatment of the able-bodied poor. Beatrice Webb was tireless in her efforts to demonstrate the social, as opposed to the individual moral causes of poverty, because she

---

[1] Report of Royal Commission of the Poor Laws and Relief of Distress, 1909, Appendix vol. I, Minutes of Evidence, questions 2230, 2366.
[2] *Ibid.* Question 3219.

thought that most of the other Commissioners, under the influence of the Charity Organization Society's views, were biassed in favour of the opinion that pauperism of able-bodied persons was caused mainly by a failing of character. By her clever cross-examination, by calling Fabians, Labour men and social investigators as witnesses, and above all by the reports of special investigators which she promoted, Beatrice Webb drove home her arguments about the social causes of unemployment.[1] The Majority Report shows the effect: though it dealt first with the 'moral causes' like drunkenness and gambling,[2] it nevertheless devoted more space to such causes as casual employment, deadend employment, unhealthy trades, low wages, and unemployment due to cyclical fluctuations.[3] Labour bureaux and unemployment insurance were recommended by the Majority as measures for dealing with pauperism resulting from social causes. Even the establishment of special works by local authorities (with the approval of the Local Government Board) in times of exceptional distress was contemplated, if only 'for a strictly limited period during the earlier years of the reforms which we suggest'.[4] Only persons receiving assistance (other than medical relief) for three months or more in a year were to be disfranchised. Thus the range of application of the 'deterrence' principle was narrowed in the Majority Report.

But an element of 'deterrence' remained. In a sense, there was an element of 'deterrence' even in the Minority Report, which agreed at least that habitual idleness, vagrancy, and mendicity should be suppressed with the full vigour of the law. But the Minority assumed that vagrants and habitual idlers were rather exceptional people, and could be dealt with by the ordinary judicial powers which the State already possessed. The Majority concluded that some special deterrent principle in the Poor Law was still necessary. The Commissioners who signed the Majority Report were more ready to assume that labour exchanges and unemployment insurance would remedy involuntary unemployment, and this may have led them to believe that, after these measures had been introduced, the able-bodied poor who were unemployed for a period longer than three months would either be slacking or would in some way be responsible; consequently their condition would need to be made 'less eligible'. Here they were being optimistic about the results of their reforms, as may be seen by comparing the Majority and Minority attitudes to public works provided by the State. The Majority thought State public works would only be necessary until their other recommendations were fully put into

---

[1] Most frequently quoted in the footnotes to the sections of the Majority Report which deal with this subject are the special reports of Mr Steel-Maitland and Miss R. E. Squire, of Mr Cyril Jackson and the Rev. J. C. Pringle.

[2] Cd. 4499 Majority Report, Sec. 531 of part IV, ch. 10.

[3] Ibid. Secs. 540, 545, 548, 549, and all of part VI. Note Jevons' explanation of cyclical crises in footnote to sec. 143 of part VI.

[4] Ibid. Recommendation 172.

force, whereas the Minority thought of State public works as a permanent institution, to be expanded or contracted with the downward or upward movement of the trade cycle, and as a *preventive* measure, in that they were to be put into operation whenever unemployment rose above a certain percentage.

In any case, there still remained the other prop of the 'less eligibility' principle, the fear that too many people would be on the rates unless State assistance were made unpleasant. The difference between the Majority and Minority on this point could not be resolved. It was the same irreducible conflict that arose so often in other fields of local politics between the policy of 'Saving the Rates' and the policy of 'High Rates and a Healthy City'. The second slogan provided the key to the Fabian attitude to poverty. Stated fairly diplomatically in the Minority Report, more directly in the Fabian Tracts, and most bluntly of all by Bernard Shaw in his plays and prefaces, it was in the last analysis that nobody should be poor. Poverty, like disease, needed to be eliminated. To such an attitude the question of individual responsibility for pauperism was almost (if not quite) irrelevant. Making people 'less eligible' meant keeping them in poverty. But it was for the welfare of the State as a whole that nobody should be allowed to fall below a certain National Minimum. The Minority Report opposed the detention of able-bodied paupers in special institutions (except those positively convicted by judicial process under the existing criminal law); it opposed the withdrawal or restriction of outdoor relief; and it insisted that adequate maintenance, without disfranchisement or other penalty, should be provided for the unemployed and their families while they were unemployed.[1] The Majority Report, with its different outlook, favoured the establishment of special institutions, not workhouses but places of detention where the able-bodied paupers would be given a course of treatment which would fit them to earn their living; it favoured the restriction of outdoor relief to a minimum of emergency cases; and it recommended generally that State relief should be rendered 'less eligible' not, it is true, than the condition of the lowest paid independent worker, but, significantly enough, than the relief given by voluntary charity; the acceptance of State relief for more than three months was to entail disfranchisement. The Minority desired the completion of the process begun by the 1905 Unemployed Workman's Act; the Majority favoured the abolition of the 1905 Act.

The recommendations in the two Reports concerning the reorganization of the machinery of poor relief followed from their different attitudes to 'deterrence' and to voluntary charity. The Majority proposed the transfer of the Guardians' functions to special Committees nominated by County Councils and County Borough Councils in part from amongst their members and in part from outside. These Committees, to be called 'Public Assistance

[1] Cd. 4499 Minority Report, pp. 1236–7. Recommendations 42 and 48.

Authorities' (to avoid the odium of the name 'Poor Law'), were to have merely supervisory functions. Actual administration was to be carried on by subordinate 'Public Assistance Committees' which were to include a certain proportion of persons nominated by the Urban and Rural District Councils, and by Voluntary Aid Committees that were to be set up to regularize and systematize voluntary charitable relief. In London the 'Public Assistance Authority' was to be a Committee of the L.C.C. of which three-quarters of the members were to be appointed by the L.C.C. (at least one quarter from outside the L.C.C.'s own members), and the other quarter nominated by the Local Government Board. On the local 'Public Assistance Committees' for London nominees of the Metropolitan Borough Councils were to replace those of the Urban and Rural District Councils of the more general scheme. Central control was to be left in the hands of the division of the Local Government Board which already dealt with poor relief, with a change of name to 'Public Assistance Division'.

The Minority described these administrative proposals as undemocratic, unnecessarily complicated and unworkable, and advocated a radical transformation from top to bottom. In its view the existing Poor Law Division of the Local Government Board was unfitted to work the new scheme, and should be replaced by a Ministry of Labour to organize the whole labour market. The complete 'break-up of the Poor Law' was recommended. The functions of the Boards of Guardians should not be transferred *en bloc* to any new Committee of local government bodies, but the services the Poor Law Guardians had administered should be divided among existing Committees of the local County or County Borough authorities. Thus the sick poor would be dealt with by the Public Health Committee of existing local authorities, the pauper children by the Education Committee, the mentally deficient poor by the Asylums Committee, the aged poor by the Pensions Committee, and other committees should be set up where desirable. The Minority argued that this arrangement would ensure more efficient administration than any special Committee dealing with 'the Poor' as a group and overlapping the functions of other Committees, and would more effectually eliminate the 'stigma of the Poor Law', since each Committee would be providing services that did not necessarily apply only to the poor. It would be left to the officers of local government to decide whether the service should be paid for or free, and thus the poor person would receive the same services and not be specially marked off from his fellow citizens.

Beatrice Webb, it may be concluded, had some considerable influence upon the Poor Law Commission, though she failed to convert the Majority to her point of view. Any more precise assessment must await a full-scale study of the Commission and the Commissioners. But there seems little doubt that her activities were partly responsible for moving the Majority further from the principles of 1834 and further towards the principles of the Welfare State than it would have gone of its own accord. Nevertheless, the difference between the Minority and Majority Reports reveals a quite deep chasm between the thinking of the Welfare State and the Liberal thought of the early twentieth century.

THE CAMPAIGN FOR THE MINORITY REPORT

The Minority Report of the Poor Law soon became a Fabian document literally as well as in spirit. The Webbs determined to conduct a large-scale national campaign for the principles of the Minority Report to influence public opinion and to force the Liberal government to accept and implement its proposals. As a first step the Fabian Society issued a cheap edition of the report. The Webbs were more successful in getting widespread circulation of the report than they anticipated, for after the Treasury had failed to restrain the Society from issuing its cheap edition, the government printer brought out one too. The report had an unexpectedly large sale. By 1910 nearly 25,000 copies of the report in both editions had been sold.[1]

This had not been the first occasion on which the Society and its members had urged the reform of the Poor Law. There had been Fabian proposals, necessarily of a less comprehensive and well-studied character, in some of their earliest Tracts. Though the same in spirit, they had not advocated such radical structural changes. During the sitting of the Royal Commission, however, a Tract drafted by E. R. Pease, *The Abolition of the Poor Law Guardians*,[2] had brought the Fabian recommendations up to date in this respect. The Society was ready and willing to provide the organizing ability behind the campaign to publicize the Minority Report, though for tactical reasons it was necessary that the campaign should not be led by the Society itself.

In April 1909, two months after the reports had been published, a broad all-party organization was formed, which took the name, 'The National Committee for the Break-up of the Poor Law'. The Rev. Russell Wakefield was its Chairman and Beatrice Webb its Secretary; and by December 1909 it had enrolled over 16,000 members. For three years its campaign was conducted with all the skill that Mrs Webb's organizing capacity and enthusiasm and Sidney Webb's experience in the Fabian Society could devise. The Committee won the support of practically all the Labour M.P.'s, but of only a few Liberals, like Sir Alfred Mond (Lord Melchett), John (Lord) Simon, and Winston Churchill, and a few Conservatives, like J. W. Hills and Gilbert Parker. A. J. Balfour, though remaining non-commital, allowed the Webbs to believe that he was not unsympathetic. An impressive list of patrons amongst academics, literary men, and ecclesiastics figured in the campaign

[1] M. A. Hamilton, *op. cit.* p. 197.
[2] Tract 126 (1906).

literature; and Beatrice Webb observed that many 'Progressives' who latterly had 'shunned . . . the Fabians are trooping in to the National Committee—Leonard Hobhouse, J. A. Hobson, G. P. Gooch, Graham Wallas, Gilbert Murray, H. G. Wells, and others'.[1] The tactics employed by the committee were those well-tried in the Fabian Society: public meetings, addressed by prominent men and women in different parts of the country; the organization of volunteer helpers in distributing leaflets and sending out circulars; the interviewing of influential people; the lobbying of M.P.'s; the writing of letters to the press. Beatrice Webb's aim was to work up a public opinion which would press upon the government a Bill to give effect to the Minority Report. The Bill had been drafted by Henry Slesser, then a young lawyer who was an active member of the Fabian Society, and its second reading was moved by Sir Robert Price on 8 April 1910.[2]

At first the National Committee for the Break-up of the Poor Law regarded the Majority Report as the chief obstacle in its path. The Majority had founded in February 1910 a body for advocating its point of view which was named The National Poor Law Reform Association, with Lord George Hamilton as its president. This Association, and the Majority Report, drew the National Committee's fire. A third organization—The National Committee for Poor Law Reform, an offshoot of the British Constitutional Association whose propaganda was summed up in the title of Sir William Chance's pamphlet *Poor Law Reform—Via Tertia—the Case for the Guardians*—was regarded as comparatively unimportant. But the Parliamentary debate on the second reading of the Prevention of Destitution Bill made it clear that the issue was not one between the Majority and the Minority—if this had not already become clear earlier. The supporters of the existing state of things regarded even the Majority Report as too radical.[3] Most of the Poor Law Guardians could obviously not be expected to favour their abolition. But it came as a great blow to the Webbs when the County Council's Association voted in favour of continuing the existing system. Though they had got a favourable resolution through the London County Council, even with its Municipal Reform majority, many of the other County Councils showed considerable unwillingness to take over the onerous and expensive functions of the Guardians. On the second reading of the Prevention of Destitution Bill the Prime Minister (Asquith) made his position clear. Speaking of both Reports he said that even

on the points on which they are agreed I am not sure whether it is possible or practicable to carry out their recommendations. They have both pronounced sentence of death on the Boards of Guardians. Let us assume they are right, I think you

[1] B. Webb, *Our Partnership*, p. 430.
[2] Hansard 5th series, vol. XIV, col. 780 *et seq.*
[3] Report of the Poor Law Conferences 1911-2, pp. 183-7.

will find that the Boards of Guardians will die very hard. They are very powerful bodies. With all their defects and short-comings they after all represent an enormous amount of gratuitous and public spirited service . . . we could ill spare from the sphere of local administration. I confess I am old-fashioned in that matter.[1]

John Burns, the ex-Social Democrat now President of the Local Government Board, still priding himself on being a 'strong man of working-class origin' but in fact completely in the hands of his officials, spoke at length to the same effect. Turning to new account some scraps of his former Marxism he solemnly assured the House that the causes of destitution were 'deep down in our social, industrial, and economic conditions', and therefore beyond the reach of any Bill, but that the better administration of the Poor Law could be satisfactorily attended to by a few regulations of his own.[2] Balfour, speaking as leader of the Opposition, dallied with logical points and really avoided a decision.[3]

From the middle of 1910 it was obvious to the propagandists of the Minority Report that their campaign, while it had been successful in enlisting the support of some political figures on both sides of the House, had failed with the leaders. It was also apparent to them that the issue lay not between the Majority and Minority proposals but between both and the *status quo*. Consequently, at the first annual meeting of the National Committee for the Break-up of the Poor Law, held in 1910, the name of the organization was changed to 'The National Committee for the Prevention of Destitution'. The reason for this change of name was not (as has been suggested)[4] to make the Committee avowedly more radical and more socialist. On the contrary, the intention was to change it from an organization devoting itself to propaganda for the Minority Report to a wider organization which could enlist some of the supporters of the Majority Report. The Webbs recognized 'that a frontal attack on the existence of the Board of Guardians . . . was, in view of the prepossessions of the Liberal Cabinet of the time, unlikely to achieve any success in the political field. More effective results might be obtained, in the long run, by promoting, through an unsectarian organization, the growth of development of the various parts of the Framework of Prevention'.[5] What they meant by the 'Framework of Prevention' is made clear in their *English Poor Law Policy*. It is there used as a wide term, covering all the methods that had been making for the prevention of destitution and for a more humane policy on the part of the Poor Law authorities over several decades.

[1] Hansard, 5th series, vol. xvi, col. 838.
[2] *Ibid.* Cols. 842–51.
[3] The Webbs, nevertheless, were grateful to Balfour for his speech for it indicated that the Conservative Party was not pledged against the Minority Report and this prevented it from being branded as an extremist Socialist document. *Our Partnership*, p. 449.
[4] M. Cole, *Beatrice Webb*, p. 105; M. A. Hamilton, *op. cit.* p. 202.
[5] S. and B. Webb, *English Poor Law Policy*, vol. II, p. 721.

The Webbs now aimed at the more gradual development of those measures of State action which they considered were gradually undermining the older conception of the Poor Law, and which they predicted would ultimately destroy it. In many of these measures there had been agreement between the Majority and Minority, and eventually at the Conference held in Whit week of 1911 the N.S.P.D. was successful in winning the sympathy of Lord George Hamilton and some of his Majority colleagues.[1]

THE FABIANS 'DISHED' BY SOCIAL INSURANCE

Once again, however, the Webbs were out-manœuvred by the Liberals, and unemployment and health insurance was the means by which it was accomplished. Social insurance schemes had been canvassed in Part VI Ch. 4 and elsewhere of the Majority Report, where cautious schemes were recommended, and they were dealt with more briefly in the Minority Report in Part II Ch. V (D). Both the Majority and Minority Reports mentioned favourably the Ghent Scheme, whereby Trade Unions were granted a subvention by the State or Municipality in order to encourage them to extend their insurance against unemployment, though the Majority thought that the growth of Friendly Societies and 'Trade Unions organized for provident benefits alone' should be encouraged by a similar scheme if it were adopted in England.[2] Both the Majority and Minority dwelt on the disadvantages of a compulsory or universal unemployment insurance scheme.[3] With regard to compulsory national health insurance the Majority and Minority were divided. The Majority declared themselves 'almost driven to the conclusion that a new form of Insurance is required, which, for want of a better name, we may call Invalidity Insurance';[4] they discussed various foreign schemes of insurance and approved a scheme which should be financed partly by contribution from the workers, partly by contribution from employers, and partly by a subsidy from the State.[5] The Minority, contemplating a vast expansion of the duties of the Public Health authorities and the numbers of the medical officers employed by them, definitely rejected any scheme for compulsory health insurance.[6]

Before the Commission's reports were issued, schemes of health and unemployment insurance were already under discussion. Lloyd George had returned from a visit to Germany in August 1908 enthusiastic about the working of the scheme of health insurance established by Bismarck in 1889. At the same time, Lloyd George and Winston Churchill were beginning to be

[1] B. Webb, *Our Partnership*, p. 473.
[2] Cd. 4499, Majority Report, part VI, ch. 4, sec. 596.
[3] *Ibid*. Secs. 579, 581; Minority Report, pp. 1199, 1200.
[4] *Ibid*. Majority Report, part VIII, sec. 10.
[5] *Ibid*. Sec. 13.
[6] *Ibid*. Minority Report, pp. 920-1.

interested in the plans for unemployment insurance which had been worked out by William Henry Beveridge in 1907 after a study of municipal schemes in a number of cities on the Continent.[1] Beveridge was then a young Radical journalist in whom the Webbs had taken an interest because of his work amongst the unemployed of London and his advocacy of labour exchanges. The Webbs incorporated many of Beveridge's notions concerning labour exchanges into their plans for Poor Law reform; they also gave Beveridge the opportunity of putting his ideas to the Poor Law Commission, and his evidence impressed the other Commissioners too. When Winston Churchill, aware of the agreement of the Commission on this subject, decided to anticipate its conclusions by introducing a Bill, the Webbs recommended 'the boy Beveridge' to him. Churchill appointed Beveridge to the Board of Trade in 1908 and made him responsible for the planning and administration of the Labour Exchanges Act 1909. Already before this appointment, however, Beveridge had been striking out in a new line of thought very different from that of the Webbs. In November 1907 he had presented to the Board of Trade a lengthy memorandum on unemployment insurance, which was read and approved by Llewellyn Smith and Winston Churchill.[2] Shortly afterwards Churchill asked Beveridge and Llewellyn Smith to work out in detail the scheme which later was embodied in Part II of the National Insurance Act 1911.

The Webbs disapproved strongly of both the Lloyd George health insurance schemes, which followed the German model, and the recommendations of the Majority of the Poor Law Commission and the new Beveridge-Llewellyn Smith-Churchill scheme for unemployment insurance.[3] They realized early that an elaborate insurance scheme was in many ways the alternative to their own proposals in the Minority Report, and they believed, or pretended to believe, that the scheme was impracticable as well as inferior. In the Minority Report they not only disapproved of compulsory contributory insurance, but also predicted that it never would be accepted. 'Any attempt to *enforce* on people of this country—whether for supplementary pensions, provision for sickness or invalidity, or anything else—a system of direct, personal, weekly contribution must, in our judgment, in face of so powerful a phalanx as the combined Friendly Societies, Trade Unions, and Industrial Insurance Companies, fighting in defence of their own business, prove politically disastrous.'[4]

[1] Lord Beveridge, *Power and Influence* (Hodder & Stoughton, London, 1953), ch. IV, *passim*. W. J. Braithwaite, a young civil servant, was sent by Lloyd George to the Continent in 1910 to study health insurance. His memoirs, edited by Sir Henry Bunbury under the title *Lloyd George's Ambulance Wagon* (Methuen, London, 1957), give the most detailed account of the framing and passing of Health Insurance.
[2] Llewellyn Smith was Permanent Under-Secretary and Winston Churchill President of the Board of Trade at that time.
[3] B. Webb, *Our Partnership*, p. 417.
[4] Cd. 4499, Minority Report, p. 921.

The Webbs dismissed as 'wasteful' the suggestion that the State should bring insurance companies, friendly societies and trade unions into the scheme, and relied on the opposition of these vested interests to wreck any Bill that would establish State competition in this field. They also felt that any insurance scheme would be used by the government as an excuse for avoiding the more urgent problems of public assistance.

Spurred on by the Webbs, the Fabian Society began by attacking the National Insurance Bill root and branch. The *Crusade* denounced it because it did not aim at prevention of ill-health (as it claimed a well-organized State Medical Service would do) nor at the prevention of unemployment, and also because the contributory system would fall more heavily upon lower-income groups. The Webbs put forward again their criticisms and alternative recommendations personally to ministers and officials and publicly in their works *The Prevention of Destitution* (1911) and *The State and the Doctor* (1910); and Bernard Shaw in 1911 wrote his well-known preface to *The Doctor's Dilemma*.

When it became apparent that Lloyd George was going to proceed with the Bill, that he was going to carry the Trade Unions with him by the powers he was prepared to accord them in the administering of it, and that some Labour Party leaders were preparing to do a deal with him over it, the Fabian criticism altered. The Society's general attitude remained critical, though two members of the Executive Committee—E. R. Pease and Sir Leo Chiozza Money—were prepared to take the complacent view that the Society's principle was that of 'accepting and making the best of' a 'Bill introduced by a strong government,'[1] and that the Society, ought therefore dissociate itself from the attacks upon the measure. The majority of the Executive, however, issued leaflets (which do not appear in the numbered series of Fabian Tracts) examining and criticising the National Insurance Bill in detail. The criticism no longer was 'root and branch': the line of attack became almost entirely concentrated upon the injustice of the contributory principle. 'You cannot mitigate the evils of poverty at the expense of the poor', declared the Fabians, as they listed their reasons for opposition. These were, first, that the 'contributory principle' amounted to a poll-tax imposed without regard to ability to pay; secondly, that some employers would lower wages or increase the prices of their goods in order to pay their share; thirdly, that the insurance services already provided by some employers would be lost, while the municipal authorities would have no inducement to extend free medical and other services; fourthly, that those who could really afford to pay contributions would, if they had wished

---

[1] Pease, *op. cit.* p. 224. Sidney Webb was inclined to acquiesce, but not Beatrice, *Our Partnership*, p. 474. An attempt by Sidney Webb to persuade Lloyd George to a compromise between the Health Scheme operated through Friendly Societies and Trade Unions and the Webbs' plan for a Medical Service administered through Local Health Authorities and the Medical Officers of Health is given in a memorandum quoted as Appendix A of *Lloyd George's Ambulance Wagon*, pp. 307-10.

to do so, already have insured themselves; and fifthly, that the benefits under the scheme which the poor would receive would amount to precious little. The remedies the Fabians proposed took the form of two main amendments (and other smaller and consequential ones): they urged that no contribution should be taken from persons receiving less than a 'living wage' (with the deficiency being made good by the State, not by the employer) and that every insured person should get a certain 'minimum benefit' which, as things stood, those who most needed it would not receive.[1]

The Fabian opposition in both its forms proved quite unavailing. The National Insurance Act of 1911 became law and the Webbs' campaign for the Minority Report, as John Burns gleefully announced, was 'dished'.[2] The Webbs' energetic but rather old-fashioned appeal at the hustings to enlightened public opinion was no match for the flamboyant demagogy of Lloyd George, with his skilful manipulation of the press. Public attention was diverted from the Minority proposals to the question of national insurance, and the issue was one calculated to divide once more the people whom the Webbs were trying to unite in their 'Prevention of Destitution' campaign. Should national insurance be regarded as part of the 'Framework of Prevention'? Differing answers to this question separated off the supporters of the Majority proposals, and even divided the Webbs' own followers. Disagreements about the role of medical men, and about contributory finance opposed to finance out of general taxation all helped to cause 'the steam to go out of' the Prevention of Destitution movement. The N.C.P.D. dwindled from a wide organization to a smaller and more radical body. Its propaganda became more controversial and though its work continued in this new form, though the younger and more radical elements even became more enthusiastic for it, the Webbs already knew when they left for a holiday abroad in June 1911 that their campaign was declining, and when they returned to England in April 1912 they realized it was all but dead. An attempt was made to continue the struggle in 1912, and a second annual conference of the N.C.P.D. was held, but it was decided in that year to reduce the office staff and no longer to make appeals for subscriptions. The monthly journal of the N.C.P.D., the *Crusade*, appeared for the last time in March 1913. The defeat was not simply a personal defeat for the Webbs and the Fabians: they realized that it meant also the defeat of more fundamental, socialist change by a galvanized Liberalism. Beatrice Webb wrote in her diary: 'The issue is fairly joined—complete state responsibility with a view of prevention, or partial state responsibility by a new form of relieving destitution unconnected with the Poor Law, but leaving the Poor Law

---

[1] *The National Insurance Bill: Issued by order of the Executive Committee of the Fabian Society* (leaflet n.d.); also, for more detailed criticism of the Bill, *The Insurance Bill and the Workers: Criticisms and Amendments of the National Insurance Bill prepared by the Executive Committee of the Fabian Society*, June 1911.

[2] B. Webb, *Our Partnership*, p. 475.

for those who fall out of benefit. It is a trial of strength between the two ideas.'[1] And the attacks which the Fabians made on the contributory principle adopted in the National Insurance Act indicate that they were aware of a deeper conflict even if they did not realize its full implications at that time.[2] Hitherto the Fabians had tended to identify advances towards the welfare state with advances towards socialism. The contributory principle, together with the subsidies to private enterprise provided for in the Insurance Act, showed that this identification was no necessary one, and that there were ways of establishing a welfare state which did not involve greater equality or complete social control.

Over the section in their *English Poor Law History* which recounts the events of these years the Webbs have placed the heading 'A Campaign that Failed?' So far as the immediate result was concerned, the query might be removed from that heading. The Webbs' campaign had failed. Nothing less than the great depression of 1929-33 was necessary to force the government to introduce any large-scale changes into the Poor Law, and the Local Government Act 1929 of the Conservative government followed more the lines of the Majority Report of 1909 than those suggested by the Minority. The Beveridge Report incorporated and restated many of the Webbs' ideas, but by the time the last remnant of the Poor Law was finally abolished in July 1948 when the National Assistance Act 1946 came into effect, the Webbs' campaign for the Minority Report had been forgotten by the public. Nevertheless, in another sense, the Webbs' query in their heading is well justified. Perhaps the agitation of the National Committee for the Prevention of Destitution had done something to change the sentiments of thinking people about the cure for poverty. And Fabian propaganda and influence did not cease with the ending of that campaign. The Fabian Research Committee undertook analyses of the National Insurance Act and the Insurance Companies, the reports of which appeared as *New Statesman* supplements on 14 March 1914 and 13 March 1915; they have been described as 'the Webbs' revenge for their Poor Law defeat'.[3] Much to their ironical amusement, the Webbs' advice was sought by Lloyd George after these supplements appeared concerning financial troubles arising out of the operation of the Insurance Act.[4] During the First World War, a Ministry of Labour was created in 1916, mainly for administrative reasons, which took over from the Board of Trade the control of all labour matters, thus incidentally carrying out one of the proposals of the

[1] *Ibid.* p. 476.
[2] It may be doubted too whether the Liberals realized the full implications: it is more likely that the contributory principle was adopted largely because it was thought to involve less large-scale budgetary policy in an age wary of such innovation.
[3] M. Cole, *Beatrice Webb*, p. 120. See these Reports and Alban Gordon, *Social Insurance: What it is and what it might be*, (Fabian Society and Allen & Unwin, London, 1924), for later Fabian attitude to insurance.
[4] M. Cole (ed.), *Beatrice Webb's Diaries* 1912-24 (Longmans, London, 1952), pp. 19, 22.

Minority Report. Beatrice Webb also urged other Minority Report proposals upon the wartime advisory committees of which she was a member; she had the satisfaction of getting most of these proposals adopted by the Local Government Committee of the Reconstruction Committee in 1917,[1] but its recommendations were shelved after the war. She put forward her arguments to the public once again in the Fabian Tract *The Abolition of the Poor Law* in 1918.[2] This quiet and steady propaganda, though devoid of immediate effect, did something to keep the problem before the minds of administrators.

Much more important were the indirect effects of the Poor Law campaign upon the Fabians themselves, and upon the Webbs in particular. It changed their view of political tactics, and marked the beginning of the end of permeation of the Liberal Party. The party divisions became more rigid when obvious reforms, that had been demanded for many years by Radicals and humanitarian Conservatives, became exhausted. Already some of the Fabians' more effective influence on the pre-war Liberal government had been exercised through the Labour Party, and as the Webbs and the older Fabians became disillusioned with their attempts to influence the Liberals, the Fabian Society began to move into the Labour Party's ambit exclusively. Out of the ashes of the *Crusade* arose the *New Statesman* in 1913. Certainly the leader of the first issue of this new journal disavowed connection with the Labour Party and announced its complete independence; but it entered the journalistic field as a rival of the *Nation* and other Liberal periodicals, and its advent marked a change from the days when the Fabians were scornful of running a paper of their own and were confident of permeating the Liberal 'capitalist press'.[3] The move of the Fabian Society away from the Liberals to a definite affiliation with the Labour Party might have taken place earlier if the Labour Party had not sunk into political lassitude and factional confusion during the years immediately before the First World War.

[1] *Ibid.* p. 99.
[2] Tract 185.
[3] Tract 70.

CHAPTER X

THE INFLUENCE OF THE FABIANS UPON THE INDEPENDENT LABOUR PARTY

THE INAUGURAL CONFERENCE OF THE I.L.P.

GEORGE BERNARD SHAW and W. S. De Mattos attended the inaugural conference of the Independent Labour Party at Bradford as representatives of the London Fabian Society, on the conditions laid down in its letter to the *Workman's Times*.[1] The conference was also attended by representatives from the Bradford, Carlisle, Halifax, Huddersfield, Jarrow-on-Tyne, Leeds, Liverpool, Nottingham, Preston, and Ramsbottom provincial Fabian Societies, and from the Yorkshire Fabian Federation. None of these provincial Fabian Societies made conditions similar to those of the London group; in fact, a Liverpool Fabian protested at the conference against the London Society's attitude.[2] The anger of many of the delegates expressed itself in a challenge to the London Fabian Society's credentials. Hostile delegates interpreted the Society's letter to the *Workman's Times* (rightly) as meaning that the Society would refuse to be bound by I.L.P. conference decisions, and (wrongly) that the London Society as a whole wished to prevent a national I.L.P. from coming into existence. One speaker, who was ruled out of order, began a general protest about the way Sidney Webb had helped John Morley at Newcastle in the teeth of the Newcastle Labour Party. Shaw, who was required to withdraw from the body of the hall while his credentials were being discussed, but who immediately took up a 'strong enfilading position'[3] in the gallery, attempted to justify the Fabian attitude, but the conference refused to hear him until the vote was taken. The credentials of the London Fabians were accepted, but only by the narrow margin of two votes: forty-nine delegates voted for acceptance, and forty-seven against.

This vote was not, of course, an expression of disfavour of Fabian policy in general; it was merely a protest against their sceptical or lukewarm attitude to 'independent' tactics. As Shaw declared later: 'It was a curious division. Gallant opponents voted for us, whilst fellow Fabians and men who had the most signal proof of our sincerity and straightness to the Labour movement voted against us. . . .'[4] And he claimed that though he (in his capacity as the

---

[1] See ch. IX, p. 249 above.
[2] Report of the First General Conference of the I.L.P. held at Bradford, 13 and 14 January 1893. The material used in this section, unless otherwise stated comes from this source.
[3] J. Sexton, *Sir James Sexton, Agitator: Life of the Dockers' M.P.: an Autobiography* (Faber & Faber, London, 1936), for a vivid, if inaccurate, account.
[4] *Workman's Times*, 28 January 1893.

representative of the London Fabians) was the most unpopular man at the conference, and though Robert Blatchford was undeniably the most popular, yet Blatchford merely got all the applause, while the Fabians got all the votes.[1] In any case, the Fabians had more than one string to their bow. If the London Society was unpopular, there remained the representatives of the practically-autonomous provincial Fabian Societies, in disagreement concerning tactics, but agreed on fundamentals, who could persuade the conference and obtain positions of influence in the new organization.

It must be recognized at the outset that certain principles and policies adopted by the inaugural conference of the I.L.P. which were in conformity with Fabian views, and which were claimed as evidence of Fabian influence,[2] were, to all practical intents, accepted before ever the conference met, and did not in the least depend on the Fabian Society's popularity or persuasion at Bradford. As the conference was called with the specific object of establishing a new party to fight parliamentary elections, the Anarchists, and all those fundamentally opposed to the use of parliamentary methods did not attend. Representatives of some S.D.F. branches were there (though the London S.D.F. had refused to co-operate), and so was Edward Aveling, the representative of the Bloomsbury Socialist Society[3] and at that time virtually the spokesman of Friedrich Engels, but the question whether the change to Socialism could ultimately be effected without revolution was not discussed at the conference; 1893 was no such revolutionary period as the middle 'eighties had been, and even the S.D.F. was prepared to fight for 'palliatives' in non-revolutionary periods. All the delegates wished to secure the co-operation of trade unions and of local Labour Leagues, many of them as yet not Socialist, which nevertheless were interested in fighting local elections on an independent platform. Even the London S.D.F. had expressed its 'benevolent neutrality'[4] to such an aim; and the picture of Aveling which emerges from the first Conference Report is that of a man whose purpose is to get a national party established at all costs: a careful diplomat, an angel of sweet reasonableness—both unusual roles for him. In these circumstances, the Fabians did not need to exert themselves to secure that the I.L.P. would take part in the parliamentary game, or that it would adopt a programme of immediate reforms. Amongst such general agreement, specific Fabian influence must be discounted.

In what matters, then, did the Fabians succeed in influencing the I.L.P. against some opposition? The Fabian representatives were not completely agreed in their views on the chief questions before the conference, but a

[1] Letter from Shaw printed in J. Sexton, *op. cit.* p. 136.
[2] Shaw's extravagant claims of Fabian influence in e.g. *Workman's Times*, 28 January 1893 must be discounted by the historian as they were at the time.
[3] And also of the Legal Eight Hours League and the International Labour League.
[4] *Justice*, 13 August 1892.

general pattern may be discovered. For the most part, and insofar as they accepted the lead of the London delegates, their spokesmen were opposed to the word 'Socialist' appearing in the name of the new party, but were in favour of a socialist objective being affirmed in its constitution; they desired a federal basis for the new organization, not an amalgamated or unified one; they were opposed to the election of a Secretary, and wanted him to be a paid employee; they resisted attempts to deny membership to those who were also members of any other party; and they fought Blatchford's 'Manchester Fourth Clause', a policy (so called from its place in the constitution of the Manchester I.L.P.) which required members to abstain from voting for the Liberal or Conservative Parties, even where there were no I.L.P. candidates in the field. In all save one of these things, the Bradford Conference decisions concurred with Fabian views. Does this not indicate that the Fabian Society influenced the I.L.P. very considerably in its beginnings?

This conclusion must not be accepted too hastily. Although the Fabians did advocate these things, and although they were, all but one, accepted by the conference, we must still ask whether the result would have been different if the Fabians had not been present. This is always a difficult question to answer in history, where there is but one instance to consider. It is especially difficult here, where in the last resort the answer may depend on the most difficult task of all: on assessing the influence of Fabian propaganda prior to the conference itself. But some evidence can be produced.

Take first the question of the name: it was overwhelmingly agreed that the name should be Independent Labour Party and not Socialist Labour Party. The principal speech against the inclusion of 'Socialist' in the title was made by Ben Tillett, who was at that time a member of the Fabian society though not one of its actual representatives at the conference. His was a powerful speech, of a type to become more familiar at Labour conferences of later years, mixing sound commonsense tactical points with ignorant chauvinism of a 'British Bulldog' variety. The speech was well received at the conference; but did it really convince the delegates, or did it merely express pungently a verdict at which they had already arrived? The overwhelming vote suggests the latter. To the minds of most, if not all, of the delegates must have been present the question whether the new organization was to attempt to win the support of the Trade Unionists who were not Socialists, and so become an 'independent' party of Socialists and Trade Unionists, or to become purely a Socialist Party on the Continental model. Emerging, as the new party was doing, hard upon the heels of the victories of the New Unionism, with the example of the S.D.F. to discredit the 'Continental' idea, there really could have been little doubt of the choice of the vast majority of delegates.

The conference required as little persuasion from the Fabians to write Socialism into its objectives as to exclude it from its title. An amendment limiting the objective to that of securing 'the separate representation and protection of Labour interests on public bodies' was defeated by ninety-one votes to sixteen. A further amendment to insert the word 'ultimate' before 'objective' was turned down by fifty-six votes to thirty-six. The reasons for these decisions seem to have been, first, that the majority of the delegates at the Bradford Conference were in fact Socialists and, although they were prepared as a matter of tactics not to flaunt the red flag in the party's title, they nevertheless desired to win the Trade Unionists for Socialism; and secondly, there was a feeling that a socialist objective would enable them to distinguish their party more satisfactorily from the 'Lib-Labs', the Labour men content to remain as the tail of the Liberal Party. In the discussion on the objective, Shaw declared that, as a Socialist, he would vote for the original resolution, and he suggested that all who were not Socialists should vote against it, thereby revealing the strength of Socialism at the conference. And another delegate supported the original resolution with the argument that the 'Lib-Labs' would capture the I.L.P. and destroy it—as they had destroyed the Labour Electoral Association and earlier bodies—if the I.L.P. had no criterion for excluding them.

Only on the relatively minor issues did the Fabians need to make any sort of fight for their views. They sustained one defeat—in their proposal to have a paid employee as Secretary rather than an elected Secretary (though, ten years later, the I.L.P. found by experience that this Fabian suggestion had been a good one, and changed its elected Secretary for a paid and employed one). They also had one victory—Blatchford was the main champion of the policy of the 'Manchester Fourth Clause', and Shaw and Aveling its most vehement opponents; in the midst of the controversy, the Bradford Fabian, Paul Bland, was able to move the successful compromise resolution, that where there were no I.L.P. candidates 'the members of the Party in that district shall act as directed by the local Branch'. Bernard Shaw also took an active part in the debate on the resolution, moved by F. W. Jowett of Brad-ford, that 'no member of any organization connected with the Liberal, Liberal Unionist, Irish Nationalist, Conservative, or any other party opposed to the principles of the I.L.P. shall be eligible for membership'. He defended the Fabian policy of permeation; but the conference was less impressed by his claims for London Progressivism than by other difficulties which might have been caused by the resolution. Even those who disagreed with the permeation tactic recognized the close links between Trade Unions and the Liberals, and the suggestion was put forward that the resolution could be made to apply to delegates to the I.L.P. conference but not to the membership as a whole. Eventually, it was Aveling who produced the compromise amendment, that 'no person opposed to the principles of the I.L.P. shall be eligible for member-ship'. This was carried by a large majority with the understanding that it left local parties free to impose additional restrictions if they desired to do so.

The Fabians had no considerable share in deciding the programme or the organization of the I.L.P. The programme, drawn up by a widely representative committee and presented in its original draft by Aveling, was in fact (especially in its amended form after discussion) a compound of the programmes of all the Socialist groups represented. It included demands for the extension of the factory acts; for a legal eight hours day and forty-eight hours week; for pensions for sick, disabled, aged, widows and orphans; for collective ownership of the land and all means of production, distribution and exchange; for free unsectarian education; and for 'properly remunerated work for the unemployed'. The more controversial aspects of the political part of the programme, such as the question of the abolition of the monarchy, or the adoption of the referendum, were avoided by the omnibus amendment declaring 'the I.L.P. is in favour of every proposal for extending electoral rights and democratizing the system of government'. The only feature of the programme which may certainly be attributed to the Fabians was the addition suggested by Bernard Shaw of the words 'and taxation, to extinction, of unearned incomes' to the fiscal proposals in Aveling's report, where the abolition of indirect taxation, and a graduated income tax were recommended. This was designed to replace a proposal to add 'and taxation of ground values', for, Shaw explained, 'they ought to have grown out of' the 'very undesirable distinction between incomes arising out of Rent and those coming from Interest'. His amendment was accepted with one dissentient. On the question of a federal versus a unified or amalgamated organization, the London Fabian representatives approved federation but abstained from voting, as the London Fabian Society decided not to join the I.L.P.[1] However, the federal arrangement had the support, in this formative period, of most of the delegates: it is interesting, in view of the organizational changes which occurred soon afterwards, that the unification plan secured only two votes at the conference.

When the elections to the National Administrative Council of the I.L.P. were being made, the London section of the Fabians decided to stand out of the list of nominees of their own accord. Yet later, *Fabian News* claimed that a number of the English members of the N.A.C. were members of provincial Fabian Societies.[2] Only one accredited representative of a Fabian Society was elected, G. S. Christie of Nottingham, but it is true that seven of the fifteen members of the N.A.C. were members of provincial Fabian Societies. The only objections the London Fabians could make to the first I.L.P. Executive were that the absence of John Burns and Tom Mann from it meant

[1] *Workman's Times*, 28 January 1893.
[2] *Fabian News*, February 1893.

that leaders of London Progressivism were not included in the party, that Aveling was not a proper representative of London Socialism, and that Shaw Maxwell was 'not a perfect appointment' as Secretary because he had quarrelled with Burns. The London Fabians also took the view that the Executive should have been a body of London men, for reasons of economy and efficiency, whereas the provincial delegates were all strongly opposed to this suggestion.[1]

What, then, may be concluded of Fabian influence on the inaugural Conference of the I.L.P.? The Fabian influence was not negligible; but some reasons have been advanced for not exaggerating it. The kind of policy the Fabians approved was adopted in the main by the conference because this policy had the 'tact of the possible', because it was in accord with the nature of the situation. If it be said that this is characteristic of policies which 'influence' such bodies, we must then ask where the distinction comes between leading and following a general body of opinion? We have seen that many of the items of the Fabian policy were so generally accepted as almost not to be in dispute at the Bradford Conference. Let us suppose Shaw and De Mattos had not been present, or had been excluded by the vote on their credentials. What would have been different? All that can be said for certain is that there would have been no dispute about 'permeation', and the slight amendment to the fiscal clause in the I.L.P. programme might not have been made. Suppose all the *representatives* of all the Fabian societies had not been present: what then? Then, it is just possible that, in addition, the compromise resolution about voting at elections might not have been moved. The real difficulty arises if these questions were pushed to the point of asking what might have happened if no *members* of any Fabian Society had been present. It is not possible to answer that question here, partly through lack of information about membership of local Fabian Societies, and partly because of the perplexity arising from the division of opinion between the London and local Societies and even within the London Society itself. Blatchford, for instance, was at this time a member of the Manchester Fabian Society and Keir Hardie a member of the London Society. We may assume that there were enough Fabians at the Bradford Conference for their absence to have made some considerable difference. But the inspiration in founding the I.L.P. was almost as little specifically Fabian as it was S.D.F. Only the complete lack of doctrinal orthodoxy in the Fabian Society enabled those Fabians who played a chief part in the founding of the I.L.P. to belong also to the Society; and it is significant that the Society soon began to lose its provincial groups to the I.L.P. The national I.L.P. initially owed more to ex-Radicals like Keir Hardie, to ex-S.D.F. men like H. H. Champion, to ex-Socialist Leaguers like F. W. Jowett, to the followers of Friedrich Engels, like Edward Aveling and

---

[1] *Workman's Times*, 28 January 1893.

Eleanor Marx and to local Labour men like Joseph Burgess than it did to the Fabians. It was in fact an amalgam created by those who were dissatisfied by the existing political sects. Its policy aspired to surmount sectarian divisions and the Fabian element in it was only one of several; if the I.L.P.'s policy appeared more akin to the Fabian than to the S.D.F.'s, that was merely a reflection of its practical and undogmatic approach. Certainly the I.L.P. always considered itself very much a separate organization from the Fabian Society in nature and spirit. Its relation to the Fabian Society resembled the relation of the Fabian Society in its earliest days to the Democratic Federation: drawing something from the earlier body but becoming a separate, and in some ways even a hostile organization. We must consider how far the I.L.P. developed away from the Fabians, and what links remained.

WAYS IN WHICH THE I.L.P. DRIFTED APART FROM THE FABIANS

By the time of its second conference, which was held at Manchester in February 1894, the I.L.P. began to drift further apart from the Fabians in some important ways. The main change was the abandonment of the policy of federation for that of unification.[1] This departure from the organization approved by the Fabians was a consequence of the Trade Unions' refusal to support the I.L.P. The federal basis had been adopted at the inaugural conference for the purpose of winning the adhesion of Trade Unions and Trades Councils rather than with any thought of accommodating provincial Fabian Societies or S.D.F. branches. The winning of Trade Union support had been the main objective of the I.L.P. men from the beginning, and the foundation of the national I.L.P. in 1893 had followed as a direct consequence of the passing by the 1892 Trade Union Congress of Keir Hardie's resolution calling upon the Parliamentary Committee to prepare a scheme for labour representation, dealing especially with the financial difficulty—a resolution that had been strengthened by an amendment submitted by an Aberdeen delegate inserting the word 'independent' before 'labour representation'.[2]

At the following Trade Union Congress, held at Belfast in September 1893, the I.L.P. men suffered a defeat, even though the Socialists appeared to be in even a stronger position than in the previous year. A scheme for financial assistance of Labour candidates at local and parliamentary elections (to which, however, contributions were to be optional) was accepted, on the motion of Ben Tillett.[3] More than that: a resolution put forward by James Macdonald of the S.D.F. making it necessary for the candidates receiving support from the fund to declare themselves in favour of the collective

[1] Report of the Second Annual Conference of the I.L.P. held at Manchester, 2 and 3 February 1894.
[2] T.U.C. Annual Report, 1892, p. 43.
[3] T.U.C. Annual Report, 1893, p. 44.

ownership of the means of production, distribution and exchange was carried by 137 votes to 97, amidst the cheers of the Socialists.[1] But this victory for Socialism did not mean a victory for the I.L.P. men. When Keir Hardie proposed a furtherre solution that the candidates supported by the fund should also declare themselves independent of both Liberal and Tory parties, his resolution was rejected by 119 votes to 99,[2] after John Burns, who was hostile to the politics of the I.L.P. and jealous of Hardie, threw his vehement weight against it, joining his opposition with that of the 'Lib-Labs'. It represented a major defeat for the I.L.P., which had failed to win exclusive Trade Union support. If any Trade Unions chose to subscribe to the fund, it was possible that the I.L.P., along with other organizations, might get some of it for its candidates. But after the 1893 Trades Union Congress it was plain that the I.L.P. was to be considered not *the* organization for putting up working-class candidates, but only one amongst others. Its hopes of securing direct Trade Union affiliation were, at least for the moment, at an end. Worse was to follow, when at the 1894 Congress it became clear that there was little response to the proposal for voluntary subscriptions to the fund, which, in any case, the 'Lib-Lab' Parliamentary Committee was deliberately sabotaging by a policy of inaction.

The events of the 1895 Congress, which was held after the I.L.P.'s debacle at the 1895 elections, merely confirmed the swing of the pendulum against Hardie and his followers. They were blamed for causing the Liberal party's defeat, for which they were not really responsible, and for the reduction of 'Lib-Lab' representation from sixteen to twelve, for which in part they were. The 'Lib-Labs' took steps to eliminate as many socialists and I.L.P. men as possible from future Congresses; the Webbs and the Fabians, who equally disapproved of Hardie and his tactics, were disgusted when John Burns lent his assistance and sanction to these anti-socialist manœuvres.[3] The new standing orders which were adopted by Congress excluded the representatives of the trade councils, where the socialists were strong, and made it necessary for all delegates to be working trade unionists or minor officials; in addition the new orders introduced the card vote, which meant that a delegate's vote counted for the number of unionists he represented, and so established the dominance in Congress of the great Coal and Cotton Unions, both opposed to independent representation.[4] After this crushing defeat, there remained no alternative for the I.L.P. but to fall back upon its own resources and to

[1] *Ibid.* p. 48.
[2] *Ibid.* pp. 48-9.
[3] B. Webb, *Our Partnership*, p. 48.
[4] The miners, concentrated in particular areas, could and did elect their own representatives to Parliament; lacking a socialist outlook, their leaders did not see why they should bother about independent representation. Many cotton operatives voted Conservative, and their union leaders preferred to keep party divisions out of union affairs.

287

become a unified political party. And the change to this policy meant a development along lines different from those the Fabians had desired the I.L.P. to follow.

The rise and repulse of the I.L.P. in the early 'nineties reflected the upsurge and recession of the New Unionism. The oldest and most firmly established of English Trade Unions, especially those in Coal and Cotton, were unions of skilled workmen, and they had through their own efforts secured satisfactory conditions under capitalism; their policies had become those of caution and collaboration with the existing parties. The uprush of the New Unionism at the end of the 'eighties and the beginning of the 'nineties appeared, momentarily, to have made a considerable change. The New Unions were fighting organizations mainly of the unskilled with a different spirit, and led by Socialists. In the early 'nineties they challenged the older tradition of Trade Unionism, and shook it severely, and, by forcing the older Unions to widen their membership, bade fair to transform them. But the new movement did not last sufficiently long. The New Unionism had fought and won its initial victories in the period of reviving prosperity from 1888 to 1890. While the New Unionists and their allies the Independent Labourites were still riding on the crest of the political wave which had resulted from this elemental movement of the rising tide of trade, the tide had changed beneath them. From 1891, until the revival in 1896, the movement of the trade cycle was downward; it was a period of increasing unemployment; it was a period when strikes and lock-outs almost invariably resulted in defeats for the workers; yet, withal, it was not a period of hunger-revolt, for the cost of living continued to decline until 1896, so real wages, for those in employment, rose. In the circumstances, New Unionism suffered a severe set-back. The Unions began to lose the increased membership, and some of the older 'Lib-Lab' Union leaders predicted that the New Unions would collapse. This did not happen. But after the 1895 Trade Union Congress, the older type of Unionism was back in power, without recapturing all the ground which the New Unionists had gained in the early 'nineties. This, then, presented the alternative to Socialists. If, like the Fabians, they took their cue from the attitude of Trade Union Congresses of 1895 and the next few years they followed the path of moderation that was dangerously near to 'Lib-Labism'. Alternatively, they could, like the S.D.F., choose the path wherein Socialism remained pure and undefiled, but it meant a retreat into the political wilderness.

The I.L.P. stood, hesitating, between the Fabians and the S.D.F. From 1894, the I.L.P.'s first move was, perforce, in the same direction as the S.D.F. —towards a unified party, built up on the basis of individual membership, on the Continental model. For the Fabian Society, the decision meant that the provincial Fabian Societies had to choose between preserving their connection with the Society and sinking their identity in the I.L.P. The majority of them preferred to go over to the I.L.P.[1] The S.D.F. Branches which had co-operated with the I.L.P. at the time of the inaugural Conference were likewise presented with the alternative of changing their allegiance or withdrawing. Thus the I.L.P. established itself as a separate organization, a new socialist group in competition, at least to a certain extent, with the S.D.F. and the Fabian Society.

The disadvantages of this state of affairs were recognized at the second conference, and from the time of that conference onwards, and chiefly under the inspiration of Tom Mann who was then elected Secretary of the I.L.P., negotiations were commenced for forming a national socialist party by unifying the I.L.P., S.D.F., and Fabian Society. These negotiations were destined to be protracted over many years, and in the end unsuccessful.[2] At first the S.D.F. made difficulties at a time when Mann might have been able to carry the I.L.P. with him; later, when Mann had resigned his Secretaryship, and MacDonald, Glasier, and Snowden had joined the I.L.P. Executive it was the S.D.F. which became anxious for unity, and the I.L.P. leadership which had grown cold about the scheme. As for the Fabian Society, Webb and Shaw were opposed to Socialist Unity, but because other members in the Society were strongly in favour the Society as a whole stood aside, awaiting developments of negotiations between the S.D.F. and I.L.P. In a letter to the I.L.P. it declared that while it was 'in favour of the principle that there should be some form of United Socialist Party', it thought 'that at present the difficulties in the way are formidable'.[3]

Along with the movement away from the policy of federation the I.L.P. showed a tendency to revert to another policy which the Fabians hoped they had vanquished at the Bradford Conference. The 'Manchester Fourth Clause', though it was never carried, not only gained an increased number of votes in 1894, but also became in fact the policy followed by the I.L.P. at the 1895 election. At Bradford, the action to be taken at elections was left to the Branches, and a conference of Branch delegates before the general election decided in effect that only I.L.P. and S.D.F. candidates should receive I.L.P. support, and that members should abstain from voting in other constituencies. This was the outcome of high feeling between the Liberals and I.L.P. men before the election. As the Fabians predicted, it meant the withdrawal of all Liberal support, and was partly the cause of the I.L.P.'s complete failure at

---

[1] See ch. VII, pp. 166, 169 above.

[2] At the second Conference of the I.L.P. a Lancashire delegate moved that an approach be made by the N.A.C. to the Executives of the S.D.F. and Fabian Society, for Socialist Unity. W. Johnstone and Enid Stacy moved that the Fabian Society be omitted as 'the Fabian Society declined to adopt any settled policy on labour questions'. This resolution was defeated by 'the previous question', moved by B. Turner and B. Tillett.

[3] I.L.P. Annual Conference Report, 1896, p. 16. For the attitude of Webb and Shaw see *Workman's Times*, 26 November 1892, 13 May 1893, 12 August 1893.

the 1895 election, and in particular the cause of Hardie's losing his seat in South West Ham.

During the 'nineties the I.L.P. leaders were very conscious of their separateness from the Fabian Society. Bruce Glasier probably expressed their point of view most clearly when he said, in 1898, that the I.L.P. stood at 'the centre of a triangle formed by S.D.F., Fabian, and Idealist Socialism'.[1] I.L.P. propaganda, too, developed an emotional quality which Fabian rationalism rather carefully avoided: a quality which derived partly from a more immediate sense of working-class grievances and partly from the background of north country working-class Nonconformity. I.L.P. propaganda, though it profited a good deal from Fabian criticism of S.D.F. propaganda, and though it drew upon and used Fabian facts, developed a character of its own—one which appealed to a wider audience than either Fabian or S.D.F. writing did. Sacrificing, no doubt, something of theoretical accuracy and academic wit, abandoning, certainly, pedantic dogmatizing, Keir Hardie by solid, honest pulpit-punches in the *Labour Leader*, and still more, Robert Blatchford and the brilliant journalists of the *Clarion* with their infectious enthusiasm and bright, clear writing became the propagandists who really brought Socialism to the masses.

During the 'nineties the I.L.P. also developed a completely different attitude to international matters from that of the majority of the Fabian Society. Its attitude here derived chiefly from Marxist sources and from Left-wing 'Little England' Liberalism; the distinctively I.L.P. synthesis of this combination included a strong advocacy of Free Trade, a hostility to Imperialism, and a belief in international working-class solidarity extending almost, if not quite, to pacifism, and to some consideration of the General Strike as a means of preventing war.[2]

FABIAN LINKS AND INFLUENCES WHICH REMAINED

(1) *Personal links*

Having observed the drift of the I.L.P. away from Fabian influence, it is now necessary to look at the other side of the case, and see what ties remained. First, there were personal ones. Members of the Fabian Society continued to be strongly represented on the National Administrative Council of the I.L.P. The size of the N.A.C. was reduced to nine at the 1894 I.L.P. Conference, and of those nine, at least six were also members of the Fabian Society in 1894,

[1] I.L.P. Annual Conference Report, 1898, p. 26. H. Russell Smart, writing in *Workman's Times*, 26 May 1893, spoke of the 'middle course' pursued by the I.L.P. between the Fabians on the one hand and the S.D.F. on the other.
[2] This development occurred from the time of the second I.L.P. Annual Conference, when the resolution of the Zurich Conference was adopted (Report, pp. 7–8). Hardie and other I.L.P. leaders were always internationally-minded and preserved I.L.P. contacts with Continental Socialists.

1895, and 1896;[1] of the nine N.A.C. members appointed at the 1897 Conference, five were Fabians; in 1898, six; while in 1899 and 1900 the number of Fabians on the N.A.C. had fallen to three.[2] However, these figures do not give a completely accurate guide to the degree of Fabian influence. These figures include such men as Keir Hardie, who from 1890 always remained nominally a member of the Fabian Society, Tom Mann, who remained a member of the Fabian Society active in London Progressivism all the time he was Secretary of the I.L.P., and J. Ramsay MacDonald, who was a member of the Fabian Society from 1886 to 1900 and who was elected to the N.A.C. in 1897. These men, who impressed their personalities so strongly upon the I.L.P., can hardly be regarded as typical Fabians.

Tom Mann, in the early 'nineties, was working closely with the Webbs. His sympathies and attitude of mind were fundamentally more Marxist-Anarchist than Fabian. But at the time of the Dock Strike, Mann was in disagreement with the leaders of the S.D.F. in matters of tactics, and this disagreement caused him to come into a fairly intimate association with leading Fabians. He joined the Society, and he became the first Secretary of the London Reform Union when the Webbs decided to harness his organizing abilities in the cause of London Progressivism. Mann, like John Burns, did not attend the inaugural Conference of the I.L.P., but soon after its formation he became actively associated with it, and he was unanimously elected Secretary of the Party when he put in an appearance at its second Conference in 1894. As I.L.P. Secretary, Mann undertook the task of welding all the Socialist bodies in which he had been interested into a Party of 'Socialist Unity'. During the years of his Secretaryship of the I.L.P., he continued to work with the Webbs in the London Reform Union, and in 1894 he and Sidney Webb were collaborating in the Minority Report of the Royal Commission on Labour—Webb was drafting the Report for Mann, and they both were engaged in persuading Mawdsley, the veteran Tory-Labour leader, to accept it.[3] However, soon after this, Beatrice Webb was noting in her diary that it was 'melancholy to see Tom Mann reverting to the old views of the S.D.F., and, what is worse, to their narrow and sectarian policy . . . as Shaw remarked, he is deteriorating. This stumping the country, talking abstractions and raving emotions is not good for a man's judgment. . . .'[4] This caustic

---

[1] *Fabian News*, May 1895 says six members of the *London* Fabian Society. The London Fabians, who had stood out of the first elections to the N.A.C., joined it in force at the elections at the Second Annual Conference in 1894. See also *Fabian News*, May 1897 for retrospect of 1896.

[2] *Fabian News*, May 1897, May 1898, May 1899, May 1900. In 1900, MacDonald had resigned from the F.S., but Hardie and Penny remained members. *Fabian News*, May 1900 mentions only the election of Shallard. At that time he was the only 'real Fabian' on the N.A.C., though Hardie and Penny still retained nominal Fabian membership.

[3] B. Webb, *Our Partnership*, pp. 36, 42.

[4] *Ibid.* p. 122.

entry was partly provoked by the tactics the I.L.P. adopted, under the guidance of Keir Hardie and Mann, at the 1895 elections. In 1896 Mann caused an uproar in I.L.P. ranks by openly declaring his sympathies with the expelled Anarchist section at the International Socialist Congress,[1] and at the following conference of the I.L.P. in 1897 he announced his resignation of the Party Secretaryship to devote himself to the organization of the dockers. The beginning of Mann's discovery of the new creed of Anarchist-Syndicalism necessarily ended his influence with the I.L.P., which was based on an acceptance of political methods.

Mann's withdrawal from the I.L.P. coincided with the election of J. Ramsay MacDonald to its National Administrative Council. The Secretaryship fell to John Penny, a Fabian and Co-operator, who filled the post efficiently but unobtrusively until 1903. The dominating role was quickly assumed by MacDonald. At the time of his election to the N.A.C., MacDonald had but recently become antagonistic to the Webbs, although he still remained a member of the Fabian Society. Earlier, his relations with the Webbs had been exceedingly cordial: he had joined the Fabian Society in 1886, and in 1894 had been elected to its Executive; in 1895 Webb appointed him one of the Society's touring lecturers under the Hutchinson Trust. MacDonald at that time was anxious to bring the Fabians and the I.L.P. into closer harmony, and a conference of the leaders of the two groups was arranged at the Webbs' house in January 1895.[2] Nothing came of this; but at the end of the same year MacDonald was still listed by Mrs Webb among the 'young people' who were 'more or less devoted to the Fabian junta'.[3] In the following year, however, relations between MacDonald and the Webbs, if not other members of the Fabian Society, became strained. Beatrice Webb attributed a great deal to personal grievance. MacDonald was piqued at Webb's refusal to appoint him to a lectureship at the newly-founded London School of Economics; Webb did not think him 'good enough' for such an appointment.[4] But there was also a division of opinion between them on certain matters of policy. MacDonald was strongly opposed to the use of the Hutchinson Trust for purely educational purposes. He considered Webb's use of the money inconsistent with the promotion of Socialism, which was the expressed desire of the benefactor: Webb had even insisted that the lectures on the provincial tours should be of an educational rather than a propagandist nature, and he was steadfastly opposed to MacDonald's suggestion that some of the funds should be used to pay an 'organizer' of 'branches' (which would inevitably have become branches of the I.L.P.).[5] Again, MacDonald, though he had once been a Liberal Party agent, became a strong opponent of the Fabian Society's

---

[1] P. Verhaegen, *Socialistes Anglais* (Englcke et Larose, 1898), p. 191.
[2] B. Webb, *Our Partnership*, p. 121.   [3] *Ibid.* p. 128.
[4] *Ibid.* p. 132.   [5] *Ibid.*

policy of 'permeating' the Liberals after his conversion to the I.L.P. in 1894; he led the attack on this policy when it was reaffirmed in Tract 70. After 1896, MacDonald was a strong critic of Sidney Webb both inside and outside the Fabian Society: Beatrice Webb's journals record constant friction between MacDonald and Webb on the L.C.C. after MacDonald had been successful at a bye-election in 1900. Their antagonism had become greater when the I.L.P. and Fabian Society took different attitudes to the Metropolitan Borough Councils Act, the Boer War, and the Education Acts. MacDonald resigned from the Fabian Society in 1900 as a result of its attitude to the Boer War. Relations between MacDonald and the Webbs never again became completely cordial, despite their association in the Labour Party after the First World War.

Because MacDonald became the principal 'official' theorist of the I.L.P. in the pre-war years, it is necessary to estimate the extent to which his ideas remained distinctively Fabian. The account of MacDonald's disagreements, personal and political, with the Webbs must not be allowed to obscure their agreement in the theoretical sphere, for it is impossible to read MacDonald's books and speeches without realizing how extensive this agreement is, and how strongly he was influenced by Fabian ideas during his membership of the Society. MacDonald's political theory was, in its main essentials, that of *Fabian Essays*, strengthened with some arguments from the Continental Revisionists, and furnished with a greater wealth of biological metaphor. There was the same emphasis on the 'organic' nature of society;[1] on the slow,[2] evolutionary inevitability[3] of social change and the unimportance of mere political revolutions;[4] the same criticism of Marxist theories of economic determinism,[5] class-war,[6] and the State,[7] with nevertheless the same 'turning to the wage-earners'[8] because they are the oppressed class; the same State-Socialist attitude,[9] with the same insistence on the importance of municipal socialism,[10] and on the interventionism of the positive, welfare

---

[1] J. R. MacDonald, *Socialism and Society* (I.L.P., London, 1905), pp. xvi, 11–18 and elsewhere.

[2] *Ibid.* p. 63 ' . . . gradual surrenders to which day and date can hardly be assigned'.

[3] *Ibid.* pp. 62–3 and elsewhere. Also *The Socialist Movement* (Williams & Norgate, H.U.L.), pp. 103–4.

[4] *Socialism and Society*, p. 20: 'Few real organic changes were effected by the hurricanes of the French Revolution'.

[5] *Ibid.* p. 121; *Socialism* (T. C. & E. C. Jack, London, 1907), pp. 123–4; *The Socialist Movement*, p. 146.

[6] *Socialism and Society*, pp. 110–7 (criticism of concept of class); p. 121 ('No constructive value' in class-war).

[7] *Socialism and Government*, pp. 109–14 (criticism of 'withering away of the state'); *ibid.* p. xxi, and pp. 3–7 (necessity of state); *Socialism and Society*, p. 134 ('positive state').

[8] *Socialism and Society*, p. 129.

[9] *Ibid.* p. 74 (criticism of Utopias); *Socialism and Government*, p. xxi (criticism of Anarchists); *Syndicalism*, passim.

[10] *Socialist Movement*, pp. 101, 157.

State; the same presenting of Socialism as the 'completion' of Liberalism;[1] the same reliance on democracy and British constitutional methods;[2] the same economic theory;[3] the same 'tolerant agnosticism' towards religion and other 'indifferent' subjects. . . .[4] Against the huge area of agreement, the differences between MacDonald's political theory and that of the early Fabians seems almost superficial. They disagreed in their attitude to Imperialism—but even here MacDonald was not completely hostile, but occupied a middle position between the Fabians and the more intransigeant I.L.P. views.[5] They were on opposite sides concerning 'independence' and 'permeation'—but here again MacDonald by no means took up an extremist position: he declared that what was required was not a Socialist Party, but a Socialistic Party, which would 'have on occasions to co-operate in a bloc, either refusing or accepting the responsibility of office'.[6] There were differences also in the extent of MacDonald's and leading Fabians' acceptance of existing British institutions of government, but this was for the most part merely a difference of degree.[7] More significant was an elusive but definite difference in 'tone' between the writings of MacDonald and the Fabians: a little more of the Noncomformist clergyman and a little less of the teacher;[8] a call for moral regeneration rather than purely a call for intelligence; a shade more of 'historicism' and a shade less of positivism; and an elusive but important element of pacifist defeatism which appears occasionally in MacDonald,[9] and contrasts with the fundamental energetic confidence of the Fabian leaders.

[1] *Socialism and Society*, p. 165.

[2] *Socialism and Government, passim.* A love of liberty which 'springs from a reverence of Parliamentary institutions' (*ibid.* p. xxv).

[3] *Socialist Movement*, p. 62, (note same difficulty about 'pure interest'); *ibid.* p. 112, piecemeal changes; *Socialism and Society*, pp. 124–5, 'Socialism is inevitable, not because capitalism is to break down, but because man is a rational being.'

[4] Lord Elton, *The Life of James Ramsay MacDonald* (Collins, London, 1939), p. 38.

[5] *Socialism and Government*, pp. 74–107. Of course, MacDonald's attitude *was* different from the Fabian, and he did leave the Society over it. But whereas most I.L.P. men believed in self-government, and the Fabians approved benevolent progressive Western rule, Mac-Donald's criterion is vaguer: he would inquire whether the native society were developing along its 'natural path' (which may not necessarily be democratic) and he would approve white rule if the whites were helping the natives along their 'natural' path.

[6] *Socialism*, pp. 120–1; *Socialism and Society*, pp. 143–9; *Socialism and Government*, vol. II, pp. 12–15. Cf. Ensor's remark that MacDonald would never have joined the I.L.P. if the Liberal Party had adopted a more generous policy towards 'Lib-Lab' candidates, *England 1870–1914* (Oxford University Press, 1936), p. 223.

[7] *Socialism and Government, passim.* The area of agreement is very great, and the general attitude of acceptance of representative democracy and existing British Parliamentary Institutions is similar. In some details, MacDonald is more conservative than the Fabians: he speaks of 'reverence' for British Parliamentary Institutions; he was opposed to a second ballot; and he defended the Cabinet system against Committee system of government.

[8] As in much I.L.P. writing the emphasis on morality is carried to the point of moralising. See *Socialism and Society*, pp. 37–8.

[9] 'The attacking army has become dispirited, or content with things as they are. "The enemy" is not so bad after all. The spirit of Labour Radicalism of the seventies has gone

James Keir Hardie from 1890 until his death remained nominally a member of the Fabian Society. There was always a certain antagonism between him and the Webbs, though he was on friendly terms with Bernard Shaw and other leading Fabians. Hardie's type of mind was as antipathetic to the Webbs as it was to Friedrich Engels. The Webbs, like Engels, hoped much at first of John Burns, and not only dismissed his rival as woolly-minded, but also suspected his motives and ambitions.[1] It is not strange that these founders of different schools of Socialism should have made similar judgments of Hardie. Both judgments were 'intellectualist', both mistook Hardie's uncompromising, and not always carefully expressed, moral fervour and the touch of harmless theatricality in his appearance and manner for careerism and a desire for notoriety. In fact, Hardie was a man of intense and passionate feeling on certain guiding principles of political conduct, but he found a great deal of difficulty in formulating them into a coherent system which could compete with the Marxist, the Fabian, or the Anarchist creeds. As a result, he floundered unhappily between them, agreeing consistently with none of them, but unable to justify himself in his rivals' eyes, and so creating the worst impression. His guiding principle of political tactics was a belief in the need for building up an independent party of Labour. He had no faith in the policy of 'permeating' or persuading the older parties: he believed firmly that any real concessions they granted to the working-class were given under pressure of one kind or another, and that the Liberals in this respect were no better than the Tories. He was convinced that the independent party of Labour needed to secure the active co-operation of the Trade Unions and to base itself on them. And recognizing the English Trade Unions for what they were Hardie was far from wishing his new party to be a revolutionary one: he desired its tactics to be 'as constitutional as the Fabians'.[2] Constitutional, but (his conduct in the House of Commons showed) not too respectful of parliamentary procedure when his feelings were aroused to protest against injustice. Hardie was behaving in his most characteristic manner in the days when he was the 'Member for the Unemployed'. The Right to Work, the Eight Hours Day, Old Age Pensions, Equal Rights for Women, the International Solidarity of Labour—these were the other principles, steps towards Socialism, for which Hardie fought with all the passion of a deeply religious nature. It could well be argued (pandering to the English taste for muddling through) that his straight-forward political tactics proved, in the event, at least as adequate as those of his critics: one instance where a man of instinct

out of us.' (*Socialism and Society*, p. 142). Role of individual in change (*ibid*. p. 22). Counter-Revolution 'would conquer us' in the event of a revolution or crisis. (Speech at I.L.P. Conference, I.L.P. Annual Report, 1909).

[1] B. Webb, *Our Partnership*, p. 122, cf. letter of Engels to Sorge, 10 November 1894, quoted Allen Hutt, *This Final Crisis* (Gollancz, London, 1935), p. 129.

[2] Verhaegan, *op. cit.* pp. 181–2.

was justified against the men of intellect. But Hardie's lack of a social philosophy made him liable, within certain limits, to fall under the influence of others who were better equipped.[1] Ramsay MacDonald came in time to supply Hardie's need exactly, and from the late 'nineties, he fell as much under MacDonald's influence as his turbulent spirit and his steadfast principles would allow—or even more, perhaps, for he later defended MacDonald's conduct in circumstances where his natural sympathies were on the other side, and when he was noticeably uneasy in doing so. Hardie's frequent laudatory descriptions of MacDonald as 'the biggest intellectual asset which the Socialist movement has in this country today'[8] leave no doubt of the esteem in which he held him, and of the sense of relief he felt at the provision for the I.L.P. of a statement of its position in theoretical terms. Hardie himself even attempted, not very successfully, a few essays in theory along MacDonaldite lines. But for our purpose it is chiefly necessary to observe that, while there was little personal sympathy between the Webbs and Hardie, yet there was some co-operation; Hardie always thought it worth while to preserve his membership of the Fabian Society, and there were always others among the Fabians—notably Shaw and the younger members—who remained on the friendliest terms with him.

Robert Blatchford was neither a platform orator nor a great political figure in the I.L.P.; but he was its outstanding journalist in the 'nineties, and it has been claimed that he made more converts to Socialism through his paper, the *Clarion* and through his booklet *Merrie England* (which appeared first as a series of articles in the *Clarion* and achieved a phenomenal circulation in pamphlet form) than any other propagandist of his time. The views which he expressed with such clarity, strength, and human appeal were remarkably eclectic; what novelty there was in them lay merely in his particular selection and combination, not at all in their originality. In 1890 Blatchford joined the Fabians and became President of the Manchester Fabian Society, and his debt to Fabian ideas is plain as can be: he not only drew heavily on Fabian statistics and facts, but his collectivism, with a strong emphasis on municipal enterprise, was essentially Fabian; and he had the same general expectations of peaceful and constitutional methods. Nevertheless, Blatchford also levied other schools of Socialism for a contribution to his views, and a large measure of his appeal came from his combination of their not always compatible elements. He drew from William Morris and Kropotkin a hatred of industrial towns and an aspiration towards a 'merrie

[1] These 'limits' were drawn by the things he felt passionately about. The direct influence of the Fabians upon him was less great than it might have been because of their repudiation of 'independence'.

[2] I.L.P. Annual Conference Report, 1909, p. 49. There were, of course, other reasons too for Hardie's respect for MacDonald; MacDonald had a mastery of parliamentary procedure and tactics which Hardie never achieved.

England' where modern urban life could be brought into a more harmonious relationship with a revived agriculture; he also got from them his belief that propaganda activity, the making of Socialists, was the main task. With the S.D.F. Blatchford shared at least a bitter rejection of the established parties, and a tendency to attack, not merely to ignore, orthodox religion. His broad unsectarian tastes in socialist theory were reflected in the campaign for Socialist Unity and Labour Federation which the *Clarion* organized in the 'nineties. The more religious and serious-minded members of the I.L.P., like Keir Hardie, were rather shocked by the levity, gaiety and somewhat bibulous habits of the 'Clarionettes', but Blatchford's influence with the young was great. That influence did not really decline until after 1906, when Blatchford's predilections for militant agnosticism, for protection in tariff policy, and for bellicose nationalism became prominent in a way that offended considerable sections of the I.L.P.

These were the leaders who dominated the I.L.P.; of the others it is not necessary to speak at length. J. Bruce Glasier was not a member of the Fabian Society,[1] though he was at one time employed by the Fabian Executive as a Hutchinson lecturer. His socialism derived from William Morris, and though he departed from the anti-parliamentary principles of his master, his interest remained chiefly in the propaganda, educational aspect: he looked upon all the institutional changes (including 'Municipal Socialism' which Morris had heartily despised) as so many manifestations of the 'change-of-heart', and he was also quick to point out that socialist institutions, unless continually animated by the socialist spirit, could become empty shells. His emphasis on the ethical aspect of Socialism enabled him to make many shrewd observations concerning the moral claims which lie at the basis of Socialism and of much other economic reasoning, but it also frequently led him into a form of sentimental moralizing exhortation repellant to the hard-headed.[2] In general, he was friendly to the Fabians, and hostile towards the S.D.F. His speech at the 1898 Annual Conference of the I.L.P. helped to defeat the move for fusion with the S.D.F.[3]

Philip Snowden came into the I.L.P. after the time when real danger of Marxist influence upon it had passed away.[4] Although he was frequently in conflict with MacDonald, personally and politically, he never moved outside the general bounds of I.L.P.-Fabian doctrine. He was closely connected with the Fabians, a member of the Society,[5] and much more 'Fabian' in his out-

---

[1] Mrs Glasier, however, was a Fabian.

[2] His work *The Meaning of Socialism* (I.L.P., London, 1925), reveals both aspects very well.

[3] I.L.P. Annual Conference Report 1898.

[4] Snowden confessed he had never read Marx; Snowden, *An Autobiography* (Ivor Nicholson & Watson, London, 1931), vol. I, p. 62.

[5] Mrs Snowden was also a member, and served on the Fabian Executive 1908-9.

look than most of the I.L.P. men. Thus, for instance, he stood for Socialism against mere 'Labourism' inside the Labour Party, and unlike many of his I.L.P. colleagues he was a strong upholder of the principle of compulsory arbitration. Always a formidable, acid-tongued orator, he acquired, under Fabian influence, another accomplishment—the detailed knowledge of public finance, which was to prove the strength and the bane of his parliamentary career.

Fred Jowett was a staunch socialist working-man who had formerly been a member of the Bradford Branch of the Socialist League. Although he was not a member of the Fabian Society, he had a thorough training in 'Municipal Socialism' as an I.L.P. representative on the Bradford City Council, and this experience led to a development of his ideas in a direction similar to the Fabians'. In some matters, particularly in his views concerning the reform of parliamentary procedure, Jowett's opinions seem to have been arrived at independently of the Fabians, despite this close resemblance. Jowett consistently represented the moderate left-wing within the I.L.P.[1]

Other prominent I.L.P. leaders can merely be mentioned. In the early days of the I.L.P., Shaw Maxwell, Curran, Burgess, Kennedy, Buttery, Lister, Drew, Dr Pankhurst, and Katherine Conway (later Mrs Bruce Glasier) were all members of the Fabian Society, though they were at that time mostly in conflict with the Fabian leaders, and of them only Lister and Miss Conway had actually come into the Socialist movement through the Society.[2] The names of Brocklehurst, Enid Stacy, Russell Smart, Mrs Pankhurst, Penny, Shallard, Ensor, Snell, and Margaret Bondfield also need to be added to the list of those on the National Administrative Council of the I.L.P. who were at one time or another members of the Fabian Society. Ben Tillett, in the early days an enthusiastic Fabian, later drifted far to the Left. George Lansbury was also a member of the Fabian Society, though he was still more closely connected with the S.D.F. Of course, a mere list of this kind does not do justice to the relation of these men and women to Fabianism, but the very number of prominent I.L.P. names in the list is significant. And as for the few other I.L.P. leaders whose names do not appear on this list, it would be possible in most cases to demonstrate, by reference to their speeches, close resemblances between their general outlook and Fabianism.[3]

(2) *Organizational links*

In addition to the personal links between the I.L.P. and the Fabian Society there were organizational ones. The most important and permanent of these arose from their mutual concern with local government. The I.L.P. had of

[1] Fenner Brockway, *Socialism over Sixty Years: The Life of Jowett of Bradford* (George Allen & Unwin, 1946), *passim*.
[2] *Workman's Times*, 11 February 1893.
[3] e.g. J. Parker and W. C. Anderson.

course always been interested in local government affairs for the party had been formed by a union of local organizations; but after the 1895 General Election defeat, it was obliged to make the most of its opportunities in the municipalities to offset its failure in national politics. Consequently the I.L.P. was very willing to avail itself of the expert knowledge of the Fabians in local government matters. The Fabian Tracts circulated widely among the I.L.P. membership, and on Fabian initiative a special committee was established with the object of pooling Fabian and I.L.P. experience of local affairs, and of giving guidance to their elected representatives. This Committee was set up following a 'Conference of Elected Persons'—a conference between Fabians and I.L.P. representatives on public bodies—held in conjunction with the I.L.P. Annual Conference at Leeds in 1899, by which year nearly 250 members of the I.L.P. had been elected to positions of local authority of one kind or another throughout Great Britain.[1] At the 'Conference of Elected Persons'[2] prominent Fabians read papers on different aspects of local government and, as a result, it was decided to establish the permanent joint Committee—the 'Socialist and Labour Elected Persons Association'—to act as an advice and information bureau. The Committee consisted of J. R. MacDonald and John Penny from the I.L.P. and E. R. Pease and F. Whelen from the Fabian Society.[3] A few months later, the name of this committee appears to have been changed to 'The Local Government Information Bureau', and its function expanded to take over some of the work which the Fabian Society had been doing informally for several years: no longer was its advice and information confined to Labour members of local authorities, but was made available to anyone who paid a small annual subscription. It was 'managed virtually by the secretaries of the two societies'[4] and performed the useful and typically Fabian function of preparing abstracts of Bills and Acts of Parliament and providing other information of interest to its members. It continued in existence until 1911, when its duties were taken over by the Joint Standing Committee which was then established (under the Chairmanship of W. C. Anderson) to co-ordinate all joint activities of the two organizations, and which consisted of four members and the secretary of each the Fabian Society and the I.L.P. From the time of the formation of the Joint Standing Committee until the outbreak of war in 1914, the relation between the I.L.P. and the Fabian Society, and their co-operation in domestic policy was exceedingly close—especially in the campaigns for the 'Prevention of Destitution' and against the Lloyd George Insurance Act, and in the adult suffrage demonstrations.[5] So active were the Fabians on behalf of the Joint Committee when it

---

[1] The I.L.P.'s largest representation was on the School Boards, which partly explains I.L.P. hostility to their abolition.
[2] Sidney Webb was Chairman. *Fabian News*, May 1899.
[3] *Ibid*. June 1899.   [4] Pease, *op. cit*. p. 207.
[5] Annual Reports of Fabian Society 1912–4.

was first established, that a series of lectures delivered under its auspices were for a short time allowed to replace the ordinary lectures of the Fabian Society.

Thus the organizational links between the Fabian Society and the I.L.P. in the local government sphere were close from 1899 until 1914, and especially close after 1911. And, although the Local Government Information Bureau was the most permanent organizational link, yet there were others of an important, though less continuous kind. The I.L.P. and Fabian Society were associated from time to time in Unemployed Committees and Housing Committees;[1] Fabian members constantly gave lectures to I.L.P. Branches and Clubs; Fabian Book Boxes were in constant demand by I.L.P. Branches; the Fabian Society conducted correspondence classes in economics and history for members of the working-classes (chiefly I.L.P. men) in which its instructors discouraged 'Socialist teaching of an extreme type',[2] although these study classes were not established on a regular basis with the I.L.P. until 1913;[3] and last, but not least, the Fabian Society provided financial assistance for I.L.P. leaders, sometimes by engaging them as touring lecturers, occasionally by assisting them financially in electoral contests.

I.L.P. PROGRAMMES EXAMINED FOR FABIAN INFLUENCE

How far were the specific doctrines and practical proposals of the Fabians accepted by the I.L.P. in its programmes and statements of policy? A statement of the I.L.P. programme more detailed than the one adopted at its inaugural conference did not appear until the third Annual Conference, which was held at Newcastle-on-Tyne in April 1895. The new programme did not differ essentially, however, from the earlier one. The fiscal, educational and social, industrial and political demands remained substantially unaltered. To the demand for free education was added proposals for 'free maintenance' of schoolchildren, and for the raising of the school leaving age to fifteen years; an addition to the demand for old age pensions required that pensions should commence at fifty years; a novel item was the demand for the 'municipalization of the drink traffic'. These additions went further than Fabian demands at that time, even if some Fabians were sympathetic to them: leading members of the Fabian Society regarded the proposals for pensions at fifty (which followed the S.D.F. programme) as being outside the realm of practical politics,[4] and the I.L.P.'s proposals for the municipalization of the drink traffic anticipated the Fabian Tracts 85 and 86 by two years. The chief addition to the I.L.P. programme made in 1895 was an extensive agricultural section, which was adopted as a result of the reorganization of local govern-

[1] e.g. Fabian Society Annual Report, March 1900.
[2] Fabian Society Annual Report, March 1897.
[4] *Ibid.* March 1914.
[3] See e.g. the remarks of Pease, *op. cit.* p. 159, concerning the proposals of George Turner.

ment in rural areas effected by the 'Parish Councils' Act of 1894. Here the measures were similar to those being put forward by the Fabians at the same time. The socialist demands in this Programme were a typically Fabian solution of the English land question—municipal ownership and the letting out of small allotments by the municipality, with (perhaps) some larger farms directly managed by the municipal authority itself. As measures for achieving this objective, local authorities were to be encouraged to obtain and exercise powers of acquiring land compulsorily, and of taxing land values. Other more immediate remedial measures were also proposed: the establishment of a State Department of Agriculture, which would found agricultural colleges and model farms; the reclamation and reafforestation of waste land; and the establishment of some form of administrative machinery to aid the marketing of agricultural produce. The programme of the I.L.P. adopted at the third Annual Conference resembled the programme of the Fabians, and owed something to them. But then it was also similar to the immediate ('palliative') measures put forward by the S.D.F., and in certain items went beyond Fabian measures to incorporate S.D.F. ones.

The list of the Resolutions which the I.L.P. submitted to the International Socialist Congress of 1896 form an interesting contrast with the witty and provocative Resolutions drafted by Shaw as the Fabian Society's contribu-tion.[1] The I.L.P.'s Resolutions, unlike the Fabian Society's, did not raise theoretical issues, and, in fact, avoided the theoretical conflict between the Marxists and the Fabians as far as possible. Unemployment and other social evils were declared capable of being abolished only by 'the complete over-throw of the capitalist system' but could be 'limited in proportion as order and regulation are introduced into the present industrial confusion' and that therefore certain 'present measures' were necessary.[2] These 'present measures' were identical with the demands of the Fabian Society, except in one case. But the phrasing made it seem that the I.L.P. leant rather to a modified version of the S.D.F.'s distinction between 'the revolution' and 'palliatives', than to the unqualified gradualism expounded by the Fabians at this time.

The practical measure upon which the I.L.P. showed itself in opposition to the Fabians concerned the eight hours day. The I.L.P. favoured the device of 'Trade Exemption', and suggested that a general Eight Hours Act should apply to all classes of workers unless two-thirds of the workers engaged in the trade demanded otherwise. The Fabian Society continued to reject 'Trade Exemption' although a sharp struggle had meanwhile taken place inside the Society about it. As we have already seen, the original Fabian proposal was the device of 'Trade Option'. This proposal gained the support of the more moderate section of Labour men, but it was rejected at the 1891 Trade Union

[1] Published subsequently as Tract 70.
[2] I.L.P. Annual Conference Report, 1896.

301

Congress in favour of 'Trade Exemption'. Following this decision, a members' meeting of the Fabian Society was held in November 1891 at which a resolution was moved for the withdrawal of Tract 9 and the substitution of 'Trade Exemption' for 'Trade Option'. The alignment was similar to that in the disputes about 'permeation' which were taking place at the same time. On this occasion, Bland was in the Chair; but Mrs Bland was one of the principal supporters of the resolution, while Webb, Pease, and Wallas defended 'Trade Option'. The resolution was carried by twenty-eight votes to twenty-six; Webb took his defeat gracefully and offered to serve on the re-drafting Committee.[1] The result, not altogether surprisingly, was a Committee dominated by Webb, of which the majority were or became opposed to 'Trade Exemption'. When the Committee reported six months later, the Society was treated to a lecture in economics explaining that the instantaneous character of 'Trade Exemption' might cause industrial dislocation, that the Act would be unworkable unless a register could be prepared, and that this would be impossible in the unorganized trades. The report reaffirmed Webb's earlier arguments that the gradualist character of 'Trade Option' would avoid these disadvantages, and promote the growth of Trade Union organization into the bargain. Angry scenes followed. Bland declared the report was 'stamped . . . with the nervous cautiousness of a certain teacher of economics at whose feet sat the majority of the Committee', and an account of the meeting describes how 'this academic tone [of the report] made one or two members, particularly Burgess, Pete Curran, and Dr Pankhurst, desperately angry'. The report was rejected.[2]

Seven months later, the dispute was settled by a compromise proposal which was carried by a considerable majority at a members' meeting. 'Trade Selection' was the name coined for the new Fabian device, and a Tract was prepared in the following year embodying it.[3] The new plan bore the marks of having been through the fire of criticism, and not only left-wing criticism. 'Trade Selection' involved the passing of a general Act for the limitation of hours of labour, leaving the application of it to particular trades to the Home Secretary under certain conditions. When requested to do so by Parliament, a County Council, a Town Council, a Trades Union, a Trades Council, or a Factory Inspector the Home Secretary was to appoint a small commission of inquiry to investigate conditions in a trade and report to him on 'the prevalent opinion of members of the trade' about a reduction of hours, on 'the probable effects on the community' of granting such a reduction, on 'what reduction was desirable' (i.e. reduction by day or week, emergency measures for seasonal trades, etc.), and whether the Home Secretary should make a regula-

[1] Report in *Workman's Times*, 21 November 1891.
[2] *Workman's Times*, 21 May 1892 and 12 November 1892.
[3] *Ibid.* 3 December 1892.

tion himself or delegate his power to do so to a local government body. Within three months of receiving the report the Home Secretary would be required either to give effect to the recommendation by making a regulation, or report to the House of Commons his reasons for taking no action.[1] The I.L.P. in 1896, however, refused to follow the Fabian lead, and reaffirmed 'Trade Exemption'.

The other main point of disagreement between the Fabian and I.L.P. Reports to the International Socialist Congress of 1896 concerned the section in the Fabian Society's Report which set forth the Society's electoral tactics:

The Fabian Society does not claim to be the people of England, or even the Socialist Party, and therefore does not seek direct political representation by putting forward Fabian candidates at elections. But it loses no opportunity of influencing elections, and inducing constituencies to select Socialists as their candidates. No person, however, can obtain the support of the Fabian Society or escape its opposition merely by calling himself a Socialist or Social Democrat. As there is no second ballot in England, frivolous candidatures give great offence and discredit the party in whose name they are undertaken, because any third candidate who is not well supported will not only be beaten himself but may also involve in his defeat the better of the two candidates competing with him. Under such circumstances, the Fabian Society throws its weight against the third candidate, whether he calls himself a Socialist or not, in order to secure the victory of the better of the two candidates between whom the contest really lies. But when the third is not only a serious representative of Socialism, but can organize his party well and is likely to poll sufficient votes to make even his defeat a respectable demonstration of the strength and growth of Socialism in the constituency, the Fabian Society supports him resolutely under all circumstances and against all other parties.[2]

Even Pease has admitted that this statement was 'extreme'[3] It is worth noting that the Liverpool Fabian Society did not accept it, but presented a separate Report to the Congress stating that it always supported I.L.P., S.D.F. and Trade Union candidates. The London Society's provocative reaffirmation of their earlier attitude encountered great opposition from the I.L.P. men in the Society. Led by Ramsay MacDonald they organized a move for the deletion of this clause, but they were voted down at a members' meeting.[4]

These programmes of the I.L.P., and particularly that of 1896, show the substantial accuracy of the view that the I.L.P. stood half-way between the Fabians and the S.D.F. In two important points of policy the I.L.P. differed from the Fabians and resembled the S.D.F. In other ways, the I.L.P. resembled the Fabians more than the S.D.F. As the N.A.C.'s Annual Conference Report said in 1898: 'We have differed from the S.D.F. almost solely

[1] Tract 48.
[2] Tract 70.
[3] Pease, *op. cit.* p. 127.
[4] *Ibid.*

because we have refused to adopt certain rigid propagandist phrases and to cut ourselves off from other sections of the Labour Movement, particularly trades unionism and co-operation, and the advanced elements in the humanitarian movements'. Equally important, though neither Report nor programmes mention it, was the fact that most I.L.P. men did not care for the outspoken atheism of many of the S.D.F. leaders. Like the Fabian Society, the I.L.P. avoided taking up a definite attitude in religious matters; many of its members and leaders were no longer members of Protestant sects, but they were still strongly influenced by the Nonconformist outlook, and patronized the 'Labour Church' movement of John Trevor.

From 1897, Fabian influence on the I.L.P. increased in some ways and declined in others. In that year, the chief personal Marxist influences on the I.L.P. disappeared with the withdrawal of Tom Mann, the suicide of Eleanor Marx-Aveling, and the final discredit of Aveling. After that time, Ramsay MacDonald and Bruce Glasier became the leading theorists of the I.L.P., and, whatever disagreements these two men may have had with some Fabians and some aspects of Fabian policy, their disagreements with Marxism were greater. In so far as Fabianism was a criticism of Marxism it was encouraged, and the Continental Revisionists and critics of Marx were translated for the I.L.P. library. The criticism of Marx was often carried to the length of fostering the idea that he was so 'wrong' or 'outdated' as not to be worth reading: in this sense, as Professor Trevelyan has shrewdly observed, 'the Fabians exonerated Socialists from the heavy obligation of reading Karl Marx'.[1] In addition, the breakdown of negotiations for unity between the I.L.P. and the S.D.F. was attended with a bitterness and mutual recrimination which produced a hostility to Marxist influence. The very existence of the I.L.P. meant a diminution of Marxist influence in that working-class men more readily than before could enter the Socialist movement without having to pass through the S.D.F. ranks. And the final years of the nineteenth century were not at all a period of social crisis, such as favours the general spread of Marxist doctrine.

This decrease of Marxist influence in itself made for the growth of 'Fabian' opinions amongst the I.L.P. But Fabianism did not flourish simply because of the decline of its opponent. It is clear that from about 1895-6 Fabian lecturing was being directed more towards I.L.P. Clubs and Branches and less towards Radical and Liberal Clubs than formerly, simply in response to the demand for the Society's speakers. Fabian 'evolutionism' and complete reliance on democratic methods, Fabian economics and views on Collectivism, Fabian 'municipal socialism' were preached to I.L.P. Branches, and found receptive audiences.

There was also one point of tactics, soon to become of great importance, in

---

[1] G. M. Trevelyan, *British History in the Nineteenth Century and After*, 1782-1919 (Longmans, London, 1937), p. 403.

which the I.L.P. returned to 'Fabian' methods. We have seen how the I.L.P. swung over to a policy of 'unification' as the only course open to it, after it had failed to secure Trade Union backing at the 1894 Trade Union Congress, and how this had led Webb and Shaw to abandon the party as hopeless. After its defeat at the 1895 election, and after some experience of the slow progress of building up a party on Continental lines, the I.L.P. leaders returned to the 'Fabian' policy of winning the Trade Unions as a quicker way to power. The Party's propaganda amongst the Trade Unions was attended with increasing success after the Engineer's Lock-out of 1897, with its attack by employers on collective bargaining.

Despite these increases in Fabian influence on the I.L.P., in other matters the I.L.P. was in disagreement with the Fabians, and some of their disagreements increased towards the turn of the century. Fabian influence was confined solely to domestic policy; and even in domestic affairs there were divergences between the two organizations. In local government policy, London Progressivism was the Fabian ideal, while the I.L.P. of course insisted on independent candidatures;[1] the I.L.P. was soon to rally to the defence of the School Boards, which Webb and the majority of Fabians desired abolished; the I.L.P. took up vigorously the demand for the 'State feeding of schoolchildren', which had once been a Fabian demand, but had been dropped by them as impracticable. But in foreign policy, especially in their reactions to imperialism and the Boer War, the majority opinions in the I.L.P. and in the Fabian Society were poles apart.

The I.L.P.'s interest in foreign affairs was greater than that of the Fabians, and this was partly due to the fact that (thanks mainly to Engels) the I.L.P. had been recognized by Continental Socialist Parties as the 'true' representative of British Socialism. The I.L.P. did not wait until the outbreak of the Boer War to reveal its attitude. In 1898 an anti-conscription resolution was passed by the I.L.P. Annual Conference, which stood in marked contrast with the attitude of prominent Fabian leaders, who always inclined towards a form of conscription. In 1899, the year of Fashoda, the I.L.P. passed a resolution expressing its opposition to war and calling for international arbitration.[2] At the Conference of 1900, when the situation had become really serious, strong resolutions were passed expressing the I.L.P.'s opposition to Imperialism, Militarism, and Conscription. The anti-imperialist resolution was in direct opposition to the resolutions adopted by the Fabian Society, because amendments to delete the word 'Imperialist' and substitute 'Militarist' or to insert 'Jingo' before 'Imperialist' were defeated; and the sentences in the I.L.P. resolution which called for the withdrawal of 'the iron and unnatural dominance of our Western political ideas', to 'allow the

---

[1] I.L.P. Annual Conference Report 1895 for resolution against 'Progressivism'.
[2] I.L.P. Annual Conference Report 1899.

development of native forms of rule' indicated that the I.L.P., unlike the Fabians, valued 'self-government' even above 'Western civilization.'[1] The anti-militarist resolution was saved by an amendment on this occasion from becoming a definitely pacifist resolution. At the succeeding Conferences of 1901 and 1902 the I.L.P. declared itself definitely 'pro-Boer'. Resolutions calling for an anti-war conference, deploring militarism, condemning 'atrocities' and 'barbarities' were passed, and a motion that the I.L.P. engage actively in peace propaganda was carried against an amendment that the Party concentrate on Socialist propaganda without 'worrying about the war', the amendment being rejected by a large majority.[2] In its attitude to foreign affairs, the Fabian Society had very little influence on the I.L.P.—but there was a minority in the I.L.P. which agreed with the Fabians, just as there was a minority in the Fabian Society which followed the I.L.P.

In the first years of the twentieth century, the Boer War and Education Act issues so dominated politics that the agreement between the I.L.P. and Fabians on other issues was obscured. They were on opposite sides in the major political alignment of that time, though their expectations of the outcome were the same. Hardie, like the Webbs, predicted the emergence of the Liberal-Imperialists as a new party, with perhaps a Rosebery-Chamberlain alliance[3] to form a 'third party' between the Old Conservatives and the 'pro-Boer' Liberals. While Webb was trying to persuade the Roseberyites to add 'Social Reform' to their other watchwords of 'Imperialism' and 'Efficiency', the I.L.P., in close co-operation with the 'pro-Boer' Liberals in the War and Education controversies, had hopes of an accession of this group to the Labour Party.[4]

[1] I.L.P. Annual Conference Report 1900.
[2] I.L.P. Annual Conference Reports 1901 and 1902.
[3] Hardie's speech in I.L.P. Annual Conference Report 1901; B. Webb, *Our Partnership*, pp. 217 *et seq.*
[4] W. Stewart, *J. Keir Hardie: a Biography* (I.L.P. Publication Dept, 1925), p. 169.

CHAPTER XI

THE INFLUENCE OF THE FABIANS UPON THE LABOUR PARTY

THE FOUNDING OF THE L.R.C.

THE Labour Representation Committee, which six years afterwards became the Labour Party, was established as a result of a meeting held in the Memorial Hall, Farrington Street, London, on 27 February 1900. Industrial conflict during the later 'nineties had convinced some powerful trade unions of the need for political action, and the persuasion and initiative of the Socialists, mainly the I.L.P. men, brought the new organization into being. The Fabians had a share in the founding of the L.R.C.; but compared with the role of the I.L.P. their part was almost insignificant. The policy adopted in the establishment of the L.R.C. resembled to some degree the policy which the Fabian Society had unsuccessfully pressed on the Labour movement in 1894 in its Tract *A Plan of Campaign for Labour;*[1] but this policy was put into force at a time when the leading Fabians had lost their enthusiasm for it.

We have seen how the I.L.P., after the defeat of its spokesman at the Trade Union Congress of 1895, was obliged to fall back upon its own resources, and attempt, like the S.D.F., to build up a Labour Party on the Continental model through individual membership. It did not make headway: so far as it is possible to estimate on very imperfect statistics, it seems that the I.L.P. declined in membership in the final years of the 'nineties.[2] The I.L.P. leaders had probably never abandoned their hopes of winning the co-operation of the Trade Unions, but the failure of the alternative method forced them to concentrate once again on that policy. Adversity had produced a chastened and less aggressive mood, more agreeable to the Trade Union Congress. Instead of demanding that the I.L.P. should be *the* political instrument of the Trade Unions, the I.L.P. leaders adopted the 'Fabian'[3] policy of attempting to draw the Trade Unions into an alliance for political action with all Socialist groups (but with reservations about 'independence'). Their endeavours were crowned with success at the Trades Union Congress of 1899.

The conditions necessary to this victory were provided mainly by events in the industrial world, although the failure of the Conservative government to grant reforms, and the apparent breaking-up of the Liberal Party provided good talking points for advocates of political action by trade unions. The

[1] Tract 49.
[2] G. D. H. Cole, *British Working Class Politics,* 1832–1914 (Routledge, London, 1941), p. 146.
[3] See Tract 49.

307

decision at the 1899 Trades Union Congress was carried, on a card vote, by the far from overwhelming margin of 546,000 votes to 434,000, and the L.R.C. was supported, at the outset, only by a small minority of unions.[1] The setting up of the L.R.C. had in fact been made possible by the swing mainly of the railwaymen, engineers,[2] boot and shoe operatives and sections of the printing, and iron trades over to the side of the New Unions. These unions had been involved in the severe strikes and lock-outs of the later 'nineties, the period of 'the employers' counter-attack', as Elie Halévy has called it. The 'lessons of the Engineering struggle' of 1897–9 in particular were discussed in the presidential speeches at both the Scottish and British Trade Union Congresses of 1898, and those Congresses mark the beginning of the turn of the tide once more in favour of the left-wing.

The decision of the British Trades Union Congress in 1899 was preluded by resolutions of the Scottish Trades Union Congress, an organization much more amenable to I.L.P. influence. The Scottish Trades Union Congress had been founded in 1896, partly for nationalist reasons, but mainly as a protest against the new standing orders introduced by the British T.U.C. in 1895, for the socialist elements excluded after 1895 from the British T.U.C. were strong in Scotland. At the initiative of the I.L.P. negotiations had already commenced between representatives of the I.L.P., the S.D.F. and the Parliamentary Committee of the Scottish Trade Unions for united political action some months before the third annual meeting of the Scottish T.U.C. in Dundee in April 1899. Keir Hardie spoke at the Congress, and a resolution was carried endorsing the moves for a conference of trade unions, trades councils, co-operative societies, the I.L.P. and the S.D.F. 'to decide upon united working-class action at the next General Election'.[3] In Edinburgh, on 6 January 1900 this conference took place and resulted in the formation of the Scottish Workers' Parliamentary Election Committee to promote independent labour representation. This development in the Scottish labour world took place without the assistance of the Fabian Society, whose organization in Scotland by the turn of the century was confined to the Glasgow and Edinburgh University groups.

The I.L.P. men pursued similar tactics with the British Trades Union Congress which was held at Plymouth five months later, but they needed to move more warily. Their resolution was much more cautiously worded than

---

[1] In March 1901 the number of unions affiliated to the L.R.C. was 41 with a membership of 353,070. At the end of 1900 the total number of trade unions in Britain was 1272, with a membership of 1,905,116.

[2] The Amalgamated Society of Engineers withdrew from the T.U.C. over a demarcation dispute before the 1899 Congress, and it did not at first affiliate with the L.R.C., but its sympathy was important and it took part in the inaugural conference which established the L.R.C.

[3] Report of the third Annual Scottish T.U.C.

the resolutions of the Scottish Congress, calling merely for a special conference of representatives of 'Co-operative, Socialistic, Trade Union, and other working organizations . . . as may be willing to take part to devise ways and means for securing the return of an increased number of Labour members to the next Parliament'.[1] When the resolution was carried against the vote of most of the Coal and Cotton unions, the next step was to ensure that it should be implemented not by the Parliamentary Committee of the T.U.C., which was largely hostile to the Socialists, but by a special committee on which the Socialists should be strongly represented. This was manœuvred. The committee appointed consisted of four members of the Parliamentary Committee—Will Thorne, a Social-Democrat, W. C. Steadman, a Fabian, and Richard Bell and Sam Woods, both 'Lib-Labs'—together with two members each from the I.L.P. (Keir Hardie and J. R. MacDonald), the S.D.F. (H. Quelch and H. R. Taylor) and the Fabian Society (Bernard Shaw and Edward Pease). Thus there were eight Socialists on the committee, and of the eight, five were at that time members of the Fabian Society.[2]

This does not mean, however, that the Fabian Society as an organization had any influence in bringing the L.R.C. into existence. The main work had been done by the I.L.P., assisted, in the later stages, by the S.D.F. It is true that a number of the I.L.P. men[3] vigorously engaged in this campaign were, as a matter of fact, members of the Fabian Society, but their work was done rather as members of the I.L.P. They were, about this time, in conflict with the majority of the Society on a number of issues, and it is clear from the publications and minutes of the Society that its main attention was directed elsewhere than towards these happenings in the Labour world. The only member of the Fabian Society not also a member of the I.L.P. who played a considerable part in the development of the L.R.C. was W. C. Steadman, of the Barge Builders. Pease and Shaw were appointed to the committee which had the task of calling the L.R.C. conference not because they had had any hand in originating this development, but because the Fabian Society was treated as a Socialist body whose co-operation was desirable. And the Fabian representatives attended, not because they thought the new development promising, but simply on the principle that any organization was worth while permeating. The Fabian Executive gave its representatives no specific instructions, and apparently Bernard Shaw took no active part in the committee's work, leaving it to Edward Pease.

When the conference was convened, W. C. Steadman was elected to the Chair. Steadman's qualifications for this position were that he was a Member

---

[1] Report of the 1899 T.U.C.
[2] MacDonald did not resign from the Fabian Society until the following year.
[3] And women: Margaret Bondfield, representing the Shop Assistants, had been a vigorous speaker in favour of the I.L.P.'s resolution before the T.U.C.

of Parliament[1] and a 'Lib-Lab', a Fabian Socialist yet favourable to the development of a Labour Party, and therefore acceptable both to the Liberal trade union leaders and to the Socialists. His election may be said to foreshadow and symbolize later Fabian influence in the Labour Party: Fabianism became the compromise position between the I.L.P. left-wing and the 'Lib-Lab' trade unionist right-wing of the party. This result was brought about by the nature of the situation, rather than by positive action on the part of the Society itself.

The official Fabian delegates to the conference were Bernard Shaw and E. R. Pease. Shaw did not go; and Pease did not speak at the conference. The Fabian Society, because of its stand-offish attitude and also because of its attitude to the Boer War, was out of favour with both the I.L.P. and the S.D.F. delegates. An I.L.P. spokesman proposed an amendment, which was carried, reducing the size of the L.R.C. from the original plan of twelve trade unionists and two representatives of each of the three Socialist organizations to seven trade unionists, one Fabian, and two members of each the I.L.P. and the S.D.F. Harry Quelch, speaking for the S.D.F., proposed the exclusion of the Fabians altogether; his proposal was not adopted, however. E. R. Pease 'appointed himself'[2] to the one seat allowed the Fabians by the I.L.P. resolution.

By tactful and diplomatic methods, and with the aid of ambiguously worded resolutions, the I.L.P. leaders preserved their control of the inaugural conference. Blatchford and his 'Clarionettes', like the Fabians, had lost influence through their attitude to the war: as a consequence, the 'Fourth Clause' did not reappear.[3] John Burns was there and made a speech, but his reputation in working-class circles had waned, and his influence at the conference was slight. For the rest, the I.L.P. was conveniently situated to throw its weight equally against resolutions it disapproved from the trade unionists on the Right of it, or from the S.D.F. on the Left, to secure their defeat. On the one hand, the I.L.P. men secured the rejection, by amendment, of a motion to restrict the L.R.C.'s activities simply to the promotion of working-class candidatures; on the other they opposed an S.D.F. resolution which sought to commit the new organization to a Socialist policy based on the class-war doctrine, and substituted for it Keir Hardie's intentionally ambiguous amendment: 'That this Conference is in favour of establishing a distinct Labour group in Parliament who shall have their own Whips and agree upon their policy, which must embrace a readiness to co-operate with any party, which, for the time being, may be engaged in promoting legislation in the direct interest of Labour, and be equally ready to associate themselves with

[1] He had won Stepney at the 1898 bye-election. He was defeated shortly after this in the 'Khaki election' of 1900.
[2] Pease, *op. cit.* p. 149.
[3] *Fabian News* commented on this in its report in the issue of April 1900.

any party in opposing measures having an opposite tendency . . .' This formula proved agreeable to the trade unionists, and the I.L.P. won recognition of its principle of 'independence' at the cost of abandoning any attempt to force the new organization to declare itself Socialist, and also at the cost of leaving undefined the precise terms upon which collaboration with the Liberal Party would be permitted. It is almost certain that at no less price could the support of the main body of trade unionists have been purchased.[1] The election of James Ramsay MacDonald as Secretary of the L.R.C. confirmed the triumph of I.L.P. diplomacy.[2]

Not much had been achieved at this inaugural conference of the L.R.C. in defining the exact nature of the new organization: most of the definition had been in the way of negation. The L.R.C. was certainly not to be a Marxist-Socialist body; it was not even Socialist; but it was not quite like the older electoral organizations which had been completely under the thumb of the Parliamentary Committee of the Trade Union Congresses. It was a federal organization, with the Socialists vastly over-represented, proportionately to their numbers, on its governing Committee, but with its purse-strings securely held by the trade unions, and their veto on its actions assured by the card vote. Initially, it had no policy, only a function: the function or organizing Labour candidatures; and the only way in which this function differed from that performed by the earlier Labour Electoral Association and by the still earlier Labour Representation League, was that, in some not altogether clear manner, the candidates promoted by the L.R.C. were to be independent of the Liberal Party.

The founding of the L.R.C. attracted very little attention at the time, and few observers expected anything important to come of it. The Fabian leaders shared this general opinion. But why were they not at least as excited about the possible developments of a link between the trade unions and Socialism as they had been in 1893-4, when they produced the *Plan of Campaign for Labour* Tract? They had grown more cynical since those days; their attention was turned elsewhere; they were 'permeating' in high official and political circles; but, not least, it also appeared to them that the L.R.C. of 1900 was obtaining trade union support at the price of its Socialism. The gain of 'independence' did not interest the Fabian 'Old Gang': they cared for Socialism and for trade unions, not at all for 'independent' tactics; that was the I.L.P.'s game.

---

[1] The I.L.P. leaders were perfectly aware that the conference represented only the left-wing elements of the trade union movement. If the Coal and Cotton unions had bothered to attend, the I.L.P. ascendency might have been seriously challenged.

[2] The story (given currency in Lee and Archbold's history of the S.D.F. and elsewhere) that J. R. MacDonald was elected in mistake for James Macdonald of the S.D.F. has little foundation. The name of another I.L.P. man, Fred Brocklehurst, was originally put forward; he declined and nominated J. R. MacDonald, who was then elected unanimously.

It must be concluded that the influence of the Fabian Society, as a Society, on the L.R.C. at the time of its foundation, was slight or negligible. But its influence was not destined to remain insignificant in the future.

THE LABOUR MEMBERS' MAINTENANCE FUND

Although the leading Fabians, and the Fabian Society as a whole, displayed little interest in the L.R.C., a few individual members of the Society were active in promoting its development, and E. R. Pease, the Society's secretary, played throughout an inconspicuous but useful role in the new organization. Pease remained the Society's single representative on the L.R.C. and Labour Party Executive from the time of its foundation until 1914, when he was replaced by W. S. Sanders. The correspondence which passed between Ramsay MacDonald and Pease in connection with the L.R.C. shows that Pease was kept constantly in touch with the Committee's work, and that he was occasionally consulted by MacDonald on special points of procedure.[1]

Pease was especially active in persuading the L.R.C. to establish itself on a sound financial basis. He and S. G. Hobson resurrected a proposal that had been made by the Fabian Society at the time of the founding of the I.L.P. for the creation of a Labour Members' Maintenance Fund, which would be contributed to by the Trade Unions at the rate of one penny per member per annum. But it was now recommended that this fund be administered by the L.R.C.[2] The proposal was discussed at L.R.C. conferences under the name of 'the Fabian scheme'. It had obvious advantages: the political advantage to the L.R.C. of making the M.P.s so maintained 'Labour representatives' rather than representatives of particular trade unions, and the financial advantage to the trade unions, particularly the smaller ones, of sharing the burden equally by all instead of leaving it entirely with the particular trade union to which the elected man happened to belong. The scheme was disliked by the Liberal leaders of the greater trade unions. The original financial provision for the L.R.C. made at its inaugural conference was a beggarly ten shillings per annum for each thousand members of the affiliated societies, and the function of the L.R.C. was said to be the recognition and assistance of candidates put forward by member organizations, not the promotion or putting forward of candidates itself. The Fabian scheme was debated, but not approved, when it was put forward by S. G. Hobson at the first annual conference of the L.R.C. held at Manchester in February 1901. Its acceptance

---

[1] The Fabian Correspondence, etc. is in the London Library of Social and Political Science, filed as 'Labour Party: Minutes, Letters and other Papers, from 27 February 1918 to 5 December 1912, and one paper of 18 August 1918, elucidating the early proceeding of the Labour Party Executive known, until 1906, as the Labour Representation Committee'. Coll. Misc. 196 M283.

[2] *Fabian News*, August 1900.

was finally made possible, like so much else, by the militancy which emerged when the trade unions realized they were unlikely to obtain a speedy reversal of the decision of the House of Lords in the Taff Vale judgment. A favourable discussion took place at the second Annual Conference, and the Fabian proposal (with an exception made in the case of trade councils) was finally adopted at the third Annual Conference of 1903.[1]

This was, then, the chief contribution of the Fabians in the early years of the L.R.C. It was, characteristically, a piece of 'machinery', but of great importance in changing the nature of the L.R.C. from a body which merely 'recognized' candidates to one which ran candidates itself. Furthermore, this demand for a political fund for the L.R.C. was urged by the Fabians at a time when the I.L.P. did not support it. At the first annual conference the I.L.P. representatives voted with the Liberal trade unionists against the scheme, whereas the S.D.F. representatives spoke in favour of it. There seem to be two possible explanations of the I.L.P. leaders' attitude on this occasion. They may have feared that, if the L.R.C. became a body capable of financing its own candidates, the I.L.P.'s importance in the movement would be greatly diminished. This explanation is plausible, but not altogether convincing,[2] for the I.L.P.'s attitude changed at the second conference, and it then supported the Fabian plan. A more likely explanation is that the I.L.P. representatives were being cautious, aware of the dangers of running ahead of trade union opinion in this matter. They showed the same attitude when, after the trade unions had come to accept the idea of the L.R.C. fund, Henderson of the Ironfounders and Weighill of the Stonemasons urged that the amount of the levy should be raised from the proposed sum of one penny per member to fourpence and one shilling respectively; the I.L.P. spokesmen were very anxious on that occasion to make it clear that these amendments did not come from the Socialists, and voted against them.[3] In the L.R.C.'s finances the Fabians were the pioneers, the I.L.P. men the diplomats, with their eyes to the 'tact of the possible'. When the Parliamentary Fund was established, E. R. Pease was elected one of its three Trustees and he continued to be reappointed until the financial arrangements of the Labour Party were reorganized at the 1912 Conference.

'BENEVOLENT PASSIVITY'

'Benevolent passivity' were the words used by Pease[4] to describe the relations between the Fabian Society and the L.R.C. and Labour Party. He is modest about his own share in the administrative work: in all his years of membership

---

[1] Contributions were made compulsory in 1904. Report of 1904 L.R.C. Conference.

[2] This explanation is advanced by G. D. H. Cole in his *British Working Class Politics*, pp. 170–1. He thinks the later change of attitude of the I.L.P. was a result of the Dewsbury incident.

[3] Report of 1903 L.R.C. Conference.   [4] Pease, *op. cit.* p. 151.

of the Executive of the L.R.C. and Labour Party, Edward Pease hardly ever missed an executive meeting. But his words describe succinctly the attitude of the Fabian Society as a whole. Not until the Newport conference of 1910 did the Society again put forward a resolution, and then it was only to urge support of the Local Government Finance Bill.[1] And neither the number of Fabians prominent in the Labour Party nor the part which the Society's representatives played at annual conferences of the Party suggest any great degree of influence separate from that of the I.L.P., at least in the early years of the Labour Party.

Apart from Pease, only two or three of the men who composed the L.R.C. (a body of fourteen members) were members of the Fabian Society, and these Fabians were also prominent I.L.P. men.[2] The proportion of Fabians amongst Labour Party members of Parliament between 1906 and 1918 was even smaller. After the 1906 election there were five Fabian members of the Parliamentary Labour Party (or six if we include W. C. Steadman, who was expelled from the L.R.C. in 1905, but who co-operated closely, particularly after 1907, with the Labour Party M.P.s); the number fell to four in the election of January 1910, but increased to eight in the election of December of the same year; it fell again to three in the 1918 election.[3]

At Labour Party conferences the Fabian Society's representatives do not seem to have exercised any outstanding personal influence. Until the Labour Party's success at the polls in 1906 the Fabian Society was content to be represented at the L.R.C. conference by Pease alone (except in 1901, when S. G. Hobson was its representative), and Pease was always a 'behind-the-scenes' man, rarely speaking at the conferences. After 1906 Fabian representation gradually increased as its growing membership entitled it to send more delegates, and Pease was joined by other prominent Fabians: at first by Bland (at the 1908 and 1910 conferences), then by Bernard Shaw (1909), and W. S. Sanders (1909 to 1914), and later by others—H. H. Schloesser (Slesser) (1911), Dr Ethel Bentham (1912), Clifford Sharp (1912), Mabel Atkinson (1913), H. Snell (1913) and finally the Webbs.[4] Bernard Shaw's appearance at the

[1] *Fabian News*, March 1910 and Report of 1910 Labour Party Conference.
[2] Viz. Hardie, Snowden, and Walter Hudson (of the Amalgamated Society of Railway Servants).
[3] Fabian members of the Parliamentary Labour Party between 1906 and 1918 were: 1906: J. Keir Hardie, Philip Snowden, Will Crooks, Walter Hudson, and James O'Grady (of the Furnishing Trades Association). Total number of Labour Party M.P.s: 30.
January 1910: Hardie, Snowden, O'Grady, Hudson. Total number of Labour Party M.P.s: 40.
December 1910: Hardie, Snowden, O'Grady, Hudson, Crooks, George Lansbury, F. W. Goldstone, and Joseph Pointer (the latter, M.P. for the Attercliffe division of Sheffield since 1909, joined the F.S. in 1910). Total number of Labour Party M.P.s: 42.
1918: Crooks, Ben Tillett, William Graham. Total number of Labour Party M.P.s: 57. However, the number of Fabian M.P.s rose spectacularly in the 'twenties to 10 in 1922 and 22 in December 1923. (Total Labour Party M.P.'s 142 and 191 respectively).
[4] Beatrice Webb at 1913, 1914, 1916, 1918 conferences and Sidney Webb at 1913, 1914,

Labour Party conference of 1909 as one of the Fabian representatives marked, in no uncertain fashion, an increase in the amount of Fabian participation, but his numerous interventions in debate were not conspicuously successful. At subsequent conferences the Fabian delegates usually had something to contribute, but as a rule they confined themselves to supplying special information or elucidating difficult points.

Is it, then, at all possible to maintain that the Fabian Society had any considerable influence on the Labour Party? At this point it becomes necessary to look at the policy that the Labour Party was gradually adopting.

THE LABOUR PARTY PROGRAMME BEFORE THE FIRST WORLD WAR

From the time of the 1901 conference, the L.R.C. adopted a series of resolutions which in effect were a party programme, though it is doubtful if the word 'programme' should be used of them, as hot debate on the question whether the L.R.C. ought to adopt a 'programme' was going on all the time these resolutions were being passed. The demand for a 'programme', which came at first from the S.D.F. men, was really a demand for a comprehensive statement of party policy, which would include socialist objectives. The opposition to it was based on the fear that a full and explicit statement of this kind would create friction between the Socialists and Liberal trade unionists who jointly made up the L.R.C. and would lead to a schism. On this ground the I.L.P. men opposed a 'programme'.

At the beginning of its existence the L.R.C. was frankly recognized by the I.L.P. leaders for what it was: an alliance, for limited purposes, between Liberal Trade Unionists and Socialists. The I.L.P. men recognized that the majority of the Trade Unionists could only be brought to accept socialistic measures by extremely gradual and cautious methods of persuasion and they were prepared, as the S.D.F. men were not, to consider labour organization more important than professions of socialist faith.[1] Thus at the first annual conference of the L.R.C. held at Manchester in February 1901 James Sexton of the Liverpool Dockers, an I.L.P. man, deprecated 'the introduction of mere party politics into the Trade Union Movement', and spoke against Socialist resolutions moved by the S.D.F. and by a fellow member of the I.L.P., saying 'that the essential purpose of this movement was to bring the scattered elements of the Labour Movement to agree on a common platform

1918 conferences. Other Fabian delegates were J. Airey (1911), C.M. Lloyd (1914), J. S. Middleton (1917 and 1918), and Emil Davies (1917).
[1] It is ironical to note that if Engels' opinion in the 'nineties be taken as Marxist orthodoxy, the I.L.P. were, in this matter, better Marxists than the S.D.F. See Engels to Sorge 12 May 1894, *Marx and Engels on Britain* (Foreign Languages Publishing House, Moscow, 1953), pp. 535–6.

of independent representation of labour. Personally he was in favour of the resolution, but he would not vote for it because he thought that in these Conferences no one side should ram their principles down the throats of the other side'. Similarly, Keir Hardie in a famous speech he made at the 1903 conference, argued that the basis of the L.R.C. was not Socialism, nor Liberalism, nor Toryism, but independent Labourism; any attempt of one section to insist that all should be Socialists or of another that all should be Liberals would split the movement; their common ground was that, when acting in the House of Commons, they should be 'neither Socialists, Liberals nor Tories, but a Labour Party'. And at the same conference he urged the delegates to be content with their measure of agreement, for 'the present was no occasion for programmes'.

The demands for a programme were voted down at L.R.C. and Labour Party Conferences; nevertheless Bernard Shaw at the 1909 conference in one of his trimming, paradoxical speeches so annoying to both sides was able to point out that the Labour Party did not need a programme because it already had one.[1] The resolutions passed by the Party conferences did in fact provide a 'programme' of some sort. It is possible to classify the main resolutions passed by the Labour Party conferences under a few broad headings, and as the Fabian Society itself very seldom put forward resolutions dealing with general policy, the problem becomes one of considering how similar the result emerging from the co-operation and conflict of the I.L.P. Socialists with the Liberal trade unionists resembled the proposals urged in the Fabian tracts.

[1] On the specific matter of the 'programme' the Fabians were divided up to 1909, and this is reflected in Shaw's speech. But already at the 1906 and 1907 conferences the Fabians Frank Smith and Ben Cooper had supported the S.D.F. demand. In 1909 the Fabian Executive yielded to the attack of the extreme 'reformers' in the Society to the extent of recommending the following quite strongly worded resolutions, which were passed by a large majority:
1. That parliamentary parties in England no longer depend for support on the strength of their names or the class from which their members are drawn, but stand or fall by their programmes.
2. That a party without a programme may influence legislation in the House of Commons, but can do nothing to influence public opinion in the country.
3. That a Labour Party, in order to justify its detachment from the two Capitalist Parties, and its calls upon the funds of the Trade Unions, must put forward a Labour programme which not only differs from the programmes of the Capitalist Parties, but consists mainly of the measures which cannot be conceivably added to those programmes.
4. That until these conditions are recognised and complied with by the Labour Party, it will be increasingly difficult for the Fabian and other definitely Socialist Societies to secure the unanimous support of their recruits for continued affiliation with the Labour Party, and to combat that tendency to break away and form new sections which has impaired the solidarity of the Labour Movement in France, and may easily do so in this country if the views of the Labour Party in Parliament remain indistinguishable from those of the left-wing of the Capitalist Parties'. (*Fabian News*, February 1909).
The Webbs in the 1920 edition of their *History of Trade Unionism* (pp. 688-9) deplored the absence of a Labour Party Programme in the pre-war years.

316

THE LABOUR PARTY AND SOCIALISM

The Labour Party was not, originally, a Socialist body. The rejection, with the connivance of the I.L.P. members, of resolutions designed to make the L.R.C. declare itself Socialist, led to the withdrawal of the S.D.F. in August 1901 and the replacement of the two S.D.F. representatives on the Executive body by two trade unionists. Individual S.D.F. men, however, continued to appear at the L.R.C. conferences, as delegates of other bodies, so resolutions designed to commit the L.R.C. to Socialism continued to be moved after the S.D.F. withdrawal. There can be little doubt that the I.L.P. could have caused the L.R.C. to declare itself definitely Socialist had it wished to do so. This was demonstrated at the 1908 conference, when an S.D.F. attempt to write the 'ultimate objective' into the L.R.C.'s Constitution was turned down by 951,000 against 91,000 votes, with the I.L.P. in opposition; but when, at the same conference, a Socialist resolution was proposed merely as a test of the conference's opinion, with I.L.P. support, it was narrowly carried, by 514,000 votes to 469,000. The I.L.P. preferred to win the Liberal trade unions and keep them united on the policy of independent Labourism. It was wary of forcing the pace of the trade unionists along the path of Socialism, which it nevertheless expected them ultimately to tread.

From 1906 the process of winning the Labour Party gradually to Socialism had been commenced;[1] particular resolutions of a Socialist character were put forward one by one for Labour Party approval. The I.L.P. men naturally began by proposing 'border-line' resolutions, which could be accepted by the Radicals, but soon their resolutions became more definite. Thus, the first 'socialist' resolution passed by the Labour Party was probably that moved by Glasier at the sixth annual conference, when he secured the Party's acceptance of the principle that taxation ought to be used for redistributing the national income on a more equal basis. At the following conference, while attempts by Quelch, Tillett and Thorne to persuade the Labour Party to adopt a socialist programme, or at least to take a ballot of the membership on the question whether the Party should be pledged to the public ownership of the means of production, were rejected as inopportune, the delegates accepted a resolution for the public ownership of 'monopolies'.

[1] Difficulties arose when the L.R.C. was persuaded by Keir Hardie to apply for membership of the Second International in 1904. The S.D.F. objected violently to a body which 'repudiated' Socialism at home representing itself as a Socialist organization on the Continent. Despite Hyndman's opposition, the International Socialist Bureau, on the motion of Kautsky, admitted the Labour Party and gave as its reason that, although the Labour Party did not officially recognize the class-struggle, it nevertheless carried it on, because being independent it was based on the class-struggle. This conflict emerged again in 1912 and 1913, when the International Socialist Bureau recognized the Labour Party secretary as *ex officio* British secretary to the International. But by 1913 somewhat less casuistry was needed to answer Hyndman's protests, and the Labour Party then claimed that it was a Socialist organization, because it had declared for the socialization of 'railways, mines, and other monopolies'.

In 1908, a more specific note was struck when the Labour Party Conference carried a resolution in favour of the nationalization of railways. This was the first demand for the public ownership of a particular service. It was at the same Conference that the general socialist resolution put forward by the Engineers for the purpose of testing the opinion of the Conference was carried by a narrow margin on a card vote. The experiment was repeated, with the same result, at the 1909 Conference. It was not, however, until the 1913 Conference that resolutions were carried adding demands for the nationalization of canals and waterways to the demand for nationalization of the railways, and also calling for the national ownership of the land and coal-mines. Another motion which won approval called for the establishment of a State Medical Service. In 1914 a further advance was made when when a resolution was carried declaring Socialism to be the aim of the Labour Party. Socialist ideas made great headway in the Labour Party during the war, but the final step was not taken until 1918, when a Socialist objective was eventually written into the Party's new Constitution.

The Fabian Society's part, compared with that played by the I.L.P., in urging the Labour Party gradually towards Socialism was only a minor one, yet it was not without some importance. The Fabians, having a less responsible position in the Labour Party than the I.L.P. leaders, were in the fortunate situation where they could criticise the Labour Party for not being socialist enough;[1] they were not necessarily obliged to incur the odium of restraining the enthusiasm of the Socialist left-wing. Yet the Fabian 'Old Guard' leaders recognized the character of the Labour Party for what it was, and they did not attempt to force the pace. Dissident Fabian members within the Labour Party however did lend support to S.D.F. and left-wing I.L.P. resolutions at conferences.[2] Presently the 'Old Guard' Fabians were facing left-wing groups within the Society itself. But the disputes within the Society did not concern the question whether the Labour Party could be forced more quickly towards Socialism, but rather the question whether it was worth while for the Society to retain its membership of so incoherent an organization as the Labour Party.[3]

The demand for a State Medical Service, which was embodied in a resolution passed by the 1913 conference, was a demand deriving from Fabian sources, and after the same conference passed the resolution for the nationalization of coal-mines the Miners' Federation and the Labour Party

---

[1] E. R. Pease, reviewing Conrad Noel's *The Labour Party, What It Is and What It Wants*, in *Fabian News*, September 1906 remarked: 'This is an excellent account of the Labour Party, its history and constitution, and above all, its ideas—not because the writer displays profound knowledge or philosophic insight, but because he is scrappy, haphazard and somewhat superficial, and this is what the Labour Party is itself'.

[2] e.g. Frank Smith at 1906 conference and Ben Cooper at 1907 Conference supported S.D.F. resolutions.

[3] See below, p. 322.

commissioned the Fabian lawyer, H. H. Schloesser (Slesser), to draw up a 'Nationalization of Mines and Minerals Bill' for presentation to Parliament.[1] Insofar as Socialism was accepted by the Labour Party before the Great War, it was Socialism of the type advocated by Fabians, but the Fabians did not need to fight for their type of Collectivist Socialism against the Syndicalists within the Labour Party. The struggle between Syndicalists and State Socialists was fought out in the trade unions and the Trade Union Congress and in the I.L.P. branches, not in the Labour Party. The leaders of both the I.L.P. and the Labour Party were convinced State Socialists, and whenever Syndicalist resolutions arose they were emphatically rejected.

MUNICIPAL SOCIALISM AND THE LABOUR PARTY

The I.L.P. had followed the Fabian Society in concentrating much of its attention in local politics. This was not the case with the Labour Party in the pre-war years. The L.R.C., and later the Labour Party, was an organization for engaging in national politics. It was a national federation, and it did not compete with other organizations in running candidates for local elections. At the fourth annual conference of the L.R.C. a specific declaration was made that the L.R.C. 'had no concern' in municipal elections, and as late as 1913 a protest that a member of the Fabian Society was standing as a Progressive for the London County Council against a Labour man was ruled out of order at the Labour Party conference on the ground that 'the Executive has no control over bodies in respect to local elections'.

This attitude was maintained, despite the emergence of bodies that became known as 'local L.R.C.s'. These bodies appear to have been of two kinds— either local federations (on the national L.R.C. model) of local Socialist and Labour organizations for the purpose of contesting elections to local government authorities, or Labour Associations formed on the basis of individual membership by particular Labour M.P.s to support them in their constituencies.[2] They were at first not encouraged: the L.R.C. preferred to work through the local Trades Councils or the machinery of its member organizations, and the I.L.P. at first looked upon the growth of these 'local L.R.C.s' with hostility as possible competitors. In 1903 they were refused affiliation to the national L.R.C., and the reason given was that they were 'really only joint committees of societies already affiliated'. But the growth of these organizations was remarkable, and in 1905 the national L.R.C. agreed that 'in constituencies which are not covered by a Trades Council, the Labour Association for the whole constituency be eligible for affiliation on the same basis as Trades Councils if it accepts the constitution and policy of the national L.R.C.'.

[1] Tract 171.
[2] There were very few of the latter, perhaps only two—at Woolwich and Barnard Castle.

The Labour Party nevertheless still declined to concern itself with municipal politics in any but its broader national aspects, until after the reorganization of the party by the 1918 Constitution. But municipal issues managed to intrude into national politics. The L.R.C. rallied to the defence of the principle of 'Municipal Trading' in 1901, when it was being attacked vigorously in the Conservative press.[1] The Labour Party upheld the principle that the Government and the municipalities should be 'model employers', paying 'fair wages' and recognizing trade union standards.[2] It also upheld the principle of 'direct employment'[3] and, where this was impossible, the enforcing of 'model conditions' on government and municipal contractors.[4] And from time to time resolutions were passed about housing, equalization of rates in London, and the municipal taxation of land values, when these were raised as parliamentary issues. These things found general support in Labour Party ranks; they did not require special advocacy by the Fabians, but occasionally they were brought before the conference by such I.L.P. Fabians as Philip Snowden.

THE POLICY OF INDEPENDENCE

The I.L.P. had persuaded the L.R.C. to declare for the policy of 'independence', but some interpretation of this policy became necessary in the years which followed. Keir Hardie's famous speech at the 1903 Labour Party conference gave vigorous expression to the principle. It was stated quite frankly at the same conference that independent tactics were necessary because the L.R.C. was recruiting adherents from former supporters of both Liberal and Tory parties. What the principle of independence meant in precise political terms was never exactly as clear as day but it was clarified somewhat by the kind of proposals that were rejected.

In the first place, it involved a steady refusal to add the word 'Socialist' to the Party's title or to allow its candidates at elections to call themselves 'Socialist' candidates. This issue was fought over and over again. The I.L.P. leaders were conspicuous in combating these attempts. The Fabian representatives took no part in these disputes until the 1911 conference, when W. S. Sanders joined the I.L.P. in opposing the perennial resolution.

On the other hand, attempts by anti-Socialists to undermine the privileged position accorded to the Socialist organizations in the Labour Party were equally resisted. A proposal to exclude the Socialist bodies from the L.R.C. in order to 'keep it clear of parties' was rejected in 1903 'with practical unanimity'. The Radicals made their most serious attempts to capture the L.R.C. at its 1903 and 1905 conferences; after 1906 the character of the

---

[1] L.P. Annual Conference Report 1901.
[2] L.P. Annual Conference Report, 1906, 1907, 1908, 1909, 1910, 1912, etc.
[3] L.P. Annual Conference Report 1908.
[4] L.P. Annual Conference Report 1906.

Labour Party as a Trade Union—Socialist alliance appears to have been too firmly established to be shaken by them. In 1903 and 1905 a number of clever amendments to the Constitution, designed to weaken I.L.P. influence, had to be fought. Resolutions were moved for the admission to the L.R.C. of Liberal Associations having similar objects; to allow constituent organizations more freedom in their politics; to give the Executive greater freedom to support candidates of other parties who were favourable to the L.R.C.'s objects; to institute a referendum for the sanctioning of increased monetary contributions; to limit membership of the L.R.C. to trade unionists; and to elect the Executive by a ballot of the whole of the delegates at the L.R.C. conference and not on a 'federal' basis.[1] All these resolutions were rejected, and the result was to tighten control over Labour M.P.s, when the I.L.P. men, retaliating, carried a resolution making it necessary for Labour M.P.s to pledge themselves 'not to identify themselves with another party' and to vote as the Parliamentary group decided.[2]

The Fabians were placed in a somewhat difficult position by the introduction of the L.R.C. 'pledge', and the *Fabian News*[3] expressed its 'surprise' at the decision. W. C. Steadman refused to accept the pledge and his name was removed from the Labour Party's list of candidates. Two other Fabians, Will Crooks and Isaac Mitchell, avoided acceptance for over a year, but finally yielded. Officially, the Fabian Society took no action; but privately leading Fabians continued to regard the policy of independence as foolish and mistaken. After the success of the Labour Party at the 1906 election, Bernard Shaw made some sour comments on the dependence of Labour Party M.P.s on Liberal ideas and Liberal votes, and hinted that its independence was merely nominal.[4]

Indeed, the extent of the Labour Party's victory was due partly to the fact that the Liberals had allowed the majority of successful Labour candidates a clear run against Conservative or Unionist opponents. In twenty-four out of the thirty successful candidatures, there had been no Liberal opposition. The existence of a secret electoral arrangement between the Liberal and Labour Parties was suspected at the time, and has since been confirmed. If this be claimed as further evidence in support of the Fabian contention that Labour Party independence was nominal, the I.L.P. men might well have retorted that independence was a better method of 'permeation' than the Fabian way. The threat of running independent candidates had caused the Liberals to yield twenty-four seats at least to Labour representatives: what had Fabian persuasion achieved in the same direction?

[1] The first two of these resolutions were moved at the 1903 conference, the others at the 1905 conference, see Reports.
[2] L.R.C. Annual Conference Report 1903.
[3] *Fabian News*, March 1903.
[4] *Clarion*, 2 February 1906.

Immediately after the election Arthur Henderson, as Chairman of the 1906 Labour Party Conference, declared that the Labour Party would treat the new government exactly as it had treated the old one. 'We must . . . guard as a sacred right', he said, 'the basic principle of independence which has assured the success of our movement'. But after the first moment of success had faded, the Labour Party found its principle of independence became the point of appeal for those dissatisfied with the Party's leadership. From the time of the 1909 conference there were quarrels about the independence of Labour Party M.P.s who shared double constituencies with Liberals in particular, and about the Parliamentary Party's independence of the Liberals in general. In the years before the First World War it needed a good deal of double-talk on the part of I.L.P. leaders to reassure their followers about their doctrine of independence; but 'myths' are important in politics.

The Labour Party's first success had been accompanied by an upsurge of socialist enthusiasm which brought crowds of new young members flocking into the I.L.P. and the Fabian Society. When the Labour Party's advance suffered a check, and the party settled down to ordinary parliamentary routine of a minority party, the enthusiasts blamed the old leaders for frustrating their energy and turned to the more extreme methods of the S.D.F. and the Syndicalists. Within the Fabian Society the 'Old Gang' had to meet a number of challenges to its leadership between 1906 and 1914.[1] The first, led by H. G. Wells from 1906 till his resignation in 1908, called for the Fabian Society to turn itself from a study group into a middle-class Socialist party which would work in co-operation with the I.L.P. and Labour Party;[2] S. G. Hobson in 1908-9 urged the Fabians and I.L.P. to withdraw from the useless alliance with the Liberal trade unionists and to join with the Social Democrats in forming a genuinely Socialist party;[3] the I.L.P. men in the Fabian Society, led by R. C. K. Ensor, Dr Haden Guest, Clifford Allen, and H. H. Schloesser, meanwhile conducted a campaign for the Society to give its exclusive support to the Labour Party and to make ineligible for a seat on its executive committee any Liberal or Conservative M.P. or candidate;[4] and alongside all these was the growing influence of Guild Socialism with its neo-syndicalist disillusionment with all political action. The attempts to change Fabian policy were repelled by the 'Old Gang', the Webbs' campaign for the break-up of the

[1] Pease, *op. cit.* chs IX-XI, *passim;* but Pease is unfair to the Fabian reformers. He does not make clear that the 'Old Gang' were not all united—Olivier was a supporter of Wells.

[2] For some details of the Wells episode, see *Fabian Quarterly*, April 1944.

[3] *Fabian News*, February 1909; Cecil Chesterton supported S. G. Hobson.

[4] The first move in this direction was led by R. C. K. Ensor (*Fabian News*, April 1907), who proposed a moderate resolution urging Fabians to give their exclusive support to the I.L.P. When, later, Guest and others moved compulsive resolutions to the same effect Ensor opposed them (*Fabian News*, February 1908 December 1910, and August 1912). See also *Fabian News*, June 1910, Manifesto of Fabian Reform Committee, 28 November 1911, *Fabian News*, March 1912, August 1912, November 1912, and Fabian Annual Report 1912.

INFLUENCE OF FABIANS UPON LABOUR PARTY

Poor Law provided an outlet for the enthusiasm of young Fabians, and the leaders of reforming movements after that of Wells and Hobson were handled more in a spirit of toleration and compromise.

Torn by these dissentions, the Fabian Society could provide no collective lead in the difficulties which the Labour Party was facing. With their 'Old Gang' leaders preserving the somewhat nebulous *status quo*, the Fabians were more influenced by the labour unrest than influential. The differences were fought out most vigorously in the I.L.P., and the conflict was the more severe as a good case could be made out for both sides.[1] There was a similar undercurrent of criticism within the Labour Party, but much fainter, as it had little hope of success there after the 'Lib-Lab' Miners' Federation had affiliated to the Labour Party in September 1908, and thereby given the Party an even stronger Liberal bias.

The most practical aspect of the independence controversy, where the Fabians were drawn into the fringes of the argument, concerned its interpretation in terms of detailed parliamentary tactics. Here three methods competed for recognition: the first was the 'demonstration' method, used by Keir Hardie in his early days, when he was the 'Member for the Unemployed' and subsequently used by Victor Grayson after his election at Colne Valley in 1907; the second was the 'traditional parliamentary' method, of which Ramsay MacDonald made himself chief advocate; the third was the 'voting on merits' method, urged principally by F. W. Jowett of the I.L.P.

The 'demonstration method', which consisted simply in making scenes in the House of Commons for the purpose of drawing public attention to some grievance, required for effectiveness to be used with discretion; it had been approved of by the I.L.P. in the days when Labour representatives were only a tiny minority in a substantially hostile House. Its later use by Grayson, and its advocacy by the Social Democrats, however, sprang from their belief that little good could come of a diplomatic approach to the 'enemy', and the House of Commons should be used primarily as a forum for drawing attention to the workers' wrongs. It was not a method that could commend itself to those who wished to convince the public that the Labour Party was a respectable and responsible organization. Most Fabians were opposed to it. But Ramsay MacDonald was its chief opponent. In a speech which carried the day at the annual conference of the I.L.P. in 1911, he declared: 'I do not know if I am differently constituted from other people, but if I found that our representatives in the House of Commons tried to appeal to me as an outsider by making propaganda speeches in the House of Commons, I should be far more disgusted than pleased. The great function of the House of Commons is to translate into legislation the Socialism that is preached in the country, and

[1] G. D. H. Cole, *British Working Class Politics* 1832–1914, pp. 198–9 for a judicious summing up of the cases.

323

to make it effective in the law of the land'. Grayson and his followers in the I.L.P. were eventually disciplined, after Hardie, Snowden, Glasier, and MacDonald tendered their resignations from the Council of the I.L.P. as a protest against the 'movement of irresponsibility which has grown up inside the Party'. The Fabian R. C. K. Ensor moved the resolution of regret when this collective resignation was announced.[1]

The 'demonstration method', if it met with disapproval in the I.L.P. in its latter days, was even more strongly discouraged in the Labour Party. The Trade Unionist leaders were proud of their respectability and altogether approved MacDonald's leadership. Very early in the history of the Labour Party, the Chairman of the L.R.C. had praised Ramsay MacDonald in these terms: 'The Committee and the Movement were to be congratulated' (he is reported to have said) 'in having for its Secretary a gentleman so able as Mr MacDonald. Before this Conference he had not the pleasure of knowing Mr MacDonald as he did now, and he was sure he will conduct the Movement in a gentlemanly manner . . .'.[2]

Though it caused less stir, the policy advocated by F. W. Jowett had more formidable support—even in Labour Party ranks. The Fabians were divided about it, and became more so in the years between 1907 and 1914.[3] Jowett put forward three proposals. First, to ensure Labour's independence of the Liberals, he proposed that the Labour Party should vote on bills according to its view of their merits, without considering the possible effect this would have on the Liberal government. Secondly, he recommended that the Labour Party should use its influence to relax party discipline generally by advocating that M.P.s should vote on bills according to their individual view of their merits, and not according to the direction of the party Whips. As a corollary, the government was to recognize that it was not obliged to resign unless defeated on a major measure, or on a definite vote of censure. Thirdly, Jowett suggested that the committee system as used in local government should be introduced in the House of Commons in place of the cabinet system. This was to involve the allocation of all M.P.s to committees, each reflecting party strength in the House, which would be responsible for the different Departments of State. The Minister was to be chairman of his departmental committee, and cabinet was to become a kind of General Purposes Committee, made up of the chairmen of the committees.[4]

Ramsay MacDonald was the chief opponent of the Jowett scheme. Against the naive critics who attacked the Labour Party's refusal to vote against the Liberal government when it opposed Labour party measures, MacDonald advanced practical considerations of electoral expenses. But he also treated

[1] I.L.P. Annual Conference Report 1909.
[2] L.R.C. Annual Conference Report 1902.
[3] See Ensor's speech and full debate in I.L.P. Annual Conference Report 1911.
[4] Fenner Brockway, *Socialism Over Sixty Years*, p. 235 *et seq.*

Jowett's full-blown scheme with contempt, and opposed it steadily. He was a firm upholder of the existing methods of party and cabinet government, and he perhaps was acquiring a greater relish for the intricate parliamentary game, which he played very well, than for the socialist results it achieved. Keir Hardie, with some misgivings, lent his official support to MacDonald. There was no common Fabian attitude to this issue, but a number of the Fabian I.L.P. men in the Parliamentary Labour Party, including Snowden, O'Grady, Lansbury, and Pointer agreed with Jowett in being sharply critical of MacDonald's leadership; they felt that the Labour Party's interests were being sacrificed for the sake of the Liberal alliance. These M.P.s defied the party Whips on several occasions—notably in the case of Lloyd George's National Insurance Bill, when they voted against the contributory principle, and three of them voted against the third reading of the Bill as a whole.[1] Amongst the older leaders of the Fabian Society, too, as time went on, there was a tendency to move to a view closely resembling Jowett's. Similar unfavourable comparisons of the existing parliamentary system with the committee system had been expressed in Fabian circles by Bernard Shaw about the time that Jowett was formulating his ideas on the subject, although Jowett appears to have arrived at his views independently of the Fabians,[2] and it is he rather than the Fabians who must be given chief credit for propagandizing the idea in the years before the First World War.

The campaign was one mainly fought out inside the I.L.P. and in the pages of the *Clarion*. The Labour Party, under MacDonald's influence, decisively rejected the plan at its 1911 conference, and Jowett and his supporters (including some individual Fabians) wisely decided to concentrate their energies first on capturing the I.L.P. for the idea. From the time he first raised the issue in 1911, until his proposals were fully carried at the 1914 conference of the I.L.P., Jowett won a steadily increasing proportion of votes. That part of his proposals demanding the committee system for Parliament was carried at the 1912 conference, and the other parts about 'voting on merits' were carried in 1914. 'Jowett—that dear, modest, dull but devotedly pious Socialist—shone out among his cleverer brethren and carried his impractical resolution . . .' was the cynical, but not unkind, comment of Beatrice Webb, who was present at the 1914 'Coming of Age' conference of the I.L.P.[3]

THE DEFENCE AND EXTENSION OF TRADE UNION RIGHTS

The defence and extension of trade union rights was an end which all the Labour and Socialist organizations desired, but when the House of Lords

[1] Hansard, 5th series, vol. XXVII, cols. 1461–2 and vol. XXXII, cols. 1529–30. (Pointer voted with the majority of the Labour Party for the third reading and Hardie abstained).

[2] Fenner Brockway, *Socialism Over Sixty Years*, p. 234.

[3] M. I. Cole (ed.): *Beatrice Webb's Diaries 1912–24* (Longmans, London, 1952), p. 23. See Fenner Brockway, *op. cit.* pp. 235–6 for the Jowett–Laski controversy after the war.

gave its decision in the Taff Vale Case in 1901 there was some disagreement about the exact response that needed to be made to it. The trade unions were aroused to vigorous protest, for the decision of the Law Lords in allowing the Taff Vale Railway Company's claim for damages resulting from a strike against its employees' union, the Amalgamated Society of Railway Servants, seemed to open the way to a general attack on the industrial organization of the workers. The Taff Vale decision was based on the reasonable enough principle that a trade union was a corporate body at law and so liable for the acts of its servants; but it had generally been assumed that trade union funds were exempted by the legislation of the early 'seventies from actions for tort.[1] The Taff Vale case came as the culmination of a whole series of legal decisions in the last decade of the nineteenth century which undermined trade unions' right to strike;[2] and in this period of 'the employer's attack',[3] it was accompanied by expressions of general hostility to labour organization from the Bench, in Parliament, and in the Press.[4]

The fortunes of the L.R.C. were made by the fierce reaction of unionists to the Taff Vale decision, and the alacrity of the I.L.P. leaders in taking advantage of the situation. The trade unions could not get a promise of redress from the Conservative government, and, although the majority of the Liberal Opposition eventually agreed to support them, there was much shilly-shallying by Liberal lawyers—understandable enough, for there was now much doubt about the legal position, but very trying to the union leaders' patience. In the circumstances, the I.L.P.'s claim for greater labour representation in Parliament won more adherents, and the trade union membership of the L.R.C. increased steadily. 'Attended one or two meetings of the Trade Union Congress . . .', Beatrice Webb recorded in her diary in July 1902.

ominant note of the Congress is a determination to run Labour candidates on a large scale, and faith in the efficacy of this device for gaining all they require. . . . There is . . . less cleavage between trade and trade, or between Old and New Unionists than in any Congress I have before attended. Practically the Congress has been captured (so far as its formal expression of opinion is concerned) by the I.L.P.[5]

Eventually, after a more moderate measure had been rejected in the House of Commons, the Parliamentary Committee of the T.U.C., encouraged and supported by the I.L.P. men, drafted a strong Bill which simply reversed the House of Lords' Taff Vale decision, making union funds immune from civil

[1] S. and B. Webb, *History of Trade Unionism.* (1921), pp. 600–4.
[2] Temperton v. Russell (1893), Trollope v. London Building Trades Federation (1895), Lyons v. Wilkins (1896) and Quinn v. Leatham (1901) extended the range of tortious acts.
[3] E. Halévy, *Imperialism and the Rise of Labour*, p. 246.
[4] *Ibid.* p. 274, and especially the articles in *The Times*, 'The Crisis in British Industry' published between November 1901 and January 1902 and later (in 1904) reprinted as E. A. Pratt, *Trade Unionism and British Industry*.
[5] B. Webb, *Our Partnership*, p. 245.

action, but retaining the advantages of corporate legal entity. It was a bold claim for a specially privileged position for trade unions, of a kind to make a lawyer blench. Some 'Lib-Labs' and a few Socialists hesitated,[1] toying with the idea of less drastic legislation, or even with an acceptance of Taff Vale if it would help forward the cause of compulsory arbitration in trade disputes.

Among those who adopted a compromising attitude were some leading Fabians, in particular the Webbs. In their preface to the second edition of *Industrial Democracy* (1902) they proposed not the direct reversal of the Lords' decision on financial liability, but a clarification of the legal position by a Bill which would define carefully those 'acts committed' and 'the agreements, combinations or conspiracies entered into by or on behalf of an association of employers or a trade union' which should not be actionable.[2] Their attitude did not commend itself to the trade unionists, who at the 1902 Conference of the L.R.C. had already expressed considerable irritation with those who were not firm enough in their response to Taff Vale. When the Balfour government set up a Royal Commission on trade disputes in 1903 and appointed Sidney Webb one of its members, the Trade Union Congress of 1903 would not accept him as a Labour representative; it unanimously condemned 'the Government's insult to Labour in the selection of members of the Royal Commission', and ordered all trade unions to boycott it. One speaker[3] declared that Sidney Webb should not be a member because he had pre-judged the issue. The union leaders made it clear that they would accept no half-measures in handling the Taff Vale case. By the time the report of the Royal Commission was published in January 1906, few Labour men and only a minority of Liberals were prepared to take notice of its majority report (which Sidney Webb had signed) recommending that trade unions should only be liable for actions of their members if these had been expressly authorized by an executive committee.[4] Logically, the Webbs could make out a convincing case that definition would provide a clear and smooth legal alternative. But it was no matter for typical Fabian compromise. The trade union leaders preferred that the law should remain unclear but that their financial position be made unassailable. The I.L.P. leaders understood better than leading Fabians that it was a question of power—and sentiment.

The Fabian Society had little influence upon the Labour Party when it was a matter of defending trade union rights. The trade union leaders were well able to conduct their own defence. When the Society was willing to act as

---

[1] Including the 'Lib-Lab' M.P. Richard Bell and Robert Blatchford. Ben Tillett, at that time an advocate of compulsory arbitration, had expressed an unwise faith in the judges before the final decision of Taff Vale at the 1900 T.U.C.

[2] S. and B. Webb, *Industrial Democracy* (Longmans, London, 1902), pp. XXIV–XXXIV.

[3] J. Wignall of the Dock Workers.

[4] Report of the Royal Commission on Trade Disputes and Trade Combinations.

'clerks to the Labour movement', the trade unions were willing to avail themselves of their services, and some of the Fabian Tracts which were circulated most widely were those which explained the benefits of trade unionism to the public or which explained to trade unionists their rights under social service legislation.[1] But where the Society had an independent policy different from that of the trade union leaders, it was conspicuously unsuccessful; the Society's attitude to compulsory arbitration in trade disputes may be taken as another example.

The Fabian Society, impressed with Australasian experiments, became after the middle 'nineties a chief advocate of the plan of compulsory arbitration. Sidney Webb urged it in his rider to the Majority Report of the Royal Commission on Trade Disputes, and the Fabian Society as a body recommended the principle to the International Socialist Congress of 1903.[2] The Fabians also sought to persuade the I.L.P. to place compulsory arbitration in its programme, but the I.L.P. from the beginning treated their claim, that compulsory arbitration could be an effective substitute for strikes, with great reserve. At its sixth Annual Conference of 1898 the I.L.P. amended a motion deploring strikes to make it emphasize merely the need for 'supplementing trade union methods by political action'. Later Ramsay MacDonald became a strong opponent not only of compulsory arbitration, but also of minimum wage legislation (which of course was the other part of the Fabian demand), and fought the Fabians on these issues inside the I.L.P.[3] Both the I.L.P. and the Labour Party were willing to accept the demand for minimum wage legislation, and to support the establishment of wages boards and arbitration courts to enforce it, but they were quite unwilling to abandon anything of the trade unions' right to strike. Syndicalism and strikes, particular or general, for political objects made little appeal to either the I.L.P. or the Labour Party, but the Fabian Society's view that the strike was an 'obsolete weapon' in the industrial field was equally unacceptable to them. When the Fabian Society's Executive in 1907 sent a letter to the press approving Lloyd George's action in establishing trade boards for the railways after the unsuccessful railway strike of that year, on the ground that compulsory arbitration needed to be enforced by the government despite protests of either workers or employers, the Fabians fell into extremely bad odour with the trade unionists, and the incident aggravated the dispute inside the Fabian Society between the 'Old Gang' and the younger members.[4] Gradually, under pressure of Labour opinion, the Fabians at least abandoned their claim that compulsory arbitration was a substitute for strikes.

[1] See ch. vii, above.
[2] *Fabian News*, November 1902 for proposed resolutions.
[3] See, e.g., debate between MacDonald and S. G. Hobson, 1904 I.L.P. Conference.
[4] *Fabian News*, December 1907.

'NATIONAL MINIMUM STANDARDS OF LIFE'

The phrase, at any rate, was a Fabian one. It had been coined by the Webbs when they sought a descriptive expression to indicate the true end of all forms of government 'interventionism', not only of those measures which the Fabians were advocating, but also of those which had occurred before their time. Even a list of the resolutions of this kind passed by the I.L.P. and Labour Party would be formidable, but a couple of examples may serve to illustrate Fabian influence. Here again, agreement about ends frequently went along with a disagreement about means.

(1) *The eight hours day*

The disputes between the Fabians and the I.L.P. concerning the method of establishing a general eight hours day have already been discussed. The Labour Party at first proceeded cautiously, and concerned itself only with the particular issue of the eight hours day for miners. The divisions amongst the miners' unions which had prevented a united demand for an Eight Hours Bill had disappeared by the early years of the twentieth century. The Northumberland and Durham miners had gradually changed their opinion,[1] and the new Liberal government, faced with the determination of the great miners' unions to press the measure through, yielded with reluctance. The Coal Mines (Eight Hours) Act became law in 1908. Not until 1907, when the campaign for the Miners' Bill was well launched, did the Labour Party begin to advocate legislation for a general eight hours day and forty-eight hours working week. At its 1909 Conference the Labour Party accepted the Fabian method of 'Trade Selection' as the means by which the general Act should be enforced. The explanation of this victory for Fabian ideas was that the Departmental Committee which the Liberal government set up to inquire into the problem before introducing the Miners' Eight Hours Bill, and which the miners had boycotted on the grounds that it was a mere 'delaying tactic', had at least produced some interesting evidence.[2] This practical demonstration of the usefulness of the 'inquiry' method redounded to the credit of the Fabian scheme.

Although the general Eight Hours Bill remained high on the Labour Party's list of parliamentary measures thereafter, the eight hours day had to be won in England by those piecemeal industrial methods which had earlier secured the nine hours day.

(2) *Unemployment and the Poor Law*

The main story of the Fabians' campaign for the reform of the Poor Law has

---

[1] S. and B. Webb, *History of Trade Unionism*, 1920, p. 513 and S. Webb, *Story of the Durham Miners*, 1662-1921, (Fabian Society and Labour Publishing Co., London, 1921).

[2] Edouard Guyot, *La Durée du travail dans les mines de Grande-Bretagne* (Rousseau, Paris, 1908), pp. 58 *et seq.*

been told in an earlier chapter.[1] All that remains to be done here is to indicate the relation between the Society, the I.L.P. and Labour Party. The Minority Report on the Poor Law became the *point d'appui* of the whole campaign for the relief of the unemployed and the 'humanising' of the Poor Law. Yet when the Report was issued, the I.L.P. declared that it was their (the I.L.P.'s) 'old proposals paraphrased, brought up to date as to facts and experience, and issued at the public expense'.[2] This was true in the sense that, by 1909, most of the principles which it embodied were common ground of all Socialist and Labour organizations. Resolutions for the amendment of the Poor Law, for the provision of remunerative government work for the unemployed, and the recognition of the 'Right to Work', had been constantly passed by the I.L.P. and the Labour Party for years. As an abstract principle, or as a principle attached to plans for the organization of co-operative workshops, the cry for the 'Right to Work' had indeed been heard well before the time of the founding of the I.L.P. or the Fabian Society; it goes back at least to the Socialists of the 1830's. It had reappeared in England in the propaganda of the Workingmen's Association in the 'sixties and in that of the S.D.F. and the Fabian Society in the 'eighties. The I.L.P. had taken it up and made it a central issue. In the 'eighties and 'nineties 'Right to Work' demands became associated with proposals for the reform of the Poor Law, and as Fabian, I.L.P. and S.D.F. representatives gained experience on Boards of Guardians, these proposals took on a more detailed character. The Labour Party, when the Balfour government's Unemployed Workmen's Act of 1905 was due to expire in 1908, was persuaded at its 1907 conference to accept a motion moved by the Social Democrat, Harry Quelch, and backed by the I.L.P., that municipalities should provide work for the unemployed. This led to the drafting of the Labour Party's 'Right to Work' Bill of 1907 which provided for the registration of the unemployed, and placed the responsibility for remedial action on the ordinary local authorities, assisted by the national government.

There was, then, considerable agreement about the principles and the general direction of the administrative reform needed, but the detailed investigation and the detailed recommendation of the precise reorganization of government machinery required to give effect to them were the Webbs' triumph, and no one who has read the Report or Beatrice Webb's account of its preparation will doubt the great industry and hard thinking which they put into it. After the Minority Report was issued, it was immediately adopted by the I.L.P. and the Labour Party as the basis of their subsequent campaigns.[3] Only the S.D.F., claiming that the directly-elected Guardians were more

---

[1] See ch. IX above.
[2] I.L.P. Annual Conference Report 1909
[3] *Ibid.* and L.P. Annual Report 1910.

amenable to popular influence, opposed the Minority Report proposals for the reorganization of the Poor Law machinery.[1]

The campaign for the break-up of the Poor Law won back for the Fabians the respect and admiration of Labour men which they had been in danger of forfeiting. But, as we have seen, that campaign ended in defeat, and it was partly the defection of the trade unionists and the Labour Party which brought about that defeat. The Parliamentary Committee of the T.U.C. was double-faced: F. W. Chandler, its representative on the Royal Commission, signed the Minority Report, and D. J. Shackleton, its Chairman, supported the Webbs' campaign, but the Parliamentary Committee as a body was not committed, and it had in fact already let it be known that it was favourably disposed to a contributory national insurance scheme. The I.L.P. men in the House of Commons at first fought the contributory principle, but when it was clear that the Liberal government would not give way, they split. The Fabians in the House of Commons, including Keir Hardie, fought it through to the bitter end, but they were isolated: MacDonald and the majority of the Labour Party believed that no matter of principle was involved and were 'not going to quarrel with the Chancellor of the Exchequer' if 'a small contribution from the workman [was] going to lubricate the matter.'[2]

EXTENSIONS OF DEMOCRACY

(1) Extension of the suffrage

Generally speaking,[3] all the Socialist groups and the Labour Party were agreed that the suffrage should be extended until the objective of 'one person, one vote' was attained. The position, however, became complicated by the claim of the more militant groups seeking the vote for women. Their demand that the vote should immediately be extended to women on the franchise which applied to men cut across the demand for universal suffrage. Even those Socialists and Labour men most favourably disposed to the women's cause had to ask themselves whether the extension of the vote to women on the existing electoral basis would result in enfranchising mainly middle-class women who would cast their vote for Conservative or Liberal candidates. It was this question, rather than a simple issue for and against votes for women, which seriously divided Labour ranks and raised sharp dispute within all Labour and Socialist groups.

The 'Old Gang' of the Fabian Society at first endeavoured to dodge this dangerous issue but they were forced to declare for the immediate extension of the vote to women on the franchise applying to men by the action taken by the

---

[1] *Report of a Debate between Geo. Lansbury and H. Quelch on the Poor Law Minorit Report*, 20 and 21 September 1910 (Twentieth Century Press, London, n.d.).

[2] The remarks are from MacDonald's speech, Hansard, 5th series, vol. xxvii, col. 1447.

[3] i.e. Excluding individual dissentients, some of them very vocal like Belfort Bax.

FABIAN SOCIALISM AND ENGLISH POLITICS, 1884-1918

leading women members of the Society.[1] A similar dispute, with a similar result, took place inside the I.L.P. At the annual conference of the I.L.P. held at Manchester in 1905 a resolution supporting the proposed Women's Enfranchisement Bill was opposed by a number of delegates, mainly on the ground that it would delay universal enfranchisement by satisfying the demands of middle-class women. The women of the I.L.P. replied fiercely to this argument, and eventually a compromise resolution was carried, declaring that universal adult suffrage was the party's goal, but calling for an immediate extension of the vote to women on the same terms as men enjoyed. This resolution became the 'official attitude' of the I.L.P. It was reaffirmed at subsequent conferences, and finally written into the party's Constitution and Rules.[2] Even this did not satisfy the more militant suffragettes, and at the Annual Conference of the I.L.P. at Derby in April 1907 there was a scene when Mrs Pankhurst insisted that woman-suffrage should be given priority over other I.L.P. demands. In practice, this came to mean that Labour M.P.s should vote against all measures of the government (whether the I.L.P. approved of them or not) until woman-suffrage was granted. George Lansbury was the only M.P. who went to the lengths of resigning his seat and recontesting it on the Votes for Women platform. The I.L.P. as a whole repudiated his action:[3] it was willing to agree that its members should vote against any further extension of the suffrage that did not include women, but would not countenance the suffragettes' extremist tactics.

Within the Labour Party the advocates of woman-suffrage had even less success, and the combination of outright opponents with those who feared the enfranchisement only of middle-class women proved the stronger until 1913. By curious chance this gave effect to the policy recommended by a Social Democrat, for Harry Quelch had moved the amendment at the 1905 L.R.C. Congress declaring that no measure would be regarded as satisfactory which did not embody complete adult suffrage for men and women alike. Philip Snowden, speaking unsuccessfully against the amendment, declared that a year before he would have agreed with Quelch that the Women's Enfranchisement Bill would delay universal suffrage, but had since been persuaded that it would not do so. Quelch's amendment, however, was carried by 483 votes to 270, and at subsequent annual conferences of the Labour Party it was always reaffirmed, though sometimes with narrow majorities. In 1913, when the suffragettes' agitation had reached its height after the Speaker of the House of Commons had ruled out of order the Women's Suffrage Amendment (on which a 'free vote' had been promised) to the government Bill extending the male franchise, the Labour Party con-

---

[1] Pease, *op. cit.* p. 177.
[2] Printed in 1908 I.L.P. Annual Conference Report.
[3] I.L.P. Annual Conference Report 1913.

ference modified its attitude to the extent of deploring the Speaker's ruling, and resolving to oppose any extension of the franchise which did not include women. W. S. Sanders spoke strongly, on behalf of the Fabian Society, in favour of this motion.[1]

(2) Ending 'Political monopolies'; payment of M.P.s

At its first annual conference, the L.R.C., on the motion of John Penny, the I.L.P. Secretary, adopted a resolution calling for 'the abolition of all political monopolies' and for the payment of the salaries and election expenses of M.P.s. In such matters, where the I.L.P. and the Fabian Society policies were in agreement, the Fabians were happy enough to see the Labour Party taking its lead from the I.L.P. Here, the cloudy language of the first part of the resolution followed closely the statement of policy adopted at the inaugural conference of the I.L.P. in 1893, which, it has been suggested, was phrased in this way to avoid a definite pronouncement about the monarchy.[2] There was undoubtedly much more need for a cautious approach to this subject in 1901. On the other hand, there was not much question of the Labour Party's attitude to the House of Lords. At the 1908 conference a resolution for the abolition of the House of Lords was carried unanimously, and at the 1911 Conference W. C. Robinson stated in his presidential address: 'Our Party's attitude with regard to the question of the House of Lords is summed up in two words—*total abolition*'.

Payment of M.P.s was, of course, a demand common to all Socialist and Labour organizations, as it was looked upon as a means of gaining increased Labour representation in Parliament and of relieving trade unions of the financial liability of supporting their members who secured election. Not much thought seems to have been given to the danger of elevating M.P.s to the status of self-employed persons, at a time when this class was diminishing in the community, apart perhaps from some attempts to prevent M.P.s from being also members of the party executives.[3] E. R. Pease came forward in opposition to these left-wing moves.[4] The Fabians were always opposed to any hint that M.P.s were 'delegates', and to the removal of the 'best men' from positions of leadership. When payment of M.P.s was eventually achieved in 1911, it was unfortunate for the Labour Party that circumstances suggested that the Liberal government was granting the measure as a consolation for its delay in reversing the Osborne judgment of 1909 which held that the expenditure of funds by trade unions for political purposes was not a legitimate trade union activity.

---

[1] L.P. Annual Conference Report 1913.
[2] See p. 284 above.
[3] L.P. Annual Conference Report 1908; I.L.P. Annual Conference Report 1909.
[4] L.P. Annual Conference Report 1908.

(3) *Proportional representation and the second ballot*

In the early days of the revival of Socialism, the S.D.F. advocated proportional representation, while the Fabian Society recommended the second ballot. Later the Fabians definitely opposed proportional representation. The I.L.P.'s early omnibus resolution, that it supported 'every proposal for extending electoral rights and democratizing the system of government', avoided a pronouncement about either, but in 1908 the I.L.P.'s new Constitution declared in favour of the second ballot.[1] In 1913, however, the I.L.P. altered its opinion and passed a resolution accepting proportional representation and rejecting the second ballot or any system of an alternative vote. This change seems to have been due mainly to the persuasion of Philip Snowden, who had come to the conclusion that proportional representation would increase the Labour Party's representation in the House, while any form of second ballot, alternative vote or preferential system would work in favour of the other parties.[2] When these questions were raised at its 1914 conference the Labour Party refused to follow the I.L.P.'s lead, and rejected both devices. Ramsay MacDonald's influence remained supreme in the Labour Party at the beginning of 1914, though it had declined in the I.L.P., and MacDonald threw his weight against proportional representation as successfully as he had done some years earlier, when Quelch had championed its merits.[3]

EDUCATION, RELIGION, TEMPERANCE

(1) *The Labour Party and education*

At the second annual conference of the L.R.C., held in February 1902, the Fabian policy towards the Education Act suffered a defeat, when a resolution in favour of *ad hoc* School Boards moved by the I.L.P. Secretary, John Penny, was carried by a large majority. The debate, however, revealed an interesting division of opinion amongst the I.L.P. leaders. John Penny and Ramsay MacDonald expressed the opinion of the majority of the I.L.P. when they spoke strongly for the resolution. But J. Parker and Philip Snowden joined with the Fabian speakers, E. R. Pease and S. D. Shallard, in defending the Act.

Thereafter, the Labour Party annual conferences continued to carry resolutions condemning the Education Acts of 1902 and 1903, until the conference of 1906. In 1906, some misgivings were felt in Labour ranks at the Liberal Party's attitude, and the government's amending bill was referred to as 'nothing but a surrender to intolerant Nonconformity',[4] but the principle

---

[1] Constitution and Rules in I.L.P. Annual Conference Report 1908.

[2] I.L.P. Annual Conference Report 1913. See also article in *New Statesman*, 14 April 1917, pp. 30-2 during later discussion.

[3] L.P. Annual Conference Report 1914 and M. Cole (ed.), *Beatrice Webb's Diaries* 1912-24, p. 17. L.P. Annual Conference Report 1911.

[4] I.L.P. Annual Conference Report 1906.

of education 'under full popular control'[1] was still upheld. By the 1908 Labour Party conference, any demand for the restoration of School Boards had disappeared from the list of resolutions, partly no doubt because of the government's defeat on the Education issue, and partly because the Labour Party was beginning to turn its attention to other questions. But in 1909 and 1910, the problem was raised in a new form with a resolution that education be 'secular'. In 1909 this resolution was opposed vigorously by Bernard Shaw, on behalf of the Fabian Society, and also by the Roman Catholic Labour leaders, Sexton and O'Grady. But it was carried, at both the 1909 and 1910 conferences. After that time, however, it did not reappear.

In the main the education policy of the Labour Party was formulated for it by the I.L.P., and particularly by Margaret MacMillan.[2] Its policy did not differ greatly from Fabian policy, except perhaps in paying chief attention to primary education, and not enough attention, in the opinion of some Fabians, to education at the secondary and tertiary level. But such measures as free meals for schoolchildren, free education up to sixteen years, scholarships and bursaries for secondary, technical, and university education, adequate Training College facilities for teachers, school clinics, etc., were fairly 'common ground' of Socialist opinion.

So far as Parliamentary action was concerned, the Labour Party devoted itself chiefly to pressing for the provision by the State of free meals for school-children. An Act was passed in 1906, but its provisions were not made compulsory and a halfpenny rate limit was imposed. Thereafter the Labour Party tried to secure an amending Bill to permit school meals in holidays, to remove the halfpenny limit, and to make the Bill compulsory for local authorities. The two first objectives were finally achieved in 1916, but the compulsive clause was deleted before the Labour Party's Bill passed into law.

(2) *Religion and the family*

Both the I.L.P. and the Labour Party, under the influence of Ramsay MacDonald, made pronouncements very similar to the Fabian Society's earlier one, about religion and the family, stating that they had no collective views on theological beliefs, and that they did not in the least desire the break-up of the home.[3] These statements were made necessary by anti-socialist attacks, but were also designed to dissociate the I.L.P. and Labour Party from the outspoken materialism of some of the S.D.F. leaders, and the atheism of Blatchford. Needless to say, these pronouncements did not prevent the I.L.P. and Labour Party from adopting resolutions for the provision by the State of kindergartens and nurseries, and of meals for schoolchildren, which some Conservatives interpreted as 'attacks on the family' and some

[1] L.P. Annual Conference Report 1906.
[2] See L.P. Annual Conference Reports 1906, 1907, and 1909.
[3] See I.L.P. and L.P. Annual Conference Reports 1908.

Marxists regarded as a 'transformation of the family'; nor did they prevent the I.L.P. and Labour Party from showing, in various ways when politics touched on religious matters, a Nonconformist collective bias, or at least the bias of those who had recently departed from the Nonconformist faith on friendly terms.

(3) *The liquor traffic*

The control of the liquor traffic was a problem that the English Socialists were bound to encounter at some time, as Liberal Puritanism constantly occupied itself with it. In the early days, perhaps the Socialists' chief concern with it was to combat the extremely optimistic type of Liberal creed which claimed that 'everyone would be well off but for the drink'. The proposal for municipal control of the drink traffic seems to have been first put forward as part of the programme of one of the Socialist groups by the I.L.P. in its programme of 1895.[1] The Fabians devoted their attention to the problem a couple of years later, at the time when the Royal Commission of Liquor Laws was conducting its investigations.[2] E. R. Pease was chiefly responsible for leading the Fabian Society to take an interest in it, and he drafted their two pamphlets on the subject: *Liquor Licensing at Home and Abroad*, a factual statement, and *Municipal Drink Traffic*,[3] which gave the details of a scheme for municipal control. The second pamphlet expressed the Society's collective views, for it was discussed and modified at members' meetings before it was published.

The idea of 'municipalizing' the drink traffic met with warm approval in the Labour movement, and a resolution (moved not by the Fabian Society but by the Darwen Trades Council) adopting this policy was carried at the 1905 L.R.C. conference. To this was added a resolution for 'local veto' at the 1906 conference. Nothing came of it: the Party's attempts in 1908 to move amendments to the Liberal government's Licensing Bill were prevented by the use of the guillotine.[4]

INTERNATIONAL QUESTIONS

(1) *International relations: Imperialism: and war*

In these questions the Labour Party was constantly torn between the pressure from the I.L.P. to declare itself against war and Imperialism in the interests

[1] The pamphlet of Dr A. T. Gordon Beveridge, *Municipalization of the Drink Traffic* was widely advertised in the *Workman's Times* in 1893. This is one of the cases which shows that the adage 'the Fabians thought out the policies, the I.L.P. selected from them what was most likely to have a popular appeal, and the Trade Unions accepted, with more or less hesitation and watering-down, what the I.L.P. gave them, and paid the bill', needs modification. Often the I.L.P. originated proposals, though the Fabians usually worked them out in detail.

[2] The Fabian Society forwarded its opinions to the Commission. F.S. Annual Report 1897.

[3] Tracts 85 and 86.

[4] L.P. Annual Conference Report 1909.

of the unity of the working-classes throughout the world, and the tendency of the trade unions to 'mind their own business'. This was amply demonstrated at the first and second conferences of the L.R.C. At the first Annual Conference of 1901, Joseph Burgess of the I.L.P. secured the passing of anti-Imperialist and anti-war resolutions. The delegates felt strongly about these things at the time of the Boer War. But at the following Conference in 1902, when Keir Hardie attempted to interest the delegates in happenings in Spain, his motion was ruled out of order, and the strong desire of the conference to confine itself to domestic issues was made clear.

The Fabian Society, though it favoured this second attitude, did not play any part in persuading the Labour Party against the I.L.P.'s resolutions. All that can be said is that Fabian policy was based on a sound diagnosis of the patriotic and insular character of the trade unionists, which put, so to speak, the onus of proving their case on to the I.L.P. men.

Resolutions of an anti-militarist, anti-war nature became a constant feature of annual I.L.P. conferences, and the I.L.P. took pride in the fact that it had 'made itself the spokesman of oppressed people throughout the world',[1] but similar resolutions were only partially successful with the Labour Party. After 1901, no other definitely anti-Imperialist resolutions were passed at Labour Party conferences before the First World War, and only an occasional resolution which dealt with the internal affairs of another nation.[2] On the other hand, general resolutions against militarism, conscription and war were frequently passed by the Labour Party, usually as a result of resolutions submitted by the I.L.P. or its members. What was always missing from these resolutions was the sanction that the Labour Party intended to employ if its resolution should not be heeded. What was to be done in the event of a war breaking out? The proposal for a strike against war, which was approved by the I.L.P., was deleted by the Labour Party Special Conference from a resolution which Keir Hardie submitted to it in 1911.[3] Resolutions moved by I.L.P. members at the Labour Party to 'give consideration to' the proposal for a strike against war were carried, but nothing was done about them.

Other resolutions dealing with international affairs, of a more specific kind, were also passed by the Labour Party. Haldane's proposal for a 'citizen-army' (which was supported by many Fabians) was utterly rejected by the Labour Party, as well as by the I.L.P., Keir Hardie observing that a 'citizen-army' was impossible with a capitalist government.[4] Blatchford was attacked by

---

[1] I.L.P. Annual Conference Report 1912.
[2] A list can briefly be given: (a) Approval of Russian Revolution of 1905; (b) support of German miners' strike 1905; (c) protest at arrest of Socialists in Duma 1911; (d) protest at execution of Japanese Socialists 1911; (e) protest at suppression of T.U.'s in South Africa 1914.
[3] Appendix to L.P. Annual Conference Report 1911.
[4] L.P. Annual Conference Report 1909.

Labour Party members for his attitude towards Germany.[1] Sir Edward Grey's 'anti-German foreign policy' was deprecated.[2] Resolutions against 'secret diplomacy' and for 'democratizing' foreign policy were carried.[3] Anti-conscription resolutions appealed equally to Liberal-Labour men, and to that anti-State feeling always present in the I.L.P., which the Fabians often derided. Indeed, the strength of the anti-conscription sentiment amongst the Labour Party was very strong, and continued even into wartime. Even after the Labour Party had carried its resolution at its 1916 conference, pledging full assistance to the government in its prosecution of the war, it was only reluctantly brought to accept each new compulsion that was found necessary. Protesting at each step, however, it acquiesced.

During the First World War, the Labour leaders were to find the Fabians helpful in directing their activities into useful channels on the War Emergency Workers' National Committee, and similar bodies. If, before war broke out, it appeared that the I.L.P. attitude to international affairs coloured many of the resolutions of the Labour Party, nevertheless, in the crisis of the war itself, the majority of the Labour Party adopted an attitude similar to that taken up by the majority of the Fabians.

(2) *Free Trade*

The Labour leaders, both those of the I.L.P. and those of the Labour Party, remained firmly attached to the doctrines of Free Trade, even though they usually added that Free Trade in itself was not enough, and needed to be supplemented, not by the 'Protection of Mr Chamberlain', but by the 'Protection of Labour'—factory acts, eight hours legislation, etc.[4] While the Fabians were divided amongst themselves on the merits of Free Trade, the basic faith of the Labour leaders was unshaken in the policy which was supposed to have been the foundation of England's prosperity since the middle of the nineteenth century and to have meant cheap food for the masses.

Resolutions were moved by Philip Snowden and carried at the 1904 conferences of the I.L.P. and L.R.C., which supported Free Trade against 'Tariff Reform' but maintained at the same time that Free Trade by itself was no solution to the community's problems. There were only two dissentient votes at the I.L.P. conference, and at the L.R.C. conference amendments calling for Empire preferential tariffs and for a full inquiry into the Tariff system were decisively rejected. The L.R.C. followed up this resolution at its next conference by declaring Free Trade organizations 'neutral platforms', not debarred to Labour speakers when these organizations did not actually

[1] L.P. Annual Conference Report 1910.
[2] L.P. Annual Conference Report 1912.
[3] L.P. Annual Conference Report 1914.
[4] J. R. MacDonald, *The Zollverein and British Industry*, 1903, p. 164.

support Liberals against L.R.C. candidates. The I.L.P., more rigid in its 'independence', however, declined to allow its members to 'truckle to the Liberals' by lecturing under the auspices of the Free Trade League, although Snowden, Hardie, Russell Smart and others would willingly have permitted it.[1] A later attempt to get the Labour Party to 'refer back' its endorsement of Free Trade platforms as neutral, failed.[2]

SUMMING UP OF FABIAN INFLUENCE

It is often said that Labour Party policy before the First World War derived from Fabian sources. One may suspect that those who make this claim have no more evidence than the fact that the Labour Party's policy was *in general* cautious, non-revolutionary, constitutional and collectivist, and was therefore *in general* similar to that policy which the Fabian Society had recommended many years before the Labour Party came into existence. A great deal more evidence than this is required to prove that the Labour Party policy was 'influenced' by the Fabians, and even more is needed to show that it 'derived from Fabian sources'. For the very nature of the Labour Party—determined to so large an extent by the Liberal trade union leaders within it—ruled out the possibility that any kind of revolutionary creed would be accepted by it: the S.D.F. could only have remained in the Labour Party on the basis of accepting the dominance of extremely moderate policies: the choice of general policy was limited to Liberal-Radicalism or a form of Radicalized Socialism.

The claim on behalf of the Fabians could again be pressed on the ground that they first formulated a theory of Radicalized Socialism, and inasmuch as the Labour Party did come to accept this policy, it was indirectly influenced by the Fabians. This claim is by no means without foundation. The most considerable Socialist influence upon the Labour Party came from I.L.P. sources, and, as we have demonstrated elsewhere, Fabian influence upon the I.L.P. had been by no means small. Nevertheless, it is also true that the I.L.P. was no mere channel for Fabian ideas, but an independent organization, with a different 'tone' and in certain respects differing policies. A number of issues were certainly 'common ground' between the I.L.P. and the Fabian Society; there was much agreement between them on general ends and methods, but as their Socialist opponents on these general issues were only occasionally more than a negligible force, differences in detail of policy bulked more largely than this agreement.

Descending to details, and recognizing that the Labour Party was nearly always brought to accept 'common ground' measures through the immediate influence not of the Fabians but of the I.L.P. men, it appears that the Fabian Society can be regarded unequivocally as originators of Labour Party policy

---

[1] I.L.P. Annual Conference Report 1905.
[2] L.P. Annual Conference Report 1909.

only in two matters, namely, in the establishment of the Labour Members' Maintenance Fund and in the method of implementing the general eight hours day. In these things the Fabians were pioneers. Closely allied with these were the proposals for the reorganization of the Poor Law and the demand for a State Medical Service. There may be some debate whether these proposals actually originated with the Fabians, but they were early in the field and their researches were of such a character that they resulted in an important new complexion being given to these demands.

In a second order of influence could be placed those measures, such as the demand for the municipalization of the drink traffic or the drafting of the Nationalization of Mines and Minerals Bill, where it cannot be said that the proposal originated with the Fabians, but where it was elaborated by them, either by a detailed investigation of the facts, or by the drawing-up of draft legislation. This was distinctively Fabian work, and its importance, after the Labour Party entered Parliament in strength, has been stressed by Philip Snowden: 'The character of Labour propaganda had been changed by the advent of the Labour members to the House of Commons. It had now become wholly political, dealing with current questions. The old Socialist propaganda had been abandoned, and with its disappearance a good deal of the idealism had been lost . . .'[1] After 1906, the typical Fabian approach to Socialism became more useful than the typical approach of the I.L.P.

Finally, in a third order of influence must be placed the outcome of the Labour Party's attitude to international questions, where, without any important direct intervention by the Fabians, but out of the conflict of 'Lib-Lab' and I.L.P. influences, emerged a policy similar to that adopted by the majority of the Fabians. Though the Fabians cannot be said to have brought about this result, it was to be responsible for increasing their later influence.

THE GROWTH OF FABIAN INFLUENCE

From the first the I.L.P. men recognized the need to proceed with caution in their policy of bringing the Labour Party to a full Socialist position. But the progress toward this objective proved exceedingly slow. The accession of the Miners' Federation at the end of 1908 made the composition of the Labour Party more Liberal than before. 'I well remember', wrote Bernard Shaw, recollecting those years, 'Edward Pease, our secretary, telling me triumphantly that we had roped in the Miners' Federation and that the money difficulty no longer existed. But I shook my head and said: "What then becomes of Socialism?" For I knew that the miners' leaders were not socialists. They were all for seats in Parliament and State regulation of employers (not of the Trade Unions) by means of factory legislation: but they were out to exploit

[1] Snowden, *Autobiography*, vol. I, p. 151.

Capitalism, not to abolish it'.[1] This delay in the progress to Socialism, coming as it did at a time of increasing labour unrest in the pre-war years, made it difficult for the Labour-I.L.P. parliamentary leaders to keep the I.L.P. and Labour Party in harness together. Despite the prestige of these leaders, the I.L.P. was manifestly tending to run ahead of the Labour Party before the outbreak of war, on various issues—on the women's franchise issue, on the reform of Parliament issue, and on the general question of Liberal-Labour relations.[2]

The different attitude adopted by the I.L.P. and the Labour Party on the outbreak of war increased this division between them. The estrangement must not be exaggerated—the I.L.P. did not cease to be a constituent member of the Labour Party during the war—but neither must it be under-estimated. Though the leaders of both parties may have managed to work together on matters that were not immediately concerned with the actual fighting, nevertheless the fact that the I.L.P. had declared against the war meant that it more definitely than ever before ranged itself amongst the ultra-radical elements of English politics. After the split in the British Socialist Party (*ci-devant* S.D.F.) on the war issue, the I.L.P. had only the most extreme Marxists to the left of it. After the war, the I.L.P. was to preserve its pacifist and extreme-radical character.

The decision of Arthur Henderson to reorganize the Labour Party and give it a new constitution at the end of the war was to some extent motivated by the Labour Party leaders' disapproval of the I.L.P. during the war years. It was announced, as one of the reasons for opening the Labour Party organization to individual members, that the party's prestige with the general public had been increased by its 'genuine working-class diplomacy' during the war: the statement was intended as a reflection upon the I.L.P., and treated as such by it.[3] Furthermore, during the war the Labour Party, although it did not expel the I.L.P. from its ranks, amended its constitution, changing the method of the election of its executive in a way that was aimed at reducing its influence.[4] Whereas previously it had had a federal executive, the election was thereafter to be by ballot at the annual conference, with no organization nominating more than one candidate unless its membership exceeded 500,000. The attempts of the I.L.P. in 1918 to get the Labour Party to revert to the system of federal representation in its new Constitution failed.[5]

---

[1] *Fabian Quarterly*, April 1944, p. 2.
[2] From 1908 there was continual rank-and-file agitation within the I.L.P. In 1911 this culminated in a secession of left-wing (particularly *Clarion*) elements, which joined with the S.D.P. to form the British Socialist Party. This split, however, did not allay the dissatisfaction in I.L.P. ranks.
[3] I.L.P. Annual Conference Report 1918.
[4] L.P. Annual Conference Report 1917.
[5] I.L.P. Annual Conference Report 1918.

This was, however, only one of the motives which inspired the new Labour Party Constitution, and withal, not the major one. Henderson was mainly concerned to reorganize the party so as to attract those persons (and especially the newly enfranchised women) who in the later years of the war were dissatisfied with the older parties, but who were unable to attach themselves to a Trade Union or a Socialist organization. In order not to alienate completely the I.L.P., Henderson cleverly presented the new Constitution of the Labour Party as a radical and bold move, which, up to a point, it was. Advised by Sidney Webb, who had become his closest associate, Henderson was prepared to placate the critics of the Left with socialist policies and the trade unionist critics of the Right with an increased voice in party organization for trade unions. The I.L.P., with some misgivings, therefore supported the reorganization.[1] At the time, the I.L.P. recognized the possible effect of the competition of the new Labour Party's branches on its own branches, but consoled itself with the hope that the Labour Party branches would appeal to a different group of persons, even that the new Labour Party branches might 'stimulate rather than injure the local branches of the I.L.P.', and that the I.L.P. would continue to have a special propaganda role to play.[2] Although this view appeared justified during the resurgence of the I.L.P. in the 1920's, the new constitution did emerge in a period of relative decline of I.L.P. influence, and in the long run it made possible that separation in the 1930's which was to prove fatal to the I.L.P.

At the time when the influence of the I.L.P. on the Labour Party had declined in the war and post-war years, that of the Fabians was increasing. Those Fabians who supported the war drew closer to the wartime leaders of the Labour Party. In 1915 Sidney Webb became the Fabian representative on the Labour Party Executive, and became a close associate and friend of Arthur Henderson, who had replaced Ramsay MacDonald as Labour Party Chairman. Henderson, who had previously been a Liberal, had joined the Fabian Society in 1912.[3] But it was really during the war years that Webb became Henderson's expert adviser.

The Report of the 1918 Labour Party Conference at Nottingham reveals the growth of Fabian influence. The reorganization of the Labour Party envisaged in the new Constitution meant an increase in clerical and research work and the Fabian Society and the Fabian Society's offspring, the Labour Research Department, were specially drawn upon to undertake it. Special Research Committees were established on Labour problems in the post-war

---

[1] Opinion inside the I.L.P. was pretty thoroughly divided about it. *Ibid.*

[2] *Ibid.*

[3] After he was elected Secretary to the Labour Party, in order to avoid an anomaly which arose out of the International Socialist Bureau's decision that the Secretary of the Labour Party should be an ex-officio British Secretary to the International (L.P. Annual Conference Report 1912).

period, and Fabians were put in charge of them. The Fabians were thanked for the work they had already performed in working out new lines of legislation, and for their assistance with publications such as the Labour Year Book. Finally, the new Party Constitution itself, and the report *Labour and the New Social Order* that went with it, were both drafted by a committee of which Sidney Webb was the leading member. That is to say, they were drafted by Webb himself.

THE NEW LABOUR PARTY CONSTITUTION

The new Labour Party constitution and its accompanying manifesto *Labour and the New Social Order* must be considered amongst Sidney Webb's most skilful pieces of 'permeation'. The bricks of earlier Labour Party resolutions are cleverly put together with a little mortar of Fabian doctrine to produce a recognizably Fabian edifice.

The distinctive new achievement was the writing of Socialism into the party's Constitution. Though the Labour Party had been growing steadily more Socialist in the war years and the years immediately before the war, the final step had hitherto been resisted. No longer was the Labour Party to be an alliance between Socialists and Liberal trade unionists on an 'independent' platform. The Labour Party in 1918 became itself a Socialist Party. It was of course explained carefully in *Labour and the New Social Order* that this Socialism would be of a very moderate, constitutional, evolutionary kind. This was assured by the reorganization of the party on a local basis, diminishing the influence not only of the I.L.P. but also of the Trades Councils (Trades Councils were to be affiliated only when there was no local Labour Party; where there was one, the Trades Councils were to be affiliated to the local Branch, not to the party headquarters). In the circumstances Webb felt there was no harm in reversing an earlier Fabian dictum to point out to potential recruits from the Liberals that warmth as well as light was needed to build up a new civilization, in place of capitalism, which was at the point of collapse.

The 'four pillars' of the new Socialist civilization which the Labour Party would endeavour to build up were said to be The Universal Enforcement of the National Minimum; The Democratic Control of Industry; The Revolution in National Finance; and The Surplus Wealth for the Common Good. With a little difficulty, all the resolutions of past Labour Party conferences were grouped under these headings, together with an occasional additional demand which had no such endorsement. Thus, under the first heading, in addition to the old demands for minimum wages etc., the principle of equal pay for men and women for equal work was slipped in quietly. A plan was outlined also for the organization of demobilization in such a way as to provide full employment, through the maintenance of wartime controls.

'The Democratic Control of Industry' did not imply, as the words might suggest, any concession to Syndicalists or Guild Socialists. It meant, as it had always meant for the majority of the Fabians, the control of industry by a democratic State. 'Democracy in Industry' meant 'the progressive elimination of the private capitalists' control of industry', and apart from that, simply the adoption of 'those systems and methods of administration and control that may be found, in practice, best to promote, not profiteering, but the public interest'. 'Immediate nationalization' was recommended for transport and mines, as the Labour Party had formerly demanded, but to them were added electricity and life insurance, whose ripeness for nationalization had only recently been investigated by the Fabians. A programme of 'municipal socialism' on Fabian lines was now set out as the basis of the Labour Party's local work, together with a rural programme, which, starting out from a resumption of control of the land by the State, envisaged a variety of forms of tenure—national farms, municipal farms, co-operative farms, and small holdings let out by the municipality.

These demands for increased State ownership went hand in hand with demands for extension of political democracy. The Representation of the People Act was not considered sufficient, and complete adult suffrage was called for. The 'maintenance of the Empire on the basis of Home Rule all round' was declared to be the Labour Party's principle, and Webb seized the opportunity to insert in the Report the scheme which had appeared in *Fabianism and the Empire* eighteen years before: Home Rule for Ireland, legislative assemblies for Scotland and Wales, and an Imperial Parliament. In the international sphere, the League of Nations and the International Court were acclaimed.

The 'Revolution in National Finance' and 'The Surplus Wealth for the Common Good' sections likewise embodied old Labour Party demands, and new ones that the Fabian Society had recently put forward. In addition to the repudiation of protective tariffs, and the call for the removal of indirect taxes, except those on luxuries, and for the increase of death duties and supertax, the new proposals were for assessment of taxation in terms of family incomes and for a capital levy to pay off the war debt.

Labour and the New Social Order ended with a typically Fabian statement that the Labour Party would lay great emphasis on the findings of political and social science, and would encourage this science in every way.

With the publication of these two documents—the 1918 Constitution and the Report—the link was made between the Fabian Society and the Labour Party, which has remained ever since, so far as the Society as a whole is concerned, despite the tendency in the inter-war years of some individual Fabians (including the founders of the doctrine) to move further to the left. The Labour Party, founded rather by the I.L.P. than the Fabians, had come by 1918 more under Fabian than I.L.P. influence. At the price of increased trade union control over the party organization, the Labour Party had accepted Fabianism as its doctrinal basis; while on their side, the Fabians at last accepted the Labour Party as the appointed instrument for bringing about Socialism in Britain.

CHAPTER XII

GENERAL CONCLUSIONS

'I can swim too', said Roo proudly.

'Not round and round', said Eeeyore. 'It's much more difficult . . . if, when in, I decide to practice a slight circular movement from right to left—or perhaps I should say', he added, as he got into another eddy, 'from left to right, just as it happens to occur to me. . . .'[1]

Sidney Webb saw History as a great river moving slowly and inevitably towards Socialism, with the Fabians floating approvingly with the current, pointing out its direction and helping to remove obstacles to its flow. As a picture of Fabian influence it was sounder than those sometimes presented by other Fabians. Bernard Shaw in his more extravagant moments would give an impression of the Society, or more particularly of Sidney Webb, as the real manipulator of the thinking of the Labour movement, or of the Liberal government, or of the Progressive Party on the London County Council. H. G. Wells, on the other hand, in a bitter and critical mood, spoke of the Fabians as self-deceivers who claimed an influence they did not have.

Measure with your eye this little meeting, this little hall [he said], look at that little stall of not very powerful Tracts: think of the scattered members, one here, one there . . . then go out into the Strand. Note the size of the buildings and the business places, note the glare of the advertisements, note the abundance of traffic and the multitude of people. . . . That is the world whose very foundations you are attempting to change. How does this little dribble of activities look then?[2]

The river of Opinion has indeed flowed in the direction the Fabians approved, but so far in the Western world not to Socialism. It remains to be seen whether the river will run on, or whether it has emptied itself into the lake of the Keynesian Welfare State. How far the Fabians were responsible for that movement is a question which, to be answered in its full complexity, requires techniques more subtle and highly developed than history can at present deploy; but certain points have been established.

Fabian doctrine did not reach the highest level of theoretical originality: it was not the kind of doctrine which, for better or worse, introduced a new departure in social thinking, as, for example, did the doctrines of Ricardo, of Marx, or of Keynes. Fabianism was eclectic and critical rather than a new synthesis; and while this is not necessarily a reflection either on its soundness or its usefulness, it does mean that the Fabians were deficient in one kind of influence. Their ideas did not form a landmark in economics, politics or

[1] A. A. Milne, *The House at Pooh Corner* (Methuen, London, 1955), p. 97.
[2] Quoted Pease, *op. cit.* p. 165.

philosophy. The Society as a whole, in its concentration on practical detailed reforms, virtually cut itself off from the higher ranges of theoretical speculation; and individual Fabians, despite great achievements, did not succeed in storming these heights. The Webbs did not 'rewrite economics', though their *Industrial Democracy* remains a worthy monument to their attempt, and though their researches into the problems of unemployment did lay, perhaps, some of the foundations of later Keynesian theory. In politics, the Fabians were content to work out to the full the implications of Victorian Liberal Radicalism, and to analyse and describe the workings of political institutions. Graham Wallas's *Human Nature in Politics* was a brilliant introduction to a new approach, but he had parted company with the Fabians before it appeared in 1908, and he failed in his later works to create the great theory of political psychology to which this book had pointed the way. In philosophy, the Fabians had little of importance to contribute. Bernard Shaw, it is true, flashed like a comet through this as well as all the other fields, but his bright contributions were those of an artist and not of a systematiser or analyst. It is in the realm of historiography and the descriptive analysis of political institutions that we discover the true greatness of the leading Fabians; in the works of the Webbs, of Graham Wallas, R. H. Tawney, R. C. K. Ensor, and G. D. H. Cole is to be found some of the finest history written since 1890, while such Fabians as Cole, Laski, W. A. Robson, and H. Finer have written a number of the standard books of political science. So far as works of history and political science have an influence amongst thoughtful persons, we may affirm in general that Fabian influence was considerable; but it is not possible to give any accurate measure of it.

Likewise in the realm of art, where the Fabians were exceedingly fortunate to have counted in their ranks the greatest playwright and (for a while) one of the most prolific and popular novelists of the time, the historian can do little more than record the opinion that Bernard Shaw and H. G. Wells by their lively assaults on bourgeois values taught many to think critically about society, even if, as G. K. Chesterton complained, the Philistines defended themselves against the 'laborious lucidity' of their attacks by an impregnable obtuseness, or by refusing to take them seriously.[1]

The eclectic nature of Fabian doctrine makes its influence the harder to assess, for there is a danger of attributing to Fabian influence effects which are due to other and more general causes. The principal general achievement claimed on behalf of the Fabians by the secretary of the Society, E. R. Pease, in his *History* was that they were able to 'break the spell of Marxism in England'.[2] The claim is extravagant, for Marxism had cast no spell over

[1] G. K. Chesterton, *George Bernard Shaw* (John Lane the Bodley Head, London, 1910), pp. 91–2.
[2] Pease, *op. cit.* p. 236.

England. So long as Socialists clung to a rigid Marxist dogma they were doomed to remain a tiny and insignificant sect in a country which was still, in the later nineteenth century, the most prosperous country in the world, and which had made half a century of progress since the turbulence of the change to an industrial society. By the time the Fabians appeared English capitalism could afford the luxury of a conscience; and the relatively larger size of the cake to be shared between worker and capitalist, as well as the advent of democracy, made necessary a modification of rigid Marxist formulas. A more accurate claim on behalf of the Fabians would be that the Fabians were the first group in the field with a Socialism suitable for a nation so prosperous, so constitutional and so respectful of suave and confident authority as England. Only a 'Fabian' type of Socialism could have won the allegiance of English trade unionists; that such a Socialism would have made its appearance, even if the Fabians had not supplied it, seems likely; that the Fabians accomplished the theoretical task well seems established by their effective predominance in the field.

England would have been constitutional anyway; the Fabians supplied a doctrine which could enable a churchwarden, or an English trade unionist, to call himself a Socialist. But his conversion, presumably, made a difference to his fundamental assumptions about society and to his ultimate social objectives, for Fabian doctrine, if not original at the highest level, did involve a serious challenge to old-established social opinions. It involved the abandonment of the ideal of a mainly *laissez faire* society and the acceptance of its opposite, the ideal of a society consciously organized; it involved the rejection of the rights of the *rentier*, and the acceptance of a greater degree of economic equality; it demanded drastic State action to eliminate poverty. These were, of course, beliefs characteristic of Socialism in general, rather than of Fabianism in particular; but Fabianism permitted Englishmen to swallow these pills without too much shock to their constitution.

It is tempting for those who discover a fascination in political doctrine to believe that history is made by the filtering down of the thoughts of political philosophers to the realm of popular beliefs:

We are the music makers, and we are the dreamers of dreams,
Wandering by lone sea-breakers, and sitting by desolate streams,
World losers and world forsakers, on whom the pale moon gleams:
Yet we are the movers and shakers of the world forever, it seems.

'It seems' weakens the claim. The obsessive and multiplex systems of theorists appear very remote from the haphazard and chaotic beliefs of ordinary citizens. The relationship between the theorist and the historical process nearly always turns out on examination to be more complicated than it seemed at first sight. Yet there is something in the claim. Systems of theorists may not be the motive force of historical development; but neither are they mere strange epiphenomena of the historical process. A political doctrine, well formulated or well expressed, has an enduring quality and an authority not enjoyed by the great bulk of political writings and speeches. Just as past civilizations tend to be remembered by works of literature and art produced by men least typical of the ordinary citizen, so the political thinking of an earlier time is often incapsulated and conveyed to a later generation in the systems of theorists. In its time I.L.P. propaganda was certainly more widely read (and in that sense more influential) than the writings of the Fabians.[1] But I.L.P. propaganda, faded as an old photograph, remains of interest to few save historians; whereas the chief works (at least) of the Fabians have withstood pretty successfully the corrosion of time. And theirs has not been merely a posthumous authority: I.L.P. men, whenever they were pressed in argument, were always likely to appeal to the more substantial writings of the Fabian theorists.

As a group, however, the Fabian Society claimed to set more store by its immediate and down-to-earth policies. In this, more measurable, field of practical politics the Fabian record is a chequered one. It is at least as much a record of errors and self deception as of success. The Fabian Society was primarily a London group, often divided within itself on major issues, and its leaders tended too readily to generalize at the level of national politics the politics suitable to the metropolis. Its success in London politics, though real, was not entirely due to its influence, for much of its programme would in any case have been carried through by the Liberal-Progressives as London made up its leeway in municipal reform. In national politics the Fabians were deceived in their hopes of permeating the Liberals, and it seems certain that the Independent Labour Party and the Labour Party would have come into existence without their assistance, which was for the most part equivocal and not very helpful. No major political development can be attributed with certainty to Fabian influence; but few similar groups, so small and so much outside the established centres of power, can have exercised as great and as varied an influence in minor but important ways. Perhaps, after all, this is not surprising, when the Fabians numbered in their ranks some of the wisest, most learned and wittiest men and women of their age.

[1] And, as we have seen, it was not invariably the case that the I.L.P. got its ideas from the Fabians.

BIBLIOGRAPHY

DOCUMENTARY MATERIAL

Parliamentary Debates; Minutes of the Fabian Society, The London County Council and the Labour Representation Committee and Labour Party; Annual Reports of the Fabian Society, London Reform Union, Technical Education Board, the National Liberal Federation, London Liberal and Radical Union, the Trades Union Congress, the Independent Labour Party, the Labour Representation Committee and the Labour Party. Newspapers and journals referred to include *The Times, Justice, The Practical Socialist, Today, Our Corner, Fabian News, Workman's Times, Handbook of the Eighty Club, Star, Radical, Speaker, Labour Leader, Clarion, I.L.P. News, Fortnightly Review, Review of Reviews, Saturday Review, Contemporary Review, The Crusade, The New Statesman, Fabian Quarterly, Fabian Journal.*

In addition, I was indebted to members of the Fabian Society for personal reminiscences and for permission to inspect some unpublished material during my stay in England between 1946 and 1948. In revising my thesis for publication I have taken account of works published since 1949 (and I have been agreeably surprised to find that they have not substantially changed the general conclusions I had arrived at), but unfortunately I have not been able to return to England to consult the rich collections of private papers which have become available in the last ten years. I console myself with the thought that probably no general survey of the field could use all the evidence available today, yet some general picture seems necessary, if only to stimulate the research which may alter and enrich its conclusions.

LIST OF FABIAN SOCIETY TRACTS PUBLISHED TO 1920

This list of Tracts follows the list given by Pease in Appendix IV of his *History*, with one amendment. It is not a complete list of Fabian publications, but only of the numbered Tracts and leaflets. In a few cases leaflets were issued which were not part of the numbered series (the leaflets on the Insurance Acts, for instance): where these unnumbered leaflets have been referred to in footnotes to this work their title has been given in full. In the following list, if the author's name is given in brackets, the Tract was adopted and (usually) revised by the Society and it was issued without the author's name. An asterisk indicates that the Tract was written, or originally drafted, by a person who was not a member of the Society.

1884   1. *Why are the Many Poor?* (W. L. Phillips.)
          2. *A Manifesto.* (G. Bernard Shaw.)
1885   3. *To Provident Landlords and Capitalists: a Suggestion and a Warning.* (G. Bernard Shaw.)
1886   4. *What Socialism Is.* Mrs C. M. Wilson and others.
1887   5. *Facts for Socialists.* (Sidney Webb.)
          6. *The True Radical Programme.* Fabian Parliamentary League. (G. Bernard Shaw.)
1888   7. *Capital and Land.* (Sydney Olivier.)
1889   8. *Facts for Londoners.* (Sidney Webb.)
          9. *An Eight Hours Bill.* (Sidney Webb.)
       10. *Figures for Londoners.* (Sidney Webb.)

1890   11. *The Workers' Political Programme.* (Sidney Webb.)
       12. *Practical Land Nationalization.* (Sidney Webb.)
       13. *What Socialism Is.* (Bernard Shaw.)
       14. *The New Reform Bill.* (J. F. Oakeshott and others.)
       15. *English Progress towards Social Democracy.* Sidney Webb.
       16. *A Plea for an Eight Hours Bill.* (Sidney Webb.)
       17. *Reform of the Poor Law.* Sidney Webb.
       18. *Facts for Bristol.* (Hartmann W. Just.)
       19. *What the Farm Labourer Wants.* (Sidney Webb.)
       20. *Questions for Poor Law Guardians.* (S. W. Group.)
       21. *Questions for London Vestrymen.* (J. C. Foulger.)
       22. *The Truth about Leasehold Enfranchisement.* (Sidney Webb.)
1891   23. *The Case for an Eight Hours Bill.* (Sidney Webb.)
       24. *Questions for Parliamentary Candidates.* (Sidney Webb.)
       25. *Questions for School Board Candidates.* (Sidney Webb.)
       26. *Questions for London County Councillors.* (Sidney Webb.)
       27. *Questions for Town Councillors.* (Rev. C. Peach.)
       28. *Questions for County Council Candidates (Rural).* (F. Hudson.)
       29. *What to Read.* (Graham Wallas.)
       30. *The Unearned Increment.* (Sidney Webb.)
       31. *London's Heritage in the City Guilds.* (Sidney Webb.)
       32. *The Municipalization of the Gas Supply.* (Sidney Webb.)
       33. *Municipal Tramways.* (Sidney Webb.)
       34. *London's Water Tribute.* (Sidney Webb.)
       35. *The Municipalization of the London Docks.* (Sidney Webb.)
       36. *The Scandal of London's Markets.* (Sidney Webb.)
       37. *A Labour Policy for Public Authorities.* (Sidney Webb.)
       38. Welsh Translation of No. 1.
1892   39. *A Democratic Budget.* (J. F. Oakeshott.)
       40. *Fabian Election Manifesto.* (Bernard Shaw.)
       41. *The Fabian Society: What it has Done and How it has Done It.* G. Bernard Shaw.
       42. *Christian Socialism.* Rev. Stewart D. Headlam.
       43. *Vote! Vote! Vote!* (Bernard Shaw.)
1893   44. *A Plea for Poor Law Reform.* (Frederick Whelen.)
       45. *Impossibilities of Anarchism.* G. Bernard Shaw.
       46. *Socialism and Sailors.* B. T. Hall.
       47. *The Unemployed.* John Burns.*
       48. *Eight Hours by Law.* (Henry W. Macrosty.)
1894   49. *A Plan of Campaign for Labour.* (G. Bernard Shaw.)
       50. *Sweating: Its Cause and Remedy.* (H. W. Macrosty.)
       51. *Socialism: True and False.* Sidney Webb.
       52. *State Education at Home and Abroad.* J. W. Martin.
       53. *The Parish Councils Act: What it is and How to Work It.* (Herbert Samuel.*)
       54. *Humanising of the Poor Law.* J. F. Oakeshott.
       55. *The Workers' School Board Programme.* (J. W. Martin.)
       56. *Questions for Parish Council Candidates.* (Herbert Samuel.*)
       57. *Questions for Rural District Council Candidates.* (Herbert Samuel.*)
       58. *Allotments and How to Get Them.* (Herbert Samuel.*)

59. *Questions for Candidates for Urban District Councils.*
60. *The London Vestries: What they are and What they Do.* Sidney Webb.
1895　61. *The London County Council: What it is and What it Does.* (J. F. Oakeshott.)
62. *Parish and District Councils: What they are and What they can Do.* (No. 53 rewritten.)
63. *Parish Council Cottages and How to Get Them.* (E. R. Pease.)
64. *How to Lose and how to Win an Election.* (J. Ramsay Macdonald.)
65. *Trade Unionists and Politics.* (F. W. Galton.)
66. *A Programme for Workers.* (E. R. Pease.)
1896　67. *Women and the Factory Acts.* Mrs Sidney Webb.
68. *The Tenant's Sanitary Catechism.* (Arthur Hickmott.)
69. *The Difficulties of Individualism.* Sidney Webb.
70. *Report on Fabian Policy.* (Bernard Shaw.)
71. *The (London) Tenant's Sanitary Catechism.* (Miss Grove.)
72. *The Moral Aspects of Socialism.* Sidney Ball.
73. *The Case for State Pensions in Old Age.* (George Turner.)
74. *The State and Its Functions in New Zealand.* The Hon. W. P. Reeves.*
1897　75. *Labour in the Longest Reign.* Sidney Webb.
76. *Houses for the People.* (Arthur Hickmott.)
77. *The Municipalization of Tramways.* F. T. H. Henlé.
78. *Socialism and the Teaching of Christ.* Rev. John Clifford, D.D.
79. *A Word of Remembrance and Caution to the Rich.* John Woolman.*
80. *Shop Life and its Reform.* (William Johnson.)
81. *Municipal Water.* (C. M. Knowles.*)
82. *The Workmen's Compensation Act.* (C. R. Allen, junr)
83. *State Arbitration and the Living Wage.* (H. W. Macrosty.)
84. *The Economics of Direct Employment.* Sidney Webb.
85. *Liquor Licensing at Home and Abroad.* E. R. Pease.
86. *Municipal Drink Traffic.* (E. R. Pease.)
1899　87. *A Welsh Translation of No. 78.*
88. *The Growth of Monopoly in English Industry.* Henry W. Macrosty.
89. *Old Age Pensions at Work.* (J. Bullock.)
90. *The Municipalisation of the Milk Supply.* (Dr G. F. McCleary.)
91. *Municipal Pawnshops.* (Charles Charrington.)
92. *Municipal Slaughter-houses.* (George Standring.)
1900　93. *Women As Councillors.* (Bernard Shaw.)
94. *Municipal Bakeries.* (Dr G. F. McCleary.)
95. *Municipal Hospitals.* (Dr G. F. McCleary.)
96. *Municipal Fire Insurance.* (Mrs Fenton Macpherson.)
97. *Municipal Steamboats.* (S. D. Shallard.)
98. *State Railways for Ireland.* (Clement Edwards.)
99. *Local Government in Ireland.* (C. R. Allen, junr)
100. *Metropolitan Borough Councils: Their Powers and Duties.* (Henry W. Macrosty.)
101. *The House Famine and How to Relieve it.* Various.
102. *Questions for Candidates: Metropolitan Borough Councils.* (H. W. Macrosty.)
103. *Overcrowding in London and its Remedy.* W. C. Steadman, M.P.
104. *How Trade Unions Benefit Workmen.* (E. R. Pease.)

1901 105. *Five Years' Fruit of the Parish Councils Act.* (Sidney Webb.)
106. *The Education Muddle and the Way Out.* (Sidney Webb.)
107. *Socialism for Millionaires.* Bernard Shaw.
108. *Twentieth Century Politics: A Policy of National Efficiency.* Sidney Webb.
1902 109. *Cottage Plans and Common Sense.* Raymond Unwin.
110. *Problems of Indian Poverty.* S. S. Thorburn.*
111. *Reform of Reformatories and Industrial Schools.* H. T. Holmes.
112. *Life in the Laundry.* Dr G. F. McCleary.
1903 113. *Communism.* William Morris.* Preface by Bernard Shaw.
114. *The Education Act, 1902. How to Make the Best of It.* (Sidney Webb.)
115. *State Aid to Agriculture.* T. S. Dymond.*
1904 116. *Fabianism and the Fiscal Question: an Alternative Policy.* (Bernard Shaw.)
117. *The London Education Act, 1903: How to Make the Best of It.* (Sidney Webb.)
118. *The Secret of Rural Depopulation.* Lieut.-Col. D. C. Pedder.*
1905 119. *Public Control of Electric Power and Transit.* S. G. Hobson.
120. *After Bread, Education.* Hubert Bland.
121. *Public Service versus Private Expenditure.* Sir Oliver Lodge.*
122. *Municipal Milk and Public Health.* F. Lawson Dodd.
123. *The Revival of Agriculture: a National Policy for Great Britain.* Henry W. Macrosty.
124. *State Control of Trusts.* Henry W. Macrosty.
125. *Municipalization by Provinces.* W. Stephen Sanders.
1906 126. *The Abolition of Poor Law Guardians.* E. R. Pease.
127. *Socialism and Labour Policy.* (Hubert Bland, Editor.)
128. *The Case for a Legal Minimum Wage.* (W. Stephen Sanders.)
129. *More Books to Read.* (E. R. Pease.)
1907 130. *Home Work and Sweating: The Causes and Remedies.* Miss B. L. Hutchins.
131. *The Decline in the Birth-rate.* Sidney Webb.
132. *A Guide to Books for Socialists.* 'The Nursery'.
133. *Socialism and Christianity.* Rev. Percy Dearmer, D.D.
134. *Small Holdings, Allotments, and Common Pastures.* Revised edition of No. 58.
135. *Paupers and Old Age Pensions.* Sidney Webb.
136. *The Village and the Landlord.* Edward Carpenter.
1908 137. *Parish Councils and Village Life.* (Revised version of No. 105.)
138. *Municipal Trading.* (Aylmer Maude.)
139. *Socialism and the Churches.* Rev. John Clifford, D.D.
140. *Child Labour Under Capitalism.* Mrs Hylton Dale.
1909 141. A Welsh Translation of No. 139.
142. *Rent and Value.* Adapted by Mrs Bernard Shaw from Fabian Essays, The Economic Basis.
143. *Sosialaeth Yng Ngoleuni'R Beibl* (Welsh). J. R. Jones.
144. *Machinery: its Masters and its Servants.* H. H. Schloesser [Slesser] and Clement Game.
145. *The Case for School Nurseries.* Mrs Townshend.
146. *Socialism and Superior Brains. A Reply to Mr Mallock.* Bernard Shaw.

147. *Capital and Compensation.* Edward R. Pease.

148. *What a Health Committee can do.* (Miss B. L. Hutchins.)

1910　149. *The Endowment of Motherhood.* Henry D. Harben.

150. *State Purchase of Railways: a Practicable Scheme.* Emil Davies.

151. *The Point of Honour. A Correspondence on Aristocracy and Socialism.* Mrs Ruth Cavendish Bentinck.

1911　152. *Our Taxes as they are and as they ought to be.* Robert Jones.

153. *The Twentieth Century Reform Bill.* Henry H. Schloesser [Slesser].

154. *The Case for School Clinics.* L. Haden Guest.

155. *The Case against the Referendum.* Clifford D. Sharp.

156. *What an Education Committee can do (Elementary Schools).* The Education Group.

157. *The Working Life of Women.* Miss B. L. Hutchins.

158. *The Case Against the Charity Organisation Society.* Mrs Townshend.

159. *The Necessary Basis of Society.* Sidney Webb.

160. *A National Medical Service.* F. Lawson Dodd.

1912　161. *Afforestation and Unemployment.* Arthur P. Grenfell.

162. *Family Life on a Pound a Week.* Mrs Pember Reeves.

163. *Women and Prisons.* Helen Blagg and Charlotte Wilson.

164. *Gold and State Banking. A Study in the Economics of Monopoly.* Edward R. Pease.

165. *Francis Place: the Tailor of Charing Cross.* St John G. Ervine.

166. *Robert Owen: Social Reformer.* Miss B. L. Hutchins.

167. *William Morris and the Communist Ideal.* Mrs Townshend.

1913　168. *John Stuart Mill.* Julius West.

169. *The Socialist Movement in Germany.* W. Stephen Sanders.

170. *Profit-Sharing and Co-partnership: a Fraud and a Failure?* Edward R. Pease.

171. *The Nationalization of Mines and Minerals Bill.* Henry H. Schloesser [Slesser.]

172. *What about the Rates, or Municipal Finance and Municipal Autonomy.* Sidney Webb.

173. *Public versus Private Electricity Supply.* C. Ashmore Baker.*

1914　174. *Charles Kingsley and Christian Socialism.* Colwyn E. Vulliamy.

175. *The Economic Foundations of the Women's Movement.* M. A. [Mabel Atkinson.]

176. *War and the Workers. Handbook of some Immediate Measures to Prevent Unemployment and Relieve Distress.* Sidney Webb.

1915　177. *Socialism and the Arts of Use.* A. Clutton Brock.

178. *The War: Women; and Unemployment.* The Women's Group Executive.

1916　Nil.

1917　179. *John Ruskin and Social Ethics.* Edith Morley.

180. *The Philosophy of Socialism.* A. Clutton Brock.

181. *When Peace Comes. The Way of Industrial Reconstruction.* Sidney Webb.

1918　182. *Robert Owen, Idealist.* C. E. M. Joad.

183. *Reform of the House of Lords.* Sidney Webb.

184. *The Russian Revolution and British Democracy.* Julius West.

185. *The Abolition of the Poor Law.* Mrs Sidney Webb.

1919　186. *Central Africa and the League of Nations.* R. C. Hawkin.*

187. *The Teacher in Politics.* Sidney Webb.

354

188. *National Finance and a Levy on Capital.* Sidney Webb.

1920   189. *Urban District Councils: their Constitution, Powers, and Duties.* C. M. Lloyd.

190. *Metropolitan Borough Councils: their Constitution, Powers, and Duties.* C. R. Attlee.

191. *Borough Councils: their Constitution, Powers, and Duties.* C. R. Attlee.

192. *Guild Socialism.* G. D. H. Cole.*

BOOKS, ARTICLES AND THESES DEVOTED ENTIRELY OR MAINLY
TO THE HISTORY OR DOCTRINES OF THE FABIAN SOCIETY
(In chronological order)

Webb, Sidney. *The Fabian Society: its Objects and Methods.* Stafford and Co., Notts., 1891.

Shaw, G. Bernard. Fabian Tract 41, *The Early History of the Fabian Society* (first published in 1892, the earlier editions were entitled *The Fabian Society: What it has Done and How it has Done It;* it has also been reprinted in *Essays in Fabian Socialism,* Constable, London, 1932).

Clarke, William. 'The Fabian Society', *New England Magazine,* n.s. x, March 1894.

Mallock, W. H. 'Fabian Economics', *Fortnightly Review,* vol. 61, March 1894.

Pfeiffer, Edouard. *La Société Fabienne et le mouvement socialiste Anglais contemporaine.* V. Giard et E. Brière, Paris, 1911.

Pease, Edward R. *The History of the Fabian Society,* the Fabian Society and G. Allen and Unwin, London, 1st ed. 1916; 2nd ed. 1925. The publication of Pease's *History* drew interesting comments from J. R. MacDonald in the *Socialist Review,* vol. XIII, no. 78, 1916, from Graham Wallas in the *New Republic,* vol. VIII, 1916 (reprinted in *Men and Ideas,* Allen and Unwin, London, 1940), and from an anonymous Liberal reviewer in the *Nation,* 26 August 1916.

Ensor, R. C. K. 'Fifty Years of the Fabians', *Spectator,* vol. CLII, 12 January 1934.

Howland, R. D. 'Fabian Thought and Social Change in England 1884–1914' (unpublished typescript thesis in British Library of Political Science, 1942).

Cole, G. D. H. *The Fabian Society* (Fabian Tract 258, 1942).

Cole, G. D. H. *Fabian Socialism.* Allen and Unwin, London, 1943.

Cole, Margaret. 'The Fabian Society', *Political Quarterly,* vol. xv, July 1944.

Underhill, F. H. 'Fabians and Fabianism', *Canadian Forum,* vol. XXVI, no. 303, April 1946.

Irvine, W. 'Shaw, the Fabians, and the Utilitarians', *Journal of the History of Ideas,* vol. VIII, April 1947.

Murphy, Mary E. 'The Role of the Fabian Society in British Affairs', *Southern Economic Journal,* vol. XIV, July 1947.

McBriar, A. M. 'Fabian Socialist Doctrine and Its Influence in English Politics, 1884–1918' (unpublished typescript thesis in Bodleian Library, Oxford, 1949: the basis of the present work).

Hobsbawm, E. 'Fabianism and the Fabians, 1884–1914' (unpublished typescript thesis in Cambridge University Library, 1950).

Cox, W., and Gordon, H. S. 'The Early Fabians: Economists and Reformers', *Canadian Journal of Economics and Political Science,* vol. XVII, August 1951.

Lewis, G. K. 'Fabian Socialism: some Aspects of Theory and Practice', *Journal of Politics,* vol. XIV, August 1952.

Clarkson, J. D. 'Background of Fabian Theory', *Journal of Economic History,* vol. XIII, no. 4, 1953.

Wilbur, W. C. 'The Origins and Development of Fabian Socialism to 1890' (unpublished thesis, University of Ann Arbour, 1954).*

Cole, Margaret. 'The Story of the Society', *Fabian Journal*, no. 12, 1954.

Mack, Mary P. 'The Fabians and Utilitarianism', *Journal of the History of Ideas*, vol. XVI, January 1955.

Arnold, G. L. 'Notes on Fabianism', *Twentieth Century*, vol. CLIX, June 1956.

McCarran, Margaret P. *Fabianism in the Political Life of Britain* 1919–31. Heritage Foundation, Chicago, 1957.*

Milburn, J. F. 'The Fabian Society and the British Labour Party', *Western Political Quarterly*, vol. XI, June 1958.*

Melitz, J. 'The Trade Unions and Fabian Socialism', *Industrial and Labour Relations Review*, vol. XII, July 1959.

Fremantle, Anne. *This Little Band of Prophets: The Story of the Gentle Fabians.* Allen and Unwin, London, 1960.*

Amongst the early accounts of the Society Bernard Shaw's superb Tract stands in a class by itself: it is beautifully written and seems to give an accurate picture of the Society to 1891 (accuracy is not invariably a feature of Shaw's later ventures into Fabian history). Mallock's article is the one which began the famous controversy with Shaw. Pfeiffer wrote as a Liberal, but with a bias in favour of H. G. Wells; his work contains many shrewd comments, especially on Municipal Socialism, but it is marred by factual inaccuracies and unanalysed generalizations about the relation of the Fabians to the Labour Party. Pease was the 'official' historian, with a dry soul, and an 'Old Guard' bias; the gaps in his account of the Society are significant. Ensor's article, on the occasion of the fiftieth birthday of the Society, is slight. Dr Howland's thesis was a pioneering modern study of the Fabians, but it deals in rather general terms with their actual doctrine and influence, and devotes a great deal of space to their antecedents and to the effect on them and Socialism generally of the 'Great Depression' of the eighties (this aspect has been dealt with more fully and systematically since then by Dr Wilbur). Professor and Mrs Cole's book, tract and article of 1943–4 were written at the time they were reviving the Fabian Society from its sexagenarian slumbers and have a little of the quality of *pièces de circonstance*. Of the many useful critical articles on the Fabians which have appeared since the Second World War, Professor G. K. Lewis's is, in my opinion, an outstanding one. Dr Eric Hobsbawm's thesis presents a critical study of the Fabians from a Marxist point of view. Mrs Fremantle's recent book is confined pretty much to the personal aspects of Fabian history: it raises, but does not answer, the important questions about the influence of Fabian ideas.

In addition to these references, the history of the Society and its doctrine is treated in many general histories, encyclopaedias, and histories of socialism and the labour movement. A selection of these is given in the general section of this bibliography; but, because of their importance, one or two of them should be mentioned here. Sidney Webb's article on 'Fabianism' in *The Encyclopaedia of the Labour Movement*, edited by H. B. Lees-Smith (Caxton Publishing Co., London, n.d.) and Bernard Shaw's article on 'Socialism: Principles and Outlook' in the 14th edition of the *Encyclopaedia Brittanica* (reprinted in Fabian Tract no. 233) are of special interest. E. Halévy's treatment of the Fabians in the *Epilogue* volumes of his *History of the English People* gives the views of a great contemporary historian. G. D. H. Cole's chapters on the Fabians in vol. III (*The Second International*) of his

*I did not see these works until this book was completed.

History of Socialist Thought are his final judgement; they incorporate the results of recent research and supersede all earlier general histories of socialism on the subject. Some of the best recent work on the Fabians has been done by historians of the Labour Party: by Dr H. Pelling in his *The Origins of the Labour Party* (Macmillan, London, 1954), Drs H. Pelling and F. Bealey in *Labour and Politics* 1900–1906 (Macmillan, London, 1958), and Professor P. Poirier in *The Advent of the Labour Party* (Allen and Unwin, London, 1958).

The prefaces to later editions of *Fabian Essays* contain illuminating opinions; and for the earliest and formative days of the Society, the material in two Socialist journals of the 'eighties, *The Practical Socialist* and *Today*, is indispensable.

SOME AUTOBIOGRAPHIES, BIOGRAPHIES AND MEMOIRS OF FABIANS

C. R. Attlee (Lord Attlee)
    Attlee, C. R. *As it Happened*. Heinemann, London, 1954.
    Jenkins, R. *Mr Attlee*. Heinemann, 1948.
Sidney Ball
    Ball, Oona A. (ed.). *Sidney Ball, Memories and Impressions of an Ideal Don*. Blackwell, Oxford, 1933.
Annie Besant
    Besant, Annie. *An Autobiography*. T. Fisher Unwin, London, 1893.
    Besterman, T. *Mrs Annie Besant: a Modern Prophet*. Routledge, London, 1934.
    Nethercot, A. H. *The First Five Lives of Annie Besant*. Univ. of Chicago Press, 1960.
    West, Geoffrey. *Life of Annie Besant*. Howe, London, 1933.
Edith (Nesbit) and Hubert Bland
    Bland, Edith Nesbit (ed.). *Essays by Hubert Bland ('Hubert' of the Sunday Chronicle)*. Max Goschen, London, 1914. (Contains an autobiographical sketch.)
    Moore, Doris L. *E. Nesbit, a Biography*. Ernest Benn, London, 1933.
Robert Blatchford
    Blatchford, R. *My Eighty Years*. Cassell, London, 1931.
    Lyons, A. N. *Robert Blatchford*. Clarion Press, London, 1910.
    Thompson, L. *Portrait of an Englishman: a Life of Robert Blatchford*. Gollancz London, 1951.
Margaret Bondfield
    Bondfield, Margaret G. *A Life's Work*. Hutchinson, London, 1949.
    Hamilton, M. A. *Margaret Bondfield*. Leonard Parsons, London, 1924.
Joe Burgess
    Burgess, Joseph. *Will Lloyd George Supplant Ramsay MacDonald?* The Joseph Burgess Publication Depot, Ilford. n.d.
Edward Carpenter
    Carpenter, E. *My Days and Dreams, being Autobiographical Notes*. Allen and Unwin, London, 1916.
    Crosby, E. H. *Edward Carpenter: Poet and Prophet*. A. C. Fifield, London, 2nd ed., 1905.
William Clarke
    Burrows, H. and J. A. Hobson. *William Clarke: a Collection of his Writings with a Biographical Sketch*. Swan Sonnenschein, London, 1908.

Dr John Clifford
  Byrt, G. W. *John Clifford, a Fighting Free Churchman*. Kingsgate Press, London 1947.
  Clement, A. S. (ed.). *Baptists Who Made History*. Carey Kingsgate Press, London. 1955.
  Cowell, H. J. *John Clifford as I Knew Him*. Baptist Union Publication Dept., London, 1936.
  Crane, D. *John Clifford, God's Soldier and the People's Tribune*. Edwin Dalton, London, 1908.
  Marchant, Sir James. *Dr John Clifford: Life, Letters and Reminiscences*. Cassell and Co., London, 1924.
Margaret Cole
  Cole, Margaret. *Growing Up into Revolution*. Longmans, London, 1949.
Will Crooks
  Haw, G. *From Workhouse to Westminster: the Life Story of Will Crooks, M.P.* Cassell, London, 1907.
Hugh Dalton
  Dalton, H. *Call Back Yesterday: Memoirs* 1887–1931. Frederick Muller, London, 1953.
Rev. Percy Dearmer
  Dearmer, Nancy. *The Life of Percy Dearmer*. Jonathan Cape, London, 1940.
H. Hamilton Fyfe
  Fyfe, H. H. *My Seven Selves*. Allen and Unwin, London, 1935.
  —— *Sixty Years of Fleet Street*. Allen and Unwin, London, 1949.
J. Keir Hardie
  Cockburn, J. *Hungry Heart: a Romantic Biography of James Keir Hardie*, Jarrolds, London, 1956.
  Cole, G. D. H. *J. Keir Hardie* (Fabian Biographical Tract no. 12).
  Fyfe, H. H. *Keir Hardie*. Duckworth, London, 1935.
  Glasier, J. B. *Keir Hardie, the Man and His Message*. I.L.P., London, 1919.
  Hughes, Emrys. *Keir Hardie: Some Memories*. Francis Johnson, London, 1939.
  —— *Keir Hardie*. Allen and Unwin, 1956.
  Johnson, F. *Keir Hardie's Socialism*. I.L.P., London, 1922.
  Lowe, D. *From Pit to Parliament: the Story of the Early Life of James Keir Hardie*. Labour Publishing Co., London, 1923.
  Maxton, J. *Keir Hardie: Prophet and Pioneer*. Francis Johnson, London, 1939.
  Stewart, W. *J. Keir Hardie: a Biography*. I.L.P., London, 1925.
Rev. Stewart D. Headlam
  Bettany, F. G. *Stewart Headlam*. John Murray, London, 1926.
Arthur Henderson
  Hamilton, Mary A. *Arthur Henderson*. Wm. Heinemann, London, 1938.
  Jenkins, E. A. *From Foundry to Foreign Office, the Romantic Life Story of the Rt. Hon. Arthur Henderson, M.P.* Grayson and Grayson, London, 1933.
S. G. Hobson
  Hobson, S. G. *Pilgrim to the Left: Memoirs of a Modern Revolutionist*. E. Arnold and Co., London, 1938.
C. E. M. Joad
  Coates, J. B. *Ten Modern Prophets*. Frederick Muller, London, 1944.
  Joad, C. E. M. *The Book of Joad: a Belligerent Autobiography*. Faber & Faber, London, 1935.

Ben Keeling

E[mily] T[ownshend] (ed.). *Keeling Letters and Recollections.* Allen and Unwin, London, 1918.

George Lansbury

Lansbury, G. *My Life.* Constable, London, 1931.

Lansbury, E. *George Lansbury, My Father.* Sampson Low and Co., London, 1934.

Postgate, R. W. *Life of George Lansbury.* Longmans, London, 1951.

Harold Laski

Martin, Kingsley. *Harold Laski, 1893-1950: a Biographical Memoir.* Gollancz, London, 1953.

Lord Pethick Lawrence

Lawrence, F. W. Pethick. *Fate Has Been Kind.* Hutchinson and Co., London, 1943.

J. Ramsay MacDonald

Elton, Lord. *The Life of James Ramsay MacDonald.* Collins, London, 1939.

Hamilton, M. A. *James Ramsay MacDonald.* Jonathan Cape, London, 1929.

Sacks, B. *J. Ramsay MacDonald in Thought and Action: An Architect for a Better World.* Univ. of New Mexico Press, 1952.

Tiltman, H. H. *James Ramsay MacDonald: Labour's Man of Destiny.* Jarrolds, London, 1929.

Tracey, H. *From Doughty Street to Downing Street: Rt Hon. J. Ramsay MacDonald: a Biographical Study.* J. Marlowe Savage, London, 3rd ed., 1924.

Weir, L. M. *The Tragedy of Ramsay MacDonald: a Political Biography.* Secker and Warburg, London, 1938.

Tom Mann

Mann, T. *My Memoirs.* Labour Publishing Co., London, 1923.

Torr, Dona. *Tom Mann and his Times.* Lawrence and Wishart, London, 1936.

H. W. Massingham

Massingham, H. J. (ed.). *H.W.M.: a Selection from the Writings of H. W. Massingham with Introductory Essays by J. L. Hammond and others.* Harcourt, London, 1925.

Sydney Olivier (Lord Olivier)

Olivier, Margaret (Lady Olivier). *Sydney Olivier: Letters and Selected Writings, with a Memoir.* Allen and Unwin, London, 1948.

Emmeline Pankhurst

Pankhurst, Emmeline. *My Own Story.* Eveleigh Nash, London, 1914.

Pankhurst, E. Sylvia. *The Life of Emmeline Pankhurst: the Suffragette Struggle for Women's Citizenship.* T. Werner Laurie, London, 1945.

Professor D. G. Ritchie

Latta, R. (ed.). *D. G. Ritchie's Philosophical Studies, with a Memoir.* Macmillan, London, 1905.

Henry Salt

Salt, H. S. *Seventy Years Amongst Savages.* Allen and Unwin, London, 1921.

—— *Company I Have Kept.* Allen and Unwin, London, 1930.

Winsten, S. *Henry Salt and His Circle.* Hutchinson, London, 1951.

W. Stephen Sanders

Sanders, W. S. *Early Socialist Days.* Hogarth Press, London, 1927.

George Bernard Shaw

Chesterton, G. K. *George Bernard Shaw.* John Lane the Bodley Head, London, 1910.

Ervine, St John. *Bernard Shaw: His Life, Work and Friends*. Constable, London, 1956.

Harris, Frank. *Bernard Shaw*. Gollancz, London, 1931.

Henderson, Archibald. *George Bernard Shaw: His Life and Works, a Critical Biography*. Hurst and Blackett, London, 1911.

—— *Bernard Shaw, Playboy and Prophet*, 2 vols. Appleton, N.Y., 1932.

—— *George Bernard Shaw: Man of the Century*. Appleton, N.Y., 1956.

Jackson, Holbrook. *Bernard Shaw*. G. Richards, London, 1909.

Joad, C. E. M. *Shaw*. Gollancz, London, 1949.

Pearson, Hesketh. *G.B.S.: a Full Length Portrait*. Harper, N.Y., 1942.

Shaw, G. B. Prefaces to *The Irrational Knot, Immaturity*, and *London Music in 1888–9*, Standard Edition. Constable.

—— *Sixteen Self Sketches*. Constable, London, 1949.

—— *Shaw Gives Himself Away: an Autobiographical Miscellany*. Gregynog Press, Wales, 1939.

Winsten, S. (ed.). *G.B.S. 90: Aspects of Bernard Shaw's Life and Work*. Hutchinson, London, 1946.

Sir Henry Slesser (Schloesser)

Slesser, H. H. *Judgment Reserved*. Hutchinson, London, 1941.

Harry Snell (Lord Snell)

Snell, Lord. *Men, Movements and Myself*. J. M. Dent and Sons, London, 1936.

Philip Snowden (Lord Snowden)

Andreades, A. M. (trans. Dorothy Bolton). *Philip Snowden, the Man and His Financial Policy*. P. S. King, and Sons, London, 1930.

Bechhofer-Roberts, C. E. *Philip Snowden: an Impartial Portrait*. Cassell and Co., London, 1929.

Snowden, Philip Viscount. *An Autobiography*, 2 vols. Ivor Nicholson and Watson, London, 1934.

Ben Tillett

Tillett, B. *Memories and Reflections*. John Long, London, 1931.

Emily Caroline Townshend

Townshend, Emily C. *Emily Townshend 1849–1934: Some Memories for her Friends*. Curwen Press, London, 1936.

Colwyn Edward Vulliamy

Vulliamy, C. E. *Calico Pie: an Autobiography*. Michael Joseph, London, 1940.

Graham Wallas

Wallas, May (ed.). *Men and Ideas*. Allen and Unwin, London, 1940. (Contains biographical table.)

Sidney and Beatrice Webb

Beveridge, Lord. 'Sidney Webb (Lord Passfield) 1859–1947', *Economic Journal*, vol. LVIII, September 1948.

Cole, Margaret. *Beatrice Webb*. Longmans, London, 1945.

Cole, Margaret (ed.). *The Webbs and their Work*. Frederick Muller, London, 1949.

—— (ed.). *Beatrice Webb's Diaries 1912–24*. Longmans, London, 1952.

—— (ed.). *Beatrice Webb's Diaries 1924–32*. Longmans, London, 1956.

—— *Beatrice and Sidney Webb*. Fabian Tract no. 297. (1955).

Hamilton, Mary A. *Sidney and Beatrice Webb*. Sampson Low, London, 1934.

Tawney, R. H. 'Beatrice Webb 1858–1943', *Proceedings of the British Academy*, vol. XXIX (1945).

—— 'In Memory of Sidney Webb', *Economica*, November 1947.

—— *The Webbs and their Work* (Webb Memorial Lecture no. 1). Fabian Publications, London, 1947.
—— *The Webbs in Perspective* (Webb Memorial Lecture, 1952). Athlone Press, London, 1953.
Webb, Beatrice. *My Apprenticeship*, 2 vols. Pelican, London, 1938.
—— *Our Partnership*. Longmans, London, 1948.

J. C. Wedgwood
Wedgwood, C. V. *The Last of the Radicals*. Jonathan Cape, London, 1951.
Wedgwood, J. C. *Memoirs of a Fighting Life*. Hutchinson, London, 1940.
—— *Essays and Adventures of a Labour M.P.* Allen and Unwin, London, 1924.

H. G. Wells
Brome, V. *H. G. Wells*. Longmans, London, 1951.
Nicholson, N. *H. G. Wells*. Arthur Barker, London, 1950.
Wells, H. G. *Experiment in Autobiography*, 2 vols. Gollancz, London, 1934.
West, Geoffrey (G. H. Wells). *H. G. Wells, a Sketch for a Portrait*. Howe, London, 1930.

Leonard Woolf
Woolf, L. S. *Sowing: an Autobiography of the Years* 1880 *to* 1904. Hogarth, London, 1960.

Other Fabians
A great deal of useful biographical material concerning less prominent Fabians can be obtained from Joseph Edward's *Labour Annual* (called after 1900 *The Reformer's Year Book*), Clarion Publishing Co., London.

SOME OTHER AUTOBIOGRAPHIES, BIOGRAPHIES AND
MEMOIRS CONSULTED

Allen, B. M. *Memoir of Dr Garnett*. Heffer, Cambridge, 1933.
—— *Sir Robert Morant, a Great Public Servant*. Macmillan, London, 1934.
Amery, J. *The Life of Joseph Chamberlain*, vol. IV. Macmillan, London, 1952.
Amery, L. S. *My Political Life*, 3 vols. Hutchinson and Co., London, 1953-5.
Asquith, C. (with J. A. Spender). *Life of Herbert Henry Asquith, Lord Oxford and Asquith*, 2 vols. Hutchinson, London, 1932.
Asquith, H. H. *Memories and Reflections*, 2 vols. Cassell, London, 1928.
Balfour, A. J. *Chapters of Autobiography*. Cassell, London, 1930.
Barnes, George. *From Workshop to War Cabinet*. Appleton, N.Y., 1924.
Bax, E. Belfort. *Reminiscences and Reflexions of a Mid and Late Victorian*. Allen and Unwin, London, 1918.
Bernstein, Eduard. *My Years in Exile*. Leonard Parsons, London, 1921.
Beveridge, William Henry (Lord). *Power and Influence: an Autobiography*. Hodder and Stoughton, London, 1953.
Broadhurst, Henry B. *The Story of his Life, from a Stonemason's Bench to the Treasury Bench*. Hutchinson, London, 1901.
Brockway, Fenner. *Inside the Left*. Allen and Unwin, London, 1943.
—— *Socialism Over Sixty Years: The Life of Jowett of Bradford*. Allen and Unwin, London, 1946.
Bunbury, Sir Henry (ed.). *Lloyd George's Ambulance Wagon* (being the memoirs of W. J. Braithwaite). Methuen, London, 1957.
Burt, Thomas. *Autobiography*. H. W. Wilson, N.Y., 1924.
Chamberlain, Sir Austen. *Politics from the Inside*. Cassell, London, 1936.

Chesterton, Mrs Cecil. *The Chestertons*. Chapman and Hall, London, 1941.
Chesterton, G. K. *Autobiography*. Hutchinson, London, 1936.
Churchill, Winston S. *Great Contemporaries*. Thornton Butterworth, London, 1939.
Clynes, J. R. *Memoirs*, 2 vols. Hutchinson, London, 1937–9.
Cole, G. D. H. *John Burns* (Fabian Biographical Tract no. 14).
Cole, Margaret. *Women of Today*. T. Nelson and Sons, London, 1938.
—— *Makers of the Labour Movement*. Longmans, London, 1948.
Cowles, Virginia. *Winston Churchill: the Era and the Man*. Hamish Hamilton, London, 1953.
Crewe, Marquess of. *Lord Rosebery*. John Murray, London, 1931.
Dugdale, Blanche. *Arthur James Balfour*, 2 vols. Hutchinson, London, 1936.
Elliot, A. D. *The Life of George Joachim Goschen*. Longmans, London, 1911.
Gardiner, A. G. *Pillars of Society*. Dodd, Mead and Co., N.Y., 1914.
—— *Life of Sir William Harcourt*, 2 vols. Constable, London, 1923.
—— *John Benn and the Progressive Movement*. Ernest Benn, London, 1925.
Garvin, J. L. *The Life of Joseph Chamberlain*, 3 vols. Macmillan, London, 1932.
Gladstone, Herbert. *After Thirty Years*. Macmillan, London, 1928.
Glasier, J. Bruce. *William Morris and the Early Days of the Socialist Movement*. Longmans, London, 1921.
Grier, Lynda. *Achievement in Education: the Work of Michael Ernest Sadler*, 1885–1935. Constable, London, 1952.
Gwynn, S. and Gertrude M. Tuckwell. *The Life of the Rt. Hon. Sir Charles W. Dilke*, 2 vols. Macmillan, London, 1917.
Haldane, Elizabeth. *From One Century to Another*. MacLehose, London, 1937.
Haldane, R. B. (Lord). *An Autobiography*. Hodder and Stoughton, London, 1929.
Hamilton, Mary A. *Remembering My Good Friends*. Jonathan Cape, London, 1944.
Harrison, Frederic. *Autobiographical Memoirs*, 2 vols. Macmillan, London, 1911.
Harrod, R. F. *Life of John Maynard Keynes*. Macmillan, London, 1951.
Hewins, W. A. S. *The Apologia of an Imperialist*, 2 vols. Constable, London, 1929.
Hobson, J. A. *Confessions of an Economic Heretic*. Allen and Unwin, London, 1938.
Hyndman, H. M. *The Record of an Adventurous Life*. Macmillan, N.Y., 1911.
—— *Further Reminiscences*. Macmillan, London, 1912.
Jones, T. *Lloyd George*. Cambridge Univ. Press, London, 1951.
Kent, William. *John Burns: Labour's Lost Leader*. London, 1950.
Keynes, J. M. *Essays in Biography*. Macmillan, London, 1933.
—— *Two Memoirs: Dr Melchior, a Defeated Enemy and My Early Beliefs*. Rupert Hart-Davis, London, 1949.
Knight, William (ed.). *Memorials of Thomas Davidson*. T. Fisher Unwin, London, 1907.
Low, David. *Autobiography*. Michael Joseph, London, 1956.
Mackail, J. W. *The Life of William Morris*, 2 vols. Longmans, London, 1899.
Mallet, Sir Charles. *Herbert Gladstone: a Memoir*. Hutchinson, London, 1932.
Masterman, Lucy. *C. F. G. Masterman, a Biography*. Nicholson, London, 1939.
Maurice, Sir Frederick. *The Life of Viscount Haldane of Cloan*, 2 vols. Faber and Faber, London, 1937.
Mayer, G. *Friedrich Engels*. Chapman and Hall, London, 1936.
Mill, J. S. *An Autobiography*. World's Classics, Oxford Univ. Press, London, 1944.
Morley, John. *Recollections*, 2 vols. Macmillan, London, 1917.
Parmoor, Lord. *A Retrospect: Looking Back over a Life of More than Eighty Years*. Heinemann, London, 1936.

Petrie, Sir Charles. *Life and Letters of Austen Chamberlain*, 2 vols. Cassell, London, 1939.

'Raymond, E. T.' (E. R. Thompson). *Portraits of the 'Nineties*. Unwin, London, 1921.

—— *Portraits of the New Century*. Allen and Unwin, 1924.

Russell, Bertrand. *Portraits from Memory and Other Essays*. Allen and Unwin, London, 1956.

Sexton, Sir James. *Sir James Sexton, Agitator: Life of the Dockers' M.P.: an Autobiography*. Faber and Faber, London, n.d. (1936).

Spender, J. A. *The Life of the Rt Hon. Sir Henry Campbell-Bannerman*, 2 vols. Hodder and Stoughton, London, 1923.

Thompson, A. M. *Here I Lie: the Memorial of an Old Journalist* ('*Dangle*'). Routledge, London, 1937.

Thompson, E. P. *William Morris, Romantic to Revolutionary*. Lawrence and Wishart, London, 1955.

Thomson, M. (with Frances, Countess Lloyd-George of Dwyfor). *David Lloyd-George: the Official Biography*. Hutchinson, London, n.d.

Ward, Maisie. *Gilbert Keith Chesterton*. Sheed and Ward, London, 1944.

Whyte, F. *The Life of W. T. Stead*. Houghton Mifflen, Boston, 1925.

A SELECT BIBLIOGRAPHY OF WORKS BY FABIANS PUBLISHED BEFORE 1920

The Fabians were intellectually prolific, and any bibliography which attempted a comprehensive list of their works would seem like a library catalogue. But a selection of them to 1920 will serve to show how much they contributed to the intellectual climate of their age.

Alden, Percy. *The Unemployed: a National Question*. P. S. King and Son, London, 1905.

—— *Democratic England*. Macmillan, N.Y., 1912.

Atkinson, Mabel. [*See also* McKillop.] *Local Government in Scotland*. W. Blackwood and Sons, Edinburgh and London, 1904.

Attlee, C. R. *The Social Worker*. G. Bell and Sons, London, 1920.

Bennett, E. Arnold. *Works*. The Minerva Edition, Library Press, 1926.

Besant, Annie. [For a Bibliography of Annie Besant's numerous works see T. Bestermann, *A Bibliography of Annie Besant*.]

—— *Modern Socialism*. Freethought Publishing Co., London, 1886.

Bland, Hubert. [*See also* Nesbit, Edith.] *With the Eyes of a Man*. T. Werner Laurie, London, 1905.

—— *Letters to a Daughter*. T. Werner Laurie, London, 1906.

—— *The Happy Moralist*. T. Werner Laurie, London, 1907.

—— *Olivia's Latchkey*. T. Werner Laurie, London, 1913.

Bray, Reginald. *The Town Child*. T. Fisher Unwin, London, 1907.

—— *The Family*. Society for Promoting Christian Knowledge, London, 1908.

—— *Boy Labour and Apprenticeship*. Constable, London, 1911.

—— *Labour and the Churches*. Constable, London, 1912.

Brock, Arthur Clutton. *William Morris: his Work and Influence*. H.U.L. Williams and Norgate, London, 1914 [and many other works on literature and art].

Brooke, Emma. *A Tabulation of the Factory Laws of European Countries in so far as they relate to hours of labour and to special legislation for women, young persons and children*. Grant Richards, London, 1898.

—— Also a number of novels, including: *Transition*. Wm. Heinemann, London, 1895 (published anonymously) about the early days of the Socialist movement, and containing a portrait of Webb as 'Paul Sheridan'.

Campbell, Rev. Reginald J. Many works of theology including: *The New Theology*. Popular Edition: with a full account of the Progressive League, including the speeches of Hall Caine and Bernard Shaw. Mills and Boon, London, 1909.

—— *Some Economic Aspects of the Woman's Suffrage Movement*. Women's Freedom League, 3rd ed., 1913.

Carpenter, Edward. Numerous works: see *A Bibliography of the Writings of Edward Carpenter*. Allen and Unwin, 1916.

—— (ed.). *Forecasts of the Coming Century by a Decade of Writers*. W. Scott, London, 1897. [Contains essays by many Fabians and other Socialists.]

Chesterton, Cecil. *Gladstonian Ghosts*. S. C. Brown, Langham and Co., London, 1905.

—— *Party and People: a Criticism of Recent Elections and their Consequences*. Alston Rivers, London, 1910.

—— *The Prussian Hath Said in his Heart*. Chapman and Hall, London, 1914.

—— *The Perils of Peace*. T. Werner Laurie, London, 1916.

Clarke, William. *Essays Selected from the Writings of Joseph Mazzini* (ed. with introduction by Wm. Clarke). Walter Scott, London, 1887.

—— *Political Orations from Wentworth to Macaulay* (ed. with introduction by Wm. Clarke). Walter Scott, London, 1889.

—— *Walt Whitman*. Swan Sonnenschein, London, 1892.

—— [See Biography section for other work.]

Coit, Dr Stanton (ed.). *Ethical Democracy*. Society of Ethical Propaganda, 1900. [Contains essays by many Fabians and I.L.P. men; Dr Coit published many other essays on the Ethical Movement.]

Cole, G. D. H. *The World of Labour*. G. Bell and Sons, London, 1913.

—— *Self-Government in Industry*. G. Bell, London, 3rd edn., 1918.

—— *Chaos and Order in Industry*. Methuen, London, 1920.

—— *Guild Socialism Restated*. Leonard Parsons, London, 1920.

—— *Social Theory*. Methuen, London, 1920.

Crooks, Will. *Education in Connection with Co-operation*. Central Co-op. Board, 1885.

—— *An Address on the Unemployed Problem*. Political Committee of the National Liberal Club, 1905.

—— *The British Workman Defends his Home*. Whitwell Press, London, 1917.

Davies, A. Emil. *The Nationalization of Railways*. Adam and Chas. E. Black, London, 1908.

—— *The Case for Railway Nationalization*. Nations Library, 1913.

—— *The Collectivist State in the Making*. G. Bell and Sons, London, 1914.

—— *The Case for Nationalization*. G. Allen and Unwin, London, 1920.

Dell, Robert E. *The Catholic Church and the Social Question*. Catholic Press Co., London, 1899.

Dix, Gertrude. *The Image Breakers* [a novel of the early days of the Socialist movement]. Heinemann, London, 1900.

Dodd, F. Lawson. *The Problem of the Milk Supply*. Baillière and Co., London, 1904.

Drake, Barbara. *Women in the Engineering Trades*. L.R.D. Trade Union Series no. 3, 1918.

Ensor, R. C. K. (ed.). *Modern Socialism, as set forth in the speeches of Socialists*. Harper, London and N.Y., 1904.

Galton, F. W. (ed.). *Select Documents Illustrating the History of Trade Unionism.* I. *The Tailoring Trade.* P. S. King and Son, London, 1896.

—— (ed.). *Workers on their Industries.* Swan Sonnenschein and Co., London, 1895.

Guest, Leslie Haden. *Theosophy and Social Reconstruction.* Riddle of Life Series no. 3, 1912.

—— *The Nation of the Future: a Survey of Hygenic conditions and Possibilities in School and Home Life.* G. Bell, London, 1916.

Hardie, J. Keir (with others). *Labour Politics: a Symposium.* I.L.P., 1903.

—— *The Unemployed Problem with some Suggestions for Solving It.* I.L.P., 1904.

—— *Can a Man Be A Christian on a Pound a Week?* I.L.P., 3rd ed., 1905.

—— *The Citizenship of Women: a Plea for Women's Suffrage.* I.L.P., 3rd ed., 1906.

—— *From Serfdom to Socialism.* The Labour Ideal Series, 1907.

—— *India: Impressions and Suggestions.* I.L.P., 1907.

—— *My Confession of Faith in the Labour Alliance.* I.L.P., 1909.

Headlam, Stewart D. *The London School Board in* 1890. F. Verinder, London, 1890.

—— *Evening Continuation Schools in London.* Dearle Bros., London, 1901.

—— *The Place of the Public in Secular Education: an Open Letter to the Teachers under the L.S.B.* Brown Langham and Co., London, 1903.

—— *Municipal Puritanism.* F. Verinder, London, 1905.

Henderson, Arthur. *The Aims of Labour.* Headley Bros., London, 1917.

Hobson, S. G. *Guild Principles in War and Peace.* G. Bell, London, 1917.

—— *National Guilds and the State.* G. Bell, London, 1920.

Hutchins, Beatrice L. (with Amy Harrison). *History of Factory Legislation . . .,* P. S. King and Son, Westminster, 1903.

Keddell, Frederick. *The Nationalization of our Railway System: its Justice and Advantages.* Modern Press, London, 1886.

Lansbury, George. *Socialism for the Poor: the End of Pauperism.* Pass on Pamphlets no. 12, 1909.

Laski, Harold J. *Political Thought in England from Locke to Bentham.* H.U.L. Williams and Norgate, London, 1920.

Lawrence F. W. Pethick (Lord Pethick Lawrence). *Women's Fight for the Vote.* Women's Press, London, 1910.

—— *The Man's Share: Mr Pethick Lawrence's Defence of Militancy Delivered from the Dock of the Old Bailey on May 20th 1912.* Garden City Press, Letchworth, 1913.

—— *A Levy on Capital.* Allen and Unwin, London, 1918.

Lindsay, A. D. (Lord Lindsay). *The Philosophy of Bergson.* J. M. Dent, London, 1911.

MacDonald, J. Ramsay. *The Zollverein and British Industry.* Grant Richards, London, 1903.

—— *Socialism.* T. C. and E. C. Jack, London, 1907.

—— *Socialism and Society.* I.L.P., 1908.

—— *Socialism and Government,* 2 vols. I.L.P., 1909.

—— *The Socialist Movement.* H.U.L. Williams and Norgate, London, n.d.

—— *Syndicalism: a Critical Examination.* Constable, London, 1912.

Macrosty, H. W. *Trusts and the State: a Sketch of Competition.* Grant Richards, London, 1901.

—— *The Trust Movement in British Industry.* Longmans, London, 1907.

Maude, Aylmer. *War and Patriotism.* A. Bonner, London, 1900.

—— *Tolstoy and his Problems: Essays.* Grant Richards, London, 1901.

—— *A Peculiar People: the Doukhobors.* Grant Richards, London, 1904.

McCleary, G. F. *Infant Mortality and Infants Milk Depots.* P. S. King and Son, London, 1905.

McKillop, Margaret (with Mabel Atkinson). *Economics: Descriptive and Theoretical.* Allman and Sons, London, 1911.

—— *Food Values: What They Are and How to Calculate Them.* G. Routledge and Sons, London, 1916.

McKillop, Margaret (with Alister D. McKillop). *Efficiency Methods: an Introduction to Scientific Management.* Routledge, London, 1917.

Money, Sir Leo G. Chiozza. *British Trade and the Zollverein Issue.* Commercial Intelligence Publishing Co., London, 1902.

—— *Through Preference to Protection: an Examination of Mr Chamberlain's Fiscal Proposals.* Free Trade Association, 1903.

—— *Elements of the Fiscal Problem.* P. S. King, London, 1903.

—— 101 *Points against Tariff Reform.* Daily News, Manchester, 1909.

—— 50 *Industries under Free Trade.* Daily News, Manchester, 1910.

—— *Money's Fiscal Dictionary.* Methuen, London, 1910.

—— *Riches and Poverty.* Methuen, 10th ed., 1911.

—— *A Nation Insured: the National Insurance Bill Explained.* Liberal Publication Dept., London, 1911.

—— *Insurance versus Poverty* (with introduction by Lloyd George). Methuen, London, 1912.

—— *The Future of Work and Other Essays.* T. Fisher Unwin, London, 1914.

—— *The Nation's Wealth: Will It Endure?* Collins, London, 1914.

—— 50 *Points about Capitalism.* Palmer and Hayward, London, 1919.

—— *The Triumph of Nationalization.* Cassell, London, 1920.

Muggeridge, H. T. *The Housing Question in Croydon: some Facts and a Remedy.* Croydon Housing Committee, Croydon, 1901.

—— *The Labour Pilgrim's Progress.* I.L.P., 1916.

Murby, Millicent. *The Commonsense of the Woman Question.* New Age Press, London, 1908.

Nesbit, Edith (Mrs Bland) (ed.). *Essays by Hubert Bland* ('*Hubert*' of the Sunday Chronicle). Max Goschen, London, 1914.

—— [Also volumes of verse, and the well-known children's stories.]

Oliver, Sydney (Lord Olivier). *White Capital and Coloured Labour.* The Socialist Library, I.L.P., 1905.

—— *League of Nations and Primitive Peoples.* Oxford Univ. Press, 1918.

Penny, John. *The Political Labour Movement.* Clarion Pamphlet no. 41.

Phillips, Dr Marion. *A Colonial Autocracy. New South Wales under Governor Macquarie* 1810–1821. P. S. King and Son, London, 1909.

—— (ed.). *Women and the Labour Party.* Headly, London, 1918.

Podmore, Frank. *Robert Owen: a Biography*, 2 vols. Hutchinson, London, 1906.

—— *Modern Spiritualism: a History and a Criticism*, 2 vols. Methuen, London, 1902.

—— [Also several other works of critical investigation of psychic phenomena.]

Reeves, Magdalen S. (Mrs Pember Reeves). *Round about a Pound a Week.* G. Bell, London, 1913.

Ritchie, Prof. D. G. *Natural Rights: a Criticism of some Political and Ethical Conceptions.* Swan Sonnenschein, London, 1895.

—— *Darwinism and Politics.* Swan Sonnenschein, 2nd ed., London, 1891.

—— *Darwin and Hegel, with other Philosophical Studies.* Swan Sonnenschein, London, 1893.

—— *Principles of State Interference.* Swan Sonnenschein, 4th ed., 1902.

—— *Studies in Political and Social Ethics.* Swan Sonnenschein, London, 1902.

Salt, H. S. *The Life of H. D. Thoreau.* R. Bentley, London, 1890.

—— *Humanitarianism: its General Principles and Progress.* Humanitarian League, 1891.

Sanders, W. S. *Trade Unions in Germany.* Fabian Society, 1916.

—— *The Tragedy of Russia.* W. H. Smith and Son, London, 1918.

Schloss, D. F. *Methods of Industrial Remuneration.* Williams and Norgate, London, 3rd ed., 1898.

—— *Insurance against Unemployment.* P. S. King and Son, London, 1909.

Shallard, S. D. *Has Liberalism a Future?* Frank Palmer, London, 1910.

Shaw, G. Bernard. *Collected Works* (Standard Edition, Constable).

Slesser, Sir Henry (with Wm S. Clark). *The Legal Position of the Trade Unions.* P. S. King and Son, London, 1912.

Snowden, Ethel. *The Woman Socialist.* Geo. Allen, London, 1907.

—— *The Feminist Movement.* The Nations Library, 1913.

Snowden, Philip. *The Chamberlain Bubble: Facts about the Zollverein with an Alternative Policy.* I.L.P., 1903.

—— *Facts for the Workers about Protection, Free Trade and Monopoly.* I.L.P., 1904.

—— *The Christ that is to Be.* I.L.P., 1904.

—— *Old Age Pensions This Year.* I.L.P., 1907.

—— *The Socialists' Budget.* Geo. Allen, London, 1907.

—— *Socialism and the Drink Question.* The Socialist Library, I.L.P., 1908.

—— *A Few Hints to Lloyd George: Where is the Money to Come from? The Question Answered.* I.L.P., 1909.

—— *In Defence of the Conciliation Bill.* Women's Publ. Co., 1911.

—— *The Living Wage.* Hodder and Stoughton, London, 1912.

—— *Socialism and Syndicalism.* Collins, London, 1913.

—— *Labour in Chains. The Peril of Industrial Conscription.* Nat. Lab. Press, Manchester, 1917.

—— *Labour and National Finance.* Leonard Parsons, London, 1920.

Sparling, H. Halliday. [Editor of works of literature. Useful collection of newspapers and reviews relating to Socialism deposited in the British Museum 1850 d. 18.]

Standring, George. *The People's History of the English Aristocracy.* R. Forder, 1891.

Tawney, R. H. *The Agrarian Problem in the 16th Century.* Longmans, London, 1912.

—— *The Establishment of Minimum Rates in the Chainmaking Industry.* G. Bell and Sons, London, 1914.

—— *The Establishment of Minimum Rates in the Tailoring Industry.* G. Bell and Sons, London, 1915.

—— *The Sickness of an Acquisitive Society.* Fabian Society and Allen and Unwin, London, 1920.

Taylor, G. R. S. *Leaders of Socialism Past and Present.* New Age Press, London, 1908.

—— *The Psychology of the Great War.* Martin Secker, London, 1915.

—— *The Guild State: its Principles and Possibilities.* Allen and Unwin, London, 1919.

—— *Modern English Statesmen.* Allen and Unwin, London, 1920.

BIBLIOGRAPHY

Tillett, Ben (with Tom Mann). *The New Trades Unionism*. Green and McAllan, London, 1890.
—— *Trades Unions and Socialism*. Clarion Pamphlet, 1897.
—— *Dock Wharf Riverside and General Workers Union: a Brief History of the Dockers' Union*. Twentieth Century Press, London, 1910.
—— *History of the London Transport Workers' Strike*, 1911. National Transport Workers Federation, 1912.
Wallas, Graham. *The Life of Francis Place*. Longmans, London, 1898.
—— *Human Nature and Politics*. Constable, London, 1908.
—— *The Great Society: a Psychological Analysis*. Macmillan, London, 1914.
Webb, Beatrice. *The Co-operative Movement in Great Britain*. Swan Sonnenschein, London, 1891.
—— *The Relationship between Co-operation and Trade Unionism*. Co-op. Union, 1892.
—— (ed.). *The Case for the Factory Acts*. Grant Richards, London, 1901.
—— *The Wages of Men and Women, Should they be Equal?* Allen and Unwin, London, 1919.
Webb, Sidney. *What Socialism Means: a Call to the Unconverted*. Leaflet Press, 1888.
—— *Wanted a Programme: an Appeal to the Liberal Party* (1888).
—— *The Progress of Socialism*. Modern Press, London, 1888.
—— *Socialism in England*. Swan Sonnenschein, London, 1890.
—— *The Fabian Society: its Objects and Methods*. Stafford, Notts., 1891.
—— (with H. Cox). *The Eight Hours Day*. W. Scott, London, n.d.
—— *The London Programme*. Swan Sonnenschein, London, 1891.
—— *The Economic Heresies of the L.C.C.* London, 1894.
—— *The Work of the L.C.C.* L.R.U., 1895.
—— *Three Years' Work on the London County Council*. May and Goulding, Deptford, 1895. [And subsequent editions *Six Years' Work . . . , Fifteen Years' Work . . . .*]
—— *London Education*. Longmans, London, 1904.
—— *Grants in Aid*. Longmans, London, 1911.
—— (ed.) *Seasonal Trades*. Constable, London, 1912.
—— *Towards Social Democracy*. Allen and Unwin, London, 1916.
—— (with Arnold Freeman). *Great Britain After the War*. Allen and Unwin, London, 1916.
—— *Restoration of Trade Union Conditions*. Nisbett, London, 1917.
—— *The Works Manager Today*. Longmans, London, 1917.
—— *To the Men and Women Graduates of the University of London: an Open Letter*. St Clements Press, London, 1918.
Webb, Sidney and Beatrice. *The History of Trade Unionism*. Longmans, 1894.
—— *Industrial Democracy*. Longmans, 1897.
—— *Problems of Modern Industry*. Longmans, 1898.
—— *English Poor Law Policy*. Longmans, 1910.
—— *The State and the Doctor*. Longmans, 1910.
—— *English Local Government from the Revolution to the Municipal Corporations Act*, 10 vols. Longmans, various dates.
—— *Prevention of Destitution*. Longmans, London, 1920.
—— *A Constitution for the Socialist Commonwealth of Great Britain*. Longmans, London, 1920.
Wells, H. G. *Works*. T. Fisher Unwin, London, 1924. [His writings of the years

1901–11 are especially important. For bibliography see G. H. Wells ('Geoffrey West'), *The Works of H. G. Wells, 1887–1925, a Bibliography.* . . . Routledge, London, 1926.]

West, Julius. *G. K. Chesterton: a Critical Study.* Secker, London, 1915.
—— *A History of the Chartist Movement.* Constable, London, 1920.

Woolf, Leonard, S. *International Government: Two Reports.* Fabian Society, 1915.
—— *Co-operation and the Future of Industry.* Allen and Unwin, London, 1918.
—— *Empire and Commerce in Africa: a Study in Economic Imperialism.* Allen and Unwin, London, n.d. [1919].
—— *Economic Imperialism.* Swarthmore Press, London, 1920.

OTHER WORKS CONSULTED

Alden, Percy. *Aspects of Changing Social Structure.* Allen and Unwin, London, 1937.

Arnot, R. Page. *The Miners, 1889–1910.* Allen and Unwin, London, 1949.

Attlee, C. R. *The Labour Party in Perspective.* Gollancz, London, 1937.

Barker, Brian. *Labour in London: A Study in Municipal Achievement.* Routledge, London, 1946.

Bateson, H. E. *A Select Bibliography of Modern Economic Theory, 1870–1929.* Routledge, London, 1930.

Bealey, F. and Pelling, H. *Labour and Politics.* Macmillan, London, 1958.

Beer, M. *A History of British Socialism.* G. Bell and Sons, London, 1929.

Beveridge, Janet (Lady). *An Epic of Clare Market.* G. Bell and Sons, London, 1960.

Blease, W. Lyon. *A Short History of English Liberalism.* T. Fisher Unwin, London, 1913.

Booth, C. *Life and Labour of the People of London,* 9 vols. Macmillan, London, 1892–7.

Bosanquet, Helen Dendy. *Social Work in London.* John Murray, London, 1914.

Bradley, F. H. *Ethical Studies.* London, 2nd ed., 1927. [First published in 1876.]

Brand, C. F. *British Labour's Rise to Power.* Stanford Univ., California, 1941.

Brown, Benjamin H. *The Tariff Reform Movement in Great Britain 1881–95.* Columbia Univ. Press, 1943.

Carpenter, Niles. *Guild Socialism: an Historical and Critical Analysis.* Appleton, N.Y., 1922.

Chamberlain, J. *The* [Unauthorised] *Radical Programme,* with a preface by ——. Chapman and Hall, London, 1885.

Churchill, Winston. *Liberalism and the Social Problem.* Hodder and Stoughton, London, 1909.

Clapham, J. H. *An Economic History of Modern Britain,* 3 vols. Cambridge Univ. Press, 1926–38.

Clayton, J. *The Rise and Decline of Socialism in Great Britain, 1884–1924.* Faber and Gwyer, London, 1926.

Cole, G. D. H. *Economic Tracts for the Times,* Macmillan, London, 1932.
—— *British Working Class Politics.* Routledge, London, 1941.
—— *A Short History of the British Working Class Movement,* 3 vols. Allen and Unwin, London, 1927.
—— *Socialism in Evolution.* Pelican, London, 1938.
—— *History of Socialist Thought,* 4 vols. Vol. 3, *The Second International.* Macmillan, London, 1956.

—— *History of the Labour Party from* 1914. Routledge and Kegan Paul, London, 1948.

—— *What Marx Really Meant.* Gollancz, London, 1934.

—— *Scope and Method in Social and Political Theory.* Clarendon Press, Oxford, 1945.

Cole, G. D. H. and R. Postgate. *The Common People.* Methuen, London, 1938.

Comte, Auguste (trans. Harriet Martineau). *Positive Philosophy,* 2 vols. John Chapman, London, 1853.

Dangerfield, G. *The Strange Death of Liberal England.* H. Smith and R. Haas, N.Y., 1935.

Davidson, J. Morrison. *The Annals of Toil, being Labour History Outlines, Roman and British.* Wm Reeves, London, 1899.

Davidson, T. *The Moral Aspects of the Economic Question.* Wm Reeves, London, 1888.

Davies, A. Emil. *The Story of the London County Council.* Labour Publishing Co., London. 1925.

—— *The London County Council* 1889–1937: *a Historical Sketch* (Fabian Tract no. 243).

Davies, Ernest. *National Enterprise: the Development of the Public Corporation.* Gollancz, London, 1946.

Davis, W. J. *The British Trades Union Congress: History and Recollections,* 2 vols. Co-op. Printing Society, London, 1910–16.

Dell, R. E. *Socialism and Personal Liberty.* New Era Series no. 14, London, 1921.

De Montgomery, B. G. *British and Continental Labour Policy.* Kegan Paul, Trench, Trubner, London, 1922.

De Schweinitz, K. *England's Road to Social Security.* Univ. of Pennsylvania Press, Philadelphia, 1943.

Dicey, A. V. *Lectures on the Relation between Law and Opinion in England during the Nineteenth Century.* Macmillan, London, 2nd ed., 1914.

Dobb, M. *Political Economy and Capitalism.* Routledge, London, 1946.

Dod's L.C.C. Directory. Geo. Bell and Whittaker, 1889.

Eaglesham, E. *From School Board to Local Authority.* Routledge and Kegan Paul, London, 1956.

Ellis, R. W. *Bernard Shaw and Karl Marx: a Symposium.* Random House, N.Y., 1930.

Elton, G. *England Arise.* Cape, London, 1931.

Ensor, R. C. K. *England 1870–1914.* Clarendon Press, Oxford, 1936.

Finer, Herman. *Representative Government and a Parliament of Industry.* Fabian Society and Allen and Unwin, London, n.d.

—— *English Local Government.* Methuen, London, 1933.

—— *Municipal Trading: a Study in Public Administration.* Allen and Unwin, 1941.

—— *The Theory and Practice of Modern Government,* 2 vols. Methuen, London, 1932.

—— *The Future of Government.* Methuen, London, 1946.

Firth, J. F. B. *The Gas Supply of London.* Edw. Stanford, London, 1874.

—— *Reform of London Government and of the City Guilds.* Swan Sonnenschein, London, 1888.

—— *London Government and How to Reform It.* London Municipal Reform League, Kerby and Endeau, London, 1882.

Fyfe, H. Hamilton. *The British Liberal Party: an Historical Sketch.* Allen and Unwin, London, 1928.

George, Henry. *Progress and Poverty.* Everyman, Dent, n.d.

Gibbon, Sir Gwilym and R. W. Bell. *History of the London County Council* 1889–1939. Macmillan, London, 1939.

Glasier, J. Bruce. *The Meaning of Socialism.* I.L.P., London, 2nd ed., 1925.

Gordon, Alban. *Social Insurance: What It Is and What It Might Be.* Fabian Society and Allen and Unwin, London, 1924.

Graves, J. *Policy and Progress in Secondary Education* 1902–42. Nelson, London, 1943.

Gray, Alexander (Sir). *The Socialist Tradition, Moses to Lenin.* Longmans, London, 1946.

Guyot, E. *La durée du travail dans les mines de Grande Bretagne.* Rousseau, Paris, 1908.

—— *Le socialisme et l'évolution de l'Angleterre contemporaine,* 1880–1911. Alcan, Paris, 1913.

Halévy, Elie. *History of the English People: Epilogue.* Benn, London, 1951–2.

Harris, J. T. *An Example of Communal Currency.* P. S. King and Sons, London, 1911.

Harris, Percy. *London and its Government.* J. M. Dent and Sons, London, 1933.

Higginbottom, F. J. *Popular Guide to the Third L.C.C., the Ninth London School Board and the London Vestries and Guardian Boards.* . . . Simpkin, Marshall, Kent and Co., London, 1895.

Hobhouse, L. T. *The Labour Movement.* Unwin, London, 1893.

—— *Democracy and Reaction.* Unwin, London, 1904.

Hobsbawm, E. (ed.). *Labour's Turning Point.* Lawrence and Wishart, London, 1948.

Hobson, J. A. *Imperialism.* Nisbet, London, 1902.

—— *The Crisis in Liberalism.* P. S. King and Son, London, 1909.

Humphrey, A. W. *A History of Labour Representation.* Constable, London, 1912.

Hutchinson, K. *The Decline and Fall of British Capitalism.* Cape, London, 1951.

Hutt, A. *This Final Crisis.* Gollancz, London, 1935.

Industrial Remuneration Conference: The Report of the Proceedings and Papers read in the Prince's Hall, Piccadilly, under the Presidency of the Rt Hon. Sir Charles W. Dilke, Bart., M.P., on the 28th and 30th January, 1885. Cassell and Co., London, 1885.

Jackson, Holbrook. *The Eighteen Nineties.* Pelican, London, 1950.

Jay, Douglas. *The Socialist Case.* Faber and Faber, London, 1937.

Jephson, H. *The Making of Modern London: Progress and Reaction.* Bowers Bros., London, 1910.

Jevons, W. S. *The State in Relation to Labour.* Macmillan, London, 3rd ed., 1894.

Joad, C. E. M. *Introduction to Modern Political Theory.* Clarendon Press, Oxford, 1924.

—— *Matter, Life and Value.* Oxford Univ. Press, London, 1929.

—— *Guide to the Philosophy of Morals and Politics.* Gollancz, London, 1938.

—— (ed.). *Shaw and Society: an Anthology and Symposium.* Odhams, London, 1953.

Kaufmann, M. *Socialism and Modern Thought.* Methuen, London, 1896.

Keynes, J. M. *The End of Laissez Faire.* Hogarth Press, London, 1926.

Kirkup, T. (revised by E. R. Pease). *A History of Socialism.* A. and C. Black, London, 5th ed., 1913.

Knowlton, T. A. *The Economic Theory of G. Bernard Shaw*. Maine Univ. Press, 1936.
Laidler, H. W. *Social-Economic Movements*. Crowell, N.Y., 1946.
Lansbury, George. *The Miracle of Fleet Street: the Story of the 'Daily Herald'* Labour Publishing Co., London, 1925.
Laski, H. *Karl Marx: an Essay*. Fabian Society and Allen and Unwin, London, 1922.
—— *A Grammar of Politics*. Allen and Unwin, London, 4th ed., 1937.
—— *Liberty in the Modern State*. Pelican, London, 1937.
—— *Parliamentary Government in England: a Commentary*. Allen and Unwin, London, 1938.
—— *The State in Theory and Practice*. Allen and Unwin, London, 1935.
Laski, H. and others (eds.). *A Century of Municipal Progress, 1835–1935*. Allen and Unwin, London, 1935.
Lee, H. W. and E. Archbold. *Social Democracy in Britain*. Social Democratic Federation, London, 1935.
Lenin, V. I. *Lenin on Britain: a Compilation*. Lawrence and Wishart, London, 1934.
Levy, H. *Monopolies, Cartels and Trusts in British Industry*. Macmillan, London, 1927.
Levy, J. H. (ed.). *A Symposium on Value*. P. S. King and Son, London, n.d.
Lindsay, A. D. (Lord). *Essentials of Democracy*. Oxford Univ. Press, London, 1940.
—— *The Modern Democratic State*. Oxford Univ. Press, London, 1947.
—— *Karl Marx's Capital*. World's Manuals Oxford Univ. Press, London, 1925.
Lloyd, John. *London Municipal Government: History of a Great Reform 1880–8*. Bedford Press, London, 2nd ed., 1911.
Lowndes, G. A. N. *The Silent Social Revolution*. Oxford Univ. Press, London, 1937.
Lynd, Helen M. *England in the Eighteen-Eighties*. Oxford Univ. Press, N.Y., 1945.
Maccoby, S. *English Radicalism, 1832–52*. Allen and Unwin, London, 1935.
—— *English Radicalism, 1853–86*. Allen and Unwin, London, 1938.
—— *English Radicalism, 1886–1914*. Allen and Unwin, London, 1953.
MacDonald, J. R. *The Story of the I.L.P. and What It Stands For*. I.L.P., 1923.
Marx, K. *Capital*. Everyman, Dent, London, 1930.
Marx and Engels on Britain. Foreign Languages Publishing House, Moscow, 1953.
Marx, K. and F. Engels. *Correspondence of Marx and Engels*. National Book Agency, Calcutta.
Masterman, C. F. G. *The Condition of England*. Methuen, London, 1909.
McCleary, G. F. *The Early History of the Infant Welfare Movement*. H. K. Lewis and Co., London, 1933.
—— *The Maternity and Child Welfare Movement*. P. S. King and Son, London, 1935.
—— *National Health Insurance*. H. K. Lewis and Co., London, 1932.
McGee, J. E. *A Crusade for Humanity*. Watts, London, 1931.
McKenzie, R. T. *British Political Parties*. Heinemann, London, 1955.
Métin, Albert. *Le Socialisme en Angleterre*. Alcan, Paris, 1897.
Mill, J. S. *Auguste Comte and Positivism*. Trubner, London, 1865.
—— *Utilitarianism, Liberty and Representative Government*. Everyman, Dent, 1948.
Money, Sir Leo G. Chiozza. *Product Money: a Sequel to Riches and Poverty*. Methuen, London, 1933.
Morrison, Herbert. *How Greater London Is Governed*. Lovat, Dickson and Thompson, London, 1935.

—— *Socialization and Transport.* Constable, London, 1933.

Noel, Conrad. *The Labour Party, What It Is and What It Wants.* Unwin, London, 1906.

Ostrogorski, M. *Democracy and the Organization of Political Parties*, 2 vols. Macmillan, N.Y., 1902.

Pelling, H. M. *The Origins of the Labour Party.* Macmillan, London, 1954.

Pipkin, C. W. *Social Politics and Modern Democracies*, vol. I. Macmillan, N.Y., 1931.

Poirier, P. P. *The Advent of the Labour Party.* Allen and Unwin, London, 1958.

Popper, K. *The Open Society and Its Enemies*, 2 vols. Routledge, London, 1945.

Quelch, H. *The Social Democratic Federation: Its Objects, Its Principles and Its Work.* Twentieth Century Press, London, 1907.

Rae, John. *Contemporary Socialism.* Swan Sonnenschein, London, 2nd ed., 1891.

Reid, J. H. Stewart. *The Origins of the British Labour Party.* Univ. of Minnesota Press, Minneapolis, 1955.

Roberts, B. C. *The Trades Union Congress, 1868–1921.* Allen and Unwin, London, 1958.

Robertson, J. M. *The Future of Liberalism.* J. W. Gott, Bradford, n.d.

Robinson, Joan. *An Essay in Marxian Economics.* Macmillan, London, 1942.

Robson, W. A. *The British System of Government.* Longmans, London, 1940.

—— *The Development of Local Government.* Allen and Unwin, London, 1931.

—— *From Patronage to Proficiency in the Civil Service.* Fabian Society, London, 1922.

—— *The Government and Misgovernment of London.* Allen and Unwin, London, 1939.

Rothstein, Th. *From Chartism to Labourism.* Martin Lawrence, London, 1929.

Rumney, J. *Herbert Spencer's Sociology: a Study in the History of Social Theory.* Williams and Norgate, London, 1934.

Sabine, G. H. *A History of Political Theory.* Harrap, London, 1948.

Saunders, W. *History of the First L.C.C., 1889–91.* National Press Agency, London, 1892.

Sells, Dorothy. *British Wages Boards, a Study in Industrial Democracy.* Brookings Institution, Washington, 1939.

Shaw, G. B. *The Intelligent Woman's Guide . . .*, 2 vols. Pelican, London, 1937.

—— *Everybody's Political What's What.* Constable, London, 1944.

Skelton, O. D. *Socialism: a Critical Analysis.* Constable, London, 1911.

Slesser, Sir Henry. *A History of the Liberal Party.* Hutchinson, London, 1944.

—— *The Law.* Longmans, London, 1936.

—— *The Law Relating to Trade Unions.* T.U. Manuals, 1921.

—— *Trade Unionism.* Methuen, London, 2nd ed., 1921.

—— *Trade Union Law.* Nisbet, London, 1921.

Slesser, Sir Henry and Arthur Henderson. *Industrial Law.* Ernest Benn, London, 1924.

Smith, H. Llewellyn and Vaughan Nash. *The Story of the Dockers' Strike.* Unwin, London, 1889.

Spencer, Herbert. *Reasons for Dissenting from the Philosophy of M. Comte.* Williams and Norgate, London, 1884.

Stead, W. T. *On the Eve: a Handbook for the General Election.* Review of Reviews Publishing Office, London, 1892.

Stead, W. T. (ed.). *The Elector's Guide*. Review of Review Office Publishings, London, 1892.

Strachey, J. *What are We to Do?* Gollancz, London, 1938.

Strauss, E. *Bernard Shaw: Art and Socialism*. Gollancz, London, 1942.

Sweezy, P. M. *The Theory of Capitalist Development*. Oxford Univ. Press, N.Y., 1942.

Tawney, R. H. *The Acquisitive Society*. G. Bell, London, 1921.

—— *The Attack*. Allen and Unwin, London, 1953.

—— *Equality*. Allen and Unwin, London, 1931.

—— *The Nationalization of the Coal Industry*. Labour Party, London, n.d.

—— *Religion and the Rise of Capitalism*. Pelican, 1938.

Tracey, H. *The Book of the Labour Party*, 3 vols. Caxton Publishing Co., London, n.d.

Transactions of the National Liberal Club Political Economy Circle, vols. I and II.

Trevelyan, G. M. *British History in the Nineteenth Century and After*, 1782–1919. Longmans, London, 1937.

Ulam, A. B. *Philosophical Foundations of English Socialism*. Harvard Univ. Press, Cambridge, Mass., 1951.

Verhaegen, P. *Socialistes anglais*. Englcke et Larose, 1898.

'Villiers, Brougham' (F. J. Shaw). *The Socialist Movement in England*. Unwin, London, 1908.

Voynich, Ethel. *The Gadfly*. Foreign Languages Publishing House, Moscow, 1955—first published Henry Holt and Co., N.Y., 1897. [A novel containing a picture of Mrs Charlotte Wilson as 'Gemma'.]

Wallas, Graham. *The Art of Thought*. Cape, London, 1926.

—— *Our Social Heritage*. Allen and Unwin, London, 1921.

—— *Men and Ideas*. Allen and Unwin, London, 1940.

Webb, Sidney. *The Story of the Durham Miners*. Labour Publishing Co., London, 1921.

Webb, S. and B. *The Consumer's Co-operative Movement*. Longmans, London, 1921.

—— *The Decay of Capitalist Civilization*. Longmans, London, 1923.

—— *Soviet Communism: a New Civilization?* 2 vols. Longmans, London, 1935.

—— *Methods of Social Study*. Longmans, London, 1932.

Westminster Gazette Handbook to the Third L.C.C. Westminster Gazette Office, 1895.

Whelen, F. (ed.). *Politics in 1896*. Grant Richards, London, 1897.

Williams, F. *Fifty Years' March: the Rise of the Labour Party*. Odhams, London [1949].

Woods, R. A. *English Social Movements*. Swan Sonnenschein, London, 1892.

—— (and others). *The Poor in Great Cities*. Kegan Paul, London, 1896.

Woolf, Leonard S. *After the Deluge*. Pelican, London, 1937.

Young, G. M. *Victorian England: Portrait of an Age*. Oxford Univ. Press, London, 1936.

INDEX

Acland, A. H. D., 210, 241, 252
Adventures of the Black Girl in her Search for God, The (by G. B. Shaw), 88
agriculture, *see* land, municipal ownership of
Airey, J., 315*n*
Alden, Percy, 252*n*, 363, 369
Allen, Clifford, 140–1, 322, 352
Amalgamated Society of Engineers, 76–7, 308, 318
anarchism, 9–10, 15, 20–2, 44–6, 72–5, 82, 99–100, 281, 292, 295
Anarchist Group of Freedom, 23
Anderson, W. C., 142, 299
Androcles and the Lion (by G. B. Shaw), 88
Annals of Toil, The (by J. Morrison Davidson), 1
Anti-Sweating League, 260
Apple Cart, The (by G. B. Shaw), 81
arbitration, compulsory, 298, 328
Archer, William, 82, 129*n*
Ashley, W. J., 132
Asquith, H. H. (Lord Oxford and Asquith), 215, 242, 252, 254–6, 259, 272–3, 361
Asylums Board, 188, 194
Atkinson, Mabel, 142, 314, 363
Attlee, Clement (Lord), 201, 355, 357, 369
Australia, 120*n*, 127, 129, 215, 240, 260, 328
Austria, 140, 144–5
Aveling, Edward, 281, 284–5, 304

bakeries, municipal ownership of, 110, 223
Balfour A. J., 215, 221, 257, 263, 271, 273, 327, 330, 361–2
Balfour, Gerald, 264
Balfour of Burleigh (Lord), 228
Ball, Sidney, 74, 108*n*, 148*n*, 154–5, 168, 357
banking, nationalization of, 113–14
Banner, Bob, 245*n*
Barnes, George N., 120, 124*n*, 361
Basis of F.S., 111–12
Battersea Labour League, 256
Baum, F. C., 198, 210*n*
Bax, E. Belfort, 30, 80–1, 331*n*, 361
Beal, James, 189, 228
Beaumont, H., 182
Bebel, August, 10, 140
Beer, Max, 163, 369
Belgium, 139–40
Bell, Richard, 309, 327*n*
Belloc, Hilaire, 182
Benn, Sir John Williams, 224–5
Bentham, Dr Ethel, 314
Bentham, J., 29, 93, 150, 153, 159

Bentley, H. G., 111
Bernstein, Edward, 71, 361
Besant, Annie, not a foundation member of F.S., 3; description of, 5; associated with Democratic Federation, 9; disapproves of revolution, 16, 68; leads Radicals, 18; her sympathies with Liberal-Radicalism, 19; plays active part in early F.S., 22–4; plans for County Farms, 27, 99; Fabian Notes column in *Our Corner*, published by, 119; later religious views, 5, 147*n*, as lecturer, 179; on London School Board, 198, 206; publications of, 363; books about, 357
'betterment' (rent charge), 110
Beveridge, Dr A. T. Gordon, 336*n*
Beveridge, Sir William (Lord), 222, 275, 361
Birrell, A., 259
Bishop, Gerald, 112
Bismarck, Otto von, 98*n*, 261, 274
'Black Monday', 17
Blanc, Louis, 27
Bland, Hubert, a founder of F.S., 2–4; description of, 3–4; treasurer of F.S., 4; journalist, 7; member of S.D.F. and of F.S. executive, 9–11; becomes member of Socialist League, 15; quoted, 16; assists preparation of F.S. report on unemployment 1886, 17; modifies revolutionary views, 18; criticizes Webb, 66; view of historical evolution, 68, 70; view of democracy, 71–2, 82; repudiates republicanism, 79–81; mocks Shaw's supermen, 87; attitude to permeation, 96–7; later religious views, 4, 147*n*; journalistic activities of, 164; as lecturer, 179–80; writes Tract 120, 218; and L.S.E., 220*n*; supports I.L.P., 246; appointed F.S. representative but unable to attend inaugural Conference of I.L.P., 249; supports 'Trade Exemption', 302; attends Labour Party Conferences, 314; publications of, 353, 363; books about, 357
Bland, Mrs Hubert, 4, 15, 302, 357, 366
Bland, Paul, 283
Blatchford, Robert, 183, 245*n*, 281–3, 285, 296–7, 310, 327*n*, 335, 337, 357
'Bloody Sunday', 17
Bloomsbury Socialist Society, 20, 281
Board of Trade, 231–2, 260–1, 275, 278
Boer War, 119–26, 128–30, 135, 255, 262, 293, 305–6, 337
Bolas, Thomas, 16
Bondfield, Margaret, 142, 298, 309*n*, 357

375